Ethiopia & Eritrea

Matt Phillips
Jean-Bernard Carillet

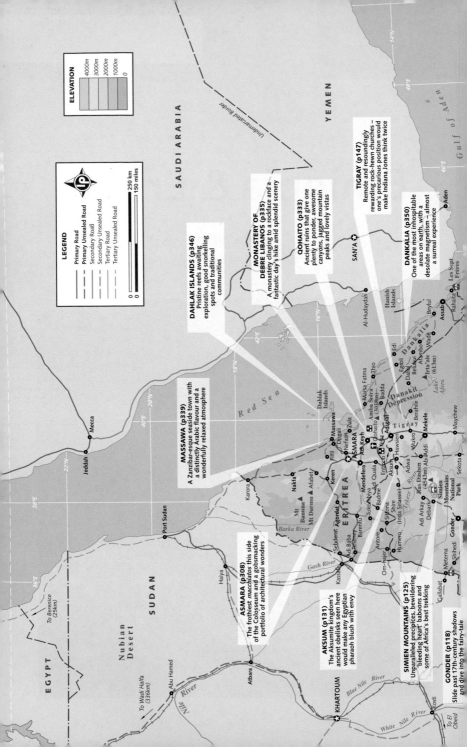

ELEVATION

4000m
3000m
2000m
1000m
0

LEGEND

Primary Road
Primary Unsealed Road
Secondary Road
Secondary Unsealed Road
Tertiary Road
Tertiary Unsealed Road

250 km
150 miles

DAHLAK ISLANDS (p346)
Pristine reefs awaiting exploration, good snorkelling spots and traditional communities

MONASTERY OF DEBRE LIBANOS (p335)
A monastery clinging to a rockface and a fantastic day's hike amid splendid scenery

QOHAITO (p333)
Ancient ruins that give one plenty to ponder, awesome canyons, jagged mountain peaks and lovely vistas

TIGRAY (p147)
Remote and resoundingly rewarding rock-hewn churches – one's precarious position would make Indiana Jones think twice

DANKALIA (p350)
One of the most inhospitable areas on earth, with a desolate magnetism – almost a surreal experience

MASSAWA (p339)
A Zanzibar-esque seaside town with a distinctly Arabic flavour and a wonderfully relaxed atmosphere

ASMARA (p308)
The frothiest *macchiatos* this side of the Colosseum and a gobsmacking portfolio of architectural wonders

AKSUM (p131)
The Aksumite kingdom's ancient obelisks seen here would make any Egyptian pharaoh blush with envy

SIMIEN MOUNTAINS (p125)
Unparalleled precipices, bewildering 'bleeding heart' baboons and some of Africa's best trekking

GONDER (p118)
Slide past 17th-century shadows and dive into the fairy-tale

LALIBELA (p155)
Take an unfathomable foray into Lalibela's rock-hewn churches: medieval Ethiopia frozen in stone

LAKE TANA (p115)
Say hello to living history today at this lake's centuries-old island monasteries

BALE MOUNTAINS NATIONAL PARK (p181)
Register for Ethiopian Endemic Wildlife 101, start your trek and study to your heart's content

LOWER OMO VALLEY (p204)
Explore Africa's last great wilderness and visit possibly the continent's most diverse and fascinating peoples

NECHISAR NATIONAL PARK (p199)
Rift Valley lakes, bleached savannah grasses, zebra herds and the odd Abyssinian lion. Safari anyone?

The international boundaries on this map serve as indications only. The Ethiopia-Eritrea border awaits formal UN demarcation.

Destination Ethiopia & Eritrea

Testing, awe-inspiring and heartbreaking – three simple words, two countries' extraordinary histories and one journey you'll never forget. You don't explore Ethiopia and Eritrea because you want a relaxing getaway, you venture here because you want to be moved. And moved you shall certainly be.

Wade through incense into a medieval Ethiopian world hewn from stone in Lalibela and watch the line between past and present blur while taking part in striking Christian ceremonies that haven't changed in 1000 years. Ethiopia's storied and sovereign history has left its wide-ranging and fertile highlands laden with historical treasures ranging from ancient Aksumite tombs and obelisks to 17th-century castles and burnt-out Russian tanks. Many, like Lalibela's magnificent rock-hewn churches, are more than a peek into the nation's past; they are a giant two-footed leap.

Ethiopia's landscapes are no less dramatic and range from the Simien and Bale Mountains, which proffer tremendous trekking and innumerable interactions with dozens of animals and birds seen nowhere else on Earth, to the Danakil Depression, an enchanting and unforgivingly hostile environment offering extreme adventure. The remote lowlands in the sultry southwest are also home to untold adventures and house some of Africa's most fascinating tribes.

Though long part of Ethiopia and home to similar Aksumite ruins, Eritrea is truly a nation of its own. Its landscapes are starkly beautiful and its Red Sea coral reefs remain rich and pristine, oozing diving potential. The coast is rich with Islamic influence while Asmara is laden with astounding Italian Art Deco architecture.

Although Eritreans are currently facing incredible hardships, Eritrea still remains one of Africa's most peaceful, secure and welcoming destinations.

FRANCES LINZEE G

Peoples & Cultures

ARIADNE VAN ZANDBERGEN

A Mursi woman (p207) wears the traditional lip plate, inserted into a slit between her lower lip and jaw

FRANCES LINZEE GORDON

A jousting competitor dresses in the style of a traditional Abyssinian warrior for the festival of Timkat (p261)

Many of the Lower Omo Valley tribes (p206) wear bright bead belts and exhibit scarification

FRANCES LINZEE GORDON

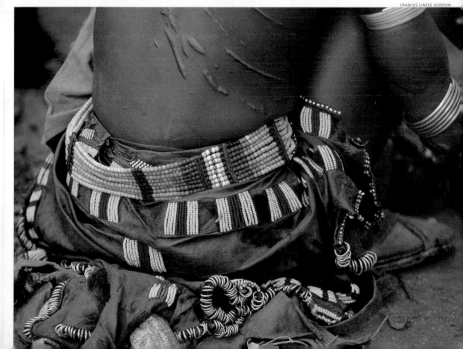

Natural Landscapes

FRANCES LINZEE GORDON

The sublime Sof Omar Caves
(p191) in Ethiopia are a wonder
to explore

ARIADNE VAN ZANDBE

Ethiopia's Danakil Depression (p154), with its barren
landscape and sulphurous pools, is other-worldly

Eritrea's Red Sea Coast (p338) has remained pristine and untouched

JEAN-BERNARD CAF

Constructed Landscapes

FRANCES LINZEE GORDON

The Irga Building (p316) in Asmara, Eritrea, is typical neoclassical architecture

MARK DAFFEY

Gidir Magala (p230) is the main market in Harar, Ethiopia, and also serves as the main meat market

A priest stands in front of Abuna Yemata Guh (p149), spectacularly located in a cliff in Tigray, Ethiopia

ARIADNE VAN ZANDBERGEN

Wildlife

FRANCES LINZEE GORDON

Nechisar National Park (p199) in Ethiopia is home to a plethora of wildlife including the Burchell's zebra

ARIADNE VAN ZANDBERGEN

The common ostrich is just one of the many bird species (p62) to be seen in Ethiopia

The intelligent gelada baboon (p61) is one of Ethiopia's most fascinating mammals

FRANCES LINZEE GO

Contents

Regional Map Contents

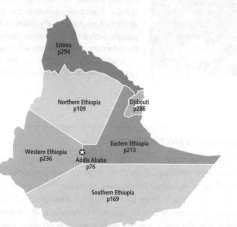

Eritrea
p294

Northern Ethiopia
p109

Djibouti
p286

Western Ethiopia
p236

Addis Ababa
p76

Eastern Ethiopia
p213

Southern Ethiopia
p169

The Authors

MATT PHILLIPS
Coordinating Author, Addis Ababa, Northern, Southern & Western Ethiopia

In 2001 Matt fell in love with Ethiopia in 1994. Strange, but according to the Ethiopian calendar, true! He'd never planned to visit but while travelling north from Cape Town he kept hearing the word 'Ethiopia' from the lips of those heading south. He aborted his Nairobi–Cairo flight and dove in. 'Ethiopia' has been leaping from his lips ever since! Matt has returned to Africa four times since then and has now been thoroughly enlightened by 22 of its amazing countries. He's co-authored Lonely Planet's *Kenya* and *West Africa* guidebooks and was thrilled to take on *Ethiopia & Eritrea*, his sixth title for Lonely Planet.

Matt's Favourite Trip

Why, with an innate fear of heights, do my favourite spots always involve big drops? With dramatic precipices and endless abysses, the Simien Mountains (p125) are my favourite. Now there's standing near cliffs and then there's hanging from them – astounding Debre Damo (p144) definitely lends itself to the latter. The priestly pull up its 15m bluff is unforgettable. Thankfully, what's on top never lets you down! Despite a narrow ledge over a 200m drop stopping me 3m short of Abuna Yemata Guh (p149), one of Tigray's amazing rock-hewn churches, the stunning climb is something I'll never forget. Beauty overcomes gravity at Lalibela, where I let the sun sink with my legs over the ledge at Bet Giyorgis (p160).

Debre Damo
Simien Mountains ○ ○ Abuna Yemata Guh
○
Bet Giyorgis

JEAN-BERNARD CARILLET
Eastern Ethiopia, Djibouti, Eritrea

A Paris-based freelance writer and photographer, Jean-Bernard is a die-hard Africa-lover. He has visited 14 nations in western, eastern and southern Africa. For this edition, he travelled from Addis Ababa to Eritrea via Somaliland and Djibouti – an epic journey in the Horn. Eritrea, his final destination, broke his heart: he found a radically different-feeling country but comfortingly unchanged people, with a fabulous inner strength. He can't think of a more agreeable city than Asmara, where he sipped more *macchiatos* than he cares to remember.

Jean-Bernard coauthored the previous edition of this book as well as Lonely Planet's *Africa on a Shoestring* and *West Africa*.

LONELY PLANET AUTHORS

Why is our travel information the best in the world? It's simple: our authors are independent, dedicated travellers. They don't research using just the Internet or phone, and they don't take freebies in exchange for positive coverage. They travel widely, to all the popular spots and off the beaten track. They personally visit thousands of hotels, restaurants, cafés, bars, galleries, palaces, museums and more – and they take pride in getting all the details right, and telling it how it is. For more, see the authors section on www.lonelyplanet.com.

Jean-Bernard's Favourite Trip

I base myself in Asmara (p308) for a couple of days. Once I have my fill of frothy *macchiatos*, Art Deco buildings and late nights in the capital, I proceed south to Qohaito (p333) and Metera (p336) for some cultural sustenance. Back to Asmara, I jump on a bus to Keren (p328) to check out its architecture and markets before stopping again in Asmara en route to Massawa (p339). After soaking up the ambience on Massawa Island and filling my tummy with Yemeni fish, I take a boat to the Dahlak Islands (p346) for some snorkelling in warm waters. From there, the lure of talismanic Dankalia (p350) is irresistible; I journey on to Assab (p351) and fly back to Asmara.

Getting Started

There's no denying that travelling in Ethiopia and Eritrea is not easy going. The roads, though improving, still batter your bottom for hours on end and hotels (both budget and midrange) are known to host a flea or two. Cheap internal flights can add years to your backside's life, but they can't save you from everything. Expecting to see the sights between lazing in first-class hotels? Please put this book gently back on the shelf for those willing to take some doses of displeasure with the bounty of treasure these countries have to offer.

Besides perusing this skookum guidebook and dreaming up an adventurous itinerary, your only compulsory pretrip planning need involve sorting visas and vaccinations (some jabs are required five or six weeks before travel). Unless you plan on coordinating your stay with one of the major Orthodox festivals (see p261), there's no point in prebooking hotels (they are best hand-picked).

WHEN TO GO
Ethiopia

There's some truth in the old Ethiopian Tourism Commission slogan '13 Months of Sunshine'. Although the famed historical circuit and the rest of the highlands receive rain between mid-March and September, most days during this period still see their fair share of sunshine. The far east and northern highlands see even more sun with significant rain only falling in July and August.

Early October, just after the rains is a particularly good time to visit. The country is wonderfully green, the wildflowers are stunning and there are fewer visitors. Trekking during this time is especially sublime, though it's pretty amazing throughout the entire dry season (October through mid-March).

If you're planning a trip to the tremendous tribes of the Lower Omo Valley, you should avoid travelling in April, May or October, when rain makes most roads impassable.

Finally, you'd do well to coincide with one of Ethiopia's very colourful festivals (p261), particularly Timkat or Meskel. Be aware, however, that domestic flights and hotels often fill up far in advance of Ethiopian festivals and European Christmas.

See Climate Charts (p257) for more information.

Eritrea

Although it is possible to visit Eritrea any time of year, the ideal time climatewise is September to October and March to April. If you are able to, avoid travelling during June to August, when it's the rainy season in the highlands and western lowlands and hot and torrid in the eastern lowlands.

See Climate Charts (p357) for more information.

With many Ethiopian Orthodox Christians in Eritrea, it's worth planning your trip to coincide with their religious festivals (see Holidays, p359). Like in Ethiopia, Timkat and Meskel are particularly special.

COSTS & MONEY
Ethiopia

For most day-to-day costs, Ethiopia is very inexpensive. Those who're willing to battle fleas in their nether regions and eat nothing but simple Ethiopian food can easily survive and get around on US$10 per day

DON'T LEAVE HOME WITHOUT...

- Small torch (headlamps are best) for finding your shoes during power failures. Oh, it's helpful exploring amazing rock-hewn churches too!
- Batteries (torch and camera).
- Updating your vaccinations (p370).
- Sun block, sunglasses and hat.
- Folding umbrella for the sun (like most Ethiopians do) or for occasional downpours.
- Flip-flops for those toe-curling bathrooms.
- Fleece sweater for chilly highland evenings.
- Mosquito repellent.
- Flea powder for cheap hotels' beds and for socks when visiting remote churches.
- Women's hygiene items.
- High-energy bars for vegetarians or those who don't take to local food.
- A water bottle and water-purification materials, needed for trekking and useful in reducing plastic waste while travelling.
- Binoculars to spot that walia ibex dancing on a distant Simien slope.
- Earplugs in case you don't agree with the bus driver's music selection.
- Sink plug – water is very precious.
- Checking visa requirements (p269 & p363).
- Saying goodbye!

(particularly outside the capital). The cheapest hotels and meals cost around US$3 and US$1 respectively.

Those keen on cleanliness and who're still on a budget can get by on US$15 per day.

On top of this are guides' fees and admissions at the national parks and historic sites, as well as one-off transportation costs such as boat trips. Even with these extra costs, budget travellers who share some expenses and ride public transport shouldn't need more than US$15 to US$20 per day in Ethiopia.

Those staying in midrange hotels and eating at hotel restaurants can expect to pay around US$50 per day. This should cover admissions, guides etc, but not internal flights or private transportation costs.

Internal flights aren't really out of anyone's budget range, costing between US$37 and US$131 – good value considering some flights save a few days of bus travel! The same can't be said for 4WD rental, which costs at least US$90 per day.

Eritrea

Although prices have more than doubled in a few years, Eritrea travel is pretty cheap too – at least by Western standards. At the budget level, plan on US$20 to US$25 per day in the capital for a decent room, meals in restaurants and public transport. Outside Asmara, you can get by on US$15 per day. Midrange travellers seeking some mod cons should plan on US$35 to US$50 in the capital, depending on the type of room you want.

More problematic are the costs of 4WD rental, which you might need to go to a number of places of interest, and the boats to the Dahlak Islands.

HOW MUCH?

Steaming *macchiato* US$0.15

100km by bus US$1.50-3

Minibus across town US$0.15

Internet per hr US$2-3

Tip for helpful priest US$0.75-1

See also Lonely Planet Index (inside front cover).

TOP TENS

Orthodox Churches

Ethiopian Orthodox churches are everywhere, rising from Addis Ababa's skyline to dotting desolate and dramatic cliffs. Here's some you'll never forget.

- Bet Giyorgis (p160)
- Debre Berhan Selassie (p122)
- Abuna Aregawi (p145)
- Bet Medhane Alem (p157)
- Bet Amanuel (p160)

- Old St Mary of Zion (p135)
- Yemrehanna Kristos (p163)
- Abuna Yemata Guh (p149)
- Narga Selassie (p116)
- Holy Trinity Cathedral (p86)

Festivals

Ethiopia and Eritrea have a phenomenal mix of vibrant festivals, both Orthodox Christian and Islamic. For additional information, see p261.

- Leddet, 6–7 January
- Timkat, 19 January
- Mawlid an-Nabi, March
- Good Friday, March/April
- Fasika, March/April

- Kiddus Yohannes, 11 September
- Meskel, 27 September
- Eid al-Fitr, September/October
- Festival of Maryam Zion, 30 November
- Kulubi Gabriel, 28 December

Coffee-Table Books

Whether delving into the striking people of the Horn or classic Italian Art Deco architecture, these books are all laden with gorgeous photographs of this unique region. Since we're a modest bunch, we'll abstain from ranking our wildly colourful, witty, authoritative and comprehensive coffee-table book that covers each and every country on the continent. *The Africa Book* hits shelves April 2007. Did we say modest?

- *Don McCullin in Africa* by Don McCullin
- *Touching Ethiopia* by J Golzábez and D Cebrián
- *Journey Through Ethiopia* by M Amin, D Willetts and A Matheson
- *Eritrean Beauty* by Anne Alders
- *Africa Ark* by C Beckworth and A Fisher
- *Bless Ethiopia* by K Nomachi
- *Asmara Beloved* by Sami Sallinen and Haile Bizen
- *Old Tracks in the New Flower* by M Batistoni and P Chiara
- *Asmara: Africa's Secret Modernist City* by E Denison, G Yu Ren and N Gebremedhin
- *Ethiopia Photographed* by R Pankhurst and D Gerard

If you're solo, this will blow your budget. Your best bet is to join a group or other travellers and share costs.

TRAVEL LITERATURE

Michela Wrong's *I Didn't Do It for You* is a compelling and at times comedic account of Eritrea's contemporary history; it helps to understand the national psyche and the failure of democracy.

In *Eating the Flowers of Paradise*, Kevin Rushby travels the old trade route from Ethiopia's highlands to Yemen. By chewing *chat* (mildly intoxicating leaf that's consumed primarily in eastern Ethiopia; it's illegal in Eritrea) at every invitation, Kevin gives a dangerously funny look into this unique drug's culture.

Part personal crusade, part celebration of all that is Ethiopia, *The Chains of Heaven* chronicles Philip Marsden's return to Ethiopia, a land that changed his life when he first visited in the early 1980s.

In *Prester Quest*, Nicholas Jubber entertainingly voyages from Venice to Ethiopia on his quest to deliver – albeit 824 years late – Pope Alexander III's famed letter to Prester John, the mythical Christian king of the East.

Sheba: Through the Desert in Search of the Legendary Queen by Nicholas Clapp successfully blends personal travel accounts with thorough academic research to shed light on one of history's most famous and least understood characters.

By following the footsteps of 19th-century French literary legend Arthur Rimbaud through Egypt, Ethiopia, Djibouti and elsewhere, Charles Nicholl's *Somebody Else* isn't only an award-winning biography, but an interesting piece of travel literature too.

Wilfred Thesiger's classic *Life of My Choice* includes reminiscences of the author's childhood and early adult years in Ethiopia, including the coronation of Haile Selassie and his renowned six-month journey through the Danakil in 1933.

Robert Kaplan's *Surrender or Starve* paints a disturbing but realistic picture of the Horn during the 1980s. Although showing some political bias, he manages to link the devastation of Ethiopia's famines to the Derg's policies.

> 'The Chains of Heaven chronicles Philip Marsden's return to Ethiopia, a land that changed his life when he first visited in the early 1980s.'

INTERNET RESOURCES

Abyssinia Gateway (www.abyssiniacybergateway.net) Provides an exhaustive list of helpful and historical links for Ethiopia, Eritrea, Djibouti, Somaliland and Somalia.

All Africa (www.allafrica.com) This site collates daily news and helpfully sorts it into country profiles.

Asmera (www.asmera.nl) A comprehensive site on Eritrea with lots of tourist information, compiled by an individual.

CyberEthiopia (www.cyberethiopia.com) Like an Ethiopian Yahoo!, CyberEthiopia has quite useful information categorised into different sections.

Eritrean Beauty (www.eritreanbeauty.com) Information on all the ethnic groups in Eritrea, with numerous photos.

LonelyPlanet.com (www.lonelyplanet.com) Includes summarised information on travelling to Ethiopia, Eritrea and Djibouti, the Thorn Tree bulletin board, travel news and helpful web links.

Itineraries

CLASSIC ROUTES

ETHIOPIA'S HISTORICAL CIRCUIT

Three to five weeks by road
(10 to 20 days by plane)

After a few days revelling **Addis Ababa's** (p75) chaos, head north to bustling palm-fringed **Bahir Dar** (p112) for a day. Spend the next day at **Lake Tana** (p115) exploring some of the lake's centuries-old island monasteries.

Next wander the extensive ruins of crenulated 17th-century castles in **Gonder** (p118). Looming 100km north, the **Simien Mountains** (p125) are home to easily visible wildlife, and days of East Africa's best trekking.

Take the long road north to **Aksum** (p131), where pre-Christian tombs underlie splendid 1800-year-old stelae (obelisks). After two days, wrangle up a 4WD and venture to the 3000-year-old ruins of Ethiopia's first capital, **Yeha** (p143), and to the cliff-top monastery of **Debre Damo** (p144).

If you didn't get your fill of heights at Debre Damo, head south and search out Tigray's precarious and stunning **rock-hewn churches** (p147).

After a short stop south in **Mekele** (p151) to view its moving museums, visit **Lalibela** (p155). Its 11 astounding rock-hewn churches and myriad of tunnels have poignantly frozen 12th- and 13th-century Ethiopia in stone. After three or so days here, it's back to Addis Ababa.

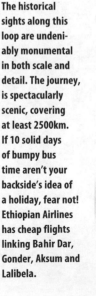

The historical sights along this loop are undeniably monumental in both scale and detail. The journey, is spectacularly scenic, covering at least 2500km. If 10 solid days of bumpy bus time aren't your backside's idea of a holiday, fear not! Ethiopian Airlines has cheap flights linking Bahir Dar, Gonder, Aksum and Lalibela.

FROM HIGH TO LOW: ESSENTIAL ERITREA

Ten days to two weeks/ Asmara to Massawa

Start by spending two full days in fascinating **Asmara** (p308), visiting its mind-blowing collection of colonial-era architectural wonders – not to mention its tantalising pastry shops. Beeline for the **National Museum** (p315) in preparation for Eritrea's archaeological sites and take a day trip to the **Debre Bizen Monastery** (p327), which offers breathtaking views.

Next, push onto **Keren** (p328), whose attractive architecture, active markets and cheerful ambience deserves a day or two. Back to Asmara, and it's time to head south. You might make a half-day stop in **Dekemhare** (p332) to recharge the batteries before spending the night in **Adi Keyh** (p333). The next day, explore the poignant ruins of **Qohaito** (p333) and expand your knowledge of Eritrea's mysterious past.

From Qohaito it's a short hop to **Senafe** (p334), where you can immerse yourself in the nearby ancient ruins of **Metera** (p336), one of Eritrea's most significant archaeological sites.

If it's not off limits to travellers (enquire in Asmara), it's well worth making an excursion to the **Monastery of Debre Libanos** (p335). It offers stunning scenery of dramatic peaks and valleys and proffers views south into Ethiopia. Having sampled the highlands' delights, head north to Asmara before proceeding east. Take the big plunge to **Massawa** (p339), on the coast, and mosey around Zanzibar-esque **Massawa Island** (p340).

Fancy a dip? Massawa is a jumping-off point for the pristine **Dahlak Islands** (p346), which are blessed with good diving and snorkelling opportunities. When you've run out of sunscreen, it's time to return to the highlands!

This is a great trip for any first-time visitor to Eritrea, taking in the country's star attractions. It's a busy but satisfying 800km journey that combines various landscapes, atmospheres and even climates. Starting off in Asmara the trip moves on through captivating sights in the highlands and ends with a sojourn in Massawa, right on the coast.

ROADS LESS TRAVELLED

LAKES, MOUNTAINS & MURSI: SOUTHERN ETHIOPIA

Two and a half to five weeks/
AddisAbaba to Omo Valley

Do what few others do in Ethiopia and point the compass south. En route from Addis Ababa to **Lake Ziway** (p171), and its hippos, birdlife and island monasteries, stop at **Tiya** (p171), a World Heritage site and one of southern Ethiopia's most important stelae fields. More impressive birdlife is found just south at **Lake Langano** (p172) and **Lake Abiata-Shala National Park** (p173).

Next it's a night lakeside at **Awasa** (p176) or up in the lush hills at **Wondo Genet** (p175), before travelling east to **Dodola** (p179) for some multiday mountain horse treks, or further east to the bounty of **Bale Mountains National Park** (p181). Treks here offer unparalleled viewing of the endangered Ethiopian wolf and mountain nyala, and countless rare bird species.

Backtrack west through Shashemene before looping south to the southern Rift Valley lakes and **Arba Minch** (p196), where gargantuan crocodiles, zebras and the odd Abyssinian lion roam nearby **Nechisar National Park** (p199).

Slip south and visit intriguing **Konso villages** (p202) around **Konso** (p201), at the gateway to the cultural riches of the **Lower Omo Valley** (p204).

Foray on the back of a truck into Hamer and bull-jumping territory at **Turmi** (p208) and into Galeb territory at **Omorate** (p209), which sits on the banks of the mighty Omo River itself. It's north from here for a respite from remoteness in **Jinka** (p202). Those with 4WDs can also descend into **Mago National Park** (p210), the home of the famed Mursi lip-stretchers.

This journey south from Addis Ababa, though the Rift Valley lakes, the Bale Mountains, Arba Minch and the Lower Omo Valley, offers some of Africa's most unique peoples and Ethiopia's best wildlife. This 1500km foray is a tough slog, and takes almost twice as long using public transport. A cheap flight from Jinka saves a two-day drive back to Addis Ababa.

ADDIS ABABA
Tiya
Lake Ziway
Lake Langano
Lake Abiata-Shala National Park
Dodola
Bale Mountains National Park
Awasa
Wondo Genet
Arba Minch
Mago National Park
Jinka
Nechisar National Park
Konso
Turmi
Omorate

DANKALIA DESOLATION   Three to five days/Asmara to Assab...or Djibouti

Starting off from **Asmara** (p308), you could either take the rickety old bus that plies the route three times weekly between the capital and Assab (ouch!) or hire a 4WD with a driver; for more freedom of movement the latter is strongly recommended. This trip will also take you through the heart of Afar country, which will yield fascinating encounters with Afar herders.

Once you've had your fill of Asmara's joys, forge east to **Massawa** (p339). Allow at least a day to visit **Massawa Island** (p340) and to stock up for your journey off the beaten track. From here you'll be leaving the asphalt on a bumpy jaunt due south. First you'll cross the town of **Foro** (p349), a base for visiting the modest, ancient Aksumite ruins of **Adulis** (p349). Continue due south to the little fishing village of **Irafayle** (p350), where Afar territory begins. The more you progress to the south, the more hauntingly bleak the landscape becomes. Take a detour to the **Buri Peninsula** (p350), where you can spot gazelles and baboons. Next is **Marsa Fatma** (p350), then **Thio** (p350), another ramshackle fishing village where you can overnight. Make it to **Edi** (p350), where you can slake your thirst before exploring the **Bay of Beraesoli** (p351) and its stunning lunar landscape. When you reach **Beylul** (p351), it's customary to share a cup of *doma* (palm wine) with Afar herders before setting off for **Assab** (p351). In Assab, at the southern extremity of the desolate Dankalia, treat yourself to a comfy room in a good hotel – you've earned it. Then decide whether Assab is your final destination or just another staging post on the way to Obock (Djibouti)...

For those with a strong sense of exploration, this itinerary is seventh heaven: you'll cross the Horn's far-flung corners and reach some of the most Inhospitable areas in the world. Be prepared for an exciting, albeit arduous, 750km ride that can take anything from three to five days – or even more, if you find the lure of Dankalia irresistible.

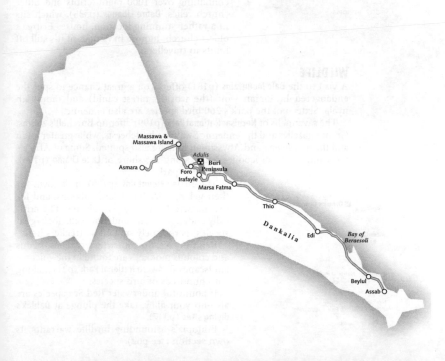

TAILORED TRIPS

ORTHODOX MONASTERIES

Ethiopian Orthodox monasteries hold some of the region's greatest treasures, whether they're brilliant illuminated manuscripts, precious crosses or vibrant murals. In most cases the monks are happy to show them off.

Unfortunately women are forbidden to visit several monasteries.

Surrounded by cliffs, atop an *amba* (flat-topped mountain), is the celebrated **Debre Damo** (p144). If you like heights, getting here is half the fun.

The **monasteries of Lake Tana** (p115) are some of the most impressive and historic. Of them, Kebran Gabriel, Ura Kidane Meret, Dega Estefanos and Narga Selassie are the most atmospheric and rich in church treasures. Although there's little to see now, Lake Tana's Tana Cherkos monastery was rumoured to house the Ark of the Covenant for over 800 years.

Debre Tsion (p171), an island monastery on Lake Ziway, is also thought to have housed the Ark in the 9th century.

Other monasteries of note in Ethiopia are **Abba Pentalewon** (p139) and **Abba Liqanos** (p139) near Aksum, **Abba Garima** (p143) near Adwa, **Ashetan Maryam** (p164) near Lalibela and **Mt Zuqualla Maryam** (p216) near Debre Zeyit.

In Eritrea, **Debre Bizen** (p327) is renowned for containing over 1000 manuscripts and other church relics. **Debre Libanos** (p335), which sits in a rather stunning location, houses Eritrea's oldest church; inquire in Asmara if it's still off limits to travellers.

Map labels:
ERITREA
Debre Bizen
Abba Pentalewon; Abba Liqanos
Debre Libanos
Debre Damo
Abba Garima
Monasteries of Lake Tana
Ashetan Maryam
Mt Zuqualla Maryam
Debre Tsion
ETHIOPIA

WILDLIFE

A visit to the **Bale Mountains** (p181) offers you a great chance to spot the endangered Ethiopian wolf (the world's rarest canid) and mountain nyala. Sixteen of the park's 260 bird species are also endemic.

The savannahs of **Nechisar National Park** (p199) offer up Burchell's zebras, Grant's gazelles and the endemic Swayne's hartebeests, while greater kudu and the odd hyena and Abyssinian lion are also spotted. Some of Africa's most impressive crocodiles bathe along the shore of **Lake Chamo** (p196), within the park.

The **Simien Mountains** (p125) are known for their gelada 'bleeding heart' baboons, and for the massive Lammergeyer vultures. The critically endangered and endemic walia ibex (goat species) is routinely spotted by trekkers here.

Beisa oryxes, Soemmering's gazelles, kudus and colobus monkeys are found in the volcanic landscapes of **Awash National Park** (p217), along with hundreds of bird species.

If bountiful underwater Red Sea species are also up your alley, take the plunge at **Dahlak's diving sites** (p347).

Ethiopia's astounding birdlife warrants its own section (see p62).

Map labels:
ERITREA
Dahlak's Diving Sites
Simien Mountains
Awash National Park
ETHIOPIA
Nechisar National Park
Bale Mountains
Lake Chamo

Ethiopia

ARIADNE VAN ZANDBERGEN

ETHIOPIA

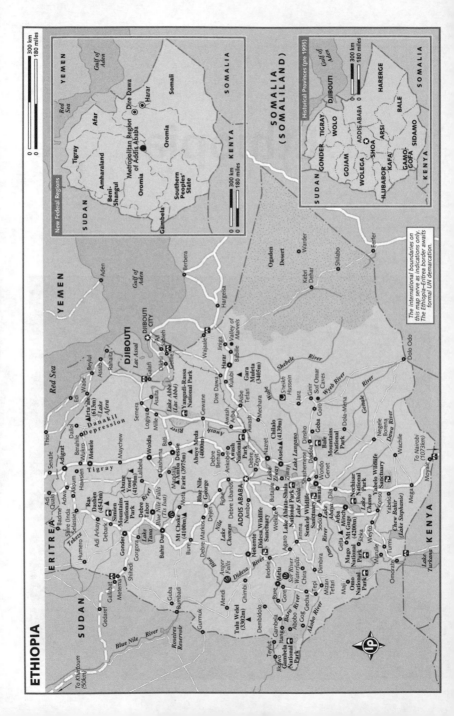

The international boundaries on this map serve as indications only. The Ethiopia-Eritrea border awaits formal UN demarcation.

Snapshot Ethiopia

Political change is once again in the Ethiopian air. The May 2005 elections showed substantial cracks in public support for Prime Minister Meles Zenawi's Ethiopian People's Revolutionary Democratic Front (EPRDF) party, which has had a stranglehold on Ethiopian government since 1991. Although Zenawi still maintains power, he must now face a country divided. Election results show a rift between rural areas that back the EPRDF, and the urban areas that back opposition parties like the Coalition for Unity and Democracy (CUD). Zenawi's strict postelection reprisals on opposition party politicians and members of the public protesting the election results, due to EU reported election irregularities, sent shock waves through the country (see p40). These controversial elections and the subsequent fallout will likely continue to be *the* hot topic among Ethiopians until they next head to the polls in 2010.

Unless you've had your head in the proverbial sand, you'll have heard of the continuing border squabbles between Ethiopia and Eritrea. Oh, you've just come from the Sahara and have actually had your head in the sand? Well, there have been no military clashes since 2000, but the continued failure to officially demarcate the border means tensions are still high. In late 2005 large military movements on both sides of the border caused international concern and the UN mission observing the no-man's-land between the nations almost pulled out before tempers finally cooled. Despite the borderland in question being barren and holding no economic, religious or historical value, many Ethiopians are passionate about getting back the land awarded to Eritrea by the 2002 border commission. Much of the anti-Eritrea sentiment is fuelled by the economic hardship faced by Ethiopia since the 1998–2000 war (see p39).

Ethiopia's inconsistent economy suffers from two major and persistent weaknesses: food insecurity and a near total dependency on coffee for foreign-exchange earnings. Agriculture provides the livelihood for 85% of Ethiopians, but drought, pests and severe soil erosion due to deforestation (see p67) continue to keep agricultural yields erratic and low. Horticulture, namely the production of fresh flowers, may soon blossom (excuse the pun). It's already a US$360-million industry in Kenya and with Kenya losing its favourable developing nation trade status with the EU in 2007, Ethiopia may take over the reigns.

Tourism is also thought to have great growth potential for Ethiopia's economy and foreign investment is now being encouraged. However, hyped media reports of famines, tensions with Eritrea and the fallout from the last election continue to hinder growth in this sector.

When Ethiopians aren't discussing politics, money or religion, they'll more than likely be talking about sports. This is one subject of conversation that you should definitely feel free to jump into. They're most passionate about running (p47), and so they should be! Their men and women are completely dominating the middle distance races these days. Like mobile phones, satellite TVs have proliferated in urban Ethiopian society of late and spawned a legion of mad Manchester United and Arsenal football fans. They must love one or the other – loving an Italian team isn't an option!

FAST FACTS

Population: 73 million

Life expectancy: 48.83 years

GDP per capita: US$800

Biggest annual exports: coffee (US$335 million) and *chat* (US$99 million)

Inflation: 6%

Average number of plaits in the Tigrayan *shoruba* hairstyle: 38

Average time taken for coffee ceremony: 28.3 minutes

Number of world records broken by Ethiopian runners: 31

24,748 days: length of time Italy took to return Aksum's obelisk.

US$7.7 million: Italy's cost of returning the obelisk (inflation's a bitch!)

History

From the ancient Aksumite civilisation's obelisks and the fascinating architectural wonders of medieval Lalibela to the castles of Gonder and the communist monuments of the Derg, Ethiopia wears its history on its sleeve. And what a history it is.

CRADLE OF HUMANITY?

In palaeoanthropology, where years are measured in tenths of millions, 40 years is less than a blink of an eye. However, 40 years worth of palaeoanthropological study can rock the very foundations of human history.

After Richard Leakey's discovery of skull 1470 near Kenya's Lake Turkana in 1972, which proved *Homo habilis* (the direct ancestor of *Homo sapiens*) had lived alongside *Australopithecus africanus* and therefore couldn't have evolved from them, the search was on for a new species that had branched into the genera *Homo* and *Australopithecus*, a species that would likely be Darwin's 'missing link'.

On 30 November 1974 Lucy was discovered in a dried-up lake near Hadar in Ethiopia's northeast. She was a new species, *A. afarensis,* and she miraculously walked on two legs 3.2 million years ago. Lucy's bipedal (upright walking) anatomy also shattered previous theories that hypothesised our ancestors only started walking upright after evolving larger brains. Lucy, the oldest and most complete hominid ever found, was famous and Ethiopia was tipped to claim the prize as the cradle of humanity.

After further finds in Ethiopia, like the 1992 discovery of the 4.4-million-year-old *A. ramidus,* whose foot bones hinted at bipedism, the ink on Ethiopia's claim was almost dry. However recent CT scans on a six-million-year-old hominid skeleton *(Orrorin tugenensis)* found in Kenya in 2001, and computer aided reconstruction of a six- to seven-million-year-old skull *(Sahelanthropus tchadensis)* in Chad seem to suggest that Lucy and *A. ramidus* may not be part of the direct line of human evolution, but rather a lateral branch of it. This is undoubtedly highly controversial – visit Lucy in Addis Ababa's National Museum (p85) and show her some support!

Regardless of what still lies beneath the soil of Ethiopia, Kenya or Chad, it's clear to the palaeoanthropologists of today that human life as we know it started in this region of Africa. Although, 40 more years of palaeoanthropology may turn things upside down, again. All it takes is the blink of an eye.

> Lucy was named after the Beatles' song *Lucy in the Sky with Diamonds*. It was playing in the archaeologists' camp when she was discovered.

LAND OF PUNT

Though this period is shrouded in darkness, Ethiopia and Eritrea are believed to have formed part of the ancient Land of Punt (p296), an area that attracted the trading ships of the Egyptian Pharaohs for millennia.

Many valuable commodities such as gold, myrrh, ivory and slaves issued from the interior of the region and were exported from the coast.

It's thought the northern coastal region saw much migration from surrounding areas, and by 2000 BC it had established strong contacts with the inhabitants of southern Arabia.

3.2 million years ago	3500–2000 BC
Lucy collapses and awaits discovery and fame 3.2 million years down the line	As part of the Land of the Punt, natural resources and slaves are reaped from Ethiopia's interior and shipped abroad

PRE-AKSUMITE CIVILISATION

The cultural significance of the southern Arabian and the East African cultures mixing was enormous. One consequence was the emergence of a number of Afro-Asiatic languages, including Ge'ez which laid the foundation for modern Amharic (much like Latin did for Italian). Amazingly, Ge'ez script is still read by many Christian priests in Ethiopia and Eritrea.

Most significant was the rise of a remarkable civilisation in Africa's Horn in 1500 BC. The fact that the influence of southern Arabia was so clear (the Sabaean script and in the worship of Sabaean gods), that the civilisation appeared to mushroom overnight and was very localised, and that it benefited from specialist crafts, skills and technologies previously unknown in the area, led many scholars to believe that the civilisation was spawned by Arabian settlers and not Africans.

However, scholars of late argue with great conviction that this civilisation was indeed African and while undoubtedly influenced by Sabaean ideas, it developed from within from local effort and initiative. If proved correct, histories of the Horn will have to be completely rewritten.

Whatever the origin, the civilisation was a very important one. The most famous relic of the times is the extraordinary stone 'temple' of Yeha (p143).

KINGDOM OF AKSUM

The Aksumite kingdom, which grew to rank among the most powerful kingdoms of the ancient world, was the next civilisation to rise in present-day Ethiopia. The first written evidence of its existence (*Periplus of the Erythraean Sea*, written by a Greek-speaking Egyptian sailor) was from the 1st century AD, but by this point its realm of influence was wide, suggesting it rose to prominence much earlier. New archaeological evidence hints it may have emerged as early as 400 BC.

Aksum, its capital, is thought to have owed its importance to its position, lying at an important commercial crossroads. To the northwest lay Egypt, and to the west, near the present-day Sudanese border, were the rich, gold-producing lowlands. To the northeast, in present-day Eritrea, was the Aksumite port of Adulis, positioned at the crux of an extensive trading route. Exports included frankincense, grain, animal skins, rhino horn, apes and particularly ivory (tens of thousands of elephants were reported to roam the region). Imports of dyed cloaks, cheap unlined coats, glassware, and iron for making spears, swords and axes flowed in from Egypt, Arabia and India. Syrian and Italian wine and olive oil (then considered a luxury) were also imported, as was much gold and silver plate for the king. The flourishing trade allowed the Aksumite kingdom to thrive.

Aksum also benefited from its well-watered agricultural lands, which were further exploited by the use of well-designed dams, wells and reservoirs.

During its heyday between the 3rd and 6th centuries, the Aksumite kingdom stretched into large parts of southern Arabia, and west into the Sudanese Nile Valley. Aksumite society was rich, well organised, and technically and artistically advanced. During this era, an unparalleled coinage in bronze, silver and gold was produced and extraordinary

> According to the Greek poet Homer (800 BC), the Greek gods, including Zeus himself, visited Ethiopia. Homer refers to the people as 'blameless Ethiopians'.

1500–400 BC	400 BC–AD 200
An Arabian-influenced civilisation rises in northern Ethiopia; the country's first capital, Yeha, is founded	The great Aksumite kingdom is formed and thrives on Red Sea trade and rich natural resources

monuments were built, all of which are visible in Aksum today (see p131). The kingdom also exerted the greatest influence of all on the future of Ethiopia: it introduced Christianity.

Those intrigued by the ancient civilisation of Aksum should pick up Professor David W Phillipson's *Ancient Ethiopia*. It's excellent and is an easy read.

THE COMING OF CHRISTIANITY

The Ethiopian church claims that Christianity first reached Aksum at the time of the apostles. According to the Byzantine ecclesiastical historian Rufinus, it arrived on Ethiopian shores by accident rather than by design, when a Christian merchant from Syria, returning from a long voyage to India with his two young students, stopped for water on Africa's coast.

What's certain is that Christianity didn't become the state religion until around the beginning of the 4th century. King Ezana's stone inscription (p139) makes reference to Christ, and his famous coins bear the Christian Cross – the world's first to do so.

The end of the 5th century AD brought the famous Nine Saints, a group of Greek-speaking missionaries who established well-known monasteries in the north of the country, including Debre Damo (p144). At this time, the Bible was first translated from Greek into Ge'ez.

Christianity shaped not just Ethiopia's spiritual and intellectual life, but also its cultural and social life, including its art and literature. Today almost half of Ethiopia's population is Orthodox Christian.

THE COMING OF ISLAM & THE DEMISE OF AKSUM

According to Muslim tradition, the Prophet Mohammed was nursed by an Ethiopian woman. Later, the Muslim Hadith (collection of traditions about Mohammed's life) recounts that Mohammed sent some of his followers to Negash in AD 615, to avoid persecution in Arabia.

Ethiopia was named by the Greeks, who saw the country as a far-off realm, populated by remarkable people and extraordinary animals. It means 'Land of the Burnt Faces'.

The refugees were shown hospitality and, it's said, Aksum's Christian King Armah liked them so much that he hoped they'd stay. However, when things calmed in Arabia, most refugees returned. However, Negash continues to be a crucial pilgrimage point for Ethiopia's Muslims (see p147).

Good relations between the two religions continued until at least King Armah's death. Thereafter, as the Arabs and Islam rose to prominence on the opposite side of the Red Sea, trade slowly shifted away from Christian Aksum and it eventually became isolated. The economy slumped, coins ceased to be minted and hard times set in. Aksum's commercial domination of the region was over (see the boxed text, p132).

After Aksum's decline around 700 AD, Ethiopia endured what is commonly known as its 'dark age'. Compared with the archaeological bounties left behind by the Aksumite kingdom and the architectural wonders of the Zagwe four centuries later in Lalibela, this period is almost completely devoid of history.

THE ZAGWE DYNASTY

The 12th century witnessed a new capital (Adafa) rise in the mountains of Lasta, not far from present day Lalibela. It was established under a new power: the Zagwe dynasty.

Although the Zagwe dynasty reigned from around AD 1137 to 1270, and left the astonishing rock-hewn churches of Lalibela for you to see today (see p155), this period is still shrouded in mystery. Seemingly, no

200–500	300–325
The Aksumite kingdom reaches its apogee; magnificent monuments are raised and tremendous tombs are sunk	Aksum's Great Stele collapses; the catastrophic event signals the end of paganism and the birth of Christianity in Ethiopia

---

ITINERANT COURTS

During the Ethiopian Middle Ages, the business of most monarchs consisted of waging wars, collecting taxes and inspecting the royal domains.

Obliged to travel continuously throughout their far-flung empire, the kings led a perpetually nomadic existence. And with the rulers went their armies, courtiers and servants; the judges, prison officers and priests; the merchants, prostitutes and a whole entourage of artisans: butchers and bakers, chefs, tailors and blacksmiths. The camps could spread over 20km; for transportation up to 100,000 mules were required.

The retinue was so vast that it rapidly exhausted the resources of the location. Four months was usually the maximum possible length of stay, and 10 years had to pass before the spot could be revisited.

The peasantry were said to dread the royal visits as they dreaded the swarms of locusts. In both cases, everything that lay in the path of the intruders was consumed.

---

stones were inscribed, no chronicles written, no coins minted, and no accounts of the dynasty by foreign travellers have survived.

It's not certain what brought the Zagwe dynasty to an end; it was likely a combination of infighting within the ruling dynasty and local opposition from the clergy. In 1270 the dynasty was overthrown by Yekuno Amlak; political power shifted south to the historical province of Shoa.

THE ETHIOPIAN MIDDLE AGES

Yekuno Amlak, claiming to be a descendant of King Solomon and Queen Sheba, established the 'Solomonic dynasty' that would reign for the next 500 years. His rule would also ring in the start of what's known as the Ethiopian Middle Ages, a period more documented than any other in the nation's past.

With its all-powerful monarchy and influential clergy, the Middle Ages were a continuation of the past. However, unlike the past, the kingdom's capitals were itinerant and were little more than vast, moving military camps. There was no longer minted money and trade was conducted by barter with pieces of iron, cloth or salt.

Culturally, the period was important for the significant output of Ge'ez literature, including the nation's epic, the *Kebra Negast* (p56). It was also at this time that contacts with European Christendom began to increase. With the rising threat of well-equipped Muslim armies in the East, Europe was seen as a Christian superpower.

Europe, for its part, dreamed of winning back Jerusalem from the 'Saracens', and realised the important strategic position occupied by Ethiopia. At the time, it was almost the only Christian kingdom outside Europe. Ethiopia even became a candidate for the location of legendary Prester John, an immensely wealthy and powerful Christian monarch believed to reign in a far-off land in the East. It was hoped that one day, he'd join Europe's kings in a mighty crusade against the infidel.

In the early 15th century, the first European embassy arrived in Ethiopia, sent by the famous French aristocrat Duc de Berry. Ethiopians in their turn began to travel to Europe, particularly to Rome, where many joined churches already established there.

Check out J Spencer Trimingham's *Islam in Ethiopia* for an insight into Ethiopia's second religion.

Prophet Mohammed's daughter and successor flee persecution in Arabia and eventually introduce Islam to Ethiopia at Negash	The Aksumites lose their hold on Red Sea trade and the kingdom collapses

THE MUSLIM–CHRISTIAN WARS

The first decades of the 16th century were plagued by some of the most costly, bloody and wasteful fighting in Ethiopian history, in which the entire empire and its culture came close to being wiped out.

From the 13th century, relations with the Muslim Ethiopian emirates of Ifat and Adal were showing signs of strain. With the increasing competition for control of the valuable trade routes connecting the Ethiopian highlands with the Red Sea, tension was growing.

In the 1490s animosities came to a head. After establishing himself at the port of Zeila in present-day Somalia, a skilled and charismatic Muslim named Mahfuz declared a jihad against Christian Ethiopia and made 25 annual raids into the highlands of Shoa. Emperor Lebna Dengel finally halted Mahfuz's incursions, but not before he had carried off huge numbers of Ethiopian slaves and cattle.

An even more legendary figure was Ahmed Ibn Ibrahim al Ghazi, nicknamed 'Ahmed Gragn the Left-Handed'. After overthrowing Sultan Abu Bakr of Harar, Ahmed declared his intention to continue the jihad of Mahfuz. Carrying out several raids into Ethiopian territory, he managed in March 1529 to defeat Emperor Lebna Dengel himself.

Ahmed then embarked on the conquest of all of Christian Ethiopia. Well supplied with firearms from Ottoman Zeila and southern Arabia (which he pragmatically exchanged for captured Christian slaves), the Muslim leader had, by 1532, overrun almost all of eastern and southern Ethiopia.

In 1535 the Emperor Lebna Dengel appealed in desperation to the Portuguese, who were already active in the region. In 1541 an army of 400 well-armed musketeers arrived in Massawa (in present-day Eritrea), led by Dom Christovão da Gama, son of the famous mariner Vasco da Gama. They met Ahmed near Lake Tana, where he quickly routed them before lopping off the young and foolhardy head of Dom Christovão.

In 1543 the new Ethiopian emperor, Galawdewos, and his amassed army joined ranks with the surviving Portuguese force and met Ahmed at Wayna Daga in the west. This time, the Christians' huge numbers proved too powerful and Ahmed was killed, and his followers fled. However, Muslim raids led by Ahmed's wife and nephew continued in the years following. In infuriation, and without the back-up of his main army, Galawdewos attacked the rich trading Muslim city of Harar in 1559. He met the same fate as Dom Christovão, and his head was paraded around Harar on a stick.

The Muslim–Christian wars were terribly costly. Thousands of people lost their lives, the Christian monarchy was nearly wiped out, and the once mighty Muslim state of Adal lay in ruins. Many of the most beautiful churches and monasteries in Ethiopia, along with their precious manuscripts, church relics and regalia, lay in ashes.

OROMO MIGRATIONS & THE JESUITS

A new threat to the Ethiopian empire arose in the mid-16th century, filling the power vacuum left behind by the weakened Muslims. The nomadic pastoralists and warrior horsemen of the Oromos (known to the Amharas as Gallas, a pejorative term) began a great migration northwards from what's now Kenya.

Mahfuz timed his annual raids to take advantage of Christian Ethiopia's weakened state during their 55-day-long fast before Fasika (Orthodox Easter).

1137–1270	1270
The Zagwe dynasty rises from Ethiopia's 'dark ages' and produces the astounding rock-hewn churches of Lalibela	Yekuno Amlak establishes the 'Solomonic dynasty' and Ethiopia enters its well-documented Middle Ages

For the next 200 years intermittent armed conflict raged between the empire and the Oromos. For the empire, the Oromo expansion meant loss of territory and vital tax revenue. The Oromos also challenged the old Muslim state; the old city walls seen in Harar today (see p226) were built in response to Oromo conflicts.

Early in the 17th century the Oromo threat led several Ethiopian emperors to seek an alliance with the Portuguese-backed Jesuits. Two emperors, Za-Dengel and Susenyos, even went as far as conversion to Catholicism. However, imposing Catholicism on their population provoked widespread rebellion. Za-Dengel was overthrown and, in 1629, Susenyos' draconian measures to convert his people incited civil war.

As many as 32,000 peasants are thought to have lost their lives in the bloodshed that followed, most at the hands of Susenyos' army. Eventually Susenyos backed down and the Orthodox faith was reestablished.

Susenyos' son and successor, Fasiladas, expelled the meddling Jesuits and forbade all foreigners to set foot in his empire. For nearly 130 years only one European, a French doctor Charles Poncet, was allowed to enter Ethiopia. He famously wrote about Emperor Iyasu's grandeur in *A Voyage to Ethiopia* (translation).

Though the Jesuits' interference had caused great suffering and bloodshed in Ethiopia, they left behind one useful legacy: books. Pero Pais wrote the first serious history of the country. Other writings included detailed accounts of Ethiopia's cultural, economic and social life.

With the rising Ottoman hold in the east, and the Oromo entrenchment in the south, the political authority of Shoa had become increasingly circumscribed. It was time to relocate the centre of power – again.

THE RISE & FALL OF GONDER

In 1636, following the old tradition of his forefathers, Emperor Fasiladas decided to found a new capital. However Gonder was different from its predecessors: it was to be the first permanent capital since Lalibela. Fasiladas' plan worked and Gonder flourished for well over a century.

By 17th century's close, Gonder boasted magnificent palaces, beautiful gardens and extensive plantations. It was also the site of sumptuous feasts and extravagant court pageantry, attracting visitors from around the world. Its thriving market even drew rich Muslim merchants from across the country.

Under the ample patronage of church and state, the arts and crafts flourished. Impressive churches were built, among them the famous Debre Berhan Selassie, which can be seen to this day (see p122). Outside Gonder, building projects included some remarkable churches at Lake Tana's historic monasteries (p115).

But not all was sweet in Gonder's court, and between 1706 and 1721 everyone from royal bodyguards, the clergy and nobles to ordinary citizens tried their hand at conspiracy. Assassination, plotting and intrigue became the order of the day, and the ensuing chaos reads like something out of Shakespeare's *Macbeth*. No less than three monarchs held power during this turbulent period, at least one meeting a sticky, poisonous end. Emperor Bakaffa's reign (1721–30) briefly restored stability, during

'Not all was sweet in Gonder's court... everyone from royal bodyguards... to ordinary citizens tried their hand at conspiracy.'

1490	1543
Mahfuz declares jihad on Christian Ethiopia and starts the bloody Muslim–Christian wars, the most costly in the country's history	Emperor Galawdewos, with help from the Portugal, finally defeats and kills Muslim raider Ahmend Gragn the Left-Handed

which time new palaces and churches were built, and literature and the arts once again thrived.

However, by the time of Iyasu II's death in 1755, the Gonder kingdom was back in turmoil. The provinces started to rebel. Ethnic rivalries surfaced and came to head in a power struggle between the Oromo people, who'd become increasingly absorbed into the court, and the Tigrayan ruler, Ras Mikael Sehul. Assassination and murder again followed and central government fell apart.

Between 1784 and 1855 the emperors were little more than puppets in the hands of rival feudal lords and their powerful provincial armies. The country disintegrated and civil war became the norm. After Gonder's renaissance, Ethiopia had stepped right back into the dark ages. Thankfully, much of Gonder's architectural grandeur survived and remains intact (see p118).

Ethiopian historians later referred to the time after Iyasu II's death as the period of the *masafent* (judges), after the reference in the Book of Judges 21:25 when 'every man did that which was right in his own eyes'.

EMPEROR TEWODROS

After the fallout of Gonder, Ethiopia existed only as a cluster of separate and feuding fiefdoms. That was until the mid-19th century, when a unique man dreamt of unity.

Kassa Haylu, raised in a monastery and the son of a western chief, had first been a *shifta* (bandit) after his claim to his deceased father's fief was denied. However, he eventually became a Robin Hood figure, looting the rich to give to the poor. This gained him large numbers of followers and he began to defeat the rival princes, one after another, until in 1855 he had himself crowned Emperor Tewodros.

'Kassa Haylu... became a Robin Hood figure, looting the rich to give to the poor.'

The new monarch soon began to show himself not just as a capable leader and strong ruler but as a unifier, innovator and reformer as well. He chose Maqdala, a natural fortress south of Lalibela, as his base and there he began to formulate mighty plans. He established a national army, an arms factory and a great road network, as well as implementing a major programme of land reform, promoting Amharic (the vernacular) in place of the classical written language, Ge'ez, and even attempting to abolish the slave trade.

But these reforms met with deep resentment and opposition from the land-holding clergy, the rival lords and even the common faithful. Tewodros' response, however, was ruthless and sometimes brutal. Like a tragic Shakespearean hero, the emperor suffered from an intense pride, a fanatical belief in his cause and an inflated sense of destiny. This would eventually be his downfall.

Frustrated by failed attempts to enlist European, and particularly British, support for his modernising programmes, Tewodros impetuously imprisoned some Britons attending his court. Initially successful in extracting concessions, Tewodros overplayed his hand, and it badly miscarried. In 1868 large, heavily armed British forces, backed by rival Ethiopian lords, inflicted appalling casualties on Tewodros' men, many of them armed with little more than shields and spears.

1550	1629
The Oromo migrations from the south start and plunge the country into 200 more years of intermittent armed conflict	Emperor Susenyos incites civil war by trying to force Catholicism on his people

Refusing to surrender, Tewodros played the tragic hero to the last and penned a final dramatic and bitter avowal before biting down on a pistol and pulling the trigger. The little that survived the British looting is still visible in Maqdala (p166).

Tewodros' defeat gravely weakened Ethiopia. This did not escape the watchful eyes of colonial powers, now hungry for expansion.

EMPEROR YOHANNES

In the aftermath of Tewodros' death, there arose another battle for succession. Using his weaponry gained from the British in exchange for his support of their Maqdala expedition, Kassa Mercha of Tigray rose to the fore. In 1871, at the battle of Assam, he defeated the newly crowned Emperor Tekla Giorgis.

After proclaiming himself Emperor Yohannes the following year, Kassa reigned for the next 17 years. In contrast to Tewodros, Yohannes staunchly supported the church and recognised the independence of local lords. With the latter, he struck a bargain: in exchange for keeping their kingdoms, they were obliged to recognise the emperor's overall power, and to pay taxes to his state. In this way, Yohannes secured the religious, political and financial backing of his subjects.

'But soon another power threatened: the Italians.'

Yohannes also proved himself a skilful soldier. In 1875, after the Egyptians had advanced into Ethiopia from the coastal area, Yohannes drew them into battle and resoundingly routed them at Gundat and then again at Gura in 1876. His victories not only ended any Egyptian designs on the territory, but brought much captured weaponry, turning his army into the first well-equipped force in Ethiopian history.

But soon another power threatened: the Italians. The opening of the Suez Canal in 1869 greatly increased the strategic value of the Red Sea, which again became a passageway to the East and beyond.

In 1885 the Italians arrived in Massawa (in present-day Eritrea), and soon blockaded arms to Yohannes. The failure of the British to impede the arrival of the Italians made Yohannes furious. He accused them of contravening the 1884 Hewett Treaty. Though protesting otherwise, Britain privately welcomed the Italians, both to counter French influence on the Somali coast (in present-day Djibouti), and to deter any Turkish ambitions.

Meanwhile, the Mahadists (or Dervishes) were raising their heads in the west. Dislodging the Egyptians and British, they overran Sudan before arriving in Ethiopia and eventually sacking Gonder in 1888.

Yohannes rushed to meet the Dervishes at Qallabat in 1889 but, at the close of yet another victory, he fell, mortally wounded by a sniper's bullet.

EMPEROR MENELIK

Menelik, King of Shoa since 1865, had long aspired to the imperial throne. Confined at Maqdala for 10 years by Tewodros, he was yet reportedly much influenced by his captor, and also dreamt of Ethiopia's unification and modernisation.

After his escape from Maqdala and his ascendancy in Shoa, Menelik concentrated on consolidating his own power, and embarked on an aggressive, ruthless and sometimes brutal campaign of expansion. He

1636	1706–21
Emperor Fasiladas founds Gonder, the first permanent capital since Lalibela; he also expels all Jesuits from the empire	Conspiracy abounds in Gonder and successive emperors are assassinated

Donald N Levine's imaginative *Wax & Gold* provides outstanding insight into Amharic culture, though chapter six is rather far-fetched!

occupied territories across the south, forcing various ethnic groups under his empire's yoke.

Relations with the Italians were at first good; Menelik had been seen as a potential ally against Yohannes. On Yohannes' death, the Italians recognised Menelik's claim to the throne and, in 1889, the Treaty of Wechale was signed. In exchange for granting Italy the region that was later to become Eritrea, the Italians recognised Menelik's sovereignty and gave him the right to import arms freely through Ethiopian ports.

However, a dispute over a discrepancy in the purportedly identical Amharic and Italian texts – the famous Article 17 – led to disagreement. According to the Italian version, Ethiopia was obliged to approach other foreign powers through Italy, which essentially reduced Ethiopia to a lowly Italian protectorate. Relations rapidly began to sour.

In the meantime, the Italians continued their expansion in their newly created colony of Eritrea. Soon, they were spilling into territory well beyond the confines agreed to in both treaties.

Despite the Italians' attempts to court Tigray's local chiefs, the latter chose to assist Menelik. Nevertheless, the Italians managed to defeat Ras Mangasha and his Tigrayan forces and occupied Mekele in 1895.

Provoked at last into marching north with his forces, Menelik shocked the international world by resoundingly defeating the Italians at Adwa (see the boxed text, p143). It was one of the biggest and most significant battles in African history – numbering among the very few occasions when a colonial power was defeated by a native force. To the rest of Africa, Ethiopia became a beacon of independence in a continent almost entirely enslaved by colonialism.

Menelik then set his sights on modernisation. He abandoned the Shoan capital of Ankober and soon founded Addis Ababa. During his reign, electricity and telephones were introduced, bridges, roads, schools and hospitals built, banks and industrial enterprises established.

The greatest technological achievement of the time was undoubtedly the construction of Ethiopia's railway, which eventually linked Addis Ababa to Djibouti in 1915 (see the boxed text, p220).

IYASU

Menelik managed to die a natural death in 1913. Iyasu, his raffish young grandson and nominated heir, proved to be very much a product of the 20th century. Continuing with Menelik's reforms, he also showed a 'modern' secularist, nonsectarian attitude.

The young prince built mosques as well as churches, took several Muslim as well as Christian wives, and supported the empire's peripheral populations, which had for years suffered at the oppressive hands of Amharic settlers and governors.

Iyasu and his councillors pushed through a few reforms, including improving the system of land tenure and taxation, but they faced ever-deepening opposition from the church and nobility.

Finally, after also upsetting the allied powers with his dealings with Germany, Austria and the Ottoman Empire, a pretext for his removal was found. Accused by the nobles of 'abjuring the Christian faith', the prince was deposed in 1921. Zewditu, Menelik's daughter, was proclaimed

1755	1855
Emperor Iyasu II dies and the central government in Gonder quickly collapses; Ethiopia slips back into the dark ages	Kassa Haylu outsteals, outwits and outmanoeuvres his rivals to become Emperor Tewodros; he unites a feuding Ethiopia

empress, and Ras Tafari (the son of Ras Makonnen, Menelik's cousin) was proclaimed the prince regent.

RAS TAFARI
Prince Ras Tafari boasted more experience and greater maturity than Iyasu, particularly in the field of foreign affairs. In an attempt to improve the country's international image, he succeeded in abolishing the Ethiopian slave trade.

In 1923 Tafari pulled off a major diplomatic coup by getting Ethiopia granted entry into the League of Nations. Membership firmly placed Ethiopia on the international political map, and also gave it some recourse against the grasping designs of its European, colonial neighbours.

Continuing the tradition begun by Menelik, Tafari was an advocate of reform. A modern printing press was established as well as several secondary schools and an air force. In the meantime, Tafari was steadily outmanoeuvring his rivals. In 1930 the last rebellious noble was defeated and killed in battle. A few days later the sick empress also died. Ras Tafari assumed the throne.

The 2nd edition of Bahru Zewde's widely acclaimed *A History of Modern Ethiopia 1855–1991* contains two particularly readable sections: Harlold G Marcus' *Ethiopia* and Richard Pankhurst's *The Ethiopians.*

EMPEROR HAILE SELASSIE
On 2 November 1930 Tafari was crowned Emperor Haile Selassie. The extravagant spectacle was attended by representatives from across the globe and proved a terrific public relations exercise. It even led indirectly to the establishment of a new faith (see the boxed text, p174).

The following year, Ethiopia's first written constitution was introduced. It granted the emperor virtually absolute power, his body was even declared sacred. The two-house parliament consisted of a senate, which was nominated by the emperor from among his nobles; and a chamber of deputies, which was elected from the landholders. It was thus little more than a chamber for self-interested debate.

Ever since the day of his regency, the emperor had been bringing the country under centralised rule. For the first time, the Ethiopian state was unambiguously unified.

The Emperor by Ryszard Kapuscinski offers bizarre insights into Haile Selassie's imperial court through interviews with servants and close associates of the emperor. Some historians question its authenticity though.

ITALIAN OCCUPATION
By the early 20th century Ethiopia was the only state in Africa to have survived Europe's colonial scramble. However, Ethiopia's position between the two Italian colonies of Eritrea and Somalia made her an enticing morsel. Any Italian attempt to link its two colonies would require expansion into Ethiopia. When Mussolini seized power, the inevitable happened.

From 1933, in an effort to undermine the Ethiopian state, Italian agents, well heeled with funds, were dispatched to subvert the local chiefs, as well as to stir up ethnic tensions. Britain and France, nervous of pushing Mussolini further into Hitler's camp, refrained from protests and turned a blind eye.

In 1934 a minor skirmish known as the Wal Wal incident took place between Italian and Ethiopian forces. Italy had found its pretext. Though the export of arms was banned to both countries, in Italy's case (itself a major arms manufacturer), the embargo was meaningless.

1872	1875–76
After helping the British dispose of Tewodros, Kassa Mercha wins the battle of succession and rises as Emperor Yohannes	Yohannes routes invading Egyptian forces at Gundat and Gura, thus ending their Ethiopian ambitions

Italian Invasion

On 3 October 1935 the invasion began. Italians, overwhelmingly superior in both ground and air forces, invaded Ethiopia from Eritrea. First the northern town of Aksum fell, then Mekele.

The League of Nations issued sanctions against Italy, but they proved to be little more than a slap on the wrist. If, as should have happened, the Suez Canal had been closed to the Italians, or an oil embargo put in place, the Italian advance – as Mussolini was later to admit – would have been halted within weeks. The lives of tens of thousands of innocent men, women and children would have been spared.

Campaigning

Terrified that the international community would come to its senses and impose more serious embargoes, and keen to keep Italian morale high, Il Duce pressed for a swift campaign.

Impatient with progress made, he soon replaced De Bono, his first general. Pietro Badoglio, his replacement, was authorised 'to use all means of war – I say all – both from the air and from the ground'. Implicit in the instructions was the use of mustard gas, which contravened the 1926 Geneva Convention. Also in contravention was Italy's repeated bombing of civilian targets, including Red Cross hospitals.

Despite overwhelming odds, the Ethiopians succeeded in launching a major counterattack, known as the Christmas Offensive, at the Italian position at Mekele at the end of 1935.

However, the Italians were soon on the offensive again. Backed by hundreds of planes, cannons and weapons of every type, the Italian armies swept across the country. In May 1936 Mussolini triumphantly declared: 'Ethiopia is Italian'.

Meanwhile, Emperor Haile Selassie had fled Ethiopia (some Ethiopians never forgave him for it) to present Ethiopia's cause to the world. On 30 June 1936 he made his famous speech to the League of Nations in Geneva. The league staggeringly responded by lifting the sanctions against Italy later that year. Only the USSR, USA, Haiti, Mexico and New Zealand refused to recognise Italy's conquest.

Occupation & Resistance

Soon Ethiopia, Eritrea and Somalia were merged to become the colonial territory of 'Africa Orientale Italiana' (Italian East Africa).

Hoping to create an important economic base, Italy invested heavily in their new colony. From 1936 as many as 60,000 Italian workers poured in to work on Ethiopia's infrastructure.

Ethiopia kept up a spirited resistance to Italian rule throughout its brief duration. Italy's response was famously brutal. Mussolini personally ordered all rebels to be shot, and insurgencies were put down using large-scale bombing, poison gas and machine-gunning from the air.

Ethiopian resistance reached a peak in February 1937 with an assassination attempt on the much-hated Italian viceroy, Graziani. In reprisal, the Fascists spent three days shooting, beheading or disembowelling several thousand innocent people in the capital. Addis Ababa's poignant Yekatit 12 monument (p87) stands in honour of those slaughtered.

It wasn't until 1996 that the Italian Ministry of Defence finally admitted to the use of mustard gas in this war.

1889	1896
Yohannes' successor, Emperor Menelik, grants Italy the region that later becomes Eritrea in exchange for the right to import arms	Tired of Italy's expanding ways, Emperor Menelik stuns the world by thrashing the Italian army in the Battle of Adwa

The 'patriot's movement' (the resistance fighters) was mainly based in the historical provinces of Shoa, Gonder and Gojam, but drew support from all parts of the country; many fighters were women. Small underground movements worked in Addis Ababa and other towns; its members were known as *wist arbagna* (insider patriots).

Graziani's response was simple: 'Eliminate them, eliminate them, eliminate them' (a statement that uncannily echoes Kurtz' 'Exterminate all the brutes' in Conrad's *Heart of Darkness*). But Ethiopian resolve stiffened and resistance grew. Although in control of major towns, Italy never succeeded in conquering the whole country.

The outbreak of WWII, particularly Italy's declaration of war against Britain in 1940, dramatically changed the course of events. Britain at last reversed its policy of tacit support of Italy's East African expansion and initially offered Ethiopia assistance on the Sudan–Ethiopia border. Later, in early 1941, Britain launched three major attacks.

Though not then widely recognised, the Ethiopian patriots played a major role before, during and after the liberation campaign, which ended on 5 May 1941 when the emperor and his men entered Addis Ababa.

'The outbreak of WWII, particularly Italy's declaration of war against Britain, dramatically changed the course of events.'

POSTLIBERATION ETHIOPIA & THE DERG

The British, who'd entered Ethiopia as liberators, initially seemed to have simply replaced Italy as occupiers. However, Anglo-Ethiopian treaties in 1942 and 1944 eventually marked Ethiopia's resumption of independence.

The 1940s and '50s saw much postwar reconstruction, including (with US assistance) the establishment of a new government bank, a national currency, and the country's first national airline, Ethiopian Airlines.

New schools were developed and, in 1950, the country's first institution of higher education was established: the University College of Addis Ababa (now Addis Ababa University).

In 1955 the Revised Ethiopian Constitution was introduced. Although for the first time the legislature included an elected chamber of deputies, the government remained autocratic and the emperor continued to hold all power.

Ethiopia's long-standing independence, untarnished but for the brief Italian occupation, also gave it a new-found diplomatic authority vis-à-vis other African states. In 1962 Addis Ababa became the headquarters of the Organisation of African Unity (OAU) and, in 1958, of the UN Economic Commission for Africa (ECA).

Discontent

Despite modernisation, the pace of development was slow and dissatisfaction with it, and with the emperor's autocratic rule, began to grow. Finally, taking advantage of a state visit to Brazil in December 1960, the emperor's imperial bodyguard staged a coup d'etat. Though put down by the army and air force, it signalled the beginning of the end of imperial rule in Ethiopia.

Discontent simmered among the students too, who protested in particular against land tenure, corruption and the appalling famine of 1972–74 in which an estimated 200,000 peasants died.

1915	1930
The Djibouti–Addis Ababa rail line is completed, expanding Ethiopian trade and ushering in rapid development of Addis Ababa	After years of careful posturing, Ras Tafari is crowned as Emperor Haile Selassie and dubbed the Chosen One of God

The emperor, now an old man in his eighties, seemed more preoccupied with foreign affairs than with internal ones. Additionally, his government was slow and half-hearted in its attempts at reform.

Meanwhile, international relations had also been deteriorating. In 1962 Ethiopia abrogated the UN-sponsored federation with Eritrea and unilaterally annexed the Eritrean state.

Then war broke out in 1964 with Somalia over joint claims to Ethiopia's Somali-inhabited region of the Ogaden Desert.

The 1974 Revolution & the Emperor's Fall

By 1973 an increasingly powerful and radical military group had emerged. Known as the Derg (Committee), they used the media with consummate skill to undermine the authority of the emperor himself. They famously flashed striking footage of starvation from Jonathan Dimbleby's well-known BBC TV report on the Wolo famine in between clips of sumptuous palace banquets.

The result was an unprecedented wave of teacher, student and taxi strikes in Addis Ababa. Even army mutinies began to be reported. At crisis point, the prime minister and his cabinet resigned and a new one was appointed with the mandate to carry out far-reaching constitutional reforms. But it was too late.

On 12 September 1974 the emperor was deposed, unceremoniously bundled into the back of a Volkswagen, and driven away to prison. Ministers, nobles and close confidants of the emperor were also arrested by the Derg. The absolute power of the emperor and the divine right of rule of the century-old imperial dynasty were finished forever.

The Derg soon dissolved parliament and established the Provisional Military Administrative Council (PMAC) to rule the country.

However, bitter clashes of ideology soon splintered the Derg, culminating in the famous Death of the Sixty on 23 November 1974 when 57 high-ranking civilian and military officials were executed.

Emerging from the chaos was Colonel Mengistu Haile Mariam who rode the wave of popular opposition to Selassie's regime, as well as the Marxist-Leninist ideology of left-wing students.

And what happened to the emperor? It's thought he was murdered by Mengistu himself in August 1975. Evidence for the crime? The ring of Solomon, rumoured to have been plucked from the murdered emperor's hand, was spotted on Mengistu's middle finger.

The Socialist Experiment

On 20 December 1974 a socialist state was declared. Under the adage *Ityopya Tikdem* or 'Ethiopia First', banks, businesses and factories were nationalised as was the rural and urban land. Over 30,000 peasant associations were also set up. Raising the status of Ethiopian peasants, the campaign was initially much praised internationally, particularly by Unesco.

In the meantime, the external threats posed by Somalia and secessionist Eritrea were increasing. In July 1977 Somalia invaded Ethiopia. Thanks to the intervention of the Soviet Union, which flooded socialist Ethiopia with Soviet state-of-the-art weaponry, Somalia was beaten back. In Eritrea, however, the secessionists continued to thwart Ethiopian offensives.

> 'The absolute power of the emporer and the divine right of rule of the imperial dynasty were finished forever.'

1935	1941
Italy invades Ethiopia; illegal use of mustard gas and bombing of civilian targets kills 275,000 Ethiopians; Italy loses 4350 men	British and Ethiopian forces liberate Ethiopia from Italian occupation

Internal political debate also degenerated into violence. In 1977 the Red Terror campaign was launched to suppress all political opponents. At a conservative estimate, 100,000 people were killed and several thousand more fled abroad.

The Demise of the Derg

Red Terror only cemented the stance of those opposing the Derg. Numerous armed liberation movements arose, including those of the Afar, Oromo, Somali and particularly Tigrayan peoples. For years, with limited weaponry, they fought the military might of the Soviet-backed Derg.

In 1984–85 another appalling famine followed a drought, in which hundreds of thousands more people died. Failed government resettlement campaigns, communal farms and 'villageisation' programmes aggravated the disaster in many areas, while Mengistu's disinclination to help the province of Tigray – the worst affected region and home to the powerful Tigrayan People's Liberation Front (TPLF) – caused thousands more to die.

The various opposition groups eventually united to form the Ethiopian People's Revolutionary Democratic Front (EPRDF), which in 1989 began its historic military campaign towards Addis Ababa.

Doubly confronted by the EPRDF in Ethiopia and the Eritrean People's Liberation Front (EPLF) in Eritrea; with the fall of his allies in Eastern Europe; and with his state in financial ruin as well as his own military authority in doubt, Mengistu's time was up and he fled the country on 21 May 1991. Seven days later, the EPRDF entered Addis Ababa and the Derg were done.

Mengistu received asylum in Zimbabwe, where he remains to this day.

THE ROAD TO DEMOCRACY (1991–95)

After the war of liberation, Ethiopia and Eritrea's leaders showed a similar determination and zeal to rebuild their countries.

In July 1991 a transitional charter was endorsed, which gave the EPRDF-dominated legislature a four-year, interim rule under the executive of the TPLF leader, Meles Zenawi. First and foremost, Mengistu's failed socialist policies were abandoned, and de facto independence was granted to Eritrea.

In 1992 extensive economic reforms began and in 1995 the country was divided into new linguistic-ethnic based regions.

In August 1995 the Federal Democratic Republic of Ethiopia was proclaimed, a series of elections followed, and the constitution of the second republic was inaugurated. Meles Zenawi formed a new government. Soon the leaderships of both Ethiopia and Eritrea were hailed, in US President Clinton's words, as belonging to a 'new generation of African leaders'.

THE ETHIOPIA–ERITREA WAR

Despite being friends and having fought against the Derg side by side for over a decade, Meles Zenawi and Eritrea's President Isaias soon clashed. Amazingly, all it took for the relationship to sour was Eritrea's introduction of the nakfa currency to replace the Ethiopian birr in November 1997. Heated disputes over Eritrea's exchange-rate system followed as did bickering over bilateral trade relations.

In 1992 the body of Haile Selassie was finally discovered. It had been unceremoniously buried beneath Mengistu's old presidential office toilet.

When the Ethiopian People's Revolutionary Democratic Front (EPRDF) rolled into Addis Ababa they were navigating with photocopies of the Addis Ababa map found in Lonely Planet's Africa on a Shoestring.

1962	**1974**
Haile Selassie unilaterally annexes Eritrea; separatist Eritreans launch a bitter guerrilla war	On 12 September, Haile Selassie is unceremoniously deposed as emperor; the Derg declare a socialist state on 20 December

---

OLD DOGS & NEW TRICKS

After fighting for freedom, Ethiopia's leaders emerged well schooled in the art of warfare, but less well versed in the skills of modern government. After deciding that you can teach old dogs new tricks, 20 senior government officials enrolled for an MBA at the well-known British distance-learning institution, the Open University.

As they sat for the final exams, a certain Meles Zenawi was gripped by nerves. On spying the 'no smoking' sign in the examination room, he exclaimed, 'I've spent the last 17 years fighting a civil war but I've never been so frightened as I am now. There's no way I'll sit the exam without a fag!'

Declaiming the newly learnt philosophy of 'participative decision making', the prime minister insisted on a vote and smoking was permitted during the exam.

Fourteen of the 20 government officials graduated, and Meles – demonstrating true leadership by example – took third place out of 1400 worldwide candidates in one exam.

In May 1998 Eritrea upped the stakes by occupying the border town of Badme. Just when it seemed things couldn't get worse, Eritrea bombed a school in Mekele in June, killing 55 people, many of whom who were children. Ethiopia followed suit by bombing military installations outside Asmara, only to have Eritrea cluster-bomb civilians in Adigrat.

In February 1999 a full-scale military conflict broke out that left tens of thousands dead on both sides before it finally ceased for good in mid-2000. During this time there were fruitless peace settlements proposed by the OAU, as well as mass exportations of Eritreans from Ethiopia and Ethiopians from Eritrea.

Although Ethiopia had agreed to peace earlier, it wasn't until Ethiopia recaptured all territory and went on to occupy parts of central and western Eritrea that Eritrea finally agreed to a ceasefire. This settlement included the installation of an OAU-UN buffer zone on Eritrean soil.

In December 2000 a formal peace settlement was signed in Algiers. In April 2001 a 25km-deep demilitarised strip, which ran the length of the internationally recognised border on the Eritrean side, was set up under supervision of the UN Mission in Ethiopia and Eritrea (UNMEE).

ETHIOPIA TODAY

Today, Ethiopia is again at a poignant period in its long history. The 15 May 2005 elections have cast doubts on Ethiopia's democracy and the world's eyes are once again hoping they're not seeing a democratic free-dom fighter turning into a dictator grasping for lifelong rule.

While the election run-up and the voting polls were witness to few irregularities, there were numerous reports by EU observers about questionable vote counting at the constituency level and the announcing of the results by state-run media.

Despite pre-election polls showing that it would be the tightest race in Ethiopian history, the EPRDF officially claimed victory over the CUD on 16 May, before any results could have possibly been calculated. Election results then trickled out over the next four months, thanks to controversial repeat elections in 32 constituencies. In the end, the 'official' results showed the EPRDF won 327 of the 548 seats to maintain their majority.

1991	1995
The Derg are defeated by the rebel EPRDF and Ethiopia's experiment with communism ends	The Federal Democratic Republic of Ethiopia is proclaimed and the first fair elections are held

Despite EPRDF losing 209 of the 536 seats they had held since the 2000 election, including all 23 in Addis Ababa, these results (and news of election irregularities) were not well taken, especially in the capital.

The initial government-released results in June led to mass protests in Addis Ababa, where government troops arrested thousands of opposition party members and killed 22 unarmed civilians. Similar protests and mass strikes occurred in early November, which resulted in troops killing 46 civilians and arresting thousands more. Leaders of the CUD, as well as owners of private newspapers, were also arrested and charged with inciting the riots. The government's actions were condemned by the EU and many Western governments.

If internal political turmoil wasn't enough, relations with Eritrea also heated up in late 2005. Stating unhappiness with the UN for refusing to force Ethiopia to accept the Boundary Commission's 2002 decision to award Badme to them, Eritrea suddenly refused to allow UNMEE helicopters to observe their troop movements. Ethiopia responded to this news by amassing its forces along the border. With fear of impending war, there was talk of the UNMEE pulling out of the demilitarised strip between the two countries.

However, at the time of writing, tensions had eased slightly and the UN had just extended the UNMEE's stay. The border still has yet to be officially demarcated.

Although only published locally, *Eritrea's War* by Paul Henze delves into the 1998–2000 Ethiopia–Eritrea War.

1998
Likened to two bald men fighting over a comb, Ethiopia and Eritrea's leaders go to war over a sliver of barren wasteland

2005
After controversial 15 May elections, mass protests turn deadly when government troops fire on unarmed demonstrators

The Culture

Encompassed on all sides by the enemies of their religion, the Aethiopians slept near a thousand years, forgetful of the world, by whom they were forgotten.

Edward Gibbon, The History of the Decline and Fall of the Roman Empire, *1776–88*

THE NATIONAL PSYCHE

Religion and an intense pride in their country's past resonate loudly within most Ethiopians. To them, Ethiopia has stood out from all African nations and proved itself to be a unique world of its own – home to its own culture, language, script, calendar and history. Ethiopian Orthodox Christians and Muslims alike revel in the fact that Ethiopia was the only nation on the continent to successfully fight off colonisation.

It must be said that some of the younger Ethiopians who've grown up in the midst of high-profile international aid efforts lack the patriotism seen in older generations. Their Ethiopian pride and self-reliance has been undermined, albeit unintentionally.

The highlands have been dominated by a distinctive form of Christianity since the 4th century. Although undeniably devout and keen to dispense centuries worth of Orthodox legends and tales dating back to Aksum and the Ark of the Covenant, Christians nonetheless still cling to a surprising amount of magic and superstition.

Belief in *zar* (spirits or genies) and *buda* (the evil eye with the power to turn people into mischievous hyenas by night) is rife and as such even Christians adorn their children, from baptism, with charms or talismans around their necks to deter such spirits and terrible diseases.

Yet, this apparent religious contradiction is quite natural to Ethiopians. In a historically isolated area where rhetoric and reasoning have become highly valued and practiced, where eloquent communication and sophisticated wordplay are considered an art form and where the ability to argue a case in point while effectively sitting on the fence is now aspired to, ambiguity and complexity are as much a part of the highland peoples' psyche as it is a part of their religion.

In the past, the causes of famine have had less to do with environmental factors – Ethiopia has abundant natural resources – and more to do with economic mismanagement and inequitable and oppressive government.

LIFESTYLE

Other than religion, which undoubtedly plays the biggest role in all Ethiopians' daily life, it's agriculture and pastoralism that fills the days of well over 80% of the country's population. Everyone is involved, right down to stick- and stone-wielding four-year-old children who are handed the incredible responsibility to tend and herd the family's livestock.

With almost everyone toiling out in the fields, it's not surprising that only 38.5% (World Bank figures) of the population is literate. Since young children are needed to help with the family plots and animals, only 52% of children attend primary school. Older children are even more in demand in the workforce, which means secondary schools sadly only see only 12% of kids. If all children under 16 were forced to attend school, Ethiopia's workforce would be ravaged and almost half of the country's entire population would be attending classes.

Families are incredibly close and most Ethiopians live with their parents until marriage. After marriage, the couple usually join the household of the husband's parents. After a couple of years, they will request a plot of land from the village on which to build their own house.

Divorce is relatively easy in Ethiopia and marriage can be dissolved at the request of either party (adultery is usually given as justification). In theory, each partner retains the property he or she brought into the marriage, though sometimes allowances are made for the 'wronged' partner.

Although women continue to lag behind men economically, they are highly respected in Ethiopian society. The same can't be said for gays and lesbians. Homosexuality is severely condemned – traditionally, religiously and legally – and remains a topic of absolute taboo.

Social Graces

Mixed in with religion and survival, numerous social graces also play a large part in people's daily lives. For example, a nod or head bow accompanying greetings shows special respect, thanks or appreciation. Deference is also shown by supporting the right arm (near the elbow) with the left hand during shaking. When Ethiopians enter a room they try and shake hands with everyone (including children). If hands are dirty or wet, limp wrists are offered. They also believe it's polite to kiss babies or young children, even if you've just met them.

Kissing on the cheek is also very common among friends and relatives of either sex, but in Ethiopia, three kisses are given (right, left, right). The cheek is touched rather than kissed, though kissing noises are made. 'Long-lost' friends may kiss up to five times.

Names are also important in Ethiopia, and the exchange of first names (surnames are rarely used) is the first important stage in forming a friendship. To address someone formally, they add the following prefixes to first names: *Ato* for men, *Weizero* for married women and *Weizerit* for unmarried women.

When receiving a gift, Ethiopians extend both hands as using only one is seen as showing reluctance or ingratitude.

While this etiquette isn't likely second nature to you, learning it will help you slip a little more comfortably into the daily nature of life in Ethiopia.

WHAT'S IN A NAME?

Ethiopian Christian names usually combine a religious name with a secular name.

Common male secular names include Hagos (Joy), Mebratu (The Light) and Desta (literally 'Pleasure'; it's also a woman's name). For women, names include Ababa (Flower), Zawditu (The Crown) and Terunesh (You're Wonderful).

Some Ethiopian names have particular meanings. Names like Mitiku or Mitke (Substitute) and Kassa (Compensation) are given to children after the death of a brother or sister. Masresha, roughly meaning 'Distraction', is given after a family misfortune. Bayable means 'If He Hadn't Denied It', and is given to a bastard-child whose father refuses to acknowledge it. Tesfaye (meaning 'My Hope') is often given to a child by a poor or single mother who looks forward to her child's future success in life. Other names can mean 'That's the Last!' or 'No More!' after a long string of children.

Many Christian names are compounds made up of two names. Wolde means 'Son of', Gebre 'Servant of', Haile 'Power of', Tekle 'Plant of', Habte 'Gift of'; so that Gebre-Yesus means 'Son of Jesus', Habte-Mikael' Gift of Michael', etc.

If you're a male, you'd better like your Christian name. Why? Because it will be the surname of all your children!

GOVERNMENT

Government consists of a federation of regional states that are governed by two assemblies: the 548-member Council of Peoples' Representatives (CPR), which is the legislative arm of the federation, and the smaller 108-member Federal Council (FC), which serves as the senate, with a merely supervisory role. The president has a mainly ceremonial role. The prime minister is the head of state and appoints the 18-member cabinet.

Under the new republic's principle of 'ethnic federalism', the old provinces were divided into 11 new regions, including the city-state of Harar and the metropolitan regions of Addis Ababa and Dire Dawa. Each has its own autonomous council and holds its own elections. The regions are demarked largely along linguistic lines, and five of Ethiopia's largest ethnic groups (the Oromo, Amhara, Tigrayan, Somali and Afar) now have their own regional states.

RESPONSIBLE TRAVEL: CULTURE

The mixing of vastly different cultures can be easier said than done. To help things along, we've compiled some tips.

- Ethiopians are conservative in their dress and it's appreciated if visitors follow suit. Ethiopian women traditionally never expose their shoulders, knees, cleavage or waist in public.
- Couples (even married ones) shouldn't display affection in public.
- Never take a photo if permission is declined (see the boxed text on p266 for more information).
- Making rude noises of any sort is considered the height of bad manners by most Ethiopians. If you do breach this strict rule of social conduct, a quick *yikerta* (excuse me) is probably the best way out!
- Punctuality is important as tardiness is seen as a sign of disrespect.
- Support local businesses, initiative and skills by shopping at local markets, buying authentic crafts and giving to local charities. Don't give directly to begging children (see p258).
- Resist the temptation to buy any genuinely old artefacts, such as manuscripts, scrolls and Bibles, sold in shops and by hawkers around the country. Ethiopia has already lost a vast amount of its heritage.
- For tips on preserving Ethiopia's environment while travelling, see the boxed text on p67.
- Remember that some Africans see Westerners as arrogant and proud; a smile works wonders.

Church Etiquette

Churches in Ethiopia are very hallowed places. The following tips should be followed when visiting them.

- Always remove shoes before entering a church.
- Try and wear clothing that covers all parts of the body.
- Never try to enter the inner Holy of Holies, which is reserved strictly for the priests.
- Avoid smoking, eating or drinking in a church, or talking or laughing loudly.
- Be sensitive when taking photos.
- Resist the temptation to photograph old manuscripts in sunlight, even if the priests offer to move the manuscripts into the sun for you. Sunlight can cause great damage.
- During prayer time, try not to stray into the areas reserved for the opposite sex.
- A contribution to the upkeep of the church is greatly appreciated after a visit.

ETHIOPIAN HAIRSTYLES

Hairstyles in all societies form an important part of tribal identification. Reflecting the large number of ethnic groups, Ethiopian hairstyles are particularly diverse and colourful. Hair is cut, shaved, trimmed, plaited, braided, sculpted with clay, rubbed with mud, put in buns and tied in countless different fashions. In the Omo Valley, hairstyles are sometimes so elaborate and valued that special wooden headrests are used as pillows to preserve them.

In rural areas, the heads of children are often shaved to discourage lice. Sometimes a single topknot or tail plait is left so that 'God should have a handle with which to lift them unto Heaven', should he decide to call them!

POPULATION

Ethiopia's population just squeezed past the 73-million mark, an astounding figure considering the population was just 15 million in 1935. If the 2.5% growth rate continues, Ethiopia will be bursting with almost 120 million people in 2025. AIDS, which affects 12.6% of the urban population, will inevitably slow this future growth.

Though a trend of urbanisation is starting to emerge, 84% of the people still live in rural areas.

Although 83 languages and 200 dialects are spoken in Ethiopia, the population can be broken down into eight broad groups, which are detailed in the following pages. For details about the Lower Omo Valley's unique peoples, see p206.

The Oromo

Although most of the Oromo in the past were nomadic pastoralists, it was skilled Oromo warrior horsemen that put fear into Ethiopians when they migrated north from present-day Kenya in the mid-16th century. It was the Oromo who inspired Harar's leaders to build a wall around the city and even led Ethiopian emperors to accept Catholicism just in order to gain Portugal's military support.

Today, most are sedentary, making a living as farmers or cattle breeders. The Oromo are Muslim, Christian and animist in religion, and are known for their egalitarian society, which is based on the *gada* (age-group system). A man's life is divided into age-sets of eight years. In the fourth set (between the ages of 24 and 32), men assume the right to govern their people.

They are the largest ethnic group in the country, making up 40% of its population. Over 85% of the massive 350,000-sq-km Oromia region's population are Oromo. Many Oromo resent the Tigray-led national government and the Oromo Liberation Front (OLF) continues to lobby for separation from Ethiopia.

The Amharas

As great warriors, skilful governors and astute administrators, the Amhara have dominated the country's history, politics and society since 1270, and have imposed their own language and culture on the country. In the past this was much resented by other tribal groups, who saw it as little more than a kind of colonialism.

Amhara tend to be devoutly Christian, although there are some Muslim Amhara. They're also fanatical about their land and 90% of them are traditional tillers of the soil: they produce some of the nation's best *tef* (endemic cereal grain used for *the* national staple, *injera*).

Making up 21% of Ethiopia's population, they're the second-largest ethnic group. Over 90% of Amharaland region's people are Amhara.

The Tigrayans

Every Ethiopian emperor (bar one) since Yekuno Amlak established the Solomonic Dynasty in 1270 has been Amhara. Yohannes (r 1872–89), who was Tigrayan, is the only exception.

Much like the Amharas, the Tigrayans are fiercely independent and zealously attached to their land. They disdain all manual labour with the single exception of agriculture – DIY is a notion completely lost on the average Tigrayan!

Most live in the Tigray region, where both Christianity and Islam were introduced to Ethiopia. Amazingly 95% of Tigrayans are Orthodox Christian, and most devoutly so. Tigrayans are Ethiopia's third-largest ethnic group, comprising 11% of the population.

As a result of the Tigrayan People's Liberation Front (TPLF) playing the major roll in the bringing down the Derg (see p39), many Tigrayans play a major roll in Ethiopia's government, including Prime Minister Meles Zenawi. This has caused resentment among other groups.

The Sidama

The Sidama, a heterogeneous people, originate from the southwest, and can be divided into five different groups: the Sidama proper, the Derasa, Hadiya, Kambata and Alaba. Most Sidama are farmers who cultivate cereals, tobacco, *enset* (false-banana tree found in much of southern Ethiopia, used to produce a breadlike staple also known as *enset*) and coffee. The majority are animists and many ancient beliefs persist, including a belief in the reverence of spirits. Pythons are believed to be reincarnations of ancestors and are sometime kept as house pets. The Sidama social organisation, like the Oromo's *gada* system, is based on an age-group system.

The Sidama comprise about 9% of Ethiopia's population and most live in the Southern Nations, Nationalities and People's region.

The Somali

The arid lowlands of the southeast dictate a nomadic or seminomadic existence for the Somali. Somali society is 99% Muslim, strongly hierarchical, tightly knit and based on the clan system, which requires intense loyalty from its members. In the harsh environment in which they live, ferocious competition for the scant resources leads to frequent and sometimes violent disputes (thanks to an abundant supply of AK-47s) over grazing grounds and sources of water.

The Somali make up 95% of the Somali region's people, and 6% of Ethiopia's population.

The Afar

The Afar, formerly also known as the Danakils, inhabit the famous region of Dankalia, which stretches across Ethiopia's east, Djibouti's west and into Eritrea's southeast. It's considered one of earth's most inhospitable environments. Rightly or wrongly, they've proudly latched onto Wilfred Thesiger's portrayal of themselves as famously belligerent and proud. Thesiger talked about them winning social prestige in the past for murdering and castrating members of an opposing tribe.

The Afar comprise 4% of Ethiopia's population.

The Gurage

Semitic in origin, the Gurage practise herding or farming, and the enset plant is their favoured crop. Known as great workers, clever improvisers (even counterfeiters!) and skilled craftspeople, the Gurage will apply themselves to any task. Many work as seasonal labourers for the highlanders. Their faith is Christian, Muslim or animist, depending on the area from which they originate.

AIDS IN ETHIOPIA

There's no denying that AIDS is a serious problem in Ethiopia, though infection rates have thankfully slowed fractionally in urban areas over the past few years. Addis Ababa has the country's highest rate of AIDS, with 14.6% of its population infected. Percentagewise there are fewer infected in rural areas, but the rates of infection are sadly increasing. Currently the worst affected rural regions are Gambela and Amhara, with 8.0% and 6.1% of their respective populations infected.

AIDS is now the single greatest threat to economic development in Ethiopia. The government continues to use hard-hitting warnings on TV and radio, as well as the ubiquitous posters around the country.

They comprise only 2% of Ethiopia's population, but make up more than 10% of the population in the Southern Nations, Nationalities and People's region.

The Harari

Also Semitic in origin are the Harari people (sometimes known as Adare), who have long inhabited the walled Muslim city of Harar. The people are particularly known for their distinct two-storey houses, known as *gegar* (see the boxed text, p231), and for the very colourful traditional costumes still worn by many Harari women today. In the past, the Harari were known as great craftspeople for their weavings, baskets and bookbindings. They're also renowned Islamic scholars.

SPORT
Running

The popularity of running took off in the 1960s when the marathon runner Abebe Bikila won gold medals at the Tokyo and Rome Olympics (famously running barefoot at the latter). Things were taken to another level by Haile Gebreselassie, one of the world's greatest distance runners of all time. Since 1992 he's managed to win two Olympic golds, eight World Championships and set at least 19 world records over distances between 3000m and 25km. The 25km record was his most recent, set on 16 March 2006.

At Helsinki's 2005 World Championships the 5000m and 10,000m distances were dominated by Ethiopia, winning nine of the 12 possible medals. The women took six of six! Tirunesh Dibaba was top of the heap, winning gold in both women's events. Kenenisa Bekele (current world-record holder in the 5000m and 10,000m) took home the gold in the 10,000m.

The annual 10km Great Ethiopian Run (p90) attracts over 20,000 participants and is the largest mass participation run in Africa.

Football

Ethiopian's do love their football (soccer). Throughout the country you'll see children chasing footballs – constructed of everything from plastic bags to rubber bands – through clouds of dust to the cheers of all.

Adults and kids alike have a passion for the English Premiership, with urban crowds piling around TVs to watch their two favourites, Manchester United and Arsenal.

There are 15 formal football teams in Addis Ababa alone, and another 29 across the country. See p103 for information on attending football games at Addis Ababa's national stadium.

Other Sports

Ethiopia also boast its own indigenous sports. *Genna* is a variety of hockey without boundaries, traditionally played at Leddet (p261). *Gugs* – a physical (and sometimes fairly violent) game of tag on horseback – is also most commonly seen at festivals, including Ethiopian New Year and Meskel (p261). In the past, the games prepared young warriors for war. Addis Ababa's Jan Meda Sports Ground (p103) is the best place to catch both *genna* and *gugs*.

Although entirely un-Ethiopian, table tennis and table football enjoy fanatical support. Even in the most obscure towns, tables line the dusty streets and are always in use. Don't step in unless you're pretty good and don't mind losing some money!

Carambula, which is cueless version of pool (introduced by Italians) is also very popular.

> Want to woo the locals and have some serious fun streetside? Hone your table-tennis and table-football skills before arriving!

MULTICULTURALISM

Ethiopia's mix of cultures has been pretty stable over the past few centuries, with only the expulsion of Eritrean citizens after the recent Ethiopia–Eritrea War and influxes of Sudanese refugees into the western lowlands shifting the status quo.

Despite the nation's regions being divided along ethnic lines in 1995, there's still some resentment, particularly among the Oromo, that the minority Tigrayan and Amhara people maintain control of the national government.

Many travellers also notice that some Ethiopian highlanders, regardless of their ethnic background, seem to show a slight distain for Ethiopians from the lowlands.

MEDIA

Ethiopian TV, Radio Ethiopia and the country's most widely circulated newspapers, the *Addis Zemen* and the *Ethiopian Herald,* are state controlled. You'll even notice that the Ministry of Information shares a building with Ethiopian TV!

After the May 2005 elections, the EU had harsh criticism of the state-owned media for regularly releasing unofficial results that highlighted the government's victories and virtually ignoring the victories of opposition parties. They blasted Radio Ethiopia and Ethiopian TV for 'completely ignoring' the press conferences and important statements given by opposition parties, information that CNN and BBC thought newsworthy.

When government forces opened fire on unarmed protesters in June and November 2005, state-owned media also severely underreported civilian casualties.

Private media in Ethiopia have a short string and government censorship is still present. In 1992 a Press Law came into effect and since then numerous journalists have been arrested without trial for publishing critical articles of the government. The editor of *Agere* died untried in prison in February 1998. Several owners of private media were arrested and their newspapers shut down during the postelectoral violence in 2005.

RELIGION

Faith is an extremely important part of an Ethiopian's life. Orthodox Christians bring religion into everyday conversation just as much as their Muslim counterparts. Although Orthodox only slightly outnumber Muslims (45% to 35%), Christianity has traditionally dominated the country's

---

KNOW YOUR ETHIOPIAN SAINTS

There's hardly an Ethiopian church not adorned with colourful, vibrant and sometimes very beautiful murals. In most cases the paintings follow a set pattern, depicting again and again the key personalities of Ethiopia's peculiar pantheon of saints. Here's a quick key:

Abuna Aregawi One day, while wandering at the foot of a cliff, Abuna Aregawi spotted a large plateau high above him. Deciding it was the ideal spot for a nice, quiet hermit's life, he prayed to God for assistance. Immediately, a large python stretched down from above and lifted him onto the plateau. The famous monastery of Debre Damo was then founded. The saint is usually depicted riding up the snake – much like a game of snakes and ladders, only in reverse.

Abuna Samuel He lived near the Takezze River, where he preached and performed many miracles, accompanied by a devoted lion. He is usually depicted astride his lion.

Belai the Cannibal Although not a saint, he's a favourite theme in religious art. Devouring anyone who approached him including his own family, Belai yet took pity one day on a leper begging for water in the Virgin's name. After Belai died – some 72 human meals later – Satan claimed his soul. St Mikael, the judge, balanced Belai's victims on one side, the water on the other. However, the Virgin cast her shadow on the side of the scales containing the water, and caused them to tip. Belai's soul was saved.

Equestrian Saints They are usually depicted on the north wall of the Holy of Holies and may include Fasiladas, Claudius, Mercurius, Menas, Theodorus and George.

Mary Very popular and little known outside Ethiopia are the numerous and charming legends and miracles concerning Mary, as well as the childhood of Jesus and the flight to Egypt. A tree is often depicted hiding the holy family – and the donkey – from Herod's soldiers during the flight to Egypt; the soldiers are confused by the sound of the donkey braying. Sometimes a furious Mary is shown scolding Jesus, who's managed to break a clay water jug. He later redeems himself a bit by fixing it.

St Eostateos Also known as St Thaddeus, he's said to have arrived in Ethiopia borne up the Nile from Egypt on three large stones. Apparently water continued to obey him: whenever the saint chose to cross a river or a lake, the waters parted conveniently before him.

St Gabriel God's messenger is usually represented cooling the flames of a fiery furnace or cauldron containing three youths condemned by Nebuchadnezzar: Meshach, Shadrach and Abednego.

St Gebre Kristos This Ethiopian prince sacrificed all his belongings to lead a life of chastity, and ended up a leprous beggar. He's usually depicted outside his palace, where only his dogs now recognise him.

St Gebre Manfus Kiddus One day, while preaching peace to the wild animals in the desert, this saint came across a bird dying of thirst. Lifting it, he allowed the bird to drink the water from his eye. Usually depicted clad in furs and girded with a hempen rope. Leopards and lions lie at his feet, and the bird flaps near his head.

St George The patron saint of Ethiopia features in almost every church. He's depicted either as the king of saints, with St Bula – who at first refused to recognise his kingship – looking on petulantly in the background, or as the great dragon slayer on his horse. In Ethiopia, the archetypal damsel in distress has a name: she's known as Brutawit, the girl from Beirut.

St Mikael The judge of souls and the leader of the celestial army, St Mikael evicted Lucifer from heaven. In most churches, the portals to the Holy of Holies are guarded by a glowering Mikael, accompanied by Gabriel and Raphael, fiercely brandishing their swords.

St Raphael He apparently once rescued an Egyptian church from the tail of a thrashing whale beached on the land. He's usually depicted killing the hapless whale with his spear.

St Tekla Haimanot The saint prayed for seven years standing on just one leg, until the other finally withered and fell off! Throughout, a bird brought him just one seed a year for sustenance. For his devotion, God awarded him no fewer than three sets of wings. The saint is normally depicted in his bishop's attire, surrounded by bells; sometimes the detached leg is shown flapping off to heaven, or else brandished by an angel.

St Yared Ethiopia's patron saint of music is sometimes shown standing before his king with an orchestra of monks along with their sistra (sophisticated rattles, thought to be directly descended from an ancient Egyptian instrument used to worship Isis), drums and prayer sticks. In the background, little birds in trees learn the magic of music.

---

past. The vast majority of highlanders are Orthodox and the religion continues to heavily influence the highlands' political, social and cultural scene. Most Muslims inhabit the eastern, southern and western lowlands, but there are also significant populations in the country's predominantly Christian towns, including Addis Ababa.

THE TABOT & THE ARK OF THE COVENANT

According to Ethiopian tradition, the Ark of the Covenant was carried off from Jerusalem and brought to Ethiopia in the 1st millennium BC by Menelik. It's now believed to sit in Aksum's St Mary of Zion church compound (see p135).

Today, every other Ethiopian church has a replica of the Ark (or more precisely the Tablets of Law that are housed in the Ark) known as the *tabot*. Kept safe in the *maqdas* (Holy of Holies or inner sanctuary) it's the church's single most important element, and gives the building its sanctity (rather as the tabernacle does in the Roman Catholic church).

During important religious festivals, the *tabot* is carried in solemn processions, accompanied by singing, dancing, the beating of staffs or prayer sticks, the rattling of the sistrum (a sophisticated rattle, thought to be directly descended from an ancient Egyptian instrument used to worship Isis) and the beating of drums. It's a scene that could have come straight out of the Old Testament.

> They carried the Ark of God on a new cart...David and all the house of Israel were dancing before the Lord with all their might, with songs and lyres and harps and tambourines and castanets and cymbals.
>
> *2 Sam. vi. 3-5*

Ethiopian Orthodox Christianity

The official religion of the imperial court right up until Emperor Haile Selassie was deposed in 1974, this church continues to carry great clout among the Ethiopian people and is regarded as the great guardian and repository of ancient Ethiopian traditions, directly inherited from Aksum (p27).

Ethiopia was the second country (after Armenia) to adopt Christianity as its state religion and it's been a truly unifying factor over the centuries. By the same measure, it's also legitimised the oppression of the people by its rulers.

Ethiopian Orthodox Christianity is thought to have its roots in Judaism. This explains the food restrictions, including the way animals are slaughtered. Even the traditional round church layout is considered Hebrew in origin. Ancient Semitic and pagan elements also persist.

Circumcision is generally practised on boys, marriage is celebrated in the presence of a priest, and confession is usually only made during a grave illness.

Islam

Ethiopia's connection with Islam is as distinguished as its connection with Christianity. Though bloody religious wars were fought in Ethiopia in the past, Ethiopia's Christian and Muslim inhabitants coexist in harmony. Fundamentalism is rare in Ethiopia, and it's uncommon to see women wearing the *hijab* (veil), though the majority wear either headscarves or *shalmas* (a gauze-thin length of fabric draped around the head, shoulders and torso).

Negash, in Tigray, where Islam was introduced in 615 AD and the shrine of Sheikh Hussein in the Bale region are both greatly venerated and attract national and international pilgrims.

The famous walled city of Harar is also an important Islamic centre in its own right and is home to an astonishing number of shrines and mosques. In the past, it was renowned as a centre of learning.

Traditional African Beliefs

Traditional African beliefs are still practiced by an estimated 11% of Ethiopia's population, particularly in the lowland areas of the west and south. These range from the Konso's totemism (see the boxed text, p203) to animism (associated with trees, springs, mountains and stones etc), in which animals are ritually slaughtered and then consumed by the people. Elements of ancestor worship are still found among the Afar (p46). The Oromo (p45) traditionally believe in a supreme celestial deity known as Wak, whose eye is the sun.

The Falashas

Falashas (Ethiopian Jews) have inhabited Ethiopia since pre-Christian times. Despite actively engaging in wars over the years to defend their independence and freedom, few now remain: war, some persecution (though much less than seen elsewhere) and emigration in the latter part of the 20th century have greatly reduced their numbers.

Tiny populations of Falashas remain north of Lake Tana in the northwest; their beliefs combine a fascinating mixture of Judaism, indigenous beliefs and Christianity.

WOMEN IN ETHIOPIA

Legally, women in Ethiopia enjoy a relatively equitable position compared to some African countries. They can own property, vote and are represented in government, though there are still some cases where women's rights are impeded. One high profile and extremely important example of such is female genital cutting (see the boxed text, below).

If you want to learn more about women in Ethiopia or get in touch with them, contact the excellent Addis Ababa–based **Ethiopian Women Lawyers Association** (EWLA; Map pp80-1; ☎ 0116 612511; ewla@ethionet.et), which campaigns for women and their rights.

For information about travelling in Ethiopia as a woman, see p270.

A SCREAM SO STRONG IT WOULD SHAKE THE EARTH

The practice of female genital mutilation, or female genital cutting as it's now officially known, is particularly rampant in the eastern part of Africa's Horn as well as in other parts of Africa and Asia. It's believed two million women are cut each year worldwide; in other words 6000 women every day.

Modern sociologists believe it's just the 'natural continuation of the ancient patriarchal repression of female sexuality'. Past examples include Romans using genital rings, Crusaders using chastity belts and 19th-century doctors in Europe and America operating on female genitalia to cure antisocial conditions like nymphomania, insanity and depression. However, nowhere else has female genital cutting taken more hold than in Africa.

Reasons given in the Horn for mutilation vary from hygiene and aesthetics to superstitions that uncut women can't conceive. Others believe that the strict following of traditional beliefs is crucial to maintaining social cohesion and a sense of belonging, much like male circumcision is to Jews. Some also say that it prevents female promiscuity.

In theory there are three types of mutilation. 'Circumcision' (the name often given confusingly to all forms of mutilation) involves the removing of the clitoris' hood or prepuce. 'Excision' makes up 80% of the cases and involves the removal of some or all of the clitoris and all or part of the inner genitals (labia minora). 'Infibulation' is the severest form and requires the removal of the clitoris, the inner genitals and most or all of the outer genitals (labia majora). The two sides of the vulva are then stitched together with catgut, thread, reed or thorns. A tiny opening is preserved for the passage of urine by inserting a small object, like a twig. The girl's legs are then bound together and she's kept immobile for up to 40 days to allow the formation of scar tissue.

There's no doubt that female genital mutilation brings enormous physical pain and suffering. An estimated 15% of girls die postoperatively. Those who survive suffer countless ongoing complications and pain, as well as untold psychological suffering. As one doctor put it, 'These women are holding back a scream so strong, it would shake the earth.'

PROSTITUTION IN ETHIOPIA

The social stigma attached to prostitution in the West is lacking in Ethiopia. Many prostitutes are students trying to make ends meet. Others are widows, divorcees or refugees, all with little or no hope of finding other forms of employment. With no social security system either, it's often their only means of survival. Though not exactly a respected profession, prostitution is considered a perfectly viable means of making a living for these women. Some very beautiful or accomplished prostitutes even become well-known figures in society.

Visiting a prostitute is considered a fairly normal part of a young boy's adolescence and bachelor life, at least in the cities. Once married, it's considered shameful, however, and married men who can afford it often keep permanent mistresses or girlfriends instead.

Men should be warned that outside Addis Ababa almost 100% of women in bars are prostitutes. AIDS rates among prostitutes is thought to be reaching 50%.

ARTS

The church, traditionally enjoying almost as much authority as the state, is responsible both for inspiring Ethiopia's art forms and stifling them with its great conservatism and rigorous adherence to convention.

Long neglected and ignored, the cultural contributions of Ethiopia's other ethnic groups are only now receiving due credit and attention.

Music

Whether it's the solemn sounds of drums resonating from a church, the hilarious ad-libbing of an *azmari* (see the boxed text, opposite) or Ethiopian pop blaring in a bus, Ethiopian music is as interesting as it's unavoidable.

Ethiopian music CDs are available throughout the country. Music stalls are everywhere – keep an ear out. Older cassette versions are usually only found in Addis Ababa.

CHURCH MUSIC

Yared the Deacon is traditionally credited with inventing church music, with the introduction in the 6th century of a system of musical notation.

Church music known as *aquaquam* resonates with the use of a drum, in particular the *kabaro*, as well as the *tsinatseil* (sistrum; a sophisticated rattle, thought to be directly descended from an ancient Egyptian instrument used to worship Isis). Percussion instruments are primarily used since their function is to mark the beat for chanting and dancing. The *maquamia* (prayer stick) also plays an essential role in church ceremonies and, with hand-clapping, is used to mark time. Very occasionally a *meleket* (trumpet) is used, such as to lead processions.

You'll get plenty of opportunities to hear church music in Ethiopia. In the solemn and sacred atmosphere of the old churches, with the colour of the priestly robes, and the heady perfume of incense, it can be quite mesmerising.

SECULAR MUSIC

Strongly influenced by church music, secular music usually combines song and dance, emphasises rhythm, and often blends both African and Asian elements. The Amharas' and Tigrayans' highland music, as well as that of the peoples living near the Sudanese border, is much influenced by Arab music, and is very strident and emotive.

Wind as well as percussion instruments are used. The *begenna* is a type of harp similar to that played by the ancient Greeks and Romans. The most popular instrument in Ethiopia is the *krar*, a five- or six-stringed lyre, which is often heard at weddings, or to attract customers to traditional pubs or bars.

In the highlands, particularly the Simien and Bale Mountains, shepherd boys can be found with reed flutes. The *washint* is about 50cm long, with four holes, and makes a bubbling sound that is said to imitate running water. It's supposed to keep the herds close by and calm the animals.

Modern composers and performers include Tesfaye Lemma, Mulatu Astatike and Tefera Abunewold.

SONG

Traditionally passed down from generation to generation, every ethnic group has their own repertoire of songs, from *musho* (household songs) and *lekso* (laments for the dead) to war songs, hunting songs and lullabies for the cradle and caravan.

Ethiopian male singing in the highlands is often in falsetto. The most characteristic element of female singing is the high-pitched trilling. The tremulous and vibrating ululations can be heard on solemn, religious occasions.

Modern, traditional singers to look out for include Habtemikael Demissie, Yirga Dubale, Tadesse Alemu and the female singer Maritu Legeese.

MODERN MUSIC

Ethiopian modern music is diverse and affected by outside influences, and ranges from classical Amharic to jazz and pop. Modern classical singers and musicians include the late Assefa Abate, Kassa Tessema and the female vocalist Asnakech Worku. The latter two are known for their singing and *krar* playing. Girma Achanmyeleh, who studied in England, is known for his piano playing. The composer Mulatu Astatike is well known for his jazz.

Amharic popular music boasts a great following with the young. Unlike many other African countries, it's generally much preferred to Western music, and can be heard in all the larger town's bars and discos. For visitors, it can take a little time to get used to, particularly when played at full volume through unsympathetic speakers on buses.

The most famous Ethiopian pop singers have huge followings both in Ethiopia and among the expat populations abroad. Many record and live or spend time in America. Among the best known (and those to listen out for) are Ephrem Tamiru, Tsehaye Yohannes, Berhane Haile, Argaw

---

MINSTRELS & MASENKOS

An ancient entertainment that continues to this day is that provided by the singing *azmari* (wandering minstrel) and his *masenko* (single-stringed fiddle). In the past, the *azmari* accompanied caravans of highland traders to make the journey more amusing.

At court, resident *azmaris,* like the European jesters, were permitted great freedom of expression as long as their verses were witty, eloquent and clever.

During the Italian occupation, the *azmaris* kept up morale with their stirring renditions of Ethiopian victories and resistance. So successfully, in fact, that many were executed by the Italians.

Today, *azmaris* can be found at weddings and special occasions furnishing eulogies or poetic ballads in honour of their hosts.

In certain bars *(azmari beats)* of the larger towns, some *azmaris* have become celebrities in their own right. They prance around grass-covered floors and sing about everything from history and sex, to your funny haircut. Although you won't understand a word (it's all in Amharic), you'll end up laughing; the locals' laughter is simply that contagious. And remember these two things: it's all done in good fun and hair always grows back!

OUR TOP FIVE MODERN MUSIC CD PICKS

- *Gigi* by Ejigaheyehu Shibabaw
- *Ebo* by Aster Aweke
- *Zeritu* by Zeritu Kebede
- *Yasstesseriyal* by Tewodros Kassahun
- *Zion Roots* by Abyssinia Infinite

Bedasso and Ali Bira, as well as the old-timers Tilahun Gessesse and Mohammed Ahmud. Blasting onto the scene of late is Tewodros Kassahun (known as 'Teddy Afro').

Female artists more than hold their own and Gonder-born, American-based Aster Aweke has produced 20 albums since the late 1970s. She's popularly known as Africa's Aretha Franklin. Her early works are only found in cassette form in Addis Ababa. Hot on Aster's tail for international fame is Ejigaheyehu Shibabaw (known as 'Gigi'), who rose to prominence after her 1997 album *Tsehay*. Her singing was heard in the Hollywood movie *Beyond Borders*. Recently bursting onto the female singing scene (and our particular favourite) is Zeritu Kebede (also known as 'Baby').

Some albums are available for download at www.emusic.com. Francis Falceto, an Ethiopian music expert, compiles popular Ethiopian contemporary music into great CDs known as 'Ethiopiques'. Twenty-one volumes have been produced to date; pick them up from www.budamusique .com or download tracks at www.emusic.com.

Dance

Dance forms an extremely important part of the lives of most Ethiopians, and almost every ethnic group has its own distinct variety. Although the *iskista* (below) movement is the best known, there are myriad others.

Dance traditionally serves a variety of important social purposes: from celebrating religious festivities (such as the *shibsheba* or priestly dance), to celebrating social occasions such as weddings and funerals and, in the past, to motivating warriors before departing for battle.

Still found in rural areas are dances in praise of nature, such as after a good harvest or when new sources of water are discovered, and dances that allow the young 'warriors' to show off their agility and athleticism. Look out for the *fukara* ('boasting' dance), which is often performed at public festivals. A leftover from less peaceful times, it involves a man holding a spear, stick or rifle horizontally above his shoulders while moving his head from side to side and shouting defiantly at the 'enemy'.

Among the tribes of the Omo Valley in the south, many dances incorporate jumping and leaping up and down, a little like the dances of Kenya's Maasai. All dancing is in essence a social, communal activity,

---

DANCING THE ISKISTA

When dancing the famous *iskista*, the shoulders are juddered up and down, backwards and forwards, in a careful rhythm, while the hips and legs are kept motionless. Sometimes the motion is accompanied by a sharp intake of breath, making a sound like the word 'iskista', or alternatively by a *zefen*, a loud, high-pitched and strident folk song. If you're not in practice, the dance is a greedy chiropractor's dream!

and you'll often be expected to join in. If you do give it a go, you'll win a lot of friends! Declining to dance can infer a slight.

Literature

Inscriptions in Ge'ez (the ancestor of modern Amharic) date from Aksumite times. It was during this early period that the Bible was translated from Greek into Ge'ez.

The year 1270 is considered to mark the golden age of Ge'ez literature, in which many works were translated from Arabic, as well as much original writing produced. It's thought that in the early 14th century the *Kebra Negast* (p56) was written.

During the 16th-century Muslim–Christian wars, book production ground to a halt and copious amounts of literature were destroyed. By the 17th century Ge'ez was in decline as a literary language and had long ceased to serve as the vernacular.

Amharic, now Ethiopia's official language was the Amharas' language. It was Emperor Tewodros who encouraged the local language in an attempt to promote national unity. In a continuation of the trend begun in the 14th century, Tewodros and other emperors right up to Haile Selassie funded writers whose compositions and poetic laudatory songs were written to praise the ruler's qualities and munificence.

ORAL LITERATURE – TALES TALL & TRUE

Every time an old person passes away, it's as if a whole library were lost.

Ethiopian-Somali saying

In the West, culture is usually defined in terms of grandiose monuments, works of art and sophisticated customs. In some countries, however, and particularly where the climate dictates a nomadic existence for its people, culture manifests itself not in enduring buildings and great writings, but in the spoken word, passed down from generation to generation.

Many languages in Africa are in the process of disappearing along with the cultures that support them. And while vast amounts of time, effort and money continue to be invested in excavating tangible evidence of past civilisations, the intangible evidence – the oral patrimony, which is just as important and certainly as fragile – is allowed to disappear forever.

The oral tradition of many African societies is rich, and particularly so in Ethiopia. Here, literally thousands of proverbs, maxims and tales are in circulation, having been told and retold for centuries by nomads, cattle herders and traders.

Among the nomadic people of East Africa, the tale serves as a kind of bedtime story. After the heat and work of the day, when the animals have been fed, watered and safely penned, families gather around the fire outside the tent. Storytellers are usually the older members of the family; among the Ethiopian Somalis, it's the grandmother who plays the part of narrator.

The tales are told to teach as well as to entertain. Children are taught not only morals and the difference between right and wrong, but useful lessons about the world they live in, and about human nature. The stories teach children to listen, to concentrate and to make judgements based on the dialogue of the characters, as the story unfolds. It encourages them to think and to analyse, and it develops their power of memory.

Tales also serve the adult population. Sometimes they are employed to clarify a situation, to offer advice tactfully to a friend, or to alert someone diplomatically to trouble or to wrongdoing. Like poetry, the tale can express a complex idea or situation economically and simply. The tale has also been used to attack latently corrupt leaders or governments without fear of libel or persecution.

In Ethiopia, there's said to be a tale for every situation. You'll be surprised how often the locals resort to proverbs, maxims or stories during the course of normal conversation. It's said that the first Ethiopian-Somali proverb of all is: 'While a man may tell fibs, he may never tell false proverbs.'

KEBRA NEGAST

Written during the 14th century by an unknown author(s), the *Kebra Negast* (Glory of Kings) is considered Ethiopia's great national epic. Like the Quran to Muslims or the Old Testament to Jews, it's a repository of Ethiopian national, religious and cultural sentiment.

It's notoriously shrouded in mystery, perhaps deliberately so. Some controversially suggest it may even represent a massive propaganda stunt to legitimise the rule of the so-called 'Solomonic kings', who came to power in the 13th century and who, the book claims, were direct descendants of the kings of Israel.

Its most important legend is that of Solomon and Sheba (see the boxed text, p139).

Under the Derg (p37), both writing and writers were suppressed. Be'alu Girma is a well-known example of one of the many artists who disappeared during their reign.

POETRY

Written in Amharic as well as other Ethiopian languages, poetry, along with dance and music, is used on many religious and social occasions, such as weddings or funerals. Rhymed verse is almost always chanted or sung in consonance with the rhythm of music.

Poetry places great stress on meaning, metaphor and allusion. In Ge'ez poetry, the religious allusions demand an in-depth knowledge of Ethiopian religious legends and the Bible.

FOLK LITERATURE

Perhaps the source of the greatest originality and creativity is the vast folk literature of Ethiopia, most of it in oral form and existing in all languages and dialects. It encompasses everything from proverbs, tales and riddles to magic spells and prophetic statements.

Architecture

Ethiopia boasts some remarkable historical architecture. Though some monuments, such as the castles of Gonder, show foreign influence, earlier building styles, such as those developed during the Aksumite period, are believed to be wholly indigenous, and are of a high technical standard.

ASKUMITE ARCHITECTURE

The 'Aksumite style' of stone masonry is Ethiopia's most famous building style. Walls were constructed with field stones set in mortar, along with sometimes finely dressed corner stones. In between came alternating layers of stone and timber, recessed then projected, and with protruding ends of round timber beams, known as 'monkey heads'. The latter are even symbolically carved into Aksum's great obelisks (see p134), which may just be the nation's greatest architectural achievements. The Aksumites were undoubtedly master masons.

The best examples of Aksumite buildings are seen at Debre Damo and the church of Yemrehanna Kristos (p163).

The Aksumite style is additionally seen in Lalibela's rock-hewn churches, as well as in modern design today. Keep an eye out for the ancient motifs in new hotel and restaurant designs.

ROCK-HEWN ARCHITECTURE

Ethiopia's rock-hewing tradition probably predates Christianity and has resulted in nearly 400 churches across the country. The art form reached its apogee in the 12th and 13th centuries in Lalibela, where the Zagwe dynasty produced 11 churches that continue to astound. They're considered among the world's finest early Christian architecture.

The churches are unique in that many stand completely free from the rock, unlike similar structures in Jordan and Egypt. The buildings show extraordinary technical skill in the use of line, proportion and decoration, and in the remarkable variety of styles.

The rock-hewn churches of the Tigray region, though less famous and spectacular, are no less remarkable.

GONDER ARCHITECTURE

The town of Gonder and its imperial enclosure represent another peak in Ethiopian architectural achievement. Although Portuguese, Moorish and Indian influences are all evident, the castles are nevertheless a peculiarly Ethiopian synthesis. Some have windows decorated with red volcanic tuff, and barrel- or egg-shaped domes.

Painting

Ethiopian painting is largely limited to religious subjects, particularly the life of Christ and the saints. Every church in Ethiopia is decorated with abundant and colourful murals, frescos or paintings.

Much Ethiopian painting is characterised by a naive realism. Everything is expressed with vigour and directness using bold colour, strong line and stylised proportions and perspective. Like the stained-glass windows in European Gothic churches, the paintings served a very important purpose: to instruct, inspire and instil awe in the illiterate and uneducated.

Though some modern artists (particularly painters of religious and some secular work) continue in the old tradition (or incorporate ancient motifs such as that of the Aksumite stelae), many artists have developed their own style. Borrowing freely from the past, but no longer constrained by it, modern Ethiopian painting shows greater originality of expression and is now a flourishing medium.

Until recently, the artist was considered a mere craftsperson, but as Western influence has spread the artist has attained a more professional standing, and works of art can be found for sale not only in modern art galleries, and cultural institute exhibitions, but also in hotels and restaurants.

Among the young painters to look out for are Behailu Bezabeh, an acute observer of everyday life in the capital; Daniel Taye, who is known for his darker more disturbing images; Geta Makonnen, whose artwork addresses social issues; the sculptor Bekele Makonnen, with his thought-provoking installations revolving around moral and social values; and Tigist Hailegabreal, a versatile young woman artist who's concerned with women's issues such as prostitution and violence against women.

ETHIOPIAN HOUSES

Ethiopian houses are famously diverse; each ethnic group has developed its own design according to its own lifestyle and own resources.

In general, the round *tukul* (hut) forms the basis of most designs. Circular structures and conical thatched roofs better resist the wind and heavy rain. Windows and chimneys are usually absent. The smoke, which escapes through the thatch, fumigates the building, protecting it against insect infestations such as termites.

Sometimes the huts are shared: the right side for the family, the left for the animals. Livestock are not only protected from predators but in some regions they also provide central heating!

The vast stained-glass window in Addis Ababa's Africa Hall (p87) is the work of one of Africa's best-known painters, Afewerk Tekle (see the boxed text, below).

Arts & Crafts

Ethiopia boasts a particularly rich tradition of arts and crafts. This is partly due to the wide range of raw materials available, from gold to good hardwood and fine highland wool. Additionally, the number and diversity of the country's ethnic groups (64 according to some reckonings), and the differing needs arising from the different environments, has ensured this.

Traditional arts and crafts include basketware (Harar is considered the centre), paintings, musical instruments, pottery, hornwork, leatherwork and woodcarving. The best woodwork traditionally comes from Jimma in western Ethiopia, where forests of tropical and temperate hardwoods once flourished. The Gurage and Sidamo also work wood.

Other crafts include metalwork (materials range from gold and silver to brass, copper and iron, and products include the famous and diverse Ethiopian crosses) as well as weaving. The Konso are known for their woollen products; the Gurage and Dorze for their cotton products, which include the famous *kemis* (traditional women's dresses) and *shamma* (togas) of the highlander men. Special skills are particularly required for making the ornate and beautifully coloured *tibeb* (borders) of the women's *natala* (shawls). Debre Berhan is considered the capital of rug making.

Remember if you're buying authentic crafts, ensure that they aren't made from indigenous woods or wildlife products. For more information, see the boxed text on p256.

Theatre

Ethiopia boasts one of Africa's most ancient, prolific and flourishing theatrical traditions. Because theatre is written mainly in Amharic, however, it's practically unknown outside the country. Having largely resisted European influence, it's also preserved its own very local flavour and outlook.

Ethiopian theatrical conventions include minimal drama, sparse characterisation (with actors often serving as symbols) and plenty of extended speeches. Verse form is still often used and rhetoric remains a very important element of Ethiopian plays. Audiences tend to be participatory. Modern playwrights include Ayalneh Mulatu.

AFEWERK TEKLE

Born in 1932, Afewerk Tekle is one of Ethiopia's most distinguished and colourful artistic figures. Educated at the Slade School of Art in London, he later toured and studied in continental Europe before returning to work under the patronage of Emperor Haile Selassie. A painter as well as a sculptor and designer, he's also a master fencer, dancer and toastmaster.

Proud to have 'survived three regimes' (when friends and peers did not), his life has hardly been without incident. In almost cinematic style, a 'friendly' fencing match turned into an attempt on his life, and a tussle over a woman led to his challenging his rival to a duel at dawn. In the royal court of the emperor, he once only just survived an assassination attempt by poisoned cocktail.

The artist famously makes his own terms and conditions: if he doesn't like the purchaser he won't sell, and his best-known paintings must be returned to Ethiopia within a lifetime. He's even turned down over US$12 million for the work considered his masterpiece, *The Meskel Flower*.

ILLUMINATED MANUSCRIPTS

Without doubt, illuminated manuscripts represent one of Ethiopia's greatest artistic achievements. The best quality manuscripts were created by monks and priests in the 14th and 15th centuries. The kings, the court and the largest and wealthiest churches and monasteries were the main patrons. The manuscripts were characterised by beautifully shaped letters, attention to minute detail, and elaborate ornamentation. Pictures included in the text brought it to life and made it more comprehensible for the uneducated or illiterate.

Bindings consisted of thick wooden boards often covered with tooled leather. The volume was then placed into a case with straps made of rough hides so that it could be slung over a shoulder.

On the blank pages at the beginning or at the end of the volume, look out for the formulae *fatina bere* (literally 'trial of the pen') or *bere' sanay* (literally 'a fine pen'), as the scribes tried out their reeds. Some are also dated and contain a short blessing for the owner as well as the scribe.

Sadly, due to the Muslim and the Dervish raids of the early 16th and late 19th centuries respectively, few manuscripts date prior to the 14th century. Modern times have seen huge numbers being pillaged by soldiers, travellers and explorers.

Don't miss your chance to see what treasures remain – church priests are usually only too happy to show you.

There are usually a few productions put on each week in Addis Ababa (see p102 for venues).

Cinema

Ethiopia, which was never colonised, missed out on the 'benefit' of colonial support for setting up a film industry enjoyed by other African countries in the mid-1950s and '60s.

Solomon Bekele was one of the pioneers of Ethiopian cinema and is best known for his Amharic feature film *Aster*. Ethiopia's most famous English-speaking film-maker is Haile Gerima, whose latest film *Adwa* (released in early 2000) deals with a recurring theme, the Ethiopian defeat of the Italians at Adwa (see p143).

Environment

The farmer who eats his chickens as well as all their eggs will have a bleak future.

Tigrayan proverb

THE LAND

With a land area of 1,098,000 sq km, Ethiopia measures five times the size of Britain or about twice the size of Texas. Ethiopia's topography is remarkably diverse, ranging from 20 mountains peaking above 4000m to one of the lowest points on the Earth's surface: the infamous Danakil Depression, which lies almost 120m below sea level.

Two principal geographical zones can be found in the country: the cool highlands and the hot lowlands that surround them.

Ethiopia's main topographical feature is the vast central plateau (the Ethiopian highlands) with an average elevation between 1800m and 2400m. It's here that the country's major peaks are found including Ras Dashen at 4543m (4620m according to some estimates and maps), Ethiopia's highest mountain and Africa's tenth.

The mountains are also the source of four large river systems, the most famous of which is the Blue Nile. Starting from Lake Tana and joined later by the White Nile in Sudan, it nurtures the Egypt's fertile Nile Valley. The other principal rivers are the Awash, the Omo and the Wabe Shebele.

Southern Ethiopia is bisected diagonally by the Rift Valley. Averaging around 50km wide, it runs all the way to Mozambique. The valley floor has several lakes, including the well-known chain south of Addis Ababa.

The northern end of the East African Rift Valley opens into the Danakil Depression, one of the hottest places on Earth.

WILDLIFE

Like its geography, Ethiopia's ecosystems are diverse, from high Afro-alpine vegetation to desert and semidesert scrubland. Filling in this spectrum's gap are six more unique ecosystems: dry evergreen montane forest and grassland; small-leaved deciduous forests; broad-leaved deciduous forests; moist evergreen forests; lowland semi-evergreen forests; and wetlands.

The massive Ethiopian central plateau is home to several of these ecosystems and a distinctive assemblage of plants and animals. Isolated for millions of years within this 'fortress environment' and unable to cross the inhospitable terrain surrounding it, much highland wildlife evolved on its own. Many species are found nowhere else in the world.

Animals

Simply because it lacks large crowds of cavorting elephants, giraffes and rhinos, Ethiopia is mistakenly written off by many ignorant Westerners as simply a historical destination. What they don't know is that Ethiopia

---

FUNNY FROGS

During a scientific expedition to the Harenna Forest in the Bale Mountains a few years ago, biologists discovered four entirely new frog species in the space of just three weeks. Many of the frogs appear to have made peculiar adaptations to their environment. One species swallows snails whole, another has forgotten how to hop and a third has lost its ears!

currently hosts 277 mammal species, 200 reptile species, 148 fish species and 63 amphibian species. And that's not even including the birds!

To date, 862 species have been recorded (compared with just 250 in the UK). Of Africa's 10 endemic mainland bird families, eight are represented in Ethiopia; only rockfowl and sugarbirds are absent. Families that are particularly well represented are falcons, francolins, bustards and larks.

More noteworthy is the fact that of all the species in Ethiopia, 31 mammals, 21 birds, nine reptiles, four fish and 24 amphibians are endemic (found only in Ethiopia). The biggest kicker of all is the realisation that you have a pretty good chance of spotting some of the rarest species, including the Ethiopian wolf, which is planet's rarest canid (dog family member).

The Afro-alpine habitat, within the Bale and Simien Mountains National Parks, boasts the largest number of endemic mammals and hosts mountain nyala, walia ibex, Ethiopian wolves, gelada baboons, Menelik's bushbuck and giant molerats. Incredibly 16 of Ethiopia's endemic birds are also found in these lofty confines (see the boxed text on p62 for the lowdown on Ethiopia's endemic birdlife and birding itineraries).

At the opposite end of the elevation spectrum, the lowly confines of the desert and semidesert scrublands host the endangered African wild ass and Grevy's zebra, as well as the Soemmering's gazelle and beisa oryx. Birds include the ostrich, secretary bird, Arabian, Kori and Heuglin's bustards, Abyssinian roller, red-cheeked cordon bleu and crested francolin.

The wide-ranging but sporadic deciduous forests play home to greater and lesser kudus, hartebeests, gazelles, De Brazza's monkeys and small populations of elands, buffaloes and elephants. Limited numbers of Grevy's zebras and beisa oryx also inhabit these areas. Birdlife includes the white-bellied go-away bird, superb starling, red-billed quelea, helmeted guinea fowl, secretary bird, Ruppell's long-tailed starling, gambaga flycatcher, red-cheeked cordon bleu, bush petronia and black-faced firefinch.

Wandering the evergreen forests in the southwestern and western parts of the country are bushpigs, forest hogs, Menelik's bushbucks and more De Brazza's monkeys. Around Gambela, in the lowland semi-evergreen forest, are rare populations of elephants, giraffes, lions and the hard-to-spot white-eared kob, a beautiful golden antelope found in larger numbers in southern Sudan. The colourful birdlife includes the

Endemic Mammals of Ethiopia, by Jill Last and published by the defunct Ethiopian Tourism Commission, gives decent descriptions of the appearance and behaviour of Ethiopia's mammals. It's usually available in Addis Ababa.

A Guide to Endemic Birds of Ethiopia and Eritrea by Jose Luis Vivero Pol is an excellent companion for birders.

THE BLEEDING HEART BABOON

The gelada baboon *(Theropithecus gelada)* is one of Ethiopia's most fascinating endemic mammals. In fact not a baboon at all, it makes up its own genus of monkey.

Of all the nonhuman primates, it's by far the most dexterous. It also lives in the largest social groups (up to 800 have been recorded), and is the only primate that feeds on grass and has its 'mating skin' on its chest and not on its bottom – a convenient adaptation, given that it spends most of its time sitting!

The gelada also has the most complex system of communication of any nonhuman primate and the most sophisticated social system: the females decide who's boss, the young males form bachelor groups, and the older males perform a kind of grandfather role looking after the young.

Although the males sport magnificent leonine manes, their most striking physical feature is the bare patch of skin on their chest. This has given rise to their other popular name: the 'bleeding heart baboon'. The colour of the patch indicates the sexual condition not just of the male (his virility), but also his female harem (their fertility), like a kind of communal sexual barometer.

Although its population is shrinking, the gelada population is the healthiest of Ethiopia's endemic mammals. Its current population is thought to number between 40,000 and 50,000. See also the boxed text, p128.

ETHIOPIA'S ENDEMIC BIRDS

There's no denying that the diversity and beauty of Ethiopia's astounding 862 recorded bird species could convert even the most die-hard nonbirder into a habitual and excited twitcher. Besides the relative ease of spotting over a hundred bird species in a few weeks, it's the endemic bird species that really set Ethiopia apart.

An amazing 21 species are found nowhere else in the world. Thirteen more are semi-endemic, shared only with Eritrea.

The best time to visit Ethiopia for birding is between November and February, when some 200 species of Palaearctic migrants from Europe and Asia join the already abundant African resident and intra-African migrant populations. The most likely time to spot birds is from dawn to 11am and from 5pm to dusk, although birds can be seen throughout the day.

The Birding Circuit

If you're a passionate birder then the circuit suggested here could suit your fancy. If you don't have 10 days to two weeks or a 4WD, then you can pick and choose your spots from the itinerary.

Start off by spending a couple of days touring the northern Rift Valley lakes. Explore the shores of Lake Ziway (p171) for marsh species, before continuing on to Lake Langano (p172), where over 300 species have been spotted. Nearby is Lake Abiata-Shala National Park (p173), which hosts abundant acacia-related bird species.

Stop at Wondo Genet (p175) to check out the forests, which host several endemics like the yellow-fronted parrot and the white-backed tit.

From there head east and spend two days in the Bale Mountains (p181), where no less than 16 of Ethiopia's 21 endemics are found. Next head east to Sof Omar (p191) and search for Salvadori's seedeater or serin. Then double back towards the Bale Mountains before crossing the Sanetti Plateau (where you have a good chance to spot the Simien wolf) and descending into the heat of the southern lowlands. The long and bumpy ride between Dola-Mena (p192) and Negele Borena (p192) is rich in birdlife and there are several endemics visible, like the Degodi lark, Prince Ruspoli's turaco and the Sidamo long-clawed lark.

Head west to the Yabelo Wildlife Sanctuary (p193) and take in two of the world's most range-restricted species, the Stresemann's bush crow and white-tailed swallow.

If you have a few days to kill and want to live on in infamy as the first person to see a Nechisar nightjar alive, head west from Yabelo and then north at Konso to visit Nechisar National Park (p199). If not, take the long road back north towards Addis Ababa and complete your birdwatching bonanza at Awash National Park (p217), where six endemics live, including the white-winged cliff chat, the banded barbet and the goldenbacked or Abyssinian woodpecker.

Endemics of Ethiopia

- Abyssinian catbird *(Parophasma galinieri)* – juniper forests within the Bale Mountains (p181).
- Abyssinian longclaw *(Macronyx flavicollis)* – Afro-alpine grassland in the Bale Mountains (p181).
- Abyssinian slaty flycatcher *(Dioptrornis chocolatinus)* – highland woodlands bracketing the southern Rift Valley.
- Ankober seedeater or serin *(Serinus ankoberensis)* – around Ankober (p167) and in Simien Mountains (p125).
- Black-headed siskin *(Serinus nigriceps)* – Afro-alpine grassland and heather forests in the Bale Mountains (p181).
- Blue-winged goose *(Cyanochen cyanopterus)* – Gefersa Reservoir (p237) and Sanetti Plateau in the Bale Mountains (p181).

- Degodi lark *(Mirafra degodiensis)* – around Negele Borena (p192).
- Erlanger's Lark *(Calandrella erlangeri)* – common in the highlands.
- Ethiopian cliff swallow *(Hirundo)* – Lake Langano (p172).
- Harwood's francolin *(Francolinus hardwoodi)* – in the Jemma Valley, northeast of Debre Libanos.
- Nechisar nightjar *(Caprimulgus nechisarensis)* – Nechisar National Park (p199).
- Prince Ruspoli's turaco *(Tauraco ruspolii)* – around Negele Borena (p192).
- Salvadori's seedeater or serin *(Serinus xantholaema)* – Sof Omar (p191) and around Negele Borena (p192).
- Sidamo long-clawed lark *(Heteromirafra sidamoensis)* – near Negele Borena (p192).
- Spot-breasted plover *(Vanellus melanocephalus)* – found near rivers and streams in the Bale Mountains (p181).
- Stresemann's or Abyssinian bush crow *(Zavattariornis stresemanni)* – Yabelo Wildlife Sanctuary (p193).
- White-cheeked turaco *(Tauraco leucolophus)* – common in highlands.
- White-tailed swallow *(Hirundo megaensis)* – Yabelo Wildlife Sanctuary (p193).
- White-throated seedeater *(Serinus xanthopygius)* – around Ankober (p167) and the Blue Nile Falls (p118).
- Yellow-fronted parrot *(Poicephalus flavifrons)* – Wondo Genet (p175), Menagesha Forest (p237) and Bale Mountains (p181).
- Yellow-throated seedeater or serin *(Serinus flavigula)* – Awash National Park (p217) and near Ankober (p167).

Semi-Endemics of Ethiopia & Eritrea

- Abyssinian woodpecker *(Dendropicus abyssinicus)* – Awash National Park (p217); rare but widespread.
- Banded barbet *(Lybius undatus)* – Awash National Park (p217) and in southern Rift Valley.
- Black-winged lovebird *(Agapornis swinderiana)* – common in highland woodlands.
- Brown sawwing *(Psalidoprocne oleagina)* – Yabelo Wildlife Sanctuary (p193).
- Ethiopian cisticola *(Cistocola lugubris)* – common in montane grasslands.
- Rouget's rail *(Rougetius rougetii)* – associated with marshes and river systems in highlands. Common in Bale Mountains (p181).
- Rüpell's black chat *(Myrmecocichla melaena)* – common in rock highlands of Tigray (p147).
- Thick-billed raven *(Corvus crassirostris)* – common in highlands.
- Wattled Ibis *(Bostrychia carunculata)* – common in highlands.
- White-backed black tit *(Parus leuconotus)* – Wondo Genet (p175) and Bale Mountains (p181). Also in Addis Ababa (p76).
- White-billed starling *(Onychognathus albirostris)* – in and around Lalibela (p155).
- White-collared pigeon *(Columba albitorques)* – common in highlands, including Addis Ababa (p76).
- White-winged cliff chat *(Myrmecocichla semirufa)* – common in rock highlands of Tigray (p147) and Awash National Park (p217).

The Nechisar nightjar
(Caprimulgus solala) was
discovered from a mere
wing found squashed on
the road near Nechisar
National Park in 1990.
None have been seen
since – sad but true.
'Solala' in its scientific
name means 'single
winged'.

Abyssinian black-headed oriole, Abyssinian hill babbler, white-cheeked turaco, scaly throated honeyguide, scaly francolin, emerald cuckoo and the yellow-billed coucal.

Hippos and crocodiles are also found around Gambela in the wetlands along the Baro River. They also populate some of the Rift Valley lakes in the south – Lake Chamo is famous for its massive crocodiles. Rouget's rails and white-winged flufftails are found in the wetland swamps, while the Senegal thick-knee and red-throated bee-eater live in riverbank habitats.

The odd leopard, gazelle, jackal and hyena still roam the dry evergreen montane forest and grassland found in Ethiopia's north, northwest, central and southern highlands. Birds of note include black-winged lovebirds, half-collared kingfishers and several endemic species (for more information, see p62).

ENDANGERED SPECIES

The International Union for the Conservation of Nature and Natural Resources (IUCN) lists seven species in Ethiopia as critically endangered; one is Ethiopia's endemic walia ibex. Amazingly, you have a pretty good chance of spotting this rare animal in the Simien Mountains National Park.

A further 19 species in Ethiopia are listed as endangered by IUCN. These include the endemic mountain nyala and Ethiopian wolf, both easily viewed in Bale Mountains National Park. Nechisar National Park holds the endangered African hunting dog and what's likely Ethiopia's rarest endemic bird, the Nechisar nightjar. Both are notoriously hard to view.

Vulnerable bird species are Prince Ruspoli's turaco (see below), Salvadori's serin, Stresemann's bush crow, the Sidamo long-clawed lark, the Degodi lark, the Ankober serin and the white-tailed swallow. For more information, see p62.

Plants

Ethiopia's flora is no less exceptional for the same reason. Ethiopia is classed as one of world's 12 Vavilov centres for crop plant diversity, and is thought to possess extremely valuable pools of crop plant genes. Between 600 and 1400 plants species are thought to be endemic; an enormous 10% to 20% of it's flora.

THE STRANGE CASE OF THE VANISHING TURACO

In a remote patch in the deep south of Ethiopia lives one of the country's rarest, most beautiful and most enigmatic birds – the Prince Ruspoli's turaco, first introduced to the world in the early 1890s. It was 'collected' by an Italian prince (who gave his name to the bird) as he explored the dense juniper forests of southern Ethiopia.

Unfortunately, the intrepid prince failed to make a record of his find, and when he was killed shortly afterwards near Lake Abaya following 'an encounter with an elephant', all hope of locating the species seemed to die with him.

In subsequent years, other explorers searched in vain for the bird. None were successful until the turaco finally reappeared in the 1940s. Just three specimens were obtained, then the turaco disappeared again. It wasn't until the early 1970s that the bird was rediscovered.

Today, recent sightings in the Arero forest, east of Yabelo, around the Genale River off the Dola-Mena–Negele Borena road, suggest that the bird may not, after all, be as elusive as it would have us believe.

SPOT THE ENDEMIC FLORA

Ethiopia has more unique species of flora than any other country in Africa. In September and October, look out particularly for the famous yellow daisy known as the Meskel flower, which carpets the highlands; it belongs to the Bidens family, six members of which are endemic.

In towns and villages, the endemic yellow-flowered *Solanecio gigas* is commonly employed as a hedge. Around Addis Ababa, the tall endemic *Erythrina brucei* tree can be seen. In the highlands, such as in the Bale Mountain and Simien Mountain National Parks, the indigenous Abyssinian rose is quite commonly found. Also in the Bale Mountains, look out for the endemic species of globe thistle *(Echinops longisetus).*

The small-leaved deciduous forests can be found all over the country apart from the western regions, at an altitude of between 900m and 1900m. Vegetation consists of drought-tolerant shrubs and trees with either leathery persistent leaves or small deciduous ones. Trees include various types of acacia. Herbs include *Acalypha* and *Aerva*.

The western and northwestern areas of Ethiopia host the broad-leaved deciduous forests, while tall and medium-sized trees and understorey shrubs of the moist evergreen forests also occupy the west as well as the nation's southwest. Even further west are the lowland semi-evergreen forests around Gambela. Vegetation there consists of semi-evergreen trees and shrub species as well as grasses.

Covering much of the highlands, and the north, northwest, central and southern parts of the country, is the dry evergreen montane forest and grassland. This habitat is home to a large number of endemic plants. Tree species include various types of acacia, olive and euphorbia. Africa's only rose, the *Rosa abyssinica,* is here.

Within the Afro-alpine vegetation habitat, you'll see the endemic giant lobelia *(Lobelia rhynchopetalum)*, an endemic species of globe thistle as well as the so-called 'soft thistle'. Heather grows into large trees of up to 10m. On the high plateaus at around 4000m are many varieties of gentian.

Look out for fig and tamarind trees along the Baro River in the west as well as along river banks or *wadis* (seasonal rivers) in the highlands and the northwest.

The Dankalia region, Omo delta and Ogaden Desert contain highly drought-resistant plants such as small trees, shrubs and grasses, including acacia. Succulent species include euphorbia and aloe. The region is classified as desert and semidesert scrubland.

NATIONAL PARKS & WILDLIFE SANCTUARIES

There are nine national parks and three wildlife sanctuaries in Ethiopia. They range from the unvisited Kuni-Muktar Wildlife Sanctuary to the famed Simien Mountains National Park, a Unesco World Heritage site.

Most parks were delineated in the 1960s and 1970s during the time of Emperor Haile Selassie to protect endangered or endemic animals. In the process, land was forcefully taken from the peasants, a measure much resented by locals. When the Derg government fell in 1991, there was a brief period of anarchy, when park property was looted and wildlife killed.

Park borders continue to overlap with local communities, and conflicts over conservation continue, despite wildlife authorities trying to encourage locals' participation in the conservation of wildlife. For instance, trees in Lake Abiata-Shala National Park continue to fall victim to the needs of its growing human population. The opposite is true in Nechisar

TOP PARKS & SANCTUARIES

Park	Features	Activities	Best time to visit
Southern Ethiopia			
Bale Mountains National Park (p181)	steep ridges, alpine plateaus; Ethiopian wolves, mountain nyala and 16 endemic birds	trekking, bird-watching	Oct-Jan
Lake Abiata-Shala National Park (p173)	crater lakes, hot springs; red-billed hornbills, Didric's cuckoos, Abyssinian rollers, superb starlings	bird-watching, walking	Nov-Dec
Mago National Park (p210)	savannah, open woodland; elephants, hartebeest, buffaloes, many birds	visiting Mursi tribes, wildlife drives	Jun-Sep & Jan-Feb
Nechisar National Park (p199)	savannah, acacia woodland; Burchell's zebras, Swayne's hartebeest, crocodiles, greater kudu, 320 bird species	wildlife drives, boat trips	Nov-Feb
Omo National Park (p211)	savannah, open woodland; elephants, buffaloes, lions	visiting Mursi, Dizi & Surma tribes	Jun-Sep & Jan-Feb
Senkele Wildlife Sanctuary (p176)	open acacia woodland; Swayne's hartebeest, Bohor reedbucks, spotted hyena, greater spotted eagles	wildlife drives	Nov-Feb
Yabelo Wildlife Sanctuary (p193)	acacia woodland, savannah grasses; Stresemann's bush crows, white-tailed swallows, Swayne's hartebeest, gerenuks	bird-watching, wildlife drive	year-round
Northern Ethiopia			
Simien Mountains National Park (p125)	dramatic volcanic escarpments and plateaus; walia ibexes, gelada baboons, Simien wolves, lammergeyers	trekking, bird-watching, wildlife viewing	Oct-Jan
Eastern Ethiopia			
Awash National Park (p217)	semiarid woodland; beisa oryxes, Soemmering's gazelles, kudu, 6 endemic bird species	bird-watching, wildlife viewing	Oct-Feb
Western Ethiopia			
Gambela National Park (p250)	semiarid woodland, deciduous forests; savannah Nile lechwe, white-eared kobs, elephants	rugged wildlife drives/treks	Dec-Mar

National Park, where lengthy negotiations have led to the park finally being settlement-free.

Nechisar and Omo National Parks, long neglected by the government, are now run by a nonprofit organisation which has successfully rehabilitated parks in other African countries. The African elephant, black rhinoceros, giraffe and other exterminated species will probably be reintroduced.

ENVIRONMENTAL ISSUES

Despite civil wars taking their toll on the environment, Ethiopia's demographic pressures have been the main culprit. About 95% of it's original forest is believed to have been lost to agriculture and human settlement.

Ethiopia's population has almost quintupled in the last 70 years and continues to grow at 2.5%; the pressures for living space, firewood, building materials, agricultural land, livestock grazing and food will only further reduce natural resources, and wipe out larger areas of wildlife habitat.

The deforestation has resulted in soil erosion, an extremely serious threat to Ethiopia as it exacerbates the threat of famine. Although hunting and poaching over the centuries has decimated the country's once large herds of elephant and rhino, deforestation has also played a role.

Wildlife and forests were both victims of the most recent civil war, where whole forests were torched by the Derg to smoke out rebel forces. Additionally, large armies, hungry and with inadequate provisions, turned their sights on the land's natural resources and much wildlife was wiped out.

Up until recently, armed conflict between tribes in the Omo and Mago National Parks continued to impede wildlife conservation efforts.

Today, things are more under control. Hunting is managed by the government and may even provide the most realistic and pragmatic means of ensuring the future survival of Ethiopia's large mammals. Poaching, however, continues to pose a serious threat to some animals.

In late 2005 a new conservation action plan and a new wildlife proclamation were accepted by the government and sent to parliament for approval. Besides bringing stricter environmental regulations, these new programmes are designed to unite the government's previously unrelated portfolios of wildlife, biodiversity and environmental protection.

For more on wildlife conservation, contact the **Ethiopian Wildlife Conservation Department** (Map pp80–1; ☎ 0115 504020; Ras Desta Damtew St, Addis Ababa).

RESPONSIBLE TRAVEL: ENVIRONMENT

Although there are a few sustainable ecotourism projects popping up across Ethiopia, the concept is still not widely known. Some effort on your part is a good step in the right direction.

- Water is an extremely precious and scarce resource in some parts of Ethiopia (including Gonder, Aksum and Lalibela). Try not to waste it by letting taps and showers run unnecessarily.
- If you're buying authentic crafts, ensure that they aren't made from indigenous woods or wildlife products.
- Be sensitive to wildlife.
- If a campfire is necessary, ensure the wood used is eucalyptus and be sensitive to the fire's location as it can disturb wildlife.
- Never litter.
- Always crush your water bottles after use to minimise waste. Better yet, take a water bottle and chemically treat local water. **Pristine** (www.pristine.ca) or Katadyn MicroPur MP1 water treatment tablets are good choices.
- Avoid driving off-road as it can harm or disturb animals and nesting birds.

Advice on responsible travel from a cultural standpoint is available on p44. For tips on responsible trekking, see p255.

An excellent organisation in the UK that can provide more information for concerned travellers is London-based **Tourism Concern** (www.tourismconcern.org.uk).

Food & Drink

Ethiopia's food is much like Ethiopia, completely different from the rest of Africa. Plates, bowls and even utensils are replaced by *injera*, a unique pancake of countrywide proportions. Atop its rubbery confines can sit anything from spicy meat stews to colourful dollops of boiled veg and cubes of raw beef.

Whether it's the spices joyfully bringing a tear to your eye or the slightly sour taste of the clammy *injera* sending your tongue into convulsions, one thing's for sure, Ethiopian fare provokes a strong reaction in all.

Ethiopian cooking is quite varied and complex, so it's worth experimenting to find something that tickles your tongue in the right way – prices are so cheap, you can afford to make the odd mistake.

STAPLES & SPECIALITIES

Popular breakfast dishes include *enkulal tibs* (scrambled eggs made with a combination of green and red peppers, tomatoes and sometimes onions, served with bread), *ful* (chickpea and butter purée) and *yinjera fir fir* (torn-up *injera* mixed with butter and *berbere*, a red powder containing as many as 16 spices or more).

At lunch and dinner the much heralded Ethiopian staples of *wat*, *kitfo* and *tere sega* come out to play with the ever-present *injera*.

> If you want to save yourself some embarrassment (unlike us), never inhale as you're placing *injera* laden with *berbere* into your mouth.

Injera

You'll never forget your first *injera* experience.

It's the national staple and the base of almost every meal. It is spread out like a large, thin pancake, and food is simply heaped on top of it. An American tourist once famously mistook it for the tablecloth. Occasionally, *injera* is served rolled up beside the food or on a separate plate, looking much like a hot towel on an airplane.

Slightly bitter, it goes well with spicy food. Like bread, it's filling; and like a pancake, it's good for wrapping around small pieces of food and mopping up juices. It's also easier to manipulate than rice and doesn't fall apart like bread – quite a clever invention, really.

Although *injera* may look like old grey kitchen flannel, grades and nuances do exist. With a bit of time and perseverance, you may even become a connoisseur.

Low-quality *injera* is traditionally dark, coarse and sometimes very thick, and is made from millet or even sorghum. Good-quality *injera* is pale (the paler the better), regular in thickness, smooth (free of husks) and *always* made with the indigenous Ethiopian cereal *tef*. Because *tef* grows only in the highlands, the best *injera* is traditionally found there, and highlanders tend to be rather snooty about lesser lowland versions.

Wat

The favourite companion of *injera*, *wat* is Ethiopia's version of stew.

In the highlands, *bege* (lamb) is the most common constituent of *wat*. *Bure* (beef) is encountered in the large towns, and *figel* (goat) most often in the arid lowlands. Chicken is the king of the *wat* and *doro wat* is practically the national dish. Ethiopian Christians as well as Muslims avoid pork. On fasting days various vegetarian versions of *wat* are available.

Kai wat is a stew of meat boiled in a spicy (thanks to oodles of *berbere*) red sauce. *Kai* sauce is also used for *minchet abesh*, which is a thick minced-meat stew topped with a hard-boiled egg – it's one of our favourites, particularly with *aib* (like dry cottage cheese).

If you want something much milder, ask for *alicha wat* (it's a yellowish colour).

Kitfo

Kitfo is a big treat for the ordinary Ethiopian. The leanest meat is reserved for this dish, which is then minced and warmed in a pan with a little butter, *berbere* and sometimes *tosin* (thyme). It can be bland and disgusting, or tasty and divine. If you're ravenous after a hard day's travelling, it's just the ticket, as it's very filling. A tip? Ask for a heap of *berbere* on the side.

Traditionally, it's served just *leb leb* (warmed not cooked), though you can ask for it to be *betam leb leb* (literally 'very warmed', ie cooked!). A *kitfo special* is served with *aib* and *gomen* (minced spinach).

In the Gurage region (where it's something of a speciality) it's often served with *enset* (*kotcho;* false-banana 'bread'). *Kitfo beats* (restaurants specialising in *kitfo*) are found in the larger towns.

> If you become a massive fan of *kitfo* or *tere sega*, best get tested for tape worms (see p375) when you get home. Hopefully there'll be no pain to go with your tasty gain.

Tere Sega

Considered something of a luxury in Ethiopia, *tere sega* (raw meat) is traditionally served by the wealthy at weddings and other special occasions.

Some restaurants also specialise in it. Not unlike butcher shops in appearance, these places feature carcasses hanging near the entrance and men in bloodied overalls brandishing carving knives. The restaurants aren't as gruesome as they sound: the carcass is to demonstrate that the meat is fresh, and the men in overalls to guarantee you get the piece you fancy – two assurances you don't always get in the West.

A plate and a sharp knife serve as utensils, and *awazi* (a kind of mustard and chilli sauce) and *berbere* as accompaniments. Served with some local red wine, and enjoyed with Ethiopian friends, it's a ritual not to be missed – at least not for red-blooded meat eaters. It's sometimes called *gored gored*.

> Contrary to the myth started by 18th-century Scottish explorer James Bruce, Ethiopians don't carve meat from living animals. Whether it occurred in ancient times, remains uncertain.

DRINKS

Ethiopia has a well-founded claim to be the original home of coffee (see the boxed text, p243), and coffee continues to be ubiquitous across the country. As a result of Italian influence, *macchiato* (espresso with a dash of milk), cappuccino and a kind of café latte known as a *buna bewetet* (coffee with milk) are also available in many of the towns. Sometimes the herb rue (known locally as *t'ena adam*, or health of Adam) is served with coffee, as is butter. In the western highlands, a layered drink of coffee and

---

TRAVEL YOUR TASTEBUDS

With raw meat being a staple in Ethiopia, what dishes could possibly constitute a radical departure for those wishing to truly travel their tastebuds?

High on the yuck factor would have to be *trippa wat* (tripe stew), which still curls our toes and shakes our stomachs. And if an unleavened bread that's been buried in an underground pit and allowed to ferment for at least a month suits your fancy, order some *enset* with your *kitfo*. Enset is made from the false banana plant and closely resembles a fibrous carpet liner.

Fermentation of an entirely different sort can lead you down a very different path. If you're not catching an early bus the next morning, try the local *araki*, a grain spirit that will make you positively gasp. The Ethiopians believe it's good for high blood pressure! *Dagem araki* is twice-filtered and is finer. It's usually found in local hole-in-the-wall bars.

tea is also popular. If you want milk with coffee, ask for *betinnish wetet* (with a little milk).

In lowland Muslim areas, *shai* (tea) is preferred to coffee, and is offered black, sometimes spiced with cloves or ginger.

Most cafés also dabble in fresh juice, though it's usually dosed with sugar. If you don't want sugar in your juice or in your tea or coffee, make it clear when you order. Ask for the drink *yale sukkar* (without sugar). Bottled water is always available, as is the local favourite Ambo, a natural sparkling mineral water from western Ethiopia.

If looking for quality *tej*, ask a local. They'll know who makes it with pure honey and who cheats by adding sugar.

One drink not to be missed is *tej*, a delicious – and sometimes pretty powerful – local 'wine' or mead made from honey, and fermented using a local shrub known as *gesho*. *Tej* used to be the drink of the Ethiopian kings and comes in many varieties. It's served in little flasks known as *birille*.

There are several breweries in Ethiopia that pump out decent beers like Harar, Bati, Meta, Bedele, Dashen and Castel. Everyone has a different favourite, so explore at will!

Though no cause for huge celebration, local wine isn't at all bad, particularly the red Gouder. Of the whites, the dry Awash Crystal is about the best bet. Unless you're an aficionado of sweet red, avoid Axumite. Outside Addis Ababa, wine is usually only found in midrange hotels' restaurants.

CELEBRATIONS

Food plays a major role in religious festivals of both Muslims and Ethiopian Orthodox Christians. During the month of Ramadan, Muslims fast between sunrise and sunset, while Ethiopian Orthodox abstain from eating any animal products in the 55 days leading up to Ethiopian Easter.

Orthodox Ethiopians also abstain from animal products each Wednesday and Friday. There are a very large number of Orthodox feast days, of which 33 honour the Virgin Mary alone.

While it has no religious connotations, Ethiopians have even taken to celebrating the serving of coffee (see the boxed text, below).

WHERE TO EAT & DRINK

Outside Addis Ababa and major towns, there isn't a plethora of eating options. You're usually constrained to small local restaurants that serve one pasta dish and a limited selection of Ethiopian food. If there's no menu, use the Eat Your Words section (p72) to inquire what's available. In

---

THE COFFEE CEREMONY

The coffee ceremony typifies Ethiopian hospitality. An invitation to attend a ceremony is a mark of friendship or respect, though it's not an event for those in a hurry.

When you're replete after a meal, the ceremony begins. Freshly cut grass is scattered on the ground 'to bring in the freshness and fragrance of nature'. Nearby, there's an incense burner smoking with *etan* (gum). The 'host' sits on a stool before a tiny charcoal stove.

First of all coffee beans are roasted in a pan. As the smoke rises, it's considered polite to draw it towards you, inhale it deeply and express great pleasure at the delicious aroma by saying *betam tiru no* (lovely!). Next the beans are ground up with a pestle and mortar before being brewed up.

When it's finally ready, the coffee is served in tiny china cups with at least three spoonfuls of sugar. At least three cups must be accepted. The third in particular is considered to bestow a blessing – it's the *berekha* (blessing) cup. Sometimes popcorn is passed around. It should be accepted with two hands extended and cupped together.

Enjoy!

ETHIOPIA'S TOP FIVE RESTAURANTS

■ Serenade (p99) – although up a dark alley, it is a vibrant and flavourful place. Heaven for vegetarians.

■ Habesha Restaurant (p95) – serving is an art form at this quality Ethiopian eatery.

■ Shangri-la Restaurant (p96) – sit by the fire and cosy up to your *tere sega* (raw meat).

■ Ristorante Castelli (p97) – in a country where almost every restaurant serves spaghetti, Castelli's is the first prince of pasta.

■ Bahir Dar Hotel (p114) – although entirely outgunned by Addis Ababa's options, it's a genuine, low-key place to enjoy a local meal beneath the stars.

---

larger towns, local restaurants and hotels both offer numerous Ethiopian meals. The hotels' menus also throw some Western meals into the mix.

Kitfo beats are specialist restaurants in larger towns that primarily serve *kitfo*. Similarly *tej beats* are bars that focus on serving *tej*.

Unlike Addis Ababa, where restaurant hours very widely, most restaurants elsewhere are open daily from around 7.30am to 10pm. *Tej beats* tend to open later (around 10am), but also close about 10pm.

Quick Eats
Cafés and pastry/cake shops *(keak beats)* both make perfect spots for quick snacks, breakfasts and caffeine top-ups. Fresh juices are usually available at each too.

Outside town, roadside snacks such as *kolo* (roasted barley), *bekolo* (popcorn) and fresh fruit make great in-between-meal fillers.

VEGETARIAN & VEGANS
On Wednesday and Friday, vegetarians breathe easy as these are the traditional fasting days, when no animal products should be eaten. Ethiopian fasting food most commonly includes *messer* (lentil curry), *gomen* (collard greens) and *kai iser* (beetroot).

Apart from fasting days, Ethiopians are rapacious carnivores and vegetables are often conspicuous by their complete absence. If you're vegetarian or vegan, the best plan is to order alternative dishes in advance. If not, some dishes such as *shiro* (chickpea purée) are quite quickly prepared. Note that fancier hotels tend to offer fasting food seven days a week.

If you're concerned about available vegetarian food, you may even want to consider travelling during a fasting period, such as the one before Fasika (p261).

HABITS & CUSTOMS
Eating from individual plates strikes most Ethiopians as hilarious, as well as rather bizarre and wasteful. In Ethiopia, food is always shared from a single plate without the use of cutlery.

In many cases, with a simple *Enebla!* (Please join us!), people invite those around them (even strangers) to join them at their restaurant table. For those invited, it's polite to accept a morsel of the food to show appreciation.

In households and many of the restaurants, a jug of water and basin are brought out to wash the guests' outstretched hands before the meal. Guests remain seated throughout (though it's polite to make a gesture of getting up if the person serving is older).

DO'S & DON'TS

Do

- Bring a small gift if you've been invited to someone's home for a meal. Pastries or flowers are good choices in urban areas, while sugar, coffee and fruit are perfect in rural areas.
- Use just your right hand for eating. The left (as in Muslim countries) is reserved for personal hygiene only. Keep it firmly tucked under the table.
- Take from your side of the tray only; reaching is considered impolite.
- Leave some leftovers on the plate after a meal. Failing to do so is sometimes seen as inviting famine.
- Feel free to pick your teeth after a meal. Toothpicks are usually supplied in restaurants.

Don't

- Be embarrassed or alarmed at the tradition of *gursha,* when someone (usually the host) picks the tastiest morsel and feeds it directly into your mouth. The trick is to take it without letting your mouth come into contact with the person's fingers, or allowing the food to fall. It's a mark of great friendship or affection, and is usually given at least twice (once is considered unlucky). Refusing to take *gursha* is a terrible slight to the person offering it!
- Put food back onto the food plate – even by the side. It's better to discard it onto the table or floor, or keep it in your napkin.
- Touch your mouth or lick your fingers.
- Fill your mouth too full. It's considered impolite.

When eating with locals, try not to guzzle. Greed is considered rather uncivilised. The tastiest morsels will often be laid in front of you; it's polite to accept them or, equally, to divide them among your fellow diners. The meat dishes such as *doro wat* are usually the last thing locals eat off the *injera,* so don't hone in on it immediately!

When attracting someone's attention, such as a waiter or porter, it's polite to call *yikerta* (excuse me) or to simply clap your hands. Whistling or snapping your fingers, by contrast, is considered rude. Don't be offended if waiters snatch away your plates the moment you've finished; it's considered impolite to leave dirty dishes in front of customers.

EAT YOUR WORDS

Want to get your fill of *ful*? Tell your *kekel* from your *kai wat*? Do yourself a favour and learn a little of the local lingo. For pronunciation guidelines see p378.

Useful Phrases

breakfast	*kurs*
lunch	*mësa*
dinner	*ërat*
Is there a cheap (restaurant) near here?	*ëzzih akababi, rëkash (mëgëb bet) alleu?*
I want to eat...food.	*yeu...mëgëb ëfeullëfallö*
Ethiopian	*itëyopiya*
Arab	*arab*
Italian	*talyan*
Western	*faranji*

If you already know your *kekel* from your *kai wat* and want to learn more Amharic, pick up Lonely Planets' *Amharic Phrasebook.*

I'm vegetarian/I don't eat meat.   *sëga albeullam*
Can I have it mild?   *alëcha yimëtallëny?*

Do you have...   *...alle?*
   bread/bread rolls   *dabbo*
   round bread   *ambasha*
   chips   *yeu dënëch tëbs*
   salad   *seulata*
   sandwich   *sandwich* (usually spicy meat between plain bread)
   soup   *meureuk* (usually a spicy lamb or beef broth)
   yoghurt   *ërgo*

water   *wuha*
water (boiled)   *yeu feula wuha*
water (sterilised)   *yeu teutara wuha*
sparkling mineral water   *ambo wuha*
bottled 'flat' water   *highland wuha*
soda/soft drink   *leuslassa*
juice   *chëmaki*
milk   *weuteut*
tea   *shai*
coffee   *buna*
strong/weak   *weufram/keuchën*
with/without   *beu/yaleu*
honey   *mar*
sugar   *sëkwar*
beer   *bira*

Food Glossary

Most of the following are served with good-old *injera*.

NONVEGETARIAN

alicha wat	mild stew (meat and vegetarian options)
asa wat	freshwater fish served as a hot stew
bege	lamb
beyainatu	literally 'of every type' – a small portion of all dishes on the menu; also known by its Italian name *secondo misto*
bistecca ai ferri	grilled steak
bure	beef
derek tibs	meat (usually lamb) fried and served *derek* ('dry' – without sauce)
doro	chicken
doro wat	chicken drumstick or wing accompanied by a hard-boiled egg served in a hot sauce of butter, onion, chilli, cardamom and *berbere*
dulet	minced tripe, liver and lean beef fried in butter, onions, chilli, cardamom and pepper (often eaten for breakfast)
fatira	savoury pastries
figel	goat
kai wat	lamb, goat or beef cooked in a hot *berbere* sauce
kekel	boiled meat
kitfo	minced beef or lamb like the French steak tartare, usually served warmed (but not cooked) in butter, *berbere* and sometimes thyme
kwalima	sausage served on ceremonial occasions
kwanta fir fir	strips of beef rubbed in chilli, butter, salt and *berbere* then usually hung up and dried; served with torn-up *injera*
mahabaroui	a mixture of dishes including half a roast chicken

melasena senber tibs	beef tongue and tripe fried with *berbere* and onion
minchet abesh	minced beef or lamb in a hot *berbere* sauce
scaloppina	escalope
tere sega	raw meat served with a couple of spicy accompaniments (occasionally called *gored gored*)
tibs	sliced lamb, pan fried in butter, garlic, onion and sometimes tomato
tibs sheukla	*tibs* served sizzling in a clay pot above hot coals
trippa	tripe
wat	stew
zilzil tibs	strips of beef, fried and served slightly crunchy with *awazi* sauce

VEGETARIAN

aib	like dry cottage cheese
atkilt-b-dabbo	*vegetables with bread*
awazi	a kind of mustard and chilli sauce
bekolo	popcorn
berbere	as many as 16 spices or more go into making the famous red powder that is responsible for giving much Ethiopian food its kick; most women prepare their own special recipe, often passed down from mother to daughter over generations, and proudly adhered to
dabbo fir fir	torn up bits of bread mixed with butter and *berbere*
enkulal tibs	literally 'egg *tibs*', a kind of Ethiopian scrambled eggs made with a combination of green and red peppers, tomatoes and sometimes onions, served with *dabbo* (bread) – great for breakfast
enset	false-banana 'bread'; a staple food (also called *kotcho*)
ful	chickpea and butter purée eaten for breakfast
genfo	barley or wheat porridge served with butter and *berbere*
gomen	minced spinach
injera	large Ethiopian version of a pancake/plate
kai iser	beetroot
kolo	roasted barley
messer	a kind of lentil curry made with onions, chillies and various spices
shiro	chickpea or bean purée lightly spiced, served on fasting days
sils	hot tomato and onion sauce eaten for breakfast
ye som megeb	a selection of different vegetable dishes, served on fasting days
yinjera fir fir	torn-up bits of *injera* mixed with butter and *berbere*

Addis Ababa
አዲስ አበባ

On first observing Ethiopia's capital over a century ago, one foreigner called it 'noisy, dusty, sprawling and shambolic'. Over the next century the tented camp morphed into a modern African business centre and the continent's fourth-largest city, yet travellers still utter the same phrase. If that isn't reason enough to discount first impressions, we don't know what is!

If you give 'Addis' a few days you'll come to appreciate its bizarre blend of past and present: old imperial statues and emblems alongside hammer-and-sickle placards of the former Marxist regime; wattle-and-daub huts with austere Italian Fascist buildings and luxurious high-rise hotels. Lift the city's skin and the same contrasts apply: *tej beats* still serve traditional golden honey wine and *azmaris* (wandering minstrels) sing centuries-old songs, while a few blocks on, martinis glow and modern beats rain down in hip new bars and nightclubs. On the wide boulevards, priests in medieval-looking robes mix with African bureaucrats, Western aid workers, young Ethiopian women with mobile phones, and the odd herd of goats.

The capital contains Africa's most important museums, vibrantly painted cathedrals and cosmopolitan cuisine unseen elsewhere in Ethiopia. Addis Ababa also boats the nation's best Ethiopian restaurants, many of which host traditional shows of music and dance.

For such a large city, Addis Ababa is remarkably friendly and laid-back. And compared with other African (and Western) capitals, it's remarkably safe too. Surprised? You shouldn't be. We've already told you to ignore your initial inklings! Addis Ababa is no ordinary African capital – dig in and enjoy.

HIGHLIGHTS

- Catch a quiet kip in the gardens outside the **Ethnological Museum** (p84), before the exhibits inside really open your eyes

- Bend your head down and look up to Lucy, our pint-sized ancient ancestor at the **National Museum** (p85)

- Indulge your tongue and tummy with a range of cuisine types in Ethiopia's best **restaurants** (p94)

- See snapshots of Addis' brief but bloody history at the monuments **Yekatit 12** (p87) and **Derg** (p87)

- Dodge dung and pilfering pickpockets and claim a prize to call your own at the massive **Merkato** (p87)

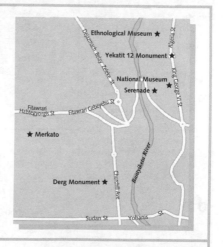

- POPULATION: 2.8 MILLION

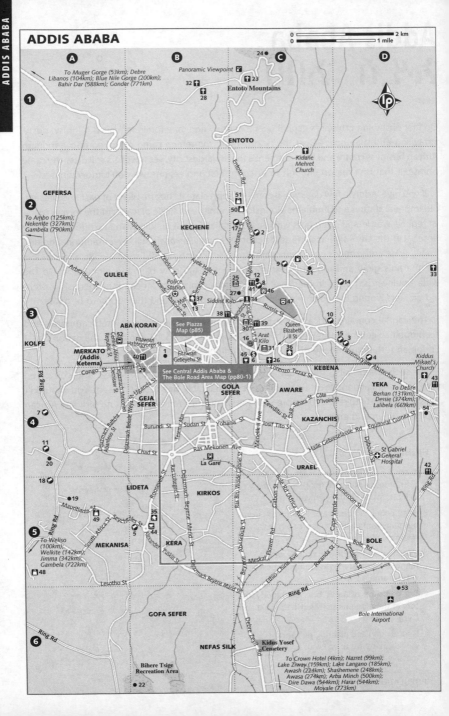

ADDIS ABABA

0 _____ 2 km
0 _____ 1 mile

A **B** **C** **D**

1

To Muger Gorge (53km); Debre
Libanos (104km); Blue Nile Gorge (200km);
Bahir Dar (588km); Gonder (771km)

Panoramic Viewpoint

24

32 23

28

Entoto Mountains

ENTOTO

Kidane
Mehret
Church

GEFERSA

2

To Ambo (125km);
Nekemte (327km);
Gambela (790km)

KECHENE

51

50

17

2

GULELE

9

21

14

33

Police
Station

37

13

Siddist Kilo

25

12

27

8

41

46

34

47

3

ABA KORAN

See Piazza
Map (p85)

38

39

10

KOLFE

52

Fitawrari
Hablegyorgis St

16

30

Arat
Kilo

Queen
Elizabeth
II St

15

3

36

**MERKATO
(Addis
Ketema)**

40

1

Fitawrari
Gebeyehu St

31

26

4

Kiddus
Mikael's
Church

29

45

6

43

See Central Addis Ababa &
The Bole Road Area Map (pp80-1)

**GOLA
SEFER**

KEBENA

YEKA

To Debre
Berhan (131km);
Dessie (374km);
Lalibela (669km)

54

**GEJA
SEFER**

AWARE

KAZANCHIS

7

Burundi St

Sudan St

Yohanis St

4

11

20

Ras Mekonen Ave

La Gare

St Gabriel
General
Hospital

42

18

LIDETA

19

KIRKOS

49

35

URAEL

5

44

5

To Weliso
(100km);
Welkite (142km);
Jimma (342km);
Gambela (722km)

MEKANISA

KERA

Bole
Rd

BOLE

48

Lesotho St

53

GOFA SEFER

Bole International
Airport

6

Ring Rd

NEFAS SILK

Kidus Yosef
Cemetery

To Crown Hotel (4km); Nazret (99km);
Lake Ziway (159km); Lake Langano (185km);
Awash (224km); Shashemene (248km);
Awasa (274km); Arba Minch (500km);
Dire Dawa (544km); Harar (544km);
Moyale (773km)

Bihere Tsige
Recreation Area

22

HISTORY

Unlike Addis Ababa's numerous predecessors, the locations of which were chosen according to the political, economic and strategic demands of the days' rulers, Addis Ababa was chosen for its beauty, hot springs and agreeable climate. Why the drastic (and pleasant) change of convention in the late 19th century? Perhaps it was the first time a woman had any say in the matter! Yes, it was the actions of Taitu, the consort of Menelik II, which led to the birth of Addis Ababa.

Menelik's previous capital, Entoto, was in the mountains just north of present-day Addis Ababa and held strategic importance, as it was easily defended. However, it was unattractive and sterile, leading Taitu to request a house be built for her in the beautiful foothills below in an area she named Addis Ababa (New Flower). In the following decade, after Menelik's power increased and his need for defence waned, he moved his court down to Taitu and Addis Ababa.

A lack of firewood for the rapidly growing population threatened the future of Addis Ababa in 1896 and Menelik even started construction of a new capital, Addis Alem (New World), 50km to the west. In the end, it was the suggestion of a foreigner (thought to be French) to introduce the rapidly growing eucalyptus tree that saved the new capital.

Since 1958 Addis Ababa has been the headquarters of the UN Economic Commission for Africa (ECA) and, since 1963, the secretariat of the Organisation of African Unity (OAU). Many regard the city as 'Africa's diplomatic capital'.

ORIENTATION

Addis Ababa is massive and incoherent. It could be likened to a sprawling 250-sq-km *injera* adorned with sporadic piles of *tibs*, spaghetti, *mahabaroui* and Sichuan noodles! To navigate the city, it's best to break it down into these distinct dishes/districts.

The mound of smoking *tibs*, representing the central (or meaty) part of the city, is at the southern end of Churchill Ave, now named Gambia St. Here you'll find many government and commercial buildings.

The steaming heap of spaghetti would symbolise Piazza, a district whose legacy and architecture is owed to the Italian occupation. Piazza is found atop the hill at Churchill Ave's north end and houses budget hotels, as well as many cafés and bars.

To the east of Piazza is Addis Ababa University, several museums and the landmark roundabouts of Arat Kilo and Siddist Kilo. South from there is Menelik II Ave, which boasts National Palace, Africa Hall, a series of new urban parks and at its southern end, the huge and ugly Meskal Sq. This melange of attributes must be likened to a meal of this, that and everything *(mahabaroui)*.

Thanks to the new ring road built by the Chinese, the southeast of the city, on and around Bole Rd between Meskal Sq and the airport, is thriving with exciting development that contrasts sharply with the rest of the city. You guessed it – the Sichuan noodles!

Maps

No new maps (besides ours!) have been produced since the radical renaming of streets in 2005. If names aren't important to you, the most accurate map of Addis Ababa's convoluted street layout is the *City Map of Addis Ababa* (2003, scale 1:25,000) produced by the **Ethiopian Mapping Authority** (Map pp80-1; Menelik II Ave; 8.30am-12.30pm & 1.30-4.30pm Mon-Thu, 8.30-11.30am & 1.30-4.30pm Fri). The EMA charge a paltry Birr23.

INFORMATION
Bookshops

The big hotels such as the Ghion, Hilton and Sheraton all sell a good, but pretty pricey selection of books, magazines and newspapers.

Africans Bookshop (Map p85; Hailesilase St; 9am-1pm & 2.30-7pm Mon-Sat) The best place for secondhand books on Ethiopia, particularly those out of print. Selection is very limited.

Bookworld Friendship City Center (Map pp80-1; Bole Rd; 9am-9pm Mon-Sat, 11am-8pm Sun); Haile Gebreselassie Rd (Map pp80-1; Haile Gebreselassie Rd; 8am-9pm); Lime Tree Restaurant (Map pp80-1; Bole Rd; 7am-11pm); Piazza (Map p85; Wavel St; 8am-8pm Mon-Sat) The best place for books in English (as well as some in French). There's also a small section on Ethiopia and some European and US magazines. Prices are more than you'd pay at home, but much cheaper than the hotels.

Cultural Centres

Alliance-Ethio Français (Map p76; ☎ 0111 550213; www.allianceaddis.org; 8am-noon & 2-6pm Mon-Fri) Besides having Internet facilities and a library, this centre has pleasant gardens and a café. Check its website for concerts and cultural events. It's off Dejazmach Ummar Semeter St.

British Council (Map p85; ☎ 0111 115496; bc.addisababa@et.britishcouncil.org; Hailesilase St; 2-7.30pm Tue-Fri, 10am-6pm Sat) The library has English newspapers and 21 Internet stations.

Goethe Institut (Map p76; ☎ 0111 242345; www .goethe.de/af/add; 10am-6pm Mon-Fri) This German cultural centre houses a library, Internet café and exhibition hall. It's off Algeria St.

Instituto Italiano di Cultura (Map p76; ☎ 0111 553427; icc.addisababa@ethionet.et; Dejazmach Belay Zeleke St; 8.30am-2pm Mon-Fri, 3.30-6.30pm Tue & Thu) Occasionally hosts live performances. The Sofia Philharmonic orchestra were playing when we were in town.

Emergency

Emergency 24-hour numbers:

Fire brigade (☎ 993)

Police (☎ 991)

Red Cross Ambulance service (☎ 992)

Internet Access

Although Internet is everywhere, fast connections are still elusive. Some convenient outlets are listed here.

Cyber Easy Internet Cafe (Map pp80-1; Bole Rd; per hr Birr21; 9am-9pm Mon-Sat) The quickest connections on Bole Rd.

Internet Cafe (Map pp80-1; Bole Rd; per hr Birr15) It's an ADSL broadband connection, though not as fast as you'd wish. One of the few open on Sunday (8.30am to 9pm).

Kibsol (Map p76; Adwa Ave; per hr Birr12) One of many Internet options on this stretch of street near Arat Kilo.

STRANGE STREET SPELLINGS

Prior to 2005, finding a street sign in Addis was truly an art form. Today, finding a street sign is easy...it's finding one spelled correctly that's an art form!

Rumour has it that the shiny new signs were bequeathed by the Chinese contractors after they finished the ring road. Who's responsible for the misspellings is anyone's guess. Some of the many gaffes include Haile Selassie becoming Hailesilase, Joseph Tito becoming Josif Tito, Ras Makonnen becoming Ras Mekonen and Meskel Sq becoming Meskal Sq.

It's not all bad news though, the new naming concept involved the removal of many colonial names and the introduction of many correctly spelt African ones, including each member state of the Organisation of African Unity (OAU).

To stay consistent and limit confusion, we're using the creative new spellings on the actual street signs for our maps and text.

ADDIS ABABA IN...

Two Days

Start in Piazza with a steaming *macchiato* (espresso with a dash of milk) at **Tomoca** (p100), before visiting **St George Cathedral & Museum** (p86). Next, extract yourself from a minibus at Arat Kilo and meet legendary Lucy in the **National Museum** (p85). From there, stroll north and absorb the magnitude of the **Yekatit 12 Monument** (p87).

After lunch and ice cream at **Blue Tops Restaurant** (p97), marvel at the brilliant **Ethnological Museum** (p84). Finish the day dining and drinking *tej* (honey wine) at a **traditional Ethiopian restaurant** (p94), while enjoying a show of song and dance.

After spending the first day viewing things you can't have, fill your second day with spending! Meander **Entoto Market** (p103) before diving inside Churchill Ave's shops; don't miss **Hope Enterprises** (see the boxed text, p84). Lastly, explore the massive **Merkato** (p87), before escaping for a sunset drink and meal at **Top View** (p98).

Four Days

With four days, you could complete the two-day itinerary at a slower pace (more *macchiatos!*), squeezing in extra sights like the **Holy Trinity Cathedral** (p86) and **Natural History Museum** (p87), both near Arat Kilo. Art-lovers should visit **Asni Gallery** (p89) and **Afewerk Tekle's home and studio** (p89), while food-lovers simply must savour **Serenade** (p99) and **Ristorante Castelli** (p97).

Megel Internet Service (Map pp80-1; Ras Desta Damtew St; per hr Birr15) Central, but on the slow side.

Nina Internet Service (Map p85; Mundy St; per hr Birr15) Of the several Internet cafés around here, Nina is the most comfortable and images can be burnt to CD with USB connections (Birr4). A new CD is Birr5.

Sheraton Business Center (Map pp80-1; Itegue Taitu St; per hr Birr180) Extortionate, but furiously fast connections.

Internet Resources

WhatsUp! Adddis (www.whatsupaddis.com) A great site highlighting upcoming cultural events and the entertainment scene in Addis.

Laundry

Every hotel does laundry and their service is inevitably cheaper and quicker than the laundries that line Bole Rd.

Libraries

Institute of Ethiopian Studies (Map p76; ☎ 0111 239740; www.ies-ethiopia.org; Addis Ababa University, Algeria St) This institute boasts the world's best collection of books in English on Ethiopia. It's free for a half-day's casual use.

National Archives & Library of Ethiopia (Map pp80-1; ☎ 0115 516532; ☒ closed morning Mon) Shelves moan under the weight of 20,000 books on Ethiopia. The English-language section is quite good. It is located off Sudan St.

Media

Several English-language publications can be of use, especially *Time Out Addis* and the monthly *What's Up!* These list restaurants, shopping venues, nightclubs and events. They're available (haphazardly) at large hotels, smart restaurants and art galleries.

Medical Services

Bethzatha Hospital (Map pp80-1; ☎ 0115 514141; ☒ 24hr) This quality private hospital, off Ras Mekonen Ave, is recommended by most embassies.

Ethio-Swe Dental Clinic (Map pp80-1; ☎ 0116 614932; Bole Rd) Likely the city's most respected dental office.

Ghion Pharmacy (Map pp80-1; Ras Desta Damtew St) Central and well stocked.

Hayat Hospital (Map pp80-1; ☎ 0116 624488; Ring Rd; ☒ 24hr) A reliable option near the airport. A consultation will set you back Birr40.

St Gabriel Hospital (Map pp80-1; ☎ 0116 613622; Djibouti St; ☒ 24hr) This private hospital has good X-ray, dental, surgery and laboratory facilities. A consultation only costs Birr50.

Zogdom Pharmacy (Map pp80-1; Bole Rd) Convenient for Bole-goers.

Money

You will have no trouble at all finding a bank to change cash or travellers cheques. However, being able to find an ATM that

ADDIS ABABA

CENTRAL ADDIS ABABA & THE BOLE ROAD AREA

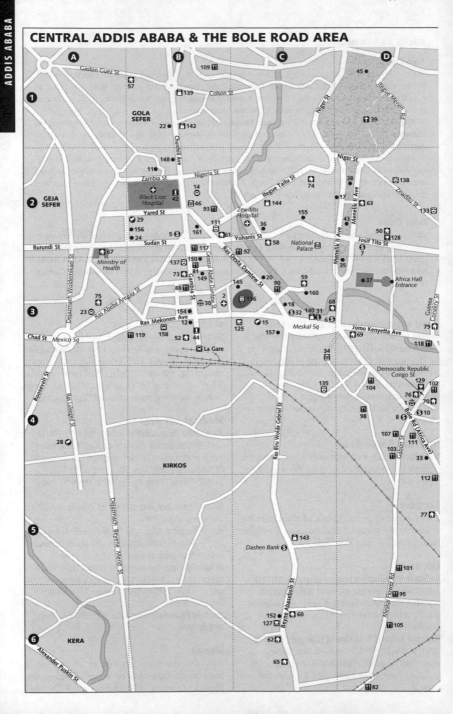

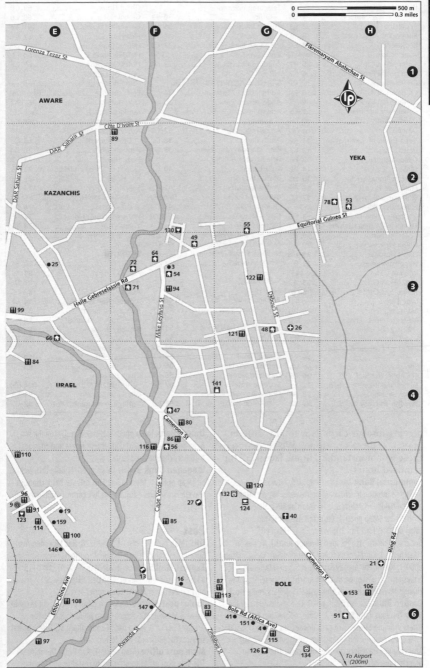

ADDIS ABABA

INFORMATION	
Air's Business Center	1 D4
Bethzatha Hospital	2 B3
Bookworld	3 F3
Bookworld	4 G6
Bookworld	(see 41)
Commercial Bank	5 B2
Commercial Bank	6 C3
Commercial Bank	7 D2
Commercial Bank	8 D4
Commercial Bank	(see 75)
Cyber Easy Internet Cafe	9 E5
Dashen Bank	10 D4
Dashen Bank	(see 74)
Department of Immigration	11 B2
DHL	12 B3
Djibouti Embassy	13 F6
EMS	14 B2
Eritrean Embassy (closed)	15 C3
Ethio-Swe Dental Clinic	16 F6
Ethiopian Mapping Authority	17 D2
Ethiopian Wildlife Conservation Department	18 C3
Ethiopian Women Lawyers Association	19 E5
Ghion Pharmacy	20 C3
Hayat Hospital	21 H6
Hope Enterprises	22 B1
Internet Cafe	(see 113)
Junior Post Office	23 A3
Junior Post Office	(see 6)
Lime Tree	(see 41)
Main Post Office	(see 14)
Megel Internet Service	(see 20)
Ministry of Culture & Tourism	24 B2
Ministry of Labour & Social Affairs	25 E3
Sheraton Business Center	(see 74)
St Gabriel Hospital	26 G3
Somaliland Representation	27 F5
Sudanese Embassy	28 A4
Swedish Embassy	29 B2

Telecommunications Office	30 B3
Tourist Information Centre	31 C3
United Bank	(see 63)
Wegagen Bank	32 C3
Wegagen Bank	(see 8)
Zogdom Pharmacy	33 D4

SIGHTS & ACTIVITIES	
Addis Ababa Museum	34 C3
Addis Ababa Park	35 D3
Addisu Filwoha Hotel & Hot Springs	36 C2
Africa Hall	37 D3
Africa Park	38 D2
Beta Maryam Mausoleum	39 D1
Bole Medhane Alem Cathedral	40 G5
Boston Day Spa	41 G6
Derg Monument	42 B2
Desalegn Hotel	(see 56)
Ethiopia Park	43 D2
Ghion Hotel	(see 59)
Hilton Hotel	(see 63)
Lion of Judah Monument	44 B3
Menelik Imperial Palace	45 D1
National Postal Museum	46 B2
Sheraton Hotel	(see 74)

SLEEPING	
Atlas Hotel	47 F4
Awraris Hotel	48 G3
Axum Hotel	49 F3
B & G	50 D2
Bole International Hotel	51 H6
Buffet de la Gare	52 B3
Central Shoa Hotel	53 H2
Classic Hotel	54 F3
Debre Damo Hotel	55 G2
Desalegn Hotel	56 F4
Extreme Hotel	57 B1
Finfine Adarash Hotel & Restaurant	58 C2

Ghion Hotel	59 C3
Global Hotel	60 C6
Harambee Hotel	61 B2
Hawi Hotel	62 C6
Hilton Hotel	63 D2
Holiday Hotel	64 F3
Hotel Concorde	65 C6
Hotel De Leopol International	66 E3
Leah's House	(see 106)
Lido Hotel	67 A2
Meridian Hotel	(see 16)
National Hotel	68 C3
Novotel/Ibis Hotel Development	69 D3
Pension Rita	70 D4
Plaza Hotel	71 F3
Queen of Sheba Hotel	72 F3
Ras Hotel	73 B3
Sheraton Hotel	74 C2
Wabe Shebelle Hotel	75 A3
Wanza Hotel	76 D4
Weygoss Guest House	77 D5
Yonnas Hotel	78 H2
Yordanos Hotel	79 D3

EATING	
17 17	80 F4
Addisu Pastry	81 B3
Agelgil	82 D6
Aladdin	83 F6
Almendi Restaurant	84 E4
Antica Restaurant	85 F5
Blue Drops Restaurant	86 F4
Bombay Brasserie	87 G6
Café Miru	88 B3
Canapé International Restaurant	89 F2
China Bar & Restaurant	90 C3
China Paradise Restaurant	(see 65)
City Café & Pastry	91 E5
Cottage Restaurant & Pub	92 C2

accepts foreign cards is a totally different matter – there are none! We've denoted those with nonstandard hours (see p257 for standard hours).

Commercial Bank Arat Kilo (Map p76; Adwa St; ☼ open through lunch); Bole International Airport (Map p76; Bole Rd; ☼ 24hr); Bole Rd (Map pp80–1; Bole Rd); Churchill Ave (Map pp80–1; Churchill Ave); Josif Tito St (Map pp80–1; Josif Tito St); Lower Piazza (Map p85; General Wingate St; ☼ open through lunch); Meskal Sq (Map pp80–1; cnr Menelik II Ave & Meskal Sq); Mexico (Map pp80–1; Ras Abebe Aregay St); Upper Piazza (Map p85; Hailesilase St; ☼ open through lunch) All these branches change travellers cheques and cash (US dollars and euros).

Dashen Bank Bole Rd (Map pp80–1); Sheraton Hotel (Map pp80–1; Itegue Taitu St; ☼ 7-11am, noon-7pm & 8-11pm) Offers Visa and MasterCard cash advances of up to US$500 for a 5.5% commission (minimum charge of US$12.50). Also changes travellers cheques and cash. The Bole Rd branch is just off Bole Rd.

United Bank (Map pp80–1; Hilton Hotel, Menelik II Ave; ☼ 6am-10.30pm) Convenient hours and changes travellers cheques and cash.

Wegagen Bank Bole Rd (Map pp80–1; Bole Rd); Meskal Sq (Map pp80–1; Meskal Sq) This private bank changes travellers cheques (slightly higher commissions) and cash.

Post

DHL (Map pp80–1; ☎ 0115 526220; Ras Mekonen Ave) Speedy and reliable international courier service.

Express Mail Service (EMS; Map pp80–1; ☎ 0115 512999; ems@ethionet.et; Ras Desta Damtew St) A reasonably priced government-run courier service.

Junior post offices Meskal Sq (Map pp80–1; cnr Menelik II Ave & Meskal Sq); Mexico (Map pp80–1; Ras Abebe Aregay St); Piazza (Map p85; Cunningham St) Offers postal services for postcards and letters only.

Main post office (Map pp80–1; Ras Desta Damtew St) The only post office to offer poste restante and international parcel services (see p265 for international shipping rates).

Telephone & Fax
The yellow public phone boxes around town take Birr0.10 coins; many also accept phonecards.

Air's Business Center (Map pp80–1; Democratic Republic Congo St) Offers cheap international calls of decent quality over the Internet. Calls to landlines/mobiles cost Birr4/5 per minute.

Telecommunications office (Map pp80–1; ☎ 0115 514977; Gambia St) International calls at standard rates (see p267).

Tourist Information
Tourist Information Centre (Map pp80–1; ☎ 0115 512310; Meskal Sq; 🕐 8.30am-12.30pm & 1.30-5.30pm Mon-Thu, 8.30-11.30am & 1.30-5.30pm Fri) This helpful office does its best to provide information about the city

and itineraries elsewhere. It also has some informative brochures about the rest of Ethiopia.

Travel Agencies
For information on travel agencies in Addis Ababa, see Tours (p282).

Visa Extensions
Department of Immigration (Map pp80–1; ☎ 0111 553899; 🕐 8.30am-12.30pm & 1.30-5.30pm Mon-Fri) Issues single-/multiple-entry extensions for US$20/30.50. Multiple-entry extensions are for those on business or for travellers with exceptional circumstances (ie making a return air trip to Tanzania where there is no Ethiopian diplomatic representation). The process takes 24 hours. The office is off Zambia St.

DANGERS & ANNOYANCES
Violent crime in Addis Ababa is fortunately rare, particularly where visitors are

HOPE SPRINGS ETERNAL

Wanting to help Addis Ababa's many street children is natural. However, giving them money or food (which in most cases is quickly exchanged for money) isn't recommended, as it invariably leads to more problems for them and their community. To solve this dilemma, **Hope Enterprises** (Map pp80-1; ☎ 0111 560345; Churchill Ave) was created. It sells meal tickets (eight for Birr4) that you can distribute to needy children. Each day an average of 660 children redeem the tickets for a 'simple but nourishing meal' at the centre.

concerned. However, petty theft and confidence tricks are problematic.

The Merkato has the worst reputation, as pickpockets abound – targeting not just *faranjis* (foreigners, especially Western ones) but Ethiopians as we. An old ploy is for someone to step blindly into you, while another gently lifts your belongings in the subsequent confusion. A less subtle tactic now being used involves someone diving at your feet and holding your legs while another pilfers your pockets.

Both times this latest manoeuvre was tried on us (once at Merkato, the other near the national stadium), the perpetrators were sent scurrying by us fighting back a little and shouting *leba!* (thief!). You are advised to leave hand luggage and jewellery in your hotel if you plan on visiting the Merkato.

Other spots where you should be vigilant include the Piazza, Meskal Sq, minibus stands, outside larger hotels, and Churchill

Ave, where adult gangs have been known to hang around the National Theatre. Common gang ploys are to feign a fight or argument and, when one man appeals to you for help, the other helps himself to your pockets.

SIGHTS

Most sights are pretty scattered throughout the city centre and Piazza, though there is a concentration of major museums and other sights in the vicinity of Arat Kilo and Siddist Kilo, which sit east of Piazza and north of the city centre.

Ethnological Museum

Set within Haile Selassie's former palace and surrounded by the beautiful gardens and fountains of Addis Ababa University's main campus is the enthralling **Ethnological Museum** (Map p76; Algeria St; adult/student Birr20/10; ☺ 8am-5pm Mon-Fri, 9am-5pm Sat & Sun).

The show starts before you even get inside: look for the intriguing set of stairs spiralling precariously skyward near the palace's main entrance. Each step was placed by the Italians as a symbol of Fascist domination, one for every year Mussolini held power (starting from his march to Rome in 1922). A small Lion of Judah (symbol of Ethiopian monarchy) sits victoriously atop the final step, like a jubilant punctuation mark at the end of a painfully long sentence.

Within the entrance hall you'll find a small exhibition dedicated to the history of the palace, and the doorway to the Institute of Ethiopian Studies Library (p79).

This contemporary museum truly comes into its own on the 1st floor, where superb

SIREN SCAM

One scam that still seems to be snagging tourists is the 'siren scam'. It takes various forms, including offering you a 'cultural show' or a traditional coffee ceremony.

The venue is usually somebody's living room, where a hostess will promptly dish copious quantities of *tej* (honey wine) and, perhaps, traditional dancers and musicians will perform.

Suddenly the 'entertainment' comes to an end and between Birr700 and Birr1000 is demanded. Approaches are made to couples or groups as well as to single males. Most commonly, the person approaching you is a young, well-dressed Ethiopian male, often claiming to be a student.

If you end up in a situation like this, offer to pay for anything you've consumed (a litre of quality *tej* shouldn't be more than Birr12), and if it's not accepted, threaten to call the police. The area around the hotels in the Piazza and Churchill Ave seem to be prime hunting grounds for potential victims.

artefacts and handicrafts from Ethiopia's peoples are distinctively displayed. Instead of following the typical static and geographical layout that most museums fall into, these displays are based upon the life cycle. First comes Childhood, with birth, games, rites of passage and traditional tales. We particularly enjoyed the 'Yem Tale', a story of selfishness, dead leopards and sore tails! Adulthood probes into beliefs, nomadism, traditional medicine, war, pilgrimages, hunting, body culture and handicrafts. The last topic is Death and Beyond, with burial structures, stelae and tombs. The exhibition gives a great insight into Ethiopia's many rich cultures.

Other rooms on this floor show the preserved bedroom, bathroom and exorbitant changing room of Emperor Haile Selassie, complete with a bullet hole in his mirror courtesy of the 1960 coup d'etat.

The 2nd floor plays home to two drastically different, but equally delightful displays. The vibrant hall focuses on religious art, with an exceptional series of diptychs, triptychs, icons, crosses and magic scrolls.

Magic scrolls, like the Roman lead scrolls, were used to cast curses on people or to appeal to the gods for divine assistance. The collection of icons is the largest and most representative in the world. Senses of another sort are indulged in the small cavelike corridor that sits next to the hall. Inside, traditional music gently fills the air and the black surrounds leave you nothing to look at besides the instruments – brilliant.

National Museum ብሔራዊ ሙዚየም

Although slightly less visually stimulating than the Ethnological Museum, the **National Museum** (Map p76; ☎ 0111 117150; King George VI St; admission Birr10; ☾ 8.30am-5pm) is no less thought provoking. Its collection is ranked among the most important in sub-Saharan Africa.

The palaeontology exhibit on the basement level contains fossilised evidence of some amazing extinct creatures, like the massive sabre-toothed feline *Homotherium* and the gargantuan savannah pig *Notochoerus*. However, the stars of the exhibit are

---

PIAZZA

0 _____ 300 m
0 _____ 0.2 miles

INFORMATION
Africans Bookshop...................1 D2
Bookworld..............................2 B3
British Council.........................3 D2
Commercial Bank......................4 C3
Commercial Bank......................5 C3
Junior Post Office......................6 B3
Nina Internet Service.............(see 10)

SIGHTS & ACTIVITIES
St George Cathedral
& Museum..........................7 C2

SLEEPING
Baro Hotel..............................8 C3
Itegue Taitu Hotel....................9 C3
Wutma Hotel..........................10 C3

EATING
Addis Ababa Restaurant.........11 C1
Cafe Chaud............................12 C3
Isola Verde Pizzeria.................13 C3
Raizel Café.............................14 C3
Ristorante Castelli...................15 C3
Seranade................................16 D1

DRINKING
Terrace Café...........................17 C2
Tomoca.................................18 C3

ENTERTAINMENT
Cinema Empire...................(see 14)
Cinema Ethiopia......................19 C3
City Hall Theatre & Cultural
Centre..............................20 C2
Hager Fikir Theatre.................21 C2

TRANSPORT
Bahir Dar Tour & Travel
Agency.............................22 C3
Ethio-Der Tour & Travel.......(see 9)
Ethiopian Airlines....................23 C3
Ethiopian Rift Valley Safaris.....24 B3
Red Jackal Tour Operator.....(see 9)
Sunrise Travel & Tour..............25 B3

two remarkable casts of **Lucy** (see p26), a fossilised hominid discovered in 1974. One lays prone, while the other stands much like she did some 3.2 million years ago, truly hitting home how small our ancient ancestors were. The real bones are preserved in the archives of the museum.

The periphery of the ground floor focuses on the pre-Aksumite, Aksumite, Solomonic and Gonder periods, with a wide array of artefacts, including an elaborate pre-1st-century-AD bronze oil lamp showing a dog chasing an ibex, a fascinating 4th-century-BC rock-hewn chair emblazoned with mythical ibexes, and ancient Sabean inscriptions. The middle of the room hosts a collection of lavish royal paraphernalia, including Emperor Haile Selassie's enormous and rather hideous carved wooden throne.

On the 1st floor, there's a vivid display of Ethiopian art ranging from early (possibly 14th-century) parchment, to 20th-century canvas oil paintings by leading modern artists. Afewerk Tekle's massive *African Heritage* and Abebe Zelelew's *Genital Mutilation* are some of the most moving pieces.

The 2nd floor contains a collection of secular arts and crafts including traditional weapons, jewellery, utensils, clothing and musical instruments.

English-speaking guides are available and worthwhile.

Holy Trinity Cathedral
ቅዱስ ስላሴ ቤተ ክርስቲያን
Off Niger St, this massive and ornate **cathedral** (Map p76; ☎ 0111 564619; admission Birr25; 7am-6pm Mon-Fri, 9am-6pm Sat & Sun) is believed to be the second-most important place of worship in Ethiopia, ranking behind only the Old Church of St Mary of Zion in Axum (p135). It's also the celebrated final resting place of Emperor Haile Selassie and his wife Empress Menen Asfaw. Their massive Aksumite-style granite tombs, complete with lions' feet, sit inside and are a sight indeed.

The exterior, with its large copper dome, spindly pinnacles, numerous statues and flamboyant mixture of international styles provides an interesting and sometimes poignant glimpse into many historical episodes of Ethiopia's history.

Inside, there are some grand murals, the most notable being Afewerk Tekle's depiction of the Holy Trinity, with Matthew (man), Mark (lion), Luke (cow) and John (dove) peering through the clouds. There are also some brilliant stained-glass windows and two beautifully carved imperial thrones, each made of white ebony, ivory and marble.

To the south of the cathedral is the memorial and graves of the ministers killed by the Derg (p37) in 1974. Due to the prime minister's compound being behind this memorial, photographs are strictly forbidden.

The churchyard also hosts the graves of many patriots who died fighting the Italian occupation, including the great Resistance fighter Ras Imru. West of the cathedral is the tomb of the famous British suffragette Sylvia Pankhurst. Sylvia was one of the very few people outside Ethiopia who protested Italy's occupation; she moved to Addis Ababa in 1956.

Tickets can be bought at the administration office 20m west of the main gate. Self-appointed guides charge Birr10 per person.

St George Cathedral & Museum
ቅዱስ ጊዮርጊስ ቤተ ክርስቲያንና ሙዚየም
Commissioned by Emperor Menelik to commemorate his stunning 1896 defeat of the Italians in Adwa, and dedicated to St George (Ethiopia's patron saint), whose icon was carried into the battle, this Piazza **cathedral** (Map p85; Fitawrari Gebeyehu St) was completed in 1911 with the help of Greek, Armenian and Indian artists. The Empress Zewditu (in 1916) and Emperor Haile Selassie (in 1930) were both crowned here.

Thanks to its traditional octagonal form and severe neoclassical style, the grey stone exterior is easily outdone by the interior's flashes of colour and art. Sections of ceiling glow sky-blue and boast gilded golden stars, while the outer walls of the Holy of Holies are covered in paintings and mosaics by artists such as the renowned Afewerk Tekle.

In the grounds just north of the cathedral is the **museum** (admission Birr20; 9am-noon & 2-5pm Tue-Sun). It's well presented and contains probably the best collection of ecclesiastical paraphernalia in the country outside St Mary of Zion in Aksum. Items include beautiful crowns, hand crosses, prayer sticks, holy scrolls, ceremonial umbrellas and the coronation garb of Zewditu and Haile Selassie. The free tour, which includes the cathedral, is interesting and helpful in demystifying the peculiarities of the Orthodox church.

Yekatit 12 Monument
የካቲት 12 ሐወ-ልት

Rising dramatically from Siddist Kilo is this moving **monument** (Map p76; Siddist Kilo) to the thousands of innocent Ethiopians killed by the Italians as retribution for the attempt on Viceroy Graziani's life on 19 February 1937. Graphic depictions of the three-day massacre are captured in bronze and envelop the lower half of the marble obelisk.

Derg Monument ድሳችን

Nothing in the capital is as poignant a reminder of the country's painful communist rule as the towering **Derg Monument** (Map pp80-1; Churchill Ave). Topped by a massive red star and emblazoned with a golden hammer and sickle, the cement obelisklike structure climbs skyward in front of Black Lion Hospital.

Merkato መርካቶ

Wading into the market chaos just west of the centre known as **Merkato** (Map p76; 8.30am-7pm Mon-Sat) can as rewarding as it can be exasperating. You may find the most eloquent aroma wafting from precious incense. You may also find your wallet has been stolen and that you've got stinky shit on your shoe.

Some people say it's the largest market in Africa, but as its exact boundaries are as shady as some of its characters, we'll refrain from adding our name to that list – let's just say it's mighty, mighty huge.

The mass of stalls, produce and people may seem impenetrable, but on closer inspection the market reveals a careful organisation with different sections for different products. If you search long enough, you can find everything from Kalashnikovs to camels for sale. Not interested in leaving Merkato on the back of your own humped, frothymouthed beast while firing live rounds into the air? Well, you can spend your birr on pungent spices, silver jewellery or anything else that takes your fancy. There's even a 'recycling market', where sandals (old tires), coffee pots (old Italian olive tins) and other interesting paraphernalia can be found.

We could tell you that bargaining is the order of the day and that you should be vigilant with your valuables, but you're

seasoned travellers and you already know that!

To find what you're looking for while avoiding *delallas* (surreptitious commission agents), simply ask shopkeepers for directions; there's little risk they'll follow you to collect commissions.

Merkato is at its liveliest on Saturday, when people from all over the country (including tourists) flock in.

Natural History Museum
የተፈጥሮ ታሪክ መ-ዝየም

Go eye to eye with a bloated leopard in this **zoological museum** (Map p76; ☎ 0111 571677; Queen Elizabeth II St; admission Birr10; 9am-5pm Tue-Sun). Yes, sometimes the stuffers just don't know when to stop stuffing! Don't let the poor leopard scare you off; most animal specimens here are rather remarkable and there's no better way to spot nature's amazing intricacies. Besides magically iridescent butterflies, you'll see an impressive walia ibex, numerous antelopes and an astounding bird collection comprising 450 species common to Ethiopia.

Addis Ababa Museum
አዲስ አበባ መ-ዝየም

Despite only being founded on the centenary of the city in 1986, the **Addis Ababa Museum** (Map pp80-1; ☎ 0115 153180; Bole Rd; admission Birr10; 9am-5.30pm Tue-Sun) is the town's scruffiest museum. That said, perusing candid portraits of the redoubtable Empress Taitu, rakish Lej Iyassu, and the very beautiful Empress Zewditu, along with pictures of the capital in its infancy, is still worth an hour or so. It's unbelievable that the raucous city outside was nothing more than tents on a hill just over a century ago.

There's also a 'first-in-Ethiopia room' with a picture of the first telephone in Ethiopia and another of Menelik with Bede Bentley in Addis Ababa's first motor car (1907).

And we'd be remiss if we didn't mention the chummy (and over-inflated) lion and leopard near the entrance. Will somebody let the Natural History Museum know they've escaped?!

Africa Hall አፍሪካ አዳራሽ

Built in 1961 by Emperor Haile Selassie, **Africa Hall** (Map pp80-1; ☎ 0115 445098; Menelik II Ave), near Meskal Sq, is the seat of the UN's

ECA. The Italian-designed building isn't very interesting, apart from the friezelike motifs that represent traditional Ethiopian *shamma* (shawl) borders.

Far more interesting is *Africa: Past, Present and Future*, a monumental stained-glass window inside by the artist Afewerk Tekle. Measuring 150 sq metres, it fills one entire wall and is one of the biggest stained-glass windows in the world. During some hours of the day, the white marble floor of the foyer is flooded with colour. It's well worth a visit (by appointment only). See the boxed text, below for some intriguing interpretations and anecdotes.

National Postal Museum
ብሔራዊ የፖስታ ሙዚየም

Stamps don't usually float our boat, but the collection within the **postal museum** (Map pp80-1; Ras Desta Damtew St; admission Birr5; 9-10.30am & 2-4.30pm Mon-Fri) held us here

longer than we had expected. Trace Ethiopia's modern history through its colourful and international award-winning stamps, which date back to 1894, or get lost looking for historic stamps from your own country in many well-lit displays hosting beautiful examples from around the globe. Some of the Russian stamps are particularly lovely.

Beta Maryam Mausoleum
ቤተ ማርያም መቃብር

Also known as Menelik's Mausoleum, the **Beta Maryam Mausoleum** (Map pp80-1; Itegue Menen Rd; 8am-5pm) is located just south of Menelik's palace and offers an enchantingly eerie experience. After the priest has rolled up the carpet and pried open the large metal door in the floor, you will descend into the thick air of the creepy crypt. There you will find the four elaborate marble tombs of Empress Taitu, Emperor

---

A KEY TO 'AFRICA: PAST, PRESENT AND FUTURE'

Inside Africa Hall is a monumental stained-glass window by Afewerk Tekle. The following interpretation of the work comes from two interviews with the artist.

The first panel represents 'Africa: Past'. Red is the predominant colour, symbolic of Africa's struggle against both ignorance (symbolised by the heavy shadow) and colonialism (the smug-looking dragon). The disintegrating state of Africa is represented by the disunited family and the lost child. The skeleton with the whip shows evil driving the African continent – carried by a group of Africans – further and further into backwardness. The black chain framing the picture symbolises slavery.

The panel on the right represents 'Africa: Present'. The predominant colour is green, and Africa, symbolised by the man wielding a heavy double-handed sword, is struggling to slay the dragon of colonialism. In the background, a new sun rises; from it emerges all the peoples, religions and races of Africa. Above, the powers of evil, represented again by the skeleton, are taking flight, banished at last.

The middle panel shows 'Africa: Future'. Yellow is the predominant colour. In the foreground a family advances bearing torches, symbolic of a reawakening and the illumination brought by knowledge. Rallying behind are the other African countries, united and resolute in their aim for advancement. On the left, the knight in armour represents the UN holding out the scale of justice. In the background, a more serene landscape depicts an African Arcadia, in which peace and harmony reign on the continent at last.

Besides using artistic flare and hard work, Afewerk required masterful diplomatic skills to complete his vision. On one side, he faced harsh criticism from within the Economic Commission for Africa (ECA) over his decision to make the torch-bearing family in 'Africa: Future' Ethiopian (note the clothing). And on the other, he had the emperor's advisors demanding the father of the Ethiopian family be depicted as Haile Selassie himself. He defused the ECA by asking them to pick a replacement nation that represented African freedom more than Ethiopia, the only African country to have fought off colonisation. To outmanoeuvre the emperor's advisors, he simply concurred, then continued with his original plan using an anonymous face. How did he get away with it? He ensured the glass pane bearing the much-debated face was placed just before the unveiling, thus denying the emperor any chance to protest. While Afewerk Tekle won the battle of artistic license, the emperor had the last laugh – he was the one who decided what the artist's final fee would be!

Menelik, Empress Zewditu and Princess Tsehai Haile Selassie.

A self-appointed guide should set you back about Birr10 per person.

Asni Gallery
አስኒ ጋለሪ (የሸእል አዳራሽ)
Housed in the 1912 villa of Lej Iyasu's minister of justice, the **Asni Gallery** (Map p76; ☎ 0111 238796; admission free; ☑ 10am-5.30pm Tue-Sat, closed Jul & Aug) annually hosts six or seven splendid contemporary art exhibitions of emerging and established Ethiopian artists. Other events include workshops and lectures; look for announcements in the *Addis Tribune*.

For details of the Saturday vegetarian buffet, see p95.

The turn-off is about 4km northeast of town centre, just north of the French embassy. Take a minibus from Arat Kilo heading to 'Francey' and get off at the Total petrol station. It's a short walk from there.

Afewerk Tekle's Home & Studio
የአፈወርቅ ተክሌ ቤት ና ስቱዲዮ
A member of several international academies and with a drawer full of international decorations – about 100 at last count, including the British Order of Merit – Afewerk Tekle is considered among Africa's greatest artists.

A 90-minute tour of **Villa Alpha** (Map p76; ☎ 0113 715941; www.afewerktekle.org; admission per person US$25; ☑ closed 1 Jul-15 Sep), Afewerk's home and studio, is offered by the artist himself (by appointment only). Besides gazing at his most famous paintings, *The Meskel Flower, Mother Ethiopia* and *The Simien Mountains,* you'll also see striking works like *The Chalice and Cross* and hear stories about his life and Villa Alpha itself – all quite fascinating.

If you're thinking of souvenirs, signed and numbered reproductions on canvas are a snip at US$200 to US$350, while vivid tapestries climb into the thousands. The artist is particular about being addressed by his formal title 'Maître Artiste World Laureat', though 'Maître' will do for short!

Photography is permitted in the compound, but not in the house.

The house and studio is west of the centre in a side street off the Ring Rd, 200m from the Ghanaian embassy.

For more information on Afewerk Tekle see the boxed texts, p51 and opposite.

Lion of Judah Monument ጥቀር አንበሳ
Long the symbol of Ethiopia's monarchy, the Lion of Judah is ubiquitous throughout the country. Although images of the almighty animal abound in Addis Ababa, it's the storied history of the **Lion of Judah Monument** (Map pp80-1; Gambia St) that makes this statue significant.

After being erected on the eve of Haile Selassie's coronation in 1930, it was looted by Italians in 1935 and placed in Rome next to the massive Vittorio Emanuelle Monument. In 1938, during anniversary celebrations of the proclamation of the Italian Empire, Zerai Deress, a young Eritrean, spotted the statue and defiantly interrupted proceedings to kneel and pray before it. After police verbally and physically attempted to stop his prayers, he rose and attacked the armed Italians with his sword whilst screaming 'the Lion of Judah is avenged!'. He seriously injured several officers (some reports say he killed five) before he was shot. Although he died seven years later in Italian prison, his legend lives on in Ethiopia and Eritrea.

The Lion of Judah Monument was eventually returned to Addis Ababa in the 1960s.

Addis Ababa, Ethiopia & Africa Parks
Straddled by Menelik II Ave and climbing sequentially northwards from Africa Hall, these three new **urban parks** (Map pp80-1; Menelik II Ave) opened in early 2006. Lovely landscaping, with winding walkways, churning channels of cascading water, tidy trees and green grass, unite the three parks and make a pleasant respite in the city centre. It looks like outdoor cafés may join the fun soon.

Bole Medhane Alem Cathedral
ቦሌ መድኃኒአለም ቤተክርስቲያን
When this massive **cathedral** (Map pp80-1; Cameroon St) was completed in 2005 it surpassed the Holy Trinity Cathedral as Ethiopia's largest church. The only reason to wade through the throng of worshippers is to see the vibrant mural in the massive central dome.

Menelik Imperial Palace
የምኒልክ ቤተ መንግስት
South of Holy Trinity Cathedral, and surrounded by a stone wall, is the old **Menelik**

Imperial Palace (Map pp80-1; Lorenzo Tezaz St), which is now the government's main headquarters. Beneath the toilet in the president's personal office was where the body of Haile Selassie was discovered buried in 1992! This fascinating building is currently closed to visitors.

ACTIVITIES

Thanks to hosting the UN's ECA, activities are more catered to businesspeople than backpackers. Though, after returning from a tough slog out on the Ethiopian roads, many travellers indulge in a heavenly massage, steam bath or sauna. Cooling swims are also justifiably popular.

Massage, Steam Bath & Sauna

The new **Boston Day Spa** (Map pp80-1; ☎ 0116 636557; Bole Rd; ☼ 8am-7pm) has already gained a great reputation. A 30-/60-minute massage costs Birr75/100. A session in the sauna, steam bath and Jacuzzi is Birr100 and includes a free hand and foot massage.

A sublime half-/full-body massage at the **Sheraton Hotel** (Map pp80-1; ☎ 0115 171717; Itegue Taitu St; ☼ 5am-11pm) will set you back Birr120/200. Use of the sauna and Jacuzzi is a steep Birr185.

Sliding into the sauna, steam bath and Jacuzzi at the **Hilton Hotel** (Map pp80-1; ☎ 0115 518400; Menelik II Ave; ☼ 5am-9pm) will leave you Birr99 lighter. Your sore muscles will sing/scream to the tune of Birr90 per 45 minutes of massage.

While not as sophisticated as the previous three options, the **Addisu Filwoha Hotel & Hot Springs** (Map pp80-1; ☎ 0115 510902; ☼ 6am-8pm) complex is powered by Addis Ababa's original *raison d'être*, its natural hot springs. A public bath in the steaming mineral water is only Birr6 to Birr12, while a sauna is Birr24. A full-body oil massage and oddly exhilarating jet-wash is Birr60. The complex is off Yohanis St.

Readers recommend the steam baths (Birr50) and massages (Birr50 for 45 minutes) at **Desalegn Hotel** (Map pp80-1; ☎ 0116 624524; Cape Verde St).

Swimming

Beat the heat with some underwater action. The sweetest swims in town are to be had at the **Sheraton Hotel** (Map pp80-1; Itegue Taitu St; nonguest admission weekday/weekend Birr85/145) and **Hilton Hotel** (Map pp80-1; nonguest admission weekday/weekend Birr75/90; Menelik II Ave). A dozen laps back in the posh pool parade is the **Ghion Hotel** (Map pp80-1; nonguest admission Birr20), off Ras Desta Damtew St. The Ghion is cheap but gets overcrowded on weekends.

Golf

The **Addis Ababa Golf Club** (Map p76; ☎ 0113 201893) has a nine-hole course in the town's southwest. Weekday/weekend green fees are Birr140/180, plus Bir50 for club rental. A thwack on the driving range costs Birr20 plus Birr20/35 for 50/100 balls. It's off Ring Rd.

Other Sports

The **Hilton Hotel** (Map pp80-1; ☎ 0115 518400; Menelik II Ave) offers up everything from table tennis, tennis, squash, minigolf, aerobics and weightlifting. Costs range from Birr16 to Birr75 per day.

COURSES

Institute of Language Studies (Map p76; ☎ 0111 239702; Addis Ababa University, Algeria St) teaches three Ethiopian languages (Amharic, Tigrinya and Orominya). Classes start in early December and early April, lasting three to four months (48 hours of lectures). There's a one-time application fee of US$50 and each subsequent course costs US$300.

Head immediately left after entering the main university gates. The office is on the 2nd floor, room 210.

TOURS

There are no scheduled tours of Addis Ababa itself, but if you contact one of Addis Ababa's many travel agencies (see p282), most can usually arrange something.

FESTIVALS & EVENTS

Although Addis doesn't boast any major festivals of its own, it's a great place to catch some of the national festivals. For Leddet and Timkat head to Jan Meda Sports Ground where the most exuberant celebrations take place. During Leddet the festivities also include a traditional game of *genna* (hockey without boundaries). When the festival of Meskel is underway, Meskal Sq is one of the best places to be in the country. For more details on these festivals see p261.

Inaugurated in 2001, the 10km **Great Ethiopian Run** (www.ethiopiarun.org) is now the biggest mass participation race on the continent. It takes over the city on the last Sunday of November, and attracts over 20,000 runners. Whether spectating or running, it's a fun time and it's a great chance to see some of East Africa's elite athletes in action.

For minor festivals and upcoming cultural events check out www.whatsupaddis.com.

SLEEPING

Accommodation runs the gamut in Addis – brandish your flip flop and do battle with almighty insects, or sink into your sumptuous suite at the Sheraton. It's all up to you, your budget and the strength of your flip flops.

Budget hotels (and the best nightlife) are concentrated around Bole Rd and Piazza, whereas the best top-end options are found in the city centre. The midrange hotels in the north and southwest tend to offer the greatest value. Nightlife apart, sights are pretty spread out so there's no right or wrong area to stay.

All hotels listed here have parking facilities unless mentioned otherwise.

Budget
CENTRE
Lido Hotel (Map pp80–1; ☎ 0115 533247; lido@ethionet .et; Sudan St; s Birr144-213, d Birr161) Set behind some doum palms and cactus plants off Sudan St, this pleasant and clean hotel has 11 reasonably priced rooms. Rooms 8 and 9 (Birr161) are the brightest of the bunch. Room 9 has the only double bed, though couples can get cosy in the single rooms for no extra cost.

Buffet de la Gare (Map pp80–1; ☎ 0115 536288; s/tw Birr90/160) Thanks to being hosted in an old colonial building near the railway station, rooms have some character. They're pretty simple and small, with blue linoleum floors and soft springy mattresses. On the downside, it can be noisy and we've had complaints about the manager's temper.

B & G (Map pp80–1; d Birr80) Just north of Josif Tito St, behind the famous Old Milk House (p101), is this simple and cleanish spot. The rooms are quite stark, but the floors are carpeted, the sheets are nice, and hot water is plentiful. The only things lacking are sinks in the bathrooms.

BOLE RD AREA
Wanza Hotel (Map pp80–1; ☎ 0115 504893; Democratic Republic Congo St; d Birr70) Despite sporadic

flowing hot water and the continued presence of the odd crawly insect hiding behind the boilers (they're getting smaller though!), this place, with cosy rooms, comfortable beds, clean bathrooms and helpful owner is one of Addis Ababa's best budget options.

Pension Rita (Map pp80–1; ☎ 0115 530979; pen@ethionet.et; d Birr90-120) Set down a dirt lane off Democratic Republic Congo St, this option has spick-and-span rooms surrounding its quiet compound. Rooms and beds vary in size and some options have satellite TV, so check out a few. Although nobody seems to be in charge, it runs smoothly enough.

Leah's House (Map pp80–1; Ring Rd; s with shared bathroom Birr100) Known more for her restaurant's pies and Cornish pasties (see p98), Leah now has 12 simple smallish rooms for rent. Leah's House is a friendly Rastafarian joint, with each room symbolising one of Israel's 12 tribes.

PIAZZA & NORTH
Itegue Taitu Hotel (Map p85; ☎ 0111 560787; exod 2005@yahoo.com; tw with shared bathroom Birr46-115, tw Birr115-167) Just south of De Gaulle Sq is the country's first government hotel, built by Empress Taitu in 1907. Rooms range from small, stark and skanky in the rear annex to large and historic, with high ceilings and satellite TVs, in the original building. It's charming but well worn.

Wutma Hotel (Map p85; ☎ 0111 562878; wutma@ yahoo.com; Mundy St; d Birr60) Perhaps it's our fault that Wutma always played second fiddle to Baro Hotel, but we say NO LONGER! No, it doesn't have Baro's garden atmosphere or cosy nook to watch satellite TV, but its smallish grey-walled rooms outshine all but a few of Baro's. There are no parking facilities.

Baro Hotel (Map p85; ☎ 0111 551447; barohotel@ ethionet.et; Mundy St; s/tw Birr65/75) Across from Wutma, Baro has a wide assortment of grubby rooms. Yes, there are some reasonable options, but they're easily outnumbered by dimly lit cubicles, with stained walls, saggy mattresses, grimy carpets and ever-gurgling toilets.

SOUTHWEST
Hawi Hotel (Map pp80–1; ☎ 0114 654499; Beyene Abasebsib St; d Birr100) Although offering less value than the top Bole Rd options, this low-key place isn't a bad choice. The rooms and loos are a bit of a squeeze, but they're clean

ADDIS ABABA

and that's what really matters. If same-sex couples want to share a room, prices will rise. There's also no secured parking.

EAST

Yonnas Hotel (Map pp80-1; ☎ 0116 633988; fax 0116 632027; d/tw Birr151/181; 🖳) With squeaky clean loos, new linoleum floors (no grotty carpet here!), satellite TVs and Juliet balconies, this is a midrange option with a budget price. It's found up a dirt lane 50m north of Equatorial Guinea St.

Debre Damo Hotel (Map pp80-1; ☎ 0116 612630; fax 0116 622920; s/d with shared bathroom Birr76/97, d Birr115-150; 🖳) Debre Damo's rooms, all boasting baby blue walls, are clean but on the dark side. Most have aged carpet floors, with the exception of the Birr150 rooms, which have laminate tiling to go with their tiny TVs. The shared bathrooms are decent. It's off Haile Gebreselassie Rd.

Midrange
CENTRE

Ras Hotel (Map pp80-1; ☎ 0115 517060; fax 0115 517327; Gambia St; s/tw incl breakfast Birr178/200) Set squarely in the town centre, this place is government-run and tidy but has as much character as a newly paved footpath. Rooms possess green carpets, low ceilings, decent mattresses and satellite TVs. Its best asset is the terrace café.

National Hotel (Map pp80-1; ☎ 0115 515166; Menelik II Ave; s US$29-36, d US$38-44; 🖳) The greyish Soviet-style exterior is downright depressing, but its swinging '70s orange carpets and naff wall coverings add some humour to the big bright rooms. Some upper-floor rooms have views.

Harambee Hotel (Map pp80-1; ☎ 0115 514000; Ras Desta Damtew St; s/tw Birr140/200) This well-positioned and somewhat tacky hotel offers some nice views. The carpeting is passable and tiny TVs spurt out BBC. Some bathrooms are brilliant, some are losing the mildew battle.

Wabe Shebelle Hotel (Map pp80-1; ☎ 0115 517187; washo.et@ethionet.net; Ras Abebe Aregay St; s/tw US$45/54, ste US$76; 🖳) A towering building west of the centre. It's fairly overpriced but the rooms are well furnished and clean, with balcony, satellite TV and telephone.

Finfine Adarash Hotel & Restaurant (Map pp80-1; ☎ 0115 514711; fax 0015 524344; Yohanis St; d incl breakfast Birr260) Sitting atop the hot springs that led

to the founding of Addis Ababa, this hotel is a classic among Ethiopia tourists. However, unless you're really into history or frilly bedspreads, it's seriously overpriced.

Yordanos Hotel (Map pp80-1; ☎ 0115 515711; Guinea Conakry St; d US$26-36, ste US$42-46; 🖳) This place has been a perennial favourite of tour groups, but its popularity won't last much longer unless it pulls its socks up. The midrange rooms are bright and some have balconies, but it's hard to overlook the dog-eared state and the decaying carpets.

BOLE RD AREA

Weygoss Guest House (Map pp80-1; ☎ 0115 512205; www.weygoss.com; s/d/tw incl breakfast US$26/35/43) Lacking a sign and hidden up an alley just north of Ethio Supermarket, this five-storey guesthouse represents great value and is perfect for families. The bright doubles have parquet floors, balconies, satellite TVs and a separate kitchen. It's off Bole Rd.

Meridian Hotel (Map pp80-1; ☎ 0116 615050; meridian-hotel@ethionet.et; Zimbabwe St; d incl breakfast US$48, ste incl breakfast US$58-78) Sure, this place is well located and has bright, comfortable and spacious rooms, but the posted rates are outrageous. Fortunately, discounts of up to 40% are offered. It's one of the few with queen-sized beds.

Bole International Hotel (Map pp80-1; ☎ 0116 633000; fax 0116 627880; Cameroon St; s/d/tw incl breakfast US$35/40/50) It's old but clean and a stone's throw from the airport. Rooms have decent carpet, Juliet balconies and satellite TVs.

PIAZZA & NORTH

Semien Hotel (Map p76; ☎ 0111 550067; semien hotel@ethionet.et; Dejazmach Belay Zeleke St; s/d/tw incl breakfast US$32/38/43, ste US$54-60) Thanks to its lofty location above Piazza, this multistorey hotel offers some sweet vistas. The cosily compact rooms don't have much character, but they boast balconies, satellite TVs and spotless surrounds. The suites are size large and very comfortable. Throw in a 7th-floor lounge with a panoramic view and you have one of Addis Ababa's best-value midrange options.

Extreme Hotel (Map pp80-1; ☎ 0111 553777; epis touch@ethionet.et; Gaston Guez St; s US$20-29, tw US$28-35) A hotel of extremes it is. Great 1st-floor rooms have shiny tile floors, contemporary furnishings, satellite TVs, free breakfasts and are utterly spotless. Cheaper 2nd- and

3rd-floor rooms have stained carpets and none of the 1st floor's modern charm; they also don't include breakfast.

SOUTHWEST

King's Hotel (Map p76; ☎ 0113 711300; kingsho tel@ethionet.et; Roosevelt St; d incl breakfast US$37) With great service and large, bright rooms hosting vibrant coloured walls, balconies and satellite TVs, this hotel is a perfect pick. The furniture, like the bathrooms, is nowhere near new but perfectly preserved.

Addis Ababa Golf Club (Map p76; ☎ 0113 201893; s/d/ste incl breakfast US$35/41/47) Surrounded by lawns, these contemporary rooms, with telephones, hair dryers, satellite TVs and marble bathrooms, are excellent value, comfortable and very quiet…'FORE!!' OK, pretty quiet. It's off Ring Rd.

Hotel Concorde (Map pp80-1; ☎ 0114 654959; hotelconcorde@ethionet.et; Beyene Abasebsib St; d US$$22-29) Offering better value than most budget hotels in eastern Addis Ababa, this place offers sizeable clean rooms, with balconies, satellite TVs and shiny bathrooms. Downstairs there's a good Chinese restaurant and piano bar.

EAST

Holiday Hotel (Map pp80-1; ☎ 0116 612081; holiday hotel@ethionet.et; Haile Gebreselassie Rd; s/d/tw incl breakfast for 1 person Birr144/175/198) Sitting at the bottom end of the midrange bracket, this hotel is good value. It has simple but bright and tidy rooms with satellite TVs (CNN and movie channel) and small balconies.

Classic Hotel (Map pp80-1; ☎ 0116 613598; fax 0116 610946; Mike Leyland St; d/tw incl breakfast Birr155/185) It's a tough call between this hotel and the nearby Holiday Hotel. Classic's rooms are quieter and have more character, but they're a little more rundown. Angle for an upstairs room here, as flowering vegetation darkens the ground floor.

Plaza Hotel (Map pp80-1; ☎ 0116 612200; plaza hotel@ethionet.et; Haile Gebreselassie Rd; d US$30-35) Not an architectural gem, but it's clean, well run and has comfortable rooms with satellite TV and telephone. It's in good shape and is the most central option in eastern Addis Ababa, though it lacks balconies.

Atlas Hotel (Map pp80-1; ☎ 0116 613661; Cameroon St; s/tw incl breakfast Birr298/317) Possessing frilly bedspreads that will curl most men's toes, The rooms are best described

as clean and cosy. They host satellite TVs, telephones, tiny toilets and, if you're facing the road, balconies.

Axum Hotel (Map pp80-1; ☎ 0116 613916; fax 0116 614265; Haile Gebreselassie Rd; s/d/tw incl breakfast US$30/34/38, ste US$45-67) Similar specs to Plaza Hotel, with dated bathrooms, satellite TV and clean, carpeted rooms. The suites offer more room and balconies. A new more deluxe wing should be finished by the time you read this. Credit cards are accepted for a 6% commission.

Awraris Hotel (Map pp80-1; ☎ 0116 614933; Djibouti St; d/tw Birr170/220) New carpets, large sunny surroundings and satellite TVs make rooms here a downright decent option. Its location east of the centre and away from convenient minibus routes is its only real downfall.

Central Shoa Hotel (Map pp80-1; ☎ 0116 611454; fax 0116 610063; Equatorial Guinea St; d/tw Birr165/196; 🖳) Rooms here are on the small side, but they're bright and have communal balconies (not so good if you want to keep your curtains open!). The bathrooms are aged, but clean.

Top End

Most of the following hotels tack on a 15% VAT and 10% service charge to the bill. That's an extra US$2020.25 per night if you're staying in a Sheraton villa – ante up cowboy!

CENTRE

Sheraton Hotel (Map pp80-1; ☎ 0115 171717; www .sheraton.com/addis; Itegue Taitu St; s/d from US$265/313, deluxe ste US$3817, villa US$8081; 🗶 🖳 🖳) One of the Africa's most elite hotels, the Sheraton is astounding and the epitome of class. Neoclassical in style, it incorporates lots

---

THE AUTHOR'S CHOICE

Ras Amba Hotel (Map p76; ☎ 0111 228088; rahot@ethionet.et; Queen Elizabeth II St; s/d/ste US$36/48/60; 🖳) Tucked quietly away east of Piazza and affording superb views over much of the city is this charming choice. There's a gorgeous rooftop terrace and rooms are relatively modern and comfortable. Most have balconies and all have satellite TVs. If there's a downside, some rooms are a little too pretty in pink.

of Ethiopian traditional designs, architectural features and tonnes – yes tonnes! – of Ethiopian marble. No expense has been spared: from Persian carpets and original Ethiopian paintings to furnishings plated with 24-carat Ethiopian gold. DVD players, satellite TVs, personal safes and three phones (at desk, bed and toilet!) are found in each of its 392 rooms. Four rooms are wheelchair accessible. It also boasts half a dozen restaurants, posh shops, a swish pool, a modern nightclub and a spectacular fountain light show each Tuesday, Thursday and Friday at 7pm. Prices even include daily golfing for up to four people!

Hilton Hotel (Map pp80-1; ☎ 0115 518400; hilton .addis@ethionet.et; Menelik II Ave; s/d from US$130/145; 🍴 🖳 🏊) Although lacking the Sheraton's panache, the high-rise Hilton still makes a splendid stay and won't break the bank. With banks, travel agencies, airline offices, restaurants, pool, health club, spa (p90) and numerous sports facilities (see Other Sports, p90 for more details), it's almost a clubhouse for the expat business community and is always alive with action. The 402 rooms each have a balcony (some with grand views) and are very comfortable, though they do show their age in places. Some rooms are wheelchair accessible.

Ghion Hotel (Map pp80-1; ☎ 0115 513222; ghion@ ethionet.et; s US$55-81, tw US$68-95, ste US$110; 🖳 🏊) Set in serene gardens smack dab in Addis Ababa's centre, off Ras Desta Damtew St, Ghion is something of an Ethiopian institution and is usually full. Though the surroundings can't be beat, the old but well-kept rooms, with slightly shaggy carpet, satellite TV and telephone, are overpriced. Credit cards are accepted.

A new Novotel/Ibis Hotel development was underway next to Meskal Sq during our visit, so check their respective websites (www.novotel.com and www.ibishotel.com) for details.

SOUTHWEST

Global Hotel (Map pp80-1; ☎ 0114 664766; global hotel@ethionet.et; Beyene Abasebsib St; d incl breakfast, sauna & steam bath US$58-66, ste incl breakfast, sauna & steam bath US$120; 🖳) If there's anything wrong with this high-rise hotel, it's that the rooms are too big. Bright windows and balconies offer views aplenty, and prices include saunas and steam baths downstairs.

EAST

Desalegn Hotel (Map pp80-1; ☎ 0116 624524; desa legne@ethionet.et; Cape Verde St; s/d/ste incl breakfast US$55/60/65; 🖳) Despite being at the low end of the top-end spectrum, service here is first class. The bathrooms are more modern than most and rooms are spotless and large, though they're stretched at the seams with furniture, satellite TVs and fridges. Balconies come complete with lounge chairs and, if you're on the upper floors, views. There's a terrace bar with panoramic views, a free gym and reasonably priced steam baths (Birr50) and massages (Birr50 per 45 minutes).

Queen of Sheba Hotel (Map pp80-1; ☎ 0116 180000; queenshebahotel@ethionet.et; Haile Gebreselassie Rd; d/ste US$69/79) Although a little impersonal, this hotel is pretty good value. The beds are queen-sized and each room has a sitting area with a sofa and satellite TV. The modern bathrooms are spotless and suites contain a small kitchen with fridge. Ask for a room facing north; they have views of the Entoto Mountains.

Hotel De Leopol International (Map pp80-1; ☎ 0115 507777; www.hoteldeleopolint.com; s US$55-75, d US$85-120, ste US$160; 🖳) This high-rise has a wide range of rooms and all boast satellite TVs, spotless bathrooms, kitschy leopard-print duvet covers and balconies with views. It's located off Jomo Kenyatta Ave.

EATING

You lucky lucky souls…you've either just stepped off a plane (Welcome to Ethiopia! Lucky you!) and can indulge in a feast of gastronomic pleasures for a fraction of what it would cost at home, or you've just arrived from several weeks in Ethiopia's wilds (How amazing was that?! Lucky you!) and now have what looks like Manhattan's menu on your doorstep. Italian or Indian? Middle Eastern or Mexican? French or Ethiopian? Eat what you choose and enjoy.

Many restaurants, particularly the smarter ones, add a 15% tax and 10% service charge to their bills; check before you order.

Ethiopian

Many places offer a 'traditional experience': traditional food (called 'national food') in traditional surroundings with traditional music in the evening. You sit in short traditional Ethiopian chairs, eating from a communal plate, on a *mesob* (Ethiopian table).

If you feel more adventurous, try the *kitfo beats* (pronounced 'kitfo bet'), which are typically ignored by tourists. These restaurants usually serve little other than *kitfo* (minced beef or lamb like the French steak tartare, usually served warmed – but not cooked – in butter, *berbere* and sometimes thyme).

If meat isn't your thing, you'll love Wednesday and Friday because fasting food (a variety of vegetarian dishes) is served by all Ethiopian restaurants.

Check out Food & Drink (p68) for more information about Ethiopian cuisine and eating etiquette.

CENTRE

Dashen Traditional Restaurant (Map pp80-1; mains Birr15-40; ☺ noon-2pm & 6-10pm) From the outside, this Ethiopian eatery doesn't look promising. However, if you venture in past the courtyard, you'll find a lovely low-key dining area, with stone walls, local art and bamboo furniture. The soft lighting and intimate surrounds are perfect for your first awkward attempts at *injera* (large Ethiopian version of a pancake/plate). It saved us from embarrassment after accidentally inhaling *berbere* – don't ask! Its fasting food is particularly good (it's also available with fish). The restaurant is off Itegue Taitu St.

Ghion Hotel (Map pp80-1; ☎ 0115 513222; meals Birr28; ☺ noon-2pm & 6-11pm) Sitting behind this hotel's boring Western restaurant is a popular and attractive traditional restaurant. On Tuesday, Thursday and Saturday there's traditional music between 8pm and 11pm; order some *tej* (honey wine) and enjoy the action. It's off Ras Desta Damtew St.

Finfine Adarash Hotel & Restaurant (Map pp80-1; Yohanis St; mains Birr11-24; ☺ noon-11pm) Housed in the former home of a nobleman, this traditional restaurant is known for its vegetarian or 'fasting food' buffet (Birr20) on Wednesday and Friday. The meaty dishes, like *minchet abesh* (a thick minced-meat stew topped with a hard-boiled egg), are also well prepared. Eat inside or within little niches in the garden.

Girma Kitfo Beat (Map pp80-1; Jomo Kenyatta Ave; kitfo Birr20; ☺ noon-midnight) Just east of Guinea Conakry St, this *kitfo beat*, with cowskin chairs and private booths, is more comfortable than most – no plastic chairs to be seen! The *kitfo* is slightly above average.

BOLE RD AREA

Habesha Restaurant (Map pp80-1; Bole Rd; mains Birr20-27; ☺ noon-3pm & 6pm-2am) For an Ethiopian meal that looks as good as it tastes, come to this fashionable Bole eatery where serving seems to be an art form. After a flurry of fast handwork, our *injera* was beautifully laden with everything from *gored gored* (raw beef cubes with *awazi*, a kind of mustard and chilli sauce) to vegetarian fasting food. There's also live music and traditional dancing every night at 8pm. This is the perfect place for your first taste of Ethiopia.

Fasika Restaurant (Map pp80-1; mains Birr35-38; ☺ 11.30am-3pm & 6pm-midnight Mon Sat) Although less sophisticated than Habesha, Fasika also has a great atmosphere, with an exotic interior and live music most nights from 8pm. Its kitchen is equally apt and produces fine Ethiopian fare. It's located 150m up a dirt lane off Bole Rd's north end.

Kal Kitfo (Map pp80-1; Bole Rd; mains Birr12-20; ☺ 6.30am-8.30pm) Although it scores a zero in traditional ambience, this modern *kitfo beat* is a safe and pleasant place to try *kitfo*.

PIAZZA & NORTH

Addis Ababa Restaurant (Map p85; mains Birr11-22; ☺ noon-10pm) With sloping plank floors, weathered furniture and aged memorabilia on the walls, this former aristocrat's residence feels more like a neglected museum. It's a long-standing favourite and continues to churn out great Ethiopian dishes and quality *tej* (it has its own brewery). Partial proceeds benefit Ethiopia Women's Development Fund. There's live music Thursday and Saturday at 8pm. It's off Benin St.

Asni Gallery (Map p76; veg buffet Birr50; ☺ 1pm Sat, closed Jul & Aug) This great art gallery (p89) serves a large vegetarian buffet of Ethiopian fasting food each Saturday. Afterwards coffee and biscuits are served in the garden.

SOUTHWEST

Agelgil (Map pp80-1; mains Birr22-55; ☺ 11am-midnight) Off Meskal Flower Rd, tucked down a dirt track next to the railway tracks, is this great option. It's famous for *agelgil* (go figure!), which is a combination of *doro wat* (chicken drumstick or wing accompanied by a hard-boiled egg served in a hot sauce of butter, onion, chilli, cardamom and *berbere*), *gomen besiga* (boiled greens with beef and seasonings), *alocha fit fit* (tender

ADDIS ABABA

lamb pieces sautéed with ginger and curry and mixed with *injera*) and *bozena shiro* (organic pea flour mixed with diced beef). There's live dancing and music every night, except Wednesday, at 7pm.

Enset (Map pp80-1; Meskal Flower Rd; mains Birr14-35; ⏰ 5pm-midnight) Despite its namesake dish, *enset* (false-banana 'bread', looking much like a fibrous carpet liner), this new restaurant and bar manages to produce some decent traditional food. Don't worry, *enset* always looks like that! It's best served with *kitfo*.

EAST

Shangri-la Restaurant (Map pp80-1; Cape Verde St; mains Birr17-50; ⏰ noon-2pm & 6pm-midnight) Shangri-la has quickly earned a reputation as an atmospheric place for great Ethiopian food, especially *tere sega* (raw meat), which is available on Thursday, Saturday and Sunday. There's an outdoor dining area with an open fire, and a cosy bar serving quality *tej*.

Yohannis Gurage Kitfo Beat (Map pp80-1; kitfo Birr19; ⏰ noon-10pm) Hidden down an alley off a dirt road between Mike Leyland St and Djibouti St, this place is likely Addis Ababa's best *kitfo beat*. It's large and unpretentious with seating indoors and outdoors.

17 17 (Map pp80-1; Cameroon St; mains Birr8-12; ⏰ noon-midnight) Come dinner and lunch, this local option is alive with action. Tables spill from inside out to a large courtyard topped by flowering vegetation. The food isn't the best, but it's filling and cheap and the atmosphere is enjoyable. There's no sign by the gate, so look for a string of lights in a tree next to a well-lit butcher.

Tenshwa Bet (Map pp80-1; Cameroon St; mains Birr30-50; ⏰ 6pm-midnight) You wouldn't know it from the street, but the interior of this eatery is pretty plush. Beneath the cloth canopy, colourful cushions line benches and sheer fabric hangs between wee wood tables. There's no proper menu, so just ask what's in store for the evening.

Elsa Restaurant (Map pp80-1; Mike Leyland St; meals Birr10-30; ⏰ noon-10pm) This simple outdoor restaurant has received high marks from expats for its quality fare. The *yetsom beyaynetu* (variety of fasting foods) is perfect for vegetarians, while *yedoro arosto* (roasted chicken) and *gored gored* assuage carnivorous cravings.

Italian
Due to il Duce's imperial ambitions and many an Italian immigrant, Addis Ababa boasts some extraordinary Italian cuisine.

CENTRE

Stagion (Map pp80-1; ☎ 0115 171717; Sheraton Hotel, Itegue Taitu St; mains Birr59-280; ⏰ noon-3pm & 7-11pm) If *risotto alle vongole e verdurine fresche dell'orto* (rice simmered with clams and garden vegetables) or *cartuccio di pesce persico del Nilo con patate e pinoli* (fillet of Nile perch with pine seeds and potatoes) makes your stomach quiver with excitement, slide into this great Italian restaurant.

Central Pastry (Map p76; Merkato; meals Birr10-15; ⏰ 8am-7pm) The perfect place to slaughter mid-Merkato shopping-spree hunger. It pumps out Ethiopian eats as well as spicy vegetarian pizza bread. The lasagne and pasta are filling, but taste like the stuff you get from a can at home. It can be hard to locate, so ask at the local bus station in Merkato.

BOLE RD AREA

Makush Art Gallery & Restaurant (Map pp80-1; Bole Rd; mains Birr28-48; ⏰ noon-2pm & 6-10pm) Surrounded by vivid paintings, woodcarvings, candlelit tables, attentive waiters and elevator music (hey, nothing's perfect!), the ambience of this restaurant almost outdoes the food. Italian ingredients pervade the menu; most meals hit the spot. The ravioli receives rave reviews from expats. It's in an office tower above Ethio Supermarket.

Antica Restaurant (Map pp80-1; mains Birr30-40; ⏰ noon-2.30pm & 6-10pm) Watch chefs manoeuvre airborne dough while you wait for your delectable thin-crust pizza at this upscale Italian option. There are two-dozen varieties and toppings range from anchovies and capers to prosciutto and Italian sausage. It's off Cape Verde St.

Little Italy (Map pp80-1; Gabon St; mains Birr28-40; ⏰ 11.30am-2.30pm & 7-10pm, closed lunch Sun) This smart Italian restaurant has a more imaginative menu than some places, mixing in various delicacies from across Europe. The quality is consistent and pleasing.

Hassy Restaurant (Map pp80-1; Democratic Republic Congo St; mains Birr10-22; ⏰ 8.30am-9pm) If you want Italian on the cheap and are tired of typical spag and tomato sauce, this is your place. Choose from four pastas and eight different sauces. Birr16 landed us salad, warm buns and *tortellini* oozing with Gorgonzola. It wasn't great, but it was far from bad.

PIAZZA & NORTH

Ristorante Castelli (Map p85; ☎ 0111 571757; Mahatma-Gandhi St; mains Birr50-80; ❤ noon-2.30pm & 7-10.30pm Mon-Sat) Hung behind the imposing and friendly Italian owner are the mugs of Swedish royalty, Bob Geldoff, Brad Pitt, Angelina Jolie and ex-US presidents, some of the more famous people who've come here for Addis' best Italian food. The pasta is homemade and excellent. We devoured the divine *fettuccine al tartufo* (fettuccini in truffle sauce). The gleaming woodwork gives the place a historic nautical feel. Reservations are wise.

Blue Tops Restaurant (Map p76; King George VI St; mains Birr24-50; ❤ 8.30am-10pm Tue-Sun) Opposite the National Museum and a favourite haunt of expats, this bright and airy restaurant serves flavourful pastas (some vegetarian options), calzones and heavenly ice-cream sundaes. Two-dozen varieties of pizza join the parade during the evenings and at lunch Sunday.

Oroscopo (Map pp80-1; General Wingate St; mains Birr14-22; ❤ noon-2pm & 6-10pm) The cheap bill, smiley staff and tasty Italian selections will have you forgetting about your cholesterol counts – yes, it's a little greasy at times.

Isola Verde Pizzeria (Map p85; Mahatma-Gandhi St; pizzas Birr13-22; ❤ noon-8pm) This tiny place serves 17 varieties of pizza. The quality isn't earth shattering, but neither is the bill.

SOUTHWEST

Le Jardin (Map pp80-1; Meskal Flower Rd; mains Birr25-43; ❤ noon-3pm & 6-10pm) As you'd imagine from the name, this restaurant has some nice garden seating. Our friends at the Canadian embassy swear it makes Addis Ababa's best pizza, and we won't argue. If pizza and pasta aren't doing it for you, delve into Greek treats like moussaka and dolmades.

EAST

Canapé International Restaurant (Map pp80-1; Côte D'Ivoire St; mains Birr25-55; ❤ noon-3pm & 6-9pm Mon-Sat) Northeast of the centre, in a brick house, is this popular Italian place serving a long list of selections like antipasto, pasta, risotto, meat dishes and fish. It's not the best you'll find in town, but prices are reasonable.

Blue Drops Restaurant (Map pp80-1; Cameroon St; mains Birr12-35; ❤ noon-2pm & 6-10pm) This simple place is popular with locals because it's particularly cheap, offers a wide range of pastas and sauces, and shows European football games on the TV. The *putanisca* [sic] sauce (tomatoes, black olives and capers) is a pretty good choice.

Other Western
CENTRE

Les Arcades (Map pp80-1; ☎ 0115 171717; Sheraton Hotel, Itegue Iaitu St; mains Birr47-158; ❤ 7-11pm Mon-Sat) If fine French fare tickles your fancy, you can't do better than Les Arcades. Let the pastry coating the baked tilapia melt in your mouth, or sink your teeth into the gorgeous pan-seared duck. A serious selection of wines stands at your beck and call.

Kaffa House (Map pp80-1; Hilton Hotel, Menelik II Ave; meals Birr26-70; ❤ 6-10.30am, noon-2.30pm & 6.30-10.30pm) There are burgers that pass for burgers in Addis and then there are burgers in Addis that would pass for burgers anywhere. Kaffa House burgers will bring a smile to the most disgruntled Texan tourist and take him back to a happy place, a place he wasn't dragged by his adventuresome wife. Oh, there are also some healthy options for his wife, like the grilled chicken with eggplant and roasted pepper caviar.

Cottage Restaurant & Pub (Map pp80-1; Ras Desta Damtew St; mains Birr21-36; ❤ noon-2pm & 6-10pm) This cosy cottage is an expat favourite for a smart lunch. While the menu is varied, ranging from Madras chicken curry and pizza to veal medallions in a *morille* (mushroom) sauce, its speciality is the beef fondue (Birr105 for two). Few leave disappointed.

Summerfields (Map pp80-1; Sheraton Hotel, Itegue Taitu St; mains Birr47-158; ❤ 7am-11pm) Tuck into Wiener schnitzel, tender beef sirloin or a fine burger, or just dive face first into their massive buffets.

Sunrise Restaurant (Map pp80-1; Ras Mekonen Ave; mains Birr15-32; ❤ noon-2pm & 6-10pm) Dine on Nile perch, veal cutlet and other Western fare at this popular restaurant. Sit in the garden or climb the colonial steps and dine inside.

BOLE RD AREA

Lime Tree (Map pp80-1; Bole Rd; mains Birr17-34; ❤ 7am-11pm) This casual, bright and open-plan eatery is great for its atmosphere and fresh food. Tuck into a pita stuffed with *tabouleh* or falafel, or savour a chicken coconut curry. It's also well known for its creative and healthy juices.

Leah's House British Restaurant (Map pp80-1; Ring Rd; mains Birr15-20; 8am-10pm Mon-Sat) Wield your fork like a Brit possessed and massacre a Cornish pasty, a full English breakfast or a steak-and-kidney pie. It's the real deal – enjoy!

Family Restaurant (Map pp80-1; Ethio-China Ave; mains Birr18-45; 11am-10pm Mon-Sat, 9am-10pm Sun) Run by the US embassy's former cook, this restaurant produces gargantuan servings of great Tex-Mex fare. To test our shrunken stomach's capacity, we overlooked the fajitas, *quesadillas*, burgers and steaks and chose a bean-and-cheese burrito, complete with rice, salsa and guacamole, off the 'Vegetarian Corner' – it fit, but barely!

Street Café & Grill (Map pp80-1; Jomo Kenyatta Ave; mains Birr15-28; 7am-8pm) This cute little place is perfect for a hot breakfast. Options include omelettes, pancakes, bacon and eggs and hash browns. We dove into the French toast with syrup – it was spot on.

Loti Restaurant (Map pp80-1; Ethio-China Ave; mains Birr19-43; 11.30am-2pm & 6.30-10pm) This new French restaurant hasn't reached its stride yet, but it's slowly building a reputation with fine dishes like *lapin á la moutarde* (rabbit in mustard) and fried tofu with vegetables. Its location sucks, hidden three floors up the back of large brick shopping centre.

Rico's Restaurant, Pizzeria & Bar (Map pp80-1; Bole Rd; mains Birr22-34; noon-10pm) A stylish, brightly lit new place serving everything from Moroccan kebabs to blackened Cajun fish and buffalo wings dripping with Texan BBQ sauce.

Satellite Restaurant (Map pp80-1; Bole Rd; mains Birr30-95; noon-2pm & 6-10pm) Despite being housed rather incongruously in a plane fuselage jutting from the front of a building and having waitresses in air hostesses' garb, this restaurant is actually an upmarket joint offering international food. The fillet of fish in white wine or the ravioli Genoa style are worth a try.

PIAZZA & NORTH

Raizel Café (Map p85; Hailesilase St; meals Birr9-18; 7am-9.30pm) The mezzanine section of this slick modern café speedily serves tasty cheese burgers, tuna melts, French fries and breakfast omelettes. Despite always being

chock-full, waiters craftily (and rapidly) find seats for you.

SOUTHWEST

Hamlet Steak House (Map pp80-1; Meskal Flower Rd; mains Birr17-45; 11am-midnight Mon-Fri, 9am-midnight Sat & Sun) Perhaps the best place in Addis Ababa to get a quality steak for a reasonable price. Cuts include New York, top sirloin and T-bone. During pre-meal festivities, lube the stomach with South African, Spanish, Portuguese or Italian wine. On weekend mornings, French toast, waffles, pancakes and the all-important syrup enter the mix.

Addis Ababa Golf Club (Map p76; mains Birr17-44; 7am-10pm) Known for its weekend BBQs and serene surrounds, this is a decent pick for a long lunch (service is slow). Choose from homemade pasta, steak and pizzas. It's off Ring Rd.

EAST

Top View (mains Birr24-52; 10am-10pm Tue-Sun) We could talk about the cannelloni stuffed with cottage cheese and spinach, or the Parma ham and fresh seafood, but we'd prefer to talk about the gorgeous view. Perched on a hill above the Ring Rd's junction with Equatorial Guinea St, it offers an unspoilt panorama of Addis Ababa, truly spectacular at sunset. Sit sheltered behind its glass walls or take a seat out on the spacious deck.

Zebra Grill (Map pp80-1; Djibouti St; mains Birr16-33; 8am-midnight) An aberration in eastern Addis, Zebra Grill is known for grilled food, with imaginative and well-prepared dishes such as chicken Montego Bay or Jamaican-style chicken. Less creative but equally tasty are the chicken wings, masala chips and Mexican burritos. The atmospheric and thatched pavilions inside hide behind an ugly tin roof and zebra-striped exterior.

Hill Belt (Map p76; Ring Rd; mains Birr15-32; 8am-midnight) Award-winning restaurant serving a variety of reasonably prices dishes, from beef stroganoff to a mixed fruit kebab with honey and mint sauce. The only downside is its loud Ring Rd location.

Indian

The Bole Rd area is king (or should we say maharajah?) when it comes to Indian, with three of Addis Ababa's top four Indian restaurants.

THE AUTHOR'S CHOICE

Serenade (Map p85; ☎ 0911 200072; mains Birr45-75; ☾ 7pm-midnight Wed-Sat, 10am-3pm Sun) Just east of Piazza, off Tewodros St, and tucked up a dark cobblestone alley is this magnificent Mediterranean eatery. It's a vibrant place, with lush walls, hardwood floors, great service and food that will leave you and your stomach in a heavenly daze. Peruse the creative menu, laden with succulent treats like braised lamb with caramelised onions, lentils, lemon and *raison orange* couscous. The carrot cumin soup seasoned with ginger (lovely!) and Tuscan Skillet (zucchini, onion, celery, bell pepper, tomato, mozzarella and spinach cooked with olive oil, fresh oregano and thyme) are just two of several vegetarian options that any meat-lover would equally devour. Full or not, you'll end up ordering dessert after you see the selections. The cardamom and saffron ice cream is oh so divine.

Shaheen (Map pp80-1; ☎ 0115 171717; Sheraton Hotel, Itegue Taitu St; mains Birr43-160; ☾ noon-3pm & 7-11pm) Set within the Sheraton's confines, Shaheen is Addis Ababa's most sophisticated Indian restaurant. The décor in the restaurant is grand and the melange of Indian curries and tandooris is vast. The *hadrabi muchi* (south Indian fish curry) is particularly lovely.

Sangam Restaurant (Map pp80-1; Bole Rd; mains Birr20-40; ☾ 11.30am-3pm & 6.30-10pm) If you have developed a craving for a cracking curry, try this atmospheric eatery. Here you can wrap your lips around *mughali biryani* (fragrant rice), tandoori dishes or, as we did, some butter chicken masala – absolutely delicious! There are also great lunchtime *thalis* (mixed meals) available for Birr40 every day but Sunday.

Jewel of India (Map pp80-1; Gabon St; mains Birr25-72; ☾ 11.30am-3pm & 6.30pm-midnight) This place is above average, and offers a menu featuring more than 150 dishes. It focuses on traditional Indian specialities, including vegetarian delicacies like *paneer tikka masala* (barbecued cottage cheese in spicy gravy). If roasted chicken stuffed with minced lamb takes your fancy, ask for a *Kerala kebab*. There's a good-value express set menu at lunchtime from Monday to Friday (Birr45).

Bombay Brasserie (Map pp80-1; mains Birr18-48; ☾ 11.30am-3pm & 6.30-11pm) With friendly service and divine dishes like *reshmi chicken kebab* (boneless chicken marinated in cashew paste and spices) and Mohan's special mutton curry, it is very easy to see why we have received readers' letters boasting about Bombay Brasserie. There are plenty of vegetarian options. The restaurant is found off Bole Rd.

Middle Eastern

Aladdin (Map pp80-1; Zimbabwe St; mains Birr18-42; ☾ noon-3pm & 7-10pm) An upmarket Armenian restaurant that serves mouth-watering hummus, *tabouleh*, *foul medames* (fava beans flavoured with lemon and garlic), *kuefteh* (spicy meatballs) and kebabs. Sit beneath the canopied ceiling or on the attractive lawn.

Almendi Restaurant (Map pp80-1; mains Birr15-75; ☾ 7-10pm) You'll leave this excellent Arabian-style eatery as full as an egg. We ordered a simple shish kebab and it arrived with flat bread, soup, salad and various meats in sauces – all tasty and very filling! The *mendi* (sheep) is also great and the *fetira* (bread with honey) makes a perfect accompaniment. It's 100m down a dirt lane leading off Democratic Republic Congo St.

Armenian Sporting Association (Map p76; Welete Johanis St; mains Birr15-30; ☾ 7-11pm Mon-Sat) This simple clubhouse northeast of the Piazza is a friendly place for some savoury Armenian dishes such as mint soup, *basturma* (pressed beef, preserved in spices), *derevi dolma* (vine leaves stuffed with meat and bulgur wheat), shish kebab and delicious homemade *madzoun* (yogurt). Nonmembers pay a 20% surcharge.

Asian

China Bar & Restaurant (Map pp80-1; Ras Desta Damtew St; mains Birr15-60; ☾ 11.30am-10.30pm) Some say nay. Some say yay. No that's not phonetic Chinese 101, rather it's expats' opinions of this restaurant and its large selection of seafood, meat and vegetarian dishes. The décor is quite attractive, with a remarkable relief ceiling.

China Paradise Restaurant (Map pp80-1; Beyene Abasebsib St; mains Birr15-80; ☾ noon-2pm & 6-10pm) While less flashy than China Bar &

ADDIS ABABA

Restaurant, this place consistently produces decent Chinese fare. It's southwest of the centre, below the Hotel Concorde.

Cafés & Pastry Shops

Cafés and pastry shops are omnipresent in Addis and you'll find them perfect for an afternoon or early morning pick-me-up. Places that stand out for their drinks are found right, while those that make the grade in the edible end of the spectrum are found here.

CENTRE

Café Miru (Map pp80-1; Gambia St; meals Birr11-17) Besides having great pastries, cakes and coffee, the upper section of this café serves some decent burgers, pastas and Ethiopian dishes.

Addisu Pastry (Map pp80-1; Gambia St; cakes Birr2-3) This place looks dead from the outside, but step in and it's standing room only. Locals love the pastries, cakes and coffee.

BOLE RD AREA

City Café & Pastry (Map pp80-1; Bole Rd; pastries Birr2-4; 7.30am-9pm) Educated in the art of apple strudel and other delicious delicacies while in the States, this café's owner produces some of the town's best pastries.

Pasticceria Gelateria – Roby's Pastry (Map pp80-1; Bole Rd; desserts Birr4-7; 7am-8pm) Doles out refreshing homemade ice cream and mouth-watering cakes.

Purple Café (Map pp80-1; Bole Rd; desserts Birr3-5; 8am-8pm) Unmistakably purple and usually packed with students, this café is known for its delicious *millefeuilles* (layered pastry).

Saay Pastry (Map pp80-1; Bole Rd; desserts Birr3-5; 8am-8pm) Saay has a tempting selection of treats, including freshly baked croissants and doughnuts, as well as ice creams and fruit juices. It also does a wonderful *macchiato*.

PIAZZA & NORTH

Dibab Recreation Services (Map p76; Algeria St; meals Birr3-10; 7am-8pm) Did the Ethnological Museum make your tummy rumble? Head for this quaint little place in the middle of a small square, just across from the university entrance. It's an ideal place to unwind in the sun over a pastry and a cup of coffee. It also serves simple Ethiopian fare.

Cafe Chaud (Map p85; Dejazmach Jote St; dishes Birr3-8; 8am-8pm) Sweet tooths will be satisfied at this spot. It doesn't really impress from the outside, but you'll be surprised to

discover the trendy interior. Besides cakes and coffee, there's savoury pizza bread.

Self-Catering

Novis Supermarket (Bole Rd area Map pp80-1; Bole Rd; 8am-10pm Mon-Sat, 9am-9pm Sun; southwest Map p76; Roosevelt St; 8am-9pm Mon-Sat, 9am-8pm Sun) Boasting the likes of Brie, Taleggio, Gorgonzola and Gouda, this supermarket is heaven for cheese-lovers. There's also a great selection of Italian prosciutto, wine and chocolate.

Shi Solomon Hailu Supermarket (Map pp80-1; Gambia St; 8am-8pm) Well stocked with Western faves, ranging from cereals and biscuits to mineral water and tomato sauce.

Ethio Supermarket (Map pp80-1; Bole Rd; 24hr) It never closes and is well stocked – enough said.

DRINKING

You won't go thirsty in Addis Ababa. Sip some of the world's best (and cheapest) coffee, down a healthy juice or simply sway home after swallowing your share of *tej*.

Cafés

There are hundreds of cafés serving great coffee in Addis; following are a few that caught our attention.

Tomoca (Map p85; Wavel St; coffees Birr2) Coffee is serious business at this great old Italian café in Piazza. The beans are roasted on site and Tomoca serves what's likely the capital's best coffee. Beans are also sold by the kilo (Birr38).

Kaldi's Coffee (coffees Birr3-14; southwest Map p76; Roosevelt St; east Map pp80-1; Cameroon St) While corporate lawyers may eventually kibosh Kaldi's Starbucks-like sign, logo, interior, uniforms and menu, thirsty expats willing to drop Birr14 for a fabulous frappuccino will ensure Kaldi's contagious coffee lives on in Addis Ababa.

La Madeline (Map pp80-1; Ras Mekonen Ave; coffees Birr1.50-2) This new city-centre café, splashed with lime green and decorated with rod iron and glass furniture, is extremely popular. The coffee is great and the treats aren't bad either.

Ras Hotel (Map pp80-1; Gambia St; coffees Birr4-5) This central hotel's terrace is a perfect place for a late afternoon coffee.

Friendship Café (Map pp80-1; 3rd fl, Friendship City Center, Bole Rd; coffees Birr1.50-3) Although new and fairly sterile, it has a great terrace overlooking town.

Terrace Café (Map p85; Fitawrari Gebeyehu St; coffees Birr1.50-3) West of St George Cathedral, this café's elevated terrace is a pleasant spot to take in Addis Ababa.

Mille Foglie Pastry (Map pp80-1; Beyene Abasebsih St; coffees Birr1.50-2.50; ☺7am-8pm) With a large streetside terrace and great coffees and juices, it's little wonder this place in southwestern Addis Ababa is usually packed.

Juice Bars

Most of Addis Ababa's cafés also serve freshly squeezed juices or slushy blends of everything from strawberries to avocado (Birr3 to Birr6).

Lime Tree (Map pp80-1; Bole Rd; juices Birr6-10; ☺7am-11pm) With luscious *lassies* and creative juices, Lime Tree is the premier place to indulge in liquid treats of the chilly variety. We downed a lime juice with mint and it refreshingly pummelled our thirst.

Pubs & Bars

With the recent addition of several chic bars that would feel at home in London or Paris, Addis Ababa's bar scene is more diverse than ever. The Bole Rd area boasts most of the new arrivals and major players, and targets well-to-do locals and expats, while Piazza oozes with dozens of smaller unnamed places that cater to locals just wanting to let loose. The area of Kazanchis, east of the centre, is much like Piazza, with down-to-earth but authentic bars often turning to impromptu dance floors late in the evening. The key to Piazza and Kazanchis is to simply let your ear do the walking.

Small local drinking holes charge Birr3 for a bottle of beer, while established bars can charge up to Birr12. Most places are open until 2am during the week, and 5am on the weekend.

Virgo Lounge (Map pp80-1; Cameroon St; ☺closed Mon) This hip new drinking den sits above Kaldi's Coffee in southeastern Addis Ababa. With colourful contemporary furniture, modern lighting and mellow music, this is an ideal place to kick back and chill out.

Black Rose (Map pp80-1; Bole Rd; ☺closed Mon) Hiding in a modern building above the Boston Day Spa, this plush bar possesses a cool vibe and a refined clientele. Candles, lush fabric, artwork and some traditional furniture call it home. Music ranges from Ethiopian to Western and Indian.

Temptation Lounge & Bar (Map pp80-1; Democratic Republic Congo St) This slick, new, lined-with-leather place was reverberating with UB40 when we were here. Its colour scheme will have you seeing red.

Mask Bar (Map pp80-1) This tiny bar is as gaudy as it is cool. Above the glowing green beer bottles that comprise the bar hang masks of all sorts; some historical, some clearly not. The crowd ranges from expats to well-heeled locals. It's well signposted off Bole Rd.

Old Milk House (Map pp80-1; Josif Tito St) Moving house has done nothing to dampen the crowds at this popular Dutch-owned bar, which sits just east of Menelik II Ave. If you don't want to mingle with the expat men chatting with local ladies, there are usually chairs around the courtyard campfire.

Top View (☺10am-10pm Tue-Sun) Enjoying a sunset drink on this remarkable restaurant's deck in eastern Addis is escapism at its best. The views west over Addis Ababa are astounding.

Semien Hotel (Map p76; Dejazmach Belay Zeleke St) The panoramic 7th-floor bar in this hotel north of Piazza is another sweet spot for a sunset beverage.

Bole Milk House (Map pp80-1) Off Bole Rd, behind City Pastry, this new venue is a perfect place to warm up for an evening on the town. There's a campfire by the outdoor bar and inside there's artwork, a pool table and decent Western music that you don't have to scream over.

17 17 (Map pp80-1; Cameroon St) This local restaurant and bar, with its large outdoor courtyard, is a pleasant place to enjoy a very cheap beer and meet locals.

Tej Beats

If authentic experiences are what you're after, there's no better place than a *tej beat* (pronounced 'tedj bet') to down the famed golden elixir (honey wine). Most are open from 10am to around 10pm, but are busiest in the evening. They're the traditional haunt of men, so women should try and keep a low profile. They never have signs, so you'll have to ask locals to point them out.

Topia Tej Beat (Map pp80-1) Off Haile Gebreselassie Rd, tucked up an alley behind the Axum Hotel, this is Addis' top *tej beat* and the only one to serve pure honey *tej*.

A small flask (Birr3.50) on an empty stomach had our head spinning. A half-/full-litre bottle is Birr12/24. It's a congenial place with tables surrounding a tiny garden.

Yegebawal Tej Beat (Map p76) For a more rough-and-ready experience, head for this place east of Piazza, off Lorenzo Tezaz St. The *tej* is dirt-cheap (Birr2 per litre), but it's not pure as sugar has been added.

While not *tej beats* per se, these options produce pure *tej*: Shangri-la Restaurant (p96) and Addis Ababa Restaurant (p95).

ENTERTAINMENT

We could blow hot air up your tail pipe, like some guides do, and tell you Addis Ababa's entertainment scene is astounding and the options are endless, but we won't. What we will tell you is that there's enough going on to keep you entertained and a few things that will leave you smiling.

The publication *What's Up!* and its website (www.whatsupaddis.com) highlight upcoming events on Addis Ababa's entertainment scene.

Jazz Clubs

These clubs don't have a cover charge, but do ask a hefty Birr12 to Birr15 for a beer.

Coffee House (Map p76; Madagascar St) Located opposite the Egyptian embassy northeast of Siddist Kilo is this fancy club. Every Thursday great live jazz performances start at 10pm.

Harlem Jazz (Map pp80-1; Bole Rd) This large and mellow venue just north of the airport hosts live jazz Sunday, Tuesday and Friday from 10pm.

La Gazelle Piano Bar (Map pp80-1; Bole Rd) Head down into this dark and moody bar for live jazz every night.

Nightclubs

Nightlife in Addis Ababa is slowly starting to mature with some modern clubs joining the circuit and music almost gaining prominence over prostitution. While most nightclubs open at 11pm, there's no point in arriving before midnight. Those open during the week close around 2am; things wrap up nearer to 5am on weekends. Cover charges vary between Birr15 and Birr30 at most venues, depending on the day (but are sometimes free). Expect to drop about Birr15 for a beer and Birr20 for a cocktail.

Male travellers beware, most single Ethiopian women encountered are still prostitutes.

Divine (Map p80-1; 2nd fl, Sheger Bldg, Cameroon St) Slip into a sleek leather lounger, sip a cocktail and groove to heavy hip-hop and rap in this sleek new nightclub.

Club Illusion (Map pp80-1; cnr Ras Desta Damtew & Itegue Taitu St; ☾ Thu-Sat) This is Addis Ababa's most raucous club. It's in the basement of the Ambassador Theatre.

D-Cave Club (Map pp80-1; Beyene Abasebsib St; ☾ Thu-Sat) This new nightclub, which lurks beneath the Global Hotel in southwest Addis Ababa, hosts well-known DJs most weekends. Music ranges from Ethiopian to hip-hop and drum and base.

Gaslight (Map pp80-1; Sheraton Hotel, Itegue Taitu St; ☾ Thu-Sat) As you'd expect at the Sheraton, the décor is lavish, the music is loud and the dance floor is large. However, thanks to a Birr40 cover charge (Birr60 for couples) and dress code (you must look reasonably smart), the atmosphere is often lacking.

Memo Club (Map pp80-1) About 200m west of Bole Rd, this is another of Addis Ababa's hot spots. Cosy seats, red lights and the odd full-length mirror surround the circular dance floor, which usually reverberates with African and Western tunes. Sadly, it's also popular with expats shopping for prostitutes.

Addis Live (Map pp80-1; Cape Verde St) Attracts a younger crowd (mainly Ethiopian) and plays a good mix of hip-hop and reggae. It's pretty quiet during the week.

Azmari Beats

What in the world is an *azmari beat*? Check out Minstrels & Masenkos, p53.

Yewedale (Map pp80-1; Zewditu St) Thanks to some of the city's best *azmaris* performing here, it's resoundingly popular and you may have trouble finding a seat. There's no sign, so just look for the thatched twin-peaked roof above its entrance.

Fendika Azmari Beat (Map pp80-1; Zewditu St) This *azmari beat* rivals Yewedale and is only a few minutes' walk down the street. It's littered with Ethiopian cultural items and is always home to a good time.

Traditional Music, Dance & Theatre

Amharic theatre is hard to come by these days, with venues only hosting shows once or twice a week. Traditional music and dance is much more accessible, with many restaurants putting on traditional shows in the evenings. *Azmari beats* (see previous section) are also atmospheric places to catch both. For general information on Ethiopian theatre, music and dance see p58.

National Theatre (Map pp80–1; ☎ 0115 514577; Gambia St; tickets Birr10) This impressive but ageing building, with its massive marble and bronze entrance hall (and odd pigeon), hosts theatre at 5pm on Saturday and Sun day.

City Hall Theatre & Cultural Centre (Map p85; ☎ 0111 112516; Fitawrari Gebeyehu St; tickets Birr15) A plush 1000-seat place in the Piazza, which shows productions Tuesday and Friday. Sometimes there's traditional Ethiopian music during public holidays.

Hager Fikir Theatre (Map p85; ☎ 0111 111268; John Melly St; tickets Birr15) Hager Fikir occasionally stages theatre, musicals and dancing.

Crown Hotel (☎ 0114 341444; Debre Zeyit Rd) This hotel's restaurant is renowned for its excellent traditional shows in its giant *tukul* (traditional cone-shaped hut with thatched roof; like South Africa's rondavel). Dancing from as many as 13 different ethnic groups takes place each night at 7pm, though it's better on weekends. Crown Hotel is located south of the city.

Other restaurants that are well known for their traditional shows: Agelgil (p95); Habesha Restaurant (p95); Fasika Restaurant (p95); Ghion Hotel (p95); and Addis Ababa Restaurant (p95).

Cinema

Cinema is more popular than ever; even pushing theatre out of most theatres! Most films are in English or have English subtitles (some have both!).

Ambassador Cinema (Map pp80–1; Ras Desta Damtew St; admission Birr5) An institution, this central cinema puts on the usual diet of action-packed and slightly passé Hollywood movies. Films are shown daily in three sessions.

Cinema Empire (Map p85; Hailesilase St; admission Birr4) Evening screenings at this Piazza cinema are Western favourites, while matinees are Amharic productions (Birr15).

Cinema Ethiopia (Map p85; De Gaulle Sq; admission Birr3) This Piazza cinema has evening viewings and shows everything from Hollywood to Bollywood.

Sport

Besides gawking at the fitness level of budding long-distance runners zooming back and forth on Meskal Sq's steps in the evenings and up and down Menelik II Ave in the early mornings, there aren't many opportunities for watching sports in Addis Ababa.

National stadium (Map pp80–1; Ras Mekonen Ave; tickets Birr7–20) This 27,000-seat stadium hosts national league football games most Sundays at 4pm. Sometimes athletics, cycling and boxing events are held here. Events are advertised in the *Ethiopian Herald*.

Jan Meda Sports Ground (Map p76) With the bed of the horse-race track in bad shape, few races still take place here. However, every second weekend the **Ethiopian Equestrian Association** (☎ 0111 232204) holds either polo, show jumping or dressage competitions; admission is free. It's off Russia St.

See Festivals & Events (p90) for information about the Great Ethiopian Run.

SHOPPING

Spend some spare change, spend your kid's college fund; the spectrum of prices and quality of goods for sale in the capital is simply that vast. You'll find most of the cheap souvenir stalls along or around Churchill Ave and in Piazza – haggling is always the way of the day!

Haileselassie Alemayehu (Map pp80–1; Churchill Ave) Although known for its silver jewellery and mix-and-match bead counter, this shop sells a wide array of items, like paintings, baskets, icons, woodcarvings and traditional clothing. Thanks to fixed (and fair) prices, there's no hassle here. It's also a good place to get your bearings on what items should cost elsewhere.

Entoto Market (Map p76; Entoto Ave) If you're interested in blankets or traditional clothing like a *shamma*, head to this group of stalls lining Entoto Ave a few hundred metres north of Botswana St and the Spanish embassy. Unlike Churchill Ave or Piazza, this is where locals do their shopping.

Ato Basket shop (Map p76; Mauritania St) Southwest of the centre, just on the side of the road, is the best place in town for baskets. This shop sells everything from hats and pots to *mesob* (woven Ethiopian tables), chairs and huge laundry baskets.

Gallery 21 (Map pp80–1; Churchill Ave) Of all the shops/stalls north of Haileselassie Alemayehu on Churchill Ave, this has the biggest selection (if you ask to see the back room) and the best-quality pieces, though the prices are higher than most.

K Design (Map pp80-1; Beyene Abasebsib St) If fine fabrics are what you're after, head no further. This place also sells elegant shawls and custom makes clothing with the cloth of your choice.

St George Interior Decoration & Art Gallery (Map pp80-1; Itegue Taitu St) This is located near the Sheraton for one obvious reason, nobody staying elsewhere can afford to shop here! However, the artwork and traditionally inspired modern furniture are exquisite and it's worth a wander.

Goshu Art Gallery (Map pp80-1) Southeast of the city centre, off Mike Leyland St, Goshu has some more unusual items including *washint* (traditional flutes), as well as skin and canvas paintings (from Birr3000).

Makush Art Gallery & Restaurant (Map pp80-1; Bole Rd) Has an excellent, carefully selected collection of high-quality furniture and paintings from various Ethiopian artists.

Gift Shop (Map pp80-1; ☎ 0115 150371; Meskal Sq) Beside the Tourist Information Centre, the Gift Shop is particularly good for books on Ethiopia and usually sells the old Ethiopian Tourism Commission map of the country (1987, 1:2,000,000). The map is often sold out, so call ahead.

Shopping for a Cause

These shops are a great way to support the city's hard-working less fortunates.

Alert handicraft shop (Map p76; ☎ 0113 211518; ☽ 8.30am-noon & 1.30-5pm Mon-Fri, 8.30am-noon Sat) Here, the Berhan Taye Leprosy Disabled Persons Work Group produces and sells beautiful handbags, pillow covers and wall

hangings, each emblazoned with vibrant embroidery. The items are so Ethiopian, yet they wouldn't feel out of place in a Kathmandu or Bangkok market. The shop is off Ring Rd, southwest of the city centre in the Alert Hospital compound; follow the signs to the canteen.

Former Women's Fuelwood Carriers Project (Map p76; ☽ 9am-4.30pm Mon-Sat) This modest shop found off Entoto Ave sells colourful hand-woven shawls (Birr40) and supports former women firewood carriers. It's tucked in a back street about 300m west of Entoto Market; look for the signs. For more information on firewood carriers, see the boxed text, left.

GETTING THERE & AWAY
Air
DOMESTIC FLIGHTS

All domestic flights are operated by **Ethiopian Airlines** (www.flyethiopian.com; Bole Rd Map pp80-1; ☎ 0116 633163; Bole Rd; Gambia St Map pp80-1; ☎ 0115 517000; off Gambia St; Hilton Hotel Map pp80-1; ☎ 0115 511540; Menelik II Ave; ☽ 8am-8.45pm Mon-Sat, 8am-noon Sun; Piazza Map p85; ☎ 0111 569247; Hailesilase St). All of these offices are open daily from 8am to 6pm unless stated otherwise. There are several more offices scattered across the city.

Schedules change quite frequently and flight durations vary depending on which stopovers the plane is making en route.

Flights leaving from Addis Ababa are listed in the following table.

THE FIREWOOD CARRIERS

An all-too-familiar sight in and around Addis Ababa is the firewood carrier. Many of these women walk up to 30km to gather bundles that weigh an average of 35kg – close to some of their own body weights. Bent like question marks under their loads, the majority of these women earn less than US$12 a month. Yet their work is their only means of survival; usually they're the only income earners in the family.

Destination	Fare (US$)	Duration (hours)	Frequency
Aksum	131	2-3½	daily
Arba Minch	81	2½	Tue, Sun
Bahir Dar	78	½	2 daily
Dessie	61	1	Tue, Sun
Dire Dawa	99	1	daily
Gambela	100	2	Wed, Fri, Sat
Gonder	102	1½	daily
Jijiga	144	1¾	Tue, Fri, Sat
Jimma	63	1	daily
Jinka	94	2¼	Wed, Sat
Lalibela	102	2-2½	2 daily
Mekele	125	1½	daily
Mizan Tefari	91	1¾	Thu
Shire	141	2½	Mon, Wed, Thu, Fri
Tepi	91	2¼	Thu

INTERNATIONAL FLIGHTS

For information regarding international flights and international airlines serving Addis Ababa, see the Getting There & Away section on p271.

Bus

Buses to Debre Zeyit (Birr4, 45 minutes), Lake Langano (Birr23, 4½ hours), Nazret (Birr11, two hours), Shashemene (Birr26, five hours) and Ziway (Birr17, three hours) leave from the **short-distance bus station** (Map pp80-1; Ras Mekonen Ave). Shashemene is also serviced from the long-distance bus station.

Long-distance buses depart from **Autobus Terra** (Map p76; Central African Republic St), northwest of Merkato. Buses for the following destinations leave officially at 6.30am.

Destination	Fare (Birr)	Duration
Aksum	109.70	2½ days
Arba Minch	51.50	12 hours
Awasa	28.75	6 hours
Bahir Dar via Dangala	60.75	1½ days
Bahir Dar via Mota	56.35	12 hours
Dessie	41	9 hours
Dire Dawa	52.65	11 hours
Gambela	85.55	2 days
Goba	49.85	13 hours
Gonder	82.50	2 days
Jijiga	66.35	2 days
Jimma	35.25	9 hours
Jinka	84.35	2 days
Lalibela	75	2 days
Mekele	82	2 days
Moyale	79	1½ days
Robe	48	12 hours
Shashemene	26.85	5 hours

There are several services to Shashemene and Awasa after the first 6.30am departure, though they all leave before noon.

Car & 4WD

Although it's possible to hire a self-drive car (see Getting Around, p106), you're usually restricted to the capital. Hiring a chauffeured 4WD, although expensive, removes most limits on where you can travel. Four-wheel drives are rented by almost all of Addis' travel agents (see p282). For more details on hiring, licence requirements and such, see p276.

Minibus

With sealed roads now all but connecting Addis Ababa with Bahir Dar and Gonder, private minibus services are starting to crop up. They're very fast (not always a good thing!) and cut journey times down to six hours for Bahir Dar and 10 hours for Gonder. There's no station per se, but commission agents tend to patrol for customers near the Wutma Hotel in Piazza. Prices are negotiable; note locals pay Birr120 to Birr150 for Bahir Dar and Birr150 to Birr180 for Gonder.

Train

Addis Ababa's train station, Chemin de Fer Djibouto-Ethiopien, is simply known as **La Gare** (Map pp80-1; ☎ 0115 517250; Gambia St). The only railway line in Ethiopia runs from Addis Ababa to Djibouti City via Dire Dawa.

Trains used to be scheduled to depart for Dire Dawa (Birr75/55/41 in 1st/2nd/3rd class) at 3pm Wednesday, Friday and Sunday, though they rarely ever left on time – now they're not leaving at all. Currently only the Dire Dawa-Djibouti City section is operating. If it gets going again, tickets go on sale two hours prior to departure. For details about crossing the border by train see p274.

GETTING AROUND

Though a sprawling city, Addis Ababa is fairly easy to get around. The most useful option for travellers is the cheap and efficient minibuses. Taxis abound and are another possibility, especially in the evening.

To/From the Airport

Bole International Airport lies 5km southeast of the city centre; both international and domestic flights depart from here.

Minibuses from Piazza, Mexico Sq and Meskal Sq serve the airport daily from 6am to 8pm (Birr1.20). Some charge an additional Birr2 or Birr3 for excess luggage.

Blue city taxis to the airport should cost Birr25 from anywhere south of Meskal Sq to around Birr40 if leaving from Piazza; add Birr15 at night or early in the morning. From the airport, prices should be similar, though you'll be asked for at least double or triple this (see p258). A taxi association has a booth at the airport's exit and charges a 'fixed rate' (negotiable) of Birr45 (Birr50 at night). Taxi drivers belonging to this association have yellow taxis.

NTO (Map pp80-1; ☎ 0115 151722; Hilton Hotel, Menelik II Ave) offers airport pick-ups and drop-offs in a Mercedes-Benz for a reasonable Birr44 (Birr55 after midnight).

Bicycle

Bicycles can be hired informally from beside the national stadium for around Birr10 per hour or Birr30/50 per half/full day. Make sure you get one with a lock.

Bus

Buses in Addis Ababa are considered poor man's transport. They're cheap but slow, run less regularly than the minibuses and are notoriously targeted by pickpockets; the minibuses are a much better bet.

Car

Rainbow Travel (p283) and Galaxy Express Services (p282) are the only travel agencies in Addis that rent self-drive cars.

Parking isn't usually too much of a problem in Addis Ababa. Most of the larger hotels and restaurants have guarded parking spaces and don't usually mind you leaving your car there. In other places, it's worth paying for a guard.

Minibus

Addis Ababa is served by an extensive network of little blue and white minibuses, which are fast, efficient, cheap and a great way of getting around.

Minibuses operate from 5.30am to around 9pm (till 8pm Sunday). Journeys cost from Birr0.55 to Birr1.25 depending on distance.

Minibus stops can be found near almost every major intersection. Major ones include Arat Kilo, De Gaulle Sq in Piazza, Meskal Sq, Ras Mekonen Ave near La Gare and in front of the main post office on Churchill Ave.

To catch the right minibus, listen to the destinations screamed by the *woyala* (attendants) hanging out the windows. 'Bole!', 'Piazza!' and 'Arat Kilo!' are the most useful to travellers. If confused, ask and someone will point you in the right direction.

Taxi

Most taxis operate from 6am to 11pm. Short journeys (up to 3km) usually cost foreigners Birr20 (more at night). Medium/long journeys cost Birr30/50. If you share a taxi, the normal fare is split between each person.

If you want to visit a lot of places in Addis Ababa, negotiate with a driver for a half- or full-day fare (Birr250 for a full day is pretty reasonable). A 'city tour' lasting a couple of hours should cost around Birr100.

Taxis can be found outside larger hotels, as well as the National Theatre, national stadium, and on De Gaulle Sq in the Piazza. At night, many line up outside the nightclubs.

NTO (Map pp80-1; ☎ 0115 151722; Hilton Hotel, Menelik II Ave) has a fleet of yellow Mercedes-Benz that charge Birr74 for the first hour (maximum 15km) and Birr58 for each additional hour. They're great for trips to the airport (see p105).

AROUND ADDIS ABABA

The cacophonous sounds of traffic can chase the most ardent Addis Ababa adorer into the hills occasionally. Lucky for them, the hills contain some historic churches (one hewn from rock in the 12th century) and some remote wilderness. For those too tired to tackle the hills, there's always an escape southward to the verdant Bihere Tsige Recreation Centre.

As well as the places listed here, sights further afield outside Addis Ababa that can still make good day trips include the crater lakes of Debre Zeyit (p214), Menagesha National Forest (p237), Ambo (p237), Mt Wenchi (p238) and the stelae field at Tiya (p171).

ENTOTO MOUNTAINS
የእንጦጦ ተራሮች

North of town are the Entoto Mountains, the site of Menelik's former capital. There's a terrific but windy panoramic view of Addis Ababa below. Near the summit is the octagonal **Entoto Maryam Church** (Map p76; ☉ Sun), which hosted Menelik's coronation in 1882. Inside are some mural paintings. Next to the church is a **museum** (admission Birr20; ☉ 9am-12.45pm & 2.30-5.30pm), which contains a large collection of religious garb mostly dating from Emperor Menelik's time.

Behind the Entoto Maryam complex stretches the newly minted 130-sq-km **Entoto Natural Park** (Map p76; admission free). Although it's said to boast everything from spotted hyenas to soaring lammergeyers, it has absolutely no infrastructure yet, meaning people spend most of their time looking for the park instead of looking for animals!

About 1km west of Entoto Maryam Church is **Kiddus Raguel Church** (Map p76; admission Birr20). Nearby is the old **rock-hewn Kiddus Raguel Church** (Map p76; admission Birr20). In theory, these sites should be open daily, but they usually only open on St Raguel Day. Check with the Tourist Information Centre (p83) in Meskal Sq for details.

To get to Entoto, take a taxi or minibus to the terminus of Entoto Ave from Arat Kilo. From there another minibus will take you to Entoto Maryam Church.

WUSHA MIKAEL CHURCH
ኡሻ ሚካኤል ቤተ ክርስቲያን

The **Wusha Mikael Church** (Map p76; admission Birr30) is a 30-minute walk up a hill behind the Kiddus Mikael's church, which is a couple of kilometres east of the town centre.

Though local priests date it back to the 3rd century AD, it most probably dates back to the 12th century. If you're not planning to visit the churches at Lalibela or Tigray in the north, it's definitely worth a peek as an example of this extraordinary building tradition. Unfortunately, from July to October it's usually flooded with rainwater.

The church is tricky to find, so ask locals en route (most know it as Tekle Haymanot).

BIHERE TSIGE RECREATION CENTRE
የእንጦጦ ተራሮች

The large and wooded **Bihere Tsige Recreation Centre** (Map p76; admission Birr1; ⏱ 8.30am-5.30pm) covers a large area of over 400 sq km. Its gardens contain 6000 varieties of flowers, shrubs and trees. It's a very pleasant place for a late afternoon walk or picnic. It lies 5km southwest of the centre off the Debre Zeyit road. A minibus from Meskal Sq will drop you off around a 20-minute walk from the entrance.

Northern Ethiopia

The bounty of northern Ethiopia's historical African treasures is only rivalled by that of Egypt's. In Aksum, elaborate pre-Christian tombs underlie ancient obelisks; in Lalibela a medieval maze of rock-hewn churches lies frozen in stone. The wealth of history continues in Gonder, where grand 17th-century castles overlook the celebrated source of the Blue Nile, Lake Tana. The lake's waters host centuries-old island monasteries and countless religious artefacts.

Northern Ethiopia's landscape is equally captivating and is unparalleled in Africa in both scale and beauty. Although the amazing backdrop of endless canyons, chasms, gorges and high plateaus covers most of the north, there's no better way to absorb it than trekking the Simien Mountains. You'll also be able to experience some of Ethiopia's endemic wildlife.

Nature takes on hostile tones in the Danakil Depression, where harsh conditions make molten lava feel more at home than you. At over 100m below sea level it's one of the lowest, hottest and most inhospitable places on Earth.

Depending on your mood and budget, getting around northern Ethiopia can be as easy as hopping a plane or as difficult as wedging your big toe into a precarious cliffside crevice.

Intrepid travellers have been returning from here for centuries with incredible tales of adventure, ancient civilisations, marvellous buildings and enchanting legends. Don't you think it's time you do the same?

HIGHLIGHTS

- Question time, history and reality while wandering dumbfounded through the rock-hewn maze of churches in **Lalibela** (p155)

- Descend into the darkness of ancient Aksumite tombs or let your eyes follow 1800-year-old stelae skyward at **Aksum** (p131)

- Exercise your eyes while trekking the sublime **Simien Mountains** (p125), home to magnificent wildlife and unparalleled panoramas of endless Abyssinian abysses

- Share **Lake Tana** (p115) with patrolling pelicans and centuries-old island monasteries

- Catch the sun's last light kissing the abled remains of 'Africa's Camelot' in **Gonder** (p118)

- Flirt with gravity and reach new heights at **Abuna Yemata Guh** (p149), one of the rock-hewn churches of Tigray

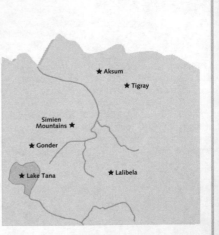

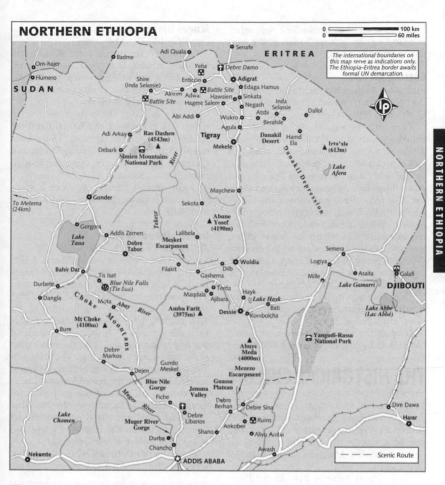

NORTHERN ETHIOPIA

Climate

The central and northern highlands are fairly mild with average daytime temperatures of 18°C. The bulk of the rain falls between May and September, with July and August being the wettest. The region of Tigray and parts of northeastern Amharaland are drier, only receiving significant rain in July and August.

The Danakil Depression, with elevations cracking 116m below sea level, regularly surpasses 50°C.

National Parks

If northern Ethiopia was devoid of astounding historical finds, Simien Mountains National Park would truly be on the world map. It's home to rare endemics, like the walia ibex and Ethiopian wolf, as well as large populations of the intriguing gelada baboon, and offers Ethiopia's best trekking and some of Africa's most astounding panoramas from its 4000m plateaus and peaks.

Getting There & Away

Ethiopian Airlines (www.flyethiopian.com) connects Addis Ababa with Bahir Dar, Gonder, Lalibela, Aksum, Shire, Mekele and Dessie.

Most people who enter northern Ethiopia overland are travelling by bus from Addis Ababa, which sits conveniently at the bottom of the historical circuit. Although possible, few people access the Addis Ababa–Bahir Dar road from the western highland town of Nekemte. The only other overland option is from Sudan at the Metema crossing (p275).

Getting Around

Ethiopian Airlines has flights interconnecting Bahir Dar, Gonder, Lalibela and Aksum. Flights also link Mekele with Aksum.

Road construction is booming and freshly sealed sections of road now connect Addis Ababa with Bahir Dar and Gonder (though still expect a few older potholed sections!). In the east, new sections of sealed road now all but link Adigrat, Mekele and Woldia. The old sealed road connecting Addis Ababa to Woldia is currently being overhauled. While fresh roads have reduced the extensive bus network's travel times, journeys are still lengthy due to the massive distances being covered. Expect at least 10 solid days of bus journeys to complete the 2500km-long historical circuit.

The only area you'll have trouble finding regular public transport is around the rock-hewn churches of Tigray.

To visit the Danakil Depression, you'll have travel by private or rented 4WD.

THE HISTORICAL CIRCUIT

The historical circuit stretches over the entire breadth of northern Ethiopia and covers all the major historical sites and provides access to natural attractions like the Simien Mountains and Danakil Depression.

Most visitors move in a clockwise direction, travelling through Bahir Dar, Gonder and Aksum, before looping back southwards. This leaves what's arguably the best for last – lovely Lalibela.

ADDIS ABABA TO THE BLUE NILE GORGE

The road north to the Blue Nile Gorge offers some historical and natural sights for those wishing to break up the long journey to Bahir Dar.

Even if you don't plan on stopping, keep an eye out for the shepherds in their delightful reed 'raincoats', the Amhara women in their pleated highland skirts, and the men carrying their indispensable *dula* (see right).

Muger River Gorge
የሙገር ወንዝ ሸለቆ

The Muger River Gorge, some 50km north of Addis Ababa, is a good spot for a bit of rambling and wildlife-watching. The endemic gelada baboon is often seen here, as are a good variety of birds.

Access is from the village of Durba, which sits 17km west of Chancho and the Addis Ababa–Bahir Dar road. There are a couple daily share-taxis linking Durba and Chancho (Birr5, 45 to 60 minutes), though more run on Saturday. To continue north or south from Chancho, you can hop on the buses running between Addis Ababa and Bahir Dar.

Debre Libanos & Fiche
ደብረ ሊባኖስና ፍቼ

Lying 104km north of Addis Ababa, 4.2km off the main Addis Ababa–Debre Markos road, is one of Ethiopia's most holy sites. The monastery of **Debre Libanos** (admission Birr50, personal video cameras Birr50) was founded in the 13th century by a priest credited not only with the spread of Christianity throughout the highlands, but also with the restoration of the Solomonic line of kings. The priest was Tekla Haimanot, today one of Ethiopia's most revered saints (see the boxed text, p49).

Although no trace of the ancient monastery remains (a casualty of the Muslim–Christian wars), the site is impressively set beneath a cliff on the edge of a gorge and is a peaceful place to wander.

Since the saint's time, Debre Libanos has served as the principal monastery of the old

---

THE DEADLY DULA

The *dula* is the chosen travelling companion of almost every Amhara man. The 1m-long hardwood staff serves a variety of purposes: to carry loads to and from market, to brace the shoulders on long treks, to lean on during never-ending church services, and to defend oneself when needed.

In the past, every Amhara was skilled in its use. The *gabi* (toga) was spun around the left arm to make a shield, and the right arm brought the *dula* crashing down on the adversary's cranium – sometimes with devastating consequences. Today its most common use is fending off unfriendly dogs.

Shoa region, and remains one of Ethiopia's largest and most important. Today, five religious schools are found here.

Many Ethiopians continue to make pilgrimages and some still seek out the area's curative holy waters – said to be good for evil spirits and stomach disorders!

The present **church**, the latest in a succession of structures, was built in 1961 by Haile Selassie after a priest apparently prophesied that a new church would ensure a long reign. It's built in the emperor's peculiar style: monumental and pretty hideous.

Besides what's believed to be the saint's tomb, the church interior isn't too interesting. The stained-glass windows and mural paintings aren't by Afewerk Tekle, as church literature claims.

Five minutes up the hill from the monastery is Tekla Haimanot's **cave**, where the saint is said to have done all his praying. It's also the source of the monastery's holy water.

If you climb past the cave, there's a marvellous view of the monastery in its dramatic setting. The cross-shaped tomb near the car park is dedicated to those executed by the Fascists (see the boxed text, right).

Near the turn-off to the monastery is the so-called **16th-century Portuguese Bridge**, in fact built at the 19th century's end by Emperor Menelik's uncle, Ras Darge. However, like Debre Libanos, the scenery and atmosphere make up for the lack of tangible historical remains. Look out for the gelada baboons, which are often seen here, as are the huge and soaring lammergeyer vultures.

Two buses run daily from Addis Ababa to Debre Libanos (Birr10, two to 2½ hours). Another option is to take a bus to the nearby town of Fiche (Birr10, 2½ hours). Minibuses connect Fiche to the monastery, 16.5km to the south (Birr3, 30 minutes, three or four minibuses daily).

If you get stuck in Fiche, the **Alem Hotel** (r with shower Birr35), on the Addis Ababa–Debre Markos road, is still the best bet. From Fiche, there are numerous buses plying the Addis Ababa–Bahir Dar route.

Blue Nile Gorge አባይ ሸለቆ

North of Fiche, around 200km from Addis Ababa, begins one of Ethiopia's most dramatic stretches of road. It serpentines to the bottom of the Blue Nile Gorge, 1000m below.

> **DEATH AT DEBRE LIBANOS**
>
> During the Italian occupation, Debre Libanos witnessed some of the worst excesses of Fascist brutality. Following the attempt on the life of the infamous viceroy Graziani, the monastery, long suspected as a hotbed of rebel activity, was singled out for reprisal.
>
> On 20 May 1937, 267 monks – 'all without distinction' – were executed; a week later, Graziani ordered the execution of all of the 129 young deacons as well. Satisfied at last, he wrote to Mussolini, 'The monastery is closed – definitively'.

Before the Italians built the bridge with their usual civil engineering flair, the Blue Nile River separated the historical provinces of Shoa and Gojam. Although your eyes will undoubtedly be drawn downward to the bridge and gorge, don't forget to look up – lammergeyer vultures regularly soar the gorge's thermals.

The **Alem Hotel** (☎ 058/ 760010; s with shared bathroom Birr30, s/d Birr70/80) in Dejen, on the gorge's northern rim, is the nearest sleeping and eating option. The rooms are clean and bright, but prices are seriously *faranji*-fied. Running water is in short supply (check the taps before settling on a price). The hotel lurks behind an unnamed petrol station.

NORTH TO BAHIR DAR

There are now two ways of reaching Bahir Dar from the Blue Nile Gorge: via Mota, along the shorter but bumpier unsealed road; or via Debre Markos (100km longer) along a slightly potholed section of sealed road.

Most Addis Ababa buses travel through Mota as it saves fuel and allows them to reach Bahir Dar in one day. Private vehicles should travel via Debre Markos – your backside will thank you and it only takes six hours to link Addis and Bahir Dar.

If you're driving and want to split the journey, Debre Markos' **Shebel Hotel** (☎ 0587711410; s/d Birr50/80) is the best option. Most rooms are bright and boast new carpets and hot showers. Some even offer balconies with views

Those on a bus travelling the Debre Markos route will usually end up spending the night in Dangla, 78km south of Bahir Dar. Dangla's **Ha-Hu Hotel** (☎ 0582 210849; d Birr30) has comfortable rooms with clean bathrooms. It's behind the NOC Mart petrol station.

BAHIR DAR ባህር ዳር
pop 166,928 / elev 1880m

Despite Bahir Dar being one of Ethiopia's most attractive towns, you'll have a hard time not turning your back on it. Just like the rest of us, you'll helplessly gravitate down the wide palm-lined boulevards to Lake Tana's gorgeous shore and once there, you'll nary look over your shoulder.

It's a great place to spend a few days. Besides some sights around town, you're on the doorstep of Lake Tana's mystical monasteries.

Although geared up to tourism, Bahir Dar is a booming business centre in its own right. It's also capital of the Amharaland region.

In the 16th and 17th centuries, various temporary Ethiopian capitals were established in the vicinity of Lake Tana. It was here where Jesuits attempted – with disastrous consequences – to impose Catholicism on the Ethiopian people. One Jesuit building, which was built by the well-known Spanish missionary Pero Pais, can still be seen today in the compound of St George's church.

In the 1960s Haile Selassie toyed with the idea of moving his capital here.

Information

INTERNET ACCESS
Ghion eDrums (Map p113; per hr Birr18)
Global Computer (Map p113; per hr Birr18) Can also burn images to CD using USB connection (Birr15).

MEDICAL SERVICES
Gamby Higher Clinic & Pharmacy (Map p113; ☎ 0582 202017; ⏰ 24hr) Town's best medical facility, complete with satellite TV in the waiting room.

MONEY
Commercial Bank (Map p113; ⏰ 8am-4pm Mon-Fri, to noon Sat) Of Bahir Dar's three Commercial Bank branches, this is the only one that changes travellers cheques and cash (US dollars and euros).
Dashen Bank (Map p113; ⏰ 8am-noon & 1-4pm Mon-Fri, 8am-noon Sat) Changes cash and travellers cheques.
Wegagen Bank (Map p113; ⏰ 8am-5pm Mon-Fri, to 4pm Sat) Only changes US dollars and euros cash.

POST
Bahir Dar is served by its obligatory post office.

TELEPHONE
Telecenter (Map p113; ⏰ 8am-9pm) This outdoor kiosk lacks a sign, but only charges Birr15 per minute for reasonably sounding international calls.
Telecommunications office (Map p113; ⏰ 8am-noon & 2-6pm Mon-Fri, 8am-noon Sat) International calls. Standard rates (p267).

TOURIST INFORMATION
ANRS Tourism Commission (Map p113; ☎ 0582 201686; ⏰ 8.30am-12.30pm & 1.30-5.30pm Mon-Fri) Although staff are keen to help, it offers little more than brochures on the area (Birr3).

TRAVEL AGENCIES
The follow agencies are noted for arranging boat trips onto Lake Tana.
Exodus Boat Tour Agent (☎ 0918 760056; Tana Hotel) Catering to well-heeled travellers. It's northeast of town.
Dib Anbessa Hotel (Map p113; ☎ 0582 201436) A bit pushy saleswise, but reliable enough.
Ghion Hotel (Map p113; ☎ 0582 200111) Less polished but best for budget travellers looking to share costs.
Tis Abay Tour & Travel Agency (Map p113; ☎ 0582 208541, 0918 762307; Papyrus Hotel) Offers quality service in either 25HP or 40HP boats.

Dangers & Annoyances
Malaria is endemic, particularly in May and from mid-September to mid-October. Take adequate preventive measures (see p373 for more information).

Tourist hustlers can be a problem here, especially around the bus station. Most 'know' the best place to stay or the 'cheapest' boat operators – thankfully you know better.

Some travellers have also complained of hassle from children at the market and on the Zege Peninsula. Taking a guide would solve the problem, but it isn't essential.

Sights & Activities
Lounging lakeside and watching pelicans skirting the surface might be the most relaxing way to pass time. You may also glimpse the flimsy, yet unsinkable *tankwa* canoe. Made from woven papyrus, they can take huge loads, including oxen! On Thursday, many bring charcoal and firewood from the Zege Peninsula; have a look out. If you'd like to see them being made, head west of town to the little village of **Weyto**.

If you are allergic to scenic lakesides and love dusty action, visit the large and lively **main market** (Map p113) in the town's southwest. It's busiest on Saturday. Sure a guide would help you find things more quickly, but isn't getting lost half the fun?

Just to save you a day of unfruitful looking, we'll be kind enough to tell you the delightful *agelgil* (ingenious leather-bound lunch boxes used by local travellers) are no longer sold in the market. They're sold by streetside kiosks near the ANRS Tourism Commission. Bahir Dar's versions are funky and furry, thanks to being made from goatskin.

The famous **outlet of the Blue Nile** (Map p116) is located some 5km outside the town, around 1km north from the Blue Nile bridge. Along the river, keep an eye out for hippos and crocodiles. For more information on the outlet of the Blue Nile, see p117.

Just south of the bridge is a massive new **war memorial** (Map p116) dedicated to those who died fighting the Derg (p37). We were told it may eventually host a museum, but we couldn't confirm this. Do let us know! It's quite the sight, its fountain cascading down to the Blue Nile.

Further south of the memorial is Bezawit Hill, the summit of which hosts the former **Palace of Haile Selassie** (Map p116) and offers panoramic views over the Blue Nile River. The palace isn't currently open to visitors.

For those Lake Tana monasteries you may have heard about, see p115. Information on the Blue Nile Falls is found on p118.

Sleeping
BUDGET

Ghion Hotel (Map p113; ☎ 0582 200111; ghionbd@ethionet.et; camping Birr33, d & tw Birr75-125; ☐) Although the rooms here are as tired and worn as your favourite pair of travel socks, there's no denying Ghion's beautiful lakeside setting. Rooms vary, and size and prices are entirely negotiable, despite what the smarmy manager tells you. Mosquitos are problematic here – bring a mossie net. It's a great place to camp (free tents are occasionally available) and airport pick-ups are free.

Enkutatash Hotel (☎ 0582 204435; d/tw Birr40/50) Just west of town, this place has rooms set

---

BAHIR DAR

To Enkutatash Hotel (200m); Weyto Village (2km); Bahir Dar Resort Hotel (4km); Airport (8km); Zege Peninsula (25km)

To Island Monasteries

Lake Tana

Marine Authority Boat & Ferry Launch

St Mikael Church

St George's Church

Mulualem Cultural Centre

Mosque

Government Council Building

To Tana Hotel (1.4km); Exodus Boat Tour Agent (1.4km); War Memorial (3.5km); Outlet of Blue Nile (5km); Palace of Haile Selassie (6km); Gonder (183km); Lalibela (261km)

(Some Minor Roads Not Depicted)

Entrance to Bus Station

Main Market

To Blue Nile Falls (32km); Addis Ababa (575km)

SLEEPING	
Bahir Dar Hotel	12 A1
Dib Anbessa Hotel	13 B2
Ghion Hotel	14 A1
Papyrus Hotel	15 B3
Summerland Hotel	16 B2
Tana Pension	17 B2

EATING	
Bahir Dar Hotel	(see 12)
Dib Anbessa Restaurant	(see 13)
Enkutatash Restaurant	18 A2
Ghion Hotel	(see 14)
Hajj Adgoy Bakery	19 A2
Summerland Hotel	(see 16)
Tana Pastry	(see 17)

DRINKING	
Araki Bars	20 B2
Blue Bird Café	21 B2
Cloud Nine Café	22 A2
Delicious Juice Center	23 A3
Galaxy Café	24 B2
Mango Park	25 B1
Paradise Café	26 A2

ENTERTAINMENT	
Balageru Cultural Club	27 C2

TRANSPORT	
Bike Rental	28 B2
Bus Station	29 B3
Ethiopian Airlines	30 B2
Marine Authority Office	31 A1

INFORMATION	
ANRS Tourism Commission	1 A1
Commercial Bank	2 A3
Dashen Bank	3 B2
Dib Anbessa Hotel	(see 13)
Gamby Higher Clinic & Pharmacy	4 A2
Ghion eDrums	(see 14)
Ghion Hotel	(see 14)
Global Computer	5 B2
Post Office	6 C2
Telecenter	7 B2
Telecommunications Office	8 A1
Tis Abay Tour & Travel Agency	(see 15)
Wegagen Bank	9 A2

SIGHTS & ACTIVITIES	
Agelgil Kiosks	10 A1
Main Market	11 A3

0 ____ 400 m
0 ____ 0.2 miles

off a pint-sized quaint courtyard. They sport rugs, mosquito nets, cold-water showers and tiny 'verandas'.

Bahir Dar Hotel (Map p113; ☎ 0582 200788; d with shared bathroom Birr40, d Birr50) Hidden behind the telecommunications office, this place offers simple and clean rooms. The private showers are hot, the common ones not so. Rooms surround the ever-so-popular courtyard restaurant, which means noise may be a problem on weekends.

Tana Pension (Map p113; ☎ 0582 201302; d with shared bathroom Birr20) Its cheap rooms are big and bright and boast clean sheets. The stained Raggedy Anne red carpets and the smelly shared bathrooms are its weak points.

MIDRANGE

Summerland Hotel (Map p113; ☎ 0582 206566; www .enjoybahirdar.com; s/d/tw Birr238/361/375) What this newish place lacks in character, it makes up for in comfort and cleanliness. The Summerland Hotel has sparkling tile floors, gleaming bathrooms, satellite TVs, mosquito nets, the odd bit of marble and balconies all up for grabs.

Tana Hotel (☎ 0582 200554; ghion@ethionet.et; s/tw/ ste US$38/50/75; ☐) Sitting lakeside just north of town, this hotel's rooms offer sunset views over Lake Tana. Triangular partitions divide the somewhat stylish accommodations, which include embroidered bedding and satellite TVs.

Papyrus Hotel (Map p113; ☎ 0582 205100; fax 0582 208543; s/d Birr215/269, ste Birr322-537; ☐ ☒) Rooms here are reasonably sized and well furnished with comfortable mattresses, wardrobes, desks and mosquito nets. Some boast balconies overlooking the pool's emerald waters. However, it lacks Summerland's polished feel and Tana's location, and only the suites offer satellite TV.

Dib Anbessa Hotel (Map p113; ☎ 0582 201436; fax 0582 201818; d/tw Birr165/180) The carpeted rooms here are comfy and clean, but they aren't ageing well. For instance, our 'hot' shower was cold and the showerhead threw more water on the ceiling than our soap-covered face. Crafty negotiations can knock off around Birr50.

Bahar Dar Resort Hotel is a behemoth lakeside place that's been 'almost' ready to open for over half a decade. Don't hold your breath.

Eating

Bahir Dar Hotel (Map p113; mains Birr7-12) If you want local atmosphere and great Ethiopian fare, there's nowhere better than this hotel's courtyard. Sit under the stars, enjoy the music (and bonfires on weekends) and dine for pennies.

Dib Anbessa Restaurant (Map p113; mains Birr13-24) A wide-ranging menu, with everything from *minchet abesh* (thick minced-meat stew topped with a hard-boiled egg) to Hungarian goulash and American meatloaf. We chose the Indian curry and were pleasantly surprised.

Ghion Hotel (Map p113; mains Birr12-20) Its lakefront terrace is a pleasant spot for a meal. The tilapia (a freshwater fish) is usually well prepared.

Enkutatash Restaurant (Map p113; mains Birr12-20) Since gaining a reputation for fine fish cutlets, the prices here have doubled. The food is still good, but the restaurant has little ambience.

Summerland Hotel (Map p113; mains Birr18-25) Like its rooms, this place is bright and modern but is devoid of character. However, it does prepare some of town's best *faranji* (foreigner, especially Western) food.

Tana Pastry (Map p113; mains Birr4-12) A good place for a pastry or omelette. Locals say it's the best place for cheap fresh fish.

Hajj Adgoy Bakery (Map p113; ☖ 5am-8pm) Town's best bread – perfect for early morning bus journeys. The sign is in Amharic, so just follow your nose.

Drinking

Tana Hotel (beers Birr10) This hotel's lakefront gardens are *the* perfect place for a sunset drink.

Mango Park (Map p113; beers Birr5) Although it lacks Tana Hotel's sunset dramatics, this tiered terrace also overlooks the lake and is a cool spot for a drink. It's usually packed with local students, families and pelicans.

Delicious Juice Center (Map p113; juices Birr3) Collapse into its streetside chairs and introduce some fresh juice to your insides.

There are numerous cafés (Map p113), like Cloud Nine, Paradise, Galaxy and Blue Bird, which all serve great coffee.

If you want something that will knock you off your feet, visit the hole-in-the-wall *araki* (a grain spirit) bars near the bus station.

Entertainment

Balageru Cultural Club (Map p113; admission free; beers Birr6) If you'd like an entertaining cultural experience and a good laugh, visit this place. Various *azmari* (see the boxed text, p53) do their thing to the rapturous joy of locals. If you're brave enough to dance and do your thing, you'll win lots of friends.

Getting There & Away

AIR

Ethiopian Airlines (Map p113; ☎ 0582 200020; ⏰ 8-11.45am & 2-5.45pm) has two or three flights daily to Addis Ababa (US$78, 30 minutes), and one or two to Gonder (US$37, 17 minutes), Lalibela (US$61, 1¼ hours) and Aksum (US$86, two to three hours).

BUS & MINIBUS

One bus departs for Addis Ababa via the Debre Markos route (Birr60.35, 1½ days, 6am), while a simultaneous service departs via the Mota route (Birr56.60, 12 hours). Gonder (Birr22.15, four hours) and Debre Tabor (Birr12.70, three hours) are each served by two morning buses. Several buses a day trundle to and from Tis Isat (Birr4.20, 45 minutes) for the Blue Nile Falls. There's also the odd unscheduled service to Lalibela (Birr46, 10 hours). All buses leave from the main station.

Private minibuses also operate to Addis Ababa (Birr120 to Birr150, six hours) and Gonder (Birr30, three hours); ask at your hotel.

FERRY

A ferry sails every Sunday at 6am for Gorgora (Birr104.50, 1½ days), on the northern shore of Lake Tana. It typically overnights in Konzola (Map p116). Buy tickets the day before at the **Marine Authority office** (Map p113; ☎ 0582 200730; ⏰ 8am-noon & 1.30-5.30pm Mon-Fri, 8am-noon Sat).

There's no restaurant or café on board, though there are stops at restaurants en route.

Getting Around

Bikes are perfect for Bahir Dar; hire one just south of Tana Pension (Birr3 per hour).

If you're in a hurry, flag a passing taxi. They cost Birr10 for short hops or Birr20 to the Tana Hotel. The 8km airport trip will set you back Birr40.

LAKE TANA & ITS MONASTERIES
ጣና ሃይቅና ገዳማት

Upon first observation, Lake Tana's beauty is obvious; its blue waters lapping on lush shores, islands dotting its distant horizon and squadrons of pelicans flirting with its surface. Explore a bit further and you'll discover famous centuries-old monasteries lurking on some 20 of its 37 islands.

The lake is Ethiopia's largest, covering over 3500 sq km, and its waters are the source of the Blue Nile, which flows 5223km north to the Mediterranean Sea.

Sights & Activities

A trip out onto the lake is as obligatory as it is enjoyable. Although the obvious highlights are the monasteries, the lake also offers some prime bird habitats.

MONASTERIES

While the boat engine's buzz is anything but a throwback to ancient times, your first meetings with remarkable cross-wielding priests after stepping onto the islands just may be.

Many monasteries date from the late 16th or early 17th century, though most were founded much earlier and may even have been the site of pre-Christian shrines.

If you want help deciphering the murals adorning the monasteries' walls, check out Know Your Ethiopian Saints on p49.

Although it's possible to see all the monasteries over several long days, you'll likely have your fill after one full day. Yes, it is possible to have too much of a good thing. If you have a 40HP speedboat, 11 hours and priests who are quick with the keys, you could conceivably visit these gems: Kebran Gabriel, Narga Selassie, Daga Estefanos, Tana Cherkos and Ura Kidane Meret.

Note that women can visit only certain monasteries, although these number among the most interesting. Admission to each monastery is collected by the priests. Priests rarely have change, so bring lots of Birr1 and Birr10 notes for tips and fees. Toting a small video camera costs an additional Birr50 per monastery

For important information on church etiquette, see the boxed text on p44.

All the stated journey times are for a one-way trip from Bahir Dar in a 40HP speedboat (add about 30% more time for a

NORTHERN ETHIOPIA

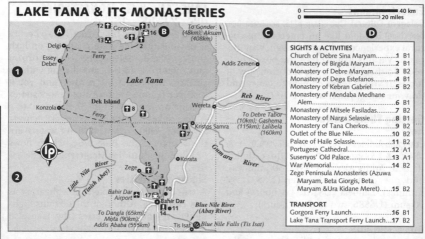

LAKE TANA & ITS MONASTERIES

SIGHTS & ACTIVITIES	
Church of Debre Sina Maryam..........1	B1
Monastery of Birgida Maryam..........2	B1
Monastery of Debre Maryam..........3	B2
Monastery of Dega Estefanos..........4	B1
Monastery of Kebran Gabriel..........5	B2
Monastery of Mendaba Medhane Alem..........6	B1
Monastery of Mitsele Fasiladas..........7	B2
Monastery of Narga Selassie..........8	B1
Monastery of Tana Cherkos..........9	B2
Outlet of the Blue Nile..........10	B2
Palace of Haile Selassie..........11	B2
Portugese Cathedral..........12	A1
Susenyos' Old Palace..........13	A1
War Memorial..........14	B2
Zege Peninsula Monasteries (Azuwa Maryam, Beta Giorgis, Beta Maryam &Ura Kidane Meret)......15	B2

TRANSPORT	
Gorgora Ferry Launch..........16	B1
Lake Tana Transport Ferry Launch...17	B2

25HP boat). See Getting Around (opposite) for boat-hire information.

One of the most beautiful and atmospheric monasteries, **Kebran Gabriel** (admission Birr20, men only) dates from the 17th century. It features a 12-columned portico and good paintings on the *maqdas* (inner sanctuary). Spot the depiction of Iyasu before Christ. It's half an hour away by boat and a short walk from the landing stage.

The original 14th-century church at **Debre Maryam** (admission Birr20) was rebuilt by Tewodros in the 19th century. It contains beautiful old manuscripts and a collection of church treasures. It's 30 minutes by boat and a short walk through coffee, mango and fig trees.

Ura Kidane Meret (admission Birr20) is the Zege Peninsula's most famous monastery and its *maqdas* is very beautifully painted. A compendium of Ethiopian religious iconography, it holds an important collection of 16th- and 18th-century crosses and crowns. The peninsula is 35 minutes by boat from Bahir Dar. Turn left from the landing stage and it's a straightforward 15-minute walk (despite what would-be guides tell you). As the most-visited monastery, it attracts the most souvenir sellers and hustlers.

Set in the middle of the lake on Dek Island, **Narga Selassie** (admission Birr20) is peaceful, atmospheric and little visited. Built in the mid-18th century, it resembles Gonder's castles. Effigies of Mentewab and James Bruce are engraved on the church's exterior, as are fine 18th-century paintings and

crosses. It's 2½ hours by boat and a two-minute walk from the landing stage.

One of the the lake's most sacred monasteries, **Dega Estefanos** (admission Birr50, men only) was rebuilt in the mid-19th century and houses a 16th-century painting of the Madonna, and mummified remains in glass coffins of five former Ethiopian emperors (13th to 17th centuries). It's set on a hill nearly 100m above the lake, 35 minutes' walk one way. The island is east of Dek Island.

It's said the Ark of the Covenant was hidden at mysterious and historic **Tana Cherkos** (admission Birr50, men only) for 800 years. The present 19th-century church is rather modest. Tana Cherkos is 2½ hours from Bahir Dar by boat. From the landing it's a 45-minute walk uphill.

Though most of the treasures of **Mitsele Fasiladas** (admission Birr20) were stolen in the 1990s, it's still worth visiting if you're in the vicinity. The setting is attractive and the old church's foundations remain. It's on an island just south of Tana Cherkos and is a short walk from the landing.

Like Ura Kidane Meret, **Beta Giorgis** (admission Birr20) and **Beta Maryam** (admission Birr20) are found on the Zege Peninsula, There's an important collection of crowns in a little 'museum' (attributed to Yohannes IV) and interesting paintings in the monasteries, probably dating from the 19th century or later. They're a short walk from the landing stage through lemon trees and coffee plants.

Also on Zege Peninsula, **Azuwa Maryam** (admission Birr20) has interesting 19th- or 20th-century paintings and a small museum. It's five minutes' walk from the landing stage.

BIRD-WATCHING

For those with an eye for birds, Lake Tana's various habitats offer up numerous species. Besides the heralded white pelicans, you may glimpse the likes of lesser flamingos, lesser kestrels, wattled cranes, bush petronia, hornbills, paradise flycatchers, kingfishers and various parrots.

Spots to peruse include the areas around Mitsel Fasiladas (popular breeding ground for wetland birds), Debre Maryam, the Blue Nile's outlet, Dek Island and Lake Tana's eastern shore.

OUTLET OF THE BLUE NILE

You don't visit the outlet of the Blue Nile to say hello to the river. You visit it to say goodbye to Lake Tana's water and wish it well on its 5223km journey to the Mediterranean. You may even see a hippo on the way.

It's about 30 minutes from Bahir Dar by speedboat. For info about reaching the outlet by road, see p113.

Getting Around

There's no shortage of boat operators in Bahir Dar, and shifty commission agents lurk everywhere.

People who've been happiest have booked boats through the travel agencies on p112.

Prices are always negotiable and range from Birr120 (one to five people) for a 90-minute trip to Debre Maryam and the Blue Nile outlet in a 25HP boat to Birr1000 (one to five people) for an 11-hour trip in a 40HP speedboat. A half-day trip to the Zege Peninsula costs between Birr250 and Birr330. Always ensure that a guide is included in the cost. Although last-minute arrangements are possible, it's best to arrange things the day before.

Before leaving, ensure your boat has life jackets and spare fuel. It's wise to bring a raincoat or umbrella and something warm.

The **Marine Authority** (☎ 0582 200730; ⊙ 8am-noon & 1.30-5.30pm Mon-Fri, 8am-noon Sat) in Bahir Dar offers a daily ferry service to the Zege Peninsula (Birr44 return). It departs Bahir Dar at 6.30am and returns at 10am, which gives you enough time (two hours) to visit the monasteries there. Zege Peninsula can also be reached by road (25km).

JAMES BRUCE: IN SEARCH OF THE SOURCE

> Half undressed as I was by the loss of my sash, and throwing my shoes off, I ran down the hill towards the little island of green sods, which was about two hundred yards distant.
> …It is easier to guess than to describe the situation of my mind at that moment – standing in the spot which had baffled the genius, industry and enquiry of both ancients and moderns, for the course of near three thousand years.
> *James Bruce*, Travels to Discover the Source of the Nile *(1790; Gregg, Godstone, 1971)*

One of the first European explorers in this part of Africa was a Scot, James Bruce, who was passionate about unknown lands.

After serving as consul general in Algiers, he set off in 1768 in search of the Nile's source – a puzzle that had preoccupied people since the time of the Egyptian Pharaohs.

After landing in Massawa, Eritrea, he made his way to the powerful and splendid court of Gonder, where he became close friends with Empress Mentewab.

In 1770 he reached the source of the Abay, the main river that empties into Lake Tana. There he declared the mystery of the Nile's source solved. He dedicated his discovery to King George III, and returned home to national acclaim.

In fact, Bruce had traced only the source of the *Blue* Nile River, the main tributary of the Nile. Not only that, but he'd been beaten to his 'discovery' – as he very well knew – over 150 years earlier by a Spanish Jesuit, Pero Pais.

Of greater interest was the account of his journey, *Travels to Discover the Source of the Nile*, published in 1790. It remains a very useful source of information on Ethiopia's history and customs. His contemporaries considered much of it as gross exaggeration, or even as pure fiction. Given his earlier claims, no wonder.

The adventurous can troll the shoreline and try to hire a *tankwa* to visit Debre Maryam.

BLUE NILE FALLS (TIS ISAT)
ጢስ እሳት

The impressive plumes of mist bellowing from the depths of the Blue Nile Falls led locals to name it Tis Isat (Water that Smokes) or Tis Abay (Nile that Smokes). Today, thanks to a hydroelectric project, the once mighty falls have withered like an aged chain smoker. How do you say 'Nile with emphysema' in Amharic?

Instead of the river's 400m width cascading over a sheer chasm to the rocks 37m below, now there is only a stream (as little as 4m wide) off the shallowest section (29m high). The remaining mafic volcanic rocks that were once cooled by the flow now bake in the sun and beg for water.

If you can manage to forget that it was once one of the most spectacular falls in Africa, a visit here is still worthwhile, particularly in wet season. It's a pretty picnic spot and you may see parrots, bee-eaters, lovebirds, touracos, white-throated seed-eaters and vervet monkeys.

The falls are located 32km southeast of Bahir Dar, just beyond Tis Isat village. The **ticket office** (admission Birr15, personal video cameras Birr100; ⏲ 7am-5.30pm) can arrange official guides (Birr30), but they aren't really necessary.

The path to the falls starts 50m west of the ticket office. From there, walk east for about 1km until you see a tiny waterfalls sign at a small junction. Go left (north) and after 400m you'll see a couple of rocky footpaths (on your left). They lead down the so-called eastern route, which crosses a 17th-century Portuguese bridge before turning west and climbing up past the little settlement towards the falls.

From the main viewpoint, continue along a path that leads over the narrow Alata River before backtracking to the base of the falls.

From here you can complete the circuit by winding up along the path to the river above the falls and crossing its banks by motorboat (following the so-called western route). The entire walk shouldn't take more than 90 minutes. The **boat service** (one way/return Birr10/20) usually operates daily from 6.30am to 6pm. Trips in local *tankwas* are forbidden. If you're here early in the morning, watch for crocs.

Less energetic and less mobile people may want to approach and return from the falls on the less steep western route.

Getting There & Away

Buses from Bahir Dar leave every few hours for Tis Isat village (Birr4.20, one bumpy hour), which is also known as Tis Abay.

From Tis Isat, the last bus travelling back to Bahir Dar leaves between 3pm and 4pm. We've sadly heard of locals trying to make travellers miss the last bus and then charging them Birr100 for a ride. Another scam we discovered was men telling us upon arrival in Tis Isat that to ensure a seat on the bus back, we'd need to pay them to hold it for us.

It's usually pretty easy to hitch back to Bahir Dar (Birr8 to Birr10) if you've missed the bus.

The **Ghion Hotel** (☎ 0582 200111) in Bahir Dar runs two daily tours (8am and 3pm) to the falls. It charges Birr300 per group for transportation and guide (up to 10 people).

GONDER ጎንደር

pop 158,019 / elev 2210m

It really isn't important whether your friends believe that you slipped beneath the shadows of grand 17th-century African castles, slid into a classic Italian Art Deco

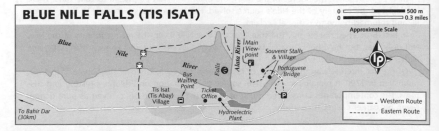

BLUE NILE FALLS (TIS ISAT)

0   500 m
0   0.3 miles
Approximate Scale

Blue
Nile
River
Main View-point
Alata River
Souvenir Stalls & Village
Falls
Bus Waiting Point
Portuguese Bridge
Tis Isat (Tis Abay) Village
Ticket Office
To Bahir Dar (30km)
Hydroelectric Plant

– – – Western Route
------- Eastern Route

café and sipped early-morning *macchiatos* while wandering Gonder one day. It's just important that you savour the surreal experience.

With several complexes laden with classical centuries-old stone castles and palaces, it's easy to see how Gonder rightfully earned the moniker 'Africa's Camelot'.

And knowing that it is (and was) surrounded by fertile land and that it was at the crossroads of three major caravan routes, it's just as easy to understand why Emperor Fasiladas (r 1632–67) made Gonder his capital in 1636. To the southwest lay rich sources of gold, civet, ivory and slaves, to the northeast lay Massawa and access to the Red Sea, and to the northwest lay Sudan and Egypt.

By Fasiladas' death, Gonder's population already exceeded 65,000 and its wealth and splendour had become legendary. Drifting through the old palaces, banqueting halls and former gardens, it's not difficult to imagine the courtly pageantry, ceremony and intrigue that went on here.

The city flourished as capital for well over a century before infighting severely weakened the kingdom (see The Rise and Fall of Gonder on p31). In the 1880s what remained of Gonder was extensively looted by the Sudanese Dervishes. Despite this and the damaged sustained by British bombs during the liberation campaign of 1941, much of Gonder remains amazingly intact.

While luck and strong construction preserved most structures from rubbly fates, local legends state a timely swarm of bees saved Debre Berhan Selassie, one of Ethiopia's most colourful and famous churches, by simply chasing the devastating Dervishes away!

Today, Gonder is a great place to spend a few days and is a convenient base to make the leap into the Simien Mountains.

Orientation

Although Gonder is fairly spread out, it's still a great place to navigate on foot or by bicycle. The piazza marks the centre of town and is laden with the most shops and services. Just south of the piazza is the Royal Enclosure and all its treasures, while the road leading north is dotted with a series of restaurants and hotels.

Information

INTERNET ACCESS

Circle Internet Cafe (Circle Hotel; per hr Birr15) Some of town's fastest connections.

Proxy Computer (per hr Birr15; ☽ 24hr) Slow connections but always open.

Star Internet (per hr Birr15) Decent connections and will burn images to your CD using USB connection (Birr15).

MEDICAL SERVICES

Birhan Tesfa Clinic (☎ 0581 115943; ☽ 24hr) Gonder's best medical facilities.

Goha Pharmacy (☽ 8am-9pm Mon-Sat) Helpful and well stocked.

MONEY

Commercial Bank (☽ 8am-4pm Mon-Fri, to noon Sat) Changes cash and travellers cheques.

United Bank S.C. (☽ 8am-4.30pm Mon-Fri, to 3.30pm Sat) Changes cash and travellers cheques.

POST

Post office (☽ 8.30am-12.30pm & 2-5.30pm Mon-Fri)

TELEPHONE

Oddly, the telecommunications office above the post office no longer offers international calls.

Telecenter (☽ 8am-9pm) This outdoor kiosk lacks a sign, but only charges Birr15 per minute for international calls.

TOURIST INFORMATION

Tourist information centre (☎ 0581 110022; amhtour@ethionet.et; ☽ 8.30am-12.30pm & 1.30-5.30pm Mon-Fri, 8.30am-12.30pm Sat) Helpful information and licensed city guides (Birr150 per day). Can arrange out-of-city 4WD tours (Simien Mountain day trips etc).

TRAVEL AGENCIES

These reliable agencies can arrange everything from city tours to Simien Mountain treks. Prices range and negotiations are always in order.

Explore Abyssinia Travel (☎ 0581 115311; explore abyssinia@ethionet.et)

Explore Simien Tours (☎ 0581 116690, 0918 770280; fasilm_675@yahoo.com; Quara Hotel)

Galaxy Express Services (☎ 0581 111546; Goha Hotel)

NTO (☎ 0581 110379, 0918 775948)

Dangers & Annoyances

Several travellers have complained about children hassling them for money with improbable 'sob stories'. The Notebook Scam (p157) is a popular ploy. A really good

NORTHERN ETHIOPIA

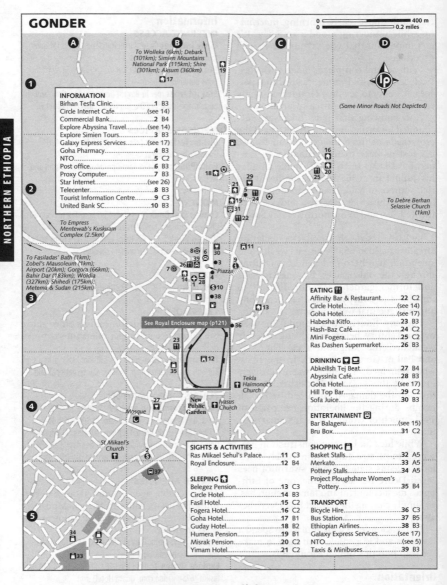

local initiative is the Peace of Mind project (which helps the genuinely hungry). Peace of Mind food tokens (Birr5 for 10) can be bought from various hotels and restaurants, including Habesha Kitfo.

Another annoyance, especially if you're left lathered at the time, is Gonder's lack of water – do your best to conserve.

Sights

ROYAL ENCLOSURE የፋሲለደስ ግቢ

It is pretty hard not to notice Gonder's impressive **Royal Enclosure** (admission Birr50, personal video cameras Birr75; 🕙 8.30am-12.30pm & 1.30-5.30pm), with its regal castles and high stone walls sitting streetside. The entire 70,000-sq-metre site (also known as Fasil

Ghebbi) was declared a World Heritage site by Unesco in 1979.

Free 90-minute guided tours (a tip will be expected) are worthwhile and available weekdays. On the weekend, you can hire a local licensed guide near the gate for about Birr30. See the Royal Enclosure Map (p121) for the following sight locations.

Almost completely restored with the aid of Unesco, **Fasiladas' Palace** (found in the compound's south) is the oldest and most impressive castle. It stands 32m tall and has a crenulated parapet and four domed towers. Made of roughly hewn stones, it's reputedly the work of an Indian architect, and shows an unusual synthesis of Indian, Portuguese, Moorish and Aksumite influences.

The main floor was used as a dining hall and formal reception area; note the recessed Star of David above several doorways, which trumpet Fasiladas' link to the Solomonic dynasty. The small room in the northern corner boasts its original beam ceiling and some faint frescoes.

On the 1st floor, Fasiladas' prayer room has windows in four directions, each overlooking Gonder's important churches. On the roof, religious ceremonies were held, and it was from here that the emperor addressed his people. Above Fasiladas' 2nd-floor bedroom was the watchtower, from where it's possible to see all the way to Lake Tana.

Behind the castle's eastern corner are various ruined buildings, including the remains of the **kitchen** (domed ceiling) and **water cistern** (thought by some to be a pool).

To the palace's northeast is the saddle-shaped **palace of Iyasu I**. The son of Yohannes I, Iyasu I (r 1682–1706) is considered the greatest ruler of the Gonderine period. Iyasu's Palace was unusual for its vaulted ceiling. The palace used to be sumptuously decorated with gilded Venetian mirrors and chairs, and gold leaf, ivory and beautiful paintings adorning the walls. Visiting travellers described the palace as 'more beautiful than Solomon's house'. Although a 1704 earthquake and British bombing in the 1940s have done away with the interior and roof, its skeletal shell reeks of history.

North of Iyasu's Place are the relics of its **banquet hall** and **storage facilities**. To the west is the quadrangular **library** of Fasiladas' son, Yohannes I (r 1667–82), which was sadly renovated and plastered over by the Italians. Although only the tower and walls remain of **Fasiladas' archive**, which sits northwest of the library, the beauty of the large arched doors and windows remains. It was once an impressive palace decorated with ivory.

The compound's northern half holds vestiges of Emperor **Dawit's Hall** and **House of Song**, in which many religious and secular ceremonies and lavish entertainments took place. Dawit (r 1716-21) also built the first of two **Lion Houses** (the second was built by Selassie) where Abyssinian lions were kept until 1992.

When Dawit came to a sticky end (he was poisoned in 1721), the Emperor Bakaffa (r 1721–30) took up the reins of power and built the huge **banqueting hall** and the impressive **stables**.

Between the stables and Dawit's Hall is the **Turkish bath** (wesheba), which apparently worked wonders for those suffering from syphilis! Inside, some of the original cowhorn clothes hooks still protrude from the walls. At the southern end you'll see the fire pit and the ceiling's steam vents.

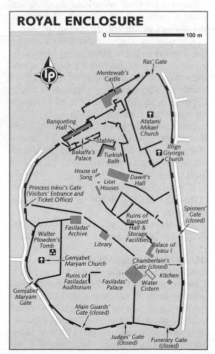

ROYAL ENCLOSURE

0 ————— 100 m

Ras' Gate

Mentewab's Castle

Banqueting Hall

Atatami Mikael Church

Stables

Ilfign Giyorgis Church

Bakaffa's Palace

Turkish Bath

House of Song

Dawit's Hall

Lion Houses

Princess Inkoi's Gate (Visitors' Entrance and Ticket Office)

Spinners' Gate (closed)

Ruins of Banquet Hall & Storage Facilities

Walter Plowden's Tomb

Fasiladas' Archive

Library

Palace of Iyasu I

Gemjabet Maryam Church

Chamberlain's Gate (closed)

Kitchen

Ruins of Fasiladas' Auditorium

Fasiladas' Palace

Water Cistern

Gemjabet Maryam Gate

Main Guards' Gate (closed)

Judges' Gate (closed)

Funerary Gate (closed)

Bakaffa's consort was responsible for the last castle, **Mentewab's Castle**, a two-storeyed structure that's now part of an Ethiopian cultural heritage project. Note the Gonder cross being used as a decorative motif.

FASILADAS' BATH ፋሲላ መዋኛ

Around 2km northwest of town centre lies **Fasiladas' Bath** (admission incl in Royal Enclosure ticket; ⏰ 8.30am-12.30pm & 1.30-5.30pm), a shady, beautiful and historical spot attributed to both Fasiladas and Iyasu I. Until the five-year project to fully restore the complex (financed by the Norwegian government at a cost of Birr6.4 million) is completed in 2008, we'll stop calling it peaceful too. That said, it's still worth a visit.

The large, rectangular sunken pool is overlooked by a small but charming building, thought by some to be Fasiladas' second residence. Almost out of Cambodia's Angkor Thom, snakelike tree roots envelop, support and digest sections of the stone wall surrounding the pool.

Although the complex was used for bathing (royalty used to don inflated goatskin lifejackets for their refreshing dips!), it was likely constructed for religious celebrations, the likes of which still go on today. Once a year, Fasiladas' Bath is filled with water for the Timkat (p261). After being blessed by a priest, the pool becomes a riot of spraying water, shouts and laughter as the crowd jumps in. The ceremony replicates Christ's baptism in the Jordan River, and is seen as an important renewal of faith.

Just east of the main compound is **Zobel's Mausoleum**. Local legend states it's named after Yohannis I's horse, which heroically brought Iyasu (Yohannis' son) back from Sudan after his father's death.

If you don't want to walk, minibuses (Birr0.85) leaving from near the piazza pass here.

You must obtain your ticket at the Royal Enclosure before visiting Fasiladas' Bath.

DEBRE BERHAN SELASSIE CHURCH
ደብረ ብርሃን ስላሴ ቤተ ክርስቲያን

Despite the walls of **Debre Berhan Selassie** (admission Birr25; ⏰ 6am-noon & 1.30-5.30pm) hosting the most vibrant ecclesiastical artwork in the nation, it's the ceiling that captures most visitors' imaginations. Think of Mona Lisa's mysterious smile and multiply it 104

times over! Yes, each of the 104 winged Ethiopian cherubs dotting the beamed ceiling seem to have slightly different, but equally quizzical expressions.

Full of all the colour, life, wit and humanity of Ethiopian art at its best, the walls provide a compendium of Ethiopian saints, martyrs and lore. The devilish Bosch-like depiction of Hell has to be our favourite. A close second is the Prophet Mohammed atop a camel being led by a devil. Although most paintings within the church are historically and happily attributed to the 17th-century artist Haile Meskel, this can't be the case because the remarkable rectangular church of today only dates back to the late 18th century. The original church was circular (its foundations are still visible) and was created in the 1690s by Iyasu I.

A large stone wall with 12 rounded towers surrounds the compound and represents the 12 apostles. The larger 13th tower (entrance gate) symbolises Christ and is shaped to resemble the Lion of Judah. If you have a keen eye, you'll be able to spot the lion's tail in the wall west of the church. Some historians hypothesise the symbolic architecture is evidence the emperor planned to bring the Ark of the Covenant here from Aksum.

Theories aside, it's clear Debre Berhan Selassie or 'Trinity at the Mount of Light' is one of Ethiopia's most remarkable churches.

Flash photography inside the church is forbidden. Priests offer tours but a small contribution for the church should be left afterwards.

The church lies around 2km northeast of the Royal Enclosure.

EMPRESS MENTEWAB'S KUSKUAM COMPLEX ቄስቋም ደብር

Although less preserved than the Royal Enclosure, this royal compound known as **Kuskuam** (admission Birr25, personal video cameras Birr75; ⏰ 8.30am-12.30pm & 1.30-5.30pm) is equally captivating. It offers an impressive mix of views over the countryside, each dramatically framed by the complex's crumbling remnants. It was built in 1730 by the redoubtable Empress Mentewab, after the death of her husband (Emperor Bakaffa).

Like the Royal Enclosure, it's made up of a series of buildings including a long, castellated palace used for state receptions and to house the royal garrison. Its exterior is decorated with red volcanic tuff; spot the figures of crosses and Ethiopian characters and animals, such as St Samuel riding his lion.

The nearby smaller building is said to have been the empress' private residence. To the residence's west used to be a fine church. However, after damage from British bombing, it had to be rebuilt. A tiny glass-roofed coffin in its crypt contains the skeletons of the empress, her son and her grandson, the Emperors Iyasu II and Iyo'as.

The complex lies in the hills 3.5km northwest of town. A taxi from the piazza should cost about Birr25 return.

RAS MIKAEL SEHUL'S PALACE
ራስ ሚካኤል ሳህል ቤተ መንግስት
Although simply a smaller version of Fasiladas' palace, this place has a slightly foreboding air. Perhaps it's because it was the residence of Ras Mikael, the dictator who usurped power at the 18th-century's end, as the monarchy became increasingly impotent and ineffectual. Later, the building was used – more chillingly – as a prison during the rule of the Derg, and is said to have been the site of untold brutality and torture.

After long being closed to the public, it should be finally open by the time you read this.

WOLLEKA (FALASHA VILLAGE) ወለቃ
Around 6km north of Gonder is the little village of Wolleka, once the home of a thriving population of Falashas or Ethiopian Jews. Before Christianity arrived, Judaism was the dominant religion of most of northwestern Ethiopia.

After the adoption of Christianity as the state religion, Falashas had their land confiscated for refusing to convert. To survive, many became skilled craftsmen. Recent research suggests Falashas may have provided the labour for the castle's construction and decoration.

From 1985 to 1991 many Falashas were airlifted to Israel, and today only a handful remain. Sadly, the pottery for which they were once famous has degenerated into clumsy, half-hearted affairs. However, the Project Ploughshare Women's Crafts Training Center, which helps disadvantaged women learn a craft, is worth supporting.

The old synagogue and Falasha homes can be visited, but a special trip can't be called worthwhile. To get here from Gonder, you can take a taxi (Birr40 return) or a *gari* (horse-drawn cart; Birr10 return).

Tours
City tours, which take in all the major sites, are easily arranged at the tourist information centre. Guides cost Birr150 per full day, and you can either walk, ride bikes, hop on local minibuses or charter a taxi for the day (around Birr30 per hour).

For Simien Mountains tours and treks, see Planning (p127).

Festivals & Events
Particularly good times to visit Gonder are during the festivals of Leddet (Christmas) and Timkat. For more information on both of these festivals, see p261.

Sleeping
BUDGET
Belegez Pension (☎ 0581 114356; d with shared bathroom Birr60, s/d Birr70/80) Simple smallish rooms surround a paved private courtyard that's perfect for parking your tired truck. The rooms are bright and clean, as are the toilets and hot showers. They have Ethiopia's best budget-hotel towels – huge and soft! Too bad the pillows are exactly the opposite! Reservations are wise.

Fasil Hotel (☎ 0581 110221; d/tw with shared bathroom Birr50/60) The top-floor rooms are huge, bright, airy and have a slight Italian feel. Ask for one that opens onto the balcony. The shared showers are hot and usually clean. It's occasionally a little noisy.

Misrak Pension (☎ 0581 110069; d Birr100) Prices are entirely *faranji*-fied but the rooms are spotless and the mattresses are comfortable. The tiny bathrooms are oh so clean. It's set off a simple garden.

Yimam Hotel (☎ 0581 110470; d & tw with shared bathroom Birr50) If next-door Fasil is full, this is a close option. The rooms are on the small and dark side, but the shared toilets (squat) are as clean as they come. Showers are sadly all cold.

Circle Hotel (☎ 0581 111991; s/tw Birr92/115) With glass exterior walls, this high-rise offers some nice views and is easily the brightest hotel in town. Sadly, all that light means you won't miss spotting the stained green carpets and occasional cockroach. Some rooms are better than others, so check a few.

NORTHERN ETHIOPIA

Other options:

Humera Pension (☎ 0581 110959; tw Birr80)
Guday Hotel (☎ 0581 110959; d/tw with shared bathroom Birr50/70)

MIDRANGE & TOP END

Goha Hotel (☎ 0581 110634; ghion@ethionet.et; s/tw/ste US$38/50/75) Perched on a high natural balcony and boasting a gorgeous garden terrace overlooking the town, this is easily Gonder's nicest hotel. While wool wall hangings, stone walls and embroidered bedding are nice touches, it's the views from rooms 201 to 209 that steal the show. The room layout, with nifty triangular partition, is identical to all other government Ghion Hotels.

Fogera Hotel (☎ 0581 110405; s/tw/tr US$20/25/35) While the rooms in the old Italian building are begging for renovations, the garden *tukuls* (conical thatched huts) have aged well and are quite attractive and comfortable. Each has high ceilings and hot-water showers.

Eating

Habesha Kitfo (mains Birr17-35) Lovingly and traditionally decked out with woven mat floor, cowhide stools and leather chairs, this is a good place for great Ethiopian food. Vegetarian fasting food is available daily.

Mini Fogera (mains Birr8-12) Although this place's cushion-covered cement stalls won't win your bottom's approval, its Ethiopian fare just might win your stomach's.

Goha Hotel (mains Birr16-23) Dine on roast lamb, fish cutlet, lentil soup or other Western favourites in this hotel's massive and bright dining room. If you order wine, ensure it's opened at the table.

Circle Hotel (mains Birr20-30) After singing 'the wheels on the bus go round and round, round and round, round...' as you make your way up the spiralling stairs, plant yourself on the rooftop restaurant and cross your fingers – *faranji* fare here is hit or miss. We happily hit a good burger.

Affinity Bar & Restaurant (mains Birr7-15) This place is popular with local businessmen for an Ethiopian meal at lunch. Dine inside or on the parking-lot-looking patio.

Hash-Baz Café (snacks Birr2) With great croissants, cakes and pastries, it's a fine spot for breakfast.

Ras Dashen Supermarket (8am-9pm) Load up on Simien Mountain supplies here.

Drinking

Goha Hotel (beer Birr7) There's nowhere better in town for a sunset drink than the hotel's lofty garden terrace.

Abyssinia Café (drinks Birr1.50-4.50) This classic Italian café in the heart of the piazza is a true throwback to the days of old. The coffee is great and the beer is cheap.

Abkeilish Tej Beat (bottles of tej Birr5) This well-known *tej beat* (purveyor of honey wine) is the best place to delve into some stiff *tej*.

Hill Top Bar (6pm-1am) American-inspired but insuppressibly Ethiopian. Try, if you dare, a *gin fir fir* (gin mixed with beer), or, less potent, wine diluted with Coca-Cola!

Sofa Juice (juices Birr3) If your insides are calling for drinks of a healthy variety, get your vitamin and fruity fix at this juice haven.

Entertainment

Mimicking the success of Bahir Dar's Balageru Cultural Club, several traditional bars have opened in Gonder. *Azmaris* (see the boxed text, p53) sing along to their *masenkos* (single-stringed fiddle), women dance and everybody has a good time.

Bar Balageru (admission free) The most fun and most packed. A glass of *tej* is Birr5.

Bru box (admission free) You'll hear the drumbeats from a block away. It's good fun but the *faranji* drink prices are stupidly steep.

Shopping

Merkato (sunrise-sunset) The obvious choice for shoppers. Within the market and on surrounding streets you'll find basket, pottery and cloth stalls.

You can support Project Ploughshare by buying pottery in Wolleka or at the unmarked stall opposite the Royal Enclosure.

Getting There & Away

For information about reaching Sudan, see p275.

AIR

Ethiopian Airlines (☎ 0581 110129) flies once or twice daily to Addis Ababa (US$102, 1½ to two hours), Bahir Dar (US$37, 17 minutes), Lalibela (US$51, 30 minutes) and Aksum (US$73, 1¾ hours).

BUS

Buses leave for Addis Ababa (Birr82.50, two days, 6am), Bahir Dar (Birr 22, four hours, three daily), Debark (Birr14.10, 3½ hours, two daily), Gorgora (Birr9.10, 1½ hours, two daily) and Woldia (Birr53.35, two days, twice weekly). For Aksum, go first to Shire (Birr40.60, 11 hours, 6am). For longer journeys, buy tickets a day in advance.

CAR & 4WD

NTO (☎ 0581 110379) and **Galaxy Express Services** (☎ 0581 111546; Goha Hotel) rent out vehicles with drivers; this should be prearranged. On short notice, **Abraham Tigabu** (☎ 0918 770386; abrahamtig@yahoo.com) and his trusty Land Cruiser will do the trick. Day trips to Sankaber in the Simien Mountains should cost no more than Birr900 with driver and fuel.

There are occasionally fuel shortages, so fill up when you can.

Getting Around

A taxi to or from the airport, which is 21km from town, costs between Birr30 and Birr40. Chartering a taxi to see Gonder's sights costs about Birr30 per hour, but you'll have to negotiate hard for this. Taxis and minibuses congregate near the piazza.

Minibuses charge between Birr0.50 and Birr1.75 for hops around town; *garis* cost around Birr1 to Birr5.

Bicycles can be hired (Birr5 per hour) outside the Royal Enclosure's northeast corner.

AROUND GONDER

Gorgora ጎርጎራ

pop 3100 / elev 1880m

The little lakeshore town of Gorgora, 67km south of Gonder, makes a pleasant excursion for those with time, particularly for travellers interested in birds (see p117).

SIGHTS & ACTIVITIES

The most interesting relic of Gorgora's former days as a temporary capital is the attractive **Church of Debre Sina** (Map p116; admission Birr25). Built in 1608 by Emperor Susenyos' son on the site of a 14th-century monastery, it's decorated with vivid 17th-century polychromatic frescoes. Ask to see the 'Egyptian St Mary'.

Emperor Susenyos (r 1607–32) built a **palace** (Map p116; admission free) on a peninsula 10km west of Gorgora, which can be reached in 30 minutes by road or boat. Compared to Gonder, it's in shambles but historical

architecture buffs should make the trip. Also in the area is the **Portuguese Cathedral** (Map p116; admission free) built by Susenyos. It's decrepit state is evidence of his failed attempt to force Catholicism on his people.

If the lake's waters are calling, you can visit Tana's northern monasteries. **Mendaba Medhane Alem** (Map p116; admission Birr20, men only) hosts ancient biblical manuscripts and some of Ethiopia's most dedicated priests, while **Birgida Maryam** (Map p116; admission Birr20, men only) is known for its 16th-century painting of Mary. Both are around 30 minutes from Gorgora by boat.

With the exception of Debre Sina, you'll need a local guide to find most of the sights. **Tesfaye Mekonnen** (☎ 0581 117732), who's usually found at the Gorgora Port Hotel, is a reliable option.

SLEEPING & EATING

Gorgora Port Hotel (☎ 0581 117732; camping Birr25, tw Birr80, 3-bedroom ste Birr180) The two massive suites scream Brady Bunch, ooze 1970s and are a little worn, but sit mere feet from the shore, allowing the sounds of lapping waves to put you soundly to sleep. The small twins are also bright and clean, but are further from shore. Electricity runs between 6pm and 10pm. The restaurant (mains Birr7 to Birr16) is good and specialises in fish.

GETTING THERE & AROUND

Two daily buses run to Gonder (Birr9.10, 1½ hours).

A ferry sails from Gorgora for Bahir Dar every Thursday at 6am (Birr104.50, 1½ days). The ferry typically overnights in Konzola, where there's food and a couple of cheap hotels. Buy tickets at the **Lake Tana Transport Enterprise office** (☉ 8am-11.30am & 2-5.30pm Mon-Fri, 8am-noon Sat). The same office rents speedboats (Birr112 per hour for one to six people) for trips to the monasteries and local ruins.

SIMIEN MOUNTAINS NATIONAL PARK
የስሜን ተራሮች ብሔራዊ ፓርክ

No matter how you look at them, the Simien Mountains will leave you speechless. For trekkers, the lack of words will be the result of their lungs screaming after slogging up a scree slope at 4200m. For animal-lovers, it will be the trepidation of sitting among a group of 100 gelada baboons that zaps their vocabulary. For everyone with a heartbeat, it will simply be standing atop a panoramic precipice and looking out over the Abyssinian abyss that takes their breath away.

Whether you come for a stroll or two-week trek, the Simien Mountains make a great break from the historical circuit's constant monument-bashing. Besides the mythical baboons (see the boxed text, p128), it's also home to a variety of endemic mammals, birds and plants, including the beautiful and massively horned walia ibex. Thanks to its wildlife, the park is a World Heritage site.

Although facilities for trekkers are few (the undeveloped state of the park is actually one of its attractions), the mountains are nevertheless easily accessible and treks can be quickly organised.

The Simien Mountains aren't to be missed – they undoubtedly rank among Africa's most beautiful ranges.

Geography & Geology

Comprising one of Africa's principal mountain massifs, the Simiens are made up of several plateaus, separated by broad river valleys. A number of peaks rise above 4000m, including Ras Dashen (4543m), which is highly touted – incorrectly so – by Ethiopian tourism officials as the fourth-highest mountain in Africa. They seem to have happily forgotten the Ruwenzori Range's Mt Speke (4890m), Mt Baker (4844m), Mt Emin (4792m), Mt Gessi (4717m) and Mt Luigi (4626m), as well as Tanzania's Mt Meru (4566m)!

The Simiens' landscape is incredibly dramatic. It was formed by countless eruptions, some 40 million years ago; layer upon layer of molten lava was poured until it reached a thickness of 3000m. The subsequent erosion produced the mountains' jagged and spectacular landscapes seen today.

The famous pinnacles that sharply and abruptly rise from the surrounding landscape are volcanic necks, the solidified plumbing of the eroded ancient volcanoes.

The 179-sq-km park lies within the 'Afro-alpine' zone, between 1900m and 4543m elevation.

Wildlife

The mountains are home to three of Ethiopia's larger endemic mammals: the walia ibex (numbers estimated at 515 in 2005), the gelada baboon (estimated to number around 6000) and the elusive Ethiopian wolf (estimated between 45 and 70). Other mammals sometimes seen are rock hyraxes, jackals, bushbucks and klipspringers.

Endemic birds include the often-seen thick-billed raven, and the less common black-headed siskin, white-collared pigeon, white-billed starling, wattled ibis, spot-breasted plover, white-backed black tit and Ankober seedeater or serin. Though common, one of the most memorable sights (and sounds!) is the lammergeyer soaring low.

Along the roadside on the approach to Sankaber, look out for the ivory-coloured, endemic Abyssinian rose.

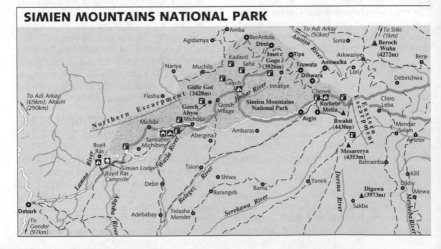

SIMIEN MOUNTAINS NATIONAL PARK

Planning

Although organising trekking yourself at park headquarters in Debark is straightforward, it still takes two hours to complete. It's best to arrive at headquarters the afternoon before you plan on starting your trek.

Organising treks through agencies in Gonder and Addis Ababa is easy, but you may end up paying more for the same trip.

WHEN TO GO

December to March is the driest time; after the rainy season in October, the scenery is greenest and the wildflowers are out.

During the main rainy season, between June and September, mist often obscures the views and trails can be slippery underfoot. But, you're still assured of several hours of clear, dry weather for walking; the rain tends to come in short, sharp downpours.

Daytime temperatures are consistently between 11.5°C and 18°C, while 3°C is typical at night. October to December nighttime temperatures can dip below freezing.

PARK FEES

All fees are good for 48 hours and are payable at the **park headquarters** (☎ 0581 113482; admission Birr50, camping Birr20, 5-seat vehicle Birr10; ☒ 8.30am-12.30pm & 1.30-5.30pm Mon-Fri, 8.30am-noon & 2-5pm Sat & Sun).

Entrance and camping fees won't be refunded once paid. However, if mules, cooks, guides and scouts aren't used (because of bad weather or acclimatisation difficulties),

> ### VANISHING WOLVES
>
> Though it derived its original name (Simien fox) from these mountains, the Ethiopian wolf is close to extinction in the area. Many have died from diseases caught from local dogs, others have died after eating rats poisoned by villagers to protect their crops, or in traps. Hybridisation with dogs is another threat to the species' survival. Fortunately, the endemic animal is faring far better in the Bale Mountains to the south (see the boxed text, p184).

their fees can be refunded; make sure this is clear before setting off.

MAPS

The most useful trekking map is produced by the well-respected Institute of Geography, University of Berne, Switzerland: the *Simen* [sic] *Mountains Trekking Map* (2003; 1:100,000). The park rents a laminated version for Birr20 per day. If you want your own copy, it's best to get it before leaving home. It can also occasionally be found in Gonder or in Debark's Simien Park Hotel (p130; Birr200 to Birr215).

EQUIPMENT

Mattresses (Birr10 per day), sleeping bags (Birr10 per day), two-person tents (Birr25 per day) and cooking equipment and gas stoves (Birr30 per day) can be hired at park headquarters. Debark's petrol station sells kerosene.

SUPPLIES

Outside Debark, there are no shops; you can buy eggs (three eggs Birr1), chickens (Birr15 to Birr20) and sheep (Birr80 to Birr150) from mountain villages. Your guide will negotiate prices. Mule handlers will gladly kill, skin and roast a sheep if they can tuck it in too. If you leave the carcass a little way from camp, it may attract a lammergeyer.

Gonder is a better place to stock up as Debark's food supplies are limited to a few tin cans, biscuits, pasta, tomato sauce and milk powder, plus some fresh fruit and vegetables. Stoves, lanterns and kerosene (paraffin) are also available in Gonder. Anything 'specialised', such as packet soups, should be bought in Addis Ababa.

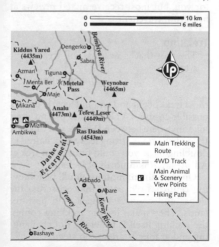

MONKEY TROUBLE

Astoundingly beautiful, and ever so slightly scary when they yawn (those are serious choppers!), gelada baboons are a favourite sight among visitors. However, the extraordinary animal is little appreciated by locals. Resented for its alleged damage to crops and pasture, it has become the scapegoat for more sinister goings-on, too. According to local police reports, gelada baboons are responsible for local thefts, burglaries, rapes and even murders – in one case bursting into a house to drag an adult man 1.5km before shoving him off a cliff face! If in doubt, blame the gelada!

Unless you want to test locals' theories, don't chase or try to feed the gelada. See also the boxed text, p61.

Water is available during the trek but should be treated. Make sure the cook, if you have one, boils the water sufficiently.

Though eucalyptus wood (sold by villagers on the mountain) is permitted for fires, it's best to bring a stove. Burning wood from indigenous trees is strictly forbidden.

If you're worried about warmth, do as the locals do: buy a *gabi* (Birr45 to Birr90 depending on the size) at Debark market, which makes a great blanket, sheet, pillow, shawl or cushion.

GUIDES, SCOUTS, COOKS & MULES

Cooks, scouts, mules and guides are all organised at park headquarters.

Official guides (Birr75 per day) are recommended and help translate while in villages. Although freelancers, they're trained by the national park on courses established by an Austrian team. Most are excellent, a few are less so. Guides work by rota, but you should not be afraid to ask for another if you're not happy with the one assigned to you.

Most people who've hired cheaper unofficial guides off the street end up regretting the decision. See p260 for more.

'Scouts' (armed park rangers) are compulsory (Birr30 per day). Few speak English, but what they lack in conversation they make up for in willingness to help.

Cooks can be hired for Birr50 per day (cooking for one to five people), a welcome and not-too-costly luxury for some.

Porters aren't available, but mules (Birr20 per day) with handlers (Birr20 per day) can be hired. The guide and scout will expect at least one mule for carrying their blankets and provisions. Check mules for tender feet (ask the owner to walk the mule up and down) and signs of saddle sores. If in doubt, ask for another.

Guides, cooks and mule handlers should bring their own food. Many bring token offerings or nothing at all and will then look to you for sustenance. Either check that they have enough or bring extra packets of rice etc.

If you plan on covering two days' worth of trekking in one, you'll have to pay your team double for the day.

See p264 for post-trek tipping advice.

ORGANISED TREKS

There are numerous tour operators or travel agencies in Addis Ababa (see p282) and several more in Gonder (p119) that can organise transport, guides, equipment rental and food. Since the agencies are just hiring the same services from park headquarters that you'd get if organising it yourself, you can use the costs mentioned previously (park fees, equipment, supplies, guides, scouts, cooks and mules etc) to judge the agencies' quotes and negotiate accordingly. See Getting There & Away (p131) and Getting Around (p131) for transportation costs.

There are also numerous freelance 'agents' in Gonder offering to organise treks for you, but most receive mixed reviews at best from travellers.

Trekking

The foot that is restless, will tread on a turd.

Ethiopian proverb

Most treks begin and end in Debark, but it's possible to use 4WDs to start or end your hike anywhere between Debark and Chenek. If you have time, strong legs and a hatred of doubling back, you could finish your trek at Adi Arkay, 75km north of Debark.

Once on the mountains you'll be following centuries-old paths that crisscross the slopes and connect villages with pasturelands. They make terrific trekking routes; the walking itself is generally not challenging and gradients aren't too steep.

Be sure to allow time for acclimatisation when planning your routes, particularly if you're aiming for Ras Dashen. Review the Safety Guidelines for Trekking (p254) and Responsible Trekking (p255) boxed texts.

CHOOSING A TREKKING ROUTE

For spectacular scenery, head for Geech. For walia ibex, Chenek is good (be sure to get here no later than 9am). Gelada baboons are best between Buyit Ras and Sankaber; Chenek and Geech aren't bad either. For pleasant walking, the stretch between Geech and Chenek is good. For lammergeyer, head to Chenek.

Ras Dashen, frankly, doesn't offer a great deal beyond the satisfaction of 'bagging it'. And thanks to an odd perspective from its summit, nearby peaks actually look higher. This has led disgruntled trekkers to drag their guides up peak after peak, repeatedly musing the 'one over there' is higher!

With two days you could walk from Debark to Sankaber and back. With four days you could reach Geech; with five you could get to Chenek, taking in Mt Bwahit; and with around 10 days you could bag Ras Dashen (these times include the return journey to Debark). If you're short on time and want to maximise your time in the mountains, using a vehicle to access Sankaber will save at least two days.

The following is a classic route; the lower camps can be bypassed using a vehicle. Times vary from person to person, and also depend on whether exact routes are followed. The following routes and times have been devised in consultation with local guides.

Debark to Ras Dashen Trek

DEBARK TO BUYIT RAS (10KM, THREE TO FOUR HOURS)

Sankaber can be reached in a single day, but many trekkers prefer to break at Buyit Ras, where there's an abundance of gelada baboons. There's also a camping spot with beautiful views, though you'll have to share the area with a new resort that opened in 2006. If you push on to Sankaber, it's another 13km (around three to four hours).

BUYIT RAS TO GEECH CAMP VIA SANKABER (25KM, SEVEN TO EIGHT HOURS)

The dirt road will take you straight to Sankaber, but the scenic route along the escarpment isn't to be missed. There are particularly good views between Michibi and Sankaber. Look out for gelada baboons.

From Sankaber to Geech it's between four and five hours' walk.

GEECH CAMP TO CHENEK VIA IMET GOGO (20KM, SEVEN TO NINE HOURS)

Geech to Chenek takes about five to six hours, but you'd be crazy not to take in Imet Gogo, around 5km northeast of Geech. It takes 1½ to two hours one way.

The promontory, at 3926m, affords some of the most spectacular views of the Simien Mountains. To make a day of it, you could continue to the viewpoint known as Saha. From Saha, you can head for the viewpoint at Kadavit (2.5km, 30 to 40 minutes), then return to camp.

You can also trek to Chenek via Imet Gogo using Saha as a starting point (eight to nine hours). Saha lies around 3km from Geech.

From Imet Gogo you have two choices: the first is to return to Geech by your outward route, then head directly south, back across the Jinbar River to where you'll eventually meet the dirt road that leads to Chenek. The alternative, which is harder but more scenic, is to follow the escarpment edge south all the way to Chenek.

Near Chenek is Korbete Metia, a stunning spot with a sinister side. It was here that some regional officials were executed. Korbete Metia loosely translates to 'the place where skin was thrown down'. Lammergeyers are often seen here.

Chenek is probably the best spot in the Simien Mountains for wildlife.

For those who want to return to Sankaber from Chenek (seven to eight hours) but avoid most of the dirt road, a scenic local trail up to Ambaras through the village of Argin can be followed. The trail affords good views of the escarpment and the foothills of Mt Bwahit.

CHENEK TO MT BWAHIT & RETURN (6KM, TWO TO THREE HOURS)

The summit of Mt Bwahit (4430m) lies to the southeast of the camp. From the top, you can see a tiny piece of Ras Dashen.

Around 20 minutes from the camp towards Mt Bwahit, there's a spot that affords one of the best opportunities for glimpsing, at long range (around 300m to 400m), the walia ibex. This animal, a member of the wild goat family, lives on the crags of the steep escarpment above 3000m. Come very early in the morning or late in the afternoon (after 4pm) with binoculars. On our last trip we were lucky enough to see two males going head to head on a precarious slope, with the crashes of their collisions echoing through the crisp air.

CHENEK TO AMBIKWA (22KM, EIGHT TO NINE HOURS)

From Chenek, a track leads eastward then southeastward up towards a good viewpoint on the eastern escarpment, to the north of Mt Bwahit. To the east, across the vast valley of the Mesheba River, you can see the bulk of Ras Dashen.

AMBIKWA TO RAS DASHEN & RETURN (17KM, EIGHT TO 10 HOURS)

Most trekkers stay two nights at Ambikwa and go up to the summit of Ras Dashen on the day in between. It's a good idea to start at first light.

At Ras Dashen there are three distinct points, and much debate about which is the true summit. Whichever peak you go for, the total walk from Ambikwa to reach one summit is about five to six hours. If you want to knock off the others, add two to three hours for each one. Returning by the same route takes about three to four hours.

Return Routes

AMBIKWA TO DEBARK (77KM, THREE DAYS)

Most trekkers return from Ambikwa to Debark along the same route via Chenek and Sankaber. If you're tired or have had enough, you may be able to hitch a lift (Birr30) with the odd truck that plies the route.

AMBIKWA TO ADI ARKAY (ABOUT 65KM, THREE TO FIVE DAYS)

One alternative return route is to trek from Ambikwa to Arkwasiye, to the northeast of Chenek, taking in the nearby peaks of Beroch Wuha (4272m) and Silki (4420m).

From Arkwasiye to Adi Arkay will take another two to three days of strenuous walking, via Sona (three hours from Arkwasiye).

From Adi Arkay, which lies 75km north of Debark, you can continue northward to Aksum.

Other Routes

There are endless alternatives for keen trekkers, such as a return route from Ras Dashen back to Ambikwa and Chenek, via the east and north sides of the Mesheba River.

One slightly more challenging route that will give you a taste of the highlands as well as the lowlands, and bags some 4000m on the way (and is much more interesting than climbing Ras Dashen), is from Debark to Adi Arkay via Sankaber, Geech, Chenek (climbing Mt Bwahit at 4430m), Arkwasiye (climbing Beroch Wuha at 4272m) and Sona (climbing Silki at 4420m). The route should take around nine to 10 days. Note that, since it takes the guides, mules and other members of your trekking entourage two further days to return to Debark from Adi Arkay, you must pay two days' extra fee.

Sleeping & Eating

DEBARK

Simien Park Hotel (☎ 0581 113481; s/d/tw with shared bathroom Birr30/40/50, tw Birr70) About 600m north of park headquarters, this place is simple and reasonably clean. Rooms come in baby blue, and showers (shared and private) are hot. Reservations are advised, particularly in January. Its bar/restaurant serves local and *faranji* food (Birr8 to Birr13) and drink.

Red Fox Hotel (☎ 0581 117807; s/d/tw with shared bathroom Birr25/35/45) This should only be an option if Simien Park Hotel is full. It has big rooms and a satellite TV in its bar, but it's not the cleanest and the shared bathrooms are rather rough. It's set a block west of the main street.

ON THE MOUNTAINS

Camping (per 48hr Birr20) The obvious choice for trekkers. It's possible anywhere, but if you're in the vicinity of an the official camp (Sankaber, Geech and Chenek) it's more convenient to drop your tent there. These camps have huts for your guides and scouts, as well as long drop loos. Besides the new block of toilets just south of Sankaber, most toilets are rather filthy.

If you don't have camping equipment (and don't want to rent it) you can do as the guides do: stay with locals (you should contribute about Birr10 per night). Don't expect luxuries. A floor or wooden platform covered with a goatskin serves as your bedroom; any number and combination of animals, children, chickens and especially fleas will be your roommates.

Simien Lodge (☎ 0116 189398, 0911 203937; www .simiens.com; dm US$15-20, d US$95-105, 4-person VIP tukul US$135-150) This new lodge opened at Buyit Ras in 2006. Dubbed northern Ethiopia's first ecolodge, it plans to promote sustainable development and encourages guests to help with charity work in Debark. The thatch-roofed *tukuls* are very comfortable and come complete with solar-powered underfloor heating. The 16-bed dormitory even has solar-powered showers, though immersion heaters help things along during the rainy season. The bar and restaurant are centred on open fires; meals must be ordered when booking the room.

Sankaber Lodge (dm Birr40) For day-trippers, there is this spartan lodge, which has a couple of nine bed dorms. Don't expect more than a rickety bed, blanket, some old bed linen and possibly the odd flea.

Getting There & Away

Two morning buses run from Debark to Gonder (Birr14.10, 3½ hours). The only bus running north to Shire (for Aksum) is the Gonder service (Birr35, 7½ hours). It typically arrives in Debark between 9am and 10am, but is usually full. If so, either head back to Gonder or hitch a lift north. From Shire, take the Gonder bus (Birr40.60) and ask to be dropped at Debark.

It's possible to arrange 4WDs in Gonder to drop you off at Debark (Birr450, two hours), Sankaber (Birr850, 3½ hours) or Chenek (Birr1000, five hours). If arranged, they can also pick you up. Return costs are the same. See Car & 4WD on p125 for contact details.

If you hike out to Adi Arkay, you can try to get a seat on the Gonder–Shire bus. We had no luck, so paid Birr50 for a cab seat in a local truck heading to Shire.

Getting Around

It's possible to arrange a 4WD at park headquarters to drop you off and pick you up at Sankaber (one way/return Birr400/800 after negotiations).

Usually at least one supply truck plies the road daily to Chenek (leaving Debark at around 6am and returning the same day).

You may be able to hitch a lift in the back (around Birr30).

SHIRE ሺሬ

pop 53,195 / elev 1923m

Shire, marked on some maps as Inda Selassie, is of interest to travellers only because it provides a link with Aksum, 60km to the east. However, the journey from Debark to Shire (and in particular the stretch of road between Debark and Adi Arkay) is one of the most dramatic in Ethiopia.

The beautifully constructed Italian road cuts its way through the mountains in a series of neat loops and bends and provides impressive views. Around Adi Arkay, look out for the peak known as Awaza (occasionally represented on the back of Ethiopian Airlines tickets).

The plains on the outskirts of Shire were the scene of fighting between the Tigrayans and the advancing Italians in the 1930s, and later Mengistu's army in the civil war. Keep an eye out for war relics.

If you get stuck in Shire (and you will if you arrive here after 4pm), the **Jelly Café** (s with shared bathroom Birr15) is by far the nicest sleeping option. The rooms are small, tidy and bright (No 7 is best). The toilet and shower is basic but clean. It's 200m west of the bus station.

There are several buses and minibuses to Aksum daily (Birr10 to Birr15, 1½ hours). One daily bus serves Gonder (Birr40.60, 11 hours, 6am).

AKSUM አክሱም

pop 41,500 / elev 2130m

Sprawling, dusty, and rural – Aksum is modest almost to a fault. On first sight, it's hard to imagine that the town was ever the site of a great civilisation. Yet Aksum is one of Ethiopia's star attractions. Littered with massive teetering stelae, ruins of palaces, underground tombs (most still undiscovered) and inscriptions rivalling the Rosetta stone itself, the town once formed part of the Aksumite kingdom that Dr Neville Chittick described as 'the last of the great civilisations of Antiquity to be revealed to modern knowledge'. Aksum is undoubtedly one of the most important and spectacular ancient sites in subSaharan Africa. Justifiably, Unesco lists it as a World Heritage site.

Aksum has a vibrancy, life and continuing national importance very rarely found

---

AKSUM'S FALL

After Aksum lost its grip on Red Sea trade, due to the rise of Islamic Arabs' fortunes, the society quickly imploded and sent Ethiopia into the dark ages for five centuries. Why this happened when it was still rich in natural resources is the subject of many theories.

The environmental argument suggests that Aksum's ever-increasing population led to over-cropping of the land, deforestation and eventually soil erosion. The climatic explanation claims that a slight 'global warming' took place, which finished Aksum's agriculture and eventually led to drought and famine. The military argument claims that Aksum was undermined by continual incursions from neighbouring tribes, such as the Beja from the northwest of the country.

According to tradition, Aksumite power was usurped around the 9th century by the dreaded warrior queen Gudit (or Judit), a pagan or Jew, who killed the ruling king, burnt down the city and sabotaged the stelae (definitely the least boring explanation!). Intriguingly, this legend seems to be born out by at least two documents written at about this time.

---

at ancient sites. Pilgrims still journey to Aksum and the great majority of Ethiopians believe passionately that the Ark of the Covenant resides here.

Though no longer a wealthy metropolis, the town continues to flourish as a centre of local trade; life continues as it has for millennia. Around the crumbling palaces, farmers go on ploughing their land, women continue to wash their clothes in the Queen of Sheba's Bath, and marketgoers and their donkeys hurry past the towering stelae. You won't find pyramid-parking coaches or sound-and-light shows here. And inextricably interwoven with the archaeological evidence is the local tradition – the legends, myths and fables.

A good time to visit is during one of the major religious festivals, particularly the celebration of Maryam Zion in late November. To do the town justice, you should schedule a bare minimum of two days, or one full day if you have a vehicle.

History

According to local legend, Aksum was the Queen of Sheba's capital in the 10th century BC. More fantasy than fact that may be, but what's certain is that a high civilisation started to rise as early as 400 BC.

By the 1st century AD, Greek merchants knew Aksum as a great city and the powerful capital of an extensive empire. For close to 1000 years, Aksum dominated the vital sea-borne trade between Africa and Asia. The kingdom numbered among the ancient world's greatest states. For more information see Kingdom of Aksum (p27) and the boxed text, above.

Information

INTERNET ACCESS

Africa Hotel (Map p133; per hr Birr60) Town's fastest and most reliable Internet option (though that's not saying much!). Found in a small room off the courtyard. Ask the manager to open it for you.

Alpha Internet (Map p133; per hr Birr48) Slow but usually steady connections.

John Telecenter & Internet Cafe (Map p133; per hr Birr48) Offers slow Internet and international telephone calls (per minute Birr25).

MEDICAL SERVICES

St Mary Hospital (Map p133; 24hr) Town's only hospital, though was hard to find anyone who spoke English.

St Mary Pharmacy (Map p133; ☎ 0347 752646; 7.30am-9.30pm) Helpful and well stocked.

St Michael Clinic (Map p133; noon-2pm & 5-10pm Mon-Fri, 8am-10pm Sat & Sun) Helpful clinic and the doctor speaks decent English.

MONEY

Commercial Bank (Map p133; 8-11am & 1-3pm Mon-Fri, 8-11am Sat) Changes cash and travellers cheques.

Wegagen Bank (Map p133; 8am-4pm Mon-Sat) Exchanges cash and travellers cheques.

POST

A small and pretty reliable post office (Map p133) is next to the tourism commission.

TELEPHONE

Telecommunications office (Map p133; 7am-10pm Mon-Sat) International calls. Standard rates (p267).

TOURIST INFORMATION

Tigrai Tourism Commission (Map p133; ☎ 0347 753924; 8am-noon & 1-5pm) One of the country's most friendly and helpful offices. It has a couple of

NORTHERN ETHIOPIA

AKSUM

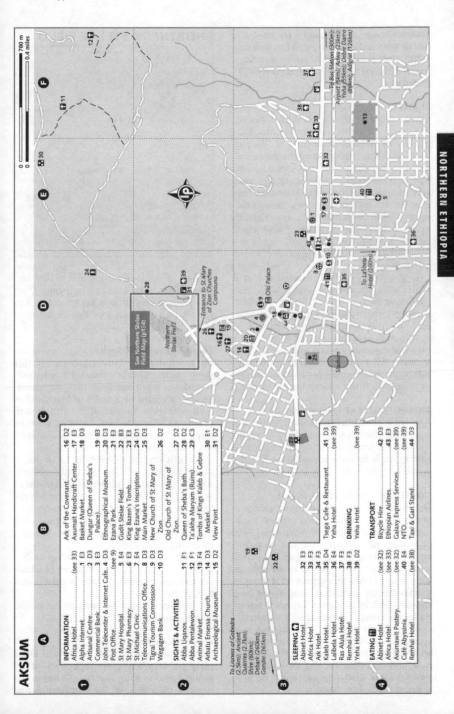

INFORMATION		
Africa Hotel..........................	(see 33)	
Alpha Internet.......................	1	E3
Artisanal Centre....................	2	D3
Commercial Bank...................	3	E3
John Telecenter & Internet Cafe.	4	D3
Post Office............................	(see 9)	
St Mary Hospital...................	5	E4
St Mary Pharmacy.................	6	E3
St Michael Clinic...................	7	E4
Telecommunications Office....	8	D3
Tigrai Tourism Commission......	9	D3
Wegagen Bank......................	10	D3

SIGHTS & ACTIVITIES		
Abba Liqanos........................	11	F1
Abba Pentalewon.................	12	F1
Animal Market.......................	13	F4
Arbatu Ensessa Church...........	14	D3
Archaeological Museum.........	15	D2
Ark of the Covenant..............	16	D2
Axumait Handicraft Center.....	17	E3
Basket Market.......................	18	D3
Dungur (Queen of Sheba's Palace).	19	B3
Ethnographical Museum.........	20	D3
Ezana Park...........................	21	E3
Gudit Stelae Field..................	22	B3
King Bazen's Tomb................	23	E3
King Ezana's Inscription..........	24	D1
Main Market..........................	25	D3
New Church of St Mary of Zion.	26	D2
Old Church of St Mary of Zion.	27	D2
Queen of Sheba's Bath..........	28	D2
Ta'akha Maryam (Ruins)........	29	C3
Tombs of Kings Kaleb & Gebre Meskel.	30	E1
View Point............................	31	D2

SLEEPING		
Abinet Hotel.........................	32	E3
Africa Hotel..........................	33	F3
Ark Hotel.............................	34	F3
Kaleb Hotel..........................	35	D4
Lalibela Hotel.......................	36	E4
Ras Alula Hotel.....................	37	F3
Remhai Hotel........................	38	F3
Yeha Hotel...........................	39	D2

EATING		
Abinet Hotel.........................	(see 32)	
Africa Hotel..........................	(see 33)	
Axumawit Pastery..................	(see 32)	
Café Abyssinia......................	40	E4
Remhai Hotel........................	(see 38)	
Tsega Cafe & Restaurant.......	41	D3
Yeha Hotel...........................	(see 39)	

DRINKING		
Yeha Hotel...........................	(see 39)	

TRANSPORT		
Bicycle Hire..........................	42	D3
Ethiopian Airlines..................	43	E3
Galaxy Express Services.........	(see 39)	
NTO.....................................	(see 39)	
Taxi & Gari Stand..................	44	D3

See Northern Stelae Field Map (p134)

Northern Stelae Field

Entrance to St Mary of Zion Churches Compound

Old Palace

Stadium

To Bus Station (800m); Airport (5km); Adwa (23km); Yeha (53km); Debre Damo (86km); Adigrat (126km)

To Lalibela Hotel (200m)

To Lioness of Gobedra (5km); Ancient Quarries (2.7km); Shire (60km); Debark (260km); Gonder (361km)

700 m
0.4 miles

official guides who give free Aksum tours on weekdays (tips are appreciated; Birr50 per group is fair). Guides are limited so arrange a time at least a day in advance. On weekends the office told us official guides charge Birr50 ·per person.

Sights

One admission ticket (adult/student Birr50/ 25) covers all sights within the immediate vicinity of Aksum, except the St Mary of Zion church compound and the monasteries of Abba Pentalewon and Abba Liqanos. The ticket is good for the duration of your stay and is sold at the Tigrai Tourism Commission. It's thought when the future Ethiopian Cultural Heritage Project museum opens behind the Northern Stelae Park, tickets will be sold there. All sights are open between 8am and 5pm unless stated otherwise.

If you can get your hands on David Phillipson's *Aksum: an archaeological introduction and guide* you'll find an excellent compendium to Aksum's history, archaeology and major sites and monuments.

Although you can see the monuments on your own, an official guide is recommended. All are trained and many are history students, so you'll get much more out of your visit. Bring a torch for the tombs.

AKSUMITE STELAE የአክሱም ሐወ-ልቶች

Ancient Aksum obelisks (stelae) pepper the area, and whether you're looking down on a small specimen or staring up at a grand tower, you'll be duly bowled over. See the boxed text, p136 for the lowdown.

NORTHERN STELAE FIELD TOMBS

Despite the grandeur above the surface, some of the Northern Stelae Field's greatest treasures are found beneath it. Amazingly, 98% of it lies undiscovered and you may find yourself hearing the sound of an unopened tomb echoing below your feet as you explore. This is part of Aksum's appeal – the thought that fascinating finds, secrets and maybe even treasures lurk in the depths. Try not to return under the cover of darkness with a shovel!

Though it's unlikely that anything as spectacular as an Ethiopian Tutankhamen will turn up, the importance of the Aksumite kingdom in the ancient world, and the potential for discovery of future excavations, shouldn't be dismissed.

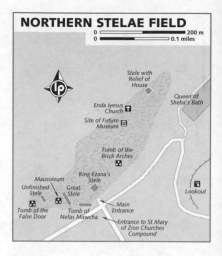

NORTHERN STELAE FIELD

Most of the tombs excavated to date had been pillaged by robbers (remember, no shovels!), so very little is known about Aksumite burial customs or the identities of those buried.

Tomb of the Brick Arches

Dating from the end of the 3rd century, this tomb (Map p134) is remarkably well preserved and contains four rock-cut chambers, subdivided by a series of brick arches built with lime mortar. If it's still closed, you'll still be able to look down its 18 stone steps to its signature horseshoe-shaped brick arch entranceway.

It's just one of two tombs so far excavated that have avoided wholesale robbery. Among the many finds were the remains of at least two skeletons, finely carved ivory including two beautiful tusks, pottery, fragments of glass vessels, and, in a pit in the first chamber, a large quantity of bronze, including decorative panels.

It was at this site that archaeologists discovered the cast plaque, the holes of which matched rivets atop one stele (see the boxed text, p136).

The tomb should be open to the public by the time you read this.

Tomb of the False Door

In 1972 the unique Tomb of the False Door (Map p134) was discovered (known locally as the Tomb of King Ramhai). It lies in the western extremity of the Northern Stelae

Field and is thought to date between the 4th and 6th centuries AD. More complex in structure, its stone blocks are also larger and more finely dressed than those found in some other tombs. Comprising an antechamber and inner chamber, it's surrounded on three sides by a passage.

Above the tomb, at ground level, a rectangular, probably flat-roofed building would have stood (measuring some 12 sq metres by 2.8m high). Above the stairs descending into the tomb's chamber was a stone slab carved with a false door almost identical to those found on the stelae. Look for the iron clamps fixing blocks of stone together like giant staples.

All the tomb's contents were stolen in antiquity and, judging from the lengths to which the robbers went to gain access, it's thought to have contained objects of great value. The much-mutilated single stone sarcophagus can still be seen.

Tomb of Nefas Mawcha

The megalithic Tomb of Nefas Mawcha (Map p134) consists of a large rectangular central chamber surrounded on three sides by a passage. The tomb is unusual for its large size, the sophistication of the structure and the size of the stones used for its construction (the stone which roofs the central chamber measures 17.3m by 6.4m and weighs some 360 tonnes!). It's believed the force of the Giant Stele crashing into its roof caused the tomb's spectacular collapse.

Mausoleum

The so-called mausoleum (Map p134) was discovered in 1974, but not excavated until the mid-1990s. A monumental portal (hewn from a single slab of granite) marked the tomb's entrance and was also carved with the stelae's curious false door motifs. The portal leads into a passageway with 10 chambers. Part of the tomb had been disfigured at some unknown date by robbers, who succeeded in digging through 1.5m of solid masonry! The mausoleum was almost set for its opening to the public during our visit – enjoy!

ST MARY OF ZION CHURCHES
የማርያም ጽዮን ቤተክርስቲያናች

Opposite the Northern Stelae Field in a walled compound lie the two churches of

St Mary of Zion (admission Birr60, personal video cameras Birr100; ☺ 8am-noon & 2-6pm).

The rectangular **old church** (Map p133) is a remarkable example of traditional architecture and was built by the Emperor Fasiladas, the founder of Gonder, in 1665. It's thought that the old podium on which it sits may well belong to Africa's first church, which was erected by King Ezana or King Kaleb in the 4th or 6th century. Unfortunately, the original church was destroyed during the incursions of Mohammed Gragn the Left-Handed in 1535.

Inside there are fine murals, including a painting of the Nine Saints (see The Coming of Christianity, p28), and a collection of ceremonial musical instruments.

A carefully guarded chapel in the church compound is said to contain the **Ark of the Covenant** (Map p133). Don't think you can take a peek: just one specially chosen guardian has access to the Ark. And many the unfortunate onlooker has 'burst into fire' just for getting close!

The little **museum** in the same building contains an unsurpassed collection of former Ethiopian rulers' crowns. Neither the chapel nor the museum is open to women, but some of the crowns can be brought out by obliging priests; you should tip them afterwards. The chapel isn't always open; try and get here early in the morning. This museum may move to the Archaeological Museum's building, when the future museum in the Northern Stele Field opens.

The huge **new church** of St Mary of Zion (Map p133) was built in the 1960s and displays Haile Selassie's usual unusual taste. We've previously awarded it the 'hideous carbuncle' prize, but we'll be kinder this time around (perhaps it's growing on us!). It does cut a dramatic silhouette on the skyline when viewed from the Yeha Hotel at sunset. Beside it, a disproportionately tall bell tower, shaped to resemble the biggest stele of all, sprouts heavenwards.

ARCHAEOLOGICAL MUSEUM
አርኪዮሎጂ መ-ዝየም

The **Archaeological Museum** (Map p133; ☺ 8am-noon & 2-6pm) contains fine and well-preserved Sabaean and early Ge'ez inscriptions, some dating back over 2500 years. There's also an interesting variety of objects found in tombs, ranging from ordinary household

A QUICK GUIDE TO AKSUM'S STELAE

For as long as 5000 years, monoliths have been used in northeast Africa as tombstones and monuments to local rulers. In Aksum, this tradition reached its apogee. Like Egypt's pyramids, Aksum's stelae were like great billboards announcing to the world the authority, power and greatness of the ruling families. Aksum's astonishing stelae are striking for their huge size, their incredible, almost pristine, state of preservation, and their curiously modern look. Sculpted from single pieces of granite, some look more like Manhattan skyscrapers than 1800-year-old obelisks, complete with little windows, doors and sometimes even door handles and locks!

Despite the stone being famously hard, Aksum's masons worked it superbly, often following an architectural design that mirrored the traditional style seen in Aksumite houses and palaces (for more details on Aksumite architecture see p56).

Metal plates, perhaps in the form of a crescent moon and disc (pagan symbol of the sun), are thought to have been riveted to the top of the stelae both at the front and back. The crescent is also an ancient pagan symbol, originating from southern Arabia. In 1996 a broken plate that perfectly matched the rusty rivet holes atop a stelae was excavated. It bore the effigy of a face, perhaps that of the ruler to whom the plate's stele was dedicated. Despite these discoveries many aspects of the stelae are still shrouded in mystery.

For one, Ethiopian traditions believe that the Ark of the Covenant's celestial powers were harnessed to transport (4km from the quarries) and raise the mighty monoliths; the largest weighed no less than 517 tonnes! While far from proven, archaeologists think that the earthly forces of elephants, rollers and winches were responsible.

NORTHERN STELAE FIELD

The Northern Stelae Field is Ethiopia's biggest and most important stelae field. It contains over 120 stelae, though the original number was higher – some have been removed, others probably lie buried.

The stelae range from 1m to 33m in height and from simple slabs of stone (the majority) to finely dressed rectangular blocks, usually with flat sides and a rounded or conical apex. Though they were undoubtedly connected with the practice of human burial, it's not yet certain if every stele marks a tomb. The three largest and most famous stelae (Great Stele, King Ezana's Stele and Rome Stele) are found here and are described in this box.

In the courtyards of **Enda Iyesus** (Map p134), a stele decorated with a disc and a crescent moon can be seen. In 1997 another huge stele (18m) was discovered near the church.

Among the various other stelae is one that boasts a unique decoration. It lies on the ground around 200m to the north of King Ezana's Stele. Measuring around 9m in length, its upper section is carved like a pointed arch. Near the top, a small houselike object is carved in **relief** (on one side of the stone, supported by a pillar; Map p134), formed by a rectangle surmounted by a triangle. Some have claimed that this is early proof of Aksum's claim to house the Ark of the Covenant!

Laying prone between the Mausoleum and Tomb of the False Door is another important stele, albeit unassuming and **unfinished** (Map p134). The fact it's unfinished is strong evidence that the final carving of stelae was finished on site and not at the quarries.

King Ezana's Stele

Although standing slightly off kilter, this magnificent 24m-high stele (Map p134) at the field's entrance has done something no other stele of similar stature has – remained standing! Henry Salt, the British traveller and first foreigner to describe it in 1805, proclaimed it 'the most admirable and perfect monument of its kind'.

It's considered by many as the most important of Aksum's stelae because it holds important religious significance. The stone platform at its base is believed to have served as an altar. Within the platform are four foot-deep cavities, which probably held sacrificial offerings. And what's the grand significance of all those little cavities? It depends on how important you think *gabeta* (a traditional board game) is! Kids will be kids no matter what century they live in.

Despite its pagan background, this stele has been embraced by the Ethiopian Orthodox church and is a centrepiece during the celebrations of Maryam Zion.

The Great Stele

Lying like a broken soldier, this massive 33m stele (Map p134) is believed to be the largest single block of stone that humans have ever attempted to erect, and overshadows even the Egyptian obelisks in its conception and ambition.

Scholars theorise that it fell during its erection sometime early in the 4th century. Comparing the unworked 'root' to the sleek, carved base and the intricate walia ibex carvings near its top gives you a vivid idea of the precision, finesse and technical competence of Aksumite's stone workers.

As it toppled it collided with the massive 360-tonne stone sheltering the central chamber of **Nefas Mawcha's tomb** (Map p134). This shattered the upper portion of stele and – according to Unesco – collapsed the tomb's central chamber, scattering the massive roof supports like tooth-picks. Seeing that no other stele was ever raised here, it's obvious the collision sounded the death knell on the long tradition of obelisk erection in Aksum. Some scholars have even suggested that the disaster may have actually contributed to the people's conversion to Christianity, like an Ethiopian Tower of Babel. More controversially, some propose it may have been sabotaged deliberately to feign a sign of God. Whatever the origin of its downfall, the stele remains exactly where it fell 1600 years ago, a permanent reminder of the defeat of paganism by Christianity.

The Rome Stele

At 24.6m high, the Rome Stele (or Aksum Obelisk to those in Rome) is the second-largest stele ever produced at Aksum and the largest to have ever been successfully raised. Like the Great Stele, its ornate carvings of multistoried windows and doors adorn all four sides. Pillagers raiding the site are believed to have accidentally caused its collapse sometime between the 10th and 16th centuries.

In 1937 its broken remains were shipped to Italy on Mussolini's personal orders. There it was reassembled and raised once more, this time in Rome's Piazza di Porta Capena. It remained in Rome until 2005, when decades of negotiations finally overcame diplomatic feet-dragging.

After its return to Aksum in April 2005, Unesco planned to raise the stele in its original position. However, while doing a geophysical survey of the site they discovered numerous new tombs surrounding the field, some even under the parking lot. Not wanting to damage these new discoveries with the massive cranes required to raise the stele, Unesco is having a rethink. Some are also worried that the original site may also not be stable enough to hold the stele. All this modern head-scratching regarding the raising of the stele throws into perspective the massive achievement of the ancient Aksumites almost 2000 years ago.

So until final decisions are made, the magnificent Rome Stele sits at the side of the road, near the park's entrance, in four neat pieces.

GUDIT STELAE FIELD

Though less immediately arresting than those found in town, the stelae in the Gudit Stelae Field (Map p133), on the south side of Dungur (Queen of Sheba's Palace), are still worth a visit.

Named after Queen Gudit (see Aksum's Fall, p132), most stelae in this field are small, undressed and lie on the ground. Locals suggest the largest stele marks the Queen of Sheba's grave.

Despite excavations in the 1970s and 1990s, little is known about the field. Though some mark graves, neither rock-hewn nor constructed tombs have been found. Finds here did include a set of fine 3rd-century glass goblets, which has led scholars to suggest the area was the burial site of Aksumite society's lesser nobles.

The walk to the complex is lovely at dusk, when you'll meet the farmers and their animals returning home before nightfall.

NORTHERN ETHIOPIA

objects such as drinking cups, lamps and incense burners, to quite sophisticated glassware including perfume bottles.

There's a particularly nice collection of Aksumite coins dating from the 4th to 6th centuries AD, though those housed in the Ethnological Museum (p84) in Addis Ababa are finer. You'll also see beautiful lion gargoyles, and the charming pot shaped like a three-legged bird. Much of the pottery was produced in ancient Aksum and the tradition continues today. An ancient amphorae from Turkey or Cyprus also provides evidence of ancient trading routes.

The free guided tours (15 to 20 minutes) are comprehensive though not wildly inspiring; tips are expected.

Everything from this museum and oodles more that's in storage will eventually be moving to a grand, modern museum (Map p134) that's to be built within the Enda Iyesus Church compound, behind the Northern Stelae Field. We were optimistically told it would be completed in 2007.

TOMBS OF KINGS KALEB & GEBRE MESKEL
የንጉስ ቃሌብና የንጉስ ገብረ መስቀል መቃብር

Set on a small hill 1.8km northeast of the Northern Stele Field and offering views of the distant jagged mountains of Adwa are these two monumental tombs (Map p133). According to local tradition, they're attributed to the 6th-century King Kaleb and his son, King Gebre Meskel. Kaleb was one of Aksum's most important rulers and succeeded in bringing southern Arabia under Aksumite rule.

Although the twin tombs' architecture resembles the Tomb of the False Door, they actually show more sophistication,

using irregular-shaped self-locking stones that don't require iron clamps. The 19th-century British traveller Theodore Bent exclaimed magnanimously that the tombs were 'built with a regularity which if found in Greece would at once make one assign them to a good period'!

Of the two tombs, Gebre Meskel (to the south) is the most refined. The precision of the joints between its stones is at a level unseen anywhere else in Aksum. The tomb consists of one chamber and five rooms, with one boasting an exceptionally finely carved portal leading into it. Inside that room are three sarcophagi, one adorned with a cross similar to Christian crosses found on Aksumite coins. While this points towards an age around the 6th century, which, very interestingly, corresponds with local tradition, many believe that Meskel was actually buried at Debre Damo.

Like Meskel's tomb, King Kaleb's is accessed via a long straight stairway. Inside you'll notice the stones are larger, more angular and less precisely joined. Of those who attribute the making of the tomb to Kaleb, few accept that he was ever actually buried here. Common theory is that his body lies at Abba Pentalewon Monastery, where he lived after abdicating his throne following his return from Arabia. The tomb's unfinished state adds credence to that theory. If you feel like a long walk, have several extra sets of batteries for your torch and, most importantly, have a knack for finding secret passages, local rumour has it that there's a secret tunnel leading from here to Arabia!

Above ground, a kind of raised 'courtyard' combines the two tombs. Some scholars have suggested that two parallel

---

AKSUMITE COINS

Aksumite coinage provides a vital and fascinating source of information on the ancient kingdom. The coins bear the names, effigies and sometimes lineage of no fewer than 20 different kings, and probably served propagandist purposes.

Beautifully struck, the coins depict the royal crowns, clothing and jewellery of the kings – even the large earrings worn by some monarchs. A curiosity still unexplained by historians is the fact that almost all the coins are double-headed: on one side the king is depicted with his crown, on the other, he dons a modest head-cloth.

In the mid-1990s a find near the little town of Hastings in southern England caused a mild sensation: an original Aksumite bronze coin was unearthed. In fact, the coin almost certainly arrived on English shores not through ancient trade with Britain, but through a modern tourist with a holey pocket.

THE QUEEN OF SHEBA

Ethiopia's most famous legend is that of the Queen of Sheba. According to the *Kebra Negast* (Ethiopia's national epic), the Ethiopian queen once undertook a long journey to visit the wise King Solomon of Israel.

While there, Solomon assured the queen that he would take nothing from her so long as she took nothing from him. However, the crafty king had placed a glass of water at her bedside. During the night, awaking thirsty after the spicy food served to her, the queen reached for a drink.

Solomon wasted little time demanding his side of the deal, and the queen returned to Ethiopia carrying his child, the future king Menelik.

Menelik later visited his father in Jerusalem in the Holy Land, but sneakily returned to Ethiopia with the Ark of the Covenant (it seems Solomon got his comeuppance after all). Menelik then established a dynasty that would reign for the next 3000 years.

Though the queen is thought to have lived a thousand years before this period, many Ethiopians believe this legend passionately, at least in parts. Haile Selassie himself, the last Ethiopian emperor, claimed direct descent from King Solomon, and therefore the divine right to rule.

churches with a basilica plan lay here, probably postdating the tombs.

KING EZANA'S INSCRIPTION
የንጉስ ኢዛና ፅሁፍ

On the way up to the tombs of Kings Kaleb and Gebre Meskel, you'll pass a little shack containing a remarkable find stumbled upon by a farmer in 1981. Inside is an Ethiopian version of the Rosetta stone, a pillar inscribed in Sabaean, Ge'ez and Greek.

It dates between AD 330 and AD 350 and records King Ezana's Christian military campaigns in Ethiopia and southern Arabia, as well as his quest to return the Ark to Aksum from Lake Tana.

The inscription (Map p133) apparently contains a curse: 'the person who should dare to move the tablet will meet an untimely death'. Needless to say, the tablet remains exactly where it was found! You should tip the guardian Birr3 to Birr5 for opening the hut.

QUEEN OF SHEBA'S BATH
የንግስት ሳባ መዋኛ

Despite the colourful legends, this large reservoir (Map p133) postdates the queen by at least a millennia. It was also more likely an important source of water rather than a swimming pool or gargantuan bath. Its large size is even more impressive considering it was originally hewn out of solid rock, no small feat in the world of ancient engineering. It's also known as Mai Shum, which translates to 'Water of Chief'.

Sadly, the outer portion of the bowl was coated with concrete in 1960s, bestowing

it with the feel of a half-hearted attempt at a modern water reservoir, instead of an impressive ancient relic.

Today, despite locals claiming that the waters are cursed (local boys occasionally drown here), you'll see lines of women fetching water and washing clothes on its steps.

ABBA PENTALEWON & ABBA LIQANOS MONASTERIES
የአባ ጴንጤሊዎንና የአባ ሊቃኖስ ገዳማት

Around 2km from the tombs of Kings Kaleb and Gebre Meskel, and thought to date from the 6th century, is the **Abba Pentalewon Monastery** (Map p133; admission Birr20, men only). Inside are some fine illuminated manuscripts, metal crosses, censers and sistra, which can usually be brought out by the priests. The site of the monastery was sacred to pagans and it's thought the monastery was built here to bolster Christianity and eradicate pagan beliefs.

From Abba Pentalewon, it's around 20 minutes by foot to the **Abba Liqanos Monastery** (Map p133; admission Birr20, men only), which boasts excellent views and contains similar religious paraphernalia. Ask to see the so-called crowns of King Kaleb and Gebre Meskel.

Neither church is a must-see, but the walk to them is pleasant.

KING BAZEN'S TOMB የንጉስ ባዜን መቃብር

Despite being the crudest of tombs, roughly hewn into solid rock instead of constructed with fine masonry, this place (Map p133) has a slightly magical feel about it. Stand in its dark depths and look up it's rock-hewn stairs through its arched entranceway and you'll see why. It's even better if explored by candlelight.

According to local tradition, King Bazen is thought to have reigned at Christ's birth. The style of the tomb is likely consistent with that period.

Near the tomb's entrance there's a rectangular pit containing a row of smaller burial chambers (including a few that appear to be unfinished). Judging from the number of tombs and stelae found nearby, the burial site may once have been quite large and important.

EZANA PARK ኢዛና መናፈሻ

Within a rather ugly tin-roofed *tukul* in this central park (Map p133) is another famous 4th-century AD stone of King Ezana. This inscription is also written in Sabaean, Ge'ez and Greek and records the honorary titles and military victories of the king over his 'enemies and rebels'. One section of script thanks the God of War, thus placing the stone's age before Ezana's conversion to Christianity.

It was moved to its present location from eastern Aksum by the Italians in the 1930s because, of all things, it stood in the way of their plan to widen the road.

TA'AKHA MARYAM ተአ ማርያም

Early excavations revealed that Ta'akha Maryam (Map p133) was a magnificent palace, probably dating from the 4th or 5th century AD. Unfortunately, much of the stone was removed and what remained was obliterated when the Italians cut a road straight through it.

Today, little more than a few piles of rubble and a couple of dressed stone blocks remain, strewn on either side of the road.

Covering a vast area of some 120m by 80m and encircled by huge stone walls, Ta'akha Maryam would have been far larger than medieval European palaces of the time, and contained at least 50 rooms.

DUNGUR (QUEEN OF SHEBA'S PALACE) ዱንጉር (የንግስት ሳባ ቤተ መንግስት)

The structure at Dungur, popularly known as the Queen of Sheba's Palace (Map p133), is similar to Ta'akha Maryam, but much better preserved (though smaller), and fully excavated (in places rather clumsily restored).

The architectural style with small undressed stones set in a timber framework and walls recessed at intervals and tapering with height are typically Aksumite. The stairwells suggest the existence of at least one upper storey. The well-preserved flagstone floor is thought to have belonged to a throne room. The palace also contains a private bathing area and a kitchen, where two large brick ovens can still be seen.

Much like Queen of Sheba's Bath, archaeologists date the palace to around the 6th or 7th century AD, some 1500 years after the Queen of Sheba.

LIONESS OF GOBEDRA ንብድራ

It was here that the Archangel Mikael fought a tremendous battle with a fierce lioness. The fight ended when the saint mustered all his strength and hurled the lion into a massive boulder. The impact had such force that the outline of the beast is still visible today. If it sounds like a story that legends are made of, you're right. It's only a legend!

Who's responsible for the work or when it was created is still anyone's guess.

It's often overlooked by visitors, but is worth the visit, especially since it's so close to the ancient quarries of Aksum. It's around 3km west of Aksum off the Shire road. It's quite a rough walk from the road over boulders and through scrub, and you'll need a guide or one of the – all too willing – local children to help you find it.

ANCIENT QUARRIES

Near the lioness, at a site on Gobedra Hill known as Wuchate Golo, are the ancient quarries of Aksum, the birthplace of the famous stelae. Mystery still surrounds the tools that were used by the master craftsmen of Aksum, but you can see clearly, in one area, the process by which they cut the hard stone from the rock. After the intended break was mapped out, a row of rectangular sockets were cut. Wooden wedges were next inserted into the sockets and made to expand either by the use of water, by percussion or by hammering in metal wedges, which caused the rock to fracture. In another place, you'll see a stele almost completely freed from the rock, but strangely abandoned.

Fascinating? Definitely.

ARTISANAL CENTRE

Although well behind schedule (it was slated to open in 2004), this Ethio-cultural heritage project (Map p133), funded by the World Bank, should finally be open by the time you read this. The traditional-style Aksumite house and compound will house local craftsmen who'll produce, exhibit and sell arts and crafts produced using ancient Aksumite techniques.

If it's still not open, check out the craftsmen at the **Axumait Handicraft Center** (Map p133), which also houses a large collection of good-quality, but not cheap (by local standards) handicrafts. Ask for the energetic and well-informed Haile, himself a carver for over two decades.

OTHER SIGHTS

Aksum has two sleepy markets that burst to life on Saturday. In the centre of town is the traditional **main market** (Map p133), with spices and the like, while to the east is the **animal market** (Map p133), ripe with camels, donkeys and fodder. A **basket market** (Map p133; Sat) takes place near the massive tree shading the taxi and *gari* stand.

An elderly woman runs the so-called **Ethnographical Museum** (Map p133; admission Birr10; 8am-noon & 2-6pm) from her home. The museum showcases eclectic arts and crafts (from her wedding dress to fine basketry and other household objects). It gives a tangible glimpse into life 'in the old days'. The museum sits next to **Arbatu Ensessa Church** (Map p133), a good example of traditional architecture.

Festivals & Events

On 30 November Aksum hosts one of Ethiopia's largest festivals, the **Festival of Maryam Zion**. In the days leading up to the event, thousands of pilgrims arrive and sleepy Aksum truly awakes. Celebrations start at King Ezana's Stele, where the monarchs of the Orthodox church line the steps and watch performers in the street below.

For an unforgettable experience make your way to the compound of the St Mary of Zion Church between 1am and sunrise on the day of the festival and witness a sea of white-robed pilgrims curled up asleep. Standing among the slowly shifting sea are a few scattered priests who are reading by candlelight.

Sleeping

Aksum suffers from water shortages so please conserve. If you don't, may you end up nicely naked and lathered when the supply runs out!

Rooms become scarce and prices rise during major festivals, especially during Maryam Zion. Reservations are wise.

BUDGET

Africa Hotel (Map p133; ☎ 0347 753700; africaho@ ethionet.et; d with shared bathroom Birr30, d/tw Birr50/70;) With an eager and omnipresent owner, this place offers a smooth stay. The rooms are simple and bright enough, the beds are soft and the bathrooms are very clean. For an extra Birr10, you can nab one with satellite TV. There's also a café and restaurant out front. Call for a free airport transfer. The doubles with shared facilities are its weak point.

Kaleb Hotel (Map p133; ☎ 0347 752222; s with shared bathroom Birr30, d/tw Birr50/70) With quiet rooms set around a garden courtyard, Kaleb is probably the nicest budget setting. The rooms are large and quite pleasant, while the pretty clean bathrooms are showing their age. There's a bar with DSTV, but no restaurant.

Abinet Hotel (Map p133; ☎ 0357 753857; d with shared bathroom Birr30, d/tw Birr50/100) Most rooms here see a fair amount of sun and boast nice wee balconies too. Some of the Birr50 options are quite small, so check out a few.

Ras Alula Hotel (Map p133; ☎ 0347 753622; d Birr50) Rooms here are on par with those at Africa Hotel, but the bathrooms are a bit cramped and it lacks any extra amenities like TVs, restaurant or Internet facilities.

Ark Hotel (Map p133; ☎ 0347 752676; d/tw Birr70/ 120;) This newish place has good-sized rooms that are bright and clean; most also offer balconies (though they aren't as private as those at Abinet). Its biggest downfalls are its lack of service and the noise emanating from chairs screeching across its floors.

Lalibela Hotel (☎ 0347 753541; d with shared bathroom Birr20) Rooms here are large, tidy and anything but dark. The foam beds are pretty comfortable and the shared bathrooms are nothing to scream at.

MIDRANGE

Yeha Hotel (Map p133; ☎ 0347 752378; ghion@ethio net.et; s/d/ste US$38/50/75) Perched atop a bluff overlooking the stelae and the Mary of Zion churches, this hotel has the most enviable location. The rooms are identical to its state-owned brothers (Bahir Dar's Tana Hotel, Gonder's Goha Hotel and Lalibela's Roha Hotel), which means they're comfortable, cosy and contain satellite TVs. Rooms 127 to 133 and 226 and suites 228, 230 and 232 are our picks as they offer sunset views.

Remhai Hotel (Map p133; ☎ 0347 751501; www.remhai-hotel.com; s Birr128-305, d Birr170-395, ste Birr475; 🖳 🖭) The expensive rooms here are huge and host king-sized beds, carpets, fridges, phone as well as the odd Juliet balcony. The cheaper options are rather dark, but are very clean and also have satellite TVs. If it weren't for the pool, terrace and upcoming sauna and gym, this out-of-the-way place would be seriously overpriced. Nonguests can patrol the pool for Birr15.

Eating

Restaurants tend to wrap things up early in Aksum, with most places being closed or out of food by 8pm.

Remhai Hotel (Map p133; mains Birr13-28) This hotel's Western restaurant, with pepper steak (our favourite), roasted chicken and even French toast, is unquestionably top dog when it comes to *faranji* fare. Tony Wheeler adds, 'their traditional restaurant had the best local food we had in Ethiopia.'

Abinet Hotel (Map p133; mains Birr12-17) If you ask locals where the best place to eat is, they'll say Remhai. But if you ask them where they like to eat, they'll say Abinet. The spaghetti and the array of Ethiopian dishes are quite good.

Yeha Hotel (Map p133; mains Birr17-25) The food is fair, the view is grand. The menu is a mix of *faranji* and Ethiopian selections.

Tsega Cafe & Restaurant (Map p133; mains Birr3-10) This is another favourite of locals (they rave about the *tibs* – sliced lamb, pan fried in butter, garlic, onion and sometimes tomato). Omelettes and scrambled eggs are on offer as well.

Café Abyssinia (Map p133; mains Birr8-12) Right in front of the hospital, this place serves as café, bar and restaurant. The Ethiopian and *faranji* fare is quite good, but you'll pay double what locals do.

Africa Hotel (Map p133; mains Birr5-10) If they didn't always run out of food early evening, this place would be more recommended.

The bread and local honey is a perfect way to start the day.

Axumawit Pastery (Map p133; cakes Birr2) Below Abinet Hotel, it's a good spot for a piece of pastry (or would that be a piece of pastery?) and sip of coffee.

Drinking

Yeha Hotel (Map p133; beers Birr8) The lofty terrace of this hotel is the perfect place for a cool beverage, especially during a scenic sunset when kites (a type of raptor) ride the fading thermals and soar low overhead.

Or for something entirely different, seek out a *tella beat* (local beer house) in the tiny streets around town; they're great places for Tigrayan dancing. The locals will help you find one.

Getting There & Away

Ethiopian Airlines (Map p133; ☎ 0347 752300) flies to Addis Ababa (US$131, two to 3½ hours, daily) via Lalibela (US$72, 40 minutes), Gonder (US$73, two hours) and Bahir Dar (US$86, 2½ hours) or via Mekele (US$40, one hour, Monday and Thursday).

For buses to Gonder and Debark (Simien Mountains), go to Shire first. There are several buses and minibuses before 4pm (Birr10, 1½ hours). There are also many services to Adwa (Birr5, 45 minutes), but only one daily bus to Adigrat (Birr20 to Birr25, five hours) and Mekele (Birr35, 8½ hours).

Numerous freelance agents rent 4WD vehicles (with driver and guide) for trips to Yeha (Birr400), Debre Damo (Birr600) and even the rock churches of Tigray (per day Birr750). These figures required lengthy negotiations. The tourism office can help arrange vehicles, or talk to NTO and Galaxy Express services at the Yeha Hotel.

Getting Around

A taxi to the new airport, 7km from town, costs Birr40, or Birr10 'shared'. From the airport, rates are set at Birr10 per person.

Contract taxis charge foreigners from Birr5 to Birr10 for short hops; longer journeys cost Birr8 to Birr15. Share-taxis cost Birr0.75 to Birr1 to cross town.

Garis cost Birr2 to Birr5 for short journeys or Birr15 for Dungur and Birr20 for the Lioness of Gobedra. You'll need to negotiate hard. *Garis* and taxis linger near the giant tree at the basket market grounds. Just

THE BATTLE OF ADWA

In September 1895, as the rains began to dwindle, Emperor Menelik II issued a decree: all the able-bodied men of his empire should gather for a march north, a march for all of Ethiopia. Behind the vast army trundled 40 cannons, hundreds of mules and 100,000 rifles. In the north, the Italians were ready.

Initial skirmishes followed and amazingly the Ethiopians and their sturdy mules captured the Italian strongholds at Amba Alage and Enda Iyesus. Serious shortages of food soon followed, leading both sides to sue for peace, but Italy's continued insistence on their protectorate claim meant an agreement couldn't be reached.

In February 1896 Crispi, Italy's prime minister, sent his famous telegram to General Baratieri. In it he declared the motherland was 'ready for any sacrifice to save the honour of the army and the prestige of the monarchy'.

In the early morning hours four days later, the Italians made their move. Stumbling in the darkness over difficult terrain, with inaccurate maps and with no communication between the three offensive brigades, the surprise attack was a disaster. Menelik, whose spies had long before informed him of the forthcoming attack, met the Italians with thundering artillery and fierce fighting on every front.

Nearly half the Italian fighting force was wiped out – over 6000 soldiers – and of the five Italian field commanders, three were killed, one was wounded, and another was captured. Finally, laying down their arms, the Italians ran. Though the Ethiopians had lost almost equal numbers, the day was clearly theirs.

To this day the battle of Adwa is justly celebrated annually and, like the Battle of Hastings in Britain or the War of Independence in America, it's the one date every Ethiopian child can quote.

---

south from there, bicycles (Birr6 per hour) can be hired.

ADWA አድዋ

pop 45,823 / elev 1907m

Like Aksum, unassuming, urban Adwa belies its status. For Ethiopians, the town holds huge significance. It was in dramatic mountains surrounding Adwa that the Emperor Menelik II inflicted the biggest defeat ever on a colonial army in Africa and Ethiopia was saved from colonisation (see the boxed text, above).

Though Adwa is a pleasant enough town, there's not much to see here besides a couple of churches (the Selassie Church contains some good murals), but you may want to use the town as a base from which to visit Yeha or Debre Damo.

About 6km due east of Adwa is the **monastery of Abba Garima** (admission Birr20; men only). Said to have been founded by one of the Nine Saints in the 6th century, it's known for its collection of religious artefacts including what may be Ethiopia's oldest manuscript. Perhaps dating to the 8th century, it's kept under lock and key and only the lucky are given a glimpse. Head 7km south of Adwa before turning east for the final 3km. It's possible to drive or hike; bring plenty of water.

The scenery around Adwa is captivating, particularly en route to Adigrat where the horizon bursts with both bulbous and jagged peaks, and endless terraced slopes climb from the road to dramatic escarpments.

Teferi Hotel (☎ 0347 711828; d with shared bathroom Birr30, d with cold/hot shower Birr40/50), next to the bus station, is the best snoozing option in Adwa. The shared bathroom rooms are actually the brightest, but they're all quite clean.

Numerous minibuses connect Adwa to Aksum (Birr5, 45 minutes). For Adigrat (Birr15, 3½ hours) three buses run daily. For Yeha, catch a bus to Enticcio (four run daily) and hop off at the Yeha signpost (Birr6, 30 to 40 minutes) on the main Adwa–Adigrat road. Unless you hop a lift with a tourist vehicle, it's a very hot and dusty 5km walk from there. Go early to ensure return transport. Contract taxis cost around Birr200 to Birr300 to Yeha and Birr400 to Birr500 to Debre Damo.

YEHA የሃ

Yeha, 58km north of Adwa, is considered the birthplace of Ethiopia's earliest civilisation nearly three millennia ago. Heated debate continues among scholars as to whether it was founded by Sabaean settlers from Arabia or by Ethiopians influenced by Sabaean ideas. We can't figure out who's screaming louder, so we'll hold off choosing sides, though the so-called temple's immense, windowless, sandstone walls do indeed look like something straight out of Yemen.

Yeha's **ruins** (admission Birr50, personal video cameras Birr100) are impressive for their sheer age, dating between the 5th and 8th century BC, and for their stunning construction. Some of the temple's sandstone building blocks measure over 3m in length and are so perfectly dressed and fitted together – without a trace of mortar – that it's impossible to insert so much as a 5¢ coin between them. The whole temple is a grid of perfect lines and geometry.

Almost 200m to the northeast are the remains of **Grat Beal Gebri**, a monumental structure distinguished for its unusual, square-sectioned, monolithic pillars (such features are also found in the Temple of the Moon in Ma'rib in Yemen). Important rock-hewn tombs have also been found in the vicinity. Amazingly, these finds and the temple are all that remains of Ethiopia's first capital.

Next to the temple is the new **Church of Abuna Aftse** (admission incl with ruins), which was built over the 6th-century original. Incorporated into its walls are stones removed from the temple. In the west wall, there's an exceptional relief of ibexes, stylised and with lowered horns. The ibex was a sacred animal of southern Arabia.

Inside there's also an outstanding collection of beautifully incised ancient Sabaean inscriptions, believed to originate from the temple, as well as some good (and unusually large) manuscripts and silver and gold crosses. There is talk of moving some

artefacts to a nearby building and creating a small museum.

Getting There & Away
See Adwa (p143) and Aksum's Getting There & Away section (p142) for transport information.

DEBRE DAMO ደብረ ዳሞ
Perched precariously atop a sheer-sided *amba* (flat-topped mountain), 86km northeast of Aksum, is one of Ethiopia's most important religious sites. **Debre Damo** (admission Birr50, men only) is thought to date back to Aksumite times and the 6th-century reign of King Gebre Meskel. It boasts what's likely the oldest standing church in the country (10th or 11th century AD), which is also a great example of an Aksumite-style building.

According to local tradition, the monastery was founded by Abuna Aregawi, one of the legendary Nine Saints, with a little help from a heavenly snake (see the boxed text, p49).

The monastery's formidable cliffs also allowed Aksumite's monarchs to coop up excess male members of the royal family here, thus removing possible threats to their reign.

Today, the 500-sq-metre monastery hosts some 80 monks, who are entirely self-sufficient. They even have their own livestock (if you could bring up a cow they'd be grateful), and water reservoirs hewn deep into the rock. Gifts of coffee, sugar or honey are also greatly appreciated.

While the monastery sits firmly entrenched on the *amba*, we said 'precariously' earlier because of the journey required to get here (see the boxed text, below).

For male travellers, a visit to Debre Damo is well worthwhile, and gives you an idea of

---

ROPE TRICKS

Your only option to reach Debre Damo, completely encircled with sheer cliffs, is to white-knuckle and red-toe it straight up over 15m! White knuckles thanks to squeezing the aging rope for dear life, and red toes from trying to madly insert your shortest digits into tiny toe holds for traction (see the boxed text, p147).

For safety, a Birr20 tip and a laugh – oh, and to help too – priests tie a leather strap around your waste and tug, tug, tug from the top.

The ascent isn't difficult, but requires some nerve and a bit of biceps. Women aren't allowed to visit the monastery, but the priests may let you have a dangle on the rope if you really want to. Shouts of *'becka, becka!'* (enough!) will soon make it clear you've come far enough!

the extraordinary artistic heritage Ethiopia might have had, had it not been for the devastation of the Muslim–Christian wars.

Sights

The remarkable **Abuna Aregawi church** is an almost prototypical example of Aksumite architecture. One window, with its wooden tracery, is virtually a replica of that depicted in stone on the largest of the Aksumite stelae. Look out for the famous Aksumite frieze: a row of false window openings constructed of wood. Also notable are the beams and ceiling, famously decorated with carved wooden panels depicting Ethiopian wild animals such as elephants, lions, gazelles, rhinos, giraffes and snakes. Various recent paintings can be seen too.

The monastery has long been used as a safeguard for religious treasures. It now has an outstanding collection of at least 50 **illuminated manuscripts**, among them some of Ethiopia's oldest surviving fragments, though they're rarely brought out to visitors (don't insist).

If you've never seen Eritrea before, the view from the monastery magnificently lays it out before you.

Getting There & Away

There's no public transport to Debre Damo, although any transport on the Aksum–Adigrat road can drop you at the well-signposted junction (5km southeast of the village of Bizet). From there it's a toasty 11km walk (around three hours); bring water, food and sunscreen.

Catching rides to Adwa, Adigrat or Aksum from the junction is hit and miss, especially in late afternoon. If there's a group of you, it's easiest to hire a 4WD in Aksum (p142) or Adigrat (p146). Contract minibuses are cheaper, but can only get you within 4km or 5km of Debre Damo.

ADIGRAT አዲግራት

pop 88,342 / elev 2473m

Adigrat is Tigray's second-largest town and is situated on what was Ethiopia's most important junction with Eritrea prior to the 1998 conflict. Today the border is still closed and with tensions remaining high after the escalation of rhetoric and troop movements in late 2005, expect to see a large UN military presence.

If border tensions ease, Adigrat makes a useful and pleasant enough stop-off point to or from Aksum. It's also a good base from which to explore some of the northern rock-hewn churches of Tigray.

At sunrise, the stratified mountains above town resemble Table Mountain in Cape Town.

Information

Commercial Bank (8.30am-12.30pm & 1-3.30pm Mon-Fri, 8.30-11.30am Sat) Changes cash and travellers cheques.

Post office (8.30am-noon & 2-5.30pm Mon-Fri, 8.30am-noon Sat)

Telecommunications office (8am-noon & 2-9pm) International calls. Standard rates (p267).

Ytbarek Internet (per hr Birr60; 7am-6pm) Adigrat's only Internet access.

Sights

Nothing is screaming to be seen here, but if you're filling in time, a couple of Orthodox churches are worth a peek: the 19th-century **Adigrat Chirkos** south of the town centre, and the 20th-century fortresslike **Medhane Alem** in the north. Early mornings are best when the grounds are full of devotees.

The large tiled dome on the skyline belongs to the **Holy Saviour Catholic cathedral**. Completed in 1916, it's Italian-designed, but with a distinctly Ethiopian flavour. Look out for the paintings by Afewerk Tekle.

There's a peaceful **Italian war cemetery** just over 4km east of town. Dante Giuseppe, Bertagna Italo and Vaudano Mario are just three of the 765 Italian soldiers commemorated here. Six hundred and fifty-nine plaques are dedicated to *caduto ignoto* (unknown fallen) who perished between 1935 and 1938. En route here you'll pass the crumbling walls of the **old Italian fort** zigzagging along a small sandstone bluff. It's now an Ethiopian army barracks, so don't go poking around!

The labyrinth of tin shacks that's now the **market** is found 500m east of Medhane Alem church. In season, you'll find locally produced pale honey, and *beles* (prickly pears), which cost just Birr1 for 10; they're deliciously refreshing.

Travelling south from Adigrat, look out for the attractive Tigrayan stone farmsteads with their **dry-stone walls**. The houses have few windows; those they do have are small to keep the interior cool.

NORTHERN ETHIOPIA

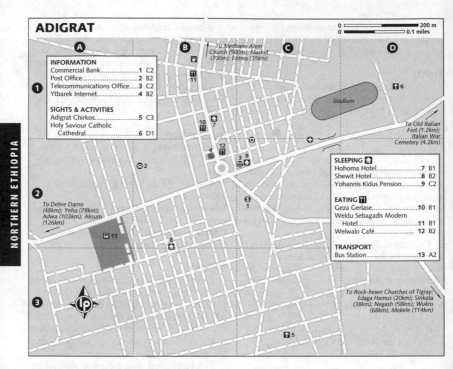

ADIGRAT

0 — 200 m
0 — 0.1 miles

INFORMATION
Commercial Bank....................1 C2
Post Office...........................2 B2
Telecommunications Office....3 C2
Ytbarek Internet....................4 B2

SIGHTS & ACTIVITIES
Adigrat Chirkos....................5 C3
Holy Saviour Catholic
Cathedral........................6 D1

SLEEPING
Hohoma Hotel........................7 B1
Shewit Hotel.........................8 B2
Yohannis Kidus Pension..........9 C2

EATING
Geza Gerlase........................10 B1
Weldu Sebagadis Modern
Hotel..............................11 B1
Welwalo Café.......................12 B2

TRANSPORT
Bus Station..........................13 A2

To Medhane Alem Church (500m); Market (700m); Eritrea (35km)

Stadium

To Old Italian Fort (1.2km); Italian War Cemetery (4.2km)

To Debre Damo (48km); Yeha (78km); Adwa (103km); Aksum (126km)

To Rock-hewn Churches of Tigray; Edaga Hamus (20km); Sinkata (38km); Negash (58km); Wukro (68km); Mekele (114km)

Sleeping & Eating

Hohoma Hotel (☎ 0344 452469; d/ste Birr50/60) Its name, inspired by Santa's brother who gave up the life of giving gifts for the cello, is just as fantastic as this hotel's value – easily Ethiopia's best deal. The modern rooms are small, but are well furnished, bright, spotless, comfortable and even boast TVs with the BBC. When we asked the price and they said *hamsa* (50), we had to ask if they meant dollars!

Shewit Hotel (☎ 0344 453028; d with shared bathroom Birr30, d Birr50) This old place is still in good shape, with its old but pristine chequered tile floors looking rather retro. The rooms are tidy, the beds are comfy and the bathrooms are clean. All but the shared showers are hot.

Yohannis Kidus Pension (☎ 0344 450284; s with shared bathroom Birr15) While it's no Hohoma (we'll never get tired of saying Hohoma – sorry), this small place with a paltry price is well looked after and is a friendly, clean choice. It's only fault: teeny rooms.

Geza Gerlase (mains Birr8-20) If you're only in Adigrat one night, head straight to this cultural restaurant. Wrap your lips around the special *tibs*, delve into the local speciality *ta'ilo* (a dough made from sorghum and dipped in spicy meat and tomato sauce) or enjoy simple spag bol under the traditional thatched roof.

Welwalo Café (mains Birr3-10) Grab a snack, juice or a tomato, onion and pepper omelette to start the day at this pleasant café.

Getting There & Away

Sealed road now connects Adigrat to Mekele, with buses (Birr14, three hours, six daily) and minibuses (Birr20, 2½ hours, four daily) covering the route. Buses also serve Adwa (Birr15, 3½ hours, three daily), Aksum (Birr20 to Birr25, five hours, two daily) and Shire (Birr30, 6½ hours, one daily). For Wukro (Birr10, 1¾ hours) and Negash (Birr8, 1½ hours), take the Mekele bus.

Minibuses run to Sinkata (Birr5, one hour), Edaga Hamus (Birr3, 30 minutes) and Wukro (Birr10, 1½ hours).

If the Eritrea border reopens, it's about a seven hour journey to Asmara.

The owner of **Welwalo Café** (☎ 0344 450218) rents his Land Cruiser (including himself as driver) for trips to Debre Damo (Birr400) and the rock-hewn churches of Tigray (per day Birr600).

NEGASH ነጋሽ

On a small hill, 56km south of Adigrat, is the tiny town of Negash, which, like Aksum and Adwa, belies its prestigious past.

Negash was the first site of Muslim settlement in Ethiopia. Fleeing persecution in Saudi Arabia in Mohammed's own lifetime, a community of Muslims, including Mohammed's daughter, took refuge here. In 2003 Ethiopia's richest man, billionaire Sheikh Mohammed Hussein Al-Amoudi (the Addis Ababa Sheraton is one of his belongings) built a new mosque here. It overshadows a small mosque that stands on the site of the 7th-century original. An ancient cemetery, also believed to date from the 7th century, was recently excavated.

To many Ethiopian Muslims Negash is the most holy Islamic site after Mecca, and thousands make a pilgrimage here each year. Despite this, just 3% of Tigray is Muslim; the mosque sits amid a sea of Christian churches.

Minibuses and buses that ply the route between Adigrat and Mekele stop here.

ROCK-HEWN CHURCHES OF TIGRAY

Although no less significant or interesting than their famous cousins in Lalibela, the rock-hewn churches of Tigray are far less famous. Lucky you.

Some of the 120-odd churches may even predate those at Lalibela, and possibly represent a crucial link between Aksum and Lalibela – chronologically, artistically and technically. The architectural features, though less perfect than at Lalibela, where the rock-hewing tradition reached its zenith, are just as remarkable and intriguing. And the stunning (and sometimes scary) cliff-face locations of some make exploring Lalibela seem like a snoozy Sunday stroll in the park.

For those who want to combine trekking with terrific art and history, this may be just the ticket. The Tigrayan churches may well prove to be Orthodox Ethiopia's best-kept secret. Bird-watchers will also love the area as it's home to the semi-endemic Rupell''s black chat and white-winged cliff chat.

History

Until the mid-1960s, the churches were almost unknown outside Tigray itself. Even today very little is known about their origins, their history or their architects. Their remote and precarious positions have led scholars to think they were being hidden from raiding Muslims.

While local tradition attributes most of the churches to the 4th-century Aksumite kings, Abreha and Atsbeha, as well as to 6th-century rulers, most historians date them between the 9th and 15th centuries.

Orientation & Information

Most churches are located in groups or clusters. Gheralta cluster, with the highest number of churches, is considered the most important, while the Takatisfi, only 3km east of the Mekele–Adigrat road, is the most accessible. Other famous clusters are the Tembien and Atsbi.

Churches are supposed to charge Birr20 for admission. If you're asked for more, simply hand over Birr20, firmly but politely. However, many priests (who receive no salary) drop work in the fields to open churches for you, so you should offer a tip of Birr5 to Birr10 after your visit.

Good walking shoes are essential. Bring a torch, lots of small notes (priests never have change) and water.

Mekele makes the best base from which to explore the churches, but Aksum and Adigrat are also viable options. The helpful staff at the Tigray Tourism Commission offices in Aksum (p132), Mekele (p151) and now **Wukro** (☎ 0344 430340; ✆ 8am-5pm) advise

NORTHERN ETHIOPIA

TOEHOLDS IN TIGRAY

Though daunting at first sight, most of the ascents up rock faces required to reach some of the Tigrayan churches aren't difficult if taken carefully. Just focus on the footholds, get a good grip, don't stop and never look down. If you're having trouble, or finding that your nerves are getting the better of you, get someone to climb in front showing you the footholds. Sometimes the holds are very small, hewn by the bare feet of generations of priests. In which case, do as they do and take off your shoes. It's amazing the grip a toe can get!

NORTHERN ETHIOPIA

on itineraries, sell maps and the informative *Tigrai: The Open-Air Museum* booklet (Birr5), and can usually wrangle up an official guide (per day Bir100). You'd be foolhardy to attempt visits without a guide, not only to locate the more remote churches, but also to act as an interpreter and for tracking down the often elusive priests, keepers of the all-important church keys.

If you're really keen, search for Ivy Pearce, David R Buxton or Ruth Plant's research on Tigray before leaving home.

Sights

Between Adigrat and Mekele there's a plethora of churches, 120 at last count. Many are pretty inaccessible, meaning visiting some churches involves steep climbs or scrambling up almost sheer rock faces using toeholds (see p147).

All this somehow adds to the churches' attraction. To come across an absolute jewel hidden for centuries in the mountains, after a long and arduous toil through Tigray's arid and rocky landscape, makes for a very rewarding excursion. Just remember that

the churches' remote locations haven't made restoration work feasible yet and several are in desperate need of repair.

Unlike many of the churches of Lalibela, which were monolithic (carved out of the ground and only left attached to the earth at the base), the Tigrayan churches are generally semimonolithic (only partially separated from the host rock) or built into pre-existing caves.

Patience is essential for your enjoyment, as it can often take up to an hour to locate some priests. With a full day, a 4WD and quick-keyed priests, you can usually see four to five churches (depending on the hikes involved).

GHERALTA CLUSTER

The drive through the Gheralta cluster is fantastic, particularly between Dugem and Megab, with stratified mountains and sharp peaks rising from the plains. Avoid visiting this cluster on Wednesday as the priests are usually at market. Minor churches of note in this cluster include Giyorgis Debre Mahar and Tekla Haimanot.

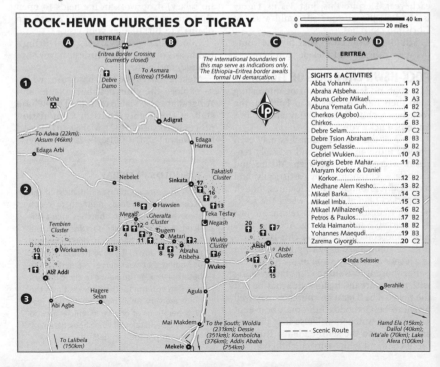

ROCK-HEWN CHURCHES OF TIGRAY

0 ——————— 40 km
0 ——————— 20 miles

Approximate Scale Only

Eritrea Border Crossing (currently closed)

The international boundaries on this map serve as indications only. The Ethiopia–Eritrea border awaits formal UN demarcation.

To Asmara (Eritrea) (154km)

SIGHTS & ACTIVITIES
Abba Yohanni	1 A3
Abraha Atsbeha	2 B2
Abuna Gebre Mikael	3 A3
Abuna Yemata Guh	4 B2
Cherkos (Agobo)	5 C2
Chirkos	6 B3
Debre Selam	7 C2
Debre Tsion Abraham	8 B3
Dugem Selassie	9 B2
Gebriel Wukien	10 A3
Giyorgis Debre Mahar	11 B2
Maryam Korkor & Daniel Korkor	12 B2
Medhane Alem Kesho	13 B2
Mikael Barka	14 C3
Mikael Imba	15 C3
Mikael Milhaizengi	16 B2
Petros & Paulos	17 B2
Tekla Haimanot	18 B2
Yohannes Maequdi	19 B3
Zarema Giyorgis	20 C2

Abraha Atsbeha አብርሃ አጽብሃ

Architecturally, this semimonolithic 10th-century church is one of Tigray's finest. It's large and cruciform in shape, with interesting architectural features such as cruciform pillars and step capitals. There's also well-preserved 17th- and 18th-century murals. The obtrusive portico was an attempt by Italians to win over locals by proving they weren't Muslims. It's easily accessible and sits just off the road, 45km west of Wukro.

Abuna Yemata Guh አቡነ የማታ ጉህ

Although less impressive architecturally, this church is likely the most rewarding in Tigray. It's spectacularly located within a cliff face, halfway up a rock pinnacle around 4km west of Megab. The first 45 minutes of the climb is mildly challenging, with a couple of tricky sheer sections requiring toe-hold action. The last two minutes require nerves of steel – our hands are sweating just thinking about it! Even if you can't make the final scramble and precarious ledge walk over a 200m drop (like us last go around!), it's still worth getting that far as the views from the baptism chamber are astounding.

Inside are beautiful and well-preserved frescoes that adorn two cupolas.

Debre Tsion Abraham ደብረ ጽዮን አብርሃም

Rectangular in shape, with six massive free-standing pillars, this church is known for its diverse architectural features, including decorated cupolas, bas-reliefs and carved crosses on the walls and ceiling. It also has beautiful, though faded and damaged, 16th-century murals and an unusual, large 15th-century ceremonial fan. It sits like a fortress on a hill about 500m south of Dugem and requires a steep 50-minute walk.

Maryam Korkor ማርያም ቆርቆር

Although an unsightly green from the outside, this impressive, cross-shaped church is known for its architectural features (cruciform pillars, arches and cupolas), fine 17th-century frescoes, and church treasures. It's also one of the largest churches in the area. The church is around 500m from Megab and involves a fairly steep 50-minute ascent. Just a couple of minutes' walk from

Maryam Korkor is the church of **Daniel Korkor**. It sits atop a paralysing precipice and offers astounding views.

Dugem Selassie ዱግም ስላሴ

This tiny, older church lies within a newer one. Its large, double-tomb chamber has three 'shelves'; look out for the beautifully carved ceiling above the *maqdas*. It was probably converted to a church later. It's on the southern edge of the village of Dugem, just off the road.

Yohannes Maequdi ዮሃንስ መኩዳይ

This rectangular chapel has six freestanding pillars that support a ceiling carved with geometrical designs. While it's best known for well-preserved murals covering the walls, it's the intense atmosphere that most visitors remember. From the village of Matari it's around a 40-minute walk (about 1km south of Dugem) via a steep footpath.

Abuna Gebre Mikael አቡነ ገብሪ ሚካኤል

Considered one of Gheralta's finest churches, this church's cruciform plan is hewn into a domelike rock. It features good frescoes and carefully carved columns, pillars, cupolas and arches. It's around 15km south of Abuna Yemata Guh and requires a steep climb, negotiating a few obstacles on way.

TAKATISFI CLUSTER
Medhane Alem Kesho መድኃኔዓለም ከሾ

Also known as Adi Kesho, this church is one of Tigray's oldest and finest rock-hewn churches. Its exterior and interior walls are roughly hewn, which only makes the elaborately carved coffered ceiling that much more special. Ask if you can watch them unlock the door from the inside – rather ingenious indeed! From the end of the 4WD track, it's a leisurely 10-minute climb.

Mikael Milhaizengi ሚካኤል ምልሃይዘንጊ

This tiny church, with its stooped doorway, is hewn into the top of a small bleached hill and is thought to date from the 8th century. It's known for its 3m-high carved dome ceiling that resembles an *himbasha* (a favourite round bread of Tigrayans). It's about 45 minutes' walk from Medhane Alem Kesho and a 15-minute walk from Petros & Paulos.

NORTHERN ETHIOPIA

NORTHERN ETHIOPIA

HEAVENLY VISIONS

One day, St Gabriel appeared in a dream to a farmer. The saint commanded the man to build a new church to replace the old one, and gave his messenger careful instructions as to its location and construction.

Yet another Ethiopian legend? Yes, only the day in question was in 1982, and the church in question was Petros & Paulos, near Sinkata.

In Ethiopia, legends are made every day.

Petros & Paulos ጴጥሮስ ና ጳውሎስ

Only partly hewn, this wood, stone and mortar church is built on a steep ledge and has delightful old murals that are very rapidly deteriorating. From Wukro, or Adigrat, take a minibus to Teka Tesfay and walk about 3km from the junction. It's a five-minute climb to the church using footholds up one precarious part.

WUKRO CLUSTER

Chirkos ጨርቆስ

This crooked cruciform sandstone church is semimonolithic and boasts beautiful cruciform pillars (notice the swirling sandstone laminae), cubical capitals, an outstanding Aksumite frieze and a barrel-vaulted ceiling. Haile Selassie oddly and unfortunately ordered the angular roof squared with concrete for aesthetic reasons in 1958. It lies around 500m from Wukro and is the most easily accessible church.

TEMBIEN CLUSTER

Avoid visiting on a Saturday, as most priests will be away at market.

Abba Yohanni አባ ዮሃኒ

Impressively located partially up a 300m-high sheer cliff face, this church has a three-aisled and four-bayed interior, eight finely hewn cruciform pillars that support the ceiling, and 10 vaults. It's also home to interesting church treasures and sits 15km from Abi Addi, including a 1km walk and a short climb with footholds.

Gebriel Wukien ገብርኤል ውቄን

Architecturally interesting, this church has three aisles and four bays. It features well-carved, interesting details; six massive, finely hewn freestanding pillars and three cupolas. It's 16km northwest of Abi Addi and involves a 15-minute easy walk, then a 10-minute climb up a mountain.

ATSBI CLUSTER

Like the Tembien cluster, most priests (and their keys) are away at market on Saturday. Minor churches in the Atsbi cluster include Cherkos (Agobo) and Zarema Giyorgis.

Mikael Barka ሚካኤል ባርካ

Atop a small but panoramic hill and behind an ugly 1960s façade sits this small rock-hewn church. It's cruciform in shape and probably dates from the 13th century. It's 17km from Wukro, and reaching it involves a 10-minute climb.

Mikael Imba ሚካኤል እምባ

Of all Tigray's rock-hewn churches, Mikael Imba most resembles those seen at Lalibela. A three-quarter monolith, the interior is huge (16.6m wide and 9m deep) with 25 pillars (nine freestanding) holding up the 6m-high ceiling. The view from here is great. It's 9km south of Atsbi and has an easy 20-minute ascent, which is finished with a short ladder.

Debre Selam ደብረ ሰላም

This church or 'church within a church' has exceptional architecture, with an inner rock-hewn section and interior structures constructed according to ancient Aksumite architectural style (alternating layers of rock and wood). There's a beautiful carved arch leading into the *maqdas*. The setting is lovely and there are good views from the top. It's close to Atsbi and also involves a simple 20-minute ascent.

Sleeping & Eating

To put it mildly, accommodation in the nearby villages is brutal. Most have more fleas than water and electricity.

If you're travelling with a vehicle, sleep in Aksum, Mekele or Adigrat. Without one, the best accommodation in the midst of things is Wukro's **Luwam Hotel** (☎ 0344 430126; d with shared bathroom Birr30, d Birr50). It's handily behind the tourism office and has small but very clean rooms – we hope you like aquamarine. Another option is to camp and to be fully self-sufficient.

Getting There & Around

Many of the churches are in remote places, some 20km to 30km off the main road. A private 4WD is the easiest way of reaching them, but if you have camping equipment and lots of time, an exploration by bus and foot is both possible and very enjoyable.

The villages of Hawsien, Edaga Hamus, Wukro, Atsbi, Abi Addi and Sinkata are all served by minibuses. Some villages (such as Megab and Hawsien) are only well served on market days.

Quite good gravel roads now connect the villages with most churches. Unfortunately, the road linking Megab with Abi Addi (shown on most maps) is still impassable. See Getting There & Away under Aksum (p142), Adigrat (p146) and Mekele (p153) for details on hiring 4WDs.

MEKELE noutλ

pop 157,688 / elev 2062m

Mekele, Tigray's capital, owes its importance to the Emperor Yohannes IV, who made it his capital in the late 19th century. For the traveller, it's home to two rewarding museums and provides a useful base for visits to the nearby rock-hewn churches of Tigray and the baking Danakil Depression. And unlike other large historical-circuit cities, it's almost hassle-free.

Information

There's no shortage of cheap Internet cafés (Birr8 to Birr15 per hour) along the south end of Alula and Guna Sts. The town also has its requisite post office.

Commercial Bank (Alula St; ☽ 8am-noon & 1-3.30pm Mon-Fri, 8-11.30am Sat) Changes cash and travellers cheques. There's a second branch near Lucy Park.

Dashen Bank & Western Union (☽ 8am-noon & 1-4.30pm Mon-Fri, 8am-noon Sat) Rates as per Commercial Bank.

El-Fami Business Internet Center (per hr Birr30; ☽ 8am-noon & 2-8pm) Overpriced Internet, but the only provider to offer CD burning.

Emmanuel Clinic & Dental Unit (☎ 0344 404692; ☽ 8.30am-noon & 2-5pm Mon-Fri, 8.30am-noon Sat) A reliable clinic with diagnostic laboratory. Around the corner is northern Ethiopia's best bet for dental action.

Telecommunications office (☎ 0344 410667) International calls. Standard rates (p267).

Tigrai Tourism Commission office (☎ 0344 409360; tigrai.tourism@ethionet.et; 5th fl, Commercial Bank Bldg, Alula St; ☽ 8.30am-12.30pm & 1.30-5.30pm Mon-Fri)

Helpful and can advise you on an itinerary for Tigray's rock-hewn churches.

Wegagen Bank (☽ 8am-4pm Mon-Sat) Slightly higher commissions than the Commercial Bank, but better hours.

Sights

YOHANNES IV MUSEUM

The Italian-designed stone palace built for Emperor Yohannes IV (r 1872–79) in 1873 is now an interesting **museum** (admission Birr24; ☽ 8am-5pm). Beneath the impressive vaulted juniper roof is a significant collection of Ethiopian manuscripts, crosses and icons. Many items had mysteriously formed part of a private collection in France, before being rightfully returned to Ethiopia in 2001. There's a 50kg bronze sculpture of Mussolini's head, which was brought here by Italy to adorn the palace's façade – it's now on the floor in the corner. Touché il Duce! Upstairs, in the emperor's personal quarters are some ornate gilded saddles and an audacious throne.

MARTYRS' MEMORIAL MONUMENT & MUSEUM

From a distance this **memorial** (admission Birr10; ☽ 8am-5pm) could be mistaken for the world's biggest golf ball and tee. From up close it's another story, with stirring statues flanking the towering monument and compellingly illustrating the true cost of war. A plaque nearby proudly reads, 'you completely defeated the seemingly immortal chauvinist enemies...' The enemies it's referring to are the communist, Russian-backed Derg, while the 'you' refers to the Tigray People's Liberation Front (TPLF).

Just north is a **museum** (admission currently incl with memorial) that hauntingly and proudly exalts the successes and sacrifices made by TPLF during the 1970s and '80s.

A second access road is being built to the museum from the north side of town.

OTHER SIGHTS

Thanks to this city's burgeoning economy and rapidly increasing population, the **old market** has been cast out of the town centre (in favour of a modern concrete mall) and now sits almost 1km to the west. It's definitely worth a stroll, particularly on Saturday before 10am. Witnessing salt bars brought in by camel from the Danakil Depression (see the boxed text, p154) is the unmistakable highlight.

NORTHERN ETHIOPIA

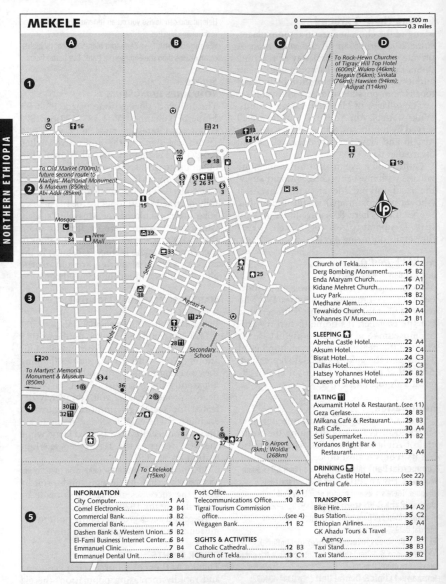

MEKELE

To Rock-Hewn Churches of Tigray; Hill Top Hotel (600m); Wukro (46km); Negash (56km); Sinkata (76km); Hawsien (94km); Adigrat (114km)

To Old Market (700m); future second route to Martyrs' Memorial Monument & Museum (850m); Abi Addi (85km)

Mosque

New Mall

Selam St

Ageazi St

Alula St

Guna St

Secondary School

To Martyrs' Memorial Monument & Museum (850m)

To Airport (8km); Woldia (268km)

To Chelekot (15km)

Church of Tekla	14	C2
Derg Bombing Monument	15	B2
Enda Maryam Church	16	A1
Kidane Mehret Church	17	D2
Lucy Park	18	B2
Medhane Alem	19	D2
Tewahido Church	20	A4
Yohannes IV Museum	21	B1

SLEEPING ☐
Abreha Castle Hotel	22	A4
Aksum Hotel	23	C4
Bisrat Hotel	24	C3
Dallas Hotel	25	C3
Hatsey Yohannes Hotel	26	B2
Queen of Sheba Hotel	27	B4

EATING 🍴
Axumamit Hotel & Restaurant	(see 11)	
Geza Gerlase	28	B3
Milkana Café & Restaurant	29	B3
Rafi Cafe	30	A4
Seti Supermarket	31	B2
Yordanos Bright Bar & Restaurant	32	A4

DRINKING ☐
Abreha Castle Hotel	(see 22)	
Central Cafe	33	B3

TRANSPORT
Bike Hire	34	A2
Bus Station	35	C2
Ethiopian Airlines	36	A4
GK Ahadu Tours & Travel Agency	37	B4
Taxi Stand	38	B3
Taxi Stand	39	B2

INFORMATION
City Computer	1	A4
Comel Electronics	2	B4
Commercial Bank	3	B2
Commercial Bank	4	A4
Dashen Bank & Western Union	5	B2
El-Fami Business Internet Center	6	B4
Emmanuel Clinic	7	B4
Emmanuel Dental Unit	8	B4
Post Office	9	A1
Telecommunications Office	10	B2
Tigrai Tourism Commission office	(see 4)	
Wegagen Bank	11	B2

SIGHTS & ACTIVITIES
Catholic Cathedral	12	B3
Church of Tekla	13	C1

About 200m southwest of the telecommunications building there's an intriguing statue rising in a roundabout. It's a **monument** dedicated to 2500 people who were killed in Hawsien by a Derg bombing raid.

There are several **churches**, both old and new, dotting the city and their large towers are visible throughout.

Sleeping

BUDGET

Hatsey Yohannes Hotel (☎ 0344 406760; s/tw incl breakfast Birr103/138) This big and bright place is opposite Lucy Park and has dozens of rooms. Most are carpeted and have balconies, satellite TVs (one English channel only) and hot-water showers. Rooms 414 to

418 and 310 to 320 (excluding 313 and 317) have nice views over the park and palace.

Queen of Sheba Hotel (☎ 0344 401387; Guna St; d with shared bathroom Birr40, d Birr50) Rooms here are spartan yet sizable, and house wardrobes, stone tile floors and clean bathrooms with hot showers. The spiral staircase isn't to be attempted after a few wobbly pops (beers).

Dallas Hotel (☎ 0344 414100; d with shared bathroom Birr20, d Birr50) A good budget bet near the bus station; the rooms here are austere but clean and comfy. They surround a vegetation-trimmed courtyard/parking area.

Bisrat Hotel (☎ 0344 401434; d with shared bathroom Birr30) Just north of Dallas Hotel, this place has simple, large rooms with clean tile floors. Some windows face the hall, making some options brighter than others. The shared bathrooms are clean and hot water is available.

MIDRANGE
Aksum Hotel (☎ 0344 405155; axum.n@ethionet.et; s/tw Birr180/210, ste Birr360-500) Everything from the chairs to the exterior screams stylised Aksum stelae at this fine hotel. The rooms here are Mekele's most comfortable and all boast satellite TVs, telephones and balconies. The hotel is well looked after and very clean.

Abreha Castle Hotel (☎ 0344 406535; fax 0344 402258; s/tw with shared bathroom US$13.75/18, s/tw US$17.50/21) This 19th-century mansion is rather regal from the exterior, but its interior is showing its age with 1970s green carpets and dated drapes. That said, rooms here have more character than any at Aksum Hotel. Rooms 203 and 204 have high ceilings and tall arched windows that offer great views over Mekele.

Hill Top Hotel (☎ 0344 405683; d/tw Birr120/240, ste Birr180-360) One of the only establishments without *faranji* prices, this slightly out-of-the-way place, 1km north of centre, represents good value. The large rooms have queen-sized beds, fridges, phones, satellite TVs and decent carpets. Sadly, only the restaurant takes advantage of the amazing view.

Eating
Milkana Café & Restaurant (mains Birr10-20) Off Guna St, Mekele's most popular café occupies the ground and 1st floors here, serv-

ing cakes, coffee, burgers and the like. The smart 2nd-floor restaurant prepares pizzas, pastas and traditional Ethiopian fare.

Yordanos Bright Bar & Restaurant (Alula St; mains Birr10-30) Simply called Yordanos I, this restaurant is known to produce the best Italian food in town. Eggplant, salami, anchovies, chillies and spinach are just some of the pizza toppings to choose from. The dining room here becomes quite atmospheric in the evenings.

Geza Gerlase (Guna St; mains Birr8-15) Although closed during our research due to a substantial fire, this great cultural restaurant and its traditional *tukul* should be back in action by the time you've arrived. Specialities include *zilzil tibs* (strips of beef, fried and served slightly crunchy with *awazi* sauce) and *kitfo* (minced beef or lamb like the French steak tartare, usually served warmed – but not cooked – in butter, *berbere* and sometimes thyme). Vegetarians steer clear.

Axumamit Hotel & Restaurant (mains Birr8-18) If you're after an interesting Ethiopian attempt at Western fare, like 'veal gorden blue' this rooftop terrace is good.

Rafi Cafe (Alula St; snacks Birr2.50) A tiny modern café with good croissants and coffee.

Seti Supermarket (☼ 5am-10pm) One of a few supermarkets for self-caterers or those stocking up for a trip to Tigray's rock churches.

Drinking
There are countless little cafés that pump out great coffee – you can't really go wrong.

Abreha Castle Hotel (beers Birr6-8) The scenic and breezy terrace of this grand old mansion is the best place for a late afternoon drink.

Central Cafe (juices Birr4) Watch them squeeze the life out of fruit, right before your eyes. Painful to watch. Delicious to drink.

Getting There & Away
Ethiopian Airlines (☎ 0344 400055) flies to Addis Ababa (US$125, 1½ hours, daily) and Aksum (US$40, 30 minutes, Monday, Wednesday and Friday).

Numerous morning buses run to Adigrat (Birr14, three hours), while one runs to Aksum (Birr28 to Birr35, 8½ hours, 6am). To Addis Ababa, you have the choice of normal service (Birr82, two days, 6am) or deluxe 'Cobra Service' (Birr150, two days, 6am). For Lalibela, take the normal Addis

Ababa bus and get off in Woldia (Birr30, 5½ hours).

For the Tigray churches, minibuses leave from the bus station daily for Abi Addi (Birr15, three hours, one daily), Wukro (Birr8, one hour, 10 daily) and, on Wednesday only, Hawsien (Birr15, 2½ hours). For Atsbi, go to Wukro first; for Sinkata, take the Adigrat bus (Birr8, 1½ hours).

There are lots of private 4WD operators who offer church trips; prices range from Birr600 to Birr1000 per day. Their reliability and quality of vehicle is unfortunately left for you to determine. The only licensed operator in Mekele is **G.K. Ahadu Tours & Travel Agency** (☎ 0344 406466; gkahadu@ethionet.et), which offers quality trucks at extortionate rates: Birr1200 per day for Tigray's churches and Birr1500 for the Danakil Depression!

Getting Around

There are several taxi stands around town. A contract taxi to the airport, 8km out of town, cost between Birr30 and Birr40. You can also take a minibus (Birr2, 20 minutes) to the village of Quiha and ask to be dropped off en route; the airport's only 200m from the highway.

Short hops in a share-taxi or three-wheeled cycle costs Birr1. Contract taxis cost Birr10 to Birr20. Bikes can be hired near the mosque for Birr4 per hour.

DANAKIL DEPRESSION ደንካል በርሃ

Say goodbye to Earth and say hello to Venus. With several points lying more than 100m below sea level, the Danakil Depression has acquired a reputation as one of the hottest, most inhospitable places on Earth. Temperatures can soar to 50°C and with its underlying continental crust pulled thin (thanks to being part of the Red Sea rift system), it's peppered with countless colourful sulphurous springs and an astonishing 25% of Africa's active volcanoes.

Irta'ale (613m), the most famous volcano, has been in a state of continuous eruption since 1967. Its small southerly crater is the only permanent lava lake on the planet. Despite gentle slopes, a night-time hike to its summit for sunrise is as captivating as it is exhausting. Taking camels is a viable option.

If you'd simply like to visit the lowest place on the continent, head for **Dallol** (-116m), which is about 25km north of the village Hamd Ela. More rewarding is a trip to **Lake Afera** (-102m), which is 30km (or five to nine hours by 4WD!) south of Irta'ale. Its waters are bright green and its salty shores have been harvested for centuries by the Afar people (p46), a nomadic ethnic group known in the past for their legendary ferocity.

An excursion into this harsh and astounding world isn't something everyone can handle. It is, however, something nobody will ever forget. It's best visited between December and February when it's at its coolest.

Trips here can be organised through tour operators in Addis Ababa (see p282) or through **G.K. Ahadu Tours & Travel Agency** (☎ 0344 406466; gkahadu@ethionet.et) in Mekele. If you're travelling with a group of private 4WDs (taking only one 4WD is suicide), you must contact the **Afar Tourism Commission** (☎ 0336 660181; fax 0336 660448) regarding permission and to arrange picking up your mandatory Afar guide (Birr100 per day) at the Afar tourist office near Berahile. If you'd like a hand with the Afar formalities, stop in at the Tigrai Tourism Commission office in

---

SALT FOR GOLD

Since earliest times and right up to the present day, salt, a precious commodity for people and their animals, has been used as a kind of currency in Ethiopia. According to Kosmos, a 6th-century Egyptian writing in Greek, the kings of Aksum sent expeditions west to barter salt, among other things, for hunks of gold!

Mined in the Danakil Depression, the mineral was transported hundreds of kilometres west across the country to the Ethiopian court in Shoa. Later, the salt was cut into small, rectangular blocks, which came to be known as *amole;* their value grew with every kilometre that they travelled further from the mine.

To this day, Afar nomads and their camels continue to follow this ancient salt route. Cutting the bars by hand from the salt lakes in western Ethiopia, they spend weeks travelling by caravan to market, where the bars will be bartered.

Wukro (☎ 0344 430340; ⏲ 8am-5pm) or Mekele (p151). Besides helping with advice on permissions and pointing you in the right direction, staff can also help plan your itinerary.

Remember, you need to treat a journey here in full expedition style; unprepared people have perished in a matter of hours.

WOLDIA ወልድያ
pop 24,533 / elev 2112m

The town of Woldia provides a springboard for visits to its famous neighbour, Lalibela, 120km to the northwest. Stock up on petrol, batteries, birr (the Commercial Bank exchanges cash and travellers cheques), and anything you might need from a pharmacy before leaving. Lalibela, despite its fame, is still the back of beyond.

Mechare Hotel (☎ 0333 310233; tw with shared bathroom Birr60, d Birr60-70) has tidy Birr60 doubles with comfy beds, linoleum floors, cold showers and the odd balcony. The Birr70 options offer hot water and larger beds. The shared showers are clean, but aren't so private. Its restaurant (mains Birr5 to Birr12) is considered Woldia's best. The hotel is 900m north of the bus station at the main junction.

Ganet Hotel (☎ 0333 310327; d with shared bathroom Birr12-15; d Birr25), north of Mechare Hotel, has spartan, smallish rooms with soft foam mattresses. The bathrooms aren't spotless, but they'll do. The price is right.

Selam Hotel (☎ 0333 311968; d Birr100) has large clean rooms that host satellite TVs, phones, dimmer lights and spotless bathrooms with hot showers and two toilets (one squat and one sit – take your pick!). Seeing that locals only pay Birr50, try negotiating (we got them to Birr80 before walking). It's on the main Addis–Mekele road between Mechare and Ganet.

Getting There & Away

The bus to Lalibela (Birr25, five to seven hours) is supposed to leave at 6am, but doesn't usually leave until 9am or 10am (when it's full). If there's a seat, the Addis Ababa bus to Lalibela also picks up at the bus station around 10am. There's usually at least one aid or government truck also making the daily journey; inquire at the Total station or around the Lal Hotel

There are also three daily buses to Dessie (Birr12, 3½ hours). For Mekele (Birr30, 5½ hours) or Addis Ababa, you should wait

for passing buses near the Shell station at the Lalibela junction on the main Addis–Mekele road.

LALIBELA ላሊበላ
pop 8484 / elev 2630m

I weary of writing more about these buildings, because it seems to me that I shall not be believed if I write more…but swear I by God in Whose power I am, that all that is written is the truth, and there is much more than what I have written, and I have left it that they may not tax me with its being falsehood.

Francisco Alvares (early-16th-century Portuguese writer) From Ho Preste Joam das Indias: Verdadera informacam das terras do Preste Joam (Lisbon 1540; Lisbon 1889)

Unlike Francisco Alvares, you'll have photos to back up your stories of Lalibela's majesty. Here, high in the rugged Lasta Mountains, is 'Africa's Petra'.

An ancient world, including 11 magnificent medieval rock-hewn churches, dimly lit passageways, hidden crypts and grottoes, was carved down into the red volcanic rock underlying this remote Ethiopian town almost a millennia ago. Today that world still remains, frozen in stone.

Descend into the tunnels and pass traditional priests and monks who float through the confines like the clouds of incense, smell beeswax candles and hear the sounds of chanting coming from the deep, cool recesses, only to find yourself standing in the sunlight, slack-jawed and staring up to a structure that defies reason.

Lalibela, a World Heritage site, undoubtedly ranks among the greatest religio-historical sites in the Christian world.

Though the town has drawn 'tourists' since the 16th century, it remains remarkably undeveloped. Sporadic electricity has just arrived and there are still no banks or pharmacies.

Lalibela also remains a very isolated place, sitting at 2630m. The journey overland continues to be quite long and arduous, with the sense of arrival feeling more like that after making a great pilgrimage. In fact, Lalibela *is* a centre of pilgrimage for many Ethiopian Orthodox Christians and being here for a major festival is unforgettable.

History

Lalibela, initially known as Roha, was the Zagwe dynasty's capital in the 12th and 13th centuries. After the death of King Lalibela, the ruler credited with the construction of the churches, the town was named after him.

Scholars and local tradition both believe (a rare consensus!) that the churches date from around Lalibela's reign in the 12th or 13th century. Legend states that King Lalibela was exiled or fled to Jerusalem in fear of persecution from his half-brother. Intrigued by the buildings he found, King Lalibela vowed to build a new holy city when he returned. Another legend claims that it was, in fact, a heavenly vision that Lalibela saw.

Perhaps King Lalibela was making a deliberate attempt to create a new Jerusalem on African soil, far from Muslim usurpers, and accessible to all Ethiopians. Even the names of Lalibela's features echo those of Jerusalem: the River Jordan, Calvary, and the Tomb of Adam. However, the buildings are so different from each other in style, craftsmanship and state of preservation that they may span a much longer period than Lalibela's reign.

The consensus between scholars and local tradition is thrown out the window when discussions about who built the churches arises. Some wizardly scholars with powerful calculators have estimated that it would have taken a workforce of some 40,000 to construct the churches, while locals claim that, toiling all the hours of daylight, the earthly workforce was then replaced by a celestial one, who toiled all the hours of darkness. In this way, the churches rose at a miraculous speed!

However, foreign intervention, whether celestial or mortal, can almost certainly be ruled out. Long a victim of the usual 'it can't be African' chauvinism, Lalibela in fact almost certainly represents the pinnacle of a very long-standing Ethiopian building tradition.

Exceptional masonry skills had long been in existence during the days of Aksum, and indeed most of the churches show clear characteristics of the ancient Aksumite style. If angels did build the churches, they were almost certainly Ethiopian angels!

Information

There are several expensive Internet options in town (up to Birr2 per minute), but they rarely ever have connections. Roha Hotel (p161) can usually change cash and travellers cheques, while the Seven Olives Hotel (p161) can change cash (US dollars) – neither give good rates.

Lalibela Health Center (☎ 0333 360416; ⊗ 8.30am-noon & 1.30-5.30pm)

Telecommunications office (⊗ 8am-8pm) International calls. Standard rates (p267). It's next to the post office.

Tourism office (☎ 0333 360167; ⊗ 8am-noon & 1.30-5.30pm Mon-Fri) This office offers some helpful advice and sells several small booklets on Lalibela.

Dangers & Annoyances

The biggest (but minor) gripe most travellers have with Lalibela are its smallest residents – fleas. They tend to be found on the rugs in churches. A little sprinkle of flea powder on your socks at the start of the day usually does the trick.

Harassment from unlicensed 'guides' can also be as irritating as a flea in your nether regions. Because unemployment is high, the prospect of money earned from guiding is attractive, to children as well as adults. Using children as guides encourages them to play truant at school, while using unlicensed guides encourages unhealthy migration to Lalibela (and more unemployed 'guides' harassing travellers). Hiring either also won't contribute to your visit, as few children or unlicensed guides know much about the churches.

Pestering from young children can also be a problem (see Notebook Scam, opposite).

Sights

Lalibela's **rock-hewn churches** (admission Birr100, personal video cameras Birr150; ⊗ 8am-5.30pm) are remarkable for three main reasons: because many are not carved into the rock, but freed entirely from it (unlike most of Petra); because the buildings are so refined; and because there are so many within such a small area.

Although time has treated the churches with remarkably gentle gloves, Unesco has built rather hideous scaffolding and roofing over most churches to protect frescoes from water seepage. They shouldn't take away from your enjoyment, but they do make photography more challenging.

NOTEBOOK SCAM

You'll undoubtedly come across a child with an improbable 'sob story' here. One child approached us and started with, 'both my parents are dead.' After briefly consoling him, we noticed he had a Chelsea FC top on so switched to happier subjects, namely football. Soon the child was excited and before he knew it, he'd asked us to his house so his mother could perform a coffee ceremony! Oops!

Most 'sob stories', whether genuine or not, usually lead to the child feigning the desperate need of school materials, particularly notebooks. Compelled by guilt, numerous travellers have purchased notebooks only to happen upon the child gleefully returning it to the vendor for cash later.

As always, never give directly to children; it only encourages them to beg and actually keeps them away from school. If you want to help with education, it's best to approach the school and find out what materials they're short of. This will allow the teachers to distribute materials to those students actually in need. No you won't see the joy in the child's face, but if you're giving for the right reason that should not be important.

Although visiting without a guide is possible – getting lost in the warren of tunnels is quite memorable and usually not permanent – you'll miss out on many of the amazing subtleties each church has to offer. We'd recommend going once with a guide and once solo, in whichever order you so choose. Local licensed guides can be arranged at the tourism office for a set fee of Birr150 per day (Birr200 for groups of five or more). However, during slow times licensed guides on the street (always ask to see their license) will occasionally drop their fees.

The **ticket office** (8am-noon & 2-5pm) lies beside the path leading to the northern group of churches and Bet Medhane Alem. Tickets give access to all churches in town for the duration of your stay.

Note that camera flashes inside churches cause great damage to the murals and frescoes, so please resist using one. Many of the priests are more than happy to show off their church's treasures and pose obligingly beside them for photos. It is customary and polite to tip them something small afterwards (Birr5).

The self-appointed shoe bearers found at each church doorway seemed to have disappeared at the time of research, but should they return a tip of Birr1 per person per church is fair.

Lastly, don't forget to bring your torch!

NORTHWESTERN GROUP OF CHURCHES

This group contains six of Lalibela's 11 churches and sits immediately behind the ticket office. From a size perspective, this group is easily the most impressive.

Bet Medhane Alem ቤተ መድኃኔዓለም

Resembling a massive Greek temple more than a traditional Ethiopian church, Bet Medhane Alem (Saviour of the World) is impressive for its size and majesty. Said to be the largest rock-hewn church in the world, it measures 33.5m by 23.5m and is over 11.5 high.

Some scholars have suggested that the church may have been a copy in rock of the original St Mary of Zion church in Aksum.

The building is surrounded by 34 large, rectangular columns (many actually replicas of the originals). The three jointed at each corner are thought to represent the Holy Trinity. There are a further 38 columns inside which support the gabled roof.

The interior consists of a barrel-vaulted nave and four aisles. Look for the three empty graves in one corner, said to have been prepared symbolically for Abraham, Isaac and Jacob. Pierced stone 'panels' fill the windows, each decorated with different central crosses. You may be allowed to see the famous 7kg gold Lalibela cross. In 1997 it was stolen by an Ethiopian antique dealer and sold to a Belgian tourist for US$25,000. Thankfully, it was recovered.

Bet Maryam ቤተ ማርያም

Connected to Bet Medhane Alem by a tunnel is a large courtyard containing three churches. The first, Bet Maryam, is small,

LALIBELA

0 _____ 500 m
0 _____ 0.3 miles

INFORMATION		
Ethio Supermarket	1	A4
Internet Café	2	C2
Lalibela Health Center	3	B3
Post Office	4	B2
Telecommunications Office	5	B2
Tourism office	6	B4
Van Internet	7	B4

SIGHTS & ACTIVITIES		
Ticket Office	8	B3

SLEEPING		
Alif Paradise Hotel	9	B4
Asheton Hotel	10	C3
Blue Lal Hotel	11	C3
Heaven Guest House	12	B4
Helen Hotel	13	B4

Jerusalem Guest House	14	A4
Lal Hotel	15	A4
Lalibela Hotel	16	B4
Mini Roha Hotel (Private Roha)	17	A3
Roha Hotel	18	A4
Seven Olives Hotel	19	C3
Tukol Village	20	B4

EATING		
Blue Lal Hotel	(see 11)	
Dirb Tezara Restaurant	21	C3
Jerusalem Guest House	(see 14)	
John Cafeteria & Lalibela Restaurant	22	C3

Megabi Cafeteria	23	A4
Megenagna Hotel	24	C2
Roha Hotel	(see 18)	
Seven Olives Hotel	(see 19)	
Unique Restaurant	25	C3

DRINKING		
Askalech Tej House	26	B3

SHOPPING		
Fine Art Gallery	27	A4

TRANSPORT		
Bus Station	28	C3
Ethiopian Airlines	29	C2

School

To Bilbila Giyorgis (32km);
Arbatu Ensessa (35km);
Bilbila Chirkos (35km);
Yemrehanna Kristos
(42km by road, 20km by mule);
Sekota (100km)

To Ashetan
Maryam (7km)

To Na'akuto La'ab
(6km); Airport (23km); Geneta
Maryam (30km); Machina Maryam
(42km); Gashema (64km); Woldia
(180km); Bahir Dar (261km)

Saturday
Market

See Enlargement

Orthodox
Cemetery

River Jordan

To airport
road (2km)

St Lalibela
Secondary School

NORTHWESTERN GROUP OF CHURCHES

0 _____ 50 m

Bet Meskel
Tomb of
Adam
Bet Golgotha, Bet Mikael
& Selassie Chapel
Bet
Danaghel
Bet
Maryam
Bet Medhane
Alem
Bet Amanuel
Bet
Giyorgis
River Jordan
Bet
Gabriel-Rafael
Bet
Merkorios
Bet Abba Libanos

SOUTHEASTERN GROUP OF CHURCHES

yet designed and decorated to an exceptionally high standard. Dedicated to the Virgin, who's particularly venerated in Ethiopia, this is the most popular church among pilgrims. Some believe it may have been the first church built by Lalibela.

On its eastern wall you'll see two sets of three windows. According to scholars, the upper set is thought to represent the Holy Trinity, while the lower three, set below a small cross-shaped window, are believed to represent the crucifixion of Jesus and the two sinners. The lower right window has a small irregular-shaped opening above it, a signal that this sinner was accepted to heaven after repenting his sins and asking for Jesus' help. The lower left window,

which represents the criminal who mocked Jesus and was sentenced to hell, has the small irregular-shaped opening below it.

Above the western porch and squeezed beneath the roof is a rare and beautifully carved bas-relief of St George fighting the dragon.

Inside, the ceilings and upper walls are painted with very early frescoes, and the columns, capital and arches are covered in beautifully carved details such as birds, animals and foliage, including a curious two-headed eagle and two fighting bulls, one white, one black (thought to represent good and evil).

At the nave's eastern end is a column that's kept permanently wrapped in cloth.

Nobody knows what lays beneath, though rumours abound – ask your guide.

Bet Meskel ቤተ መስቀል
Carved into the courtyard's northern wall at Bet Maryam is the tiny semichapel of Bet Meskel. Four pillars divide the gallery into two aisles spanned by arcades.

Keep an eye out for the cross carved in relief beneath stylised foliage on one of the spandrels of the arches.

Bet Danaghel ቤተ ድንግል
To the south of the Bet Maryam courtyard is the chapel of Bet Danaghel, said to have been constructed in memory of the maiden nuns martyred on the orders of the 4th-century Roman emperor Julian in Edessa (modern-day Turkey). Many of its features – the cruciform pillars and bracket capitals – are typical architectural features of the churches.

Bet Golgotha, Bet Mikael & Selassie Chapel ቤተ ጎልጎታ ቤተ ሚካኤል ና ስላሴ የጸሎት ቤት
A tunnel at the southern end of the Bet Maryam courtyard connects it to the twin churches of Bet Golgotha and Bet Mikael (also known as Bet Debre Sina).

Bet Mikael serves as an anteroom to the Selassie Chapel, one of Lalibela's holiest sanctuaries. It contains three monolithic altars. One is decorated with a beautiful relief of four winged creatures with their hands held up in prayer; it's thought to represent the four evangelists. Unfortunately, the chapel is very rarely open to the public.

Bet Golgotha is known for containing some of the best early examples of Ethiopian Christian art. On the so-called Tomb of Christ (an arched recess in the northeast of the church) a recumbent figure is carved in high relief; above it, in low relief, hovers an angel. Almost as amazing are the life-size depictions of seven saints carved into the walls' niches.

Close to the Tomb of Christ is a movable slab of stone, said to cover the most secret place in the holy city, the tomb of King Lalibela himself. Such is the importance and sanctity of Golgotha that a visit is said to assure your place in heaven!

Bet Golgotha also boasts some of Lalibela's most important religious treasures.

You may be shown a blackened metal cross (thought to symbolise the nails of crucifixion) and a large prayer stick (composed of wood, iron and horn), both supposed belongings of King Lalibela. Sadly women are not allowed into Bet Golgotha.

Standing in a deep trench in front of the western façade of Bet Golgotha is the so-called Tomb of Adam. It consists of a giant, hollowed-out block of stone.

SOUTHEASTERN GROUP OF CHURCHES
Although smaller in size than the northwestern group, the southeastern cluster offers one of Lalibela's most finely carved churches as well as some intrigue, with various historians debating whether some churches had pasts as prisons and palaces.

Bet Gabriel-Rufael ቤተ ገብርኤል ሩፋኤል
Its entrance flanked to the west by a sloping sliver of hewn rock known as the 'Way to Heaven', this imposing twin-church marks the main entrance to the southeastern group.

Unlike most Lalibela churches its entrance is at the top and is accessed by a small walkway, high over the moatlike trench below. This, along with its curious, irregular floor plan, has led scholars to propose that Bet Gabriel-Rufael may have been a fortified palace for Aksumite royalty as early as the 7th and 8th centuries.

Although the section of Bet Rufael's roof that collapsed has been rebuilt, services only take place in Bet Gabriel. Once inside the complex you'll realise its monumental façade was its most interesting feature.

Bet Merkorios ቤተ መርቆሪዮስ
Reached via a long, narrow and pitch-black tunnel that starts from Bet Gabriel-Rufael, this current church may have started as something altogether different. The discovery of ankle shackles among other objects has led scholars to believe that the building may have served as the town's prison, or house of justice.

Due to a large section of roof collapsing, the interior is a fraction of its former size. Don't miss the beautiful fresco thought to represent the three wise men. With their little flipper hands and eyes that look askance, they're delightfully depicted; it may date from the 15th century. The 12 apostles are also represented in a less attractive fresco, probably of a later date.

The painting on cotton fabric is believed to date from the 16th century, though the priests will claim it's 14th century. Formerly, such paintings were plastered to the church walls with a mixture of straw, ox blood and mud.

Bet Amanuel ቤተ አማኑኤል

Freestanding and monolithic, this is considered one of the Lalibela's most finely carved churches. Some have suggested Bet Amanuel was the royal family's private chapel.

It perfectly replicates the style of Aksumite buildings, with its projecting and recessed walls mimicking alternating layers of wood and stone. To appreciate this fully, you should make a day trip to Yemrehanna Kristos (p163), which is one of Ethiopia's best-preserved Aksumite structures.

The most striking feature of the interior is the double Aksumite frieze in the nave. Although not accessible, there's even a spiral staircase connecting the four-pillared walls to an upper gallery. In the southern aisle, a hole in the floor (beneath the donation box) leads to a long, subterranean tunnel (one of three) which connects the church to Bet Merkorios and Bet Gabriel-Rufael.

Outside, you may see the odd 'sacred bee' flying about. Behind a high door in the courtyard's southern wall is their hive. Throughout Ethiopia, honey produced in churches is believed to possess special healing properties.

The chambers in the walls are the old graves of pilgrims who requested to be buried here.

Bet Abba Libanos ቤተ አባ ሊባኖስ

Bet Abba Libanos is hewn into a rock face and is unique among Lalibela's churches in that it's a hypogeous church. In English, that means only the roof and floor remain attached to the strata.

Like Bet Amanuel, many of its architectural features, such as the friezes, are Aksumite. Curiously, although it looks large from the outside, the interior is actually very small. The carved corners of its cubic capitals are rather unique; some guides say they may represent angel eyes.

The church is said to have been constructed in a single night by Lalibela's wife,

Meskel Kebra, with a little help from angels. The church seems to grow from the rock and gives you a vivid idea of the work required to excavate these churches.

A tunnel leads off the church to the tiny chapel of Bet Lehem.

BET GIYORGIS ቤተ ጊዮርጊስ

Resting all on its own, south and west of the northwestern and southeastern groups, is Lalibela's masterpiece, Bet Giyorgis. Standing on the brow of its compound, you'll have little doubt that it's the most mesmerising object in all of Ethiopia.

Representing the apogee of the rock-hewn tradition, it's the most visually perfect church of all, a 15m-high three-tiered plinth in the shape of a Greek cross. Due to its exceptional preservation, it also lacks the obtrusive scaffolding seen on the other churches.

Inside, light flows in from the windows and illuminates the ceiling's large crosses – beauty in simplicity. There are also two 800-year-old olive-wood boxes; one (with the opposing corkscrew keys) is rumoured to have been carved by King Lalibela himself.

Be warned that some of the cavities in the walls surrounding the church hold unsettling mummified corpses.

See also the boxed text, above.

Festivals & Events

The most exciting time to visit is during a major festival, when thousands of pilgrims crowd in for Timkat, Leddet and Fasika.

Meskel and Kiddus Yohannes are also busy. See p261 for dates and details.

Outside these periods, try to attend at least one church's saint's day; inquire at your hotel.

Sleeping

Note that vacancies are almost nonexistent during the festival period and European Christmas, so reservations up to six months in advance aren't unheard of. However, prices for reserved rooms during these times soar – one hotel's Birr150 room jumps to US$50! If you arrive during a festival without reservations, you'll risk being forced into a dive. Conversely, if there's space, you'll end up paying a fraction of what you would have if you'd made those costly reservations.

Discounts are negotiable in most hotels from May through August.

Lalibela suffers from water shortages, particularly during dry season and high tourism season. Hotels may limit showering to early mornings and evenings or may give out buckets of warm water instead. Lengthy electrical cuts are still a problem.

Due to an increasing number of travellers visiting Lalibela, a few new hotel projects, like Tukol Village, are starting to crop up. Next on the horizon is the Yemrha Hotel, which is being built by Green Land Tours (see www.yemrhahotel.com or www.green landethiopia.com for details).

BUDGET

Asheton Hotel (☎ 0333 360030; s with shared bathroom Birr50, tw Birr100) The twin rooms, with white-washed walls, local art and embroidered bedding, have more character than other budget options. They're starting to age though – our Aksumite-inspired coat hook fell from the wall and plunged to its death on the carpet floor. The showers are hot, the service is pleasant and the prices are *always* negotiable. The spartan singles aren't as pleasing.

Heaven Guest House (☎ 0333 360075; tw with shared bathroom US$10, s/tw US$10/15) Wood ceilings look over shiny linoleum 'wood' floors, sturdy yet comfortable beds and creative Aksumite headboards. The bathrooms are tidy and put forth hot H20. This new place is very clean and the friendly owner is keen to keep it that way. Its future looks bright, especially with a small *tukul* restaurant under construction.

Lalibela Hotel (☎ 0333 360036; s/tw Birr50/100) A good-value option for singles, the rooms here are crisp and clean. And unlike most places in this price range, they aren't trying to hide dirty corners, so rooms and loos are actually lit by more than a 5-watt bulb. Heck, you can even read by it!

Blue Lal Hotel (☎ 0333 360380; d & tw Birr120-150) Although extremely austere, these rooms are bright, clean and the showers spurt hot water. Land room 2, 3 or 4 and you'll have a balcony to play on.

Mini Roha Hotel (☎ 0333 360394; s/d with shared bathroom Birr30/60) Also known as Private Roha, this is the best of the bottom feeders. Set around a patio, the dimly lit rooms are reasonably clean but have no glass windows. Open the shutters though, and you may land a view. Oddly, the toilet has quite the vista!

Other options:

Helen Hotel (☎ 0333 360053; s/tw Birr80/120)
Alif Paradise Hotel (☎ 0333 360023; s/tw Birr80/120)

MIDRANGE

Roha Hotel (☎ 0333 360009; ghion@ethionet.et; camping per 2-person tent US$12.50, s/d/ste US$38/50/75) Although the comfortable and cosy rooms are identical to its state-owned brothers (Bahir Dar's Tana Hotel, Gonder's Goha Hotel and Aksum's Yeha Hotel), its lobby, dining area and bar are a steep step up in the architectural beauty department. Rooms 220 to 229 have sunset views. Campers have access to hot showers and the hotel has its own generator.

Tukol Village (☎ 0333 360564; camping per tent US$4, s/d US$20/30) Scheduled to be open by the time you read this, this hotel has several two-storey red sandstone *tukuls*, some of which offer views over Bet Giyorgis from their balconies. It also rents quality two-person Dutch tents for US$3 per day (US$5 if you take them outside Lalibela).

Seven Olives Hotel (☎ 0333 360020; s/d US$15/27.50) Now privately run, this place has dropped its prices by US$10 despite the improved quality. The large rooms and bathrooms still feel a bit old, but the beds are new and the updated plumbing gushes hot water 24 hours a day. Its leafy terrace is its strongest asset. Rooms 10 to 16 offer the best views.

Lal Hotel (☎ 0333 360008; laltour@ethionet.et; camping Birr60, s/d US$30/36) Art-clad stone walls, small bathrooms and laminate floors call these large rooms home. Rooms 16, 20 and 57 through 65 offer views west. Discounts are usually negotiable, though all rooms cost US$48 during festivals. Free airport transfer is offered.

Jerusalem Guest House (☎ 0333 360047; camping per tent US$10, s/d US$30/40) These large, rather vacant-feeling rooms have one massive thing going for them: they all open onto private balconies that overlook the lowlands and the amazing sunsets.

Eating

Seven Olives Hotel (mains Birr16-32) Eat inside the round, modernised *tukul* or dine alfresco on the leafy terrace. An Ethiopian chef with experience in America was training the staff to make more than the usual *faranji* fare when we were in town. Most meals were already hitting their mark.

Jerusalem Guest House (mains Birr15-22) This hotel's large *tukul* restaurant serves decent Ethiopian fare and *faranji* food, such as beef stroganoff and chicken curry.

Unique Restaurant (mains Birr4-10) Opposite the Asheton Hotel, this dark and understated little restaurant, serving cheap and tasty Ethiopian dishes, has received rave reviews from a number of readers.

Blue Lal Hotel (mains Birr7-20) We'd heard this hotel's owner used to live in France, so we ordered the quiche Lorraine. Forty-five minutes later we were presented with an entire behemoth of a pie – be warned! After enjoying a fifth of it, our bulging insides forced us to move on. Small appetite? Try the crêpes with honey, we hear they're great.

Roha Hotel (mains Birr20-32) Its dining gallery, with massive hangings cascading from the ceiling, has to be the flashiest place to eat. However, the food usually underperforms.

John Cafeteria & Lalibela Restaurant (Map p158; mains Birr7-16) These neighbours share a kitchen and menu. Birr10 will get you an omelette breakfast with toast, local honey and a steaming *macchiato*.

Other local restaurants to get your fill:

Dirb Tezara Restaurant (mains Birr8-12) Ethiopian dishes. Popular with small local business crowd.

Megabi Cafeteria (mains Birr4-8) Pleasant thatched pavilions. Decent *tibs*.

Megenagna Hotel (fasting food Birr5) Locals claim it serves Lalibela's best fasting food. We were still recovering from our quiche and couldn't confirm these claims.

Drinking

Besides having a cold sunset drink on the Seven Olive Hotel's terrace, there's one other drinking experience you shouldn't miss.

Askalech Tej House (flask of tej Birr5) Also known as 'torpedo', it serves *tej* (honey wine) of varying potency. There's usually traditional music after 7pm.

Shopping

Fine Art Gallery (☯ 7am-8pm) One shop that stands out from Lalibela's throng of souvenir shacks. Inside are beautiful watercolour and sepia paintings created by Tegegne Yirdaw, a local artist who can count Princess Anne as one of his work's admirers. Small originals range from Birr150 to Birr200.

Getting There & Away

Ethiopian Airlines (☎ 0333 360046) flies at least once daily to Addis Ababa (US$102, 2½ hours), Gonder (US$51, 30 minutes), Bahir Dar (US$61, 1¼ hours) and Aksum (US$72, 40 minutes).

Overland, the best approach is currently from Woldia via Gashema. Gashema can also be reached from the west but transport is sporadic at best. With your own vehicle (or oodles of patience) it's a rewarding journey to arrive from the north via Adwa, Abi Addi and Sekota. On that note, fuel (out of the barrel) is now available in Lalibela.

Two buses depart daily at 6am for Woldia (Birr25, five to seven hours), with one continuing to Addis Ababa (Birr75, two days) after overnighting in Dessie (Birr39, 8½ to 10 hours). Sometimes there's a direct bus to Bahir Dar (Birr46, 10 hours). Tickets are best bought the afternoon before travel (after 4pm) when the buses arrive from Woldia.

Getting Around

Most midrange hotels offer airport transfer service (from Birr25 to Birr30 one way) to the airport, which is 23km south of town.

Of the midrange hotels that arrange 4WD hire to visit the churches outside town (opposite), the Seven Olives has the best prices. Possible trips include Na'akuto La'ab (Birr150), Yemrehanna Kristos (Birr500), Geneta Maryam (Birr500) and Bilbala Chirkos and Yemrehanna Kristos (Birr600 to Birr700).

If you think Landrovers are crude brutes, you can hire a mule for longer or steeper treks; ask at your hotel. A full day should set you back Birr50 to Birr70 per mule and driver. A shorter trip to Ashetan Maryam and Na'akuto La'ab will cost Birr35 to Birr40. A tip of Birr15 for short day journeys is recommended, Birr30 for longer days.

AROUND LALIBELA

Many other fascinating churches and monasteries lie within a day's striking distance of Lalibela, and a journey to them, whether by foot, mule or 4WD, is rewarding. Don't forget to look for the endemic white-billed starlings while on the go! The stunning countryside is also home to unique ecotourism treks.

Ecotreks on the Mesket Escarpment

For a real insight into the life of Ethiopian highlanders and some astounding scenery, contact the local charity **Tourism in Ethiopia for Sustainable Future Alternatives** (TESFA; ☎ 0111 140583; www.community-tourism ethiopia.com), which offers rewarding treks south of Lalibela.

TESFA's goal is 'to work in partnership with local communities to enable them to generate sustainable improvements in their livelihood through the development of their own tourism related enterprises, while also contributing to the protection of their physical and cultural environments'. Save the Children (UK) and the Royal Netherlands Embassy have helped fund the project.

Treks are typically three days long and take place along the top of the Mesket Escarpment, which houses caves, rock-hewn churches, fascinating columnar basalt outcrops and genuine local villages. Because you stay on the escarpment, gradients are quite low and you'll find the walking is fairly easy.

TESFA has two camps in local villages, each currently consisting of two traditional, yet comfortable *tukuls*. Wajela camp sits near an interesting cave complex while Mequat Maryam teeters near the escarpment edge and offers incredible vistas – even the view from the toilet is inspiring.

Treks, including guides, packing mules and drivers, accommodation, meals (breakfast, lunch, dinner and the odd snack), tea and coffee, cost Birr300 per person per day (there are discounts for children).

Transportation to/from Lalibela must be arranged privately, though TESFA recommends the local 4WD operator **Habte** (habte@ethionet.et) who has fixed rates of Birr700 for drop offs at Gashema (start of trek) and Birr800 for pick-ups at Filakit (end of trek).

Due to limited space, these treks must be booked well in advance.

Churches & Monasteries

The churches around Lalibela vary greatly in style, design and age, some are even thought to predate those in Lalibela. Quite tucked away and still absent from any modern maps, the churches require a guide to find them. Although many are in need of urgent restoration, such as Ashetan Maryam, Bilbila Chirkos and Bilbila Giyorgis, a few are in amazing states of preservation.

See Lalibela's Getting Around section (opposite) for transport details.

YEMREHANNA KRISTOS የመረሃና ክርስቶስ

Despite **Yemrehanna Kristos** (admission Birr50) being one of Ethiopia's best preserved late-Aksumite buildings, only 15 or so people reward themselves with a visit each week. A fact made even more astounding considering the church only sits 1½ hours (45km) away from Lalibela by 4WD.

The church is unusual because it's built rather than excavated. Seeing the stepped exterior façade, created from alternating wood and stone layers, you'll truly come to appreciate why so many of Lalibela's rock-hewn churches look like they do. And knowing that Yemrehanna Kristos may predate Lalibela's churches by up to 80 years, you have before you a virtual blueprint of greatness.

Incredibly, the whole church sits on a foundation of carefully laid olive-wood panels, which 'float' it perfectly above the marshy ground below. The carving and decoration are exceptional, especially the cruciform windows and the elaborate nave ceiling. Conceiving how the massive marble arches were placed so accurately in such surrounds is almost harder to grasp than the construction of Lalibela's churches.

Behind the church lies a pile of mummified pilgrims (the priests told us there were over 10,000 of them) who'd come here to die over the centuries. Most lay exposed and the expression on one face was truly shocking. Watch your step walking around the back of half of the complex – we stubbed our toe on a partially exposed skull hidden beneath the grass floor.

This entirely inspiring and slightly spooky complex sits within a cave roofed by basalt lava flows. The ugly brick wall at the front was built in 1985 to improve the church's security.

It's also possible to get here by foot or mule. Both options take about five hours to cover the shorter 20km distance.

ARBATU ENSESSA አርባቱ እንሰሳ

West of Yemrehanna Kristos, around 35km from Lalibela, is **Arbatu Ensessa** (admission Birr30). Its a three-quarter monolith church in a wild, overgrown, but rather beautiful setting. It's thought to have been built by King Kaleb in AD 518. *Arbatu ensessa* means 'the four beasts' after the four Evangelists, Matthew, Mark, Luke and John.

BILBILA CHIRKOS ቢልቢላ ጨርቆስ

Close to Arbatu Ensessa is **Bilbila Chirkos** (admission Birr30). An interesting three-quarter monolith, it's known particularly for its ancient frescoes. Also attributed to King Kaleb, it's thought to date from AD 523. It's a three-minute walk from the road.

BILBILA GIYORGIS ቢልቢላ ጊዮርጊስ

Lying to the west of Arbatu Ensessa, around 32km from Lalibela, **Bilbila Giyorgis** (admission Birr30) is another attributed to King Kaleb. It resembles Bet Abba Libanos in design.

According to tradition, five swarms of bees took up residence shortly after the church was completed. They still reside and their sacred honey is said to have curative properties, particularly for psychological disorders and skin problems. The priest will let you taste it. It's 20 to 30 minutes' walk up the hill to the church from the road.

ASHETAN MARYAM አሼታን ማርያም

Set at 3150m, atop a mountain that rises directly above Lalibela, is this **monastery** (admission Birr20). Understandably, there are commanding views in all directions. The local priests believe they're 'closer to heaven and God' here, and it's easy to see why.

The monastery's construction is believed to span Lalibela's and Na'akuto La'ab's reign; some even claim King Na'akuto La'ab lies buried in the chapel. Church treasures include parchment and some icons.

Although the architecture here compares pretty poorly with Lalibela, the journey takes you through lovely country. Listen out for the francolins' witchlike cackle resounding around the valley.

The 1½-hour climb (one way) is quite steep. Many travellers take mules, though you'll still need to walk over the rockiest parts.

NA'AKUTO LA 'AB ናቁቶ ላአብ

Lying 7km from Lalibela, just off the airport road, is this **church** (admission Birr20) attributed to Lalibela's successor. It's simple but attractive (apart from the outer security wall) and built under a natural cave. It was almost certainly the site of a much older shrine.

Empress Zewditu built the ugly inner red-brick building. Some very old stone receptacles collect the precious holy water as it drips from the cave roof.

The church boasts various treasures said to have belonged to its founder, including crosses, crowns, gold-painted drums and an illuminated Bible.

GENETA MARYAM ገነታ ማርያም

Near the source of the Tekeze River, 31km from Lalibela, lies **Geneta Maryam** (admission Birr20). It's thought to have been built around 1270 by Yekuno Amlak, who restored the Solomonic line. With its rectangular shape and 20 massive rectangular pillars that support it, Geneta Maryam resembles Lalibela's Bet Medhane Alem. It's also known for its remarkable 13th-century paintings.

On the western wall, there's a moon-shaped face of Christ, and on the southern side, very grumpy-looking elephants. Geneta Maryam is about four hours by foot from Lalibela, or 1½ hours by vehicle.

MACHINA MARYAM መቺና ማርያም

Two hours' walk from Geneta Maryam and six hours' walk (42km) from Lalibela is the remote church of **Machina Maryam** (Emachina Lideta Maryam; admission Birr20), said traditionally to have been constructed by three virgins during the reign of King Gebre Meskel in AD 537.

The church is constructed under an overhanging rock in a natural cave. It rather resembles Yemrehanna Kristos in design, and many features are Aksumite, but its beautiful frescoes, some of hunting scenes with one-eyed lions, are the main attraction.

There are many bricked-up tombs in the church. Bodies buried under the rock are said to be preserved forever. The church is little visited, but is worth the long and steep ascent. Mules are a good idea in the dry season.

DESSIE ደሴ
pop 139,936 / elev 2470m

Rusty tin roofs and eucalyptus trees carpet the hills in Dessie – no, the ex-capital of the former Wolo province wouldn't win any beauty contests. However, you may end up spending a night here because it's a major transport hub for Lalibela, Hayk and Maqdala.

Information

There are several Internet cafés (Birr18 per hour), pharmacies, a good health clinic and banks (change cash and travellers cheques) along the main drag. There are pickpockets aplenty around the bus station – be vigilant.

Sleeping & Eating

Rooms can be in short supply, especially on weekends, so call ahead.

Fasika Hotel 2 (☎ 0331 117705; s/d Birr65/95) This bright and quiet place has comfortable rooms with satellite TVs, foam beds and hot showers.

Fasika Hotel 1 (☎ 0331 112930; d with shared bathroom Birr30, d Birr50) It offers smaller and darker rooms than its brother hotel, but is equally clean and also hosts hot water.

Ambaras (☎ 0331 119118; s/d/ste Birr72/88/100) This place is past its prime, with 1970s green carpets, dated drapes and dog-eared bathrooms. However, it's pretty functional and has a comfy lounge downstairs with a satellite TV.

Royal Pension (☎ 0331 114939; d Birr25) Up a small alley behind the Shell station. The rooms at the Royal Pension outshine the exterior, though that isn't say much! While they aren't spotless and bedspreads looks like shag carpets, you do get a typically tidy bathroom.

Tossa Restaurant (mains Birr5-11) This restaurant is the best place to eat in town. The

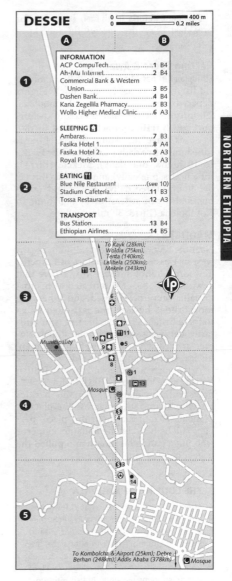

DESSIE
0 ___ 400 m
0 ___ 0.2 miles

INFORMATION
ACP CompuTech.....................1 B4
Ah-Mu Internet.......................2 B4
Commercial Bank & Western
  Union...............................3 B5
Dashen Bank..........................4 B4
Kana Zegellila Pharmacy..........5 B3
Wollo Higher Medical Clinic......6 A3

SLEEPING
Ambaras.................................7 B3
Fasika Hotel 1.........................8 A4
Fasika Hotel 2.........................9 A3
Royal Pension........................10 A3

EATING
Blue Nile Restaurant.............(see 10)
Stadium Cafeteria...................11 B3
Tossa Restaurant....................12 A3

TRANSPORT
Bus Station...........................13 B4
Ethiopian Airlines...................14 B5

To Kayk (28km); Woldia (75km), Tenta (140km); Lalibela (250km); Mekele (343km)

Municipality

Mosque

To Kombolcha & Airport (25km); Debre Berhan (248km); Addis Ababa (378km) Mosque

NORTHERN ETHIOPIA

Ethiopian fare is great and you even pay local prices! It's 150m north of the Wollo Higher Medical clinic. Ask any local to point it out.

Blue Nile Restaurant (mains Birr5-14) Just west of the Royal Pension, this is another popular local place. It also serves some *faranji* options.

Stadium Cafeteria (meals Birr4) It's great for breakfast. Try the *special ful* (chickpea purée).

Getting There & Away

Ethiopian Airlines (☎ 0331 112571) flies daily to Addis Ababa (US$61, one hour). Flights depart from the airport near Kombolcha, 23km from Dessie. Shared taxis to the airport cost Birr10, contract taxis cost Birr80.

Buses leave for Addis Ababa (Birr41, nine hours, five daily), Lalibela (Birr39, 8½ to 10 hours, one daily), Mekele (Birr41, nine hours, one daily) and Woldia (Birr12, 3½ hours, three daily). Buses and minibuses also run at least every half-hour to Kombolcha (Birr3, 30 minutes).

MAQDALA

Near the tiny village of Tenta, 140km north-west of Dessie, are the vestiges of Emperor Tewodros' hilltop fortress. It was here that Tewodros (r 1855–68) retreated as his formidable empire collapsed and where he took Britons hostage in a last-ditch effort to force Britain's hand in helping him militarily. Lets just say that when Sir Robert Napier arrived with 32,000 well-armed men, his last goal was to help Tewodros.

After such a route and heavy British looting (see the boxed text, below), it is not surprising that little remains besides a few remnants strewn across the plateau. Maqdala is rather a mournful place, perhaps still haunted by the unhappy emperor who put a gun in his mouth and pulled the trigger before being captured.

THE LOOTING OF MAQDALA

After the British troops devastated Tewodros' army and freed the prisoners in 1868, they looted everything from the amulet around the dead emperor's neck to altar slabs, ancient manuscripts and processional crosses from the nearby church. Amazingly, much of the stolen items remain in British museums and private collections, despite strong calls from Ethiopian historians for their return.

The **Association of the Return of Ethiopia's Maqdala Treasures** (AFROMET; www .afromet.org) continues to fight for the treasures' return, arguing that looting had no basis in law and that it was an act of sacrilege.

History aside, the 3½-hour hike to Maqdala from Tenta is great and there are stunning views of the surrounding countryside from the windswept top. You'll need to stop at the **administration office** (⏰ 8am-12.30pm & 1.30-5pm Mon-Fri) in Ajibara (10km before Tenta) to get papers and pick up your compulsory police escort (Birr50).

One bus runs from Dessie to Tenta each morning at around 6am (Birr35, five hours) and stops long enough in Ajibara for you to sort formalities. There are a couple of fleapit hotels in Ajibara and Tenta. With a vehicle, the journey to Tenta is possible in just under two hours.

HAYK ሃይቅ

Lying 28km north of Dessie on a peninsula is the little town of Hayk, known for its monastery and lake.

The monastery dates from the mid-13th century and was founded by Abba Iyasus Moa. Between the 13th and 15th centuries it was among Ethiopia's most important monasteries. Today it hosts the oldest known manuscript to record its own date: the book of the four gospels produced for the monastery between 1280 and 1281. It's open to men only.

The lake and its environs, 3km from town, is an excellent spot for birders.

At least 15 minibuses or buses (Birr4, one hour) run daily to the village of Hayk.

KOMBOLCHA ኮንቦልቻ

pop 100,954 / elev 1850m

The dramatic and curvaceous descent from Dessie to Kombolcha outdoes anything the twin towns have to offer. Kombolcha is less of a transportation hub than Dessie, but it's much less dirty and noisy and has better hotels, making it a more pleasant option to break your journey between Addis Ababa and Lalibela. It's also closer to the airport (2km).

Tekle Hotel (☎ 0335 510056; d with shared bathroom Birr30, d/tw Birr57/80) is set in pleasant grounds and the rooms come in all different shapes, sizes and levels of brightness. They're all clean so have a wander and take your pick. There's also a decent restaurant.

Kombolcha Wine Hotel (☎ 0335 512091; tw with shared bathroom Birr30, d Birr20-30), like Tekle, is about 2km up the hill from the bus station. If you don't want to walk, take a *gari* or share-taxi (Birr1 to Birr2). It's a quiet and clean spot with a friendly owner and a range of rooms to choose from. Try the *bazana shiro* (chickpea purée with meat) in its popular restaurant.

Ama Hotel (d with shared bathroom Birr20, d Birr30) is a cheap and simple option close to the bus station. The rooms with shared facilities are actually much brighter and quieter than the more expensive options. It's opposite the Kombolcha City Service complex.

Harego Lodge (☎ 0335 513767; d Birr60) is the most comfortable option, but only viable if you have a vehicle. It's several kilometres out of town en route to Dessie.

Hikma (snacks Birr1-2) on the piazza and the **Sport Cafe** (snacks Birr1-2) are the best pastry shops.

Frequent buses serve Dessie (Birr3, 30 minutes). One bus leaves daily for Addis Ababa (Birr38.50, 8½ hours).

BATI ባቲ

The little town of Bati, 41km east of Kombolcha, is known for its large, colourful **Monday market** (☺ 9am-3pm), which attracts up to 10,000 Afar, Oromo and Amharas from all around.

Bati's market is Ethiopia's largest after Addis Ababa's Merkato. It's interesting and lively (especially around 11am), so check it out if you're in the area. Look out for the old gallows (dating from the emperor's day). If you're planning to take photos, come armed with Birr1 notes. An Ethiopian companion is a good idea to keep curious children, as well as pickpockets, away.

At least one bus and 10 to 15 minibuses leave for, and arrive from, Kombolcha daily (Birr7 to Birr10, 1¼ hours).

DEBRE BERHAN ደብረ ብርሃን

pop 53,000 / elev 2840m

Small, yet somehow sprawling, the town of Debre Berhan sits 130km northeast of Addis Ababa. Despite being the 15th-century capital of Emperor Zara Yaqob and the site of Ahmed Gragn the Left-Handed's slaughter of the imperial army, Debre Berhan is most famous for its woollen blankets and rugs; check them out at the cooperative

near the telecommunications office. The only real nonwoolly reason to stop here is if you're planning on visiting nearby Ankober.

The drive from here north to Debre Sina, which takes you off the Guassa Plateau and down the dramatic Mezezo Escarpment, is unforgettable (watch for gelada baboons).

Eva Hotel (☎ 0116 813607; r Birr100), the pink palace at the town's entrance from Addis Ababa, has large spotless rooms with beautiful and bright bathrooms. New carpets prevent the traditional early morning greeting between warm toes and cold tiles.

Akalu Hotel (☎ 0116 811115; d 40) sits literally and figuratively between Eva and Helen, offering a bit of comfort at cheap prices. We delved into *kai wat* (goat in *berbere* sauce) at their reputable restaurant (mains Birr7 to Birr15); it was served with cheese and was delicious.

Helen Hotel (☎ 0116 811204; d with shared bathroom Birr20, d Birr40) lies at the opposite end of town and offers cheap but clean rooms.

Yabsera Café (drinks & snacks Birr1-3) will quell on-the-road tummy rumbles with coffee, juice, cakes or pastries. It's next to the bus station.

Numerous buses/minibuses serve Addis Ababa (Birr13/15, 2½ hours). One bus leaves daily at 6am for Kombolcha (Birr28, seven hours) and Dessie (Birr31, eight hours). Buses travelling north from Addis Ababa also occasionally have seats.

ANKOBER አንኮበር

The little town of Ankober lies 40km southeast of Debre Berhan. Right up until the late 19th century, when Addis Ababa was founded, it was the capital of the Shoan princes.

Set atop a hill 2km from town are the ruins of Menelik II's old palace. Though little more than a section of wall remains, the walk here is a good one and the area is renowned as a birders' haven. It's the official home of a very rare endemic bird, the Ankober serin. The white-throated seedeater and yellow-throated seedeater are often seen here too.

Three morning buses run between Debre Berhan and Ankober (Birr8, two hours).

Southern Ethiopia

Shiver under moonlight in the splendid Bale Mountains, swelter politely, slack-jawed in a Mursi village or silently savour the spotting of a rare bird. Known for its rich natural attractions, southern Ethiopia proffers captivating wildlife, scenic landscapes, great trekking possibilities and some of the continent's most diverse and fascinating peoples.

The southwest's Omo region has been called 'Africa's last great wilderness', and is home not just to Ethiopia's few remaining large mammals including lion and elephant, but also its last isolated tribes, including the famous Mursi lip stretchers and body-painting Karo.

Africa's renowned Rift Valley cuts through the south and hosts lakes, astounding birdlife, national parks and wildlife sanctuaries.

East of the Rift, the Bale Mountains tower over the surrounding pastures of the Oromo people. Within these peaks is one of Africa's largest mountain parks. The Bale Mountains National Park is the best place in Ethiopia to see endemic wildlife, including the endangered Ethiopian wolf. Trekking in the mountains, in the rain, among the heather, is fantastic.

The southeast's Oromo are predominantly Muslim and two significant Islamic shrines are found here: Sheikh Hussein, southern Ethiopia's most important annual Muslim pilgrimage site; and the mystical Sof Omar Caves.

Before putting the brakes on your northern journey to head south, know that travel here is as tough as it is astounding. We'll only make one guarantee – it will be memorable.

HIGHLIGHTS

- Baking, sweating and swearing there's nowhere you'd rather be than in the **Lower Omo Valley** (p204) while witnessing lip stretchers, bull jumpers and body painters

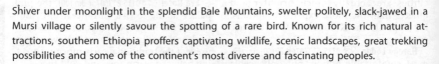

- Counting to 20 using your fingers and toes *after* visiting Lake Chamo's amazing **crocodile market** (p196)

- Breezing through bleached savannah grasses, with Burchell's zebra in the rear-view mirror and Rift Valley lakes stretched out below, at **Nechisar National Park** (p199)

- Spotting the world's rarest canid, the Ethiopian wolf, while trekking the sublime **Bale Mountains** (p181)

- Dining on fresh tilapia and doing the backstroke in the world's largest cup of tea at **Lake Langano** (p172)

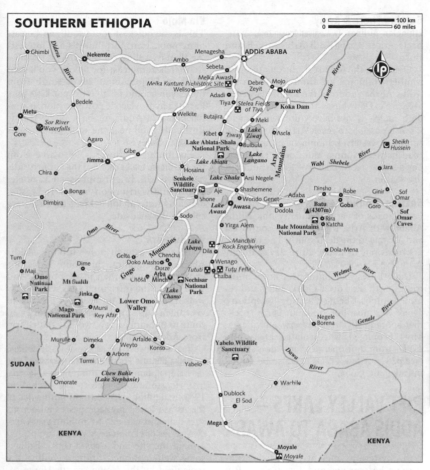

SOUTHERN ETHIOPIA

Climate

With elevations varying from 450m in the Lower Omo Valley to 4377m in the Bale Mountains, daytime temperatures in this region range from 10°C to 40°C.

Rain traditionally falls between March and October in the highlands, with July, August and September receiving the most precipitation. April, May and October are the wettest months in the Lower Omo Valley, with sporadic precipitation falling the rest of the year.

National Parks & Wildlife Sanctuaries

Offering splendid trekking, the rarest of mammals and hundreds of bird species, Bale Mountains National Park has every-

thing in spades. Nechisar National Park offers diverse scenery, Rift Valley lakes, massive crocodiles, Burchell's zebras and the odd Abyssinian lion.

Although African plains wildlife also roams Mago National Park and Omo National Park in the remote and rugged Lower Omo Valley, the real attraction in these national parks is the isolated traditional tribes.

If birds are of interest to you, head to Lake Abiata-Shala National Park, Senkele Wildlife Sanctuary and Yabelo Wildlife Sanctuary, which host a range of unique and endemic species.

For more on these parks and sanctuaries, see p66.

Getting There & Away

Ethiopian Airlines (www.flyethiopian.com) connects Addis Ababa with Arba Minch and Jinka.

Overland, the only real options to enter southern Ethiopia are from the north via Addis Ababa and from the south via Kenya at Moyale. Daily buses and minibuses serve both routes. If you have your own vehicle, it's also possible to reach Arba Minch from Jimma in western Ethiopia via an upgraded road between Jimma and Sodo. The journey's supposed to take five to six hours in dry season.

Getting Around

Paved roads of variable quality link Addis Ababa with Arba Minch in the southwest and Moyale in the deep south. The remaining roads rate from decent to devastatingly painful.

Daily buses and minibuses cover most routes, with the Lower Omo Valley and remote southeast being the only exceptions. There you must hop on or in Isuzu trucks that sporadically trundle between villages. Most people visiting isolated areas hire 4WDs from tour operators in Addis Ababa (see p282). A few 4WDs can also be rented in Jinka and Goba.

RIFT VALLEY LAKES – ADDIS ABABA TO AWASA

With mysterious ancient stelae fields, numerous hot springs and five unique Rift Valley lakes hosting everything from historical island monasteries to endangered birds, this 275km-long corridor is more than just a gateway to southern Ethiopia's riches.

SOUTH TO LAKE ZIWAY

Travellers heading to Lake Ziway from Addis Ababa have two routes to ponder: one via Mojo, the other via Butajira. Along the way you'll see countless shade houses, all part of Ethiopia's blossoming business venture. Flowers are already a US$360-million industry in Kenya and with Kenya losing its developing nation trade status with the EU in 2007, Ethiopia hopes to take over the reigns.

Via Mojo

This is the quickest route south and offers more pubic transport, but it's less interesting than travelling via Butajira.

After heading east for 94km, you'll turn south at Mojo. About 20km south from there, you should be able to spot **Koka Dam**. Part of a hydroelectric power station, it supplies most of Addis Ababa with electricity. Birdlife is good near the water and hippos can sometimes be seen.

Continuing southwards, keep an eye out for the **Oromo tombs** that dot the countryside, decorated with bright murals, some of elephants and warriors on horses. In season, delicious watermelons (Birr2 to Birr5) are sold on the roadside.

Via Butajira

With fresh asphalt now linking Addis Ababa and Butajira, this route is significantly less painful than it used to be. And with two of the intriguing sites within easy walking distance of the road, it's possible to visit them with public transport, either en route to Butajira or as a two-day return trip from Addis Ababa.

Just southwest of Melka Awash village is **Melka Kunture Prehistoric Site** (admission Birr10; ⏰ 9am-5pm), famous for the remarkable prehistoric stone-tool factory discovered in 1963. Extending over 5km on both sides of the Awash River, it encompasses numerous sites dating as early as 1.7 million years ago.

A series of explanatory panels are posted around the site and a *tukul* (hut) displays some well-captioned finds, including the tools used by the *Homo erectus/Homo sapiens* who once inhabited the area. It's a fascinating place.

The nearest accommodation is in Melka Awash. **Awash Ber Hotel** (s/tw with shared bathroom Birr12/24) has small austere rooms with shared squat toilets that are crude, but adequate.

Around 4km south of Melka Kunture, there's a signposted turn-off to the impressive rock-hewn church of **Adadi Maryam** (admission Birr30). It sits within the village of Adadi, some 12km west of the turn-off. Believed to date from the 12th or 13th century, Adadi Maryam is a semimonolithic church (only three of its four sides are detached from the surrounding strata) and is fairly crude in comparison with its counterparts in Lalibela and Tigray. However, if this is your only chance to see a rock-hewn church, you should jump at it. On Adadi's market days (Thursday and Saturday) public transport runs to and from Melka Awash.

Tiya (admission Birr10), a fascinating Unesco World Heritage site, is found further south, almost 40km from Melka Awash. The site contains around 36 ancient stelae, 32 of which are engraved with enigmatic symbols, notably swords. Despite the largest standing 2m tall, they're as intriguing and mysterious as any of the standing stones found in Europe. Tiya is the most important of several stelae clusters that dot the countryside all the way down to Dila.

Almost nothing is known about the monoliths' carvers or their purpose. French excavations have revealed that the stelae mark mass graves of individuals aged between 18 and 30.

The stelae lie 500m from the village of Tiya. A guard, who'll charge you the Birr10 and open the gate, now lives in a small building next to the fenced compound; he occasionally offers tours.

LAKE ZIWAY ዝዋይ ሐይቅ

Surrounded by blue volcanic hills, 158km south of Addis Ababa, and covering a massive 425 sq km is Lake Ziway, the largest of the northern group of Rift Valley lakes. It's an attractive enough place, but it's best known for its **birdlife**. White pelicans, black egrets, saddlebill and yellowbill storks are all seen here, as well as a variety of kingfishers and waterfowl.

One of the best spots to see birds is from the earthen 'jetty' in the town of Ziway; you'll find it about 1.5km due east of the Bekele Mola Hotel. The birds are particularly numerous here in the early morning and evening, when they gather to pick at the fishermen's castoffs. You can also take a local punt (Birr35 per person after hefty negotiation) or pay a fisherman (Birr25 to Birr30) to see the **hippo pods**, about 15 minutes by boat from the jetty.

The lake is also home to five little volcanic islands, of which three once boasted medieval churches. Tullu Gudo, 14km from Ziway and the largest island, is still home to three monasteries. **Debre Tsion**, the most famous, has a long and enigmatic history. According to tradition, it once housed the Ark of the Covenant. Priests, fleeing the

destruction of the city of Aksum at the hands of Queen Gudit in the 9th century, brought it here. The original church now lies in ruins and a new one has been built. Interestingly, the oldest written documents on Aksum were discovered here.

Tullu Gudo is a beautiful, little-visited place. The walk to the church through the *tef* (an indigenous grass cultivated as a cereal grain), wheat and barley fields is pleasant and there are very good views from the church. You can also bathe in hot springs; the islanders have created a little tub near the shorefront. A brief exploration of the island takes around two hours.

Currently rather slow (15HP) motorboats can be hired from private operators in Ziway (but they lack radios and life jackets). Head for the jetty and inquire there. Starting prices were an absurd Birr800 per person for the return trip to Tullu Gudo. Negotiations should bring that down to Birr500 for the entire boat. It takes between two and three hours one way. If you're lucky you may be able to hop on an early morning boat that takes locals to the island. Locals pay Birr5 for the trip, which means if you're honed in the art of negotiations you may only pay Birr25!

Trips to the nearer islands of Debre Sina, Galila and Bird Island cost from Birr150 each, or Birr200 to Birr300 to visit all three (for one to six people).

Information

There's a Commercial Bank on the Addis–Shashemene road in Ziway, but only cash (US dollars and euros) is exchanged.

Sleeping & Eating

Camping is permitted on Ziway's islands. If that doesn't float your boat, the town of Ziway is a pleasant, laid-back little place, with good, reasonably priced hotels, restaurants and cafés. All the following listings are found along the Addis–Shasheme road.

Brothers Hotel (☎ 0464 412609; s/d Birr22/32) Just south of the bus stand, this option is easily the best in town. The tile floors, blue walls, bed sheets and bathrooms (complete with hot showers) are all spotless. There's a popular local restaurant attached.

Bekele Mola Hotel (☎ 0464 412077; s/d Birr29/35) Behind the Shell station, Bekele Mola's aged but clean rooms surround a pleasant and peaceful courtyard that's brimful of birds.

The bathrooms are dog-eared and some mattresses are on their last legs, so poke a few before choosing. The shady terrace restaurant (mains Birr17) is nice and caters to Westerners.

Ziway Tourist Hotel (☎ 0464 413993; r 50) Towards the southern end of town, this option has a range of rooms, some much better than others. It can also be loud at times and *faranjis* (foreigners, especially Western ones) pay double. The garden restaurant (mains Birr7 to Birr15) has less ambience than its counterpart at the Bekele Mola, but it serves a wider variety of dishes.

Firehiwot Pastry (pastries Birr1.75) Just north of the bus stand, this is a perfect place for a quick breakfast.

Drinking

City Snack & Juice House (juice Birr2-3) Swig a glass of orange, papaya or blended avocado at this new spot just south of Brothers Hotel.

Getting There & Around

Buses leave for Shashemene (Birr10, two hours, four daily), Butajira (Birr7, 1½ to two hours, seven daily) and Addis Ababa (Birr17, three hours, three daily). Numerous minibuses also serve Addis Ababa (Birr20). For Debre Zeyit or Nazret, take a minibus to Mojo first (Birr10, 1½ hours).

For Lake Langano, take the Shashemene bus or a minibus to Arsi Negele (Birr7, 45 to 50 minutes); ask to be dropped at the junction to the Bekele Mola or Langano Resort (Wabe Shebele) Hotels.

Bikes can be hired near the bus station and Jemaneh Hotel in Ziway for Birr3 per hour. *Garis* (horse-drawn carts) across town cost Birr1 to Birr2.

LAKE LANGANO ለንጋኖ ሐይቅ

Lake Langano, set against the 4000m blue Arsi Mountains, is a dream come true for many Brits. They can don their swimming kit and cross 'doing the backstroke in the world's largest cup of English tea' off their list of fantasies – yes, Langano's water is on the brown side. That said, it's actually clean and is one Ethiopia's few lakes to have been declared bilharzia-free. British or not, get in and get wet!

The birding is excellent on some of the more remote sections of this 300-sq-km lake, and over 300 species have been

recorded, including the Ethiopian cliff swallow.

Lake Langano also makes a convenient and comfortable base to explore nearby Lake Abiata-Shala National Park. Visit Langano during the week; it's cheaper and you'll avoid the hoards of weekenders making the 180km trip from Addis Ababa.

Sleeping & Eating

Accommodation and dining options around Lake Langano are limited to several resorts, two of which are southern Ethiopia's premier ecolodges. More lodges are scheduled to open in coming years.

The following rates are for weekdays (Sunday through Thursday). Add about 50% for weekends.

Bishangari Lodge (☎ 0115 517533, 0911 201317; www.bishangari.com; s/tw with shared bathroom US$32/57, s/tw US$52/92, ste US$63-109) Hyped as Ethiopia's first ecolodge when it opened in 1997, Bishangari is an amazing place to stay. Sleep in one of nine beautiful *godjos* (bungalows), each nestled privately along the lake's southeastern shore in stands of fig trees (complete with hammocks). Inside, natural woods blend with local artwork in the bright surroundings. There are also 12-traditional *tukuls* (mud huts), which are more down to earth and have shared facilities (hot showers). The 12-hectare site is a peaceful place and the Tree Bar and outdoor restaurant are wonderful touches. Activities include horse riding, mountain biking, fishing, trekking, hippo spotting, bird-watching and swimming. Rates listed include breakfast (an extra US$20 per person will include a lovely lunch and dinner). Partial proceeds go to the Bishangari Community Fund, which supports sustainable development in the local community. A shuttle runs between the lodge and Addis Ababa (Birr200 return).

Wenney Eco-Lodge (☎ 0988 766249, 0911 203614; www.wenneyecolodge.com; s/tw US$42/52) Located on Langano's remote southern shore, Wenney Eco-Lodge opened in 2005. Although it offers similar serene surrounds to Bishangari (and the same activities), it's accommodation and dinning areas are less refined.

Bekele Mola Hotel (Map p173; ☎ 0981 190011, 0911 486014; camping Birr32.50, 1-/2-/3-bedroom bungalows Birr208/276/346) Unlike the secluded nature of Bishangari and Wenney's bungalows, accommodation here is densely packed along the lake's southwestern shore. Although it's popular with families (thanks to its playground and swimming area), it's the loudest and most crowded on weekends. The beach here is better than that seen at Langano Resort Hotel, though it's still coarse and pretty grey. Rooms are old and simple, yet clean and sport mosquito nets. Facilities include horse riding (Birr34.50 per hour), tour boats (Birr345 for 40 minutes; up to 30 people) and pedal boats (Birr27.60 for 30 minutes). It also hires out two-person tents (Birr92 including camping fees). The restaurant (mains Birr33 to Birr45) serves delicious tilapia (a freshwater fish). If you bring your own food, you're charged Birr100 per person per day!

Langano Resort Hotel (Map p173; ☎ 0981 190131; camping Birr25, 1-/2-/3-bedroom bungalows incl breakfast Blrr146/254/352) Like Bekele Mola Hotel, this resort only sits 3km off the main Addis Ababa–Shashemene road. The site is less attractively designed and situated than the Bekele Mola, but it's much more peaceful, particularly at weekends. Motorboats (maximum five people) can be hired (Birr2.50 per person per minute!) for visits to the hot springs (20 minutes one way) and for lake tours. Tent rental is Birr50 per person. Set two-course meals are Birr40.

Getting There & Away

To get to/from Lake Langano, take any bus plying the Addis Ababa–Shashemene road, and ask to be dropped off/picked up (just signal) at the turn-off to your hotel. Rides to Wenney and Bishangari Lodges can usually be arranged in advance.

LAKE ABIATA-SHALA NATIONAL PARK
አባያታ ሻላ ሐይቅ
ብሔራዊ ፓርክ

West of Lake Langano lie the twin lakes of Abiata and Shala, which form part of the 887-sq-km **Lake Abiata-Shala National Park** (admission per 48hr Birr50, 5-seat vehicle Birr10). Identical twins these lakes are not. Shala's 410-sq-km surface sits within a collapsed volcanic caldera and depths exceed 260m in some areas, while Abiata's highly alkaline waters rest in a shallow pan no more than 14m in depth.

Traditionally, fish thriving in Abiata's waters fed storks, cormorants and pelicans that bred in safety on volcanic islands dotting Shala's surface. Pelican Island was one of only seven nesting sites in all of Africa

for the great white pelican. We say 'was' because the last decade has seen Lake Abiata suffer greatly at the hands of humans. The thick acacia woodland surrounding it has been turned into charcoal by illegal settlers, and commercial farms and a soda-ash factory have caused pollution and a substantial drop in the water level. The lake's increased salinity has killed the fish population, resulting in the pelicans and other birds deserting their former nesting grounds. The opposite is true for flamingos, who've been lured here by the newly thriving algae population. The only problem is that the shrunken lake and flamingos sit in the middle of an impenetrable dust bowl!

The saviour of the park still has to be Lake Shala, with its scenery and its abundant acacia-related bird species, such as the weaver bird, red-billed hornbill, Didric's cuckoo, Abyssinian roller and superb starling. There are some nice **lookouts** within walking distance of the main gate, though you'll need to take a guide/scout for directions/security (Birr30/100 for short vehicle trips/whole day by foot). If you have a vehicle, don't leave it unattended; guards can also be hired at the gate.

On the northeast shore of Shala, there's a **sulphurous hot spring**, which is often crowded with locals bathing and cooking maize in the thermal waters. At Shala's southwestern shore there's a second hot spring and a stunning, though pint sized, crater lake. Looking 80m down from the rim to **Lake Chitu** and

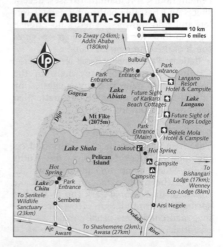

LAKE ABIATA-SHALA NP

SOUTHERN ETHIOPIA

RASTAFARIANS

Unbeknown to Ras Tafari, he gained subjects who lived far beyond the confines of his own kingdom when he was crowned Emperor Haile Selassie in 1930. In Jamaica, where Marcus Garvey's 'return to Africa' movement had been established, many saw the emperor's coronation as fulfilment of the ancient biblical prophesy that 'Kings will come out of Africa'.

Identifying themselves passionately with Ethiopia's monarch, as well as with Ethiopia's status as an independent African state, Garvey's followers created a new religion.

In it, the emperor was accorded divinity – the Messiah of African redemption. And the new faith would bear his former name.

What did the Emperor think of all this? Well, it was said that he was a bit embarrassed by it all. In 1963 he did grant them land in Shashemene though.

Rastafarians follow strict dietary taboos: pork, milk and coffee are forbidden. Ganja (marijuana) is held to be a sacrament.

Today the Rastas still patiently await the restoration of the Ethiopian monarchy. The recent Ethiopian–Eritrean War was seen by Rastafarians as a punishment visited on the country for having killed its king – the chosen one of God.

Treatment of Rastafarians by Orthodox Ethiopians ranges from a guarded tolerance to all out accusing them of spreading drugs and crime – claims Rastas dismiss as springing from prejudice. To date, no Ethiopian government has granted citizenship to any Rastafarians, including their Ethiopian born children.

---

spotting its semiresident flamingos is a sight worth the effort. The south shore is accessed via Aware or Aje. Note that admission must be paid at the main park entrance.

Sleeping & Eating

Nearby Lake Langano is the obvious place to base yourself. However, if Langano's lodges will break the bank, head south to Arsi Negele.

Tsaday Hotel (☎ 0461 160813; Arsi Negele; d Birr15) Arsi Negele's best has cleanish rooms with cement floors, soft foam mattresses, decent sheets and passable bathrooms (squat toilets and cold showers). There's no English sign, so look for the battered green gates south of the Commercial Bank.

National Park camping (adult per 48hr Birr20) Camping is permitted anywhere in the park, but two main sites are suggested by officials. Don't leave anything unattended and bring a scout for security.

Getting There & Around

The main park entrance is signposted on the highway. Any bus doing the Addis Ababa–Shashemene run can drop you off.

From the main park entrance to Lake Abiata-Shala National Park (up to the hot springs) is around 8km. If you're driving, road conditions usually make a 4WD essential.

SHASHEMENE ሻሸመኔ
pop 89,680 / elev 1700m
Shashemene is a grubby and raucous town that sits at southern Ethiopia's most important crossroads, which connects north to south and east to west. It has little to offer travellers besides transportation links, and it has sadly gained a reputation for its occasional rude and hostile treatment of travellers. A decent alternative is to stay in nearby Awasa, which has reasonable transportation links. If you just need a break, head for nearby Wondo Genet.

In February 2005 Shashemene hosted thousands during part of the 'Africa Unite' celebrations put on by Rita Marley (Bob Marley's widow), the African Union and Unicef.

Information

There's a post office, Commercial Bank and two Internet options (per hour Birr15) stretched out along the main drag, along with most of the hotels and restaurants.

Sights

Shashemene can boast one claim: it's the unofficial capital of Ethiopia's Rastafarian community. Straddling the road to Addis Ababa just north of town, the community is known to locals as 'Jamaica'. Previously reluctant to welcome tourists, they've now opened the informal **Black Lion Museum** (☯ hrs vary), which honours their Rastafarian heritage. They still don't take kindly to those looking to buy marijuana.

Sleeping & Eating

South Rift Valley Hotel (☎ 0461 105710; s/tw Birr48/138, d Birr66-138) This large terraced garden complex is quiet and comfortable. The pink 'palace' out back has the best rooms, with balconies, TVs, firm mattresses and modern bathrooms. The cheaper rooms within the hillside structure are smaller, but are equally clean and also have TVs. The restaurant is the town's best and prepares local and *faranji* fare.

Bekele Mola 1 (☎ 0461 103344; tw Birr46) Clean rooms surround a palm-fringed courtyard that's set slightly back off the main drag. The beds are comfortable and the bathrooms boast hot water. The restaurant (mains Birr14 to Birr20) serves decent Western food, but lacks atmosphere.

Bekele Mola 2 (☎ 0461 103348; r Birr35) Less charming than its sister across the street, this modern cement block of a hotel has clean but weathered rooms.

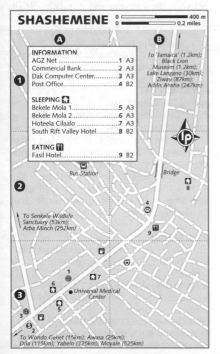

Hoteela Cilaalo (☎ 0461 103720; d with shared bathroom Birr20) The best of the bottom feeders. The medium-sized rooms are brightly lit and pretty clean. The bar can get noisy at times.

Fasil Hotel (mains Birr8-12) The best of many local Ethiopian eateries.

Getting There & Away

Shashemene is the principal transport hub of the south. There are buses servicing Addis Ababa (Birr24, five hours, four daily), Arba Minch (Birr26, six hours, one daily), Goba (Birr26, six to seven hours, two daily), Ziway (Birr10, two hours, four daily) and Moyale (Birr54, 1½ days, one daily), overnighting at Yabelo (Birr35, 12 hours).

Six minibuses run daily to Dila (Birr12 to Birr17, three hours), and leave every 15 minutes or so for Awasa (Birr4, 30 minutes).

Bekele Mola 1 hotel is a convenient spot to hitch a ride, as tourist vehicles often take breakfast or lunch there.

WONDO GENET ወንዶ ገነት

Found 15km southeast of Shashemene, and surrounded by dense forest, bird song, a variety of larger wildlife and – in season – fruit and honey, the mountain resort village of Wondo Genet is truly a breath of fresh air.

Although its hot springs pools receive the most accolades from Ethiopians due to their therapeutic powers, we have to say that the surroundings are the true attraction here. Go hiking into the bird-filled forest, catch glimpses of the Rift Valley below and search for everything from yellow-fronted parrots and white-backed black tits to bushbucks, baboons and hyenas, though we'd imagine you'd rather not meet up with the latter! A short but interesting walk is to the source of the springs, which is about 10 minutes from the resort hotel. There you'll find cowherds cooking their lunch in the springs: 17 minutes for potatoes, 35 minutes for maize!

The cement **hot springs pools** (admission Birr5; ⏱ 24hr), although soothing to swim in and surrounded by gardens, have more the feel of a water treatment plant than a resort. Things can also get awfully crowded on weekends.

Sleeping & Eating

Wondo Genet Resort Hotel (☎ 0462 203763; washo .et@ethionet.et; camping Birr37.50, s/tw incl breakfast Birr205/273) Set amid citrus orchards, flowering gardens and playful colobus and vervet

SOUTHERN ETHIOPIA

monkeys, this resort sits on a natural balcony overlooking the Rift Valley. With high prices, 1970s décor and run-down bathrooms, you're obviously paying for the location. Reservations (via email) are advised for weekends. Guests have free use of the hot springs pools. The hotel restaurant (mains Birr12 to Birr14) can prepare picnic lunches or barbecues around a campfire.

Abyssinia Hotel (d Birr40) Although *faranji* prices are in full effect, this hotel 3km down the hill in Wondo Washa is the best budget bet. Reasonable-sized rooms, set in a pleasant garden behind the hotel's restaurant, are bright and clean.

Though closed when we visited, there's a nameless rudimentary budget option just below the hot springs pools.

Delicious seasonal fruit can be bought in the area, including papaya, avocado, banana and mango. Try a local favourite, the *kazmir*. The area is also known for its *chat* (see p228).

Getting There & Away

From Shashemene, buses and minibuses run regularly (until 5pm) to and from the village of Wondo Washa (Birr4, 40 minutes), which is 3km from the springs. From there, you can walk or take a *gari* (Birr5 per person).

A contract minibus (up to 10 people) from Shashemene costs Birr250 to Birr300 return (including waiting time).

SENKELE WILDLIFE SANCTUARY
ሰንከሌ የዱር አራዊት ፓርክ

Originally established to protect the endemic Swayne's hartebeest, the open acacia woodlands of the **Senkele Wildlife Sanctuary** (admission Birr70) also hosts Bohor reedbucks, greater kudus, spotted hyenas, serval and civet cats, caracals, warthogs, common jackals and oribi antelopes. The globally threatened *Aquila clanga* (greater spotted eagle) is one of 191 bird species documented.

With a population of approximately 450, the Swayne's hartebeest is the most easily spotted species in this 36-sq-km park.

The park has had a troubled past, with large numbers of livestock and illegal settlers, but since an agreement between Aje administration, elders and park officials in 2001 things have been on the mend.

The park is 53km west of Shashemene and is worth a visit if you're in the vicinity.

There's a 65km track around the park, but it's usually only driveable between October and March. From the Borana Hill, around 6km east of the park office, there are good panoramic views. It's also possible to explore on foot.

Sleeping & Eating

Ideally, you would visit this park en route between Shashemene and Arba Minch. However, those without vehicles will have to stay in Aje as there's no camping in the park.

Zed Hotel (s with shared bathroom Birr10) The best thing we can say about this Aje option is that the sheets are clean. The dimly lit rooms aren't tidy and the shared bathrooms are pretty grim. Cold showers come in buckets. It's not signed, but it's across from the communications tower. You can eat in its restaurant.

Getting There & Away

The park turn-off lies 5km west of Aje. From there, it's at least 10km to the park headquarters. Around 20 minibuses run between Shashemene and Aje daily (Birr5, 30 minutes). In Aje, a contract minibus to the park should cost Birr250 to Birr350 return, including two hours waiting time; in the dry season, it's possible to drive around parts of the park.

AWASA አዋሳ
pop 140,999 / elev 1708m

Perfectly poised at Lake Awasa's edge, the capital of the Southern Nations, Nationalities and Peoples' region is both large and attractive. While there are no major sights, the lake and its surrounds offer a relaxing respite from the rigours of travel for a day or two. It definitely makes a more pleasurable stop on the north–south route than Shashemene, 25km to the north.

Information

The town centre has the telecommunications building, post office and other major services.

Commercial Bank (☼ 8-11am & 1-4pm Mon-Fri, 8-11.30am Sat) Changes travellers cheques, US dollars and euros.

Kibru Medical Center (☎ 0462 210950; ☼ 24hr) Awasa's best medical facility. Includes a pharmacy, clinic and diagnostic laboratory.

M-Link Internet Center (per hr Birr18) Slow and steady Internet connections.

Nardos Computer Service (per hr Birr18) As slow and as steady as M-link.

Sights & Activities

The waters of **Lake Awasa**, teeming with tilapia, catfish and barbus, attract good birdlife. Kingfishers, herons, storks, crakes, darters and plovers are among the species commonly seen on the water's edge, while weavers, hornbills and the endemic black-winged lovebird are found in the fig forest and scrub surroundings.

The easiest way to take in the lake and its wildlife is to stroll the footpath at the edge of the lake, leading north from the military post near Wabe Shebele Hotel 2. If your legs need slightly more stretching than strolling, hike up the steep and stubby **Tabour Hill**, which sits about 1km from the fish market. Your legs will have long recovered before you tire of the summit's view.

A trip onto Awasa's shimmering waters in a row boat is the best way to experience the lake. Boats, with rower, cost Birr50

per hour (one to five people) and are hired from the pier at the base of the main drag. Row row row your boat north to **Tikur Wuha** (Black Water) to see the hippos and birds (around three hours return) or south to **Amoora Gedel** (1½ to two hours return), one of the best places for birds.

If you fancy some fishing, hooks and line are cheap and easy to find in town. Otherwise, boat owners will charge Birr30 per hour to rent theirs!

The **fish market** (admission Birr10; ☀ 8am-10am), located on the shores of Crow Valley, is well worth the wander. With colourful boats lining the shore, children untangling nets, birds soaring above, massive marabou storks watching from treetops and pelicans patrolling the shallows, you'll have plenty to look at. Follow locals' lead and devour raw fish (Birr1). Come by foot, *gari* (Birr2) or row boat (three hours return).

Sleeping

Gebrekiristos Hotel (☎ 046 202780; d Birr63-76, tw Birr79) The best-value hotel in town. The Birr76 doubles are big, bright and boast

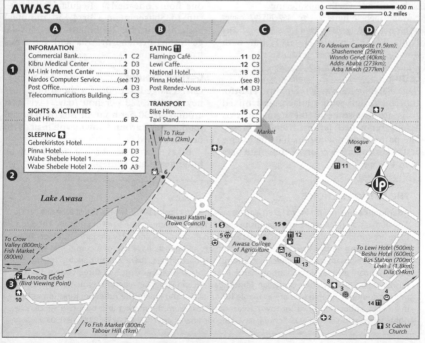

AWASA

0 — 400 m
0 — 0.2 miles

INFORMATION
Commercial Bank.........................1 C2
Kibru Medical Center 2 D3
M-Link Internet Center 3 D3
Nardos Computer Service ....(see 12)
Post Office...................................4 D3
Telecommunications Building.....5 C3

SIGHTS & ACTIVITIES
Boat Hire......................................6 B2

SLEEPING
Gebrekiristos Hotel.....................7 D1
Pinna Hotel..................................8 D3
Wabe Shebele Hotel 1................9 C2
Wabe Shebele Hotel 2..............10 A3

EATING
Flamingo Café............................11 D2
Lewi Caffe..................................12 C3
National Hotel............................13 C3
Pinna Hotel............................(see 8)
Post Rendez-Vous 14 D3

TRANSPORT
Bike Hire....................................15 C2
Taxi Stand..................................16 C3

To Adenium Campsite (1.5km);
Shashemene (25km);
Wondo Genet (40km);
Addis Ababa (273km);
Arba Minch (277km)

To Tikur Wuha (2km)

Market

Mosque

Lake Awasa

Hawaasi Katami (Town Council)

Awasa College of Agriculture

To Crow Valley (800m); Fish Market (800m)

Amoora Gedel (Bird Viewing Point)

To Lewi Hotel (500m); Beshu Hotel (600m); Bus Station (700m); Lewi 3 (1.8km); Dila (94km)

St Gabriel Church

To Fish Market (800m); Tabour Hill (1km)

SOUTHERN ETHIOPIA

balconies, satellite TVs, telephones, fridges and mosquito nets; angle for room 317 or 217. The twins and cheaper doubles are equally clean but lack TVs and fridges.

Lewi Hotel (☎ 0462 206310; d Birr70-180; ☒) Rooms range from utterly spartan and small, with linoleum floors, to incredibly comfy, with velvet sitting chairs, parquet flooring and queen-sized beds. All but the cheapest options have satellite TVs. It's 200m west of the bus station.

Pinna Hotel (☎ 0462 210336; fax 0462 202343; d/tw Birr160/192, ste Birr225-272) Well-located on the main drag, this modern option is pleasantly furnished and comfortable. Rooms have satellite TV, veranda and telephone.

Beshu Hotel (☎ 0462 206957; d with shared bathroom Birr33, d Birr56) Between Lewi Hotel and the bus station, Beshu has small, clean rooms. The doubles with private bathroom have satellite TVs, hot showers and mosquito nets.

Wabe Shebele Hotel 1 (☎ 0462 205395; 1-/2-/3-bedroom bungalows from Birr127/166/400; ☒) Lovely lakeside location and beautiful gardens, though rooms are incredibly worn and seriously overpriced. Only rooms 19 to 39 (one bedroom) are worth considering.

Wabe Shebele Hotel 2 (☎ 0462 205397; camping per tent Birr40, bungalow tw/d Birr78.25/93.75; ☒) Think Wabe Shebele Hotel 1, but with worse rooms and nicer gardens.

Eating

Pinna Hotel (mains Birr9-30) Shrimp risotto, gnocchi, ravioli with spinach, and mixed grills are just some of the items on this hotel's renowned *faranji*-friendly menu. The pastry shop downstairs has the town's best cakes and a selection of chocolate bars from Europe.

Post Rendez-Vous (mains Birr6-15) An eclectic outdoor restaurant and popular local hangout, this place is good for a variety of Western food including pasta, pizza and even veggie burgers.

National Hotel (mains Birr5-10) A local restaurant that dishes out traditional Ethiopian fare to the masses. It's usually packed.

Lewi 3 (mains Birr12-18) On the Shashemene–Dila road that skirts the town's northeast edge, this restaurant offers a wide range of dishes from curries to club sandwiches and pizza.

Options for cakes, pastries and coffee:
Flamingo Café (cakes Birr1.25)
Lewi Caffe (cakes Birr2)

Getting There & Away

The bus station lies about 1km east from the town centre. Since most southbound services will drive through town before reaching the station, simply ask to hop off in town. Otherwise, *garis* are available at the station.

Buses run to Addis Ababa (Birr28, 5½ hours, five daily), Arba Minch (Birr27, 6½ hours, one daily) and Wondo Genet (Birr9, one hour, one daily). Regular minibuses run to Shashemene (Birr4, 30 minutes) and Dila (Birr10, 2½ hours). For Moyale, go to Shashemene or Dila and get a bus from there.

Getting Around

Garis charge Birr1.50/2 for short/long journeys or Birr3/20 per hour/day. Taxis cost around Birr30 per hour, or Birr10 to Birr20 for journeys around town; you'll need to negotiate hard.

Bikes (Birr4/20 per hour/day) can be hired near Lewi Caffe.

SOUTHERN ETHIOPIA

A BALE BABY *Matt Phillips*

It was the grimmest day of my research for this book, with rain and fog obscuring everything but the road immediately ahead. Approaching Dodola, my driver and I spotted a crowd of almost 40 people carrying a bed with a blanketed body over their heads.

It seemed obvious that this pour soul was knocking on death's door, so we offered to help. The crowd was overwhelmingly distraught and tears were everywhere, my eyes included. As the body was being placed on the laps of three locals who'd piled into the back seat, a surprisingly young woman's head popped from beneath the blankets and mustered a few words. Before I knew it, the woman was whisked out and the quiet sullen air was pierced with the cries of…a newborn baby!

Worry instantaneously turned to elation and celebrations broke out amongst the crowd. I'm happy to say mother and baby are doing well.

It was undoubtedly the brightest day of my Ethiopian trip.

THE SOUTHEAST & BALE MOUNTAINS

Offering adventure, whether by foot, horseback or roaring 4WD, this unique region of southern Ethiopia fascinates those who visit.

DODOLA – HORSE TREKS IN THE BALE MOUNTAINS

Resting between Shashemene and the Bale Mountains National Park, the diminutive town of Dodola has become a base for some unique trekking. It's all due to the pioneering Integrated Forest Management Plan (IFMP), which was initiated in 1995 by the German aid organisation GTZ. Now self-sufficient, the nonprofit programme works to conserve natural Afro-alpine forest environment by offering local people an alternative income to felling the local forests.

Thanks to five simple but self-contained and comfortable lodges built along the route, it's perfect for those without tents and camping gear to explore the Bale Mountains' western range.

Due to the high altitudes and steep gradients, IMFP prefers people to trek on horseback (no riding experience is necessary), but this isn't mandatory and those with large lungs and legs of steel can trek on foot.

For information on Bale Mountains' geography, climate, plants and animals, see p181.

Planning

IFMP (☎ 0226 660036; www.baletrek.com; ⏱ 8.30am-5.30pm Mon-Sat), which is located on the main Shashemene–Dinsho road in Dodola, organises horses (Birr20 per day), horse handlers (one per four horses, Birr20 per day) and mandatory guides (Birr70 per day). Fees are paid to the service providers, not IFMP. IFMP also sells a 1:75,000 scale trekking map (US$3). The **Bale Mountain Motel** (☎ 0226 660016; gtz.ifmp@les-raisting.de), which is associated with the IFMP, can also provide the same services. The motel is located a few hundred metres east of the IFMP office.

Limited foodstuffs (pasta, rice, lentils, biscuits, cheese, tomato paste etc) can be purchased in Dodola and goats can be bought en route. Stoves, cooking utensils, beer (Birr5) and soft drinks (Birr4) are found within the lodges. Lodge keepers can provide local meals, but these are an acquired taste – bring supplies! Water is also available but requires treatment before drinking.

Trekking

Please review the Safety Guidelines for Trekking (p254) and Responsible Trekking (p255) boxed texts before embarking.

To complete the full circuit would take six days, but since every lodge is within four to five hours of a trail head, treks of even two days can be catered for. The full circuit (moving west to east) is described here. Times given are for those on horseback.

DAY ONE

Starting from Changiti (2750m), 11km south of Dodola, the trail leads 7km (2½ to 3½ hours) up the Tikiku Lensho River (very wet for those on foot) to the lodge at Wahoro (3340m). Spend the afternoon bagging Tute (3705m) and checking out Idjar Waterfall. The sunrise from Wahoro is amazing.

SOUTHERN ETHIOPIA

DAY TWO

Take the short 10km route (three to four hours) to the lodge at Angafo (3460m) or the longer 13km (four to five hours) option that offers better views and chances of spotting an Ethiopian wolf. After lunch climb Tullu Hangatu (3546m) for an astounding view.

DAY THREE

Continue 5km (1½ to two hours) east to the lodge at Andele (3350m), which is nestled within the Herero Forest, or continue 13km (or 18km depending on your route) further to the lodge at Moldicho (3349m).

DAY FOUR

If you slept at Andele, head east to the lodge at Moldicho. If you're up for it, you can visit Moldicho Waterfall.

DAY FIVE

From Moldicho, you'll skirt the Tinsich Boditi Ridge before crossing the Wageda Forest to reach the lodge at Duro (3400m). The day covers 18km (five or six hours).

DAY SIX

Descend the 11km (three hours) to the trail head at Bucha Raja (2680m) or continue 9km further (two hours) to the town of Adaba. Alternatively, you could spend a second night at Duro and explore Berenda Ridge.

Sleeping & Eating
DODOLA

Bale Mountain Motel (☎ 0226 660016; gtz.ifmp@les-raisting.de; camping Birr20, d with shared bathroom Birr20, d/tw Birr30/60) Although bare and small, the rooms here are comfortable and clean. It's a long and chilly walk to the outhouse-like loos for those with shared bathrooms. It has a homy little restaurant (meals Birr8 to Birr10) out back, but meals should be ordered in advance.

ADABA

Tourist Hotel (☎ 0226 630591; d Birr50) Located on the main Shashemene–Dinsho road, this option has two cosy Dorze huts (p201), each with comfy bed and clean bathroom. Meals and coffee are served in a massive Dorze hut.

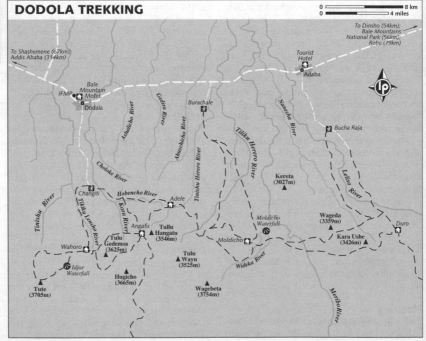

DODOLA TREKKING

ON THE MOUNTAINS

Each of the **lodges** (camping Birr15, s with shared bathroom Birr35) at Wahoro, Angafu, Adele, Moldicho and Duro has eight beds, complete with mattresses, bedding, blankets, sleeping bags and towels. The kitchen facilities can also be used by campers for a Birr5 fee. Guests and campers both must pay Birr5 for a hot shower.

Getting There & Around

From Dodola, two early morning buses serve Shashemene (Birr11, three to four hours) along a horrendous section of road. For Dinsho, take the Robe bus (Birr20, 3½ to four hours, four buses daily) and ask to be dropped off. Numerous minibuses run between Dodola and Adaba (Birr4.50, 40 minutes).

IFMP in Dodola provides 4WD transportation to and from trail heads (Birr3 per kilometre).

BALE MOUNTAINS NATIONAL PARK
የባሌ ተራሮች ብሔራዊ ፓርክ

More than any other park in Ethiopia, the Bale Mountains National Park is known for its wildlife. Over 60 mammal species and 260 bird species have been recorded here.

The scenery may be less spectacular than the Simien Mountains', but it's certainly no less beautiful. As you approach the park from Dodola, ridges to the east are punctuated with fortresslike escarpments, while those to the north are more gentle, their rounded rock pinnacles dotting the ridges like worn teeth protruding from an old man's gums. Within the park, rivers cut deep gorges; alpine lakes feed streams; and water accepts gravity's fate at several waterfalls. In the lower hills, Highlanders canter along century-old paths on their richly caparisoned horses, and the noise of shepherds cracking their whips echoes around the valley. Among the abundant wildflowers, beautiful birds such as the malachite and Tacazze sunbird flit about.

Geography & Geology

The park stretches over 2400 sq km and ranges in altitude from 1500m to 4377m.

The Harenna Escarpment splits the park in two, running fracturelike from east to west. To the northeast of the escarpment lies the high-altitude plateau known as the Sanetti Plateau (4000m). The plateau is broken by a series of volcanic plugs and small peaks, including Tullu Deemtu, which at 4377m is the highest point in southern Ethiopia.

To the south, the land gradually falls away from the plateau, and a thick heather belt gives way to heavily forested areas known collectively as the Harenna Forest.

Wildlife
PLANTS

The park can be divided into three main zones. The northern area of the park, around the park headquarters at Dinsho, consists of grassy, riverine plains and bushland of mainly sagebrush and St John's wort. From 2500m to 3300m, woodland of mainly *Hagenia abyssinica* and *Juniperus procera* is found. The abundant wildflowers in the area include geranium, lobelia and alchemilla.

Higher up, montane grassland gives way to heather. Here the plant can be found not only as little bushes, but as large and mature trees.

The second zone, the Sanetti Plateau, is home to typical Afro-alpine plants, some of which have adapted to the extreme conditions by either remaining very small or becoming very large. The best known is the curious-looking giant lobelia (*Lobelia rhynchopetalum*), which can reach 5m in height. The silver *Helichrysum* or 'everlasting' flowers are the dominant wildflowers. Keep an eye out for the indigenous Abyssinian rose, with its lovely subtle scent.

The third habitat, the moist, tropical Harenna Forest, is home to tree species such as *Hagenia, Celtis* and *Podocarpus*.

ANIMALS

The Bale Mountains are known for their endemic wildlife, particularly the Ethiopian wolf and the mountain nyala.

The sighting of an Ethiopian wolf, the world's rarest canid, is a highlight of a trip to the Bale Mountains, and is almost guaranteed on the Sanetti Plateau. But there are plenty of other no-less-remarkable endemics to be seen, including Menelik's bushbuck and the giant molerat.

Other large mammals commonly seen in the northern area include grey duikers, Bohor reedbucks and warthogs. Serval cats and Anubis baboons are occasionally seen.

In the Harenna Forest, giant forest hogs, bushpigs, warthogs, colobus monkeys and

SOUTHERN ETHIOPIA

spotted hyena are all found, as well as leopards, lions and African hunting dogs. The last three are rarely seen.

Though most of you can't wait to get trekking, the area around the park headquarters at Dinsho is, ironically, the one place where many of the larger mammals are easily seen. The animals are less shy here and the early morning and late afternoon provide great photographic opportunities.

Bale is also famous for its incredible number of endemic birds – 16 at the last count. Unusually, the endemics are very easily seen. No self-respecting twitcher should leave the mountains off their itinerary! On the plateau, sightings of endemics (the blue-winged goose, wattled ibis,

thick-billed raven, Abyssinian longclaw, black-headed siskin, spot breasted plover and Rouget's rail) are almost guaranteed. The birdlife in the juniper forests around the park headquarters is outstanding too; try to spot the elusive Abyssinian catbirds and yellow-fronted parrots.

Near the park headquarters, a 1km nature trail leads up to Dinsho Hill, from where there are quite good views of the surrounding park. The little **museum** (admission free with park entrance; 8.30am-6.30pm) below headquarters is also worth a peek. Though tiny, it's crammed with various local stuffed animals including those not commonly seen, such as the honey badger, civet cat and aardvark. There also some interesting

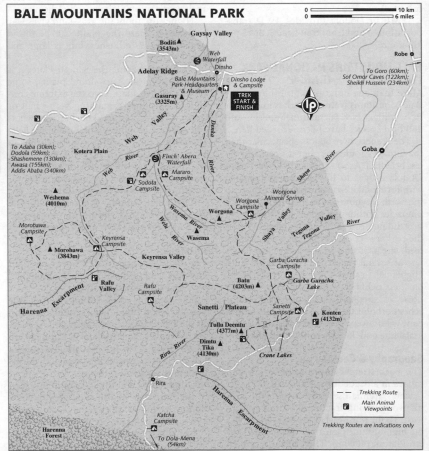

SOUTHERN ETHIOPIA

BALE MOUNTAINS NATIONAL PARK

0   10 km
0   6 miles

Gaysay Valley

Boditi ▲
(3543m)

Web
Waterfall
Dinsho

Robe ●

Adelay Ridge

To Goro (60km);
Sof Omar Caves (122km);
Sheikh Hussein (234km)

Bale Mountains
Park Headquarters
& Museum

Dinsho Lodge
& Campsite

Gasuray ▲
(3325m)

TREK
START &
FINISH

Goba ●

Web

Valley

Denka

Shaya

River

To Adaba (30km);
Dodola (59km);
Shashemene (130km);
Awasa (155km);
Addis Ababa (340km)

Kotera Plain

Web

River

Finch' Abera
Waterfall

Mararo
Campsite

River

Worgona
Mineral Springs

Sodota
Campsite

Weshema ▲
(4010m)

Wasema River

Worgona

Worgona
Campsite

Shaya Valley

Tegona   Valley

Tegona
River

Morobawa
Campsite

Keyrensa
Campsite

Web

River

Wasema

Morobawa ▲
(3843m)

Keyrensa Valley

Garba Guracha
Campsite

Batu ▲
(4203m)

Garba Guracha
Lake

Rafu
Valley

Rafu
Campsite

Sanetti   Plateau

Sanetti
Campsite

Konten ▲
(4132m)

Harenna   Escarpment

Tullu Deemtu ▲
(4377m)

Rira River

Dimtu
Tika ▲
(4130m)

Crane Lakes

Rira

Harema   Escarpment

Katcha
Campsite

Harenna
Forest

To Dola-Mena
(54km)

– – –   Trekking Route
        Main Animal
        Viewpoints

Trekking Routes are indications only

POTENT PLANTS

While trekking in the Bale Mountains, look out for the endemic plant *Kniphofia foliosa*, a member of the red-hot poker family, found quite commonly in the hills between 2050m and 4000m. The plant flowers from May to October and from December to January.

Long valued by the local Bale people for its medicinal properties, it's used to relieve stomach aches and cramps. Scientific investigation has revealed that the plant does in fact contain several anthraquinones including islandicin, which is found in fungi such as *Penicillium islandicum*!

information panels about conservation efforts, flora, fauna, and the local people.

Planning

All treks begin and end at park headquarters, which sits 2.5km from the village of Dinsho or 160km west of Shashemene.

Plan to arrive in the early afternoon, so you can sort out your trek for the following morning. A night spent in Dinsho is also a good start towards acclimatisation.

WHEN TO GO

The hottest and driest days here fall between December and February, but late September to early December is when the scenery is greenest and the wildflowers are out. Nighttime temperatures between December and January are also the coldest – frost and snow are occasionally seen.

PARK FEES & REGULATIONS

All fees are good for 48 hours and are payable at the **park headquarters** (admission Birr50, vehicles Birr10; camping Birr20; ⏲ 8.30am-12.30pm & 1.30-5.30pm Mon-Fri, 8am-12.30pm Sat). Outside these opening hours, someone can usually be summoned.

Fires are permitted only at campsites. Ensure guides and scouts only use dead erica wood or eucalyptus for their fires.

MAPS

Dinsho Lodge usually has a decent park map (Birr10) and a small Bale Mountains booklet (Birr10), which gives a good overview of the park's environment. *Bale Mountains: A Guidebook* by Ethiopian wolf expert Stuart

Williams is an excellent accompaniment; look for it in Addis Ababa.

SUPPLIES

There are a few stores in Dinsho selling bare basics (pasta, rice, tomato purée etc). If you're planning more elaborate menus, stock up in Addis Ababa. Eggs (Birr1 for three or four) and chickens (Birr20 to Birr25) can be bartered for in Dinsho or in the mountains.

Water is available in various places on the mountain but should be treated.

Bring your own camping gear or hire it in Addis Ababa – there's slim pickings in Dinsho.

GUIDES, SCOUTS & HORSES

Organising the 'team' (guide, scout, horses) is done at park headquarters and should be arranged the day before you plan to start.

All trekkers must be accompanied by a guide and an armed scout, though it's OK to walk around the woodland near park headquarters without them.

Guides work as freelancers, but by rote, so there's little point recommending individuals. Few scouts speak English, but they make willing additions to the team. Guides cost from Birr70 per day (one to three people) to Birr90 (four to 20 people); scouts Birr40 (one to 40 people).

Porters aren't available, but horses (Birr25 per day) and horse drivers (Birr30 per day) can be hired. The guide and scout will expect you to pay for at least one horse to carry their blankets and provisions.

Guides, scouts and handlers should provide food for themselves. Some bring token offerings or nothing at all and will then look to you for sustenance. Either check they have enough or bring extra. As if by compensation, the guide is happy to act as cook, and the scout to collect dead wood.

See the boxed text on p264 for post-trek tipping advice.

Trekking

Most trekking is fairly gentle and undemanding, following good, well-trodden paths or sheep tracks. But don't forget that altitude makes easy-looking terrain quite heavy going.

The trekking routes cover a relatively small area, and most treks last six days, or four days with a vehicle.

SOUTHERN ETHIOPIA

THE ETHIOPIAN WOLF

The Ethiopian wolf *(Canis simensis)* is the rarest canid (dog family member) in the world. Found only in the Ethiopian highlands, it's thought to be on the verge of extinction. Only about 600 wolves are believed to remain in the whole country.

Wolves are found on both sides of the Rift Valley, in the old provinces of Gonder, Wolo, Menz, Arsi and Bale. The Bale Mountains are home to the largest population (approximately 200). In Amharic, the wolf is known as *ky kebero* or 'red jackal'. Though the wolf does look like a jackal, its connection to the wolf family has firmly been established.

Living in family groups of around 13 animals, the wolves are highly territorial and family oriented. When the dominant female in the pack gives birth to her annual litter of between two and six pups, all members chip in, taking turns to feed, look after and play with the young. When it comes to hunting, however, the wolves forage alone. Any of the 19 rodent species found in Bale provide snacks. The giant molerats provide a feast and are the favourite food of the wolves.

The main threats to the wolves are rabies and canine distemper caught from the domestic dog population, and crossbreeding (male wolves with female dogs). In the Bale Mountains, the 1991–92 outbreak of rabies reduced the population from around 400 animals to 120. In 1995 distemper also took its toll.

Loss of habitat to livestock and cultivation (such as in north and south Wolo), and local superstition are other obstacles to be overcome. Locals believe that the antirabies vaccine changes the character of their dogs, or renders them less efficient as guard dogs. It's also considered very bad luck if a wolf crosses your path. In the past wolves have been deliberately run over or shot by truck drivers.

Current measures to try and save the animal from extinction include an antirabies vaccination, a sterilisation programme for local domestic dog populations and local education. There is still talk of starting a captive breeding programme in the future. Though it's still threatened, the Bale population of wolves now looks healthier than it has in decades.

Please review the Safety Guidelines for Trekking (p254) and Responsible Trekking (p255) boxed texts before lacing up.

The following routes and approximate trekking times have been devised in consultation with local guides.

CLASSIC ROUTE
Day One
Work your way southwest up the Web Valley towards the Finch' Abera Waterfall (two or three hours from the park headquarters), before continuing on to Mararo, where there's a pleasant campsite.

Day Two
Keep an eye out for giant molerats while trekking through the Wasema Valley. Next, start climbing up to the Sanetti Plateau as you approach Mt Batu (six to eight hours).

Day Three
Bag Mt Batu before you walk to the picturesque campsite situated in the Tegona Valley under the sheer cliffs beside the Garba Guracha Lake (six hours). The campsite is a great spot for birds of prey. Lammergeyers,

buzzards and eagles are all commonly seen here.

Day Four
Trek to the Crane Lakes (six hours; marked on some maps as the 'Alpine Lakes'). Although known for their water birds, they're a great place to glimpse Ethiopian wolves. A detour can be made to Tullu Deemtu (4377m), which affords good views from the summit. The mountain itself is little more than a monotonous scree slope. This area is close to Goba–Dola-Mena road, which means it's possible to end your trek here (if you've pre-arranged a 4WD pick-up in Goba or if you're patient enough to hitch).

Day Five
Descend off the Sanetti Plateau to Worgona (six or seven hours). A good detour from Worgona is the nearby mineral springs.

Day Six
Follow the Denka River down to Dinsho (six hours).

(Continued on page 189)

Angels painted the ceiling of Debre Berhan Selassie church (p122), Gonder, Ethiopia

Priest outside octagonal Entoto Maryam Church (p106) near Addis Ababa, Ethiopia

FRANCES LINZEE GOR

Bags filled with *berbere* (special Ethiopian blend of spices), Mekele's old market (p151), Ethiopia

Traditional Christian priest in full regalia with Ethiopian crosses outside Bet Amanuel (p160), Lalibela, Ethiopia

DAVID

FRANCES LINZEE GORDON

A guide points from the summit of Imet Gogo (p129) to the panorama of the Simien Mountains, Ethiopia

Massawa (p339) boasts quite diverse architecture, reflecting different influences, Eritrea

Coffee pot (p307) and cups seen from above, Dahlak Kebir, Eritrea

Robed priests celebrating the festival of Meskel (p261), Eritrea

PATRICK BEN LUKE SYDER

Men on the steps of the Great Mosque
(Kulafah Al Rashidin; p314), Asmara, Eritrea

FRANCES LINZEE GORDON

Intricate wood and tile work on damaged doors of
the old Imperial Palace (p341), Massawa, Eritrea

Enda Mariam Orthodox Cathedral (p315), Asmara, Eritrea

JEAN-BERNARD CA

(Continued from page 184)

THE KEYRENSA VALLEY LOOP

This six- to seven-day loop takes in Garba Guracha Lake and the mineral springs near Worgona.

Day one Dinsho–Sodota (four hours).
Day two Sodota–Keyrensa campsite (five to six hours).
Day three Keyrensa–Rafu campsite (five to six hours).
Day four Rafu–Garba Guracha campsite (five hours).
Day five Garba Guracha–Worgona campsite (five hours).
Day six Worgona–Dinsho (six hours).

ALTERNATIVE ROUTES

One-day excursions include walks up the Web Valley to Gasuray Peak (3325m) and Adelay Ridge. The Web Gorge takes around 1½ hours to reach, and is good for seeing colobus monkeys. Go early in the morning.

For a very pretty walk that includes birds and a good chance of seeing the Ethiopian wolf (and the slightest chance of spotting a leopard), go to the Finch' Abera Waterfall (two to three hours' walk one way). You could also spend the night at the nearby campsite. Another good overnight excursion is to the Kotera Plain, where Ethiopian wolves are often seen. The walk takes five hours one way.

For those who want to spend longer periods in the mountains, the almost totally unexplored Harenna Forest offers great hiking potential.

Nontrekkers

If you've limited time, or can't walk far, you can still see a great deal of wildlife, particularly in the forest around park headquarters where mountain nyala, warthogs and other species reside.

With your own vehicle, the top of Tullu Deemtu can also be reached by 4WD, via Goba and the Sanetti Plateau. If you reach the plateau by 7am, you're almost guaranteed a sighting of the Ethiopian wolf; they spend this time intently searching for food. Failing an early start, the late afternoon is your next best bet.

If you approach the wolves from downwind, you can get very close indeed. If you're lucky, you may spot a klipspringer here too.

A pleasant, short stroll from the Goba–Dola-Mena road is to the Crane Lakes, an excellent spot for birds (though in the dry season some of the lakes evaporate).

Wattled cranes often nest here during June and September.

Sleeping & Eating

DINSHO

Dinsho Lodge (tw with shared bathroom Birr50, 3-/5-/11-bed dm Birr25/15/10) Located at park headquarters and surrounded by endemic species – a stay here is a no-brainer. It feels like an abandoned ski chalet, with lots of aging rustic charm. It's usually pretty cold, but you can buy wood (make sure it's eucalyptus or dead erica) in the village to stock the lodge's fireplace and to heat the sauna. A large bundle should cost Birr20. The rooms are clean but there's little in the way of bedding, so you'll have to use your sleeping bag. Showers are cold…really cold. During the high season, reservations should be made in advance by writing directly to: The Warden, Dinsho Lodge, PO Box 107, Goba, Ethiopia.

Camping (per person per 48hr Birr20) Three basic but scenic sites sit on Dinsho Hill behind the lodge. Expect oodles of wildlife.

Hotel Tsahayi (meals Birr5-10) This hotel makes the town's best grub. Its bedrooms (Birr10) are dark and dank.

ON THE MOUNTAINS

Camping (per person per 48hr Birr20) The national park has established various sites for camping, though there are still not yet any huts, shelters or other facilities. You'll need to be fully independent with tent, sleeping bag and cooking gear.

Getting There & Away

If coming from Addis Ababa, catch an early morning bus to Robe (Birr48, 12 hours) or Goba (Birr49.85, 13 hours) and leap off in Dinsho. If the return buses to Addis Ababa are full when passing Dinsho, head to Shashemene (Birr25, seven hours) and go from there. One daily bus runs to Robe (Birr8, one hour).

By private vehicle, it's possible to reach Dinsho from Addis Ababa in a day if you make a dawn start.

Getting Around

A great way to take in a lot of the park without your own vehicle is to catch one of the buses or trucks that ply the Goba–Dola-Mena road. The road takes you right through the park, up over the Sanetti Plateau and down into the Harenna Forest. You can explore the area from the road, then hitch back, which isn't too difficult, but don't leave it too late in the day.

ROBE ሮቤ
pop 43,713 / elev 2600m

For most people, their love affair with Robe is brief and unmemorable. Feelings, sparked by an attractive eucalyptus-lined river on the northern edge of town, are typically extinguished seconds later by the sight of Robe itself. It's a mucky 1½-street town, 25km east of Dinsho, that's growing rapidly and is due to host the region's only university.

Islam is strong here and you'll notice a palpable change in the atmosphere from points further west. There's nothing here to warrant a visit, but it makes a convenient stop en route to the Sof Omar Caves.

At the Thursday market, seek out the delicious local acacia honey, the attractive basketry and the heavy cotton *buluko* (togas).

Sleeping & Eating

Bekele Mola (☎ 0226 650065; d/tw Birr40/52) On the road towards Goba, 350m north of the bus station, Bekele Mola has the town's most comfortable accommodation. Three-room blocks of rooms are set in a grassy garden with several huge acacia trees. Inside they're big and bright, but the paint is cracking and rugs are weary. The restaurant serves local fare and bland *faranji* food.

Bale Park Hotel (☎ 0226 651197; s with shared bathroom Birr12, s/d Birr20/25) Immediately north of Bekele Mola, just off the main drag, is this cheap and cheerful choice. The double rooms are the prize winners – they're reasonably sized and sport comfy beds. The cheaper singles are much smaller, though they still have access to hot showers. All toilets are of the squat variety. It's signposted as 'Parkii Baalee'.

Mana Nyaata Jeddah (meals Birr5-15) This Muslim restaurant, at the north end of the main drag, is known for *hanid*, a meal of rice, *injera*, French fries and goat meat. It tastes more Middle Eastern than Ethiopian.

Fountain Café (snacks Birr1-1.50) Cakes, coffee and smiles served here. Next to the main roundabout.

Shamshat Cafe (snacks Birr3-7) Just east of Fountain Café, Shamshat is good for a breakfast omelette.

Getting There & Away

The bus station is at the southern end of town. One bus runs daily to Dinsho (Birr8, one hour), Shashemene (Birr25.50, eight hours) and Addis Ababa (Birr48, 12 hours). Two daily buses serve Goro (Birr9, two hours). There are regular services to nearby Goba (Birr1.50, 20 minutes).

GOBA ጎባ
pop 33,000 / elev 2743m

Goba, the old capital of the Bale region, is 13km south of Robe. Goba is in a state of decline and Ethiopian Airlines has even cancelled its flights here. The only reason to visit this ramshackle town is to access the stunning Sanetti Plateau within Bale Mountains National Park.

Information

Commercial Bank (⊙ 8-11.30am & 1.30-4pm Mon-Fri, 8-11.30am Sat) Changes US-dollars cash only.

Goba Hospital (☎ 0226 610258; ⊙ 24hr) This local hospital is 1km north of town.

Nagi Shope (per hr Birr21; ⊙ 2-7pm) Its Internet connection is as sketchy as its opening hours.

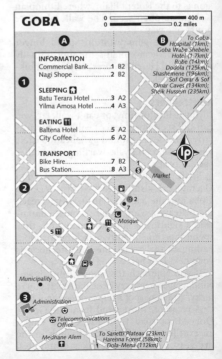

GOBA

INFORMATION	
Commercial Bank	1 B2
Nagi Shope	2 B2

SLEEPING	
Batu Terara Hotel	3 A2
Yilma Amosa Hotel	4 A3

EATING	
Baltena Hotel	5 A2
City Coffee	6 A2

TRANSPORT	
Bike Hire	7 B2
Bus Station	8 A3

To Goba Hospital (1km); Goba Wabe Shebele Hotel (1.7km); Robe (14km); Dodola (125km); Shashemene (196km); Sof Omar & Sof Omar Caves (134km); Sheik Hussein (235km)

Market

Mosque

Municipality

Administration

Telecommunications Office

Medhane Alem

To Sanetti Plateau (23km); Harenna Forest (58km); Dola-Mena (112km)

SOUTHERN ETHIOPIA

Sleeping & Eating

Goba Wabe Shebele Hotel (☎ 0226 610041; s/tw Birr135/170, ste Birr180-345) For this price, you'd expect more than just clean rooms and toilets. Only the expensive suites have any character, with most rooms being boringly bland. The restaurant is well regarded and prepares Western dishes, including three-course set meals (Birr37.50). It's almost 2km north of town.

Batu Terara Hotel (☎ 0226 610712; s Birr25) This place is bruised and battered but bright enough.

Yilma Amosa Hotel (d with shared bathroom Birr25, d Birr50) This place is past its prime and the rude owner (the joys of undercover research!) smugly charges *faranjis* more than double for everything. Make it an option of last resort.

Baltena Hotel (mains Birr6-10; ☯ 6am-midnight) This garden restaurant is the best place for a local meal.

City Coffee (snacks Birr1; ☯ 6am-9pm) Sip coffee, inhale cake and imagine what life behind bars is like in this fortified café.

Getting There & Around

Regular minibuses serve Robe (Birr1.50, 20 minutes), while two daily buses reach Goro (Birr10, 2½ hours). Robe offers more reliable services to Shashemene and Addis Ababa.

Daily Isuzu trucks (inside/outside Birr40/20, five to six hours) are the best option to Dola-Mena and the Sanetti Plateau, especially on Dola-Mena's market days (Wednesday and Saturday); inquire at the bus station.

4WDs, with driver and fuel, can usually be rented in Goba (ask around the bus station). Postnegotiation prices should be about Birr750 per day or Birr 250 for a short trip to the plateau.

Always check on the condition of the road to Dola-Mena as it's occasionally impassable after rains.

Bikes can be hired to get around town (Birr3 per hour).

SOF OMAR CAVES
የሶፍ ኦማር ዋሻዎች

If the Web River's water and its suspended sediments weren't the artists and if the sublime carvings weren't welded to the Earth's insides, sections of the Sof Omar Caves would be housed in some of the

world's finest galleries. They're simply that stunning.

Accessed from the village of Sof Omar, 122km east of Robe, the labyrinth of caverns stretches some 16km through limestone hills. Unless you intend on swimming into the darkness (never a good idea!), you can only explore the first 1.7km on foot. Luckily, the walkable portion houses the remarkable formations known as the Chamber of Columns, the dome and the balcony. With vaulted chambers, flying buttresses, massive pillars and fluted archways, these sections almost resemble an Antonio Gaudí cathedral.

The caves have been an important religious site since ancient times and despite being greatly venerated by Muslims in the area, due to Sheikh Sof Omar reputedly taking refuge here in the early days of Islam, many pagan rites and ceremonies seem to carry on.

Some Sof Omar villagers ask Birr100 for a tour, but Birr30 ought to be adequate. Wear footwear you don't mind getting wet and always bring a torch, though turning it off once in the depths is as eerie as it is extraordinary.

Once in the light of day, twitchers should search for Salvadori's serin, a rare endemic species.

Getting There & Away

From the village of Goro, about 60km east of Robe, infrequent pick-ups leave for Sof Omar (Birr22, 1½ hours). Sof Omar's market day (Saturday) is the only day there's guaranteed transport. Two daily buses connect Robe and Goro (Birr9, two hours).

SHEIKH HUSSEIN ሼክ ሑሴን

Located north of Sof Omar, Sheikh Hussein is southern Ethiopia's most important centre of Muslim pilgrimage and attracts thousands of pilgrims every year. The complex consists of an attractive little mosque, various tombs, and shrines and caves that are found within an hour's walk east. It's said Sheikh Hussein himself used the caves to seek some peace and quiet for prayer.

At least 500 years old, it's dedicated to the 13th-century holy man, who was responsible for the conversion of many Bale and Arsi Oromo to Islam. Pilgrims come here to make wishes and to offer thanks for wishes fulfilled. Feast days are during

May and October, with minor ones during February and September; the exact dates depend on the lunar calendar.

This peaceful and atmospheric place is open to people of all faiths. Local religious leaders will give you a tour. It's customary to leave a small contribution of Birr20. The most colourful time to visit is during a major pilgrimage.

Getting There & Away
Unless you time your visit with a pilgrimage, you really need your own vehicle to visit Sheikh Hussein. Daily minibuses from Robe do reach Jara (Birr25, six to seven hours), which is 57km south of Sheikh Hussein, but from there you're on your own.

DOLA-MENA ዶላ ሜና
Although Dola-Mena's intense heat, striking Somali herdsmen and camels are a novelty after the Bale Mountains, the main reason to visit this bleak town is for the captivating 110km journey south from Goba.

After leaving Goba you'll traverse the eastern part of the Bale Mountains National Park (see Nontrekkers, p189), cross the Harenna Escarpment and wind up onto the lofty Sanetti Plateau itself. The route is the highest all-weather road in Africa and must rank among the continent's most surreal.

The road takes you through the extraordinary *Podocarpus* woodland known as the **Harenna Forest**. With its twisted trunks draped in 'old man beard' lichens, mosses and ferns, and with cloud swirling all around, the forest is straight out of a Grimm brothers fairy tale.

The forest, undoubtedly one of the most remarkable in Ethiopia, is home to a whole host of endemic plants, amphibians (see the boxed text, p60) and insects, as well as wild coffee. Unfortunately local demand for firewood is now seriously threatening the forest.

After a steady descent you'll eventually find yourself in dusty Dola-Mena. The **Makuriya Mengistu Hotel** (d with shared bathroom Birr10), centrally placed on the main drag, is the best of the basic options. You'll have to dodge cows on the way to the toilet and put up with some occasional loud music, but the people are very friendly. There are some decent unnamed local restaurants near the mosque.

Getting There & Away
See Goba's Getting There & Away section (p191) for transport details to Dola-Mena.

If you don't want to backtrack, you'll have wait for a rare truck (one or two per week) heading 179km south to Negele Borena.

There is no fuel station in Dola-Mena, but a black market exists, if you're desperate.

NEGELE BORENA ነገሌ ቦረና
Negele Borena sits at an important crossroads of the remote southeast and serves as a useful transport hub. Fervent birders will undoubtedly pass through here while tracking rare endemic species like the Sidamo long-clawed lark, Degodi lark, Prince Ruspoli's turaco and Salvadori's seedeater.

The **Green Hotel** (s with shared bathroom Birr20, s Birr30), southwest of the bus station, is simple and clean. Its restaurant isn't a bad choice for local fare.

Getting There & Away
A couple of trucks per week serve Mega (Birr40, eight to 12 hours), to the southwest. There are no direct services to Dila or Yabelo, so you'll have to make short hops from village to village.

SOUTH TO MOYALE

The northern half of this route will take you through verdant *enset* plantations (false-banana tree found in much of southern Ethiopia, used to produce a breadlike staple also known as *enset*), past wild coffee and enable you to visit some of southern Ethiopia's most important archaeological sites. Travel the southern half and you may witness singing wells, salt-filled craters and a rare bird or two. Complete the journey and you'll be wiping sweat from your brow and drool from your chin as you stare across the baking plains and desolate glory that is northern Kenya.

DILA ዲላ
pop 48,348 / elev 1592m
No matter how unremarkable this administrative centre and college town is, there's no denying the importance of its surroundings. To the south sit two of southern Ethiopia's most important stelae fields and resting to its northwest are little-known ancient rock carvings.

Before visiting the sites, you must pay Birr30 at the **Gedeo tourism office** (Gede'iinxxe Zooneke; ☎ 0463 312697; ◷ 8am-12.30pm & 1.30-5.30pm Mon-Fri) in Dila. Since the archaeological sites are tricky to find, especially the rock carvings, organise a guide while you're at the office. The office is 250m west of the main drag, down the road opposite the Brook Pharmacy.

With over 80 stelae variously carved with facial features, phalluses etc, **Tutu Fella** is the most impressive site. It's accessed from an eastern turn-off, some 3km south of Wenago or 17km south from Dila.

The tapered stones at **Tututi** also mark graves, but are generally larger (up to 7.5m tall) and lack the detailed carving seen at Tutu Fella. The Tututi field rests on a hill 2.3km west of Chalba village, which sits 8.5km south of the Tutu Fella turn-off.

About 10km northwest of Dila are the remote **Manchiti rock engravings**. A vertical rock face hosts an ancient herd of some 50 stylised cows, which were chiselled over 3000 years ago.

Sleeping & Eating

Lalibela Pension (☎ 0463 312300; d with shared bathroom Birr20, d Birr40) Although the frilly bedcovers may induce convulsions in male customers, this place fits everyone's bill. Bathrooms (shared and private) are sparkling and the Birr40 rooms even have satellite TV. It's signposted off the main street west of Dilla Rendez-Vous, a haven of pastries.

Zeleke Hotel (☎ 0463 312834; d with shared bathroom Birr15, d Birr25) The Birr25 rooms are clean, and have large beds with soft foam mattresses. The shared bathrooms are on the smelly side. It's at the south end of town, near the bus station.

Aregash Tourist Lodge (☎ 0462 251136; alltour@ ethionet.et; d Birr300) Located in the village of Yirga Alem, midway between Dila and Awasa, this new lodge is a brilliant choice. Accommodation is housed in elaborately woven Dorze huts, which sit in garden surroundings.

Warka Hotel (mains Birr5-7) The spot for tasty Ethiopian fare in Dila. It's found one block west of the post office.

Getting There & Away

At 6am a bus departs for Yabelo (Birr25, four hours) and Moyale (Birr34, seven hours). Four or five buses run daily to Shashemene (Birr14, three hours) via Awasa (Birr10, 2½ hours). A few minibuses also serve these four destinations.

YABELO ያበሎ

Yabelo, 5km west of the main Moyale–Shashemene road, makes a convenient base for a visit to Yabelo Wildlife Sanctuary. It's also the southern gateway to the Omo Valley via Konso.

Sitting at the Yabelo junction on the main Moyale–Shashemene road, **Yabello Motel** (☎ 0464 460237; tw/d with shared bathroom Birr25/50, d Birr100) is the town's only tourist-class hotel. The pricey doubles, with mosquito nets and satellite TV, are clean and comfortable. The cheaper options aren't nearly as special and *faranji* prices are in full effect. The restaurant pumps out expensive Western fare (up to Birr30).

With glass windows instead of wood shutters, **Girooserii Hawwii** (s/d with shared bathroom Birr15/20) is the brightest of the cheap hotels. It's found just north of the market.

On Yabelo's main street, **Girooserii Salaami** (mains Birr5-10) is the most popular local restaurant.

A few minibuses leave daily for Moyale (Birr25, 3½ hours), while only one bus and one minibus serve Dila (Birr30, five hours). If you're out of luck in Yabelo, head to the Shashemene–Moyale road and try to hop on the buses heading north or south. A few daily Isuzu trucks run to Konso (Birr25, three hours).

YABELO WILDLIFE SANCTUARY ያበሎ የዱር አራዊት ፓርክ

Covering an area of 2496 sq km, the **Yabelo Wildlife Sanctuary** (admission free) was originally created to protect the endemic Swayne's hartebeest. However, it's now better known for two truly unique range-restricted bird species. Although commonly seen within

---

COWS & CROWNS

Cattle rearing is the mainstay of the southeast's economy, and cows are greatly prized. Cows supply meat, milk, butter and blood for food, as wells as dung for fuel and for building houses. Ownership of cattle confers great social status on Oromo men: traditionally, if a herdsman owns more than 1000, he's entitled to wear a crown.

the sanctuary, the Stresemann's bush crow and white-tailed swallow are not found anywhere else in the world. Why they never stray more than 100km from here is still anyone's guess. The semi-endemic brown sawwing is also found here.

The 25 mammal species inhabiting the acacia woodland and savannah grass include Burchell's zebras, dik-diks, greater and lesser kudus, gerenuks and Grant's gazelles, all quite commonly seen. The golden jackal and ostrich are sometimes spotted.

Only visitors with a park scout are allowed to enter. Scouts (per day Birr50) are available from the **park office** (☎ 0464 460087; ⏱ 8.30am-12.30pm & 1.30-5.30pm Mon-Fri) in the town of Yabelo.

YABELO TO MEGA

The 100km between Yabelo and Mega offers up an interesting array of cultural and physical phenomena.

Delve into Borena territory near Dublock, about 70km south of Yabelo, where several of the famous *ela* or **'singing wells'** (below) have been operating for more than a century.

To find them you'll need a guide from Dublock. Borena chieftains now charge entrance fees, which vary widely depending on how many people they bring to work the well. Expect to pay about Birr80 per group. To see the real water gathering (rather than a performance), come during dry season (January through March) when the cattle come to drink. Getting to some wells involves quite long walks.

The village of **El Sod**, around 20km south of Dublock, lies beside one of Ethiopia's largest salt deposits. Known as the **House of Salt**, it's famed for its 100m-deep crater lake, one of four in the region. The lake is about 800m across and is so dark, it looks like an oil slick. Valuable, muddy, black salt has been extracted from the lake for centuries. Today, donkeys laden with the mud continue to toil up the steep sides of the crater.

From the village, it's a 30-minute walk into the crater and a one hour walk up (admission Birr50 per person and per vehicle, Birr100 for two compulsory guides). It's best to visit during the morning's cooler temperatures.

A couple kilometres north of Mega, you'll see vestiges of an old **Italian fort** overlooking the distant plains below. Though impressive from the road, there's little to see within.

At least nine buses ply the Addis Ababa–Moyale road from towns north and south of Dublock and can drop you off at the various turn-offs. Hitching is usually required to reach the House of Salt.

MOYALE ሞያሌ
elev 1090m

There's only one truly compelling reason to visit Moyale: Kenya.

Although a seemingly porous border cuts the one-street town of Moyale in two, the difference in feel between the two sides is immediately palpable. The Kenyan side, with dust-swept dirt streets, expensive petrol being served from barrels and ragtag vehicles trundling in from the punishing northern plains, has a true wild frontier atmosphere.

THE SINGING WELLS OF THE BORENA

The Borena are seminomadic pastoralists who occupy lands that stretch from northern Kenya to the dry, hot plains around Yabelo. Their lives revolve entirely around their cattle and during the long dry season, it's a constant struggle to keep their vast herds alive. To combat the problem, the Borena have developed their own peculiar solution: a series of wells dug deep into the earth. Each Borena family and each clan is assigned its own well.

A series of water troughs are dug close to each well's mouth. Approaching them is a long channel that drops to about 10m below the ground level, which funnels the cattle to the troughs. It's just wide enough to allow two single columns of cattle to pass one another.

When it's time to water the cattle, the men create a human ladder down the well (which can be up to 30m deep), tossing buckets of water between one another from the bottom up to the top, where the troughs are gradually filled. The work is very strenuous, and the men often sing in harmony to encourage one another as well as to reassure the cattle. Several hundred or even thousand cattle come to drink at a time; it's a memorable and unique sight.

Information

Black market moneychangers hang around the border and change Birr and Kenyan shillings (KSh). For convenience, Birr1 is about KSh8.50.

ETHIOPIA

Commercial Bank (☽ 8am-noon & 1.30-4pm Mon-Fri, 8am-noon Sat) Changes travellers cheques and cash. It doesn't exchange Kenyan shillings or buy back unused Ethiopian birr. It's 2km north of the border.

KENYA

Kenya Commercial Bank (☽ 9am-3pm Mon-Fri, to 11am Sat) Changes cash (US dollars, euros and pound sterling) and travellers cheques (KSh50 charge per leaf, plus KSh300 commission). Ethiopian birr are not accepted.

Post office (☽ 8am-5pm Mon-Fri, to noon Sat) With Internet and cardphones.

Sleeping & Eating

ETHIOPIA

Gihon Hotel (☎ 0464 440065; d with shared bathroom Birr15, d Birr20) This place is cheap, clean and has one of Moyale's best restaurants. The bathrooms (shared and private) are weak but passable. It's 2.2km from the border.

Bekele Mola Hotel (☎ 0464 440030; camping Birr20, d Birr40) Located 150m north of Gihon, this dog-eared hotel has large rooms with private bathrooms and mosquito nets. Sadly, there's no running water so showers come in buckets.

Tourist Hotel (s with shared toilet Birr15) Sheltered behind its cool Rasta-inspired bar, this sleeping option just over the Ethiopian border has decent rooms with private showers. The shared toilets are nothing to sing about, but thankfully they're nothing to scream about either.

Hagos Hotel (meals Birr8-12) Have your last Ethiopian meal here. There's a terrace out back and some shady seating below a flowering tree. It's just up from the border.

Ethio-Kenya (breakfast Birr3-6) Across from the Hagos Hotel, Ethio-Kenya's leaf-laden terrace is a great place for breakfast and an animated location for drinks later in the day.

KENYA

Tawakal Hotel & Lodging (s/tw with shared bathroom KSh150/200) This place, with a relaxing TV lounge, has comfortable beds in large, rather dark rooms. Unfortunately the toilets are a cockroach committee room during the evenings, so go during daylight hours! If that last bit didn't turn you off, the restaurant (meals KSh80 to KSh150) serves decent local meals. It's off the main drag and is northeast of the bank.

Baghdad Hotel II (meals KSh80-150) On the main drag just south of the post office, this is a popular place to eat – sit down, swipe some flies and get stuffed.

Prison Canteen (meals KSh70-150) This kitsch place, with its zebra motifs and thatched pavilions, is the canteen for prison workers and makes an atmospheric place for a meal and cold beer. It lurks west of the police station on a side street.

Getting There & Away

Two early morning buses depart daily for Addis Ababa (Birr79, 1½ days), one overnighting at Dila (Birr40, seven hours), the other at Shashemene (Birr48, 11½ hours). A few minibuses leave daily for Yabelo (Birr25, 3½ hours).

For those driving, fill up on the Ethiopian side – petrol is half the cost and more reliable.

For details about heading south into Kenya, see p275.

ARBA MINCH & AROUND

Bordered by verdant mountains and home to Ethiopia's two largest, and arguably most beautiful, Rift Valley lakes, this region offers an eyeful. Ogle zebras in the resurgent Nechisar National Park and watch your fingers and toes at Lake Chamo's crocodile market, where they're the ones doing the shopping.

While travelling to the region from Shashemene, you'll pass through some of the most fertile land in Ethiopia, where abundant fruit and cotton are grown. Don't miss the bananas – no bigger than your middle finger, but as sweet as honey. The local *gishta* fruit is worth tasting!

ARBA MINCH አርባ ምንጭ

pop 73,072 / elev 1400m to 1600m

Arba Minch is southwestern Ethiopia's largest city. Although its grubby streets and chaotic atmosphere won't immediately endear it to you, one drink on the terrace of Bekele Mola Hotel's lofty terrace and you'll start to see the city's charm. Stretched scenically below is the Rift Valley and waters of nearby lakes.

Considering Arba Minch is also on the doorstep of the rejuvenated Nechisar National Park and the highland towns of Dorze and Chencha, you'd do well to base yourself here for a few days.

Orientation & Information

The town consists of two settlements connected by a 4km stretch of asphalt: Sikela, to the north, and Shecha, perched on the hill overlooking the lakes to the south.

There are countless private telecentres that charge Birr25 per minute for international calls. Cheaper is Shecha's telecommunications office, which charges standard international rates (see p267).

Arba Minch Hospital (Map p197; ☎ 0448 810123; 🕑 24hr) The region's best hospital, just south of Sikela.

Commercial Bank (Map p197; Sikela; 🕑 8.30am–noon & 2-3.30pm Mon-Fri, 8.30am–noon Sat) Changes American Express travellers cheques and cash (euros and US dollars).

ESA Business Center (Map p197; per hr Birr30) Sikela's best Internet connections.

Sol Internet Caffe (Map p197; per hr Birr30) Shecha's only Internet option.

Tourism office (Map p197; ☎ 0468 810127; Shecha; 🕑 8.30am-12.30pm & 1.30-5.30pm Mon-Fri) Bring any question to the excellent and indefatigable Kapo Kansa. He can also suggest treks in the park, surrounding forests and Guge Mountains as well as bird-watching expeditions. He can organise everything from guides (within/outside town Birr50/100) to boats.

Sights & Activities

LAKES ABAYA & CHAMO

Ringed by savannah plains and divided by the 'Bridge of God', Lakes Abaya and Chamo (Map p199) are truly beautiful. Measuring 1160 sq km, Lake Abaya is the Rift Valley's largest lake. If out on the Abaya's waters, try to spot the Hararus in their high-prowed *wogolo* boats. Made of *isoke* (a very

lightweight local wood), the boats are capable of carrying quite heavy loads (including cattle).

The lake's peculiar red waters are a result of the massive crocodile population's regular feeding frenzies on unfortunate cattle. No, we're not serious! Elevated natural concentrations of suspended ferrous hydroxide is the lacklustre and all-too-boring answer of science.

If you impulsively bellowed 'cool' when you thought hungry crocs coloured Lake Abaya, you'll love Lake Chamo. Check out its massive crocodiles at the aptly named crocodile market (see following).

The colour of Chamo? An unadventurous blue.

CROCODILE MARKET

Where the Kolfo River empties into Lake Chamo, you'll find oodles of fat and famous crocodiles sunning themselves. The area, simply known as the crocodile market (Map p199), is truly one of Africa's best crocodile displays.

The safest and most rewarding way to visit is by boat. The launching point is 8km southeast of Shecha, down a dirt track leading east of the Konso road. Although it's only a 15- to 30-minute boat ride to the spot, a minimum of 1½ hours should be allowed for the trip. It's best to visit during late afternoon or early morning. Remember to keep your limbs in the boat! Keep an eye out for hippos and birdlife.

The crocodile market can also be approached by land through Nechisar National Park (p199). However, be very careful and bring an armed park scout (Birr30); you won't find it otherwise. Scouts are typically mandatory; park rangers are wary of you being lost to the crocs (as still happens with local fishermen).

Whether you're visiting by water or land, you'll need to pay park entrance fees (Birr70 per person) at park headquarters (p200) prior to your visit.

See Getting Around (p199) for boat-hiring information.

FORTY SPRINGS

Arba Minch or 'Forty Springs' (Map p199) derives its name from the innumerable little springs that bubble up in the evergreen forest covering the flats below the town.

The semipluvial vegetation is home to good birdlife and a variety of mammals. It's a nice hike from town and you can bathe in the pools around the springs. It's also a great place for a picnic.

A visit to the springs (the town's main water supply) requires a permission paper from the **Arba Minch Water Supplies Service** (Map p197; ☎ 0468 810252; ☺ 8am-noon & 1-4pm Mon-Fri), halfway between Sikela and Shecha. It's a simple, quick and free procedure. It's not worth trying to sneak into the springs – guards have fired warning shots at travellers doing so!

The springs lie within the Nechisar National Park and there's talk that park entrance fees may be charged in the near future; inquire at the tourism office.

To get here, take the road towards Nechisar National Park; stay right when the road forks. The springs are a further 2.8km.

ARBA MINCH CROCODILE RANCH
The government **crocodile ranch** (Map p199; admission Birr20; ☺ 8.30am-noon & 1.30-6.30pm) currently contains around 10,000 crocs and serves four purposes: to boost the crocodile industry, to educate the public about the economic and ecological importance of crocodiles, to conserve crocs, and to attract tourism. Of the 10,000 crocs, 8000 are less than a year old and are still hidden within incubators. The remainder are kept in cramped quarters with others of the same age.

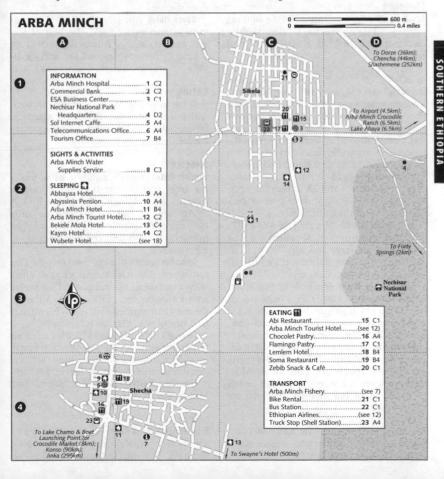

ARBA MINCH

0 — 600 m
0 — 0.4 miles

To Dorze (36km);
Chencha (44km);
Shashemene (252km)

Sikela

To Airport (4.5km);
Arba Minch Crocodile
Ranch (6.5km);
Lake Abaya (6.5km)

To Forty
Springs (2km)

Nechisar
National
Park

Shecha

To Lake Chamo & Boat
Launching Point.for
Crocodile Market (8km);
Konso (90km);
Jinka (295km)

To Swayne's Hotel (500m)

Although it's slightly exciting to walk over the open compounds, a visit here is more depressing than inspiring. Most of the hapless crocs are killed at the age of five (when the skin is the best quality), and will end up as handbags or belts in Middle Eastern markets.

More enjoyable is the rickety platform by the lake's edge. It's good for spotting hippos in the late afternoon.

The guided tour (20 to 30 minutes) is free, but you should tip afterwards.

The farm is situated off the Addis Ababa road, about 7km from the Sikela. Walk, bike, hitch or get a contract taxi (Birr50 one way, Birr80 to Birr100 return).

Sleeping

Most of Shecha's accommodation options outgun Sikela's. Shecha is also slightly cooler, quieter and has a better choice of restaurants.

SHECHA

Swayne's Hotel (☎ 0468 811895; www.swayneshotel .com; camping Birr50, s/tw Birr200/250) Woven Dorze huts envelop half of this hotel's bungalows and give the place a quirky, yet traditional feel. Colourful local artwork hangs from the modern rooms' walls, hand-carved wooden furniture sits on spotless floors and colourful lamps shine light on it all. Book a room number between 4 and 22, as they have private terraces boasting stunning lake views. The hotel is southeast of Shecha.

Abyssinia Pension (Map p197; ☎ 0468 810381; d Birr125) A quiet option, Abyssinia has new rooms that are large and very clean. Considering it lacks hot showers, it's a little bit expensive – try negotiating.

Bekele Mola Hotel (Map p197; ☎ 0468 810046; camping per tent Birr40, s Birr179-225, d Birr266-312) Its terrace is a city highlight, but the rooms are very plain, well worn and overpriced (despite rates including breakfast and dinner).

Wubete Hotel (Map p197; ☎ 0468 811629; d with shared bathroom Birr20, d Birr40) This place is pretty friendly and rooms are quite clean. Mosquito nets are the norm and most toilets even don seats! For doubles, the beds are rather small.

Other options:

Arba Minch Hotel (Map p197; ☎ 0468 810206; s with shared bathroom Birr30, s/tw Birr40/60) Simple, spartan and reasonably clean. Quieter than others.

Abbayaa Hotel (Map p197; ☎ 0468 810181; d Birr40) Best of the worst. Do the dozen 'Roach Killer' bottles at reception tell you there's a problem, or does it show they care?

SIKELA

Arba Minch Tourist Hotel (Map p197; ☎ 0468 812171; fax 0468 813661; s Birr150, d Birr170-200) Since it lacks any views and charges *faranjis* double, the new Arba Minch Tourist Hotel tries to distract you with spotless modern rooms boasting satellite TVs, bright windows and quality furnishings. The doubles have comfortable queen-sized beds and built-in wardrobes. The compound contains coffee and juice bars, a leafy seating area and a pizza restaurant. They even have plans for an outdoor theatre.

Kayro Hotel (Map p197; ☎ 0468 810323; d with shared bathroom Birr15, d Birr25) The best of Sikela's budget choices. Although the beds are a squeeze for couples and the bathrooms are a bit grungy, it's still decent value.

Eating

Fish has long been a staple in the diet here, with *asa kutilet* (fish cutlet) being a particular speciality. Sadly, overfishing means it's harder to come by these days.

SHECHA

Lemlem Hotel (Map p197; mains Birr7-16) Sit under the trees and devour the best Ethiopian food in Arba Minch. The menu is only in Amharic, so just ask for your favourite (see Eat your Words, p72). We indulged in *minchet abesh* (minced beef or lamb in a hot sauce).

Soma Restaurant (Map p197; mains Birr7-100) This restaurant, aimed at tourist groups, offers some great meals like *asa gulash* (fish served with a tomato and chilli sauce). Although the *asa filetto* (grilled fish) is lovely and may feed two of you, Birr100 is ludicrous.

Swayne's Hotel (mains Birr25-35) This open-air restaurant prepares the best Western fare in town. Pick from the menu or enjoy a set meal (breakfast/lunch or dinner Birr22/44).

Chocolet Pastry (Map p197; pastries Birr2) Mmmmm…tasty pastries.

SIKELA

Arba Minch Tourist Hotel (Map p197; mains Birr6-20) This hotel opened the day we arrived (good timing!), but the restaurants hadn't yet opened. Judging by its impressive kitchen and pizza oven, food should be top notch.

Abi Restaurant (Map p197; mains Birr5-17) The *asa kutilet* and *asa gulash* are the top picks at this local eatery. Eat streetside or in the courtyard out back.

Flamingo Pastry (Map p197; pastries Birr2) Sikela's best pastries, cakes and fruit juices.

Zebib Snack & Café (Map p197; pastries Birr3) Now in a modern two-storey building, Zebib has literally grown up. The pastries are as good as ever.

Getting There & Away

Ethiopian Airlines (Map p197; ☎ 0468 810649) now flies between Addis Ababa and Arba Minch on Tuesday and Sunday (US$81, 2½ hours). The office is located near the gate that leads into the Arba Minch Tourist Hotel, along with a line of other shops.

One or two daily buses leave Sikela's bus station for Addis Ababa (Birr51.50, 12 hours), Awasa (Birr27, 6½ hours), Shashemene (Birr23.35, six hours), Jinka (Birr33, eight hours), Konso (Birr11, 3½ hours) and Weyto (Birr20, five hours).

Trucks also run south to Konso, Weyto and Jinka. They pick up passengers at Shecha's Shell station. They typically charge 10% more than buses.

Getting Around

Frequent minibuses connect Sikela and Shecha (Birr1.50) from around 6am to 9pm. To reach the airport grab a contract taxi (Birr20 to Birr40) near Flamingo Pastry in Sikela.

The tourism office rents 4WDs for Birr600 to Birr700 per day (including fuel and driver) for trips to Nechisar National Park.

Bikes are a good way to get around. New specimens are rented near Sikela's post office (Birr5 per hour).

Boats for the crocodile market or Lake Abaya are available through the tourism office (Birr300 for 1½ to two hours, one to five people) and the **Arba Minch Fishery** (Map p197; ☎ 0468 810197), which charges between Birr240 and Birr670 for 1½ to two hours, depending on numbers of passengers. Readers also recommend the boat of **Berhane-Wolde Mariam** (☎ 0468 811257), a charismatic and knowledgeable ex-fisherman. He charges Birr250 for 1½ to two hours.

NECHISAR NATIONAL PARK
ኔጭ ሳር ብሔራዊ ፓርክ

Spanning the narrow, yet mountainous 'Bridge of God' that separates Lakes Chamo and Abaya, Nechisar National Park ranks among the most scenic – yet least visited – in East Africa.

Although only 514 sq km, the park contains diverse habitats ranging from wide-open savannah and acacia woodland to thick bush and sections of riparian forest. The bleached savannah grasses actually spawned the park's name, which means 'white grass' in Amharic.

Reflecting the diversity of habitats is the diversity of birds and animals – and this is what makes Nechisar special. Ninety-one mammal species are found in the park. In the forest, bushpigs, warthogs, Anubis baboons, thumbless colobus monkeys, genets, bushbucks and vervet monkeys are found. On the savannah plains (where animals are most easily seen), the Burchell's zebra is the most conspicuous animal, sometimes seen in unusually large herds of 100 animals or more. They're a beautiful sight, bucking defiantly or baying as they canter off before your 4WD. And let's not forget the massive crocodile population in Lake Chamo! They're best seen at the crocodile market (p196).

Of the antelopes, the most commonly seen is the greater kudu in the cover of the bush, with its beautiful spiralling horns, and the monogamous Guenther's dik dik, which is often seen in pairs. The Grant's

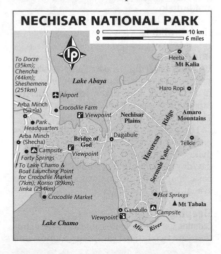

NECHISAR NATIONAL PARK

0 — 10 km
0 — 6 miles

To Dorze (35km); Chencha (44km); Sheshemene (251km)

Lake Abaya

Airport

Arba Minch (Sikela)

Crocodile Farm

Viewpoint

Nechisar Plains

Park Headquarters

Arba Minch (Shecha)

Bridge of God

Dagabule

Campsite

Forty Springs

Viewpoint

To Lake Chamo & Boat Launching Point for Crocodile Market (7km); Konso (89km); Jinka (294km)

Crocodile Market

Viewpoint

Lake Chamo

Gandullo

Mio River

Hot Springs

Mt Tabala

Campsite

Telkie

Amaro Mountains

Ridge

Haro Ropi

Heetu

Mt Kalia

Harenesa

Sermule Valley

gazelle, with its horns pointing forward, is easy to spot on the plains, as is the endemic Swayne's hartebeest.

If you're very lucky you may get to see an endangered African hunting dog, a spotted hyena, leopard, black-backed jackal or one of the few Abyssinian lions inhabiting Nechisar.

Like the mammals, the birds here are diverse: 320 species have been counted including hornbills and bustards. It's also the home of the Nechisar nightjar, Ethiopia's rarest endemic bird (see the sidebar on p64).

Up until recently the local Guji and Koira people (and thousands of their cattle) also inhabited the park, much to the detriment of wildlife. Finally, after a government-negotiated settlement in 2004, the Koira successfully resettled 15km south. By the time you read this, the Guji should have followed suit. Although negotiated, these resettlements have been highly controversial and many Guji and Koira accuse the government of using heavy-handed tactics.

In 2005 park management was taken over by the nonprofit organisation **African Parks Conservation** (APC; www.africanparks-conservation.com), which has successfully rehabilitated neglected parks in several African nations. Besides ensuring the park's ecological and financial sustainability, they plan on reintroducing some of the animals exterminated by humans, namely the African elephant, black rhinoceros, giraffe, eland, gerenuk, beisa oryx, Grevy's zebra, cheetah and buffalo.

It looks like happy days ahead for Nechisar's wildlife.

Information

Whether entering the **park** (Map p199; admission Birr70, vehicle Birr20) by land or water, you must first pay park fees at the **park headquarters** (Map p197; 6am-7.30pm), which is located 1km southeast of Sikela.

The park is not keen on letting visitors on foot enter, but they've been known to make exceptions if an armed scout (per day/day and night Birr30/50) is taken. A basic map and information sheet are also available at headquarters.

Sleeping

Camping (per tent Birr30) Possible anywhere, but there are two official camping grounds: one

beside the Kulfo River, south of park headquarters, and the other in the Sermule Valley. Most travellers sleep in Arba Minch.

Getting There & Around

Being only a stone's throw from Arba Minch, the park is easily accessible. However, the roads within the park can be treacherous, making a 4WD necessary.

There's a 120km-long complete circuit, as well as a shortened 85km version that covers an excellent variety of landscapes, viewpoints, animals and birds. The shortened version takes between five and seven hours to complete (including stops). If you're pushed for time, there's a reasonable three-hour circuit.

See Getting Around under Arba Minch (p199) for details about 4WD and boat rental.

DORZE & CHENCHA
ዶርዜ ና ጨንቻ

High up in the **Guge Mountains**, to the northwest of Arba Minch, is the cold and cloudy Dorze territory. The journey up here affords some spectacular views over Arba Minch and the Rift Valley lakes and is worthwhile in itself.

The Dorze belong to one of the many Omotic peoples of the southwest and are famous for their huge huts (see the boxed text, opposite). Some fine examples can be seen around 30km from Arba Minch in the village of Dorze. The people are skilled farmers who prevent soil erosion of the mountainside with ingenious terracing.

Some of Ethiopia's best woven cotton comes from Chencha, which sits 8km northwest of Dorze village. Fine cotton *shammas* (cotton togas) and *gabis* (thicker *shammas*) can be bought here. Interestingly, men weave and women spin. You can visit the **weaving cooperative** (9am-5pm Tue-Sun) at the village of Gambela Doko, 1.2km from Chencha. You'll be expected to pay at least Birr10 to Birr20 if you want to take photos. *Gabis* cost Birr30 to Birr80, depending on their size.

There's a very colourful **market** (Tuesday and Saturday) at Chencha, and at Dorze (Monday and Thursday). Woven blankets (around Birr100), honey (Birr7), traditional woven Dorze trousers (Birr40 to Birr80) and decorated gourds (Birr15 to Birr20)

DORZE HUTS

Standing up to 12m high, the famous Dorze hut resembles a giant beehive. Constructed with vertical hardwood poles and woven bamboo, it's topped with a thatched roof of *enset* (false-banana tree) leaves. On the outside, a section juts out, which serves as a small reception room.

Though fragile-looking, huts can last up to 60 years. Thanks to the structure's vertical poles, huts are easily transported to new locations. When rot or termites get the better of it, huts are eventually abandoned.

Most Dorze huts also boast their own little garden containing vegetables, spices, tobacco and *enset*.

---

can all be bought there. The piles of white, mushy dough wrapped in green leaves are *enset* (see the boxed text, p69).

The Guge Mountains are also home to Ethiopia's most underrated trekking possibilities. One option would be a five- or six-day cultural journey from Doko Masho to Chosa via Mt Guge (4000m). The best time is late September during the Meskel festival. For details, inquire at Arba Minch's tourism office (p196).

Getting There & Away

In the early mornings, a couple of Landrover taxis (Birr12) leave Arba Minch's Sikela bus station for Dorze (Birr12, two hours) and Chencha (Birr12, 2½ hours). They return around lunchtime.

If you're driving, check the condition of the road in advance as rains turn the road into a steep and slippery quagmire.

KONSO & THE LOWER OMO VALLEY

If there's anything in southern Ethiopia that can rival the majesty of the north's historical circuit, it's the people of this region. Whether it's wandering through traditional Konso villages, watching Hamer people performing a Jumping of the Bulls ceremony or witnessing the Mursi's mystical stick fights and mind-blowing lip plates, your visit here will stick with you for a lifetime.

KONSO ኮንሶ
elev 1650m

For those in a hurry to the Omo Valley, Konso is little more than the place they down a cold Coke and top up on fuel. For those who have some time to invest, Konso may just be the sleeper sight that steals the southern Ethiopia show.

While the town is unequivocally unattractive, despite its lofty ridge-top setting, it's the ancient, complex and fascinating culture of the Konso people (see the boxed text, p203) and their architecturally inspiring villages that really take the cake.

If you're interested in visiting some of the sights around Konso (p202), you must visit Konso's **tourism office** (☎ 0468 811755; ⏲ 8.30am-noon & 1.30-5.30pm Mon-Fri) to pick up visitation forms. A Birr30 fee (whether you intend to visit one village or 12) must then be paid at the revenue office. You're also encouraged to take a trained guide (up to Birr50 per day).

The tourism office is a slight sight itself, with a room holding dozens of famous Konso *wagas* (carved wooden sculptures raised in honour of Konso warriors after their death). It's about 200m northwest of town's main roundabout; ask a local to point it out (or to find the staff on weekends).

A walk to the **market** (⏲ Mon & Thu), which sits 2km west along the ridge, is worthwhile as it proffers grand views over the Rift Valley. Once there, you'll find tea, millet, tobacco, raw cotton, sweet potatoes, butter, incense and cassava. Locally woven cotton blankets (Birr15 to Birr160) make a good souvenir. The giant two-handled pots are for making *tella* (home-brewed beer). If you're lucky, you may find some lovely old Konso glass beads.

Around Konso, keep an eye out for the traditional lozenge-shaped beehives placed in the acacias. On the road to Jinka, you'll see young boys selling tennis-ball sized clumps of *etan* (incense used in coffee ceremonies).

Sleeping & Eating

Hotels still rely on their generators for power, so don't expect electricity between midnight and 6pm.

Green Hotel (camping Birr30, d Birr50) This newish hotel is found on the left, just as you enter town from Arba Minch. The clean rooms are neither small nor spacious and have oversized foam mattresses, mosquito nets and cold showers. Campers must pay Birr15 for a shower!

Edget Hotel (s/tw Birr30/50) Set on the town's only roundabout, Edget has its rooms surrounding its popular courtyard restaurant and bar. Rooms are well worn, but will do for a night's kip. Most toilets lack seats and plumbing is sketchy at times. The food is the best Konso has to offer.

Unnamed Hotel (s with shared shower Birr30) Too new for a name, this spartan place has clean and bright rooms in a tiny garden compound on offer. The cement squat loos are smelly, but clean. The shower stall dividers are a bit low for female patrons. Look out for the rust-coloured gates 100m east of Edget Hotel.

Tourism office camping (Birr10) Behind the tourism office, there's a reasonably flat (albeit pebbly) section to pitch tents. The tin-shack toilets are grim and there's no water, but the views are amazing.

Getting There & Away

One daily bus from Arba Minch picks up passengers here en route to Jinka (Birr25, 5½ hours, departing between 9am and 10am), via Weyto (Birr7, two hours) and Key Afar (Birr18, four hours). The bus from Jinka does the same while travelling to Arba Minch (Birr11, 3½ hours, departing between 11am and noon).

Isuzu trucks depart daily for Yabelo (Birr20 to Birr25, three hours), Weyto (Birr15) and Arba Minch (Birr15). For Turmi, go to Key Afar first (as Weyto has no accommodation if you get stuck).

AROUND KONSO

If you have a vehicle, a great excursion is the traditional Konso village of **Machekie**. Although it sits atop a rusty bluff and offers astounding views, you'll likely prefer wandering through the narrow maze of stone-walled walkways, *Moringa oleifera* trees and thatch-roofed homes. Despite many thefts, Machekie still has some wonderful *wagas*, some more than 150 years old.

Local children, like many of those in this region are prone to '*faranji* frenzy' (p259), but the village's guide (Birr50 per day) keeps them in check. The longer you stay, the less attention you'll draw and the more you'll enjoy the experience. Some people

are even offered the chance to spend the night in the community house (Birr10).

If you want to enter the clan compounds, you'll likely be charged Birr20 per person. Pictures of people cost Birr1 per person, while pictures of houses are free.

To reach Machekie, head 5km west from Konso towards Jinka, before turning south and following the dirt track another 5km. From there, you'll see the village on the hill 3km to your east. A single track will lead you to the outer rock walls.

Other interesting Konso villages are **Busso** (7km south of Konso) and Gesergio (17km southwest of Konso). **Gesergio** (gas-*ag*-ee-yo), with its bizarre landscape of entrancing sand formations, is the most famous. Thanks to the towering pinnacles resembling skyscrapers, the town is now more commonly known as 'New York'.

While local legend states that the landscape is the result of God's hands digging in search of a chief's stolen sacred drums, science chalks it up to wind and water.

Sadly, our latest trip to Gesergio was spoiled by hundreds of children attacking – yes, attacking – our 4WD when we wouldn't hand out pens or bottles of water. Either they've been spoiled by thoughtless tourists, or they'd recently been given a crate of Starbucks' chocolate-covered coffee beans (can you say hyper?) from someone visiting from Seattle. Although giving children gifts may feel good at the time, it often ends up leaving them worse off; see Begging & Giving, p258.

To reach Gesergio, follow the directions to Machekie but continue 7km southward instead of turning east along the 3km single track to Machekie.

A sight of an entirely different nature is the Konso-Gardula Project's **archaeological excavations**, which have unearthed many unique fossils (human and animal) dating back 1.9 million years. The area is currently on Unesco's tentative list of future World Heritage sites. If you're a closet archaeologist, inquire at Konso's tourism office (p201).

JINKA ጂንካ

pop 18,000 / elev 1490m

Set in the hills above Mago and Omo National Parks, Jinka offers a cool respite from the lowland's steamy confines. Although its services are limited and its central

KONSO CULTURE & CONSTRUCTION

The pagan Konso society boasts a rich culture, and a highly specialised and successful agricultural economy.

Beautifully constructed, buttressed stone terraced fields have allowed the Konso to eke out a living from the dry, unyielding land around them. Villages typically adorn hill tops and are surrounded by sturdy stone walls, which serve as a defence against intruders, as well as protecting against straying cattle. Visitors must enter a Konso house on hands and knees, via a wooden tunnel – a compromising position should the visitor turn out to be a foe.

Traditional villages are divided into nine separate compounds, one for each of Konso's clans. Within each compound there's a *pogala mugla* (representative of the clan chief), a *mora* (thatched two-storey communal house where adolescent boys spend their nights) and a ceremonial square where generation polls stand tall (one poll is raised every 18 years).

The squares also contain the famous Konso *wagas*, carved wooden sculptures raised in honour of Konso warriors after their death. Designed according to a strict formula, the 'hero' is usually distinguishable by the phallic ornamental *khalasha* worn on the sculpture's forehead, or by its slightly larger size.

Placed on either side of the hero are between two and four of his wives (identifiable by necklaces and breasts) and the hero's slain enemies (usually smaller and without phallic symbols), or animals (such as leopards) that the hero has killed. Occasionally a monkeylike figure stands at the feet of the hero, and sometimes his spears and shields are included. The eyes of the figures are usually represented with shells or ostrich eggshells, the teeth with the bones of goats.

Unfortunately, *waga* erection is dying out. The widespread theft and removal of the statues to Addis Ababa for sale to diplomats and tourists, as well as the work of missionaries who are against ancestor worship, has discouraged the continuance of this ancient tradition.

Some traditions continue to live on though, like bans on marriages between members of the same clan, and clan chiefs (and their families) living lives of amazing solitude, just so they can be impartial with intraclan conflicts. Traditions of the truly bizarre include secretly embalming clan chiefs after death, sitting them up in their favourite chair and telling clan members that they're simply sick and unable to talk for up to nine years after death.

airstrip doubles as a grazing ground for local cows and sheep, Jinka can feel downright sophisticated if you're arriving from a foray into the Omo Valley.

Jinka is known for its vibrant Saturday **market**, which sits around 400m northwest of the airstrip. It attracts a variety of ethnic groups, among them the Ari, Hamer and Banna (see the boxed text, p206); most charge Birr1 per photo. The fruit market, 300m further west, is a tasty excursion – try the delicious *fruitish* (passion fruit), also known locally as 'fashion fruit'!

The German-funded **South-Omo Museum & Research Centre** (☎ 0467 750149; admission Birr10; 🕑 9am-noon & 3-5pm Tue-Sat) is also worth exploring. It's perched on a hill northeast of town (look for the green roof halfway up the hill) and hosts an interesting exhibition on the material culture of the peoples of the region. There's even a library with ethnographic DVDs; evening showings can be requested. They're planning on building a

traditional Ari house out front, which will display and sell local artwork.

From Jinka, you can do a day trip to Mursi territory, around 60km west of the town.

Sleeping & Eating

Jinka, like most of this region, charges foreigners up to double for everything. Reservations are advised June through September.

Jinka Resort (☎ 0467 750143; camping Birr35, s/d/ tw Birr150/173/230) Opened in 2003, this hotel is set in a lovely section of forest just east of the town centre. Easily Jinka's most cushy option. Rooms here are large, bright and spotless. The camping area is beautiful and closer to town than Rocky Campsite, but there's no cooking facilities and it's twice the price. The restaurant (mains Birr12 to Birr20) prepares cheese burgers and spaghetti, but service can be very slow.

Goh Hotel (☎ 0467 750033; d/tw Birr100/120) Goh's rooms are aged in comparison to Jinka Resort's, but they're still bright and clean. The

SOUTHERN ETHIOPIA

twin rooms have hot showers and are larger than the doubles. It's worth negotiating in low season. Goh Hotel is immediately east of the airstrip. It has a large satellite TV that shows movies and European football.

Orit Hotel (☎ 0467 750045; s/d/tw Birr100/120/150; 🖳) This hotel's double rooms, with sparkling bathrooms, hot water and comfy mattresses, easily outshine its southerly neighbour (Goh Hotel). However, the opposite is true with Orit's twin rooms, which have cold showers and are rather small. Its restaurant (mains Birr8 to Birr12) serves Jinka's best pasta.

Rocky Campsite (camping Birr15) About 1.5km east of Jinka's Total station, this campsite is quite pleasant. Hedges separate tent sites and there are a couple of thatch-roofed cooking areas.

Hannah Maryam (mains Birr8-10) The spot to enjoy fine Ethiopian fare. It's 150m north of the runway; look for the blue tents with orange fringe.

Tsion Restaurant (mains Birr5-8) Inhale an early morning omelette or guzzle some fresh juice. It's just north of Orit Hotel.

Cheap local hotels that will do for a night's kip:

Mengistu Pension (☎ 0467 750419; s with shared bathroom Birr20) Often full and usually clean, it's found down a lane north of the airstrip.

Omo Hotel (☎ 0467 750067; s/d with shared toilet Birr40/50) Set west of the airstrip; rooms here are reasonably clean, but not pleasant.

Getting There & Away

Ethiopian Airlines (☎ 0467 750126) flies between Addis Ababa and Jinka (US$94, 2¼ hours) on Wednesday and Saturday. During wet season, flights are sometimes postponed because of poor conditions. The office is west of the airstrip.

Currently buses arrive and depart near the police station. A bus leaves daily for Addis Ababa (Birr84.35, two days) via Key Afar (Birr7, 1½ hours), Weyto (Birr12, 3½ hours), Konso (Birr25, 5½ hours) and Arba Minch (Birr33, eight hours).

Four or five Isuzu trucks depart daily (near the Orit and Omo Hotels) for Key Afar (Birr12) and Weyto (Birr20). Trucks also serve Omorate (Birr55, 10 hours), via Dimeka (Birr35, 5½ hours) and Turmi (Birr50, eight hours). *Faranji* prices are in full effect, so negotiate hard.

Various government and missionary cars also roam the region; they usually give lifts, but a contribution towards fuel should be made. The Mobil and Total petrol stations are good places to troll for rides.

The **NTO** (☎ 0467 750154) has an office near the airstrip and rents 4WDs (US$110 per day). This includes driver, fuel and 100km (US$0.75 per additional kilometre). Private vehicles are also available, though they carry their own risks. Ask at your hotel.

LOWER OMO VALLEY
ዝቅተኛው የአሞ ሸለቆ

With the Lower Omo Valley hosting some of Africa's most fascinating and colourful ethnic groups, as well as Ethiopia's worst roads, a trip here is as captivating as it is uncomfortable.

The landscape is diverse, ranging from dry, open savannah plains to riverine forests bordering the Omo and Mago Rivers. The vast Omo River meanders for nearly 1000km, from southwest of Addis Ababa all the way to Kenya. There it's the sole feeder of Kenya's massive Jade Sea (Lake Turkana). The river also bisects Ethiopia's largest, wildest and most inaccessible national parks: Omo and Mago.

Undisturbed and little visited, the parks boast a remarkable mixture of wildlife and remote tribes. It's here that ancient customs and traditions have remained almost entirely intact. Animism is still the religion, and some still practise a purely pastoral economy. Hostility between neighbouring tribes is still high and internecine warfare is common.

Culturally, the best time to visit is from June to September, when many celebrations take place, including harvest-home dances, marriage ceremonies, and initiation ceremonies including the famous bull-jumping. The driest period (January and February) increases the odds of animal sightings in Omo and Mago National Parks. Avoid coming in October or between mid-March and early June when rains are traditionally the worst. Be aware just one day of rain can render the roads temporarily impassable, so keep your itinerary flexible.

Or you can avoid the roads all together and river raft through the region (see White-Water Rafting & Kayaking, p255).

When visiting the villages of the Lower Omo Valley, try and coincide with at least one market day (see p209). Otherwise, a good time to visit the villages is between 5pm and 6.30pm, when the workers return from the fields or from market.

Dangers & Annoyances

Tsetse flies continue to be a problem in some areas, particularly Mago National Park after the rains. Malaria is also prevalent, so precautions are essential. For more information, see p373.

For many ethnic groups, raiding is a part of life – a means of survival in a very harsh environment. Camps should never be left unattended, and all jewellery, including watches, is best removed before you mingle with some groups such as the Mursi.

Recently, groups have given wrong directions to inexperienced drivers. No sooner is the vehicle stuck in mud, than a fee of up to Birr1000 is demanded to help pull it out!

Oddly, photography here can be rather stressful; see Tips for Photographers in Ethiopia on p266. If you don't want to deal with the photography shemozzle, the coffee-table book *Don McCullin in Africa* contains stunning photographs from the Lower Omo Valley.

Omo Valley Villages

A good itinerary that gives you a glimpse of diverse ethnic groups, as well as diverse scenery, begins in Konso and takes you through the little villages of Weyto, Arbore, Turmi, Omorate, Dimeka and Key Afar, before finishing at Jinka. An alternate route from Omorate could be to pass through Mago National Park, stopping at the villages of Kolcho and Dus.

If you plan on staying in any of these villages, know that accommodation is bare-bones budget at best and electricity is only at establishments with generators (usually between 6pm and 10pm).

WEYTO ወይቶ

This little village lies at the junction to Arbore, roughly halfway between Konso and Key Afar. The Tsemay, part farmers, part

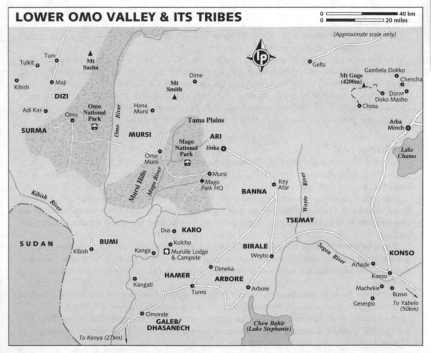

LOWER OMO VALLEY & ITS TRIBES

0   40 km
0   20 miles

(Approximate scale only)

pastoralists, inhabit the region. Besides the Sunday market and the popular **Mihirat Restaurant** (mains Birr5-10), there's little reason to stop here.

It's possible to camp at the restaurant, but at Birr30 it's quite the rip-off.

Arba Minch–Jinka buses stop here, but there are rarely empty seats. Daily Isuzu trucks serve Konso (Birr15, two hours), Key Afar (Birr12, 1½ hours) and Turmi (Birr25, four hours) via Arbore (Birr12, 1½ hours).

PEOPLES OF THE LOWER OMO VALLEY

The Lower Omo Valley is unique in that it is home to so many peoples in such a small area. Historians believe that the south served for millennia as a kind of cultural crossroads, where Cushitic, Nilotic, Omotic and Semitic peoples met as they migrated from the north, west, south and east.

Described here are some its most notable peoples. The map on p205 illustrates the geographical distribution of all tribes.

The Ari ኣሪ

Almost 120,000 Ari inhabit the northern border of Mago National Park. They keep large numbers of livestock and produce large amounts of honey, often used for trade. The women wear skirts made from the *enset* tree.

The Banna ባና

Numbering around 45,000, the Banna inhabit the higher ground east of Mago National Park. Most practise agriculture, though their diet is supplemented by hunting. After killing a buffalo, they decorate themselves with clay for a special celebration and feast for the whole village.

The Bumi በ-ሚ

Inhabiting the land south of the Omo National Park are around 8000 Bumi. They occasionally invade the southern plains when fodder or water is scarce.

The Bumi are agropastoralists, growing sorghum by the Omo River as well as fishing and rearing cattle. They also hunt and smoke bees out of their hives for honey. Known as great warmongers, they're regularly doing battle with the Karo, the Hamer and the Surma.

The Bumi use scarification for cosmetic purposes, tribal identification and as indications of prowess in battle. Both men and women use little *pointilles* or dots to highlight their eyes and cheekbones. The women also scarify their torsos with curvilinear and geometrical designs.

The Hamer ሃመር

The Hamer, who number around 50,000, are subsistence agropastoralists. They cultivate sorghum, vegetables, millet, tobacco and cotton, as well as rearing cattle and goats. Wild honey is an important part of their diet.

The people are known particularly for their remarkable hairstyles. The women mix together ochre, water and a binding resin before rubbing it into their hair. They then twist strands again and again to create coppery-coloured tresses known as *goscha*. These are a sign of health and welfare.

If they've recently killed an enemy or dangerous animal, men are permitted to don clay hair buns that sometimes support magnificent ostrich feathers. With the help of special headrests *(borkotos)* for sleeping, the buns last from three to six months, and can be 'redone' for up to one year.

The Hamer are also considered masters of body decoration. Every adornment has an important symbolic significance; earrings, for example, denote the number of wives a man has.

The women wear iron coils around their arms and bead necklaces, and decorate their skin with cowrie shells. The *ensente* (iron torques) worn around the necks of married and engaged

ARBORE አሬቦሬ

Arbore rests 50km south of Weyto on the Turmi road. The Arbore people are a mixed bunch, with ancestry linking back to the Omo Valley and Konso highlands. With their beads and aluminium jewellery, they almost resemble the Borena people. To escape the area's notorious mosquitoes many Arbore sleep on 5m-high platforms; locals outside the village know it as 'mosquito town'.

South of Arbore, off the main Arbore–Turmi road, tracks lead to the strange saline

---

women indicate the wealth and prestige of their husband. Unmarried girls wear a metal plate in their hair that looks a bit like a platypus' bill.

The iron bracelets and armlets are an indication of the wealth and social standing of the young girl's family. When she gets married, she must remove the jewellery; it's the first gift she makes to her new family.

The Hamer territory stretches east to Chew Bahir, south to the Kenya border and north to Banna territory.

The Karo ካሮ

With a population of about 1500 people, the Karo people are thought to be the Omo Valley's most endangered group. Inhabiting the Omo's eastern bank, many of these traditional pastoralists have now turned to agriculture after disease wiped out their cattle.

In appearance, language and tradition, they slightly resemble the Hamer, to whom they're related. The Karo are considered masters of body painting, particularly when preparing for a dance, feast or celebration. Most famously, chalk is used to imitate the spotted plumage of the guinea fowl.

The Karo are also great improvisers: Bic biros, nails, sweets wrappers and cartridges are all incorporated into jewellery and decoration. Yellow mineral rock, black charcoal and pulverised red iron ore are traditionally used.

The Mursi መ-ርሲ

The 6500 or so Mursi are mainly pastoralists who move according to the seasons between the lower Tama Plains and the Mursi Hills in Mago National Park.

Some Mursi practise flood retreat cultivation, particularly where the tsetse fly prohibits cattle rearing. Honey is collected from beehives made with bark and dung. The Mursi language is Nilo-Saharan in origin.

The most famous Mursi traditions include the fierce stick fighting between the men, and the lip plate worn by the women. Made of clay and up to 15cm in diameter, the plates are inserted into a slit separating their lower lip and jaw. Due to the obvious discomfort, women only wear the lip plates occasionally, leaving their distended lips swaying below their jaw. Anthropologists offer several theories to explain the practice: to deter slavers looking for unblemished girls; to prevent evil from entering the body by way of the mouth; or to indicate social status by showing the number of cattle required by the wearer's family for her hand in marriage.

The Surma ሱ-ርማ

Formerly nomadic pastoralists, the Surma now largely depend upon the subsistence cultivation of sorghum and maize. The Surma have a fearsome reputation as warriors, in part inspired by their continual search for grazing lands. Fights against the Bumi, their sworn enemies, still occur.

It's believed that the Surma once dominated the area, but their territory has been reduced to the western edges of Omo National Park. The population of 45,000 is split into three subgroups: the Chai, Tirma and Bale. The Surma hunt in the park and make beehive huts. Like the Mursi, the Surma men stick fight and the women don distending lip plates.

The Surma are also known for their white, almost ghostlike body painting. White chalk is mixed with water to create a kind of wash. The painting is much less ornamental than that found in other tribes and is intended to intimidate enemies in battle. Sometimes snake and wavelike patterns are painted across the torso and thighs.

SOUTHERN ETHIOPIA

SOUTHERN ETHIOPIA

BODY DECORATION

The people of the Omo have developed art forms that allow them not just great artistic expression, but also serve important social and cosmetic purposes. The practice of body painting and scarification developed by the tribes is among the most ornate and extravagant seen anywhere in the world.

For most tribes, scarification serves as a distinction for brave warriors; the men are not allowed to scarify themselves until they have killed at least one foe. For women, the raised texture of the skin is considered highly desirable, and is said to hold sensual value for men.

Scarification is achieved using a stone, knife, hook or razor blade. Ash is then rubbed into the wound, creating a small infection and promoting scar tissue growth. As the wound heals, the raised scar creates the desired knobbly effect on the skin's surface.

---

lake of **Chew Bahir** (also known as Lake Stephanie). From Arbore to the junction of the main track is a 35km drive. From the junction to the lake is 60km. Oryx and gazelles are sometimes found near the lake. The ground around the lake is notoriously unstable, so take a police-guide from Arbore. They'll ask for up to Birr200 for the day, but Birr80 to Birr100 is plenty. January to December is the best time to visit.

Daily Isuzu trucks ramble past en route to Weyto (Birr12, 1½ hours) and Turmi (Birr15, two hours).

TURMI ቱርሚ

Although tiny **Turmi** (admission per vehicle Birr50) is indistinguishable from other towns in the region, it's surrounded by several traditional Hamer villages. On Monday, Hamer people descend on Turmi and pack its famed **market**.

Hamer women, with their shimmering coppery-coloured tresses, sell vegetables, spices, butter, milk and traditional items like incised calabashes, head stools, metal arm bracelets and fantastically smelly goatskins decorated with beads and cowrie shells.

The region around Turmi is known for the famous Hamer and Banna **Jumping of the Bulls ceremony** (see right). Admission fees of Birr100 per person are asked (minimum Birr300); the ceremony lasts all day (from 11am to 6pm). The *evangadi* (Hamer night dance) can also be seen or organised. It usually costs Birr10 per person and lasts three hours. Ask locally.

Sleeping & Eating

Turmi has the Omo Valley's best range of accommodation.

Greenland Lodge Campsite (camping Birr30, tw with shared bathroom Birr200) Despite the hefty price tag, these rooms are nothing special. They're housed in old semipermanent tents, with tarp floors and camp beds. The star of the site (even beating out the acacia trees) is the sparkling block of loos.

Tourist Restaurant (☎ 0911 190209; s with shared bathroom Birr30) Simple cement-floored singles host ageing foam mattresses and futile mosquito nets. The squat toilet stall is clean enough, though the holey shower shack is less than private. The restaurant (meals Birr4 to Birr10) is popular with tour operators and serves simple omelettes, pastas and Ethiopian fare.

Buska Restaurant (s with shared bathroom Birr20) Spartan rooms with small beds, clean cement floors and mosquito nets. The shared toilets are a bit of a fly feast (ughh!). The food here is similar to the Tourist Restaurant's.

JUMPING OF THE BULLS CEREMONY

Whipping, teasing, screaming and a whole lot of leaping are part of this infamous ceremony. It's a right of passage into manhood for all young Hamer and Banna boys and is truly a sight to behold. After 15 to 30 bulls have been lined up side by side, each naked boy taking part must leap down the line of bulls jumping from back to back. If they fall, they're whipped and teased by women. If they succeed, they must turn around and complete the task three more times!

During the ceremony young female relatives of the boys beg to be whipped; the deeper their scars, the more love they show for their boy. It's as disturbing as it's intriguing.

Ceremonies typically take part between late February and early April, July through September and the first half of December.

Kaske Campsite (camping Birr20) Chuck your tent in the heavenly shade provided by the canopy of lush mango trees. There are also thatched pavilions for cooking and rudimentary toilets. The site sits next to the Kaske River, 3.9km north of Turmi, just off the road to Weyto. There's a risk of flash flooding here, so check conditions before making camp.

Camp Kaina (camping per tent Birr15-25) This makeshift campsite is also set on the Kaske River, but is accessed from the town centre along a 2.5km dirt track that leads behind the police station. The bush toilet and shower are comically crude, but do the job. It rents reasonable one- and two-person tents, complete with mattresses, for Birr25.

Getting There & Away
Set at an important crossroads, daily Isuzu trucks leave for Omorate (Birr15, two hours), Arbore (Birr15, two hours), Weyto (Birr25, four hours), Dimeka (Birr15, two hours), Key Afar (Birr30, six hours) and Jinka (Birr35, eight hours).

OMORATE አሞራተ
Omorate is nestled along the baking eastern bank of the **Omo River**, 72km southwest of Turmi. For those without a vehicle, Omorate is the only place you can actually lay eyes on the mighty river. During our most recent trip, we stood onshore and watched silhouettes paddle across the silver waters at sunset – truly transcendent.

The town itself is rather unsightly, but you can hop across the river in a dugout canoe and visit traditional Galeb (also known as Dasanech) villages. Local 'guides' loitering around the hotels insist you go with one of them (Birr50) and pay an additional Birr100 for the boat and village admission – rubbish. After shaking off all these pesky guides, we walked south along the bank and hired a canoe for Birr10 return (generous but fair). The driver acted as our guide and the village chief only requested Birr15 for admission.

Once in the villages, you'll be mobbed by colourful locals fishing for photographs. The going rate is Birr1 per person per photo.

There's not much difference between Omorate's **Tourist Hotel** (s with shared bathroom Birr30), **Park Hotel** (s with shared bathroom Birr30) and **National Hotel** (s with shared bathroom Birr30). Spread

---

MARKET DAY IN THE OMO VALLEY
A terrific way to see the Omo's people is at local markets. Since most people have long journeys to and from the towns, markets are best visited between 10.30am and 2pm. The most interesting markets include the following:

Town	Day
Arbore	Fri
Dimeka	Tue & Sat
Jinka	Tue & Sat
Key Afar	Thu
Konso	Mon & Thu
Turmi	Mon
Weyto	Sun
Yabelo	Sat

The markets at Dimeka, Key Afar and Turmi (in that order) are probably the most colourful.

---

around the police station, they all charge inflated *faranji* rates for grubby, small single cells (rooms is too kind a word). National is the loudest option, but its restaurant has the best food.

It's possible to camp for free within the police compound.

Getting There & Away
Despite rumours, you don't need permission from the tourism office in Konso or the Ministry of Culture & Tourism in Addis Adaba to visit Omorate.

There's usually a couple of daily trucks heading north to Turmi (Birr15, two hours).

The turn-off for Kolcho, Dus and Mago National Park is 9km north of town.

For details about crossing into Kenya, see p275.

DIMEKA ዲሜቃ
Like Turmi, which sits 28km to its south, **Dimeka** (admission per car Birr50) is a Hamer village. However, since it borders on Banna territory its Tuesday and Saturday **markets** (Tuesday is best) attract locals from both tribes.

The **Tourist Cafeteria** (s with shared bathroom Birr15) is the best of a few weak sleeping options. Its small rooms are tidy and have clean sheets, holey mosquito nets, squishy foam mattresses and tin ceilings.

Passing Isuzu trucks pick up people heading for Turmi (Birr15, two hours) and Key Afar (Birr20, four hours).

KEY AFAR ቀይ አፋፋ

A haven of cool compared to Turmi or Omorate, Key Afar rests on a lush plateau along the Konso–Jinka road. Lacking the traditional atmosphere seen in other villages, Key Afar's Thursday **market** more than compensates, attracting Ari, Hamer and Banna people.

The **Abebe Kebede Hotel** (s with shared bathroom Birr15) and **Getay Hotel** (s with shared bathroom Birr10) offer crude rooms with cement floors, old sheets and toe-curling tin-shack toilets. Abebe Kebede has a makeshift 45-gallon drum shower, while showers at Getay come in buckets.

Arba Minch–Jinka buses can drop you here, but there are rarely empty seats if you want to get on. Daily Isuzu trucks head to Dimeka (Birr20, four hours), Turmi (Birr30, six hours), Weyto (Birr12, 1½ hours) and Jinka (Birr12, two hours).

KOLCHO, KANGA & DUS

These three villages all sit between Omorate and Mago National Park. Minuscule Kolcho is arguably the most beautiful, with its lofty views over the Omo River and traditional Karo dwellings. It's also a great place for traditional dancing, though it'll cost you (Birr300 to Birr700 per group depending on size). Dances last around one hour and usually take place at sunset.

Around 1km from Kolcho is **Lake Deepa**, which is a great spot for bird-watching. The Bumi village of Kanga, which lies across the river further south, can also be visited.

It's also possible to arrange traditional dancing at the large village of Dus, north of Kolcho (same prices as Kolcho).

About 6km south of Kolcho is the amazing Murulle camp built by **Ethiopian Rift Valley Safaris** (☎ 0111 552128; www.ethiopianriftvalley safaris.com). To stay at its amazing lodge, you'd have to be on one of their pricey package tours. However, it's possible to camp here for US$9.20 per person per night.

The only way to access Kolcho, Kanga, Dus and Murulle is with a private 4WD.

South of Murulle is a beautiful savannah plain where oryx and Grant's gazelles are frequently seen. Oddly there are far more animals reported here than at Mago National Park! There are also 340 bird species in the region. Watch out for the delightful carmine bee-eaters, which fly alongside your vehicle and snap up the insects stirred up by the wheels. The clouds of little quail-like birds that explode like popcorn from the grass as vehicles pass are red-billed queleas.

Mago National Park
ማጎ ብሔራዊ ፓርክ

Not for the pusillanimous, a visit to this 2162-sq-km **park** (admission Birr70, vehicle Birr100) is a two-footed leap into true African wilds. You'll battle roads that eat Landrovers for brunch, wage war with squadrons of mosquitos and tetsi flies, and sweat more than you thought humanly possible. The payoff? It's more adventure than you can shake a stick at! You'll also have the chance to visit **Mursi villages** along the Mago River and spot some animals too. One thing is for sure, you'll never forget your time here.

Most of the park is below 500m elevation, so temperatures can soar over 40°C. Landscapes range from thick acacia forest and dense riparian vegetation to typical African savannah.

Although the park was originally created to protect lions, leopards, buffaloes, elephants and giraffes, widespread poaching means you stand little chance of spotting them. Expect the Serengeti or Masai Mara and you're in for one major disappointment. Mammals you can expect to spot are Burchell's zebra, greater and lesser kudu, the defassa waterbuck and the ever so elegant gerenuk. Topis and Lelwel hartebeest are also sometimes seen. Occasionally, large herds of buffalo are reported congregated at sources of water during dry periods. The driest time is January through February.

The tiny visitors centre at the park headquarters contains some information panels, maps and the usual animals' skulls and skins. The headquarters also provides mandatory armed scouts (Birr40/60 per 12/24 hours).

It's possible to camp (Birr30 per person), but there are no facilities.

Headquarters can be reached from Jinka, 40km (two to four hours) to the north, or Kolcho, 115km (six to eight hours) to the south. There's no public transport, so you'll have to rent a 4WD from a tour operator in Addis Ababa (see p282) or Jinka (p204).

Always try and go in convoy with another vehicle and ensure both have good tyres, a shovel, pick axe and a metal cable (a winch is even better).

When the going is heavy, you'll only average 6km/h and burn serious fuel, so plan on carrying plenty of extra fuel (some guides recommend a total capacity of 230L). A knowledgeable driver or guide is essential; sometimes the roads are little more than tracks that lose themselves in the savannah, or clearings through the jungle. Be aware that roads can become impassable after rain.

Omo National Park
አሞ ብሔራዊ ፓርክ

If Mago National Park is for the adventurous, **Omo National Park** (admission Birr70, vehicle Birr100) is for the masochists. To state the obvious, travelling in Ethiopia's most remote park is incredibly tough.

Although hosting similar wildlife to Mago National Park, Omo's ecological environment is quite different. Although the reduced forest cover actually makes it easier to spot the remaining animals, you'd still need to spend a few days to maximise your chances.

In December 2005 **African Parks Conservation** (APC; www.africanparks-conservation.com), the same nonprofit international organisation that's rehabilitating Nechisar National Park and several other parks in Africa, signed an agreement with the Ethiopian government to take over park management.

Over the next decade, APC and their social anthropologists plan to work with the Mursi, Dizi and Surma tribes who live in the park to protect the wildlife, and will eventually start to reintroduce endemic animals such as elephants, rhinos, giraffes and lions. Until APC believes the locals can handle increased numbers of visitors, infrastructure within the park will be kept at a bare minimum.

Although the APC states that it has no intention of resettling the tribes outside the park's boundaries, many are worried because the APC refused to put a 'no eviction' clause in its contract with the government. This, combined with the fact that the APC won't make this contract available to the people of the Omo Valley, worries many in the region and some activists abroad. Even if resettlement does not take place, it's crucial the APC allows tribes to retain access to vital subsistence resources so that they can continue to obtain a sustainable livelihood.

To check on the park's progress or to find information about visiting, log onto APC's website or talk to a tour operator in Addis Ababa (see p282). To further inform yourself on the potential resettlement issues (and determine if you want to spend your money in APC's park) check out www.iucn.org and plug Omo National Park into its search engine.

SOUTHERN ETHIOPIA

Eastern Ethiopia

A trip to eastern Ethiopia is a journey that tickles the heart, boggles the mind and challenges the soul – no less than that. In stark contrast to the green, densely populated, Christian highlands, the east is largely arid, wild, low-lying and Muslim. In it lies eastern Ethiopia's *piéce de résistance*: the old walled city of Harar, which seems straight out of a story from the *Arabian Nights*. This gem of a place is shrouded with a palpable historical aura that will appeal to culture vultures. And after nightfall, the hard-to-believe ritual feeding of the Harar hyenas will leave you gasping in awe.

True, if you're an outdoor enthusiast, you might find eastern Ethiopia is a bit low on active pursuits. There is potential, but it's still largely undeveloped. But the Awash National Park, with its outstanding birdlife, offers ample compensation. Be sure to squeeze it into your itinerary.

For wannabe National Geographic wanderers, the seemingly endless ribbon of bitumen leading northeast to Asaita offers opportunities for remote exploration. Follow Wilfred Thesiger's steps and head to the mesmerisingly desolate area known as the southern Danakil region, which is home to the fascinating Afar people and remains adamantly off the beaten track.

But if all you want is to please your palate, the east could also prove your Shangri-la: it is known as the home of the best coffee in the world – we agree. Or you could unleash your inner rebel and dare to try chewing *chat,* the mildly intoxicating stimulant.

So go ahead, dive in!

EASTERN ETHIOPIA

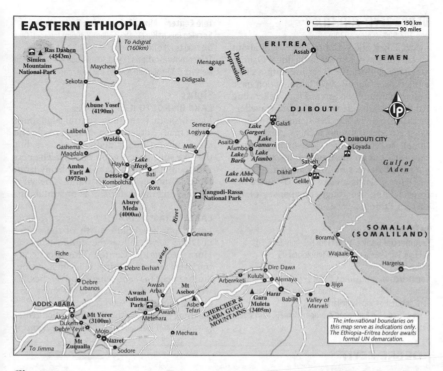

EASTERN ETHIOPIA

The international boundaries on this map serve as indications only. The Ethiopia–Eritrea border awaits formal UN demarcation.

Climate

The lowlands around Asaita and Awash are baking hot (up to 45°C) from May to September and receive little rain. They are also prone to severe droughts. The climate in Debre Zeyit and Nazret is similar to the conditions that prevail in Addis Ababa. The highlands around Dire Dawa, Harar and Jijiga are hot and dry. The main rains fall from July to September.

National Parks

While you can easily dismiss the Yangudi-Rassa National Park, where the wildlife is as abundant as in Manhattan, make sure you don't skip Awash National Park. The park has enough species of birds to keep twitchers happy, and a fair share of other wildlife.

Getting There & Away

Ethiopian Airlines (www.flyethiopian.com) connects Addis Ababa with Dire Dawa and Jijiga. Most people who enter eastern Ethiopia overland travel by bus or by train from Djibouti City and disembark in Dire Dawa.

It's also possible to travel from Hargeisa (Somaliland) to Jijiga by bus. For more information see p275.

Getting Around

Good sealed roads connect the main cities, including Asaita to the far northeast. Most cities in this part of Ethiopia are well served by public transport, except for the long stretch from Awash to Asaita where buses are infrequent. To visit Awash National Park, you will have to travel by private or rented 4WD.

ADDIS ABABA TO AWASH

The long stretch of road between Addis Ababa and Awash is a gentle introduction to eastern Ethiopia. Most foreign visitors rush straight through without stopping, which is a bit of a shame. Although there's nothing really jaw-dropping (be patient!), there are enough attractions and notable towns to keep you busy for a few days. Get your bearings and enjoy!

EASTERN ETHIOPIA

DEBRE ZEYIT ደብረዘይት
pop 107,000 / elev 1920m

Lakes, lakes, lakes. Debre Zeyit is all about lakes. The town, known in the local Oromo language as Bishoftu, is strung with a dishevelled necklace of crater lakes, which have been a longtime playground for weekending Addis Ababans. However, most travellers pass through Debre Zeyit, lured by more magnetic destinations such as Awash National Park or Harar. It's a shame because they miss out on these superb lakes. Sure, it ain't the Bahamas but the countrified town of Debre Zeyit is a tasty hors d'oeuvre before tackling the rougher expanses of far eastern Ethiopia.

Information
Commercial Bank (8-11am & 1-4pm Mon-Fri, 8-11am Sat) Changes cash only (euros and US dollars).

Construction & Business Bank (8-11am & 1-3pm Mon-Fri, 8-11am Sat) On the road to lake Hora. Changes cash only (euros and US dollars).

Post office (8am-noon & 3-6pm Mon-Fri, 8am-noon Sat) Off the road to Lake Hora.

Tele Center – Almaz Information Technology Service (per hr Birr21; 8.30am-8.30pm) Internet. On the road to Lake Hora.

Telecommunications (8.30am-noon & 1.30-5.30pm Mon-Fri, 8.30-noon Sat) Next to the post office.

Sights

LAKE BISHOFTU ቢሾፍቱ ሐይቅ

Lake Bishoftu is the most central lake, south of the main Addis Ababa–Nazret road. The area is almost totally denuded of trees, but the lake still attracts good birdlife. The best way to appreciate the lake is probably from Hotel Bishoftu, drink in hand. The view overlooking the crater rim is breathtaking.

LAKE HORA ሆራ ሐይቅ

Lake Hora lies 1.5km north of the centre of Debre Zeyit; follow the signposts to the Hora Recreation Center. The lake is attractively set and its birdlife is outstanding. Storks, pelicans, shovellers and grebes, as well as brightly coloured kingfishers, are among the species seen here.

Along the shore, the **Hora Recreation Center** (admission Birr4) has opened. At the weekend it

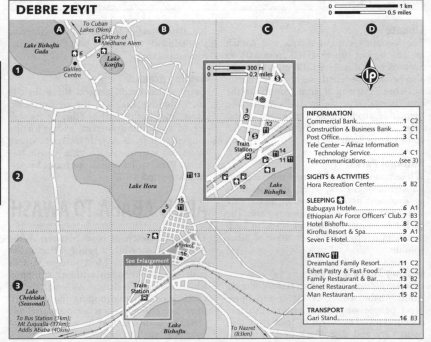

DEBRE ZEYIT

0 ━━━━ 1 km
0 ━━━━ 0.5 miles

To Cuban Lakes (9km)

Church of Medhane Alem

Lake Bishoftu Guda

Galileo Centre

Lake Koriftu

Lake Hora

0 ━━━━ 300 m
0 ━━━━ 0.2 miles

Train Station

Lake Bishoftu

See Enlargement

Market

Train Station

Lake Chelelaka (Seasonal)

To Bus Station (1km);
Mt Zuqualla (37km);
Addis Ababa (40km)

Lake Bishoftu

To Nazret (83km)

INFORMATION	
Commercial Bank	1 C2
Construction & Business Bank	2 C1
Post Office	3 C1
Tele Center – Almaz Information Technology Service	4 C1
Telecommunications	(see 3)

SIGHTS & ACTIVITIES	
Hora Recreation Center	5 B2

SLEEPING	
Babugaya Hotele	6 A1
Ethiopian Air Force Officers' Club	7 B3
Hotel Bishoftu	8 C2
Kiroftu Resort & Spa	9 A1
Seven E Hotel	10 C2

EATING	
Dreamland Family Resort	11 C2
Eshet Pastry & Fast Food	12 C2
Family Restaurant & Bar	13 C2
Genet Restaurant	14 C2
Man Restaurant	15 B2

TRANSPORT	
Gari Stand	16 B3

can get a bit noisy, but it's easy enough to escape the crowds: just follow the footpath around the lake as it winds through the forested slopes of the crater. A circumnavigation of the lake takes around 1½ hours. You should go accompanied, as hassle (and even theft) has been a problem.

There are plans to build a luxury hotel here.

OTHER LAKES
If you feel lake addicted after visiting Lake Bishoftu and Lake Hora, and need another lake fix, follow the road to the north. Walk past the Defence Engineering College and the Agriculture Research Centre until you reach a fork. Take the right fork and follow the dirt road until you reach the Galileo Centre. Continue straight on for about 400m, until a dirt road to your left leads down to the shore of the scenic and peaceful **Lake Bishoftu Guda**.

To get to the milky-looking **Lake Kiroftu**, backtrack to the Galileo Centre and take the road on the left leading to the Kiroftu Resort & Spa. Lake Kiroftu is known particularly for its tilapia (freshwater fish) and its varied birdlife.

There are other lakes dotted around Debre Zeyit, including the **Cuban Lakes**, but they lie much further away and are not easily accessible unless you have private transport.

Sleeping
Hotel Bishoftu (☎ 0114 338299; fax 0114 339655; s/d Birr50/70) All's shipshape at the welcoming Bishoftu. The adjoining rooms are set around a sun-dappled courtyard, and the restaurant overlooks the lime-green waters of Lake Bishoftu. It's in a quiet street off the main drag.

Kiroftu Resort & Spa (☎ 0911 248213, in Addis Ababa 011-6636557; s/d Birr300/500; ☒) Need an escape hatch? Travel no further. This ambitious outfit, opened in 2006, fits the bill with 18 spacious, comfy cottage-style units with thatched roofs, wooden beds, spick-and-span bathrooms, a sauna, a pool and spectacular lake views thrown in for good measure. It's about 4km north of the centre, perched above Lake Kiroftu.

Babugaya Hotele (☎ 0114 331155; r Birr50) This family-run place has a low-key, easy-going appeal and the well-tended garden encourages light-hearted chatter. The six rooms are in good nick although the fixtures in the

bathrooms leave something to be desired. One thing is for sure: the views over Lake Bishoftu Guda are jaw-dropping. It's in the same area as the Kiroftu, just after the Galileo Centre (look for the brown and black metal portal with the letters AA on it).

Ethiopian Air Force Officers' Club (☎ 0114 338035; s/d Birr200/400; ☒) If spending some time with army officials is your idea of a nice retreat, you can bunk down in this characterless yet airy complex. The general feel is a bit faded but the killer here is the Olympic-sized pool (Birr15).

Seven E Hotel (☎ 0114 339888; d Birr25-35) Although décor is not its strong point, this nonetheless good-value option is an acceptable crash pad if the other ones are full. Its best feature is the refreshing garden compound. It's just off the main road from the Shell station.

Eating
Eshet Pastry & Fast Food (pastries Birr2-5; ☒ 6am-9.30pm) With loud TV, smiling waitresses, thick pineapple juices (Birr4), strong *macchiatos* (Birr2) and shady terrace, this lively den is a perfect spot to soak up the atmosphere. You can't miss it; it's near the main square, on the road to Lake Hora.

Genet Restaurant (☎ 0114 640542; mains Birr8-15) Just down the road from Hotel Bishoftu, this modest but pleasant and popular eatery serves good Ethiopian staples at puny prices. The menu is not translated in English; just ask for *tibs* (sliced lamb, pan fried in butter, garlic, onion and sometimes tomato) or *misto* (a combination of various types of meat served with *injera*, a large Ethiopian version of a pancake/plate) and you should depart happy and buzzing.

Dreamland Family Resort (☎ 0114 339498; mains Birr15-25) The selling point of this restaurant is its unbeatable position, with such a breathtaking view over the lime-green waters of Lake Bishoftu that it's hard to tear yourself away. The garden is really enchanting, with lots of greenery. Foodwise it dishes up the usual suspects at reasonable prices.

Family Restaurant & Bar (☎ 0114 338066; mains Birr25-45; ☒ weekend) Surprise: this place is modelled on an American bar and serves Tex-Mex grub. It may push the budget but where else could you grab invigorating nachos, tacos and guacamole cheeseburgers? It's next to the Defence Engineering College.

EASTERN ETHIOPIA

Man Restaurant (☎ 0114 339858; mains Birr8-15) About 300m past the junction for the Recreation Centre, on the main road. Choice is limited (pastries, chicken dishes and spaghetti) but there's a tacky mural to keep you smiling ('Donuts are fancy', whatever that might mean). Grab a seat in the leafy compound.

Getting There & Around

Buses and minibuses leave every 15 minutes for Addis Ababa (Birr4, one hour) and Nazret (Birr8, one hour).

A *gari* (horse-drawn cart) is a great way to visit the lakes. They can be hired at the market, about 800m from the main roundabout. Expect to pay around Birr30/60 per half/full day. Hops about the town in a local minibus cost Birr0.90.

MT ZUQUALLA ዝቄላተራራ

Debre Zeyit also makes a good base from which to explore the extinct volcanic cone of Mt Zuqualla. Though only rising to just over 600m, the mountain dominates the landscape for miles around. On a clear day, the views from the top are stunning. You can see the Rift Valley to the east and the lakes to the south; Addis Ababa and the Entoto Mountains are just discernible to the northwest.

The crater, measuring 2km across and over 60m deep, contains a lake that has long been held holy by the monks of the nearby monastery.

The **monastery of Mt Zuqualla Maryam** (admission Birr50) is traditionally thought to have been founded by St Gebre Manfus Kiddus (see the boxed text, p49) in the 12th or 13th century. The site may actually date to the 4th century, when a hermit community may have been established here by St Mercurios.

In March and October large festivities are held at the monastery, and pilgrims come from miles around to attend them. Try to have your visit coincide with the festivities.

You're welcome to spend the night at the monastery, but don't expect the Ritz. The 'guesthouse' more closely resembles a stable spread with straw. You can also camp in the church compound. Any gifts are greatly appreciated by the monks. Bring your own food.

Getting There & Away

The nearest village to Mt Zuqualla is Maryam Wember, which lies at the foot of the mountain, around 25km southwest of Debre Zeyit.

Usually one to two 4WD vehicles travel daily to Maryam Wember (Birr10, up to two hours) from Debre Zeyit (more on market day on Thursday). From Maryam Wember, it's a 12km walk (three hours up and 2½ hours down).

If you're not watching the pennies, your best bet is to rent a 4WD in Addis Ababa (see p282.

NAZRET ናዝሬት

pop 224,000 / elev 1712m

Great churches, ancient monasteries and sacred relics? You'd be forgiven for thinking that Nazret has it all. But its name, derived from Christ's birthplace in Israel, is a misnomer, and you certainly won't wax mystical in this large, commercial and bustling town, lying just 100km from the capital. Its attractions are much more secular: it flaunts good accommodation options, so if you want to break up your journey, this is a convenient stopover. It's also a popular weekend retreat for frazzled Addis Ababans in search of tranquillity.

Information

Commercial Bank (☎ 0221 111952; ◷ 8am-noon & 2-5pm Mon-Fri, 8-11am Sat) On the main roundabout.
Millenium Internet Cafe (per hr Birr15; ◷ 7.30am-9.30pm) Opposite Frank Hotel, in a shopping centre.

Sleeping & Eating

Safari Lodge Adama (☎ 0221 122011; r Mon-Fri Birr250, Sat & Sun Birr281; ⊠) Surprise! The hippest venture in town is not beyond your financial reach. All the perks of a mellow retreat: ideal location, restaurant, Jacuzzi, swimming pool and well-designed gardens where you can flake out. And did we mention the two well-stocked bars? Just one grumble – although it's off the main road, the traffic noise is still audible.

Bekele Molla Hotel (☎ 0221 112312; d Birr70-116) On the eastern approach to town, the Bekele Molla surprises guests with well-furnished bungalows, prim bathrooms and plenty of verdant surrounds to mooch around in. Some rooms are also housed in a yellowish building that resembles an elementary school. The dining room boasts unusually bright splashes of colours.

Palace Hotel (☎ 0221 113800; s Birr75-115, d Birr105-150) 'Palace' may be stretching it a tad but it's brilliant value and ideally positioned, opposite the bus station. Rooms are nothing fancy but are well scrubbed and serviceable. Plus, there's a large garden to unwind in.

Pan-Afric Hotel (☎ 0221 122720; fax 0221 126888; Addis Ababa Rd; d Birr75-85) The closest thing Debre Zeyit has to a business hotel, with well-looked-after rooms equipped with satellite TV and prudish bathrooms. If you find that the carpets show signs of wear and tear, focus your attention on the cheesy bunches of fake flowers. Aim for one of the brighter and quieter rooms at the rear.

Adama Makonnen Hotel (☎ 0221 110880; Addis Ababa Rd; s/d Birr95/140) Almost next door to the Pan-Afric, on the main Addis Ababa road. This concrete blob is certainly not a paean to futuristic architecture but at least it's functional, well maintained and tidy. Some rooms are more luminous than others, so ask to see a few.

Frank Hotel (☎ 0221 112196; Addis Ababa Rd; mains Birr10-20) Not far from the main square, the Frank is indisputably the most popular eatery in town – it can be a squeeze finding a table come dinnertime. It's a little timewarpish (neon lighting, reddish tablecloth) and the *faranji* (Western foreigner) food is certainly not gourmet but we can't fault the *chicken cutlete* (chicken wing) and service is as smooth as its papaya juice. Ignore the hotel section – it's shabby.

Sunrise Bakery (pastries Birr3-5) Hmm, those damn little 'corrasants' (croissants), eye-catchingly displayed, continue to torment us! Spellchecking aside, this snappy place is ideal to recharge the batteries, sip a *macchiato* (Birr2) and watch the world go by. It's a 200m jog away from the main square, to the north.

BM Pastry (Addis Ababa Rd) The day we dropped by, the large dining room was chock-full with a rambunctious young crowd watching English-league football on a large TV screen. It's a good stop any time of the day for a cup of coffee or a snack.

Getting There & Away

At least 20 buses leave daily for Addis Ababa (Birr11, 2½ hours). One bus and frequent minibuses leave daily for Awash

(Birr15, 2½ hours). For Debre Zeyit (Birr8, one hour), it's best to go to Mojo first and change, as buses leave there every 15 minutes (Birr4, 15 minutes).

When heading south for Bale Mountains National Park, go to Asela (Birr7, two hours) first and change. For Ziway and the Rift Valley lakes, go to Mojo (Birr4, 15 minutes) and change.

AWASH NATIONAL PARK
አዋሽ ብሔራዊ ፓርክ

Easily accessible from Addis Ababa, **Awash National Park** (admission per person per 48hr Birr50, per vehicle up to 5 seats Birr10; ☻ 6am-6pm) is one of eastern Ethiopia's star attractions and one of Ethiopia's most visited parks. But don't expect Kenyan-style safaris; if you come here to experience the thrill of staring slack-jawed at lions crunching through bones, you'll be seriously disappointed. This park is much lower-key. Nevertheless, for those with patience and some time, it offers quite good wildlife viewing and outstanding birdlife viewing. It also contains an interesting range of volcanic landscapes.

The park takes its name from the Awash River, the longest river in Ethiopia. The river marks the park's southern boundary, then veers north before disappearing into the remote and desolate confines of the Danakil region. The salt lake, Lake Abbe (Lac Abbé) on the Ethiopia–Djibouti border, is the river's last gesture.

Wildlife
BIRDS

Twitchers, rejoice! The park lies on an important migratory route between the north and the south and is littered with an astonishing amount of birdlife. More than 400 bird species have been recorded in the park, among them six endemics: the banded barbet, golden-backed woodpecker, white-winged cliff chat, white-tailed starling, thick-billed raven and wattled ibis among others.

Two especially good spots to observe birds are around Filwoha Hot Springs, and around the camping grounds near Awash River, where doves, barbets and hoopoes are all seen.

Near the river itself, kingfishers and bee-eaters are found. On the plains, bustards are quite easily spotted, and sometimes secretary birds and ostriches. Among the many raptors are tawny and fish eagles, dark chanting gos-hawks and pygmy and lanner falcons.

MAMMALS

In the south of the park lies the grassy Illala Sala Plains, which attracts most of the larger mammals. The beautiful beisa oryx is easily seen here (in particular between the park gate and Kereyou Lodge), as are Soemmering's gazelles. Salt's dik-diks prefer the acacia bushes.

In the bushland areas, particularly in the rocky valleys to the north, around the park headquarters and in the area known as 'Kudu Valley', greater and lesser kudus, defassa waterbucks (though few in numbers now) and warthogs can be seen. Anubis and hamadryas baboons are found in the east side of the park as well as around the Filwoha Hot Springs and Fantale Crater.

The colobus monkey is found in the riverine forest. Leopards, lions, black-backed and golden jackals, caracals, servals and wildcats are also found in the park, but thank your lucky stars if you manage to spot one of them – they are seen pretty rarely. Striped and spotted hyenas are often heard at night. The nocturnal aardwolf is also present.

Orientation & Information

The park covers an area of 756 sq km and mostly lies at around 1000m above sea level. The exception is the dormant volcano of Fantale, which at 2007m dominates the centre of the park.

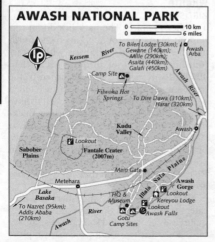

AWASH NATIONAL PARK

The main gate is around 14km after the town of Metehara, 16km before Awash, if you're coming from Addis Ababa. The park headquarters lies 10km southeast of the main gate.

Dangers & Annoyances

Walking is 'discouraged' (not allowed) in the park. The official explanation is because of the carnivores that inhabit the area but, in reality, robbery from local tribespeople poses the greater risk. Even if you're with a vehicle, armed scouts (from Birr50 for the whole day) are recommended. They can also act as guides.

If you're planning to travel in the northern region of the park (including the Filwoha Hot Springs), the scouts are compulsory. Tribal conflicts between the Kereyu, Afar and Itu pastoralist tribes are still common.

Be aware that many of the locals are sensitive about cameras, and may become very aggressive if you take photos without permission. See p266 for tips for photographers in Ethiopia.

An armed scout is a good idea if you leave the campsite during the day, as well as providing extra security during the night (Birr50 per night). Leaving the vehicle to take photos or approach birds is permitted, but it is better to do so with a scout.

Malaria here is a major problem; make sure that you take adequate precautions (see p373). You'll also need to bring all drinking water with you.

Watch out for both the baboons and the grivet monkeys, which have become adept camp pillagers.

Sights

To see the greatest number of animals, come first thing in the morning or late in the afternoon. At noon, many animals retire to the shade of the trees.

In the same complex as the park headquarters is a small **museum** (6am-6pm) filled with the usual stuffed animals, plus some mildly interesting 'interpretative materials' on the area's flora, fauna and people, and some useful animal locator maps. Nearby, there's a viewpoint over the **Awash Falls**, which are a good spot for bird-spotting. In season, when there's enough water, you can have a dip in the falls.

FANTALE CRATER ፋንታሌ

Towards the west of the park lies Fantale Crater. With its terrific vistas, total quiet and cool air, it is a great place for a picnic. At the top the 360-degree view is phenomenal and the elliptical caldera, which measures an enormous 3.5km in diameter, is an eerie sight. The local Kereyu people can be seen grazing their animals and growing crops far below.

The crater rim lies around 25km from headquarters; it's a two-hour drive as the dirt road is very steep and rough in parts – it's motorable by 4WD only. Hamadryas baboons are easily seen.

FILWOHA HOT SPRINGS ፍል ወኃ

Fancy a dip? Head to the Filwoha Hot Springs, in the far north of the park, around 40km from the park headquarters. You can swim in the turquoise-blue pools. They're not as refreshing as they look: temperatures touch 36°C! In the cooler areas of the springs, as well as in the Awash River, crocodiles are found (but they are not present in the hotter areas). Hippos also haunt the Awash River, though they are shy.

Around the springs, look out for the doum palms, much appreciated by the local Afar people (who use them to make mats as well as a kind of wine). After 5pm, the area comes alive with birds. Lions can sometimes be heard at night. Waterbucks and hamadryas baboons are also seen here.

You'll need a 4WD to get to the springs.

Sleeping & Eating

Camping (Birr20) The shady sites along the Awash River in the area known as 'Gotu', 400m south of the park headquarters, are attractive. Of the six spots, the Gumarre (Hippo) site is considered the most engaging. At night you can often hear the noises of hippos, hyenas and jackals, which come to the river to drink. Crocodiles are also seen here, sunbathing on the banks of the river. Bring everything you need because there are no facilities. Another option is the area around the Filwoha Hot Springs in the northern extreme of the park, with its shady fig trees. Note that camping outside these two areas is forbidden.

Kereyou Lodge (caravan s/d Birr150/200) This 'lodge' is a (sad) joke and, at this price, a rip-off. The setting is absolutely sublime – it is perched on the edge of a plummeting gorge,

12km from the park gate – but facilities are rudimentary. This is more a decrepit caravan site than a lodge, with a row of 16 neglected caravans with cold 'showers' (in fact buckets). However, the restaurant (mains Birr15 to Birr20) has a terrace that boasts phenomenal views over the gorge and the Arba River. After some early-morning wildlife viewing, it's a fabulous place for a coffee, a goulash or a surprisingly well-crafted shish kebab while ogling the fabulous chasm below your feet.

Getting There & Around

Walking is not allowed in the park, nor are bikes or motorcycles. Most visitors hire vehicles or come with a tour, both from Addis Ababa (see p282).

A 4WD is necessary for the Fantale Crater and the Filwoha Hot Springs, or during the rainy season (July to September).

AWASH አዋሽ

pop 5886 / elev 900m

Halfway between Addis Ababa and Dire Dawa, Awash is a good place to get out of the bus and stretch. Though Awash won't win the award of tourist destination of the year, this haphazard town will hold your attention for a short stroll. Wax nostalgic at the derelict railway station – the railway is still its *raison d'être* – and spend a night at the historic hotel nearby. If you're in town when the old Djibouti–Addis Ababa train pulls in, it's definitely worth a peek.

On Monday there is a very colourful market that attracts both Kereyu and Afar people. Look out for the Kereyu women in skins and sandals and with braided hair. The men prefer a carefully shaped Afro, often ornamented with combs. Animal fat (like a kind of Ethiopian Brylcreem!) is used to give it a chic gloss and to keep it in condition.

Around 600m behind the station lies the giddy-deep Awash Gorge, also worth a small detour to soak up the vertigo-inducing views.

Sleeping & Eating

Buffet d'Aouache (☎ 0222 240008; d with shared bathroom Birr20-50, 'presidentielles' r Birr100) There's something delightfully timeless about this zany old relic of French railway days (1904). It's utterly without frills but it's high on atmosphere, with whitewashed walls, birds

EASTERN ETHIOPIA

THE TRIUMPH OF MAN OVER TOPOGRAPHY

In the 1890s a man had a dream: to build a railway that would link Ethiopia with French Somaliland (present-day Djibouti) 800km to the east. Carved through some of the most inhospitable terrain in Ethiopia, the railway was planned to end forever the old isolation of the Ethiopian highlands.

Each kilometre of line demanded no less than 70 tonnes of rails, sleepers and telegraph poles, as well as massive quantities of cement, sand and water, and food and provisions for an army of workers. To keep the costs down, a narrow gauge of just 1m was used.

To cross the difficult terrain, several viaducts and 22 tunnels (one nearly 100m long) had to be built. In the meantime the local Afars, whose territory the 'iron monster' was penetrating, ran horrific raids on the line at every opportunity, stealing building materials and killing workers. It took no less than 20 years to complete.

Since the Eritrean–Ethiopian border dispute of the late 1990s, the railway has carried a significant part of the country's imports and exports to and from the Red Sea port of Djibouti City. However, its importance is fading these days because of the development of lorry transport, which is considered much more reliable, and the lack of maintenance.

Still, this bone-shaking iron horse will appeal to train enthusiasts. Indeed, it's exactly this uniquely ramshackle quality that is the main source of its charm – perversely!

humming in the rambling garden and a bougainvillea-draped courtyard. The rooms with shared bathrooms are pretty spare; better treat yourself to a generous-sized 'presidentielle' room, equipped with fan and a giant bath on legs. Meals come in for warm praise (mains Birr12 to Birr30), and Greek, Italian or French-style dishes can be ordered in advance.

Genet Hotel (☎ 0222 240040; d with shared bathroom Birr40-80, d Birr120) At the eastern end of town, a stone's throw from the bus station. The Genet features a decent restaurant and four different types of rooms arranged around an airy courtyard where goats and other farmyard animals can be seen pottering about. May we suggest you opt for the more expensive, but salubrious, rooms?

Awash Meridian (☎ 0222 240051; d with shared bathroom Birr15-30, d Birr80) Almost a carbon copy of the Genet. Steer clear of the cheaper rooms; rather, hole up in the more expensive ones, with fan, mosquito net and private bathroom. There's an on-site restaurant.

Getting There & Away

One bus leaves daily for Gewane (Birr17, two hours), three buses go weekly to Logiya (Birr43, eight hours) via Mille (Birr35, seven hours), and two buses leave daily for Nazret (Birr11, three hours).

For Dire Dawa (Birr 43, nine hours), try to find a seat on one of the 10 buses that pass through Awash from Addis Ababa and Nazret.

AWASH TO ASAITA

If you're looking for thunderous waterfalls, great rivers and verdant meadows, you've come to the wrong place. The endless road north to Asaita is more like an American highway in Arizona. Think severely parched terrain, vacuous plains, ferocious sun, negligible shade, barren scenery that can send the perpetually curious into a free-fall of boredom, and a fistful of unassuming towns. Be prepared for an almost meditative drive that needs a damn-good supply of Amharic pop cassettes.

But this remote part of Ethiopia is definitely not to be sneezed at. Crossing this dry-as-a-bone expanse is a fascinating experience. The journey might be low on highlights, but it's strong on atmosphere, as it takes you through the heart of Afar country. The hauntingly bleak landscape has a peculiar appeal. It's a bit like penetrating a forgotten world.

THE ROAD NORTH TO ASAITA

From the junction with the Addis Ababa–Dire Dawa road, you'll first cross **Awash Arba**, about 14km to the north, then the featureless town of **Gewane**. It doesn't warrant a lengthy stop but you'll be overwhelmed by the stark allure of the dramatic volcano that lords over the surrounding plains. After Gewane, the country resembles Djibouti more and more: arid and desolate.

EASTERN ETHIOPIA

The road passes through the **Yangudi-Rassa National Park** but, frankly, don't expect much wildlife; there is probably less here than in any national park in Ethiopia. If you're lucky, you might spot ostriches, bustards and Soemmering's gazelles.

About 150km north of Gewane, the town of **Mille** won't leave you awestruck but makes a convenient stop if you feel the urge to quaff a lukewarm soda and recharge the batteries. Around Mille, look out for the little domed Afar huts, made from the interwoven leaves of the doum palm, which are light and easy to transport. As for the rolled-up objects sold along the roadside, they are mattresses made from local rushes. About 10km south of town lies the junction with the road that heads west to Bati and Dessie.

Continuing north the road takes you through **Logiya**, a surprisingly bustling town where Ethiopian truck drivers usually overnight. Don't expect airs and graces: it's a rough-and-ready town, with a herd of seedy hotels, brothels and restaurants lining the main drag. About 8km northeast of Logiya, it's a shock to come suddenly upon **Semera**, the new regional capital of Afar. With its quirky mix of barracks, modern apartment blocks and soulless administrative buildings, it looks like a microscopic version of Brasília emerging incongruously in the middle of the desert – except that it's a completely botched attempt at creating a new town. Should you want to explore the lakes around Asaita (see p222), you'll have to stop here to hire a compulsory guide and get a permission paper at the **tourist office** (☎ 0336 660488; ✆ 8-11.30am & 3-5pm Mon-Fri), near the Justice building. For some places, you'll also have to hire an armed policeman (Birr100 per day). Disputes over land ownership in the region sometimes result in violence between the different clans.

About 10km north of Semera along the main road, an easy-to-miss asphalt road branches off to the right and leads to Asaita.

Sleeping & Eating

If you need to break your journey, the choice of reliable accommodation is very limited. Most hotels are spartan and cater primarily to Ethiopian truck drivers on their way to and from Djibouti port. Foodwise, if you find yourself missing *haute cuisine*, remember what you're here for: adventure, darlings. The following places are your best bets.

Bilen Lodge (in Addis Ababa ☎ 0111 508869; Bilen; tukul s/d US$40/50) If you're in the mood for hush and seclusion, nothing can beat this hideaway on the edge of Awash National Park. The 16 traditional-style huts are perched on a mound and boast private bathrooms and electricity. Add US$25 per person per day for full board. Various activities can be organised in the vicinity, ranging from a visit to Afar villages to wildlife-watching excursions. You'll need a private vehicle to get here. It's 52km past Awash Arba. Drive 40km to the north from Awash Arba, then take a track on the left for another 12km; it's signposted. Reservations are necessary. Contact the Village Ethiopia agency (p283) in Addis Ababa.

Parki Hotelli (☎ 0332 230113; Mille; r with shared bathroom Birr45) A ramshackle building with cell-like, ultrabasic rooms with fan and shared bathrooms that, er, seem to see the occasional mop. There's an on-site 'restaurant' serving cheap fare.

Nazret Hotel (☎ 0332 500222; Logiya; r with shared bathroom Birr20) This is usually where UN officials bunk down when in town, which is enough to recommend this place on the main street. Ask for the more recent rooms in the second compound at the back. The beds are as lumpy as Thanksgiving's mashed potatoes but a fan and a mosquito net are *de rigueur*. The ablution block is in decent shape. The food is pretty varied (read: pasta, rice and *tibs*) and you'll sample your meal sitting in front of faded posters featuring Sydney's Opera House. Isn't it cute?

There are also several shops selling basic supplies in most towns.

Getting There & Away

From Awash, with your own wheels, follow the Dire Dawa road for about 5km then turn left at a well-signposted junction. This is not the road less travelled: countless Ethiopian trucks ply this route to and from Djibouti, so be vigilant. The road is in excellent condition.

Bus services are fairly infrequent and not really reliable on this long stretch. One bus departs Awash daily for Gewane (Birr17, two to three hours). Buses run three times weekly from Awash to Logiya (Birr43, eight hours) via Mille. From Logiya or Semera to Asaita, services are more frequent; there

EASTERN ETHIOPIA

OGLING THE AFARS

On the journey north, look out for Afar men striding along in simple cotton *shirits* (sarongs), with their famous *jile* (the curved knives described by the writer Wilfred Thesiger) hanging at their side. Many also carry gourds which act as water bottles.

Many Afars still lead a nomadic existence, and when the herds are moved in search of new pasture, the huts in which the Afars live are simply packed onto the backs of camels and carted away. Look out for the wooden boughs used for the armature, which resemble great ribs curving upwards from the camels' backs. In the relatively fertile plains around the river, some Afars have turned to cultivation, growing tobacco, cotton, maize and dates. Interclan rivalry is still alive; conflict occasionally breaks out.

are several daily departures in the morning (Birr12, about two hours).

From Awash to Logiya, your best bet is probably to hitch a lift with one of the many trucks travelling that way. In Awash, ask around at the petrol stations. The ride should set you back about Birr40.

From Mille, there's at least one daily bus to Dessie (Birr20, four hours). From there you can catch a bus to Addis Ababa (see p166).

There's no public transport to Galafi (the Djibouti border) or to Djibouti City, but it's quite easy to hitch a lift (front seats only) with one of the legions of trucks that overnight in Logiya. The prices we were quoted ranged from Birr150 to Birr200 to Djibouti City (about eight hours).

ASAITA አሳይታ

pop 14,392 / elev 300m

Gosh, it's a gruelling ride to get to Asaita, a cul-de-sac, end-of-the-world town about 70km east of Logiya. Here you'll instantly feel a 'last frontier' ambience and an overpowering sense of exoticism and adventure. At the heart of Afar territory, Asaita prides itself on being the bastion of Afar identity and culture.

Come prepared. The heat is unbearable for nine months of the year. At first glance, the town is not especially alluring, with no obvious attractions, but it will grow on you sooner than you'd think, with its chirpy,

coloured façades, its buzzing atmosphere in the evening and its magnificent, proud Afar inhabitants. It's also a convenient base from which to explore the 30 salt lakes in the area, the volcanic springs and the Danakil Depression.

Tuesday is Asaita's market day – a must if you're in town.

Information

Note that to visit the surrounding attractions (including the lakes), you'll need to get a permission paper as well as hiring a compulsory guide in Semera (see p220).

Commercial Bank (☼ 7-11.30am & 3-5pm Mon-Fri, 7-11.30am Sat) Changes cash (euros and US dollars).

Sights

Do you *really* want to get back to nature? Then the **salt lakes** that are scattered around Asaita are your promised land. This area remains one of the most inhospitable corners of the Horn, appearing much the same as when explorer Wilfred Thesiger first laid eyes upon it in the 1920s. The scenery, straight out of Dante's *Inferno*, can't be more forbidding. There's a stark, desolate, almost surreal beauty. For serious adventurers, this little-explored territory is something of a holy grail. Birdlife is another attraction: storks, flamingos, ibises, vultures and raptors can be seen. The journey to the lakes also takes you through very remote Afar country. With their dagger slung around their waist in a long thin leather pouch, or their rifle poised over the shoulder, the Afar people, almost the only ones capable of surviving in these harsh conditions, have acquired the patina of myth. They have long fascinated European travellers and explorers, including Thesiger himself, whose account of the Afar peoples (then known as the Danakils; see p46) encountered along the way has become something of an epic. It greatly fuelled the Afars' already legendary reputation for ferocity.

For those with time and stamina, this remote region can be explored on foot. You'll need to hire an Afar guide (see p220). Several agencies based in Addis Ababa also organise tours in the area (see p282).

Note that it takes time to reach the lakes and sometimes access is limited because of security concerns. A minimum of three days is usually required. Check the situation when you get there.

Lakes in the region that can usually be visited include **Lake Gamarri** (around 30km from Asaita – known for its hundreds of flamingos); **Lake Afambo** and **Lake Bario** (both near the town of Afambo); and **Lake Abbe**, on the border with Djibouti. Lake Abbe can also be approached from the Djibouti side.

Sleeping & Eating

You won't face a dilemma in Asaita.

Basha Hotel (☎ 0336 550119; d with shared bathroom Birr20) The best option by far is this hotel, a coin's toss from the Commercial Bank (there's no sign, so ask around). The hutlike entrance is a bit off-putting, but the swing-a-cat-sized rooms at the rear are set around a pretty courtyard and boast immaculate sheets, surprisingly back-friendly beds, working (though rattling) fans and tolerable shared toilets. The last room at the back is the best, with sweeping views over the Awash River. At night, you can hear the hyenas, and the camels in the camps of the Afar nomads below. Omelettes, *tibs* and fresh yogurt are available in the modest restaurant at the front.

Lem Hotel (☎ 0336 550050; r with shared bathroom Birr20) If the Basha is full, this place makes an acceptable plan B, but the bar at the front is noisy.

Getting There & Away

Buses and minibuses leave from the main square. At least five minibuses leave each day for Logiya (Birr10, two hours). There are also regular services to Semera (Birr12, 2½ hours). One bus leaves daily for Dessie (Birr33, eight hours).

For Djibouti, you'll have to take a bus back to Logiya. From there, try to hitch a lift (front seats only) on the steady stream of trucks travelling from Addis Ababa to Djibouti.

At the time of writing there were no 4WDs available for hire in Asaita, and no contract taxis.

AWASH TO JIJIGA

This is what you were looking for. Here's the menu: cities filled with character and mystery, majestic landscapes that capture the mind, and a pervading sense of exploration. If one place had to be singled out, it would be Harar, the jewel in the crown. As you travel further east towards the Somali border, the sense of adventure is even more pronounced. Nature-lovers, city types and budding adventurers will all have their slice of heaven in this corner of Ethiopia.

THE ROAD TO DIRE DAWA

Going east, the landscape seems to get drier and drier, the temperature hotter and hotter. It's not too long, though, before the road once again starts to snake upwards from the arid lowlands.

This is the heart of Oromo country. The men gathered under ancient trees are attending the village assembly. Around the Chercher Mountains, the first signs of *chat* cultivation appear; look for the little bushes with shiny, dark-green leaves planted in neat rows.

What majesty! As scenic drives go, this road is awesome. As the road begins to climb, you're taken through some very beautiful scenery with stunning views; the last 120km or so of road before the turnoff to Dire Dawa (at Alemaya) is one of the prettiest in Ethiopia. At sunset, eye-popping hues saturate the landscape and ignite the imagination of photographers. Other highlights include the markets along this route – they are among the most colourful in the country. Don't miss them. The Thursday market at **Asbe Tefari** is probably the most eye-catching. Saturday is market day for many villages in the region – if you can travel east on this day, do. Many women don their best finery: very colourful skirts, headbands, waistband and beads. Unforgettable!

DIRE DAWA ድሬዳዋ

pop 260,000 / elev 1200m

The second-most populous town in Ethiopia, Dire Dawa never fails to elicit strong reactions. Some travellers rave about its remarkably spacious and orderly layout (a rarity in Ethiopia, as you'll soon realise), its tree-lined streets, neat squares and colonial buildings, while others think it's the definition of utilitarian and self-contained.

Sure, it does lack the charisma of nearby Harar, and in the eyes of most visitors it will always play second fiddle to Harar, but you'll soon discover that it has its fair share of beguiling sights and some inviting

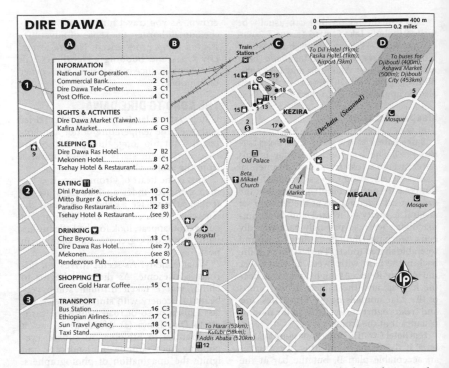

DIRE DAWA

0 — 400 m
0 — 0.2 miles

INFORMATION
National Tour Operation.............1 C1
Commercial Bank.......................2 C1
Dire Dawa Tele-Center...............3 C1
Post Office...............................4 C1

SIGHTS & ACTIVITIES
Dire Dawa Market (Taiwan)........5 D1
Kafira Market...........................6 C3

SLEEPING
Dire Dawa Ras Hotel..................7 B2
Mekonen Hotel.........................8 C1
Tsehay Hotel & Restaurant.........9 A2

EATING
Dini Paradaise.........................10 C2
Mitto Burger & Chicken.............11 C1
Paradiso Restaurant.................12 B3
Tsehay Hotel & Restaurant........(see 9)

DRINKING
Chez Beyou............................13 C1
Dire Dawa Ras Hotel................(see 7)
Mekonen................................(see 8)
Rendezvous Pub......................14 C1

SHOPPING
Green Gold Harar Coffee...........15 C1

TRANSPORT
Bus Station............................16 C3
Ethiopian Airlines...................17 C1
Sun Travel Agency..................18 C1
Taxi Stand.............................19 C1

Train Station

To Dil Hotel (1km);
Fasika Hotel (1km);
Airport (3km)

To buses for
Djibouti (400km);
Ashqwa Market
(500km); Djibouti
City (453km)

KEZIRA

Dechatu (Seasonal)

Mosque

Old Palace

Beta
Mikael
Church

Chat
Market

MEGALA

Mosque

Hospital

To Harar (53km);
Kulubi (58km);
Addis Ababa (520km)

quarters. So rather than dismiss it, pack an open mind and investigate the possibilities.

History
The great Addis Ababa–Djibouti railway was supposed to pass through Harar, but with ever-burgeoning costs, the project was falling into difficulties. Then a momentous decision was taken: to bypass the great Cher-cher Mountains and keep to the lowlands. Instead of passing through the old commer-cial town of Harar, the railway would pass through a new town, which Menelik chose to call New Harar. In 1902 Dire Dawa – as it was known locally – was born.

Orientation
Despite it being a fairly sprawling town, your chances of getting lost in Dire Dawa are vir-tually nonexistent. It's simply laid out and is a breeze to navigate. The town is made up of two distinct settlements, divided by the Dechatu wadi (seasonal river). Lying to the north and west of the Dechatu is the 'new town' known as Kezira. On the southern and eastern side of the wadi is the 'old town'

known as Megala, which, with its Arab-ooking houses, has a distinctly Muslim feel.

Information
Commercial Bank (Kezira; 7.30-11am & 2.30-5.30pm Mon-Fri, 7.30-10.30am Sat) Changes cash and travellers cheques.
Dire Dawa Tele-Center (0251 120908; Kezira; per hr Birr18; 7am-9pm) Diagonally opposite Mitto Burger & Chicken. An Internet café that also doubles as a telephone centre.
National Tour Operation (NTO; 0251 111119; Kezira; 2-5pm Mon-Fri) Serves as a tourist office.
Post office (Kezira; 8am-noon & 3-6pm Mon-Fri, 8am-noon Sat) Opposite the railway station.

Sights
Dire Dawa's main highlights are its thriving markets. With its Babel-like ambience, the enormous **Kafira Market**, in Megala, is the most striking one. Delving into the organ-ised chaos of its narrow lanes is an assault on the senses. This market attracts people from miles around, including Afar herd-ers, Somali pastoralists and Oromo farm-ers; sometimes, around dawn, large camel

caravans march in from the Somali desert. A large variety of spices are sold here. There is also a thriving contraband market; merchandise is brought in from Djibouti either by night caravans across the remote frontiers, or carefully concealed in trucks. The best time to go is around 10am. It has some distinct 'Moorish-style' architectural features; look out for the striking horseshoe arches that serve as entrances.

Ashawa Market, on the outskirts of town, sells everything from beard trimmers to 'designer watches' and baby powder. The nearby **Dire Dawa Market** (also known as Taiwan), as its name suggests, specialises in cheap electronic goods. Both are worth a peek.

Foreign influence is still in evidence. Look for Arab, French and Italian styles in some of the architecture and design.

Sleeping

Mekonen Hotel (☎ 0251 113348; Kezira; r with shared bathroom Birr40) A good deal that won't hurt the hip pocket. This faded glory is housed in an old Italian colonial building opposite the train station. Most rooms (especially room 2) have plenty of space to really strew your stuff around, and some have balconies overlooking the square. Shared bathrooms (with cold showers) are a tad scummy but still do the trick. The proximity of cafés and restaurants is another bonus.

Tsehay Hotel & Restaurant (☎ 0251 110023; Kezira; r Birr60) The Tsehay is a bit of a trek from the centre but features cleanish rooms set in pleasant, hedged gardens. When we dropped by, plumbing seemed to be on the brink

of agony but was still functional. Best asset is the restaurant.

Fasika Hotel (☎ 0251 111260; Kezira; r Birr100) Off the airport road (follow the sign), this is one of the best midrange places, with neat common areas, a façade dripping with bougainvillea, quiet gardens and simple yet serviceable rooms.

Dil Hotel (☎ 0251 114181; Kezira; r Birr150-250) Remember the boarding school when you were young? Well, this sharp-edged, concrete lump lying 1.3km from the train station on the airport road was probably designed by the same architect. Not really the best place to curl up with your beloved, but the bathrooms are the most sparkling in town and rooms are well equipped.

Dire Dawa Ras Hotel (☎ 0251 113225; Kezira; r Birr88-220; 🏊) If you're into design history, this government-run hotel is definitely worth a peek. It was built in 1964 and nothing seems to have changed since then. The outdoor pool is a (sad) joke, but the large garden (full of birds) is a great spot to chill out.

Eating & Drinking

Paradiso Restaurant (☎ 0251 113780; Kezira; mains Birr15-20) Haven't had a slap-up meal for a while? Don't look past Paradiso, the most respected restaurant in town. The menu roves from palatable Italian dishes to more traditional gut-busters, such as *kitfo* (minced beef or lamb like the French steak tartare, usually served warmed – but not cooked – in butter, *berbere* and sometimes thyme) and *tibs*. Add in friendly staff, wallet-friendly prices and an enticing setting – an old-world mansion and a veranda – and you have a winner.

Tsehaye Hotel & Restaurant (Kezira; mains Birr11-22) The hotel is thoroughly undistinguished,

GENUFLECT AT KULUBI GABRIEL

Every year in December, tens of thousands of pilgrims converge on the little town of Kulubi and its cathedral, Saint Gabriel, perched on a hill above town. Pilgrims come to express thanks after the fulfilment of a wish, or in the hope of a miraculous cure. If you're in the area during the festival, it's well worth a stop.

Frequent minibuses and Peugeot contract taxis connect Kulubi with Dire Dawa (Birr10, 1½ to two hours).

but the food shines out at this sprightly outfit. Besides tummy-filling pasta, aim safely for Ethiopian delicacies such as the palate-blistering *kwanta firfir* (strips of beef rubbed in chilli, butter, salt and *berbere* then usually hung up and dried; served with torn-up *injera*), *zilzil tibs* (strips of beef, fried and served slightly crunchy with *awazi* sauce), or the delicious vegetarian combo on Wednesday and Friday. The menu is in Amharic only, which is not a bad sign (use p72 to decipher). The leafy garden is an added bonus. The waiters are pretty in turquoise and inky blue, too.

Mitto Burger & Chicken (☎ 0251 111206; Kezira; mains Birr10-25) With its wrought-iron chairs with tacky upholstery, (loud) satellite TV tuned to CNN, blondwood fittings and a nifty mezzanine for a little flirting, this is the closest thing Dire Dawa has to a snug fast-food joint. If you're pining for Western snacks, including pasta and burgers, this is the place to go. Its mango juice, served with a slice of lemon, kicks like a mule.

Dini Paradaise (Kezira; mains Birr5-10) Set in a large garden dripping with bougainvillea, Dini Paradaise (no typo) is a great place to escape the heat and dust of the town, relax over a cup of coffee or dig into inexpensive munchies.

Rendezvous Pub (Kezira) For a tipple, this rough-and-ready pub near the train station is worth a try.

Mekonen (Kezira) The shady terrace of the Mekonen is an excellent vantage point from where, drink in hand, you can watch the world go by.

Chez Beyou (Kezira) After a glass of whisky? Head to this tiny bar, almost next door to Mitto Burger.

Dire Dawa Ras Hotel (Kezira) The garden of this hotel is a pleasant place for a drink in the evening.

Shopping
Green Gold Harar Coffee (☎ 0251 101860; Kezira; ☻ 7.30am-noon & 3-5.30pm Mon-Sat) Are you a caffeine-addict? This is the place to stock up. It sells 1kg packets of excellent-quality Ethiopian coffee for Birr25.

Getting There & Away
AIR
Ethiopian Airlines (☎ 0251 113069; Kezira) flies between Dire Dawa and Addis Ababa at least once daily (Birr883 one way). It also operates four weekly flights to Jijiga (Birr480 one way).

Sun Travel Agency (☎ 0251 114059; Kezira) is an agent for Djibouti Airlines. Flights depart four times weekly for Djibouti City and cost Birr780 one way, plus US$20 for departure tax.

BUS
Four buses run daily to Addis Ababa (Birr54, 12 hours) via Awash (Birr43, nine hours), Nazret (Birr43, 10 hours) and Debre Zeyit (Birr46, 11 hours). Minibuses run every 15 minutes to Harar (Birr10, one hour); around five to 10 Peugeot contract taxis run daily to Kulubi (Birr10).

For Djibouti, a company runs daily buses from Dire Dawa to Djibouti City via Gelille (see p274 for more details).

TRAIN
Trains head east from here for Djibouti City. There are three weekly departures (see p274). Tickets can be bought at the train station.

In principle, the train also runs to Addis Ababa but this leg was indefinitely out of service at the time of research.

Getting Around
A contract taxi to or from the airport should set you back around Birr40.

HARAR ሐረር
pop 91,000 / elev 1856m
Harar is a place apart. Off the southern edge of the Chercher Mountains, this sensational city will shake up and blast your senses. With its 368 alleyways squeezed into just 1 sq km, its countless mosques and shrines, its coffee scents meandering through the streets, its animated markets, its superb architecture, its charming people and its uniquely unforgettable ambience, the old walled city will make you feel like you're floating through another time and space. As if it wasn't enough, an otherworldly ritual takes place every night outside the walls: men feed hyenas. Don't be confused: it's not a touristy show, it's a tradition.

A bit like Zanzibar, Harar is a place that appeals to both spiritual seekers and hedonists. Despite its shortcomings (read: poverty and minor hassles), you'll fall

HARAR

0 ———— 500 m
0 ———— 0.3 miles

INFORMATION
Canal Internet Cafe..............(see 27)
Commercial Bank.........................1 B3
Internet Cafe Ras Hotel ....(see 23)
Speedy Laundry...........................2 A4
Tourist Office..............................3 B3

SIGHTS & ACTIVITIES
Asma'addin Bari Market (New
  Market).................................4 C4
Emir Nur's Tomb..........................5 C3
Gidir Magala (Main Market)..........6 D3
Handicraft Museum......................7 D3
Harari National Cultural
  Centre..................................8 D3
Hyena Feeding Site.......................9 D3
Hyena Feeding Site.....................10 C2
Jamia Mosque............................11 D3
Medhane Alem Cathedral............12 C3
Oromo Market............................13 D3
Ras Makonnen Statue.................14 B3

Ras Makonnen's Palace.............(see 7)
Ras Tafari's House.......................15 C3
Recycling Market.......................16 B3
Rimbaud's House & Museum.......17 D3
St Mary Catholic Church.............18 D3
Sheikh Abadir's Tomb.................19 D4
Smugglers' Market......................20 B3
Tomb of Said Ali Hamdogn..........21 C3

SLEEPING
Belayneh Hotel..........................22 C4
Ras Hotel...................................23 A3
Rewda Guesthouse.....................24 C3
Tewodros Hotel..........................25 B3

EATING
Alpha Cafeteria & Restaurant.....26 A3
Canal Cafe.................................27 B3
Hirut Restaurant........................28 B3
Ice Cream Mermaid....................29 C3
Rose Cafe & Restaurant 30 A3

DRINKING
Ali Bal Café...............................31 C3
Bar Cottage...............................32 C3
GC Pub..................................(see 33)
Samsun Hotel............................33 C3

ENTERTAINMENT
National Hotel...........................34 B3
Tourist Hotel.............................35 B3

SHOPPING
Fatuma Safir Ahmed...................36 D3
Nure Roasted Harar Coffee........37 D3
Zeituna Yusuf Grille's Shop........38 D3

TRANSPORT
Bus Station................................39 B3
City Taxi Stand...........................40 C3
Selam Cafe................................41 C3

EASTERN ETHIOPIA

in love with this gem of a city – at least we did.

History

Harar is steeped in history. Situated just a few hundred kilometres east of the staunchly Christian highlands, Harar, like an exotic bird, might have been blown off course, either from across the waters of the Red Sea or from the northern deserts of Muslim North Africa.

For centuries, as a crossroads for every conceivable commerce, the town boomed, great dynasties of rich and powerful merchants grew up and the arts flourished. Harar became a kind of commercial meeting point of Africa, India and the Middle East. Right up until 1850, it was home to the most important market in the Horn.

Harar also spearheaded Islam's penetration into the Horn. In the 17th and 18th centuries, Harar become known as an important centre of Islamic scholarship. It still holds very special significance for Ethiopia's Muslim population. For years, the city was closed to Christians. In 1854 Richard Burton, the famous British explorer, was the first non-Muslim to penetrate the city. Later the bustling commercial town attracted many foreign merchants from India, Armenia, England and France. The famous French poet Arthur Rimbaud (p229) spent some of his last years here. In 1887 the city surrendered to the Emperor Menelik, who

CHAT, ANYONE?

Some travellers love it, others loathe it. To be frank, we loathe it, as the unpleasant bitterness and texture of *Catha edulis Forskal (chat)* continues to haunt us. A natural and mildly intoxicating stimulant, *chat* has been consumed for centuries in many eastern and southern African countries as well as on the Arab peninsula. Good news: it is legal in Ethiopia. An evergreen shrub averaging around 2m in height, it is found on warm, humid slopes between 1500m and 2800m and is actively cultivated in Yemen (where it's known as *qat*), Kenya (where it's called *miraa*) and Ethiopia. Some of the best *chat* is cultivated around Harar and it's exported the same day or so by truck or by plane to Djibouti and Somaliland.

It's an important pastime in eastern Ethiopia, but not on the same scale as, say, Somalia or Djibouti where chewing *qat* has become a national addiction, with serious socioeconomic consequences. For more information, read *Eating the Flowers of Paradise*, by Kevin Rushby, who followed the ancient route of *qat*.

During your stay in eastern Ethiopia, it's not a bad idea to give it a go. Don't expect to be stoned, however, and take antidiarrhoeal tablets, just in case. At least you'll impress the locals and, more importantly, your friends when you're back home. But if you just want to get tipsy, believe us: nothing beats a good Harari beer.

---

sought to expand and unify his highland empire.

Harar's economic fortunes suffered a serious blow at the end of the 19th century when the Addis Ababa–Djibouti railway was diverted to Dire Dawa. To this day, the city retains a somewhat isolated, inward-looking feel. The Hararis have their own ethnic identity, language and culture.

With the new government and the new federal constitution of 1995, Harar won a new victory: a kind of independence, with legal recognition as a city-state within the Federal Republic of Ethiopia.

Orientation

Fear not: you can't get lost. Harar's old walled town is so compact you'll eventually come to a major street or wall that will lead you back to Harar Gate, the main gate. There are six gates in total. Streets lead from each gate and converge in the centre at a bustling square, known as Feres Magala (Horse Market). Radiating out from the square are a maze of little alleyways and passages. The main thoroughfare in the walled city runs from Harar Gate to Feres Megala.

New town sprawls west of Harar Gate.

Information

Canal Internet Cafe (new town; per hr Birr21; ☾ 8.30am-noon & 2.30-8pm) Above Canal Cafe.
Commercial Bank (new town; ☾ 8-11.30am & 1.30-4.30pm Mon-Fri, 8-11am Sat) Near Harar Gate. Changes cash (euros and US dollars) and travellers cheques.

Internet Cafe Ras Hotel (new town; per hr Birr24; ☾ 8am-noon & 2.30-8pm) In the Ras Hotel.
Speedy Laundry (new town; ☾ 8am-noon & 1-6pm Mon-Sat)
Tourist office (☎ 0256 661763; new town; ☾ 8am-noon & 2-5.30pm Mon-Fri) Housed in the Harari People National Regional State Trade & Industry building. Mildly useful. Some English is spoken.

Dangers & Annoyances

Water shortages are a major problem in Harar and can affect the city for two or three days at a time. Try not to waste it. A new project to pipe water from Dire Dawa is underway, but it will take until 2009 to complete it. Power cuts are also a problem; city quarters are supplied by rota and do without one day a week.

Some travellers have written to complain of hassle from children in the walled city. Hiring a guide is the best deterrent (see following). Watch your wallet in the market areas.

GUIDES

For your first foray into Harar, it's quite a good idea to hire a guide and take a turn round the town's main attractions. Guides also know the location of less-visited corners and the best Harari houses and arts and crafts shops. Hiring a guide also deters other would-be guides. Later, you can return to wander unaccompanied.

Currently five official guides work in Harar (and many more unofficial ones). If you're in doubt ask to see ID. There's no official price, but Birr100/200 per half/full day is fair. One guide that can be particularly recommended is Abdul. If he is not available, he will direct you to other competent guides.

Sights

You can see the major attractions in a day (and a night), but two days is better.

INSIDE THE WALLED CITY

Harar's old walled town is a fascinating place that begs exploration. The thick, 5m-high walls around town, which stand to this day, were erected in the 16th century by an emir, in response to the migrations northwards of the Oromo. Within the walls the city is a maze of narrow, twisting alleys and lanes, replete with historic buildings, including 82 small mosques, numerous shrines and tombs, as well as traditional Harari houses.

The magnificent Adare (Harari) women, known for their very colourful traditional costumes, add to the appeal. Their dresses – usually black, yellow, red or purple – are worn over velvet trousers. Many also wear orange headscarves. Sometimes they carry huge bundles of cloth or baskets on their heads. You should be sensitive when trying to photograph these women. See p266 for tips.

Gates

There are six gates in total; two were added by the Emperor Menelik in 1889 to the four original ones (which date from the 16th century). An exploration of the old walled town (known locally as Jugal) begins at the main gate. This is known as the **Harar Gate** or Duke's Gate, after the first Duke of Harar, Ras Makonnen. The nearby **Shoa Gate** (also known as Asmae Diin Bari in Harari) is particularly well preserved and boasts superb mosaics. It's also worth taking your weary bones to the **Buda Gate**, which is in good shape as well.

To the north, the **Fallana Gate** is said to be the one Richard Burton entered disguised as an Arab merchant.

Medhane Alem Cathedral

Lying off the main square, the rather unimpressive Medhane Alem Cathedral was originally an Egyptian mosque, but Haile Selassie 'converted it' in the 1940s.

Rimbaud's House

Near the middle of the walled city, Rimbaud's House is (yet another) building in which the poet is said to have lived. It was thoughtfully restored with the support of the Italian and French embassies. Although Rimbaud did live in the city, it is not thought to have been here. However, the building houses a new **museum** (admission Birr10; ☼ 8am-12.30pm & 2-5pm Mon-Sat) dedicated to the poet, with a series of illustrated panels (mainly in French) about his life. On the 1st floor, don't miss the excellent turn-of-the-20th-century photographs of Harar – a fantastic step back in time. Another

---

ARTHUR RIMBAUD – A MULTIFACETED GENIUS

In 1875 an unhappy young man made a decision. Discouraged both by the reception of his poetry in Paris and by increasing financial worries, Arthur Rimbaud, the great French poet, came to a bitter conclusion: to turn his back on poetry forever. He was just 21 years old.

In 1876 Rimbaud set out to see the world. In the winter of 1879, in the service of a coffee trader in Aden (Yemen), Rimbaud achieved a different kind of fame. He became the first white man to travel into the Ogaden region of southeastern Ethiopia. In October 1885 he decided to risk all his savings on a venture to run guns to King Menelik of Shoa.

While in Ethiopia, Rimbaud lived like a local in a small house in Harar. His interest in the Ethiopian culture, languages and people made him popular with the locals, and his plain-speaking and integrity won the trust of the chiefs and the governor of Harar.

In 1891 Rimbaud developed a tumour on his right knee. Leaving Harar in early April, he endured the week's journey to the coast on a stretcher. Treatment at Aden was not a success, and Rimbaud continued onto Marseilles, where his right leg was amputated.

By the time of his return, Rimbaud's poetry was becoming increasingly known in France. But he was indifferent to his fame. He died later that year at the young age of 37.

Rimbaud's poetry has won a huge popular following for its daring imagery and beautiful and evocative language. *Somebody Else*, by Charles Nicholl, is a remarkable biography of Rimbaud's life.

room holds changing exhibitions (often old photographs or paintings), and there's a small selection of traditional Adare arts and crafts. From the rooftop, there's a good view over Harar to the blue Chercher Mountains. A guide can give a 30-minute tour (he will expect a tip afterwards).

Ras Tafari's House
Within pouncing distance of Rimbaud's House is the conspicuous Ras Tafari's House. The building has now been taken over by a local family including a holy man-cum-herbal healer. A sign declares that the sheikh can cure anything from STDs to diabetes, mental illness and cancer! Past patients – apparently testifying to his success – return to look after the holy man, cooking and cleaning for him for the rest of their lives.

The house was built by an Indian trader and many of its features, such as the Hindu figures on the door, are Oriental. Haile Selassie spent his honeymoon here, hence the house bears his pre-coronation name.

Ras Makonnen's Palace
Don't expect a fairy-tale castle! This 'palace' on the main drag is a sharp-edged, charmless, whitish building but it houses a **Handicraft Museum** (admission Birr3; 8am-noon & 2-5pm Mon-Fri) on the 1st floor – nothing flash but it's worth popping your head in. You can also climb to the top floor and soak up the views.

Jamia Mosque
The Jamia Mosque located just south of the central square is Harar's great mosque. The mosque was originally built in the 16th century, though according to local tradition, a mosque has stood on the site since the 12th century, long before the foundation of Harar. These days it has a modernish appearance but remains an appealing sight in its own right.

Gidir Magala
Down from Mekina Girgir you'll stumble upon the arcades of the Gidir Magala, the main market (previously known as the Muslim market); it's definitely worth a stroll. It also serves as the city's meat market – consider yourself warned if you're squeamish. On Mondays, Oromo and some Somali people come in from the surrounding areas (it is the most busy from 2.30pm to 5.30pm).

St Mary Catholic Church
Almost opposite Jamia Mosque, St Mary Catholic Church is a haven of peace and a good spot if you need to unwind. It's a Catholic mission dating from the late 19th century. The woodcarved door is particularly attractive.

Mekina Girgir
Leading southeast from Feres Magala, there is a narrow street called Mekina Girgir (Machine Rd). Ambling down this atmosphere-laden lane you'll quickly understand why it was given this name: it's jam-packed with tailors' workshops, hence the name, in reference to the sewing machines. If you were thinking of a wedding suit, this is the place!

Traditional Adare Houses
Visiting a traditional Adare house is a must (see opposite), but you'll probably need a guide to find one. The easiest house to find, not far from the Erer Gate (known locally as Argobari), houses the **Harari National Cultural Centre** (admission Birr10; 8am-noon & 2-5pm Mon-Fri). This typical Adare house contains examples of traditional arts and crafts.

Several Adare houses also double as family-run souvenir shops (see p233). If you don't buy anything, it's customary to tip the owner for the tour.

Shrines & Tombs
Shrines devoted to local holy men or religious leaders are even more numerous: over 300 inside and outside the walls – no-one has yet managed to count them. Many are very peaceful, beautiful and well-kept places open to both sexes and all religions.

Southwest of Gidir Magala is the **Tomb of Said Ali Hamdogn**, a former religious leader of the town. The tomb looks a little like a miniature mosque without the minaret. Local legend has it that below his tomb there lies a well that can sustain the whole city in times of siege. The sheikh who lives here will probably show you some fragile ancient Islamic manuscripts. He expects a tip.

Another tomb that can be visited is **Sheikh Abadir's Tomb**, near the southeastern point of the old town. The sheikh was one of the most important preachers of Islam in the region and his tomb still attracts worshippers seeking solutions to daily struggles: financial concerns, illnesses, family crises and infertility. If their prayers are answered, many devotees return to make gifts to the shrine: usually rugs or expensive sandal wood. The tomb has become an important centre of pilgrimage, especially for those who cannot afford a trip to Mecca.

Emir Nur's Tomb, north of central square, is devoted to the ruler who built the city's walls. It resembles a spiky beehive.

OUTSIDE THE WALLS
Hyena Feeding

Are you ready for the thrill of a lifetime? Possibly Harar's greatest attraction is the hyena men of Harar. As night falls (from around 7pm), the last remaining hyena men (about four) set themselves up just outside the city walls. Sometimes the hyena men risk feeding the animals from their own mouths – you can have a go at this, too, if you like! We didn't… The hyena men know the animals as individuals and call them by the names they have given them.

Though the tradition of feeding spotted hyenas like this has existed for no more that 35 years, the ritual is less of a tourist show than some travellers imagine. The Hararis have long had a strange relationship with the hyena, and some rituals remarkably similar to this one have existed for at least 700 to 800 years.

If you want to see the feeding, just let your guide know. One feeding takes place near Sanga Gate in the east of the old town. The other one takes place about 200m north of Fallana Gate. Be sure to establish the fee in advance; in principle, you'll be charged about Birr50 for the 'show', more if you have a video camera (usually Birr100). If there are a few of you (say five) Birr25 is sufficient. Usually you can expect to see between 15 and 20 hyenas. Be there from around 7pm to 8pm to be sure of seeing the spectacle (though it can go on to 9pm). If you just turn up, you'll still be expected to contribute something.

Some guides recommend hiring a taxi to provide a kind of floodlight for the show (and to assist taking photos).

Other Attractions

No visit to Harar would be complete without wading through the shambolic markets that sprawl outside Harar Gate and Shoa Gate. At first sight this minicity appears to be an impenetrable latticework of tiny streets and alleys; on closer inspection it reveals a careful organisation with different sections. It's a great place to ramble. You could start with the **Smugglers' Market**, southeast of Canal Cafe; it's chock-full with goods from Asia. The adjoining **Recycling Market** is a stunner: witness the workmanship and watch men beating metal into every single useful utensil or spare part. Then elbow your way through the **Asma'addin Bari Market** (New Market; also known as the Christian Market), near Shoa Gate. Look out for the *etan* (incense) from Jijiga; it's sold for the famous coffee ceremonies (see p70). The odoriferous spice market is filled with bark,

EASTERN ETHIOPIA

ADARE HOUSES

A distinct architectural feature in Harar, the *gegar* (traditional Adare house) is a rectangular, two-storey structure with a flat roof. The house is carefully constructed to remain cool whatever the outside temperature: clay reinforced with wooden beams is whitewashed. Sometimes bright green, blue or ochre murals adorn the façades. A small courtyard conceals the interior of the house from curious passers-by.

The upstairs room used to serve as a storeroom; today it acts as a bedroom. The main living room consists of five raised platforms of different levels, which are covered in well-made rugs, cushions and stools. Guests and members of the household sit on the platform befitting their status.

The walls are usually painted bright red or ochre, said to symbolise the blood that every Harari was prepared to shed during the resistance against Menelik. Hung on the walls are woven cloths or carpets. Eleven niches are carved into the wall. In these, cups, pots and plates made by the Adare women themselves are proudly displayed.

After marriage, newlyweds retire to a tiny, windowless, cell-like room that lies to the side of the living quarters. They remain there for one whole week, during which time they are passed food and water through a hatch by relatives.

roots and twigs used in the preparation of traditional medicine. Make sure you save energy for the no-less-animated **Oromo Market**, off Erer Gate. With its heaps of vegetables, it's exotic and colourful by the bucketload.

After all this sightseeing, you might need a stimulant to keep your spirits high. What about chewing a leaf (or two) of *chat*? *Chat* markets can be found around most of the city gates, except the Buda Gate, as well as to the south of Feres Magala.

In the centre of Ras Makonnen Sq stands an Italianate equestrian **statue** of the *ras* (duke), cast in bronze by the well-known Amhara artist Afewerk Tekle.

Sleeping

Most commendable places are outside the walled town.

Tewodros Hotel (☎ 0256 660217; new town d Birr50-70) Room with a hyena view… No joke – you won't believe your eyes! At night, from the windows of rooms 15, 16, 117 and 18 (if not renumbered by the time you pop in), you can watch hyenas rummaging in a garbage dump behind the hotel. It's your very own hyena show and a memorable experience. Oh, and the rooms are well kept and serviceable; some have hot showers. Ship out if offered the grotty rooms downstairs at Birr25. The hotel is just a wee walk from Harar Gate.

Rewda Guesthouse (☎ 0256 662211; old town; r with shared bathroom incl breakfast Birr200-300) Enter here at your own risk: you may never feel like leaving again! This cocoonlike guesthouse occupies an old Harari house at the absolute heart of the old town (ask somebody to show you the way at Weber Stationary shop, as it's tucked away in a side street). Rest your head in one of the two well-kept rooms, and marvel at the thoughtfully decorated common areas. Throw in the warm welcome of Rewda, your congenial host, and you have a winner. Reservations are crucial.

Belayneh Hotel (☎ 0256 662030; fax 0256 666222; new town; s/d Birr115/138) Popular place with tour groups, near the bus station. A little mundane, it offers sizable rooms equipped with bathrooms that won't have you squirming. If you can snaffle a room with a view of the Christian market, how can you possibly complain? Steer clear of the restaurant – the fodder is as bland as the dining room.

Tana Hotel (☎ 0256 668482; new town; r Birr50) This outfit west of the new town is a good

example of resurrection, with spotless, bright rooms with clean bathrooms (hot showers) and satellite TV. There's a bar and restaurant specialising in Ethiopian dishes (raw meat, anyone?). Brilliant value.

Rewda Hotel (☎ 0256 669777; new town; s with shared bathroom Birr70, d Birr120-150) This recent pile won't win any style awards but features well-organised rooms. For budgeteers, the singles are pokey but will do for a night's kip. Feeling peckish? There's a pastry shop on the ground floor.

Abadir Guest House (☎ 0256 660721; new town; r with shared bathroom Birr50-70, r Birr80) Family-run Abadir is nothing fancy but is good value if you're not too choosy.

Ras Hotel (☎ 0256 660027; new town; s/d Birr125/163; 🖵) The government-run Ras is a cross between a boarding school and a psychiatric institution. Think Soviet-style décor, overpriced rooms, bare corridors and dour staff. Nab a table on the terrace and keep up your spirits with a Harar beer at hand.

Eating

Hirut Restaurant (☎ 0256 660419; new town; mains Birr15-25) A cheery, authentic place to savour Ethiopian dishes as well as pasta and various grills. Sink your teeth into a superfilling *kwanta firfir* and knock it all down with a bottle of Gouder wine, if you're game. The dining room is cosy but the shady terrace is a sure winner. Service was a tad amateurish the day we popped in.

Rose Cafe & Restaurant (new town; mains Birr10-15) The closest thing Harar has to a hip café. Chow down on various snacks, including pasta and burgers, or start the day with an omelette or scrambled eggs. It also has bait for the sweet-toothed. The wait-staff in pink complete this very rosy picture.

Rewda Café (new town) Drool over the devilish display of cakes and pastries in this sleek venture. It's also a good for breakfast, with a choice of eggs, omelettes and sandwiches.

Canal Cafe (new town) Near Harar Gate, this is another treasure-trove for carb-lovers, although the setting is more down-at-heel.

Alpha Cafeteria & Restaurant (new town; mains Birr10-20; 😋 lunch) The best place for a cheap stodge, behind the Shell petrol station. Try its Harari soup.

Ice Cream Mermaid (old town) A peaceful refuge from the crowded strip nearby, this hole-in-the-wall place concocts some flavoursome

EASTERN ETHIOPIA

ice creams as well as filling cakes. If you need a vitamin fix, it has refreshing fruit juices.

Drinking

If you're pining for a good, fresh beer, Harar is seventh heaven. There's a smattering of buzzing watering holes around town. Among the brands to try are the light Harar beer, Hakim stout and Hakim, a kind of lager. Sofi is nonalcoholic, designed for Harar's Muslims. And of course, you'll keep everlasting memories of the Harari coffee, hailed as one of the best in the world; to buy, see Shopping, below.

Ali Bal Cafe (Feres Magala, old town) Slap bang in the heart of the old town, this is a good place to mull over a coffee or sugar-cane juice and watch life go by.

Samsun Hotel (old town) Don't be confused by the name, it's under the right heading here. Identity crisis aside, this publike venue is popular at weekends with an eclectic crowd gulping down glasses of beer. It's just past Harar Gate.

GC Pub (old town) Almost next door to Samsun Hotel, this pub-cum-bar works to the same formula of booze, reggae beats, a touch of sleaziness and tight-packed bodies at weekends. Dive in!

Bar Cottage (old town) Still haven't tried *tej* (honey wine)? It's time to get a hands-on education in this traditionally decked out, dimly lit den. It's a bit nibbled around the edges but after a few drinks you'll call this place home. It's best at weekends.

Entertainment

National Hotel (new town) Hallelujah! Live music Thursday to Sunday from around 9.30pm to 2am or 3am. The music is a mixture of Ethiopian/Middle Eastern pop, with some traditional tunes thrown in. When not playing, there's football on big-screen TV – much less exotic.

Tourist Hotel (new town) Another bar-cum-club venue, a few doors from the National Hotel. A bit brash, but take a bold approach and you should do all right.

Shopping

Nure Roasted Harar Coffee (☎ 0256 663136; ⏰ Mon-Sat) Just thinking about the scents wafting from this place makes us swoon. One step inside, and you're hooked forever. It sells 1kg packets of excellent coffee for Birr45 –

the best souvenir! There's tours of the roasting and grinding machines in the back.

In some of the Adare houses in the old town, the ever-enterprising Adares have set up souvenir shops displaying beautifully made baskets, and silver and amber jewellery. The house of Fatuma Safir Ahmed, just north of the main market, is one. Another is Zeituna Yusuf Grille's shop, south of the market; it's as good as an antique shop. Amber necklaces and baskets are on sale, but bring your sharpest bargaining skills! Because these shops are family-run, they may not always be 'open'. Knock on the doors.

Getting There & Around

All transport leaves from the bus station near Harar Gate. Minibuses leave every 15 minutes for Dire Dawa (Birr10, one hour). Around seven buses leave for Jijiga (Birr13, 2½ to three hours) via Babille (Birr8, 45 minutes). Two buses leave daily for Addis Ababa (Birr55, one day). Tickets for the capital should be bought from 10am the previous day at the bus station. There are also several minibuses a day to Addis Ababa (Birr100, nine to 10 hours). They don't leave from the bus station but pick passengers up at their hotel (ask the reception to book the ticket for you). Minibus tickets can also be bought at the Selam Cafe in the old town.

Shared/contract taxis cost Birr1/5 for a short hop about town.

HARAR TO JIJIGA

When visiting Jijiga, getting there is half the fun. The stunning 102km stretch of gravel road is one of the most scenic in eastern Ethiopia, with superb volcanic rock formations, contoured terrain and a strangely seductive, end-of-the-world atmosphere. You'll first pass through the blink-and-you'll-miss-it town of **Babille**, renowned for its elephant sanctuary, but don't expect to get up close and personal with some proboscideans. Unfortunately, the elephants have gone and you're unlikely to see any wildlife.

About 4km from Babille, the road passes through the Dakhata Valley, now better known as the **Valley of Marvels**. Here, tall rocks have been sculpted into strange shapes by the elements. Some are topped by precariously balanced boulders, including one that's formed like an arch – a very strange vista indeed. The valley stretches for some 13km.

JIJIGA ጅጅጋ

pop 60,000 / elev 1696m

Feeling adventurous? It's time to explore one of the least-visited corners of the country. Hop on a local bus from Harar and prepare yourself for a taste of mysterious Ethiopia. True, there is little to see and less to do in Jijiga, the capital of the Somali region, but its real highlights are its proud people, who are unaccustomed to travellers but are always helpful and kind (in a blunt way). This is the heart of Somali territory, and it won't take long to feel that the atmosphere is noticeably different from the rest of the country. Here you can already feel the flavour of neighbouring Somalia (sorry: Somaliland). Business, including contraband, is unexpectedly brisk, signs are written in Somali, women are veiled and Arab-style mosques dominate the skyline. There's an edgy roughness to it, but fear not, gone is the rather sullen, oppressed atmosphere that prevailed several years ago. However, it's always wise to check the situation in Harar.

Information

There's a smattering of Internet outlets in the vicinity of Adom Hotel, but connections were very slow when we visited. There's also a post office and a telecom office.

Commercial Bank (☿ 8-11am & 2-4.30pm Mon-Fri, 8-11am Sat) Changes euros, US dollars and travellers cheques.

Sights

The large **market** is definitely worth exploring. You can sometimes find intricately woven mats as well as silver jewellery and yellow amber necklaces. Most of it is little more than heaps of contraband 'junk'. The **camel and livestock market** is also very interesting.

Sleeping & Eating

Being an important administrative and commercial centre, Jijiga boasts a flurry of places to stay. Sure, it's more brash than glam but it's OK for a night's snooze.

Bade Hotel (☎ 0257 752841; fax 0257 752218; s/d Birr100/120) The neat, bricklike façade of this professionally run outfit promises great things but we found the rooms fairly unspectacular for the price and the beds a bit too unkind to our creaky joints. It's in a side street running parallel to the main Harar road.

Adom Hotel (☎ 0257 753077; r Birr80) Modest but clean rooms set round a courtyard. It

---

NEXT STOP: HARGEISA, SOMALILAND

We did it, and we won't forget it. If you want to impress your peers, go to the bus station in Jijiga and hop on a bus to Wajaale, at the border with Somaliland. Every morning a handful of rattling buses and minibuses trundle along the gravel road from Jijiga to the border. It takes about 1½ to two hours depending on the number of punctures (two, the day we were here) and costs Birr15. Be prepared to be the focus of attention: foreigners still very rarely cover this route using public transport. Fewer things will get your heart pumping faster than crossing this border and entering virtually unchartered territory.

To avoid any incident, seek local advice on the situation before setting off, both in Harar and Jijiga. For more information on Somaliland, use Lonely Planet's *Africa on a Shoestring*. See also p275.

---

lies 100m off the main road; take the first left after the Shell station if coming from Addis Ababa.

Alem Ayu Hotel (☎ 0257 752814; s/d Birr30/50) A reliable pick, on the main road, about 500m west from the bus station. The beds can be a bit spongy but the rooms fit the bill for an overnight stop.

Djibouti Restaurant (mains Birr15-20) If your stomach is in knots, this no-frills eatery tosses up decent fare. Tuck into chicken with rice while watching Al-Jazeera. It's signposted.

Rugsan House of Sweets (mains Birr5) A sure fix for blood-sugar lows, a skip and a jump from the Commercial Bank. The incongruous mural featuring the Eiffel Tower at the entrance is amusing. It also sells provisions.

Getting There & Away

AIR

Ethiopian Airlines (☎ 0257 752030) flies four times a week to Addis Ababa via Dire Dawa (Birr1250 one way). The airport is 3km out of town.

BUS

Around seven buses leave daily for Harar (Birr13, 2½ to three hours). One leaves for Addis Ababa (Birr70, 1½ days); book tickets the day before (after 1pm).

Jijiga is the gateway to Somaliland. See p275 for details.

Western Ethiopia

Western Ethiopia's Anuak people believe that if you keep walking, you'll eventually fall off the world's end. If you keep walking west in Ethiopia, you'll fall into another world. Almost 350km due west of Addis Ababa the highland plateau drops dramatically to lowland plains. The remarkable transition sees fields of golden *tef* (an indigenous grass cultivated as a cereal grain) and feral coffee giving way to plantations of verdant banana and mango; Semitic people to dark Nilotic people; and a bracing climate to the torrid humidity of the tropics. Geographically, climatically and culturally, the western lowlands have much more to do with Sudan than with Ethiopia.

Sadly, like in Sudan, the western lowlands are currently experiencing ethnic and political problems (see the boxed text, p248). For their sake more than yours, we hope peace is achieved and the doors to tourism open again.

Conversely, the western highlands are as stable as can be and a trip through the lush 'birthplace of coffee' can be richly rewarding and eye-opening (thanks to the scenery – not the caffeine!). It was this 'little bean that could' that was responsible for opening up what was once an almost impenetrable region. Some good roads now ford the great rivers and gorges, which for so long isolated the area from the rest of Ethiopia.

While visitors spoiled by countless must-see sights in other regions will be disappointed by the absence of major natural or historical attractions, those simply looking for an interesting journey through beautiful surroundings will get an engaging peek into everyday Ethiopian life.

HIGHLIGHTS

- Straddle a mule for a scenic descent into the lake-filled crater of **Mt Wenchi** (p238)
- Search for birds, colobus monkeys and Menelik's bushbuck while meandering in **Menagesha National Forest** (p237) on the slopes of Mt Wuchacha
- Savour coffee in the old kingdom of Kafa, the birthplace of the bean, before heading west to tour the verdant coffee plantations near **Tepi** (p241) and **Bebeka** (p242)
- Stare steadily at the striking scenery moving past your window while driving from **Ambo to Nekemte** (p238), from **Metu to Tepi** (p241) and from **Jimma to Welkite** (p247)

Menagesha National Forest
Nekemte ○ — ★ Ambo ★
Mt Wenchi ★
○ Metu   ○ Welkite
★   ★
○ Jimma
Tepi ★
★ Bebeka

WESTERN ETHIOPIA

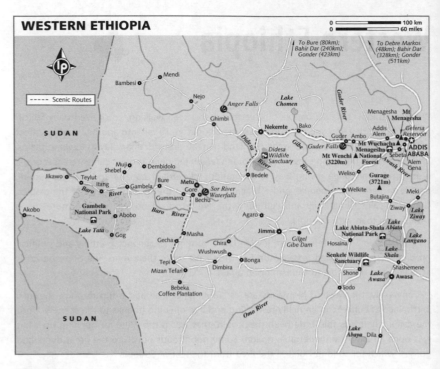

WESTERN ETHIOPIA

Climate

The western highlands receive almost 1600mm of annual rainfall. Heavy rains fall between April and September, with moderate precipitation in March and October. The highlands never exceed 29°C nor ever reach frost point.

The western lowlands receive slightly less rain than the highlands, with most falling between May and October. Unlike the moist highlands, December through February is very dry. Temperatures average 27°C but can reach 40°C in February and March.

National Parks & Wildlife Reserves

The newly delineated Didesa Wildlife Sanctuary (p240) holds some hope for future wildlife viewing in the region, while the lowlands' troubles continue to hamper the health of Gambela National Park (p250).

Getting There & Away

Ethiopian Airlines (www.flyethiopian.com) connects Addis Ababa with Jimma, Mizan Tefari and Gambela.

Most people who enter western Ethiopia overland are travelling by bus from Addis Ababa, which provides access to the southwest via Jimma and to the northwest via Nekemte.

If travelling with a vehicle it's also technically possible to reach Jimma from Sodo in the south and to reach Nekemte from the Addis Ababa–Bahir Dar road in the north.

Getting Around

Jimma and Gambela are connected with flights three times weekly by Ethiopian Airlines.

There are new sealed roads that are heading west from Addis Ababa. It is planned that these roads will reach Nekemte and Jimma in the next few years. When this happens, travel times will be cut significantly.

With the exception of remote lowlands areas, most areas are covered by regular bus services. However, during the wet season, roads and schedules can run equally amuck.

THE WESTERN HIGHLANDS

Carpeted in lush forests, dense patchworks of cultivation, shady coffee plantations and deep river valleys, the western highlands seem like an Ethiopian Arcadia.

ADDIS ABABA TO AMBO

If you are into bird-watching but won't have a chance to visit some of southern Ethiopia's birding havens, a stop at the **Gefersa Reservoir** may be warranted. Wattled ibis, endemic blue-wing geese and, occasionally, pelicans peruse its sparsely vegetated shores. The reservoir lies 18km west of Addis Ababa, and supplies the capital with its water.

Just west of the reservoir is the domed profile of **Mt Menagesha**. According to local tradition, many Ethiopian kings' coronations were held on this forested mountain.

If forested hikes and the odd antelope suit your fancy, continue west past the tiny village of Menagesha and turn left at the Tseday Farm Horticulture Development Enterprises sign. A rough road leads 18km to the forestry office on the lower slopes of **Mt Wuchacha** where you can ditch your vehicle and take to the **Menagesha National Forest** (admission Birr20). Almost a dozen trails (up to 9km in length) meander through the forest, with one even heading above the treeline to Wuchacha's 3380m summit.

On the crater's western slopes, you can get a good idea of how Ethiopia's ancient, indigenous forest must have looked before the arrival of the eucalyptus and mass settlement. Some trees, among them giant juniper and *wanza* (Podocarpus) are over 400 years old.

Colobus monkeys and Menelik's bushbuck are the most seen mammal species here, while only the lucky get to spot duikers and klipspringers. The endemic Ethiopian oriole and Abyssinian woodpecker are just two of the many bird species present here. You'll need a 4WD to get here in wet season.

On foot, the national forest is more easily accessed from the village of Sebata on the Addis Ababa–Jimma road (p247).

Addis Alem አዲስ አለም

This unprepossessing agricultural town 55km west of Addis Ababa was the site of Emperor Menelik II's future capital; Addis Alem literally means 'New World' in Amharic. He'd sent engineers and builders to start construction here when Addis Ababa was crippled by the late-19th-century firewood shortages. The introduction of eucalyptus ended up saving the new flower (Addis Ababa) and killed the new world.

Of the remaining buildings, **St Maryam Church** (admission Birr25) is the most interesting. It stands out for its lavish decoration: the basilica's exterior, as well as the *maqdas* (inner sanctuary), is entirely covered with murals of Ethiopian rulers, saints, landscapes, plants and wild animals, including four grumpy-looking lions of Judah. If you're not going to northern Ethiopia, the church is worth visiting.

Unfortunately, a fire in 1997 destroyed the adjacent museum and many of the church's old treasures that it housed. However a new **museum** (admission incl with church; ☺ 8.30am-3pm Mon-Thu, 9am-4pm Sat & Sun) opened in 2004 and displays crowns and clothing belonging to Menelik and Haile Selassie, and relics from the Battle of Adwa. The royal dining room survives nearby but it's looking rather derelict.

The site sits atop a rocky hill 600m south of the main road.

Numerous buses pass heading east to Addis Ababa (Birr6, 1½ to two hours) and west to Ambo (Birr10, two to 2½ hours). You may have to wait for one with a seat.

AMBO አምቦ

pop 41,500 / elev 2101m

Mineral water is Ambo's claim to fame; it's bottled here and sold throughout Ethiopia. It's so fizzy that it continues to sparkle even in a glass left overnight! Although you can't visit the factory, you can take a dip in the famous thermal mineral-water **pool** (admission Birr5.75; ☺ 6am-8pm Thu-Sun) run by Ambo Ethiopia Hotel. Despite the murky green colour, the pool is cleaned weekly. It's a pleasant setup, but does become manic on weekends.

The town also offers some fine Italian 1930s architecture and an interesting Saturday market where you can find the brightly coloured Ambo baskets.

WESTERN ETHIOPIA

Almost 2km west of Ambo is **Teltele Park** (admission Birr20), a new pint-sized park that encapsulates walking trails, sections of the Teltele and Huluka Rivers and a few waterfalls including the 25m-high **Huluka Falls**. Campsites and a permanent tented camp should be completed by the time you arrive. Check with the Ambo Ethiopia Hotel for details.

Sleeping & Eating

Ambo Ethiopia Hotel (☎ 0112 362007; amboethhotel@ ethionet.et; tw with shared bathroom Birr28, tw Birr52.50, d Birr46-125; 🏊) Set around well-manicured flowering gardens, this old colonial place has bundles of charm. Though it shows its age in places, it's still quite comfortable and some rooms have satellite TV. Rooms 25 and 26 overlook the garden. The classic dining hall (mains Birr11 to Birr16) serves tasty Western and Ethiopian selections. Guests have free use of the town's mineral pool.

Abebech Metaferia Hotel (☎ 0112 362365; d/tw Birr60/70) This modern tower, cascading with marble, sits just east of town and houses Ambo's most comfortable rooms. Rooms are big, bright and have new balconies. The restaurant (mains Birr20 to Birr40) is known for quality *faranji* (Western foreigner) fare, but it's a bit pricey.

Jebatna Wecha Hotel (☎ 0112 362253; d Birr25) These rooms are better value than Ambo Ethiopia's twins with shared facilities. It's clean and pretty bright, though showers are all cold.

Gimbi Restaurant (mains Birr4-12) A thriving local restaurant serving well-prepared Ethiopian selections. Try the *shekla tibs* (sautéed meat served on a hot clay pot).

Getting There & Away

A dozen daily buses serve Addis Ababa (Birr10, three hours), while only one serves Nekemte (Birr22, 5½ hours, 6am). For Guder (Birr1.50, 15 minutes) minibuses run approximately every 30 minutes.

MT WENCHI ወንጪ ተራራ

Resting within the beautiful collapsed caldera of Mt Wenchi, 31km south of Ambo, is **Lake Wenchi**, the island monastery of **Cherkos** and several **hot springs**. The crater itself is a patchwork of cultivation, and locals living here have set up boat trips (Birr40 per person return) to the island monastery. This price should also include a trip to the hot

springs, though some people have managed to talk the boat operator into also visiting a second island that's home to a local village.

At Cherkos ask to see the large 'Gonder bell', which once belonged (according to tradition) to the Emperor Fasiladas and was brought here by Menelik. Sunday services (before 10am) are classic; catch one if you can. There's no official entrance fee. A fair price is Birr10 per person, though you may well be asked much more.

Water birds are found on the lake; raptors soar above the crater. On the paths up and down, look out for the monkeys and baboons.

With a vehicle, it makes a good day trip from Addis Ababa. You can picnic at the crater before taking a dip in Ambo's mineral pool. The 3km road from Wenchi village to the crater rim typically requires a 4WD; from there you usually have to hike about 30 minutes. Climbing back takes about an hour. It's also possible to hire mules in Wenchi village. Prices are fixed at Birr15 per person each way, plus Birr60 per party for a guide. Without your own wheels, there's usually an early morning Landrover taxi running between Ambo and Weliso during dry season; ask to be dropped at Wenchi village. Unless you come on Sunday (market day), there's no return transport, so bring camping gear. A hotel on the crater is planned but has yet to be built; ask in Ambo.

Private 4WDs with driver can usually be hired in Ambo. A return trip costs between Birr300 and Birr500, depending on your length of stay at the lake. Ask at the bus station or talk to Tadessa Hailu (a reputable guide) at Ambo's Abebech Metafaria Hotel.

AMBO TO NEKEMTE

The journey towards Nekemte soon takes you through Guder, which sits only 11km west of Ambo. About 1km from Guder, after crossing the river, you'll see a gate for **Guder Falls** (admission Birr5; ⏰ 7am-6pm). It isn't spectacular, but is worth a peek in the wet season.

The Guder River is an important tributary of the Blue Nile. The ubiquitous Ethiopian red wine, Gouder, was ostensibly named after the river, and a few vineyards can still be seen covering the surrounding area.

As you climb from Guder the views open up and you'll see endless fields of quilted yellows, reds and greens. Although the views down are great, don't forget to look up too – there are some impressive columnar basalt flows along the road cut above Guder.

While winding circuitously westward through coffee, sorghum and barley crops, you'll catch glimpses of gaping northern canyons, which hammer home the lofty heights of this seemingly subdued plateau.

About 65km from Ambo, you'll reach an escarpment offering westward vistas over distant volcanic landscapes. Heading further west things start to feel less cultivated and more raw and natural. This area is part of the historical Wolega province and is home to gold reserves and precious frankincense. Both still fetch high prices in Middle Eastern and Egyptian markets.

NEKEMTE ነቀምቴ

pop 98,000 / elev 2101m

Nekemte, 202km west of Ambo, is the sprawling commercial and administrative centre for the Oromia region's East Wolega zone. Although busy, it still has a sleepy enough ambience. If you wander you'll notice many leftovers from the Marxist Derg, namely star and sickle emblems.

Although there's little besides a well-put-together museum to hold you here, Nekemte has decent facilities and makes an obvious spot to break your westward journey.

Information

Commercial Bank (8-11am & 1-3pm Mon-Fri, 8-11am Sat) The manager told us he changes travellers cheques but not cash. Play it safe and don't count on either.

Hiwot Clinic (☎ 0576 612036; 8am-7pm) A better bet than the local hospital. The doctor speaks English and there are X-ray and laboratory facilities. A malaria test is Birr7.

Post office (8.30am-noon & 2-5.30pm Mon-Fri, 8.30am-noon Sat)

Telecommunications office (☎ 0576 611090) International calls. Standard rates (p267).

Welel Pharmacy (☎ 0576 613611; 8.30am-12.30pm & 1.30-6pm Mon-Sat) Well stocked and helpful.

Sights

The remains of an Italian military plane shot down by the Black Lion Patriots in 1935 proudly sits in front of the **Wolega Museum** (admission Birr25; 8.30am-12.30pm & 2-6pm Tue-Sun). Inside, displays give a good insight into the Wolega Oromo life and culture. It contains traditional musical instruments as well as displays on the local spinning, carving and basket-weaving industries. There is also a wooden coffin; according to traditional Oromo culture, men must prepare their own. Other exhibits include a reconstruction of an Oromo hut and a good collection of arms including a traditional hippo- and buffalo-hide shield. Guided tours are available – expect a whole lot of hand waving!

Also worth a wander is Nekemte's **market**, which bustles most on Wednesday, Thursday and Saturday. Although the **Church of St Gabriel** casts a nice silhouette from town, it can be classed as good from far but far from good.

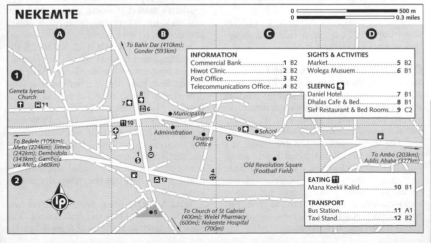

NEKEMTE

0 — 500 m
0 — 0.3 miles

To Bahir Dar (410km);
Gonder (593km)

Geneta Iyesus
Church

INFORMATION	
Commercial Bank	1 B2
Hiwot Clinic	2 B2
Post Office	3 B2
Telecommunications Office	4 B2

SIGHTS & ACTIVITIES	
Market	5 B2
Wolega Musuem	6 B1

SLEEPING	
Daniel Hotel	7 B1
Dhalas Cafe & Bed	8 B1
Sief Restaurant & Bed Rooms	9 C2

Municipality

Administration

Finance
Office

School

To Bedele (105km);
Metu (224km); Jimma
(242km); Dembidolo
(343km); Gambela
via Metu (360km)

Old Revolution Square
(Football Field)

To Ambo (203km);
Addis Ababa (327km)

EATING	
Mana Keekii Kaliid	10 B1

TRANSPORT	
Bus Station	11 A1
Taxi Stand	12 B2

To Church of St Gabriel
(400km); Welel Pharmacy
(600m); Nekemte Hospital
(700m)

WESTERN ETHIOPIA

Sleeping & Eating

Sief Restaurant & Bed Rooms (☎ 0576 612499; nonresidents of Ethiopia d Birr60) A new place with spotless rooms, large comfy beds, bedside lamps, clean bathrooms and a friendly owner. Ethiopian residents (even *faranji* ones) pay Birr35. The Ethiopian fare here is pretty good.

Dhalas Cafe & Bed (☎ 0576 611849; d with shared bathroom Birr40, d Birr50) The austere rooms are large and host beds with comfortable foam mattresses. The shared bathrooms are very clean and boast hot water and toilet seats. The only downer is knowing locals pay half.

Daniel Hotel (☎ 0576 615999; d Birr35) Although rooms here are clean and have private bathrooms (cold showers), they aren't as bright and put together as those at Dhalas. However, its restaurant (mains Birr5 to Birr15) is popular and well recommended.

Mana Keekii Kaliid (mains Birr3-5) Known locally as 'Ephrem', this is a great place for a local breakfast. Try spicy, tomato-based *sils* or puréed chickpea *ful*. There's also a selection of cakes and fruit juices. If you hear screaming inside, there's obviously a football game on TV (Birr1 per game).

Getting There & Around

One daily bus serves Addis Ababa (Birr33.50, 8½ hours, 6am), though five more pass through each morning and pick up passengers if they have free seats. Other 6am services include Ambo (Birr20, 5½ hours), Dembidolo (Birr41, 12 to 13 hours), Jimma (Birr29.60, 10 hours) and Bedele (Birr13.90, 4½ hours).

Contract taxis cost Birr10 to Birr15 for short hops about town. A ride in a share-taxi is Birr1 to Birr2.

DIDESA WILDLIFE SANCTUARY

Roughly halfway between Nekemte and Bedele is this new 1300-sq-km wildlife sanctuary. Although there's currently no access, you'll have a glimpse of its beauty when descending into the Didesa River valley. The views from the top are grand. It's thought the deciduous forest holds small populations of elephant, buffalo and lion, as well as numerous guereza monkeys, baboons and birds. Some people have been lucky enough to see hippos in the river. Future access is still being planned, so inquire about its progress in Nekemte.

BEDELE በዴሌ

pop 16,000 / elev 2162m

Bedele lies 105km south of Nekemte and sits at an important crossroads linking Metu, Jimma and of course, Nekemte. Besides a tour of the celebrated **Bedele beer factory** (☎ 0474 450134, ext 21; admission free; ☷ 8am-4pm Mon-Fri), there's little reason to even stop here. Sadly, *faranji* frenzy (unwanted attention from local children) can be really rude here.

If you're stuck here, try **Hagere Selam Hotel** (d with shared bathroom Birr20, d Birr30). Its Birr30 doubles are quiet, set at the back of the property. The Birr20 rooms aren't nearly as nice. It's signposted at the main roundabout.

For eating, head to **Hoteela Mo'aa** (mains Birr5-7), which is the best local restaurant. There are some outdoor tables out back.

Between 6am and noon four buses pass here heading for Jimma (Birr15, 3½ hours), while six head to Metu (Birr12, four hours). There's a 6am service to Nekemte (Birr13.90, 4½ hours) and another to Addis Ababa (Birr75, 12 to 13 hours) via Welkite.

METU መቱ

pop 24,000 / elev 1600m

Spreading over the slope of a small hill 115km west of Bedele is Metu, the capital of the old Ilubador province. It's far from being an ugly town, but you'll find few reasons to stick around. For travellers, Metu acts as the primary gateway for the western lowlands, as well as a springboard for trips south through some of the west's most wild and beautiful scenery to Tepi and Mizan Tefari.

Metu's **market** is worth a stroll and you can pick up everything from fresh coffee and berries to wild honey.

Antenna Hotel (☎ 0474 411002; d Birr40-70) sits only 50m from the bus station. Its *faranji*-priced upstairs options are large, clean and bright and have decent bathrooms. The downstairs Birr40 rooms aren't as nice as those at Hoteela Tinsaa'ee.

Hoteela Tinsaa'ee (☎ 0474 411557; d with shared bathroom Birr22, d Birr30), near the Commercial Bank (no forex facilities) 1.4km east of the bus station, has small, basic rooms that are reasonably clean. The shared squat toilets house a few flies but they pass the nostril test.

Snack & Bakery (snacks Birr2-5; ☷ 6.30am-9pm) is good for breakfast and fruit juices. The honey is tasty as is the local *ir'go* (yogurt).

Buses depart for Gambela (Birr22, six hours, two daily), Bedele (Birr12, four hours, six daily) and Addis Ababa (Birr64, 1½ to two days, 6am) via Jimma (Birr28, nine hours). Regular minibuses serve Gore (Birr5, around 35 minutes).

To reach Tepi take a minibus to Masha (Birr18, four hours) and go from there. If you start early enough, you can reach Tepi or Mizan Tefari in a day.

SOR RIVER WATERFALLS
ሶር ወንዝ ፏፏቴ

A worthwhile excursion from Metu is to the Sor River Waterfalls, one of the most beautiful falls in Ethiopia. It lies close to the village of Bechu, 13km southeast of Metu. The last 15 minutes of the one-hour walk from Bechu takes you through some dense forest teeming with birds and monkeys. In a small opening, the Sor River suddenly drops 20m, over the lip of a wide chasm. Amazing. Brave souls can take a dip in the pool below.

A daily Land Cruiser leaves Metu for Bechu (Birr10, one hour) around 7am. It returns as soon as it's full, which means you may have to walk back to Metu or battle a night of fleas in Bechu. To find the falls, you can enlist the help of a Bechu villager (Birr10). With a 4WD you could make the return trip from Metu in less than four hours.

METU TO TEPI

Although the first 25km south of Metu to the inconsequential Gambela-junction town of Gore is regularly travelled, the 150km gravel road south from there to Tepi rarely sees traffic (local or visitors). Around Gore the road snakes along a ridge and offers vistas over the western lowlands and flirts with sections of thick forest that have so far survived the axe. Some large trees, shrouded in vegetation, seem to have ecosystems of their very own. You may even spot a colobus monkey or two.

North of Masha you'll pass through some rolling hills carpeted in tea plantations before entering thick sections of forest and the occasional stand of bamboo south of town. We managed to spot a duiker just before the scenic descent to the village of Gecha.

After Gecha the road winds through *enset* plantations (false-banana tree, used to produce a breadlike staple also known as *enset*), traditional villages and lovely areas of forest.

As you near Tepi, you'll start to see coffee drying outside homes along the roadside.

In a private vehicle the drive takes between 4½ and seven hours depending on the season. It's also possible in a day by riding local minibuses, though you'll likely have to change minibuses at Masha and Gecha.

TEPI ቴፒ
elev 1238m

Tepi is famous for its coffee plantation. It's Ethiopia's second-largest and stretches over a huge 6290 hectares. Just over 2000 hectares lies around Tepi while the remainder, including Beshanwaka (a beautiful crater lake) is in the Gambela region about 30km away. The state-run plantation produces about 25,000kg of raw arabica coffee per year.

Because of Ethiopia's lowly latitude, the coffee requires extra protection from sunlight. The forest's natural trees (*Gravilia robusta*, *Melia*, *Cordia africana*, *Cuperessus* and rubber trees) give natural protection, providing plants with 70% shade.

The beautiful forest is brimful of birds and makes a lovely walk or drive. However, because of the plantation's size, a vehicle (your own) is really required for a proper tour. To cover the plantation, crater lake, experimental spice and fruit plantations, and the pulping and processing stations, you'll need about eight hours. A morning and afternoon tour is ideal. The coffee harvest (May through October) is a good time to visit.

Although you're welcome to turn up, it's a good idea to arrange for a proper tour in advance by calling the **Coffee Plantation Development Enterprise** (☎ 0114 168789) in Addis Ababa. Tours are currently free, but charges will be implemented in the near future.

The **plantation headquarters** (☎ 0475 560468) are signposted 400m beyond the main roundabout on the Jimma road.

Sleeping & Eating

Coffee Plantation Guesthouse (☎ 0475 560062; s/tw Birr40/80, d Birr50-60) Located at the plantation headquarters, this guesthouse is good value and is set in pleasant gardens. The large first-class doubles vaunt bright-green laminate floors, frilly bedspreads, small verandas and clean washrooms (cold showers). The bathrooms in the smaller second-class doubles and twins aren't as nice. If you order ahead, the 'workhouse club' can prepare meals.

WESTERN ETHIOPIA

Tigist Hotel (☎ 0475 560227; d with shared bathroom Birr24-32, d Birr40-50) The top-floor rooms have queen-size beds, shiny bathrooms (cold showers) and mosquito nets. Rooms 20 and 21 have views over town. The lower-floor rooms aren't as clean or bright.

Feleggion Hotel (☎ 0475 560015; d with shared bathroom Birr10) Just around the corner from the bus station, this is the most tolerable of the cheapies.

Abyssinia Hotel (mains Birr5-10) The best place to fuel up on *tibs* (sliced lamb, pan fried in butter, garlic, onion and sometimes tomato) or *kitfo* (minced beef or lamb like the French steak tartare, usually served warmed – but not cooked – in butter, *berbere* and sometimes thyme). Excuse the motor oil and woodchips on the floor – it's a novel approach to dust containment! It wouldn't be such a worry if your wobbly chair didn't seem like it was about to topple.

Getting There & Away

Three buses run daily to Masha (Birr15, three hours), while one continues to Gore (Birr30, 5½ to nine hours). Two buses serve Jimma (Birr30.40, eight hours). For Mizan Tefari (Birr10, 1½ hours), seven buses run daily.

Ethiopian Airlines flies to/from Addis Ababa (US$91, 2¼ hours) and Mizan Tefari (US$40, 20 minutes) on Thursday.

MIZAN TEFARI ሚዛን ተፈሪ

Mizan Tefari, the old capital of the Bench people, serves as a base for a visit to the nearby Bebeka coffee plantation. On Tuesday, there's quite a colourful market.

Aden Hotel (☎ 0473 330542; d with shared bathroom Birr26, d Birr40) is our top pick and sits in a leafy compound west of the main drag at town's south end. The Birr40 rooms are a decent size and sport mosquito nets, firm but comfy mattresses, bright windows and clean bathrooms. Its restaurant is good, though prices often succumb to *faranji* fluctuations.

Nuhamin Cafe (snacks & mains Birr2-4), 50m east of the Total station, is a fine breakfast spot. Perfect for a chocolate doughnut, *macchiato*, omelette or *ful*.

Buses run to Tepi (Birr10, 1½ hours, seven daily), Bonga (Birr25, five hours, two daily) and Addis Ababa (Birr63, 1½ days, one daily) via Jimma (Birr28, 7½ hours, one daily).

Ethiopian Airlines flies to/from Addis Ababa (US$91, 1¾ hours) and Tepi (US$40, 20 minutes) on Thursday.

BEBEKA COFFEE PLANTATION
በበቃ የቡና እርሻ

Twenty-eight kilometres southwest of Mizan Tefari is Ethiopia's largest and oldest **coffee plantation** (☎ 0471 118621). A tour of the 9337-hectare plantation gives a fascinating insight into Ethiopia's most important export.

As with Tepi, you should arrange for a proper visit in advance by calling the **Coffee Plantation Development Enterprise** (☎ 0114 168789) in Addis Ababa. Fees for tours will be implemented in the near future.

Around 15,000 quintals of arabica coffee are produced annually; during the harvest, up to 20,000 workers are employed. Almost 1500 hectares are devoted to honey production and experimental spice and fruit plantations. The honey is delicious and costs just Birr15 for a kilogram; pots can normally be provided. Spices grown include black pepper, cardamom and cinnamon, while bananas, oranges, jack fruits and pineapples are some of the fruits dotting the plantation's hills.

Bebeka has much more comfortable and attractive accommodation than Tepi. The **plantation guesthouses** (camping per 2-person tent Birr42, dm/d Birr10/52, 2-bedroom cottages Birr90) sit in the thick of the plantations and are surrounded by birdlife. The dorms are rough but the doubles and cottages are very comfortable. There's a nearby employee lodge with decent meals and satellite TV.

Since you require your own 4WD for a tour, there's really no point in rocking up on foot. The plantation is about an hour's drive from Mizan Tefari.

EAST TO WUSHWUSH

The road east to Wushwush from Mizan Tefari climbs through lush, intensively cultivated valleys and past neat rows of *tukuls* (traditional cone-shaped huts with thatched rooves). Stop and pick up some mangos if you can; 30 still just cost Birr5!

About 5km before the sleepy town of Wushwush, 92km east of Mizan Tefari, is the 1242-hectare **Wush Wush Tea Development plantation** (☎ 0471 112979; ☼ 8am-12.30pm & 2-5.30pm Mon-Fri, 8am-1pm Sat). A tour of the privatised plantation's tea-covered hills and its

STARBUCKS THANK KALDI'S GOATS

At some point between the 5th and 10th centuries, long before Starbucks opened its first store in Seattle's Pike Pl public market in 1971, coffee was discovered in Ethiopia. Although rumours abound of how its properties were realised, the following story is the most accepted account.

An astute herder by the name of Kaldi noticed that his goats were behaving rather excitedly each time they chewed a certain plant's leaves and berries, so he decided to give it a go himself. Sure enough, after a few chews and a couple of swallows, Kaldi was one hyper herder! Off he rushed to the nearest monastery to tell of his discovery, only to be reprimanded for 'partaking in the Devil's fruit'. However, all it took for the monks to come around was the aroma emanating from the fire where they'd thrown Kaldi's beloved beans.

Soon the monks were drying the beans for transport and shipping them to Ethiopian monasteries far and wide. There, monks would rehydrate them in water, eat the fruit and drink the fluids to keep them awake for nocturnal prayers. Surely something that helped them pray into the early hours must be the work of God and not the Devil!

Soon Arabs were importing the beans and the coffee business was well and truly underway. Although it wasn't until the 15th century in Turkey that today's style of coffee was first brewed, the name of Kaldi's kingdom stuck to the elixir of awakedness. And to what kingdom did Kaldi belong? Kafa, of course!

---

packaging factory is possible and makes an interesting excursion for those with time.

Wushwush Guest Lodge (camping free, r Birr25) is 200m off the main road. If heading towards Jimma, take the first right after passing the plantation's turn-off. It's a reasonable place and is set in pleasant grounds. You'll need to register with plantation's administration office before arriving.

You can use the lodge's kitchen or walk about 1km to a simple restaurant catering to plantation workers.

BONGA ቦንጋ
pop 10,851

Bonga used to form part of the great kingdom of Kafa, the birthplace of coffee (see the boxed text, above). In the surrounding area are a number of unexcavated historical sites, including what's thought to be an ancient burial site for kings. Various battle sites, including defensive ditches believed to date from the 14th century, and some 500-year-old churches, have also been found.

There's also terrific potential for hiking in the surrounding hills. Caves, waterfalls, natural bridges, hot springs, natural forest, wildlife and birdlife are all found close to town.

For more information on this almost unexplored but fascinating and beautiful area, visit the little **Bonga Information & Culture Office** (☎ 0473 320842; PO Box 6, Bonga, Kafa).

Kafa Development Programme Guesthouse (KDP; ☎ 0473 310195; supaks@ethionet.et; camping Birr35, r incl breakfast Birr80), set up a hill behind town, is a great choice for a rest. This NGO has several comfortable cottages, with kitchens, common areas and clean confines. It can also arrange guides for exploring the area.

National Hotel (☎ 0473 310051; d with shared bathroom Birr18) is a giant drop in quality and cleanliness from KDP, but it's also one quarter the price and much closer to the bus. Its restaurant (meals Birr5 to Birr10) is known as Bonga's best.

Jimma (Birr20, four hours), Mizan Tefari (Birr25, five hours) and Wushwush (Birr5, 30 minutes) are each served with one bus daily.

JIMMA ጂማ
pop 132,360 / elev 1678m

How you interpret western Ethiopia's largest city really depends on which direction you arrive from. Enter from Addis Ababa and it's a smaller and quirkier version of the raucous capital, with wide boulevards, lots of honking horns and a massive coffeepot rising from its main roundabout. Arrive from the wild, wild western lowlands and Jimma is a place of great sophistication and gentility. Cake shops, topiary hedges, city planning and fat policemen are among the city's attributes, and there's no shortage of decent hotels and restaurants.

For centuries, a powerful Oromo monarchy ruled the surrounding fertile highlands from its capital at Jiren (part of present-day Jimma). The region owed its wealth to its situation at the crux of several major trade routes and to its abundant crops. At its height, the kingdom stretched over 13,000 sq km. When Menelik came to power in the late 1800s, he required the region to pay high tribute.

When the Italians entered the picture in the 1930s, they had grand plans to create a modern city in the heart of Ethiopia's breadbasket and Jimma was subsequently born from Jiren. The town still boasts some good examples of Italian Fascist architecture.

Information

INTERNET ACCESS

Jiffar Computer Center (per hr Birr18) Slow and steady Internet connections.

Leo Computer Service Center (per hr Birr18) Internet as slow as the rest, but the owner is friendly.

River Tele Center (per hr Birr12) Cheap, but a slow go – bring a book!

MEDICAL SERVICES

Dr B Cossar Higer Clinic (☎ 0471 112814; ⊗ 24hr) Decent facilities and an English-speaking doctor.

Ethiopia Red Cross (☎ 0471 111257) Ambulance services.

Pharmacy (☎ 0471 116699) Helpful and well stocked.

MONEY

Commercial Bank (⊗ 8am-4pm Mon-Fri, to noon Sat) Changes cash and travellers cheques.

Dashen Bank (⊗ 8am-noon & 1-5pm Mon-Fri, 8am-noon Sat) Similar services and rates to the Commercial Bank.

POST

Post office (⊗ 8am-6pm Mon-Fri, to noon Sat)

PHOTOGRAPHY

Super Photo (⊗ 8am-8pm Mon-Sat, to 1pm Sat) Produce pictures from digital cameras (Birr2.50 per photo).

TELEPHONE

Telecommunications office northside (⊗ 8am-6pm Mon, Thu & Fri, to 4pm Tue & Wed, to noon Sat); southside (⊗ 8.30am-5pm) International calls. Standard rates (p267).

Sights

JIMMA MUSEUM ጂማ ሙ-ዚየም

The traditional culture section of the **Muuziyemii Jimmaa** (admission Birr25; ⊗ 9am-12.30pm Mon

& Wed, 9am-noon & 2-5.30pm Tue, Thu & Fri, 2-5.30pm Sat & Sun) houses examples of Jimma's traditional arts and crafts, and includes some fine examples of woodwork, musical instruments and weapons. The bark skirts and the grass raincoats on display are still worn in areas of western Ethiopia today.

The historical section plays home to numerous artefacts ranging from a rickety-looking Italian machine gun and an Italian-made walking stick-cum-gun to possessions belonging to Kafa kings, including a carved wooden throne and two massively bulbous and cartoonish nightclothes boxes. Much less regal is one king's loo, which looks like a frying pan with a hole in it.

The enormous drum (1.3m in diameter) was used to summon the people to war.

PALACE OF ABBA JIFFAR

የአባ ጂፋር ቤተ መንግስት

Looking more out of America's wild west than the Kafa kingdom, the forlorn-feeling **Palace of Abba Jiffar** (admission Birr25; ⊗ 9am-12.30pm Mon & Wed, 9am-noon & 2-5.30pm Tue, Thu & Fri, 2-5.30pm Sat & Sun) sits atop a hill 7km northeast of the town centre, near the village of Jiren.

King Jiffar (1852–1933), who was one of the most important Kafa kingdom rulers, held power at the end of the 19th century.

The palace contains a private family mosque (which is still in use) and rooms that used to serve as a library, throne room, reception chamber, king's guard room, sentry tower, courthouse and guesthouse.

The adjoining house is said to have belonged to the king's grandson, the sultan. From the balcony overlooking the courtyard, the royal family watched musicians, wrestlers, singers and poets. Almost 1.6km back down the hill lies the tomb of the king.

With the road in its current state, only 4WDs can make it up. Until it's repaired you'll have to catch one of the town's shared taxis or minibuses (Birr0.50 to Birr2) to the end of the asphalt (about halfway), from where it's a one-hour walk.

OTHER SIGHTS

In the vicinity of Jimma, there are various caves, hot springs and a hippo pool (at the Boye Dam, 5km from town) that can be visited; inquire at your hotel.

If you're a connoisseur of Italian Fascist architecture, take a peek at the cinema, post

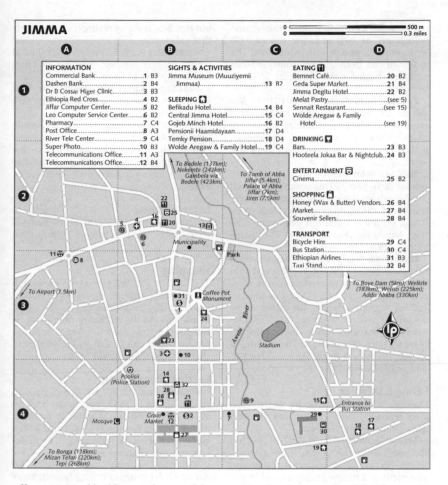

JIMMA

INFORMATION	
Commercial Bank.....................1	B3
Dashen Bank..........................2	B4
Dr B Cossar Higer Clinic...........3	B3
Ethiopia Red Cross..................4	B2
Jiffar Computer Center.............5	B2
Leo Computer Service Center....6	B2
Pharmacy..............................7	C4
Post Office............................8	A3
River Tele Center....................9	C4
Super Photo..........................10	B3
Telecommunications Office.....11	A3
Telecommunications Office.....12	B4

SIGHTS & ACTIVITIES	
Jimma Museum (Muuziyemii	
Jimma).............................13	R2

SLEEPING 🛏	
Befikadu Hotel......................14	B4
Central Jimma Hotel..............15	C4
Gojeb Minch Hotel................16	B2
Pensionii Haamidayaan.........17	D4
Temky Pension.....................18	D4
Wolde Aregaw & Family Hotel....19	C4

EATING 🍴	
Bemnet Café........................20	B2
Geda Super Market................21	B4
Jimma Degitu Hotel...............22	B2
Melat Pastry........................(see 5)
Sennait Restaurant...............(see 15)
Wolde Aregaw & Family	
Hotel..............................(see 19)

DRINKING 🍸	
Bars...................................23	B3
Hooteela Jokaa Bar & Nightclub..24	B3

ENTERTAINMENT 🎭	
Cinema...............................25	B2

SHOPPING 🛍	
Honey (Wax & Butter) Vendors...26	B4
Market................................27	B4
Souvenir Sellers....................28	B4

TRANSPORT	
Bicycle Hire.........................29	C4
Bus Station..........................30	C4
Ethiopian Airlines..................31	B3
Taxi Stand...........................32	B4

office, municipal buildings and some of the old hotels.

Sleeping

Jimma hotels have openly embraced the *faranji* price scheme – the one where you pay double! Prices listed here are *faranji* rates. Sadly, paying double doesn't make your room immune to Jimma's regular power cuts. All listings have hot showers unless stated otherwise.

Central Jimma Hotel (☎ 0471 118283; d with shared bathroom Birr51, d Birr76, ste Birr173-230; 🖥) There are some hotels you wouldn't dream of walking barefoot in. This is not one of those hotels! The Birr76 doubles and suites are spotless, comfortable and bright. The suites also have satellite TV. The rooms with shared bathrooms are smaller and don't have mosquito nets – they also aren't barefoot worthy. A swim (guest or not) will set you back Birr23.

Wolde Aregaw & Family Hotel (☎ 0471 112731; d with shared bathroom Birr51, s Birr67-78, d/tw Birr92/115, ste Birr126-184) Opposite the bus station and set in quite large grounds, this hotel's shared bathroom options are better value than Central's. The other rooms are less so. Most are large and well kept, but aren't as comfortable and feel old – the dated pink bathrooms don't help.

Temky Pension (☎ 0471 110844; d/tw with shared bathroom Birr25/35, d/tw Birr39/46) Down a dirt lane east of the bus station, this *pension* has cheap, small and tidy rooms with shared bathrooms, as well as larger rooms with mosquito nets and private bathrooms. The music in the lively garden courtyard can be a drawback for those wishing to go to bed early.

Pensionii Haamidayaan (☎ 0471 116014; d/tw with shared bathroom Birr23/40, d/tw Birr33/50) This economical place is a quieter version of its neighbour Temky, though the rooms, bathrooms and shared facilities are more worn.

Befikadu Hotel (☎ 0471 111757; d with shared bathroom Birr15, d Birr23) This is the least you'll pay for private bathrooms, though showers spurt cold water and most toilets lack seats. It will do for a night, but keep your flip-flops handy for the odd roach. The rooms at the back are less noisy.

Gojeb Minch Hotel (☎ 0471 110103; r with shared bathroom Birr40-50, r Birr80-120) We'd heard that this hotel's newly renovated rooms were something special, so we posed as tourists seeking accommodations for our parents' upcoming visit and popped in. Unfortunately the manager was entirely unhelpful (dare we say rather rude!) and he demanded we pay just to see them. So you'll have to find out for yourselves.

Eating & Drinking

Dining is not Jimma's strong point, though after returning from a foray into the west it's a culinary extravaganza.

Sennait Restaurant (mains Birr10-14) Within the confines of the Central Jimma Hotel, this is Jimma's most respected restaurant. The menu is a mix of Ethiopian and Western fare.

Jimma Degitu Hotel (mains Birr6-24) The *faranji* food here is quite good (if you remember you're in Ethiopia) and more varied than elsewhere. We happily wolfed down a cheese burger. The French fries were cold but good, as they more resembled crisps or potato chips. Pizza is also on the menu.

Wolde Aregaw & Family Hotel (mains Birr6-12) This hotel's menu is much the same as Sennait's. Dine on choices like *doro arrosto* (roast chicken), spaghetti or fish cutlet.

Bemnet Café (snacks & drinks Birr1-2) This streetside café serves great coffee and is extremely popular with local students. The chocolate-coated doughnuts look lovely,

but one bite and you realise it's more sugar that substance.

Melat Pastry (snacks & drinks Birr1-2) Its shaded terrace vaunts the best selection of cakes and fruit juices in town.

Geda Super Market (☺ 8am-8pm) The best stocked store in Jimma, though that isn't saying much!

Try tasting the local *besso* drink, made from ground barley. Some of Jimma's swinging bars – or rather dingy dives – are marked on the map. Hooteela Jokaa Bar & Nightclub is a particular favourite of locals.

Entertainment

Cinema (admission Birr2) North of Bemnet Café; shows Western movies with English subtitles.

Shopping

Thursday is the main market day; search out Jimma's famous three-legged stools. Good-quality basketware can also be found in and around the market. Jimma honey is well known and costs from Birr10 to Birr12 per kilo. You can find it in the warren of shacks opposite the grain market.

Getting There & Away

Ethiopian Airlines (☎ 0471 110030) flies daily to Addis Ababa (US$63, one hour) and on Wednesday, Friday and Saturday there are flights to/from Gambela (US$74, one hour). Note that during the rainy season, flight delays and cancellations are common.

Two early morning buses leave daily for Addis Ababa (Birr34.60, nine hours). More Addis Ababa–bound buses pick up during the day, but most will overnight somewhere en route. Tepi (Birr30.40, eight hours), Mizan Tefari (Birr28, 7½ hours), Bedele (Birr15, 3½ hours) and Nekemte (Birr29.60, 10 hours) each have one early morning service. There are up to six minibuses to Welkite (Birr20 to Birr25, five hours).

Getting Around

Garis (horse-drawn carts) cost Birr0.50 to Birr2 for hops around town depending on the distance. Bikes can be hired (Birr3 per hour) just north of the bus station.

No buses or minibuses go to the airport, so you'll need to flag a contract taxi (Birr50) or walk to a taxi stand.

JIMMA TO ADDIS ABABA

After Jimma, the road begins to wind back in a northeastern direction towards Addis Ababa. Approximately 57km out of town, the road detours around the Gilgel Gibe Dam, which, when finished, will be Ethiopia's second-largest hydroelectric plant (after the one on the Tekeze, begun in 2002). Anubis baboons are commonly seen along the road.

Much further west you'll see several impressive bulbous rock pinnacles rising from the seemingly subdued plateau in the distance. Once you pass the major outcrop, the road serpentines down into the gaping Gibe River Valley. The view west after you've ascended the opposite side is even more impressive.

If you get stuck at **Welkite**, the **Gebra Mamo Hotel** (☎ 0113 301505; d with shared bathroom Birr35, d Birr50) has large comfy beds, hot-water showers, mosquito nets and clean bathrooms. It's also home to Welkite's best restaurant.

Two buses leave daily for Addis Ababa (Birr15 to Birr20, 3½ hours) and for Jimma (Birr20 to Birr25, five hours). There's one service to Hosaina (Birr15 to Birr20, four hours).

The little town of **Weliso**, 43km northeast of Welkite, is known for its hot springs. A great naturally heated **swimming pool** (admission nonguests Birr12.50; ☒ Fri-Sun) can be found at the **Negash Hotel** (☎ 0113 410002; d & tw Birr62.50-137.50; ☒). The hotel is 1.4km from the town centre; you can hop on a gari for Birr0.50. Camping is occasionally permitted. The grounds are full of birds and vervet monkeys.

Ten buses travel daily to Addis Ababa (Birr10, 2½ hours) and to Welkite (Birr5, one hour). For Jimma, go to Welkite. There's usually one early morning Landrover taxi heading north to Ambo (for Mt Wenchi) during the dry season.

The area around Weliso is home to the Gurage people (p46). From the village of Sebeta, a solid 3½ hour trek (one way) takes you up to the top of Mogli, one of the peaks of Mt Wuchacha. With a vehicle, Mt Wuchacha is best accessed from the Addis Ababa–Ambo road (p237).

The Addis Ababa–Jimma road is currently being upgraded and when we visited the sublimely sealed sections had made it as far west as Welkite.

THE WESTERN LOWLANDS

The swampy western lowlands, comprised of the Gambela federal region, stand in stark contrast to the striking landscapes seen in the country's north and south. One breath of the region's moist, searing air and you'll quickly notice the difference too.

Unfortunately, a recent escalation in ethnic and political violence has made the region unsafe for travellers (see the boxed text, p248). For the region's people, who have to be some of the nicest in the country, we hope peace isn't too long over the African horizon.

GAMBELA ጋምቤላ
pop 45,308 / elev 526m

Set on the banks of the chocolate-brown Baro River, at a lowly altitude of 526m, Gambela is muggy, swampy and sweaty. These surroundings, mixed with lowland populations of the Anuak and Nuer peoples, makes Gambela unlike any other city in Ethiopia. Gambela is also the capital of the 25,274-sq-km Gambela federal region.

Although the recent ethnic and political violence may seem to say otherwise, the people here, although initially appearing reticent and deeply suspicious, are actually incredibly hospitable and treat visitors with more warmth than anywhere else in the country. Using 'daricho', the Anuak greeting, or 'male', the Nuer greeting, helps break the ice.

Gambela's past is as turbulent and intriguing as the city is today. Thanks to the Baro River being the only truly navigable river in Ethiopia, it was along this watercourse that raiding slave parties transported thousands of captured men.

Later, at the 19th century's end, the river's strategic and commercial importance was contemplated by the British and Ethiopians. Knowing that the Baro was navigable all the way to Khartoum (via the White Nile), Menelik II dreamed of linking Ethiopia with Egypt and Sudan. To help create the great inland shipping service, the emperor agreed to grant the British, who were already in control of Sudan, an enclave on the Baro River. In 1907 the site was chosen

SAFETY WARNING

We strongly suggest that you keep your eye on developments around Gambela before visiting the western lowlands. Since 1991 tensions have been rising between the Anuak and the Nuer peoples, who represent the vast majority of the region's population.

The long on-and-off conflict has been fuelled by a number of reasons, one being repeated incursions by the Sudanese People's Liberation Army (SPLA). Another reason seems to be the minority Anuak's historical control of local government.

Since 7 July 2002, when there was a rash of retribution Anuak killings by Nuers sparked by an Anuak police station commander's killing of several Nuer in Itang, things have taken a drastic turn for the worse. From 13 to 15 December 2003, hundreds of Anuaks were killed and over 500 homes burnt and looted in the town of Gambela after police displayed eight bodies of Nuers slain by an armed Anuak group.

The fact that Ethiopian government forces were found to have done most of the killing has led Anuak leaders to believe they are victims of systematic genocide. The subsequent arrest and torture (according to Amnesty International) of hundreds of Anuak, who the government claims were involved in the armed group responsible for the killing of the eight Nuers, and the government's attempted forced disarming of the Anuak has only thrown more fuel on the fire.

A few days before our arrival from Metu, an armed group of Anuak attacked the Gambela police station and prison. In the process they killed several officers, including the state police commissioner, and freed an unknown number of prisoners. This outbreak of violence meant we weren't able to do first-hand research of the area.

and Gambela was formally inaugurated as a port and customs station.

Soon steamers were chugging up and down the wide river, laden with valuables ranging from coffee, salt and beeswax to skins, liquors and cotton. Commerce flourished and Gambela boomed.

The Italians briefly captured Gambela in 1936 and vestiges of their fort are still visible. The British won the river port back in 1941 and amazingly made it part of Sudan 10 years later. When Sudan gained its independence in 1956, the protectorate was given back to Ethiopia. It was around this time that the old shipping service formally ceased to be.

Since the fall of the Mengistu regime, there have been talks about plans to revive the river port and boost the region's economic fortunes, but nothing has been done. In the meantime, Gambela slowly sinks back into the mud.

Information

There's currently only one Internet café and the foreign-exchange policy of Gambela's branch of the Commercial Bank is up in the air at the moment, so plan ahead.

With the closure of the tourist office, the **Gambela National Park Headquarters** (☎ 0475 510912; 7am-12.30pm & 3-5.30pm Mon-Fri) seems to have taken up the reigns in helping with

advice for those planning trips outside Gambela.

Dangers & Annoyances

If the heated security situation (see the boxed text, above) has calmed and travel is possible, your biggest concern should be mosquitos. Malaria continues to kill an extraordinarily high percentage of the population here and adequate precautions are essential (see p373 for more information). Giardia is also common.

Although much less of a risk, a much bigger thing to wrestle with are the river's crocodiles. If you do decide to take your chances, only swim where the locals do. That's no guarantee though – a local was taken not long ago.

Photographers should show even more sensitivity and caution than normal (see

THE ETHIOPIAN SLAVE TRADE

Ethiopia's slave trade was a lucrative one. From the 16th century right up to the 19th century, the country's main source of foreign revenue was from slaves. At the height of the trade, it's estimated that 25,000 Ethiopian slaves were sold every year to markets around the globe.

the boxed text, p266). It's strictly forbidden to take photos of, or from, the bridge. The Anuak and Nuer people are also notoriously camera-shy. Always ask permission before taking photos (even for people's houses and animals); if you don't, their warm hospitality may turn to real upset, anger and aggression, including stone throwing.

Sights & Activities
A pleasant walk around Gambela includes the riverside, the old steamship and pier (visible from the riverbank), the bridge and the markets. You may well come across an old colonial warehouse, bungalow or merchant villa too. This walk is marked on the Gambela map.

At sunset, many locals gather at the point where the river diverges. People come to bathe, walk or catch up on gossip. It's a colourful scene. The **Nuer villages** on the outskirts of town, known as 'New Land', can also be visited; a Nuer guide is a good idea. A **Nuer market** can be found near the Gambella Ethiopia Hotel.

In the north of the town is the **Anuak market**. Vendors sit in the shade of the trees selling cereals, firewood, large Nile perch and tobacco. To pass the time, many indulge in *akowyo* (water pipe) smoking. You can taste the *borde* (traditional 'beer'), served to thirsty market-goers from metal buckets.

Sleeping & Eating
Decent hotels and restaurants are not Gambela's forte.

Gambella Ethiopia Hotel (☎ 0475 510044; tw Birr150) Although dog-eared and dilapidated, this is by far and away Gambela's best hotel. Knowing fleapits are your only other option, prices here are now absurd. The only redeemable features are the birds and monkeys in the grounds and the cold drinks available. The restaurant (mains Birr8 to Birr15) is also one of its better traits and serves local and *faranji* food (such as steak and shish kebab).

Tourist Hotel (☎ 0475 521584; d with shared bathroom Birr20) The cleanest and quietest of the flea havens.

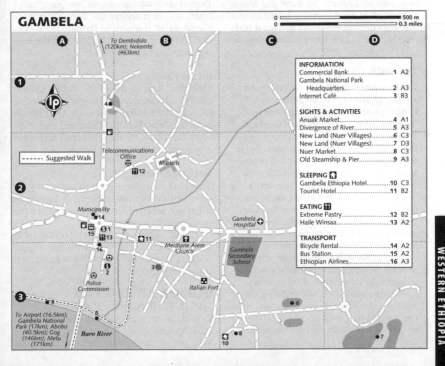

GAMBELA

0	500 m
0	0.3 miles

INFORMATION
Commercial Bank...................1 A2
Gambela National Park
  Headquarters.....................2 A3
Internet Café.........................3 B3

SIGHTS & ACTIVITIES
Anuak Market.........................4 A1
Divergence of River...............5 A3
New Land (Nuer Villages)......6 C3
New Land (Nuer Villages)......7 D3
Nuer Market...........................8 C3
Old Steamship & Pier.............9 A3

SLEEPING
Gambella Ethiopia Hotel.......10 C3
Tourist Hotel.........................11 B2

EATING
Extreme Pastry.....................12 B2
Haile Winsaa........................13 A2

TRANSPORT
Bicycle Rental......................14 A2
Bus Station..........................15 A2
Ethiopian Airlines.................16 A3

To Dembidolo (120km); Nekemte (463km)

Suggested Walk

Telecommunications Office

Markets

Municipality

Gambela Hospital

Medhane Alem Church

Gambela Secondary School

Police Commission

Italian Fort

To Airport (16.5km); Gambela National Park (17km); Abobo (40.5km); Gog (146km); Metu (171km)

Baro River

THE ANUAK

The Anuak's language closely resembles that of the Luo tribes in Kenya. Fishing is their main means of survival, though some grow sorghum. Outside Gambela most live in extended family groups, rather than villages, composed of a cluster of huts in a small compound.

Anuak huts are characterised by low doorways and thickly thatched roofs. The eaves, which stretch almost to the ground, keep out both the torrential rain and baking sun. The houses' walls are often decorated with engraved designs, including animals, magical symbols and geometrical patterns.

A common practice among many Nilotic peoples of Ethiopia and Sudan, including the Anuak, is extraction of the front six teeth of the lower jaw at around the age of 12. This is said to have served originally as a precaution against the effects of tetanus or 'lockjaw'.

Haile Winssa (mains Birr5-15) Although you'd never dream of staying here, locals swear it serves the best Ethiopian fare in Gambela.

Extreme Pastry (mains Birr3-5) It's the best cake shop in town, though the selection isn't enormous. It also does breakfast. Try the *ful* (chickpea purée) and *sils* (spicy tomatoes).

Getting There & Away

4WD

Although on a map it looks attractive to make a loop to Gambela from Nekemte via Dembidolo and return via Bure and Metu, the Dembidolo road is rather horrific (and impassable during the rains) and local traffic rarely uses it. This route is also prone to bandits (see Shifty Shiftas, opposite). It's best to stick to the Metu–Gambela road.

There are no 4WDs available for hire in Gambela.

AIR

Ethiopian Airlines (☎ 0475 510099) flies to/from Addis Ababa (US$100, two hours) and Jimma (US$74, one hour) on Wednesday, Friday and Saturday.

BOAT

During the wet season in the past, cargo boats occasionally ran the Baro River from Gambela all the way to the Sudanese border. This is no longer the case and the border is indefinitely closed.

BUS & TRUCK

One bus leaves daily for Addis Ababa (Birr85.55, two days) overnighting at Bedele (Birr31, 10½ hours) via Gore (Birr20, six hours), Metu (Birr22, 6½ hours) and Welkite (Birr78.80, 1½ days). There's no longer any regular transport to Dembidolo.

Getting Around

There are no taxis or *garis* in town, so your only option besides walking is bicycling. Bikes are rented (Birr6 per hour) near the municipality building.

To get to/from the airport, 16.5km from town, you'll have to hitch with fellow passengers or ask Ethiopian Airlines to sort something for you.

GAMBELA NATIONAL PARK
ጋምቤላ ብሔራዊ ፓርክ

Less than 50 years ago, Gambela National Park, spreading over 5061 sq km, was one of Ethiopia's richest places for large mammals.

THE NUER

The Nuer people, who are relatively recent arrivals to the region, originated in the Nilotic-speaking regions of Sudan and now form the largest ethnic group in Gambela. They're largely cattle herders, though like the Anuak, they also fish. The people's affection for their cattle is legendary and much Nuer oral literature, including traditional songs and poetry, celebrates their beasts.

Unlike the Anuak, the people like to live together in large villages on the banks of the Baro River. Very tall and dark, the Nuer women are fond of ornamentation, including bright bead necklaces, heavy bangles of ivory or bone and, particularly, a spike of brass or ivory which pierces the lower lip and extends over the chin. Cicatrising (considered sensual) is also widely practised; the skin is raised in patterns used to decorate the face, chest and stomach. Rows of dots are often traced on the forehead.

Elephants, lions, leopards, giraffes, buffaloes, topis, tiangs, roan antelopes, hartebeests and waterbucks were all found here. The park was also home to species more typical of Sudan, like the Nile lechwe and white-eared kob.

However, today's ever-growing need for shelter, firewood, food and land for farming, as well as the influx of Sudanese refugees, has dramatically reduced wildlife and their habitats. The Alwero dam project constructed in the park's core didn't help either.

The lack of funds is a big obstacle to the park, too. Despite budget increases in 2001 after national and international interest in the park, Gambela remains one of the most neglected and threatened parks in Ethiopia.

There's also little to no tourist infrastructure, meaning you have to be totally self-sufficient.

Although discomfort is guaranteed and the wildlife rewards are few, you'll definitely have stories to tell. And encounters with the fascinating Anuak and Nuer people shouldn't be underrated.

Wildlife

Vegetation consists largely of woodland and grassland, with large areas of swamp in between.

Animals you might realistically hope to see are the common bushbuck, oribi, lesser kudu and the white-eared kob. The best place to spot these animals is 180km or so west of Gambela along the banks of the Baro.

SHIFTY SHIFTAS

Some stretches of road around Gambela (such as between Shebel and Gambela) continue to be targeted by *shiftas* (bandits).

Should you be unlucky enough to encounter gun-toting shiftas, here's a quick survival guide. Stop at once, stay very calm and hand over a respectable wad of money as calmly and quickly as possible (keeping an easily accessible stash somewhere nearby is a good idea). If you're driving, don't attempt to move until the *shiftas* have disappeared back into the bush. Accidents only happen when drivers panic and try to do a runner. If you have a driver, make sure they understand the plan of action too. Tourists are not targeted; if anything, they're avoided because of the repercussions.

Poaching has limited elephant numbers and you'd be a lucky soul to see one. The last ones were spotted around 56km south of Abobo on the road to Gog. Further south, around Gog, the odd villager still complains about livestock being taken, which leads people to think there are still lions in the area.

Birdlife is plentiful, both in the forest and around the swamps. Gog is particularly good for woodland birds, and Itang for water birds (including the pink-backed pelican).

Planning

The **Gambela National Park Headquarters** (☎ 0475 510912; admission per 48hr Birr35; ◷ 7am-12.30pm & 3 5.30pm Mon-Fri) in Gambela organises guides (Birr20 per day) and obligatory armed scouts (Birr50 per 48 hours).

Sleeping & Eating

Camping (a future fee is still being pondered) is really your only option unless you want to stay in one of Gog's or Itang's dives. Camping is permitted anywhere, though you'll have to be fully self-sufficient with food and cooking gear.

Getting There & Around

For any trips within the park, you'll really need to come with your own sturdy 4WD. You also must be prepared for some long treks if you want to increase your chances of spotting animals.

Occasional public transport runs through the park between Gambela and Gog; inquire at park headquarters.

DEMBIDOLO ደንቢዶሎ

If you're bound and determined to not double back through Bure and Metu when returning to the highlands from Gambela, you'll likely end up spending at least one night in Dembidolo. The town is known for two things in particular: its goldsmiths and its *tej* (honey wine). The former can be seen at work, the latter can be tasted in any of Dembidolo's numerous bars *(tej beats)*.

Birhane Hotel (☎ 0575 550127; r with shared bathroom Birr15, r Birr25) is on the main road and has Dembidolo's cleanest rooms.

There's usually a painful daily bus to Nekemte (Birr41, 12 to 13 hours). A couple of trucks a week run to Gambela (Birr30, five hours).

WESTERN ETHIOPIA

Ethiopia Directory

CONTENTS

ACCOMMODATION

Finding accommodation in Ethiopia is easy. Finding accommodation that won't curl your toes and send you running for the doors is tiring work – thankfully we've done most of that for you.

Ethiopia's range of options is heavily slanted towards the budget end (US$1 to US$20 per night), with Addis Ababa and major tourist centres providing only a handful of midrange options (US$20 to US$50). True top-end picks (US$50 and up) are only found in the capital.

The various listings throughout this guidebook are given in the order of the author's preference.

PRACTICALITIES

■ The best-known English-language daily newspapers are the government-owned *Ethiopian Herald* and the privately owned *Monitor*. Other weekly private newspapers include the *Fortune,* the *Reporter,* the *Sun, Sub-Saharan Informer* and the *Capital*. Only the *Ethiopian Herald* is available outside Addis Ababa. The weekly *Press Digest* and *Days Update* (both Birr15) give useful summaries of the most important stories from the week's Amharic and English press.

■ Radio Ethiopia broadcasts in English from 1.30pm to 2pm and 7pm to 8pm weekdays. The BBC World Service can be received on radios with shortwave reception, though frequencies vary according to the time of day (try 9630, 11940 and 17640 MHz).

■ Ethiopia's ETV1 channel broadcasts in English from 10.30pm to midnight. Many hotels and restaurants have satellite dishes that receive BBC or CNN. Others have South Africa's multichannel DSTV system.

■ Ethiopia's electricity supply is 220V, 50 cycles AC. Sockets vary from the European continental two-pin, earth prong (two round prongs), rated at 600W to South African/Indian-style plug with two circular metal pins above a large circular grounding pin.

■ Ethiopia uses the metric system for weights and measures.

Camping

Tents are useful in Ethiopia for trekking, the exploration of remote regions and to save money on extended stays. If you're just planning a short trek, tents can be hired from Addis Ababa's tour operators (p282) or from business in Lalibela, Gonder and Debark.

In theory, you can camp anywhere, bar the obvious off-limit sites, such as military installations. 'Established' campsites have

BOOK ACCOMMODATION ONLINE

For more accommodation reviews and recommendations by Lonely Planet authors, check out the online booking service at www.lonelyplanet.com. You'll find the true, insider lowdown on the best places to stay. Reviews are thorough and independent. Best of all, you can book online.

been set up in some of the national parks and in the Omo Valley, but most lack facilities and consist of little more than a clearing beside a river. It's always essential to treat drinking water at the sites.

There are increasing numbers of upmarket hotels now allowing camping on their grounds, though prices are close to what you'd pay for nice budget accommodation.

All camping fees in this book are per person unless stated otherwise.

Hotels

Hotels will play home to everyone who's not camping. Even in the capital, there are no hostels, homestays, or university or rental accommodation available to travellers.

Pricing invariably leads to resentment from many travellers as countless hotels (many openly) charge substantially higher rates for *faranjis* (forcigners, especially Western ones). Although you make take offence to a hotel owner calling you a rich *faranji*, remember prices are still dirt-cheap, and you'll always be given priority as well as the best rooms, facilities and service. That said, we still applaud those establishments with flat rates.

Charging same-sex couples more for rooms than mixed couples is also pervasive but less justifiable.

Some hotels (particularly government-owned ones) charge a 10% service charge and 15% tax on top of room prices. We've incorporated these extra charges into the room prices listed.

In Ethiopia, a room with a double bed is confusingly called a 'single', and a room with twin beds a 'double'. In our reviews we've used the Western interpretation of singles, doubles and twins. Similarly when hotel managers say the room has a 'shared shower', they mean a shared bathroom. Note that there are rarely single occupancy rates.

Reservations are wise in Gonder, Aksum and Lalibela during the major festivals. See the relevant Sleeping sections for advice.

Although there are no left-luggage facilities in Addis Ababa, most hotels will hold your belongings for no extra charge.

BUDGET

Since our last visit, the quality of budget hotels, which make up 95% of the country's hotels, has made a notable leap. There are still countless dives, but the number of clean and comfortable options is rising, especially in the north. We definitely pulled less fleas this go around! Although an aberration, we even managed a smart room with hot shower and satellite TV for Birr50!

The vast majority of budget rooms are always spartan – think four walls, linoleum rolled over a cement floor, a bed and, if you're lucky, a plastic chair. Depending on your budget, you can typically have your pick of a shared or private bathroom.

In smaller, out-of-the-way towns hotels may double as drinking dens and brothels – bring earplugs. Many lack glass windows, only having a shutter to let air and light in.

Maintenance doesn't seem to be a high priority, so the best budget hotels are often those that have just opened. If you hear of a new hotel in town, it may be the best place to head.

MIDRANGE

Although very comfortable compared to Ethiopian budget options, most midrange hotels here would be scraping by as bare-bones budget options in the Western world. They typically include a simple room with private bathroom and satellite TV, as well as an adequate restaurant, secure parking and a garden. Though usually clean and quiet, the majority are looking tired and run-down, and very rarely offer good value for money. Many are old 'tourist' hotels that were nationalised in the 1970s and '80s under the socialist Derg, and many still host the orange shag carpets of that era!

Worth singling out, however, is the Ghion Hotel Group. Its chain of hotels along the historical circuit (Bahir Dar's Tana Hotel, Gonder's Goha Hotel, Aksum's Yeha Hotel and Lalibela's Goha Hotel) provides the best accommodation in northern Ethiopia.

Each offers exceptional settings, attractive traditional designs and great service.

Several slick new privately owned mid-range options have cropped up in Arba Minch, Bahir Dar and Lalibela, so more are sure to follow.

TOP END

There are several top-end options in Addis Ababa, including the five-star 'Luxury Collection' Sheraton Hotel that rivals anything on the continent for facilities and comfort. The nearby Hilton seems inconsolably modest in comparison.

ACTIVITIES

With two amazing 4000m mountain ranges and countless other peaks and valleys hosting unique wildlife, it's little wonder that trekking in Ethiopia has become a major activity. Rock climbing is also possible, but this sport is still in its infancy here. The waterways churning through Ethiopia's topographic delights play home to some fine rafting and fishing. Last but not least, the fact that Ethiopia's skies are blanketed with a plethora of endemic and migratory birds has led to a boom in bird-watching. If statistics are to be believed, more people come to Ethiopia to see its birds than to see anything else. Grab your binoculars and enjoy!

Bird-Watching

The birds of Ethiopia are so numerous, so diverse and so colourful that they attract twitchers from around the globe. To do the birds and the art of bird-watching

justice, we've created a special boxed text, Ethiopia's Endemic Birds (p62). It highlights some of Ethiopia's most famous birds and gives you the lowdown on where to go to find them and when. The Animals section (p60) of the Environment chapter also delves into some of the species you'll spot while travelling through the country.

Some of Addis Ababa's tour agencies (p282), as well as some excellent agencies abroad, offer great bird-watching tours.

Fishing

Ethiopia's lakes and rivers are home to over 200 species of freshwater fish, including very large catfish (up to 18kg), tilapia, large barbus, tigerfish, the brown and rainbow trout and the famously feisty Nile perch.

Fly-fishing, bait fishing with float and leger, freelining, threadline spinning and trolling are all permitted fishing practices, but you'll need to be totally self-sufficient as far as equipment is concerned.

Popular fishing spots include Lake Tana in the north and the Rift Valley lakes in the south. Fishing is permitted almost everywhere in Ethiopia, with the exception of rivers in the Bale Mountains National Park, where endemic species are found.

Rock Climbing

There's untapped potential for rock climbing, particularly around Mekele in the region of Tigray, which offers sandstone climbs in the HVS – E2 (4-5c) range, though you'll have to come fully equipped and self-sufficient, and prepared to locate your own

---

SAFETY GUIDELINES FOR TREKKING

Before embarking on a trek, consider the following points to ensure a safe and enjoyable experience.

■ Pay any fees and possess any permits required by local authorities.

■ Be sure you are healthy and feel comfortable walking for a sustained period.

■ Obtain reliable information about physical and environmental conditions along your intended route (eg from park authorities).

■ Trek only in regions, and on trails, within your realm of experience.

■ Be aware that weather conditions and terrain vary significantly from one region, or even from one trail, to another. Seasonal changes can significantly alter any trail. These differences influence what you should wear and what equipment you carry.

■ Ask officials before you set out about the environmental characteristics that can affect your trek and how you should deal with them if they arise.

RESPONSIBLE TREKKING

Trekking in Ethiopia has the potential to put great pressure on the environment. You can help preserve the ecology and beauty of the area by taking note of the following information.

- Carry out all your rubbish. Never ever bury it.
- Minimise the waste you must carry out by taking minimal packaging and taking no more food than you'll need.
- Where there's no toilet, at lower elevations bury your faeces in a 15cm deep hole (consider carrying a lightweight trowel for this purpose). At higher altitudes soil lacks the organisms needed to digest your faeces, so leave your waste In the open where UV rays will break it down – spreading it facilitates the process. Always carry out your toilet paper (Ziplock bags are best). With either option make sure your faeces is at least 50m from any path, 100m from any watercourse and 200m from any building.
- Don't use detergents or toothpaste within 50m of watercourses, even if they're biodegradable.
- Stick to existing tracks and avoid short cuts that bypass a switchback. If you blaze a new trail straight down a slope, it will erode the hillside with the next heavy rainfall.
- Avoid removing any plant life as they keep topsoils in place.
- Try to cook on lightweight kerosene, alcohol or Shellite (white gas) stoves instead of burning dead erica wood or eucalyptus. Never burn indigenous trees.
- Be aware of local laws, regulations and etiquette about wildlife and the environment.
- Never feed animals as it messes with their digestive system and leads them to become dependent on hand-outs.
- If camping, try to make camp on existing sites. Where none exist, set up away from streams on rock or bare ground, never over vegetation.

routes. Contact **Village Ethiopia** (☎ 0115 523497; www.village-ethiopia.com), which has catered to climbers in the past.

Trekking

Trekking is the highlight of many people's trips to Ethiopia. Treks from a few days up to two weeks are regularly completed in the striking 4000m surroundings of Simien Mountains National Park (p125), while treks through the rich wildlife of Bale Mountains National Park (p181) typically last four to six days.

New horse treks in the western range of the Bale Mountains are now possible out of Dodola (p179). Also new on the scene are ecotreks around Lalibela (p163).

White-Water Rafting & Kayaking

Rafting began in Ethiopia in the 1970s, when an American team rafted the Omo River in the southwest. Most Addis Ababa tour operators (p282) now run trips as do some international operators, such as the incredibly experienced **Remote River Expeditions** (www.remoterivers.com).

The Omo River rafting season is from September to October (after the heavy rains). Tours usually last from one to three weeks. The white water (classed as a comparatively tame three or four on the US scale) is not the main attraction, rather it is the exposure to wildlife (particularly birds) and tribal groups (such as those along the Omo River).

Shorter rafting trips can also be planned on the Blue Nile (a few days) and Awash (one or two days) Rivers. Although two historic expeditions have recently paddled the Blue Nile from Lake Tana to Khartoum and beyond to the Mediterranean, this journey won't be on any travel agency itinerary for a millennium or so.

In theory, excellent kayaking could be had on all the rivers mentioned earlier, but it's not for the inexperienced. Trips need to be well planned, well equipped and well backed up. In the past, some badly planned trips have gone tragically wrong. Get in touch with the Addis Ababa tour operators, which will put you in touch with experienced kayakers in Ethiopia.

IN SEARCH OF SOUVENIRS

During the last several hundred years, thousands of manuscripts and other national treasures, including gold and silver crosses and even a giant stele (!), have left Ethiopia as 'souvenirs'. Most will probably never be recovered.

Today, tourists, antique dealers, professional thieves and even diplomats are responsible for the disappearance of works of art. In 1996 a German tourist removed several items from the National Museum at Aksum, and in March 1997 a Belgian tourist almost succeeded in removing Lalibela's famous 7kg gold cross. Things became so critical that the World Bank recently funded a four-year project to try and create a nationwide, computerised inventory of Ethiopia's treasures.

At the current rate of 'souvenir' removal, it's thought that Ethiopia will be bereft of most of her treasures by 2020. If you don't want to risk wasting money on a souvenir that can't leave the country have a look at the following list of banned souvenirs.

List of Banned Souvenirs

The following list is adapted from the official catalogue of objects that are now denied export permits. Be warned that currently much parchment is being denied permission.

- Animal and plant fossils and any prehistoric items such as stone tools, bones or pottery.
- Anything of outstanding anthropological or ethnographical interest.
- Anything with an ancient inscription on it.
- Old processional or hand crosses that bear the names of kings or religious leaders; or any currently in use at churches or monasteries.
- Any items (including manuscripts, books, documents or religious objects such as chalices, crosses and incense burners) currently serving in churches.
- Any old wooden items.
- Coins and paper money not currently in circulation.
- Any endangered species or their products, such as ivory, tortoiseshell or leopard skins.
- Any items of exceptional artistic interest whether old or modern.
- Art with outstanding historical value, such as engravings with historical figures.
- Any items formerly belonging to the emperor, his family or to Ethiopian nobles

Exportation Permits

Although you may have been told that you'll need an exportation permit from the Department of Inventory and Inspection at the National Museum if you plan to leave Ethiopia with anything that looks antique, this is no longer the case.

As of late 2005 customs officials at Bole International Airport and Addis Ababa's main post office, now trained in the art of antiquities, will make the determination as to whether your souvenir can leave Ethiopia. If you haven't declared questionable souvenirs and they're discovered by officials, you'll likely have the item confiscated and have a lot of explaining to do.

BOOKS

One of the best-known books about Ethiopia is Graham Hancock's *The Sign and the Seal*. The author spent 10 years trying to solve one of the greatest mysteries of all time: the bizarre 'disappearance' of the Ark of the Covenant. Though the research and conclusions raised an eyebrow or two among historians, this detective story is very readable and gives a good overview of Ethiopia's history and culture, however tenuous the facts!

Evelyn Waugh's *Remote People,* though rather dated now, includes some wry impressions of Ethiopia in the 1930s. *Waugh in Abyssinia* is based on the author's time as a correspondent covering the Italian–Ethiopian conflict in the 1930s.

The charming *A Cure for Serpents* by the Duke of Pirajno recounts the duke's time as a doctor in the Horn and is beautifully and engagingly written. Episodes include encounters with famous courtesans, noble chieftains and giant elephants.

The newly reprinted (locally) *Ethiopian Journeys,* by the well-respected American writer Paul Henze, charts travels during the emperor's time. Recently published locally is *Off the Beaten Trail,* by John Graham, which is based on travels around the country during the author's time as an aid worker.

In Search of King Solomon's Mines entertainingly takes the reader through Debre Damo, Lalibela, Gonder and other exotic Ethiopian locations on author Tahir Shah's quest to find the mythical mines of Solomon.

Thomas Pakenham's fascination with the historical anecdotes revolving around Ethiopia's *ambas* (flat-topped mountains) is the basis of *The Mountains of Rasselas,* an engaging book on Ethiopia's history.

For the best travel literature see p16. Interesting Ethiopian history books are found in the sidebars of the History chapter (p26).

BUSINESS HOURS

In general, banks, post offices and telecommunications offices are all are open the core hours of 8.30am to 11am and 1.30pm to 3.30pm weekdays and from 8.30am to 11am Saturday, but many open earlier, close later or stay open for lunch.

Most government offices are open from around 8.30am to 12.30pm (to 11.30am Friday) and 1.30pm to 5.30pm Monday to Friday. Private organisations and NGOs open from 8am to 1pm and 2pm to 5pm weekdays. Shops usually operate half an hour later. Outside Addis Ababa, restaurants typically open between 7am and 8am and close between 9.30pm and 10.30pm. Restaurant reviews in this guide won't list business hours unless they differ from these standards.

Cafés are typically open daily from 6am or 7am through to 8pm or 9pm, while *tej beats* (honey-wine bars) usually run daily from 10am to 10pm. Bars open from 6pm to midnight.

Internet cafés are typically open 8am to 8pm Monday to Saturday. Some have limited hours on Sunday.

CLIMATE CHARTS

Compared with other equatorial nations, Ethiopia's climate on the whole is very mild. Average daily temperatures on the wide-ranging highlands are below 20°C. It's only the lowland fringes in the east, south and west where daytime temperatures can soar past 30°C.

The majority of rains traditionally fall between mid-March and early October, with the central and western highlands receiving up to 1600mm annually. The far east and northern highlands only receive significant rainfall in July and August (400mm to 1000mm). The far south breaks the trend receiving most of its rain in April, May and October.

More information on weather patterns can be found in the Climate section of each destination chapter. See also the When to Go section, p14.

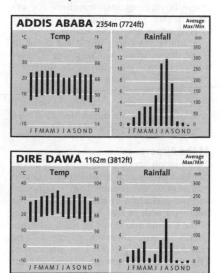

COURSES

Unless you're living in Addis Ababa, there are really no courses of note in Ethiopia. It's likely due to the lack of demand – perhaps most travellers are just too busy trying to absorb the country's history, culture and nature while on the go!

For long stays, the Institute of Language Studies at Addis Ababa University offers four-month language courses (see p90).

CUSTOMS

Upon arrival in Ethiopia, visitors must declare foreign currency. There's no limit to the amount of currency that can be brought in, but no more than Birr100 can be exported and imported. You may import 2L of spirits and 200 cigarettes or 100 cigars duty-free.

If you're bringing with you anything of value, such as a video camera or laptop computer, you may be required to register it on your passport as you enter Ethiopia at immigration (to deter black-market trading).

Leaving the country with certain souvenirs can be a problem (see the boxed text, p256).

DANGERS & ANNOYANCES

Compared with many African countries, Ethiopia and its capital, Addis Ababa, are remarkably safe places. Serious or violent crime is rare; against travellers it's extremely rare. Outside the capital, the risk of petty crime drops still further.

A simple traveller's tip? Always look as if you know where you're going. Thieves and con artists get wind of an uncertain newcomer in a minute.

Though the following list may be off-putting and alarming, it's very unlikely you'll encounter any serious difficulties – and even less likely if you're prepared for them.

At the Airport

Commission-seeking taxi touts and guides can be a problem at most airports. Unless you want to take money from your pocket and put it straight in theirs, decide on the hotel you wish to stay before you step out of the airport and don't let them take you elsewhere. And always negotiate the taxi rate *before* you get in. The majority of Ethiopian taxi drivers are helpful, charming and honest.

Begging & Giving

Many travellers find that the begging they encounter is one of the most distressing aspects of travel in poorer countries.

Ethiopia has its fair share of beggars. Some travellers resent being 'targeted' by beggars because they are foreign. However, the work of high-profile aid efforts has made this inevitable. Foreigners are often seen as dispensers of charity.

It's difficult to know when to give, to whom and how much. A good rule of thumb is to give how locals give; small coins dispensed to those who can't make a living, such as the disabled, the ill, the elderly and the blind. Handing out more only increases expectations and leads to more disappointment down the line.

If you don't want to donate money, say instead *igzabier yisteh/yistesh* (m/f; God bless you) with a slight bow of the head; this is a polite and acceptable way of declining to give.

Although it's hard, you should never give to children, whether it be money, sweets, pens, empty water bottles or food. Older Ethiopians are heartbroken seeing younger generations of children, who are no worse off than they were when they were young, begging for money, empty water bottles, food etc. Most children don't beg because they need the items, but because they can get the items. Being rewarded for this behaviour only pulls them from school, robs them of a traditional childhood and makes them believe they need hand-outs from Westerners (instead of growing up proud and self-reliant like past generations).

Yes, giving to kids puts a smile on their face, but you have to remember this is temporary and only leads to unhappiness in the future. If you really want to help children in need, you need to invest time and effort. This may involve visiting a community and finding out what materials the school needs. This allows teachers to distribute materials to those students actually in need. No, you won't see the joy on the child's face, but if you're giving for the right reason that should not be important.

Civil Disturbances

Since the controversial government elections in May 2005, there have been two isolated occasions in Addis Ababa where large opposition protests have sparked violence. On 8 June 2005 at least 22 civilians were killed when police fired into crowds of protesters throwing stones. The fallout resulted in thousands of opposition party members, journalists and protestors being jailed.

A week of similar demonstrations in November 2005 resulted in police killing 46 and arresting thousands more. Although

Addis Ababa is once again quiet, travellers should monitor local news and stay clear of any mass demonstrations.

If you're concerned, check your government's latest security reports on countries (such as those published by the British Foreign Office).

Land Mines

Most travellers have nothing to fear from mines, but those trekking in parts of Tigray or driving off-road in the Ogaden region of southeastern Ethiopia or along the Kenyan border should check with local village officials. Keep to well-worn routes when possible. A useful phrase might be *Fenjy alle?* (Are there mines here?) Popular trekking areas such as the Simien and Bale Mountains National Parks are perfectly safe.

Mobbing & Faranji Frenzy

The most wearisome annoyance in Ethiopia is the famous '*faranji* frenzy', which greets you at almost every turn. For the new arrival as much as for the old-timer, the phenomenon is distressing.

The shouts of 'You, you, you, you, YOU!' is what most raises the hackles of travellers. Bear in mind, however, that the Amharic equivalent *(Ante!/Anchee!)* is the colloquial way of catching someone's attention. In other words, it's not as rude and aggressive as it sounds in English.

It can also take the form of screaming, giggling, shouting or sniggering children. Like begging, there's no clear response. Ignoring it or, even better, treating it with humour is probably the best answer. Anger only provokes children more (there can be few things more tempting than a grumpy *faranji*!). An Amharic *hid!* (clear off!) for a boy, *hiji!* for a girl or *hidu!* for a group is the Ethiopian response, and sends children scuttling, but it can have the reverse effect, and is considered rather harsh from a foreigner.

If you're waiting for a bus and become a 'captive spectacle', trying to communicate with locals usually breaks the animal in a zoo feeling. You may just transform the howling mob into delightful and charming individuals.

Although you're never likely to get used to *faranji* frenzy, at least feel thankful that it's almost *never* aggressive or hostile.

Scams

Compared to other African countries, Ethiopia has few scams and rip-offs to boast of. Those that do exist, like the siren scam (p84) in Addis Ababa and the notebook scam on the historical circuit (see p157), are pretty transparent and rather easily avoided.

You'll also hear many 'hard luck' stories, or those soliciting sponsorship for travel or education in Ethiopia or abroad. Although most are not genuine, some stories are sadly true, so don't be rude.

Also look out for fake antiques in the shops.

Self-Appointed Guides

High unemployment has spawned many self-appointed and unofficial guides. You will be approached, accompanied for a while, given unasked-for information and then charged. Be wary of anyone who approaches you unasked, particularly at the exit of bus stations etc. Unfortunately, there's almost always an ulterior motive. Be polite but firm and try not to get paranoid!

Shiftas

In some of the more remote areas, such as the southeast's Ogaden Desert, near the Kenyan border, along the Awash–Mille road at night, and in the far west, *shiftas* (bandits) are sometimes reported. However, most of these places lie far from the main tourist trails. In fact, tourists are very rarely targeted; indeed they are positively avoided for fear of government repercussions.

Theft

Pickpocketing is the biggest concern, but is a problem mainly in Addis Ababa and other large towns, in particular Shashemene, Nazret and Dessie. For tips on thieves' tactics, see Addis Ababa's Dangers & Annoyances section (p84).

Keep an eye on your belongings at bus stations and be wary of people offering to put your bags on the bus roof. Be aware that professional thieves sometimes operate at major festivals and markets (such as Bati), targeting Ethiopians as well as foreigners.

A money belt is best for your passport and cash stash, but not for your daily spending money – keep that separate so you don't have to yank out your money belt each time you spend. It's also a good

GUIDELINES FOR GUIDES

Although more official guides exist in Ethiopia today, particularly in the cities along the historical circuit, there are still countless unofficial 'guides' waiting at every corner.

Some of them resort to aggression, hysterics or sulking to extract money from tourists; others resort to hard-luck stories or appeals for 'sponsorship'. Others claim special expertise and that this and other guidebooks are wholly or partly 'wrong'. Some 'guides' in Addis Ababa have even conned apprehensive first-time travellers into taking them along for the entire historical circuit, at a cost of US$20 per day!

Even if the unofficial guide is friendly, they'll know little in comparison to those who've been trained and will likely charge the same fee. Their lack of actual knowledge takes away from your trip and encourages unhealthy migration of potential 'guides' to towns.

Hiring children may seem like a nice way to help, but you're only giving them reason to miss school, and like unofficial guides, they have little knowledge that will benefit your trip.

If you don't want to be one of the many people writing to us with stories of a guide ruining your trip, here are a few tips:

■ If possible, hire licensed guides.

■ Choose a guide you're comfortable with. Test their knowledge of English and of the sites in advance, perhaps over a coffee.

■ Before starting ensure that your expectations are clearly understood, such as what you want to see and how much time you have.

■ Negotiate a fee in advance. Be aware that some may ask initially up to five times the going rate or more. Professional licensed guides' fees are set at Birr150 per day (one to four people) in Gonder and Lalibela. For a knowledgeable guide elsewhere, Birr10 per hour (minimum total fee of Birr20) is very fair. Check this book for quotes.

■ If the service has been good, it's fair and polite to tip a bit extra at the end, but don't be pressured into it, particularly if the tour was poor. See the boxed text, p264.

idea to keep an emergency stash of US$100 hidden somewhere.

EMBASSIES & CONSULATES
Ethiopian Embassies & Consulates

Ethiopia has diplomatic representation in the following countries:

Australia (☎ 03-9417 3419; www.consul.com.au/index .html; 38 Johnston Street, Fitzroy, Victoria 3065)

Belgium (☎ 02 77 132 94; etebru@brutele.be; 231 Ave de Tervuren, 1150 Brussels)

Canada (☎ 613-235 6637; Suite 210, 151 Slater St, Ottawa, K1P 5H3)

Egypt (☎ 02-335 3693; 6 Abdel Rahman Hussein St, El-Gomhuria Sq, Mohandiseen)

France (☎ 01 47 83 83 95; embeth@starnet.fr; 35 ave Charles Floquet, 75007, Paris)

Germany (☎ 030-772 060; Boothstr 20a, 12207, Berlin)

Ireland (☎ 01-677 7062; info@ethiopianembassy.ie; 1-3 Merrion House, Fitzwilliam St Lower, Dublin 2)

Italy (☎ 06 440 36 53; embethrm@rdn.it; 16-18 Via Andrea Vesalio, 00161, Rome)

Kenya (☎ 020-2732050; State House Ave, Nairobi)

Sudan (☎ 471156; Plot 4, Block 384 BC, Khartoum South)

Sweden (☎ 08-665 6030; ethio.embassy@telia.com; 17 Lojtnantsgatan, 115 50, Stockholm)

UK (☎ 020-7589 7212; 17 Prince's Gate, London, SW7 IPZ)

USA (☎ 202-364 1200; info@ethiopianembassy.org; 3506 International Drive, NW Washington DC 20008)

Embassies & Consulates in Ethiopia

The following list isn't exhaustive (almost every African nation has representation in Addis Ababa), but it covers the embassies most of you will likely need.

Australia See Canada.

Belgium (Map p76; ☎ 0116 611643; embel.et@ ethionet.et; Fikremaryam Abatechan St)

Canada (Map p76; ☎ 0113 713022; addis@dfait -maeci.gc.ca; Seychelles St) Also represents Australia.

Djibouti (Map pp80-1; ☎ 0116 613006; PO Box 1022) Off Bole Rd.

Egypt (Map p76; ☎ 0111 553077; egyptian.emb@ ethionet.et; Madagascar St)

Eritrea (Map pp80-1; ☎ 0115 512844; Ras Mekonen Ave) Currently closed.

France (Map p76; ☎ 0111 550066; amba.france@ ethionet.et; PO Box 1464)

Germany (Map p76; ☎ 0111 550433; german.emb
.addis@ethionet.et; PO Box 660)
Italy (Map p76; ☎ 0111 553042; italembadd@
ethionet.et; PO Box 1105)
Kenya (Map p76; ☎ 0116 610033; kenigad@ethi
onet.et; Fikremaryam Abatechan St)
Netherlands (Map p76; ☎ 0113 711100; nether
lands.emb@ethionet.et) Off Ring Rd.
Somaliland (Map pp80-1; ☎ 0116 635921; btwn Bole
Rd & Cameroon St)
Spain (Map p76; ☎ 0115 550222; embaespet@
mail.mae.es; Botswana St)
Sudan (Map pp80-1; ☎ 0115 516477; sudan.emb
assy@ethionet.et; Ras Lulseged St)
Sweden (Map pp80-1; ☎ 0115 511255; sweden.emb
assy@ethionet.et; Yared St)
Switzerland (Map p76; ☎ 0113 711107; vertre
tung@add.rep.adm.ch; Ring Rd)
UK (Map p76; ☎ 0116 612354; britishembassy
.addisababa@fco.gov.uk; Fikremaryam Abatechan St)
USA (Map p76; ☎ 0115 174000; http://addisababa
.usembassy.gov; Algeria St)

FESTIVALS & EVENTS

Islamic holidays are not particularly conspicuous in Ethiopia but they are important
events for the Muslim population. Festivals
include Ras as-Sana (Muslim New Year),
Mawlid an-Nabi (Prophet's birthday), Lailat
al-Mira'ji (Prophet's Ascension), Eid al-Fitr
(marking Ramadan's end) and Eid al-Adha
(Festival of Sacrifice).

Major Ethiopian Orthodox festivals include the following:

January

Leddet (also known as Genna or Christmas) 6–7 January.
Although less important than Timkat and Meskel, Leddet is
still significant. The faithful attend all-night church services,
often moving from one church to another. On Christmas
day, the traditional games of *genna* (a kind of hockey) and
sometimes *gugs* (a kind of polo) are played, along with
horse racing. Priests don their full regalia. Lalibela is one
of the best places to experience Leddet; Addis Ababa is
also good.

Timkat (Epiphany, celebrating Christ's baptism) 19
January. This three-day festival is the most colourful of
the year. The church *tabots* (replicas of the Ark of the
Covenant) are taken to a nearby body of water on the
afternoon of the eve of Timkat. During the night, the
priests and faithful participate in a vigil around the *tabots*.
The following morning, the crowds gather around the
water, which is blessed, then splashed onto them; religious
vows are renewed. The *tabot* is then paraded back to the
church accompanied by much singing and dancing. Gonder
is considered the best place to be for Timkat; Addis Ababa
is also good (head for Jan Meda; p103).

March–April

Good Friday March/April. From Thursday evening before
Good Friday, the faithful fast until the Easter service, which
ends at 3am on Easter Sunday.

Fasika (Orthodox Easter) March/April. Fasika marks the
end of a vegetarian fast of 55 days, in which no animal
product is eaten. Officially, nothing should be consumed
until the daily church service finishes at around 3pm. In the
past, many of Ethiopia's enemies took advantage of the
fasting period to inflict heavy casualties on its weakened
armies.

September

Kiddus Yohannes (New Year's Day) 11 September.
Ethiopian New Year (also known as Enkutatash) is an
important family and social event. Traditionally, new
clothes are bought for the occasion, particularly for the
children, and relatives and friends are visited. Special feasts
are prepared. The traditional game of *gugs* can sometimes
be seen.

Meskel (Finding of the True Cross) 27 September. This
two-day festival is the most colourful festival after Timkat.
Bonfires are built topped by a cross to which flowers are
tied, most commonly the Meskel daisy. After the bonfires
are blessed, they are lit, and dancing and singing begins
around them. Priests don their full regalia. Addis Ababa,
Gonder and Aksum are good places to experience Meskel.

November

Festival of Maryam Zion 30 November. This is one of
Ethiopia's largest festivals, though it's only celebrated in
Aksum. See p141 for details.

MAJOR ISLAMIC HOLIDAYS

Islamic year	New Year	Prophet's Birthday	Prophet's Ascension	End of Ramadan	Festival of Sacrifice
1428	20 Jan 07	31 Mar 07	10 Aug 07	13 Oct 07	20 Dec 07
1429	10 Jan 08	20 Mar 08	31 Jul 08	02 Oct 08	9 Dec 08
1430	29 Dec 09	09 Mar 09	20 Jul 09	21 Sep 09	28 Nov 09

December
Kulubi Gabriel 28 December. Although not on the official religious holiday list, large numbers of Ethiopians make a pilgrimage to the venerated Kulubi Gabriel church near Dire Dawa in the east (see the boxed text, p225). If you're in the area, don't miss it.

FOOD
For information on what you'll find heaped atop your *injera*, see p68. What's *injera*? Turn to p68! Get the picture?

Eating out in Ethiopia is ridiculously cheap, with local meals in remote areas costing you less than US$1. In large regional cities a local meal will ding you US$1.50, while a Western meal will rob you of an extra 50¢. If you pull out all the stops and dine on succulent braised lamb with caramelised onions, lentils, lemon and raison orange couscous in Addis Ababa's best restaurant, you'll be out about US$8.

In this book restaurants are listed solely in order of author preference, with Addis Ababa being the only exception. There, restaurants are ordered first by style of food (Ethiopian, Italian, Indian etc), second by neighbourhood and lastly by author preference.

If cafés are more known for their pastries and cakes, they'll fall under Eating. Conversely, if it's their coffee or juices that shine, you'll find them under Drinking.

GAY & LESBIAN TRAVELLERS
In Ethiopia and Eritrea, homosexuality is severely condemned – traditionally, religiously and legally – and remains a topic of absolute taboo. Don't underestimate the strength of feeling. Reports of gays being beaten up aren't uncommon. In Amharic, the word *bushti* (homosexual) is a very offensive insult, implying immorality and depravity. One traveller wrote to us to report expulsion from a hotel and serious threats just for coming under suspicion. If a hotel only offers double beds, rather than twins, you and your companion will pay more or may even be refused occupancy.

Women may have an easier time: even the idea of a lesbian relationship is beyond the permitted imaginings of many Ethiopians! Behave discreetly, and you will be assumed to be just friends.

Note that the Ethiopian penal code officially prohibits homosexual acts, with penalties of between 10 days' and 10 years' imprisonment for various 'crimes'. Although gay locals obviously exist, they behave with extreme discretion and caution. Gay travellers are advised to do likewise.

Information on homosexuality in the Horn is hard to come by, even in the well-known gay publications. Try the **International Lesbian & Gay Association** (ILGA; www.ilga.org) for more information.

HOLIDAYS
Ethiopia's public holidays can be divided into three categories: national secular holidays, Christian Orthodox festivals (p261) and Islamic holidays (see the boxed text, p261). During the Christian Orthodox festivals, accommodation is hard to come by in Gonder, Aksum and Lalibela, as are open seats on internal flights. While prices rise for rooms during these times, transportation costs remain the same. It's best to book flights as far in advance as possible to avoid problems. See the relevant towns' sections for more details.

National holidays include the following:
Victory of Adwa Commemoration Day 2 March
International Labour Day 1 May
Ethiopian Patriots' Victory Day (also known as Liberation Day) 5 May
Downfall of the Derg 28 May

INSURANCE
A travel-insurance policy for all medical problems is essential for travel in Ethiopia, while one to cover theft and loss really is helpful but not vital. For information on medical insurance, see p369.

Vehicle insurance is covered on p280.

Worldwide cover to travellers from over 44 countries is available online at www.lonelyplanet.com/travel_services.

INTERNET ACCESS
Internet in Ethiopia is like a pimple on your wedding day – it's always found where everyone looks and never where nobody can see. In English? Internet is everywhere in Addis Ababa, pretty easy to spot in major towns and nonexistent in places that see few tourists. Most are open 8am to 8pm Monday to Saturday. Some open limited hours on Sunday.

Connections are still on the slow side and costs range from Birr0.20 to Birr0.30 per minute in most places. The exceptions are Aksum (Birr1 per minute) and Lalibela (Birr2 per minute).

For those with laptops, only the Sheraton and Hilton in Addis Ababa have facilities for you to go online.

See also Internet Resources, p17.

LEGAL MATTERS

Remember that when in Ethiopia, you're subject to Ethiopian laws. If you're arrested, you must in theory be brought to court within 48 hours. You have the right to talk to someone from your embassy as well as a lawyer. For the most part, police in Ethiopia will show you as much respect as you show them. If confronted by the police, always maintain your cool, smile and be polite. Compared with some other African nations, police here rarely, if ever, ask for bribes (we've yet to experience it).

Alcohol

Alcohol cannot be served to anyone under 18 years of age in Ethiopia. Disturbance caused by those under the influence of alcohol is punishable by three months' to one year's imprisonment. Driving while under the influence attracts a fine of around Birr150.

Drugs

Penalties for possession, use or trafficking of illegal drugs (including hashish) are strictly enforced in Ethiopia. Convicted offenders can expect both fines and long jail sentences.

Consumption of the mildly stimulating leaf *chat* is permitted in Ethiopia, but not in Eritrea.

MAPS

For simply travelling around the country on public transport, the maps in this guidebook should suffice. For those of you venturing off into the nether regions with 4WDs, a good map is essential. Since trekking without a scout is illegal in the Simien and Bale Mountains, additional maps aren't necessary, though topographic maps (see the parks' relevant sections for details) can help you plan your routes with more precision.

In Ethiopia, the map produced by the defunct Ethiopian Tourism Commission (1987; 1:2,000,000) isn't bad and can be picked up in some Addis Ababa hotels or in the gift shop (p104) next to the Tourist Information Centre in Addis for Birr61.

A more accurate map (although it lacks distance labels between cities) of the same scale is available from the Ethiopia Mapping Authority (p78) in Addis Ababa for Birr28.75.

Of the maps currently available outside the country, the best is that produced by International Travel Maps (1998; 1:2,000,000). It's much more up to date than both maps available in Ethiopia.

The Cartographia map of Ethiopia, Eritrea and Djibouti (1996; 1:2,500,000) comes second, and isn't a bad choice for the region.

Most major map suppliers stock maps produced outside Ethiopia, including **Stanfords** (☎ 020-7836 1321; www.stanfords.co.uk) in London.

MONEY

Ethiopia's currency is the birr. It's divided into 100 cents in 1, 5, 10, 25 and 50 cent coins, and there are 1, 5, 10, 50 and 100 birr notes. Despite a weekly auction determining exchange rates, the birr is one of Africa's most stable currencies.

See the inside front cover for exchange rates and p14 for details about the costs of travel.

According to National Bank of Ethiopia regulations, all bills in Ethiopia must be paid in birr. This isn't enforced and Ethiopian Airlines, most major hotels, most travel agencies and even the Department of Immigration accept (and sometimes demand!) US currency.

One regulation that's strictly enforced is the conversion of birr to US dollars or euros; this transaction can only be done for people holding onward air tickets from Ethiopia. This means people leaving overland must budget accordingly. There are black-market traders around the borders, but rates are poor and it's risky (see below).

ATMs

There are no ATMs in the country that accept foreign cards.

Black Market

The black market is in decline as the official and free rates for the Ethiopian birr converge. It's rare to be offered a rate much above 10% more than that offered by the banks.

TIPS FOR TIPPING

Tipping can be a constant source of worry, hassle or stress for travellers. This guide has been compiled with the help of Ethiopians.

- In the smaller restaurants in the towns, service is included, and Ethiopians don't tip unless the service has been exceptional (up to 10%).
- In bars and cafés, sometimes loose coins are left. However, in the larger restaurants accustomed to tourists, 10% will be expected.
- In Addis Ababa's midrange and top-end hotels, staff will expect a minimum Birr10 per service.
- Outside Addis Ababa, midrange and top-end hotels' luggage handlers will expect a tip of around Birr2 to Birr5 per bag, and people acting as impromptu guides around Birr10.
- For the assistance of a child, Birr1 or Birr2 is plenty.
- At traditional music and dance shows in bars, restaurants and hotels, an audience shows its appreciation by placing money (around Birr10) on the dancers' foreheads or in their belts.
- Taxi drivers in Addis Ababa expect around Birr2 added to the fare; car 'guards' (often self-appointed) expect the same.
- Drivers of 4WD rental vehicles make around Birr70 per day in salary, so a tip of Birr30 to Birr50 per day is generous for quality service.
- If the service has been good at the end of the trek, a rule of thumb for tipping guides/scouts/mule handlers might be an extra day's pay for every three days' work.
- Professional English-/German-/Italian-speaking guides hired from Addis Ababa travel agencies for multiday 4WD tours make around Birr200 per day, so a nice tip would be Birr50 to Birr70 per day.

The black market is illegal; penalties range from hefty fines to imprisonment. If you do indulge, stick to the shops, and be wary of other places, particularly Merkato and the Piazza in Addis Ababa, where's there's a good chance of being swindled or robbed.

Cash

As with many African countries the US dollar is the preferred foreign currency in Ethiopia. You'll have no trouble exchanging US cash wherever there are forex facilities. Euros are gaining in popularity, but they're still more of a hassle to change and less banks accept them. The same can be said for pounds sterling.

Although more banks in Ethiopia change cash than travellers cheques, you will usually end up getting slightly worse rates for cash.

Credit Cards

Credit cards (Visa and MasterCard) are only mildly useful in Addis Ababa and completely useless (with the exception of some Ethiopian Airlines offices) outside it. The travel agencies, airline offices and major

hotels that do accept cards typically ding you 5% extra for the privilege of plastic.

Cash advances are only possible at a couple of branches of the Dashen Bank in the capital (5.5% commission). Only Addis Ababa's Sheraton can give you US dollars instead of birr.

Tipping

Tips (*gursha* in Amharic) are considered a part of everyday life in Ethiopia, and help supplement often very low wages. The maxim 'little but often' is a good one, and even very small tips are greatly appreciated. It's a great mistake to overtip: it unfairly raises the expectations of locals, undermines the social traditions and may spoil the trips of future travellers. Local guides can start to select only those tourists who look lucrative, and can react very aggressively if their expectations aren't met.

If a professional person helps you (or someone drawing a regular wage), it's probably better to show your appreciation in other ways: shaking hands, exchanging names, or an invitation to have a coffee and pastry are all local ways of expressing gratitude.

Furnishing yourself with a good wad of small notes – Birr1 and Birr5 – is a very good idea. You'll need these for tips, taking photographs etc. You should budget around Birr50 for tips per week.

Travellers Cheques

Most banks in Addis Ababa and the larger towns (but not smaller ones) exchange travellers cheques. In the capital, a few major hotels and travel agencies also accept them. Like cash, travellers cheques are best carried in US dollars.

Almost all of the banks charge from 0.5% to 1.0% commission for travellers cheques, plus around Birr8 per cheque. In general, the Commercial Bank levies the lowest charges, with private banks charging slightly more. It's always worth asking what the 'fixed fees' are (this term is better understood than 'commissions') before signing your cheques.

PHOTOGRAPHY & VIDEO

With the boom of digital photography, some Internet cafés now offer to burn your images to CD through a USB connection. They charge between Birr4 and Birr15 for the service, Birr10 more if you need a CD. We've noted which cafés offer this service in their respective reviews.

Decent print film is quite widely available in the capital and costs around Birr40 for a 36-exposure Kodak film. Some slide film is also available. Outside Addis Ababa, it's difficult to find film except in the larger towns, and products may not always be fresh.

For some helpful advice on photography in the region, see the boxed text, p266.

POST

Ethiopia's postal system is reliable and reasonably efficient. Airmail costs Birr2 for postcards; Birr2 for a letter up to 20g to Africa, Birr2.45 to Europe and the Middle East, and Birr3.45 to the Americas, Australia and Asia. Letters should take between five and eight days to arrive in Europe; eight to 15 days for the USA or Australia.

International parcels can only be sent from the main post office in Addis Ababa. Surface mail takes between five and seven months to reach Europe. Posting a small parcel of between 1kg and 2kg costs Birr13.90 worldwide.

Prices of airmail parcels are different for each country, with a 1kg parcel to Australia/Canada/UK/Italy costing Birr190.50/209.65/205.55/170.55. For each extra 500g to the same countries you'll pay approximately Birr50/51/38/24. All parcels are subject to a customs inspection, so leave them open until you've had their contents inspected at the counter.

Express courier service is available in Addis Ababa, with Express Mail Service (EMS) and DHL. See p83 for more information on this.

There's a free poste restante service in Addis Ababa (address mail to 'Poste Restante, Addis Ababa, Ethiopia') and in many of the larger towns. When you collect it, it will likely be under your first name instead of your surname.

SHOPPING

Ethiopia has rich history of arts and crafts. To get an idea of what will be sold throughout the country see p58. To see the top end of quality and artistry, visit the Ethnological Museum in Addis Ababa (p84) before hitting the markets and shops.

Good souvenir shops are found in the capital as well as major towns on the historical circuit. Quality and creativity ranges from poor to very high, so it's worth comparing shops and wares. Prices always depend on your skills of negotiation. Don't forget the export regulations (see the boxed text, p256). While not illegal, you should try and avoid buying crafts made from indigenous woods.

The *gabi* (white cotton toga worn by the highlanders) makes a great (albeit bulky) travelling companion. It serves as a blanket, pillow, mattress, cushion (on long bus journeys) and wrap against the cold.

Bargaining

Prices are usually fixed in Ethiopia. Haggling over prices can sometimes greatly offend Ethiopians. All the usual discounts apply for long stays in hotels, low season, extended car hire etc though, and you shouldn't hesitate to ask for them in these instances.

The few exceptions, where haggling is almost expected, are at the local markets and with the local taxi and *gari* (horse-drawn cart) drivers. Don't forget that haggling is meant to be an enjoyable experience. Just remember the aim is not to get the lowest

TIPS FOR PHOTOGRAPHERS IN ETHIOPIA

Many Ethiopians, particularly outside Addis Ababa, are unused to tourists pointing the camera at them. Many feel seriously threatened or compromised, especially women. Be sensitive. Always try and ask permission, even if it is only using basic sign language. Best of all, use a local as an interpreter or go-between. Never take a photo if permission is declined.

In other areas, where people are starting to depend on tourists for income, the opposite is true. In the Lower Omo Valley, you'll be chased by people demanding their photo be taken! However, their eagerness has to do with the fee they'll claim for each snap of the shutter (around Birr1 to Birr2 per person per picture). Always agree to an amount first. The whole mercenary and almost voyeuristic affair can be rather off-putting for many travellers.

People with guides typically have a more enjoyable time, as the guides can usually sort out fees for individual photos, or better yet, a lump sum for unlimited (and unpestered) shots. Some people recommend giving their camera to the guide, who'll usually have an easier time getting shots while you happily wander. Remember that the local people have a right to benefit from tourism. In fact, it's money bargained for photos instead of money bargained for crops. Tourism may even help to preserve the groups and their traditions by assisting them economically.

Be aware that it's strictly forbidden to photograph 'sensitive areas', including military and police installations and personnel, industrial buildings, government buildings, residences and royal palaces; and major 'infrastructure' such as bridges, dams, airports. Penalties for contravening this law range from confiscation of film and camera, to between three months' and one year's imprisonment!

Following is some less social and more technical advice.

- Never leave equipment or film in a car or in the hot Ethiopian sun. High temperatures can wreck equipment and play havoc with film colour.

- The morning and late afternoon are the best times to take photos in Ethiopia, ideally before 8am and after 4pm. The light is gentler and there's less contrast between light and shade.

- Spot-metering – if you have it – is great for photographing faces, particularly dark ones in difficult conditions.

- Ethiopia's many hours of sun each day permit the use of slow film (such as ISO50 for slide film or ISO100 for print film), which can yield clear, fine-grained and colour-saturated pictures.

- A flash is useful for indoor scenes such as the *azmaris* (wandering minstrels) or dance spectacles in Addis Ababa.

- A small zoom lens of some sort is great, both for wildlife and for photographing Ethiopia's colourful people (but don't forget to show sensitivity and tact).

- Bring plenty of batteries with you. Outside the capitals, batteries are often old, and of very poor quality.

- Beware dust which can wreak havoc with the electronics. A UV filter on each lens is essential as a protector as well as a filter. A dust blower (either compressed air or manual) is a must, as is a decent lens cloth.

- For the full monty on travel photography, pick up Lonely Planet's *Travel Photography*.

possible price, but one that's acceptable to both you and the seller. If you're light-hearted and polite about it, you'll end up with a much better price!

SOLO TRAVELLERS

Travelling solo in Ethiopia can be incredibly rewarding, but it can also be more expensive. There are no cheap organised tours for solo travellers to just sign up for in Ethiopia. If you have a group, you can do a trip together and share costs. If you're alone, you'll have to find people to share with or cover all the costs yourself. The biggest cost issue is transport. If you have limited time and still want to explore areas such as the Lower Omo Valley and remote rock-hewn churches of Tigray, you'll have to shoulder the cost of an expensive 4WD hire yourself.

Similar problems arise for boat trips onto Lake Tana and the Rift Valley lakes as well as with treks into the Simien and Bale Mountains, where transport, guide fees, tent rental etc must be borne individually. However, in the cases of Lake Tana and the Simien Mountains, you'll usually have an easy time locating people to share costs in Bahir Dar and Gonder respectively.

Few hotels offer single occupancy rates, so you'll be paying double what you'd be paying if you were sharing. It should be noted that double rates are still very inexpensive!

Although travelling alone puts you at greater risk for petty theft (which still isn't high), it also increases the number of Ethiopians who'll be looking out for your welfare. For specific details about travelling alone as a female, see p270.

The biggest benefit of travelling solo is that you'll unintentionally be more open to conversing with locals. A distant second-place finisher would have to be all the times you manage to get the last seat on the last bus heading somewhere special.

TELEPHONE

Ethiopia's telecommunications have started to turn the corner; there are now a couple of options for making local and international calls. In the past, the only way to make an international call was through the telecommunications offices located in almost every Ethiopian town. These offices are still the cheapest option (Birr50.50 for the first three minutes and Birr10 for each minute after, plus 15% tax), but these operator-assisted centres can have waits of up to an hour.

Now countless shops also operate as 'telecentres' and can quickly connect you anywhere worldwide for Birr15 to Birr25 per minute. These telecentres also usually boast more flexible opening hours. Some hotels offer phone services but they are usually at least 20% more expensive.

When calling abroad from Ethiopia, use ☎ 00 followed by the appropriate country code. Collect calls are only available at the telecommunications offices and can be made to the UK, USA and Canada only (Australia, Germany and France should be possible in the near future); you still have to pay a 'report charge' of Birr5 to Birr8, plus a Birr10 (refundable) deposit.

Cheap local calls can also be made from telecommunications offices, telecentres and public phone boxes. Most boxes take both coins and cards (sold at the telecommunications offices in denominations of Birr25, Birr50 and Birr100).

Note: all Ethiopian numbers were changed in 2005 to have 10 digits. The old six-digit numbers now trail a new four-digit area code that must always precede the old number, no matter where you're calling from.

Important telephone numbers and Ethiopia's country code are inside this book's front cover.

Mobile Phones

The speed with which Ethiopia's mobile phone network has expanded would make Starbucks blush. It now covers most Ethiopian cities. Depending on which mobile network you use at home, your phone may or may not work while in Ethiopia. Your best plan is to call your mobile network provider and ask. If your network isn't compatible, you can bring your phone and try to pick up a SIM card while in Addis Ababa.

TIME

Ethiopia is three hours ahead of GMT/UTC.

Time is expressed so sanely in Ethiopia that it blows most travellers minds! At sunrise it's 12 o'clock (6am our time) and after one hour of sunshine it's 1 o'clock. After two hours of sunshine? Yes, 2 o'clock. The sun sets at 12 o'clock (6pm our time) and after one hour of darkness it's…1 o'clock! Instead of using 'am' or 'pm', Ethiopians use 'in the morning', 'in the evening' and 'at night' to indicate the period of day.

The system is used widely, though the 24-hour clock is used occasionally in business. Be careful to ask if a time quoted is according to the Ethiopian or 'European' clock (*Be habesha/faranji akotater no?* – Is that Ethiopian/foreigner's time?). For the purposes of this book, all times quoted are by the European clock.

TOILETS

Both sit-down and squat toilets are found in Ethiopia, reflecting European and Arab influences respectively. You'll usually only find squat jobs in the bottom end of the budget hotel bracket.

MISSED THE MILLENNIUM PARTY?

Another great Ethiopian time-keeping idiosyncrasy that confounds many a traveller is the calendar. It's based on the old Coptic calendar, which has its roots in ancient Egypt. Although it has 12 months of 30 days each and a 13th month of five or six days, like the ancient Coptic calendar, it follows the Julian system of adding a leap day every four years without exception.

What makes the Ethiopian calendar even more unique is that it wasn't tweaked by numerous popes to align with their versions of Christianity, like the Gregorian calendar (introduced by Pope Gregory XIII in 1582) that we Westerners have grown up on.

What does this all mean? It means the Ethiopian calendar is 7½ years 'behind' the Gregorian calendar, making 11 September 2006 to 10 September 2007 '1999' in Ethiopia. If you hurry, you can say goodbye to the 1990s and ring in the year 2000…AGAIN!

If you're late, at least you can still consider yourself seven years younger!

Public toilets are found in almost all hotels and restaurants, but may not form your fondest memories of Ethiopia. In small towns and rural areas, the most common arrangement is a smelly old shack, with two planks, a hole in the ground, and all the flies you can fit in between. You may suddenly find that you can survive the next 1000km after all.

Toilet paper is very rare in any toilet; you're best advised to carry your own.

TOURIST INFORMATION
Local Tourist Offices
In 2005 the Ethiopian government unceremoniously sacked the heads of the Ethiopian Tourism Commission (ETC) and created the new Ministry of Culture and Tourism. Thankfully, this ministry will continue to keep open the ETC's ever-helpful Tourist Information Centre in Addis Ababa's Meskal Sq (see p83).

The offices of the Tigrai Tourism Commission in Aksum, Mekele and Wukro have to be the most helpful and prepared. Other tourist offices exist elsewhere, but few are worth the effort of visiting (Konso's and Arba Minch's being the exceptions).

While in Addis Ababa, the most accurate information on travel outside the capital region is available through tour operators (see p282), though naturally they will expect to sell you something. Outside Addis Ababa, hotel managers and the traveller grapevine are your best sources for up-to-date information.

Tourist Offices Abroad
No national tourist office exists abroad. The Ethiopian embassies and consulates try to fill the gap, but generally just hand out the usual tourist brochures.

An active, nonpolitical organisation in the UK is the **Anglo-Ethiopian Society** (www.anglo -ethiopian.org; PO Box 55506, London SW7 4YP), which aims 'to foster a knowledge and understanding of Ethiopia and its people'. Membership costs from £12 annually. The society holds regular gatherings, including talks on Ethiopia. A well-stocked library on Ethiopia and Eritrea is open to members. There's a tri-annual Newsfile.

TRAVELLERS WITH DISABILITIES
There's no reason why intrepid disabled travellers shouldn't visit Ethiopia. The recent civil war left many soldiers disabled, so you should expect to find at least some degree of empathy and understanding.

For those with restricted mobility, all the sites on the historical route are easily reached by internal flights. Passengers in wheelchairs can be accommodated. Car rental with a driver is easily organised (though it's expensive). Be aware that some roads can be rough, and hard on the back.

Taxis are widely available in the large towns and are good for getting around. None have wheelchair access. In Addis Ababa a few hotels have lifts; at least two (the Sheraton and Hilton hotels) have facilities for wheelchair-users. Kerb ramps on streets are nonexistent, and potholes and uneven streets are a hazard.

Outside the capital, facilities are lacking, but many hotels are bungalow affairs, so at least steps or climbs are avoided.

For those restricted in other ways, such as visually or aurally, you'll get plenty of offers of help. Unlike in many Western countries, Ethiopians are not shy about coming forward to offer assistance.

A valuable source of general information is the **Access-Able Travel Source** (www.access-able.com). This site has useful links.

Before leaving home, visitors can get in touch with their national support organisation. Ask for the 'travel officer', who may have a list of travel agents that specialise in tours for the disabled.

VISAS & DOCUMENTS

Be aware that visa regulations can change. The Ethiopian embassy in your home country is the best source of up-to-date information.

Currently, all visitors except Kenyan and Djiboutian nationals need visas to visit Ethiopia.

Nationals of 33 countries can obtain tourist visas on arrival at Bole International Airport. These include most of Europe, the USA, Canada, Australia, New Zealand, South Africa and Israel. Although the process upon arrival can occasionally be tiresome, the one-month tourist visa is only US$20, substantially less than that charged at some Ethiopian embassies abroad. Some people arriving without US dollars have managed to pay the visa in euros. Immigration officials in Addis Ababa told us that they don't require onward air tickets, though some people have been asked for them.

Ethiopian embassies abroad may require some or all of the following to accompany visa applications: an onward air ticket (or airline itinerary), a visa for the next country you're planning to visit, a yellow fever vaccination certificate and proof of sufficient funds (officially a minimum of US$50 per day). Ethiopian embassies in Africa are usually less strict.

Presently, the only multiple-entry visas issued are business visas (except for US citizens who can get two-year multiple entry tourist visas for US$70). To acquire a one- to three-month business visa at an embassy you'll need a letter from your employer in addition to the items mentioned earlier. One-month business visas (US$20) are available upon arrival at the airport, but only if your company has made arrangements (in person) with the Department of Immigration in Addis Ababa prior to your arrival.

If your citizenship isn't one of the 33 that can acquire a visa at Bole and there's also no Ethiopian diplomatic representation in your country, you may be able to ask Ethiopian Airlines or a tour operator to order you a visa before your arrival. Visas cannot be obtained on arrival without prior arrangement at immigration.

Travellers of all nationalities can obtain transit visas on arrival or at the embassies abroad; these are valid for up to seven days.

Visas (tourist and business) can be extended to a maximum of three months (see Visa Extensions, p83).

Other Documents

In theory a yellow fever vaccination certificate is mandatory as is a vaccination against cholera if you've transited through a cholera-infected area within six days prior to your arrival in Ethiopia. These are rarely checked, but you probably wouldn't want to risk it.

Documentation needed to bring a vehicle into Ethiopia is covered on p279.

All important documents (passport data page and visa page, credit cards, travel insurance policy, air/bus/train tickets, driving licence etc) should be photocopied. Leave one copy with someone at home and keep another with you, separate from the originals.

Visas for Onward Travel
DJIBOUTI

Bring US$30 and two passport photos to the **Djibouti Embassy** (Map pp80-1; ☎ 0116 613006; ✆ 8.30am-12.30pm & 2.30-4.30pm Mon-Fri) and you'll usually have your visa the same day. It's off Bole Rd.

KENYA

The **Kenyan embassy** (Map p76; ☎ 0116 610033; kenigad@ethionet.et; Fikremaryam Abatechan St; ✆ 8.30am-12.30pm & 2-5pm Mon-Fri) charges US$50 or Birr438 for three-month tourist visas. One passport photo is required. Applications are taken in the morning only, with visas being ready the following afternoon. Visas are also easily obtained at the Moyale border (p275) and at Jomo Kenyatta International Airport in Nairobi.

SOMALILAND

The **Somaliland office** (Map pp80-1; ☎ 0116 635921; btwn Bole Rd & Cameroon St; ✆ 8.30am-12.30pm & 2-3.30pm Mon-Fri) produces tourist visas for

ETHIOPIA DIRECTORY

US$40. They require one passport photo and it takes 24 hours or less to process. The office is unmarked, so call ahead and they'll send someone to meet you.

SUDAN

Obtaining a visa at the **Sudan embassy** (Map pp80-1; ☎ 0115 516477; sudan.embassy@ethionet.et; Ras Lulseged St; ⏰ 8.30am-5pm Mon-Fri) is no longer an easy task. All applications are sent to Khartoum for approval, so the process can take over a month to complete. Note that many applications come back denied. A letter of introduction from your own embassy may speed things along. Tourist visas cost US$61 and one passport photo is required.

WOMEN TRAVELLERS

Compared with many African countries, Ethiopia is pretty easy-going for women travellers. The risk of rape or other serious offences is likely lower than travelling in many Western countries. The best advice is to simply be aware of the signals your clothing or behaviour may be giving off and remember these unspoken codes of etiquette.

Drinking alcohol, smoking, and wearing excessive make-up and revealing clothes are indications to the male population of 'availability', as this is also the way local prostitutes behave. Apart from the young of the wealthier classes in Addis Ababa, no 'proper' woman would be seen in a bar.

Many cheap hotels in Ethiopia double as brothels. Ethiopian men may naturally wonder about your motives for staying here, particularly if you're alone. While there's no cause for alarm, it's best to keep a low profile and behave very conservatively – keep out of the hotel bar for example, and try and hook up with other travellers if you want to go out.

Also be aware that accepting an invitation to an unmarried man's house, under any pretext, is considered a latent acceptance of things to come. Dinner invitations often amount to 'foreplay' before you're expected to head off to some seedy hotel. Even a seemingly innocent invitation to the cinema can turn out to be little more than an invitation to a good snog in the back row!

Be aware that 'respectable' Ethiopian women (even when they're willing) are expected to put up a show of coyness and modesty. Traditionally, this formed part

---

FEMALE PHOBIA

In some of the monasteries and holy sites of Ethiopia and Eritrea, an ancient prohibition forbids women from setting foot in the holy confines. But the holy fathers go strictly by the book: the prohibition extends not just to women but to all female creatures, even she donkeys, hens and nanny goats.

---

of the wedding night ritual of every Amhara bride: a fierce struggle with the groom was expected of them. Consequently, some Ethiopian men may mistake your rebuttals for encouragement. The concept even has a name in Amharic: *maqderder* (and applies equally to feigned reluctance for other things such as food). If you mean no, make it very clear from the start.

If there aren't any other travellers around, here's a quick trick: pick a male Ethiopian companion, bemoan the problems you've been having with his compatriots and appeal to his sense of pride, patriotism and gallantry. Usually any ulterior plans he might have been harbouring himself are soon converted into sympathy or shame and a personal crusade to protect you!

Adultery is quite common among many of Ethiopia's urban population, for men as well as women. For this reason, a wedding ring on a woman traveller (bogus or not) has absolutely no deterrent value. In fact, quite the reverse!

The one advantage of Ethiopia being a relatively permissive society is that Western women (in particular white women) aren't necessarily seen as easier than local women, something that's common in many developing countries due to Hollywood cinematic 'glamour'.

With all this talk of keeping Ethiopian men's potential advances at bay, it's odd that the biggest actual hindrance to women travellers is priests! See the boxed text, above.

WORK

Travellers in Ethiopia on tourist visas are forbidden from working. If you're planning to work, you'll have to apply to the **Ministry of Labour & Social Affairs** (Map pp80-1; ☎ 0115 517080; Josif Tito St, Addis Ababa) for a work permit, and to the **Department of Immigration** (Map pp80-1; ☎ 0111 553899; Addis Ababa), off Zambia St.

Ethiopia Transport

CONTENTS

GETTING THERE & AWAY

Flights, tours and rail tickets can be booked online at www.lonelyplanet.com/travel _services.

ENTERING ETHIOPIA

Entering Ethiopia by air is painless, even if you have to pick up your visa upon arrival at Bole International airport. Important visa and document information is found on p269.

Ethiopian border officials at land crossings are more strict but equally fair. You *must* have a valid visa to enter overland as none are available at borders. Those entering with vehicles should have all the necessary paperwork (p274) and expect a lengthier process.

Passport

Make sure your passport's expiry date is at least six months past your intended departure date from Ethiopia. For visa and other document information, see p269.

AIR
Airports & Airlines

Addis Ababa's **Bole International Airport** (code ADD) is the only international airport in Ethiopia. Although modern, upon arrival there's little more than a 24-hour bank, a restaurant and a few cafés; baggage carts are free. When departing, there's an Internet lounge, a bar and duty-free shops.

Ethiopia's only international and national carrier, **Ethiopian Airlines** (airline code ET; www.fly ethiopian.com), is rated as one of the best airlines in Africa and has a good record (the US Federal Aviation Authority gave it a No 1 rating for compliance with international aviation safety standards). Ethiopian Airlines is also one of the largest African carriers, with a modern fleet of 737s, 757s and 767s. There are 50 or so offices worldwide, which sell both international and domestic tickets directly. Reconfirmation of bookings is essential.

Other international airlines currently serving Ethiopia:

British Airways Addis Ababa (airline code BA; Map pp80-1; ☎ 0115 505913; www.ba.com; Hilton Hotel, Menelik II Ave) Hub Heathrow Airport, London.

Daallo Airlines Addis Ababa (airline code D3; Map pp80-1; ☎ 0115 534688; www.daallo.com; Bole Rd) Represented by Abadir Travel & Tours. Hub Djibouti-Ambouli International Airport, Djibouti City.

Djibouti Airlines Addis Ababa (airline code D8; Map pp80-1; ☎ 0116 633702; fax 0116 614769; Rwanda St) Hub Djibouti-Ambouli International Airport, Djibouti City.

EgyptAir Addis Ababa (airline code MS; Map pp80-1; ☎ 0111 564493; www.egyptair.com.eg; Churchill Ave) Hub Cairo International Airport, Cairo.

KLM (airline code KL; www.klm.com) Bole International Airport, Addis Ababa (Map p76; ☎ 0116 650675; Bole Rd); Hilton Hotel, Addis Ababa (Map pp80-1; ☎ 0115 525541; Menelik II Ave) Hub Amsterdam Schiphol Airport, Amsterdam.

Kenya Airways (airline code KQ; www.kenya-airways .com) Bole International Airport, Addis Ababa (Map p76;

THINGS CHANGE...

The information in this chapter is particularly vulnerable to change. Check directly with the airline or a travel agent to make sure you understand how a fare (and ticket you may buy) works and be aware of the security requirements for international travel. Shop carefully. The details given in this chapter should be regarded as pointers and are not a substitute for your own careful, up-to-date research.

☎ 0116 650507; Bole Rd); Hilton Hotel, Addis Ababa (Map pp80-1; ☎ 0115 525548; Menelik II Ave) Hub Jomo Kenyatta International Airport, Nairobi.

Lufthansa Addis Ababa (airline code LH; Map pp80-1; ☎ 0111 551666; www.lufthansa.com; Gambia St) Hub Frankfurt International Airport, Frankfurt.

Saudi Arabian Airlines Addis Ababa (airline code SV; Map pp80-1; ☎ 0115 512637; www.saudiairlines.com; Ras Desta Damtew St) Hub King Abdulaziz International Airport, Jeddah.

Sudan Airways Addis Ababa (airline code SD; Map pp80-1; ☎ 0115 504724; www.sudanair.com; Ras Desta Damtew St) Hub Khartoum International Airport, Khartoum.

Yemenia Addis Ababa (airline code IY; Map pp80-1; ☎ 0115 526441; www.yememia.com; Ras Desta Damtew St) Hub Sanaa Airport, Sanaa.

Ethiopian Airlines isn't usually the cheapest option to fly into Ethiopia, but does offer some good perks: a generous baggage allowance; the option of changing your return date as many times as you wish at no extra charge; and if there's two or more of you, 50% off domestic flights (see p276).

Tickets

For Ethiopia, travel during the month of August and over Easter, Christmas and New Year should be booked well in advance. Ethiopians living abroad tend to visit their families during this time, and tour groups often try to coincide with the major festivals. Ticket prices are highest during this period.

Numerous travel agencies and online ticket sources are mentioned in the following sections under the region or country they each are located in. One truly international website that can't be categorised is www.flights.com.

INTERCONTINENTAL (RTW) TICKETS

It's possible to include Addis Ababa as part of a round-the-world (RTW) ticket. Check with one of the major airlines that form the

---

DEPARTURE TAX

The international departure tax is US$20, which must be paid at the airport. It's supposed to be paid in dollars, but we had no problem paying it in birr. Either way, try and have the exact amount as change isn't always available. Travellers cheques in US dollars are accepted, but commissions are charged.

Star Alliance (www.staralliance.com) or **One World** (www.oneworldalliance.com).

It's also possible (and usually cheaper) to arrange these tickets online; try www.airtreks.com.

Africa

Ethiopian Airlines flies to 25 African countries including Djibouti, Egypt, Sudan, Somalia, Kenya and South Africa. It also offers regular flights to eight West African countries. Fares on Ethiopian Airlines and other African couriers vary drastically throughout the year, depending on the high seasons of each individual country.

Rennies Travel (www.renniestravel.com) and **STA Travel** (www.statravel.co.za) have offices throughout Southern Africa. Check their websites for branch locations. In Nairobi, **Let's Go Travel** (☎ 020-444 7151; www.lets-go-travel.net) is reliable. **Egypt Panorama Tours** (☎ 2-359 0200; www.eptours.com) in Cairo is also good.

Australia

There are no direct flights from Australia to Ethiopia. **Qantas** (www.qantas.com.au) and its code-sharing partner **South African Airways** (SAA; www.flysaa.com) fly to Johannesburg, from where you can connect to Nairobi. You'll have to book the Nairobi–Addis Ababa flight separately. This is typically cheaper than buying separate Australia–Johannesburg and Johannesburg–Addis Ababa tickets.

Via the Middle East is usually slightly cheaper; try **Emirates Airlines** (www.emirates.com) via Dubai to Nairobi. Other routes include via Mumbai (Bombay) on Qantas, or via Mauritius on **Air Mauritius** (www.airmauritius.com). Note, these all still only get you to Nairobi.

STA Travel (☎ 1300 733 035; www.statravel.com.au) and **Flight Centre** (☎ 133 133; www.flightcentre.com.au) have numerous offices throughout Australia and are worth checking out.

For online bookings try www.travel.com.au; they found us a cheap Sydney–Bangkok–Addis Ababa flight using a combination of British Airways and Ethiopian Airlines.

Canada

There are no direct flights between Canada and Ethiopia. Currently British Airways, KLM and Lufthansa offer the easiest connections, through London, Amsterdam and Frankfurt respectively.

Canadian discount air ticket agencies tend to have fares around 10% higher than those sold in the USA. **Flight Centre** (☎ 877-967 5302; www.flightcentre.ca) is usually reliable and has 1500 Canadian outlets. **Travel Cuts** (☎ 800-667 2887; www.travelcuts.com) is Canada's national student travel agency. For online bookings try www.expedia.ca.

Continental Europe
Numerous weekly Ethiopian Airlines flights serve over two dozen European cities (many directly), including Amsterdam, Berlin, Copenhagen, Madrid, Paris, Frankfurt and Rome. KLM and Lufthansa have daily flights to Addis Ababa, but most flights make stops en route.

FRANCE
Recommended agencies:
Anyway (☎ 08 92 89 38 97; www.anyway.fr)
Lastminute (☎ 08 92 70 50 00; www.lastminute.fr)
Nouvelles Frontières (☎ 08 25 00 07 47; www.nouvelles-frontieres.fr)
OTU Voyages (www.otu.fr) This agency specialises in student and youth travellers.
Voyageurs du Monde (☎ 01 40 15 11 15; www.vdm.com)

GERMANY
Recommended agencies:
Expedia (www.expedia.de)
Just Travel (☎ 089 747 33 30; www.justtravel.de)
Lastminute (☎ 01805 284 366; www.lastminute.de)
STA Travel (☎ 01805 456 422; www.statravel.de) For travellers under the age of 26.

ITALY
One recommended agent is **CTS Viaggi** (☎ 06 462 0431; www.cts.it), specialising in student and youth travel.

THE NETHERLANDS
One recommended agency is **Airfair** (☎ 020-620 51 21; www.airfair.nl).

SPAIN
Recommended agencies include **Barcelo Viajes** (☎ 902 116 226; www.barceloviajes.com) and **Nouvelles Frontières** (☎ 902 17 09 79; www.nouvelles-frontieres.es).

Middle East
EgyptAir, Saudi Arabian Airlines and Yemenia serve the Middle East and combine to link Ethiopia with Lebanon, Israel, Saudi Arabia (Jeddah and Riyadh), the United Arab Emirates and Yemen.

In Dubai, **Al-Rais Travels** (www.alrais.com) is a good travel agent, while the **Israel Student Travel Association** (ISTA; ☎ 02-625 7257), in Jerusalem, is helpful. For Cairo, see Africa (opposite).

New Zealand
The story for New Zealand is much the same as that for Australia, with code-sharing partners Qantas and SAA only getting you as far as Nairobi. However, if you go through agents (in person or online), they should be able to combine airlines to get you straight to Addis Ababa via Bangkok.

Both **Flight Centre** (☎ 0800 243 544; www.flightcentre.co.nz) and **STA Travel** (☎ 0508 782 872; www.statravel.co.nz) have branches throughout the country. The site www.travel.co.nz is recommended for online bookings.

UK & Ireland
British Airways and Ethiopian Airlines both have daily flights between London and Addis Ababa.

Discount air travel is big business in London. Advertisements for many travel agencies appear in the travel pages of the weekend broadsheet newspapers, in *Time Out*, the *Evening Standard* and in the free online magazine **TNT** (www.tntmagazine.com). The website www.cheapflights.co.uk is helpful in finding deals.

Recommended travel agencies:
Flight Centre (☎ 0870 499 0040; flightcentre.co.uk)
Flightbookers (☎ 0800 082 3000; www.ebookers.com)
North-South Travel (☎ 01245 608 291; www.northsouthtravel.co.uk) Donates part of its profit to projects in the developing world.
STA Travel (☎ 0870 160 0599; www.statravel.co.uk) For travellers under the age of 26.
Travel Bag (☎ 0800 082 5000; www.travelbag.co.uk)

USA
Ethiopian Airlines only serves Washington DC, so you'll likely have to fly through Europe on British Airways, KLM or Lufthansa (or their American code-sharing partners).

Discount travel agents in the USA are known as consolidators (although you won't see a sign on the door saying 'Consolidator'). San Francisco is the ticket consolidator capital of America, although some good deals can be found in Los Angeles, New York and other big cities.

ETHIOPIA TRANSPORT

Peruse the following websites for the cheapest flight options:

CheapTickets (www.cheaptickets.com)
Expedia.com (www.expedia.com)
Orbitz (www.orbitz.com)
STA Travel (www.sta.com) Better for travellers under the age of 26.
travelocity (www.travelocity.com)

LAND
Djibouti
Border formalities are usually pretty painless crossing between Djibouti and Ethiopia, but you *must* have your visa prior to arriving as none are issued at the border (see Visas for Onward Travel on p269).

ROAD
There are two current road routes linking Djibouti and Ethiopia: one via Dire Dawa and Gelille, and one via Awash and Galafi.

The Gelille route is best for those without vehicles as daily buses link Djibouti City and Dire Dawa. The journey takes 10 to 12 hours, though it involves changing buses at the border. In Djibouti City, **SPB** (☎ 826573, 828838) buses depart at dawn from Ave 26; tickets cost DFr2700. In Dire Dawa, **Shirkada Gaadidka Dadweynaha Ee Yaryar Dhexe Iyo Xamuulkaa** (☎ 0251 118455) buses depart daily at a painful 3.30am from its office northeast of the 'old town' of Megala; tickets cost Birr120. In either direction, it's important to buy tickets at least a day in advance.

Although longer, the Galafi route accessed from Awash is best for those driving, as it's sealed the entire way. Even locals with 4WDs prefer this route over the Gelille

route, which is only sealed on the Djibouti side. For those coming from northern Ethiopia, this route can be accessed via a shortcut at Dessie.

Those without vehicles can also travel via Galafi. A sporadic evening bus (DFr2000) from Djibouti City reaches Galafi (5km from the border) in the morning after overnighting in Yoboki. From Galafi, you must rely on hitching a lift with one of the many trucks heading into Ethiopia. The first town with regular buses to Awash or Dessie is Mille (p221). Those using this route to leave Ethiopia can hitch a lift with trucks overnighting in Logiya (p221) right to Djibouti City (Birr150 to Birr200, eight hours).

TRAIN
A dilapidated, hot and painfully slow train also covers the Djibouti City–Dire Dawa route. Trains are supposed to leave every second day, but they're notoriously behind schedule and delays of days are common. First-class tickets costs around Birr80 in Dire Dawa and DFr3900 in Djibouti City; 2nd class' cost about half. First class is by no means comfortable, but it's a world above 2nd class. Tickets should be bought the day before travel.

In theory the train is supposed to run all the way to Addis Ababa, but this leg is currently out of commission.

Eritrea
There are three traditional entry points from Eritrea into Ethiopia: Asmara to Adwa and Aksum via Adi Quala; Asmara to Adigrat via Senafe; and Assab to Addis Ababa via Serdo and Dessie. However, all

---

ENTERING ETHIOPIA OVERLAND

The overland route from South Africa through southern Africa and East Africa to Ethiopia is quite well trodden, and should present few problems, though the last section through northern Kenya is the toughest and still suffers from sporadic banditry.

The only routes currently open from West Africa and North Africa are much rougher and relatively less travelled; they both enter Ethiopia from Sudan at Metema, west of Gonder.

Border officials can be lax or stringent, but they're usually not unfair. If you're travelling with a vehicle, make sure you have a valid international driving license, a *carnet de passage* (a guarantee issued by your own national motoring association that you won't sell your vehicle in the country you are travelling), the vehicle's registration papers and proof of third-party insurance that covers Ethiopia (see the Car & Motorcycle section on p279 for details about driving licences, road rules, road conditions etc).

For important visa and documentation information see p269.

these border crossings have been indefinitely closed since the 1998 war.

With relations on their current path, it seems sadly infeasible that the borders will be reopened during the lifetime of this book. See p290 for details about reaching Eritrea through Djibouti.

Kenya

There are usually few problems crossing between Ethiopia and Kenya. The most used crossing is at Moyale, 772km south of Addis Ababa by road. Moyale has two incarnations, one on either side of the border.

The northern version is well connected to the north and Addis Ababa by bus, along a pretty good, but often potholed section of sealed road (transport details are found on p195).

The southern side is truly in the middle of nowhere, some 600km north of the nearest sealed road and over 1000km north of Nairobi. That said, a daily bus connects Moyale with Marsabit (KSh600, 8½ hours) and Isiolo (KSh1200, 17 hours). Trucks servicing the same destinations pick up passengers near the main intersection. From Isiolo there's regular transport to Nairobi (KSh500, 4½ hours).

For those of you in your own vehicles, the road between Moyale and Marsabit is long and hard (on you and your 4WD – bring at least two spare tires), but thankfully the banditry problems of the past seem to be under control and armed convoys are no longer used along this route. The Wajir route south is still not considered safe. Either way, be sure to check the security section before setting out from Moyale. Also make sure you fill up before leaving Ethiopia as the petrol is half the price.

The Ethiopian and Kenyan borders at Moyale are open daily. Kenyan three-month visas are painlessly produced at **Kenyan immigration** (⊗ 6.30am-6pm) for the grand sum of US$50. It's payable in US dollars (some have managed to pay in euros), but not birr. Transit visas cost US$20 (valid for seven days). **Ethiopian immigration** (⊗ 8am-noon & 2-6pm Mon-Fri, 9am-11am & 3-5pm Sat & Sun) cannot issue Ethiopian visas; these must be obtained at an Ethiopian embassy prior to arrival at the border.

If you're heading south and have a serious 4WD, there's a more adventurous crossing well west of Moyale near Omorate in the Lower Omo Valley. Although there's now an **Ethiopian immigration post** (⊗ 7.30am-5pm) in Omorate that can stamp you out, there's still no Kenyan post to issue you a visa, so you must obtain one from the Kenyan embassy in Addis Ababa beforehand (see Visas for Onward Travel on p269). Once you reach Nairobi you'll have to get it stamped; immigration officials are used to this.

The remote and sandy track to Kenya is accessed along the road to Turmi, 13km north of Omorate. A long day of driving should get you to Sibiloi National Park and the Koobi Fora research base. From there, it's a tricky seven-hour drive south to Loyangalani. This route will reward you with one of East Africa's greatest sights, Lake Turkana, but it's only for the truly well-prepared and should never be attempted in wet season.

This route isn't technically possible heading north because Ethiopia requires a Kenyan exit stamp in your passport. If you don't mind being turned back, you could always try your luck – bring lots of fuel.

Somaliland

There are now daily buses running along the dusty desert track between Jijiga and the border town of Wajaale (Birr15, 1½ to two hours). Get stamped out at Ethiopian immigration (look for the MAO building on the main street) before walking to the gate where customs will perform their perfunctory search. From there, cross no-man's-land (about 200m) to Somaliland's immigration shack, where they'll stamp your passport and check your visa. The visa must have been acquired in advance, as none are issued at the border (see Visas for Onward travel on p269 for details).

Contract taxis (Birr300) and minibuses (about Birr40) run from the border to Hargeisa, Somaliland's capital, which is about 90km to the southeast. Fares can be paid in US dollars.

Sudan

The only border currently open with Sudan is the Metema crossing, 180km west of Gonder. It's imperative that you've obtained your Sudan visa in Addis Ababa (see p270) before heading this way.

From Gonder one bus leaves daily for Shihedi (Birr23, five to six hours). Buy the ticket early in the morning (around 7am) of the previous day, as the route is popular. From there, pick-up trucks (Birr8) cover the last 40km or so to Metema. Stay overnight at Shihedi, as it has better facilities than Metema. Several travellers have also written of being harassed and robbed in Metema, so keep your guard up.

After reaching Metema the next morning, you can walk across the border into the Sudanese town of Gallabat. From Gallabat, you can catch a truck to the nearest large town of Gedaref (Dinar 1500, eight to 10 hours).

If you're driving your own 4WD, put on supportive underwear before you reach the border – it's rough going on the Sudan side! In wet season even trucks get stuck between Gallabat and Gedaref, so be prepared.

If you're coming from Sudan, stay overnight in Gedaref (better than Gallabat) then catch a dawn truck straight though to Shihedi via Gallabat. The bus from Shihedi to Gonder departs at around 7am.

Formerly, it used to be possible to travel by bus from Gambela into Sudan. However, because of the current ethnic tensions in the area, the border is closed and the Gambela area is considered unsafe. Check the current situation when you arrive in Ethiopia.

GETTING AROUND

AIR
Airlines in Ethiopia
The national carrier, **Ethiopian Airlines** (www.fly ethiopian.com), uses five Fokker 50s and three DHC Twin Otters to provide the only regular domestic air service. As mentioned earlier in this chapter, they have a solid safety record.

It's well worth considering a domestic flight or two, even if you're travelling on a budget. Most flights are very reasonably priced and cut out days spent on the road. With the lower-altitude flying of the domestic planes, and the usually clear Ethiopian skies, you'll still see some stunning landscapes, too. If you want a window seat, check in early.

Standard security procedures apply at all airports, though there'll be more polite groping than screening at the remote ones. The baggage limit is 20kg on domestic

ETHIOPIAN AIRLINES' DOMESTIC DESTINATIONS

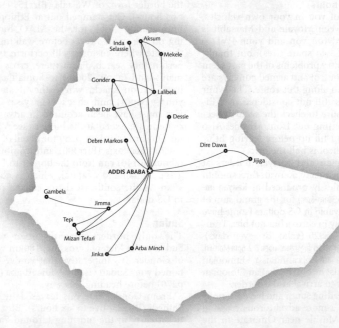

flights. Don't bring bulky hand luggage as the interiors are quite small.

Most flights leave from Addis Ababa, but they are rarely nonstop, which means you can also jump from one town to another. For instance, the daily Addis Ababa–Aksum flight stops at Bahir Dar, Gonder and Lalibela en route.

If there's two or more of you, and if you fly into Ethiopia from outside Africa on Ethiopian Airlines, Ethiopian Airlines offers you 50% off the standard domestic rates. These flights must be booked at the same time as your international ones, but you can change the exact dates later without penalty. Although you'll find Ethiopian domestic flights available for purchase at online brokers like **Expedia** (www.expedia.com), they can charge up to 300% more than the standard fares. For domestic schedules and the standard fares see the pertinent city's Getting There & Away section.

If buying tickets in Ethiopia, standard rates always apply, whether buying the ticket a month or three hours in advance. However, booking early to ensure a seat is particularly important on the historical circuit and during major festivals.

It's *essential* to reconfirm all flights. Officially, this should be done 72 hours in advance. In practice, you can normally get away with 48 hours in advance, but never leave it less than 24 hours. If you're visiting the historical route and are not spending more than 72 hours in any one place, you don't need to reconfirm each leg.

Beware that schedules are occasionally forced to change due to weather or mechanical difficulties, so try to not to plan an itinerary that's so tight it doesn't make allowances for these changes.

BICYCLE

Bicycling in Ethiopia offers a smooth way to navigate sprawling towns, and a painfully rewarding way to explore the country. If you're only interested in the first option, you'll find reasonable bikes for hire in most large Ethiopian towns (Birr3 to Birr5 per hour). If want to cycle across the country, come well prepared with a sturdy bike, plenty of spare parts, a good repair kit and the capacity to carry sufficient amounts of water. Cycles new and secondhand can be bought in Addis Ababa, but they are not

generally the type of bike you'd wish to conquer the historical circuit with!

In the past, irregular terrain and brutal roads have scared off most adventure addicts and their bicycles, but with today's greatly improving road network it may just be the right time for you to give it a try. For general road conditions see p280.

Cyclists should show the usual caution when travelling around the country: never travel after dark, be wary of thieves and keep the bicycle well maintained. Brakes need to be in good working order for the mountainous highland roads.

Be particularly wary of dogs (and the risk of rabies); sometimes it's best to dismount and walk slowly away. Cycling in the rainy season can be very hard going.

Punctures are easily repaired: just head for any *gommista* (tyre repairer) or garage. Many mechanics are also more than happy to help with cycle problems, and often turn out to be ingenious improvisers.

Note the customs regulation regarding the importation of a bicycle. A deposit must usually be left (amounting to the cycle's worth) at customs at the port of entry on arrival. When you leave, this will be returned. This is to deter black-market trading.

Cycles are accepted aboard Ethiopian Airlines international flights. On domestic flights you'll need to check first in advance as it depends on what type of plane is covering the route on that given day.

Finally, a few tips from a seasoned African cyclist: check and tighten screws and nuts regularly, take a spare chain, take a front as well as rear pannier rack, and pack a water filter in case you get stuck somewhere remote.

More advice can be found at www.owen .org/cycling/ethiopia.

BUS

A good network of long-distance buses connects most major towns of Ethiopia. One government bus association and around a dozen private ones operate in Ethiopia, though you'll rarely be able to tell the difference between any of them. The biggest differentiating trait between government and private buses is the predeparture rituals.

Government buses sell seat-specific tickets in advance and passengers must wait in line while the bus is loaded. After that's

ETHIOPIA TRANSPORT

THE JOYS OF BUS TRAVEL

Riding the buses around Ethiopia can provide some real highs and some real lows.

There are astounding cliff-top views. There are butt-clenching moments when you think you and your bus are about to be quickly introduced to that cliff's bottom.

There's the joy and honour of holding an Ethiopian's baby in your arms. There's the pleasure of cleaning that baby's bodily fluids off your only pair of trousers.

There's the common decency of everyone keeping their windows closed on a cold morning. There's the moment when it reaches 40°C inside and you realise that wasn't common decency, but rather an innate fear of deadly moving air that keeps those windows shut.

There's the smell of fresh oranges permeating through the bus after a quick stop at streetside sellers. There's the moment when you plug your nose and officially bestow upon the bus the title of Vomit Comet.

To enjoy your memorable bus jaunts, bring a sense of humour, a lot of patience and a little understanding. Oh, and if you're fond of kids, don't forget some wet wipes!

---

completed, the queue is paraded around the bus before tickets are checked and the boarding barrage occurs. Private buses simply open the doors and start selling tickets to the flood of passengers as they cram in. Needless to say, private buses are usually the first to leave. They also tend to be slightly more comfortable than government ones (though that's not saying much!).

In most cases when you arrive at the bus station there'll only be one bus heading in your direction, so any thoughts about it being private or government are a waste of time – get on and get going!

Once on the road, you'll realise that all buses are slow. On sealed roads you can expect to cover around 50km/h, but on dirt roads 30km/h or less. In the rainy season, journeys can be severely disrupted. Thankfully, rapid road construction to the tune of US$500 million is turning many troublesome dirt sections into slick sections of sealed road. The one drawback so far has been the increase in road accidents due to speed (though the rate is still low by African standards).

Unlike most African countries, standing in the aisles of long-distance buses is illegal in Ethiopia, making them more comfortable (note that we've said more comfortable, which is a far cry from saying comfortable!) and safer. On the longer journeys, there are usually scheduled 20-minute stops for meals. There are no toilets on board.

The major drawback with bus travel is the size of the country. For the historical circuit alone, you'll spend a total of at least 10 days sitting on a bus to cover the 2500km.

Although most long-distance buses are scheduled to 'leave' at 6am or earlier, they don't typically set out before 7am as most are demand driven and won't leave until full. To be safe you should make an appearance at the prescribed departure time. Remember that the Ethiopian clock is used locally (see p267), though Western time is used when quoting bus times in this book.

In remote areas long waits for buses to fill is normal – some may not leave at all. In general, the earlier you get to the bus station, the better chance you have of catching the first bus out of town.

On those journeys quoted in this book with durations longer than one day, there are overnight stops en route (Ethiopian law stipulates that all long-distances buses must be off the road by 6pm). In many cases you won't be allowed to remove luggage from the roof, so you should pack toiletries and other overnight items to take with you in a small bag on the bus.

Smaller and more remote towns are usually served by minibuses or Isuzu trucks (see p281).

Costs

Buses are very cheap in Ethiopia. Both government-run and private buses work out at around US$1.50 per 100km. There's just one class of travel.

Reservations

Tickets for most long-distance journeys (over 250km) can usually be bought in advance. If you can, do: it guarantees a seat (though not a specific seat number on private buses) and cuts out the touts who sometimes snap up the remaining tickets to resell for double the price to latecomers. Most government ticket offices are open daily from 5.30am to 5.30pm. For short distances (less than 250km), tickets can usually only be bought on the day.

If you would like a whiff of fresh air on your journey, get a seat behind the driver as he tends to buck the trend and keep his window cracked open.

CAR & MOTORCYCLE
Bring Your Own Vehicle
If you're bringing your own 4WD or motorcycle, you'll need a *carnet de passage* (a guarantee issued by your own national motoring association that you won't sell your vehicle in the country you are travelling), the vehicle's registration papers and proof of third-party insurance that covers Ethiopia.

Driving Licence
Although Ethiopian law recognises international driving licences, it fails to do so for longer than seven days. Officially, once you reach Addis Ababa you're supposed to acquire an Ethiopian-endorsed licence. To acquire one you must take a certified (by your embassy) copy of your domestic licence (or certified English translation) to the Protocol Service Division of the **Ministry of Foreign Affairs** (Map pp80-1; ☎ 0115 506561; Yohanis St), where you'll pay Birr300 for an official stamp. From there, head to the **Transport & Communications Bureau** (Map p76; Equatorial Guinea St) with all your paperwork, plus two passport photos, a copy of your passport and Birr30. After a lot of waiting and signing some things, you'll have your Ethiopian-endorsed licence.

This is rarely enforced and most overlanders we met hadn't bothered with this convoluted process and had yet to encounter any problems – roll the dice if you so please.

Fuel & Spare Parts
Fuel (both petrol and diesel) is quite widely available, apart from the more remote regions such as the southwest. Unleaded petrol is not available. Diesel costs from around Birr4.35 to Birr4.80 per litre, while petrol costs around Birr5.50 to Birr5.90 per litre. These prices are government subsidised and may leap in the near future if those in power

change policy. When this recently happened in Kenya, prices almost doubled. Note that your vehicle's fuel consumption will be 25% higher in Ethiopia than at sea level because of the increased altitudes.

While there are helpful garages throughout the country (ask your hotel to recommend one), spare parts are not abundant outside Addis Ababa. It's wise to take stock while in Addis and acquire all that you may need for the journey ahead, whether it be Sudan or Kenya. Thanks to Toyota Land Cruisers being the choice of most tour operators, their parts are more plentiful and less expensive than those for Landrovers.

Hire
Even with the recent road improvements, you still really need a 4WD to explore the country. Despite competition between the numerous tour agents in Addis Ababa (see p282) that hire 4WDs, prices are steep and range from US$90 per day for older vehicles to US$180 for luxurious newer models. Most companies include unlimited kilometres, a driver, driver allowance (for their food and accommodation), fuel, third-party insurance, a collision damage waiver and government taxes in their rates; check all these details and ask if service charges will be added afterwards and if there are set driver's hours.

Know that prices are always negotiable and vary greatly depending on the period of rental and the season. Despite the hassle, you'll always pay much less organising things yourself in Ethiopia rather than hiring an agency at home to arrange it.

Though expensive, the chief advantage of 4WD hire over bus travel is the time that can be saved. Trip durations are at least halved and there's no waiting around in remote regions for infrequent and erratic buses. Note also that some national parks can only be entered with a 4WD.

The mandatory drivers (currently no agency offers self-drive 4WD) can be very useful as guides-cum-interpreters-cum-mechanics. Although tips are expected afterwards (see the boxed text, p264), a nice gesture during the trip is to share food together (which costs very little).

Some Addis Ababa–based agencies have branch offices in towns on the historical route and can rent 4WDs, but only by prearrangement. Increasingly, private individuals

ETHIOPIA TRANSPORT

ETHIOPIA TRANSPORT

rent to tourists. Be aware of the risks, particularly regarding insurance and the condition of the car.

Self-drive cars are only hired by a couple of agencies in Addis Ababa (see Galaxy Express Services, p282, and Rainbow Travel, p283), but these companies aren't happy if their vehicles leave the capital and they forbid them to travel off sealed roads. If you're still interested in hiring one to toot around the capital you must have a valid international driver's licence and be between 25 and 70 years old. Vehicles cost between US$35 and US$50 per day with 50km to 70km free kilometres. They usually require a deposit of Birr1000 to Birr2000.

Motorcycles are not currently rented.

Insurance

Third-party vehicle insurance is required by law. Thankfully, unlike some other African countries, which demand that vehicles are covered by an insurance company based in that country, Ethiopia only requires your insurance from elsewhere is valid in Ethiopia. Although not mandatory, we'd also recommend comprehensive coverage.

If you don't have either, the numerous offices of **Ethiopian Insurance Corporation** (www .eic.com.et) sell third-party/comprehensive insurance from Birr70/600 per year.

Purchase

If you're looking to buy a quality secondhand vehicle, expect to pay a minimum of US$12,000 to US$20,000. With the large expat community that's resident in Addis Ababa, vehicles are usually easy to find there. Start by looking in the local English-language newspapers.

TRAVELLERS LORE

Once there was a dog, a goat and a donkey. They wanted to go on a journey together, and decided to take a taxi. The donkey paid and got out, the dog paid, got out but never got his change, and the goat got out but never paid.

To this day, and whenever a vehicle passes, the dog still chases his change, the goat still scatters at the first approach, and the donkey just plods tranquilly on.

Ethiopian folk tale

Road Conditions

There are 17,000km of all-weather roads and about 35,000km of dry-weather roads in Ethiopia. About one-quarter of the all-weather roads are currently sealed and an ambitious US$500-million project is either adding more sealed sections or upgrading those that are in rough shape.

From Moyale on the Kenyan border north to Awasa, and from Arba Minch to Shashemene, the roads are sealed but rather potholed, while the stretch from Awasa to Addis Ababa is much better. The unsurfaced roads connecting Jinka and the Lower Omo Valley to Arba Minch and Yabelo range from bad to tolerable. The same can be said for the roads heading east from Shashemene to Bale Mountains National Park.

Two new sections of sealed road are spreading west from Addis Ababa and should reach Nekemte and Jimma in the life of this book. The lowland roads can be diabolical in the rains.

Decent sealed roads all but link Addis Ababa to Gonder, with only the Blue Nile Gorge section still in rough shape. New sealed sections have also all but linked Woldia, Mekele and Adigrat on the historical circuit. The sealed section connecting Woldia to Addis Ababa is currently being upgraded. The rest of the northern historical circuit ranges from finely graded gravels to course corrugations.

Harar and Dire Dawa, both 525km east of Addis Ababa, are connected to the capital with good sealed roads.

Road Hazards

In the outskirts of the towns or villages, look out for people, particularly children playing on the road or kerbside. Night driving is not recommended. *Shiftas* (bandits) still operate in the more remote areas. Additionally, some trucks park overnight in the middle of the road – without lights.

In the country, livestock is the main hazard; camels wandering onto the road can cause major accidents in the lowlands. Many animals, including donkeys, are unaccustomed to vehicles and are very car-shy, so always approach slowly and with caution.

Land mines still pose a threat throughout the country; drivers should always stay on sealed roads or existing dirt tracks. During the rainy season, some roads, particularly in the west and southwest, become impassable. Check road conditions with the local authorities before setting out.

Road Rules

Driving is on the right-hand side of the road. The speed limit for cars and motorcycles is 60km/h in the towns and villages and 100km/h outside the towns. The standard of driving is generally not high; devices such as mirrors or indicators are often disregarded. On highland roads, drive defensively and beware of trucks coming fast the other way. Also keep a sharp eye out for a row of stones or pebbles across the road; it marks roadworks or an accident. Most vehicles don't have seatbelts, though we should say that people would be crazy not to use them if they are available – simply for safety reasons.

HITCHING

In the past, if someone asked for a ride in Ethiopia, it was usually assumed that it was because they couldn't afford a bus fare and little sympathy was spared for them. Many Ethiopians also suspected hitchers of hidden motives such as robbery.

However, for some towns not readily served by buses or light vehicles, hitching is quite normal, and you will be expected to pay a 'fare'. Negotiate this in advance. The best place to look for lifts is at the hotels, bars and cafés in the centre of town.

Be aware that the density of vehicles on many roads is still very low in Ethiopia; on the remote roads, you'll be lucky to see any. Non-Governmental Organisation (NGO) vehicles sometimes oblige, but you'll be expected to contribute towards fuel.

LOCAL TRANSPORT

In many of the larger towns, a minibus service provides a quick, convenient and cheap way of hopping about town (from

---

> **HITCHING**
>
> Hitching is never entirely safe, and it's not recommended. Travellers who decide to hitch should understand that they are taking a small but potentially serious risk. Hitching is safer in pairs. Additionally, try and let someone know where you're planning to go. Women should never hitch alone.

---

around Birr0.75 for short journeys). 'Conductors' generally shout out the destination of the bus; if in doubt, ask.

Taxis operate in many of the larger towns including Addis Ababa. Prices are reasonable, but foreigners as well as well-heeled Ethiopians are always charged more for 'contract services' (see the boxed text, below). Fares are usually between Birr10 and Birr20 depending on the distance. If in doubt, ask your hotel for an estimate.

Garis (horse-drawn carts) are a popular local means of getting about town. They're cheap (usually no more than Birr1 to Birr2) and are useful to travellers in two ways particularly: as cheap transport to hotels from bus stations, and for city tours. Be aware that in many towns now they are banned from operating on the principal roads and must stick to the back ones. Most drivers speak little or no English; you may have to enlist a local to act as interpreter.

MINIBUSES & ISUZU TRUCKS

Minibuses are now commonly used between towns connected by sealed roads or to cover short distances. They cost slightly more than buses, but they leave more often and cover the distances more quickly. You'll usually find them at bus stations.

In more remote regions where the roads aren't conducive to buses, like the Lower

---

ETHIOPIA TRANSPORT

> **TAXI TERMINOLOGY**
>
> In the towns, villages and countryside of Ethiopia and Eritrea, taxis offer two kinds of service: 'contract taxis' and 'share-taxis'. Share-taxis ply fixed routes, stop and pick people up when hailed and work to all intents like little buses. They become 'contract taxis' when flagged down (or 'contracted') for a private journey. The fare is then split between all passengers.
>
> Though not really 'taxis' at all, minibuses, trucks, 4WDs and various other kinds of cars can all be contracted in this way. Contracting a large minibus for yourself is seen as perfectly normal if you should want to. Before hiring a contract taxi, always negotiate the fare before you get in, or you may be asked far above the going rate at the end of the journey.

ETHIOPIA TRANSPORT

Omo Valley, Isuzu flatbed trucks carrying goods between villages are often the best way to get around. A seat in the cabin usually costs twice as much as riding in the back. Prices are always negotiable. Petrol stations or market areas are commonly the collection points.

TOURS

For the independent traveller, incorporating an organised tour into your travels in Ethiopia is useful for four things: specialised activities such as white-water rafting; access to remote regions with limited public transport such as the Lower Omo Valley or the Danakil Depression; 'themed trips' (such as bird-watching) with expert guides; and to help those with limited time who are keen to see as much as possible.

If you're interested in taking a tour, contact the agencies in advance and compare itineraries and prices. Most now have websites that you can visit first.

To reduce the cost of tours (few are cheap), hook up with a group of other travellers, or contact the agency far in advance to see if there are pre-arranged tours that you can tag onto. You'll need to be flexible with your dates.

NTO, the government-owned travel agency, once had a monopoly. Its drivers and guides have excellent reputations, but its prices remain uncompetitive. A cluster of much more competitive private operators has sprung up in the past 10 years, all based in Addis Ababa.

Agencies offer all or some of the following: guides, 4WD hire, camping-equipment hire, historical route tours, bird-watching and wildlife-viewing, white-water rafting, fishing, Omo Valley tours, photo safaris, Simien and Bale Mountain trekking, Rift Valley lake trips, and Danakil and Afar excursions. Some have branches in towns outside Addis Ababa, from where (if pre-booked) you can hire a 4WD or guide or take a tour.

Some agencies also have very attractive, 'ecofriendly' lodges and campsites, including Ethiopian Rift Valley Safaris (in the Omo Valley); Green Land Tours (Swayne's Hotel at Arba Minch and Wenney Eco-Lodge at Lake Langano, with Yemrha Hotel opening soon in Lalibela); and Village Ethiopia (in Bilen, near Awash).

Though prices are officially fixed, most are very open to negotiation, particularly during the low season. Many agencies now accept credit cards.

All 4WD hire prices listed here include mandatory driver, driver allowance and insurance. Most charge extra for guides and camping equipment, and some tack on extra fees for mileage and fuel. It's always worth negotiating, especially in the off-season.

The following list is far from exhaustive, but it includes those recommended by travellers and Ethiopians in the tourism industry.

Abyssinian Tours & Travel (Map pp80–1; ☎ 0115 519293; www.abyssiniantours.com; Ethio-China Ave) Friendly and reasonably priced, Abyssinian runs trips across the country. Prices for a 4WD with driver range from US$110 to US$130 per day depending on the state of the vehicle and distance being travelled.

Bahir Dar Tour & Travel Agency (Map p85; ☎ 0111 550546; bdtta@ethionet.et; Churchill Ave) This long-standing company offers personalised tours of northern and southern Ethiopia. Its daily rate for a new-model Land Cruiser, including fuel and mileage, is US$100. It's also an International Air Transport Association (IATA) approved flight-ticketing agent.

Ethio-Der Tour & Travel (Map p85; ☎ 0111 571157; www.ethio-der.com; Itegue Taitu Hotel, Piazza) Ethio-Der charges US$100/120 per day for an old/new 4WD, including fuel and mileage. Professional guides cost US$30 to US$50 per day, depending on the number of people. Camping equipment is US$5 per day.

Ethio-Fauna Safaris (Map pp80–1; ☎ 0115 505301; ethfauna@ethionet.et) One of the most respected agencies, with top-notch vehicles, equipment and service. A basic trip will start at US$160 per day for the 4WD. Off Gambia St.

Ethiopian Rift Valley Safaris (Map p85; ☎ 0111 552128; www.ethiopianriftvalleysafaris.com) Unlike the other agencies listed, this elite operation only offers package tours, including guides, meals and accommodation in hotels. Prices typically range from US$160 to US$200 per person per day. Count on sublime service. It's off Cunningham St.

Four Seasons Travel & Tours (Map pp80–1; ☎ 0116 613121; fsta@ethionet.et; Bole Rd) A reasonable outfit charging Birr950 per day for a 4WD. Prices include mileage, but fuel is extra.

Galaxy Express Services (Map pp80–1; ☎ 0115 510355; www.galaxyexpressethiopia.com; Gambia St) This well-run agency offers various Ethiopia tour packages. Travel is in new Land Cruisers, which cost US$170 per day including unlimited mileage, driver and insurance. It's also an Avis agent and rents self-drive cars for use in and around Addis Ababa (US$49 per day with 50km free; each additional kilometre is 45¢).

Green Land Tours & Travels (Map pp80-1; ☎ 0116 185875; www.greenlandethiopia.com; Cameroon St) Green Land is one of the biggest agencies, with various hotels and camps set up throughout southern Ethiopia. It also runs trips north. Prices for 4WD, guide, fuel and mileage range from US$130 to US$150 per day.

Hess Travel Ethiopia (Map pp80-1; ☎ 0115 520955; www.hesstravel.com; Bole Rd) A popular agency with a great reputation, Hess offers trips starting from US$130 per vehicle. Prices include mileage, fuel and equipment. It has French-, German- and English-speaking guides.

NTO (www.nto.com) Hilton Hotel (Map pp80-1; ☎ 0115 151722; Menelik II Ave); Ras Desta Damtew St (Map pp80-1; ☎ 0115 514838; Ras Desta Damtew St) This government travel agency is the most experienced and is one of the few that takes credit cards. A 4WD with 100 free kilometres per day costs US$126. Each excess kilometre costs 75¢. Well-spoken guides are US$43 per day. With offices in many cities, it can organise tours for those wishing to fly between major sights. It accepts Visa and American Express (7% surcharge).

Rainbow Travel (www.rainbowtravelplc.com) Bole Rd (Map pp80-1; ☎ 0116 615414; Bole Rd); Meskal Sq (Map pp80-1; ☎ 0115 513755; Ras Biru Wolde Gebriel St); Sheraton Hotel (Map pp80-1; ☎ 0115 173697; Itegue Taitu St) This agency organises 4WD tours with new Nissan Patrols for Birr750 per day, which includes 75 free kilometres. Each excess kilometre costs Birr2.85. Small self-drive cars can be rented for trips in and around Addis Ababa for around Birr300 per day with 75 free kilometres (Birr1 to Birr2 each additional kilometre). It also caters to those wishing to fly between major sights. Visa and MasterCard are accepted (6% surcharge).

Red Jackal Tour Operator (Map p85; ☎ 0111 560559; www.redjackal.net; Itegue Taitu Hotel, Piazza) Prices for tours to Ethiopia's south and north range from US$80 to US$120 per vehicle per day. These include fuel and mileage.

Rocky Valley Safaris (Map pp80-1; ☎ 0115 516408; Gambia St) This company sits within the Ras Hotel and offers 4WD tours for Birr750 per vehicle per day (fuel is

extra). It doesn't offer professional guides, but its drivers can arrange local guides en route.

Sunrise Travel & Tour (Map p85; ☎ 0111 578921, 0911 223246; www.sunrisetours.com; Cunningham St) This agency runs Ethiopia tours with older 1989 Land Cruisers. Prices are the lowest you'll find, with 4WD, mileage and fuel costing Birr750 per day.

Tour Ethiopia (Map pp80-1; ☎ 0115 510168; www.travelethiopia.net) This agency sits below the parking lot of the Ghion Hotel and offers Ethiopia tours starting from US$150 per vehicle per day. Trips in newer Land Cruisers cost US$180 per day. Tent rental is included. It's off Ras Desta Damtew St.

Travel Ethiopia (www.travelethiopia.com) Ghion Hotel (Map pp80-1; ☎ 0911 206976); National Hotel (Map pp80-1; ☎ 0115 525478; Menelik II Ave) A self-professed 'ecominded' tour company with multilingual guides (English, French, Italian and German) and quality 4WD vehicles. The Ghion Hotel is off Ras Desta Damtew St.

T-Tam Travel & Tour (Map pp80-1; ☎ 0111 578921, 0911 223246; www.ttamtour.com; Bole Rd) This established agency charges Birr900 per day for 4WDs, but 15% VAT and fuel are not included. It's also an IATA ticketing agent.

Village Ethiopia (Map pp80-1; ☎ 0115 523497; www.village-ethiopia.net; National Hotel, Menelik II Ave) This agency offers everything from bird-watching and ethnic tours in the south to rock climbing in Tigray. It also specialises in the Danakil Depression and has a lodge near its toasty confines.

Yumo Tours (Map pp80-1; ☎ 0115 513783; www.yumo.net; Ras Mekonen Ave) This refreshingly honest operator told us they're not very good at tours of the Lower Omo Valley. However, if birding in the south is your thing, they are your people.

TRAIN

The Addis Ababa–Dire Dawa train is indefinitely out of action, though the Dire Dawa–Djibouti City section is still chugging along (see p274).

Transitting Through Djibouti

Djibouti might be one of the tiniest, youngest and least-known nations in Africa; it could also well be the most talented or, depending on your perspective, the most opportunistic. While Eritrea and Ethiopia, its larger and more powerful neighbours, are embroiled in what seems to be a never-ending border dispute, Djibouti stands out as a haven of stability and neutrality. The country's leaders cleverly maintain good relations with their unruly neighbours. Djibouti's port is now Ethiopia's main hub for imports and exports.

As long as the border between Ethiopia and Eritrea remains closed, Djibouti is the obvious transit point for those travellers who want to visit the two countries in a single trip. It is well connected to both, whether by air or by land. But, you would miss out if you limited your experience of Djibouti to a few hours or even a full day waiting for a connecting flight, train or bus. Djibouti is much more than a stopping point on the road to Eritrea or Ethiopia. Why not settle in for a few days and enjoy its dishevelled nightlife, culinary delights and well-organised infrastructure? Or visit its surreal hinterland? Sure, Djibouti will put a dent in your wallet but if you need to recharge the batteries before (or after) a serious overland trip of Eritrea or Ethiopia, this is the place.

PRACTICALITIES

- Djibouti uses the metric system and distances are in kilometres.

- Electricity in Djibouti is 220V. European two-prong plugs are mainly used.

- Local newspapers are published weekly in French. They include *La Nation* and *Réalité*.

- TV programmes are in Somali, Afar, Arab and French.

DJIBOUTI CITY

Djibouti City is not your average African capital. Coming from Eritrea or eastern Ethiopia, many travellers are surprised to discover that it is an active and fairly cosmopolitan city that tries hard to be recognised as the little Dubai in the Red Sea. Traditionally robed Afar tribesmen, stalwart French legionnaires (and the odd GI), sensuous Somali glamour kittens and frazzled businessmen with the latest mobile phones stuck to their ear all jostle side by side.

While it's not exactly a diamond in the rough, it boasts good infrastructure but doesn't come cheap – be prepared for a financial shock. If you're into clubbing, Djibouti City offers a couple of lively options right in the centre. For more on things to do in Djibouti, see the boxed text, p288.

INFORMATION
Embassies & Consulates

Djiboutian diplomatic representation abroad is scarce, but there are embassies in Ethiopia and Eritrea (see p260 and p359). In countries without representation, travellers should head for the French embassy, which acts for Djibouti in the issuing of visas.

Most foreign embassies in Djibouti City are located on Plateau du Serpent, north of the city centre.

Canada (☎ /fax 355950; Place Lagarde)
Eritrea (☎ 354961; fax 250212; Plateau du Serpent)
Ethiopia (☎ 350718; fax 354803; ave F. d'Esperey)
France (☎ 350963; www.ambafrance-dj.or; ave F. d'Esperey)
USA (☎ 353995; www.djibouti.usembassy.gov; Plateau du Serpent)

Internet Access

There's a slew of Internet outlets in the centre. The following ones offer the best connections.

Cyber Cafe Filga Informatique (rue de Paris; per hr DFr300; ⏰ 7am-12.30pm & 4-10pm Sat-Thu, 4-10pm Fri)
Easy Internet (rue de Londres; per hr DFr400; ⏰ 7.30am-1pm & 4-11pm Sat-Thu, 4-11pm Fri)

Medical Services

CHA Bouffard (☎ 351351; Boulaos district) The best equipped hospital, south of the city.
Pôle Médical (☎ 352724; ⏰ Sat-Thu) A well-equipped clinic run by French doctors who can speak English. It's off Place du 27 Juin 1977.

Money

At the time of writing the two ATMs in Djibouti City were not functioning and there were no plans to fix them up. Your best bet is to rely on cash. If you're short of funds, the BCIMR is an agent for **Western Union** (☎ 358885; Place Lagarde; ⏰ 8.15am-12.30pm & 4-6pm Sun-Thu).
BCIMR Place Lagarde (☎ 358885; ⏰ 7.30-11.45am Sun-Thu); Plateau du Serpent (☎ 353143; ave F. d'Esperey; ⏰ 7.45-11.45am & 4-5.30pm Sun-Thu) Doesn't accept travellers cheques but can do cash advances on credit cards (Visa only). For cash transactions, a flat fee of DFr500 is charged. The ave F. d'Esperey branch is less crowded.

There are also two authorised bureaus de change around Place Lagarde and one at the airport.
Bureau de change (☎ 821970; international airport; ⏰ 7.30am-1pm & 4pm-last departure Sat-Thu, 4pm-last

---

FAST FACTS

- ATMs: two in Djibouti City but they were not functioning at the time of writing

- Best season: October to March

- Borders: Eritrea and Ethiopia open

- Capital: Djibouti City

- Languages: Arabic, French, Afar, Somali

- Money: Djibouti Franc (DFr); US$1 = DFr175.19

- Telephone: country code ☎ 253; international access code ☎ 00

- Time: GMT/UTC + 3h

departure Fri) At the airport (cash only) but the rates are slightly inferior to the ones offered in the centre.

Dilip Corporation (☎ 352857; Place du 27 Juin 1977; ⏱ 8am-noon & 4-7.30pm Sat-Thu) Changes cash (no commission) and does cash advances on Visa and Master-Card but doesn't accept travellers cheques.

Mehta (☎ 353719; Place du 27 Juin 1977; ⏱ 7.30am-7.30pm Sun-Thu) Next door to Dilip (same family), Mehta also changes cash (no commission) and usually accepts travellers cheques but charges a whopping 6% commission. It can also do cash advances on Visa and MasterCard but the rates are inferior to the ones offered by the BCIMR.

Post & Telephone

The most convenient places to make an international or a local call are the various telephone outlets scattered around the city centre.

Main post office (blvd de la République; ⏱ 7am-1pm & 4-7pm Sat-Thu) North of the centre.

Tourist Information

Tourist office (☎ 352800; www.office-tourisme.dj in French; rue de Foucauld; ⏱ 7am-1pm Sat-Thu, 4-6pm Sat, Mon & Wed) To the southeastern side of Place du 27 Juin 1977. Sells a map of the country for DFr300 and gives a free photocopy of a map of the city.

SLEEPING

Grit your teeth: the choice of budget accommodation is limited.

Hotel Ali Sabieh (☎ 353264; ave Georges Clemenceau; s DFr9400-10,500, d DFr12,700; ❄) One of

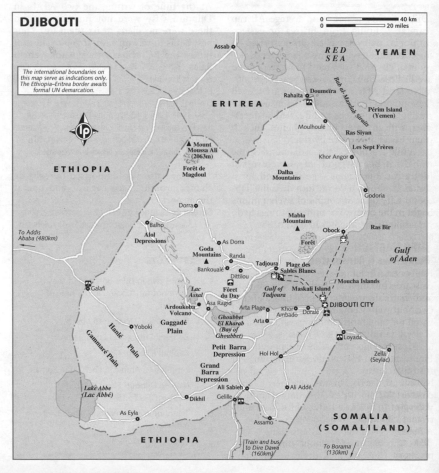

DJIBOUTI VISAS

All visitors, including nationals of France, need visas. Tourist visas cost from US$30 to US$60 and are usually valid for one month. Visas can be obtained at the nearest Djibouti embassy (including Addis Ababa and Asmara if you're in the Horn) or, where there is none, from the French embassy. Note that travellers from most Western countries can also obtain tourist visas on arrival at the airport: leave your passport at the Immigration Office and you get it stamped the next day or, if you're really lucky, within a couple of hours. It costs DFr3000 for 10 days and DFr5000 for one month.

---

the most reliable options in town. Top marks go to the clean-smelling rooms, the back-friendly mattresses and the immaculate bathrooms. Another plus is its position, right in the thick of things.

Bed & Breakfast La Maison Blanche (☎ 869935, 352176; Le Heron district; r incl breakfast DFr12,000-15,000; ❄ Aug; ✖ 🖳 🖳) La Maison Blanche is seventh heaven if you need to pamper yourself after a tiring overland trip. Picture this: a gleaming white villa that used to be an ambassador's residence, two generous rooms with all mod cons, bathrooms so scrupulously clean you could eat off the floor, a secluded garden and a nifty pool in which to cool off. It's a tad out of the action but mini buses to the centre are within easy reach.

Menelik Hotel (☎ 351177; Place du 27 Juin 1977; s/d DFr11,000/15,200; ✖) The Menelik has a certain 'could be anywhere' sensibility in its décor and standards, but its very central location is a gem, with all the bars, restaurants and clubs at your tiptoes. Amenities are solid, and the bathrooms are exceedingly clean. Credit cards (Visa only) are accepted but you'll pay a painful 10% commission.

Hotel de France (☎ 813781; blvd du Général de Gaulle; d DFr6500-8500; ✖) A short stagger from Place Lagarde, this is a reassuring choice for budgeteers with no surprises (good or bad) up its sleeves. Rooms are generous and comfortable, if a little anonymous. Handy if you want to be close to the clubs, bars and restaurants in the centre.

Auberge Sable Blanc (☎ 351163; s/d DFr6000/7000; ✖) Another good haunt for pennypinchers. Close to blvd de la République,

this converted villa boasts a mixed bag of rooms, so ask to see a few. If you're a light sleeper, be prepared to be lulled by the call to prayer emanating from the nearby mosque.

Hotel Horseed (☎ 352316; blvd du Général de Gaulle; s/d with shared bathroom DFr5000/7500; ✖) The Horseed won't feature in the pages of the *Condé Nast Traveller* and its location is not the most prepossessing, but the prices are competitive and the rooms presentable. Air-con is extra (DFr500).

EATING & DRINKING

The city is endowed with a smattering of restaurants that will please most palates – a testimony to the French presence. OK, it doesn't come cheap, especially if you come from Ethiopia, but at least it's worth every mouthful. Splurge! There's also a smattering of watering holes off Place du 27 Juin 1977.

Chez Marco (☎ 828087; mains DFr1600-2600; ❄ lunch & dinner Tue-Sun) Hmm, will it be *filet de boeuf sauce roquefort* (fillet of beef with roquefort cheese sauce) or *escalope de poulet au citron vert* (chicken with lemon sauce)? This very French outpost serves delectable fare with a Mediterranean twist in a welcoming, light-toned interior. It's off Place du 27 Juin 1977.

La Table de Julien (☎ 357355; ave F. d'Esperey; mains DFr1900-2500; ❄ lunch Sat-Thu, dinner Mon-Sat) Opposite the railway station, this terribly French venue was the flavour of the month when we visited. Creative dishes like *filet de daurade au sel du lac Assal* (sea bream

---

VISAS FOR ONWARD TRAVEL

Eritrea
Visas are valid for one month and cost DFr7200 or US$40. You need one photo. Visa applications can be received every morning from 8.30am to 10.30am except Friday, but visas are delivered on Wednesday and Sunday mornings only. Note that a same-day service is also possible (DFr9000 or US$50) if you apply early morning.

Ethiopia
Visas are valid for three months and cost DFr3600 (DFr12,600 for US nationals). You need to supply one photo. They are issued within 24 hours. Open 7.30am to 1.30pm Sunday to Thursday and 9am to 1pm Saturday.

KILLING TIME IN DJIBOUTI

If you are in transit for a couple of days, here are some suggestions on how to make the most of your stay:

- Stroll in the alleyways of the chaotic Marché Central in **Djibouti City**.
- Snorkel with whale sharks (from October to January) in the **Bay of Ghoubbet**. Contact **Dolphin Excursion** (☎ 350313; dolphinexcursions@hotmail.com) or **Le Lagon Bleu** (☎ 353036, 250297; atta@intnet.dj).
- Dive Moucha and Maskali Islands in the **Gulf of Tadjoura**. Contact **Dolphin Excursion** (☎ 350313; dolphinexcursions@hotmail.com) or **Le Lagon Bleu** (☎ 353036, 250297; atta@intnet.dj).
- Take a tour to **Lake Assal**, the lowest point on the African continent (153m below sea level). Contact **AECVETA** (☎ 354695; www.aecveta.com) or **Dankali Expeditions** (☎ 350313; dolphinexcursions@hotmail.com).
- Forget the hardships and flake out on a porcelain-sand beach at **Plage des Sables Blancs**. Contact **Agence Le Goubet** (☎ 354520).
- Windsurf on wheels across **Grand Barra**, a great salty plain. Contact **AECVETA** (☎ 354695; www.aecveta.com).
- Immerse yourself in the Martian landscape of **Lake Abbé**, where *Planet of the Apes* was filmed. Contact **AECVETA** (☎ 354695; www.aecveta.com) or **Dankali Expeditions** (☎ 350313; dolphinexcursions@hotmail.com).

---

cooked with salt from Lake Assal) as well as the restaurant's signature dessert, *fondant au chocolat* (chocolate cake), will have you gushing superlatives. Wash it all down with a glass of well-chosen wine.

Mukbasa – 7 Freres (☎ 351188; ave 13; fish dishes DFr2000; ☾ lunch & dinner) This popular joint in the African Quarter is famous for one thing and one thing only: *poisson yemenite* (oven-baked fish). It's served with a chapati-like bread and a devilish *mokbasa* (purée of honey and either dates or banana). Truly finger-licking.

Restaurant Saba (☎ 354244; ave Maréchal Lyautey; mains DFr1000-2500; ☾ lunch Sat-Thu, dinner daily) Close to the railway station, this unpretentious joint gets kudos for its wide-ranging menu and mouthwatering fruit juices. Try shark fillet, crab or shrimps. Vegetarians will plump for salads (DFr700 to DFr1200). Despite the simplicity of the setting, this place feels surprisingly cosy.

Shawarma (ave F. d'Esperey; shwarma DFr300-500; ☾ dinner) If money really matters, this cheap and cheerful eatery (no sign), a mere skip from the railway station, is the ideal pit stop. Fork out DFr500 for a shwarma (kebablike dish) and you'll leave patting your tummy contentedly.

Chez Mahad (juices DFr150-300; ☾ 7.30am-noon Sat-Thu, 7.30-11am & 4-9pm Fri) Ultrafresh fruit juices are the deal in this buzzing bolthole, so put some bounce in your step with a glass of mango mixed with milk or papaya with watermelon. It's off rue de Madrid.

Restaurant Ougoul (☎ 353652; ave Georges Clemenceau; mains DFr1600-3200; ☾ lunch & dinner) Nosh on freshly prepared fish and seafood dishes in this Djibouti classic, slap bang in the centre of town.

AROUND DJIBOUTI

Rather than heading straight to Djibouti City, you can pause in the following towns. You can't really get stuck there; they are fairly well connected to the capital.

DIKHIL

If you're coming on a truck from Ethiopia via Galafi, Dikhil, 118km west of Djibouti, might be a convenient stop to reboot your chakras before continuing on to Djibouti City. **Hôtel-Restaurant La Palmeraie** (☎ 420164; r DFr6000) is the best place to stay. There is also a restaurant attached.

Getting There & Away

There are regular bus services between Dikhil and Djibouti City (DFr600, 2½ hours).

ALI SABIEH

If proceeding from Dire Dawa, either by bus or by train, it's not a bad idea to break up your journey in Ali Sabieh. It's an active yet intimate town with a distinct Somali flavour. If it's your first exposure to Djibouti, you'll find it pretty relaxing and, to a certain extent, photogenic and full of attitude.

You don't have to pay a king's ransom to bunk down at the **Hotel Gogareh** (☎ 825308; s with shared bathroom DFr1000), just off the main square (ask around, because there was no sign when we visited). It features shoe-box-sized yet functional rooms set around a courtyard.

If your purse strings are a little more relaxed, **La Palmeraie d'Ali Sabieh** (☎ 426198; r DFr6000; 🗷), on the outskirts of town, has well-appointed rooms, pathogen-free bathrooms and a leaf-dappled courtyard, as well as a decent on-site restaurant.

For a cheap and tasty meal, nothing can beat **Restaurant du Mont Arrey** (☎ 426191; mains DFr1000-2000; 🕑 lunch & dinner), with pasta dishes, steaks, couscous and, in the evening, freshly-prepared sandwiches.

Getting There & Away

The most convenient way to get to Djibouti City is by bus. There are daily services (DFr700), mostly in the morning. You can also hop on the train (DFr1500) that runs three times a week from Dire Dawa to Djibouti City via Ali Sabieh.

To get to Dire Dawa in Ethiopia, you'll first have to take a bus to Gelille at the Ethiopian border (DFr600) then change to another bus heading to Dire Dawa.

OBOCK

The last significant town before the border with Eritrea, Obock exudes a kind of 'last frontier' feel that is not devoid of charm. Although it doesn't have many facilities, it's an obvious staging post for those who want to travel to Eritrea or those who come from Assab, in Eritrea's south. If you decide to stay, you can lay your head at the basic **Campement de Ras Bir – Ougef** (☎ 816034, 822446; huts with full board DFr8000), about 5km east of the centre. Location is top-notch – it's right on the beach. Accommodation is in traditional huts and the shared bathrooms are rudimentary. About 2km west of the centre, a more upmarket option was under construction when we visited. Ask around.

Getting There & Away

The most convenient way to get to Djibouti City is by speedboat or dhow. They leave daily to L'Escale, a small marina northeast of the centre early in the morning (DFr1500 by speedboat, about 1½ hours; DFr700 by dhow, about three hours). If travelling by road, there are irregular bush taxis that trundle along the dirt road between Tadjoura and Obock (about DFr2000, three hours). From Tadjoura there are morning buses to Djibouti City (about DFr1500, 3½ hours).

There's also a small plane that flies on a twice-weekly basis between Obock and Djibouti City (DFr2000, 30 minutes).

TRANSPORT IN DJIBOUTI

GETTING THERE & AWAY
Entering Djibouti

Djibouti has one international gateway for arrival by air, **Ambouli Airport** (☎ 341646), about 5km south of Djibouti City. There are also several land borders with neighbouring Eritrea, Ethiopia and Somaliland.

Disembarkation at the airport is usually simple, with only the usual arrival form to fill in. You might be asked for an address or contact in the country; in this case, mention a hotel in Djibouti City. Crossing at land borders is relatively easy too, but be sure to have your passport stamped with an entry/exit stamp if you enter/leave the country.

PASSPORT

To enter Djibouti you must have a valid passport and a visa.

Air
AIRPORTS & AIRLINES

The only airport handling international traffic is Ambouli Airport. All airlines flying to/from Djibouti have an office or a representative in Djibouti City. They are closed on Friday.

Air France (☎ 351010; www.airfrance.com; Place du 27 Juin 1977)

Daallo (☎ 353401; www.daallo.com; rue de Paris)

Djibouti Airlines (☎ 351006; www.djiboutiairlines.com; Place Lagarde)

Ethiopian Airlines (☎ 351007; www.flyethiopian.com; rue de Marseille)

Globe Travel (☎ 250297, 353036; Place Lagarde) Agent for Eritrean Airlines and Kenya Airways.

DEPARTURE TAX

The airport departure tax is DFr3000 for neighbouring countries and DFr5000 for further-flung destinations. In some cases it's included in the cost of your ticket; check with any airline while in Djibouti.

Yemenia Yemen Airways (☎ 356579; www.yemenia .com; rue Marchand)

TICKETS
Eritrea

The only airline connecting Djibouti with Eritrea is Eritrean Airlines, Eritrea's national airline. It has a twice-weekly flight between Djibouti and Asmara (US$290 return, one hour).

Ethiopia

Ethiopian Airlines connects Djibouti and Addis Ababa four times a week (US$195/280 one way/return). Djibouti Airlines has three weekly flights to/from Dire Dawa (DFr15,000/22,000 one way/return) and one weekly flight to/from Addis Ababa (DFr25,000/36,000 one way/return).

Land
ERITREA

Travel overland to Eritrea is possible, but it might be time-consuming and there's the risk of getting stuck either in Obock (Djibouti) or in Assab (Eritrea) for a few days – consider yourself warned. The main cause of headaches for travellers is the lack of reliable transportation scheduled between Assab and Obock. Traffic is limited to shared taxis (usually Land Cruisers) from Obock to Moulhoulé, the last town before the border. Then other taxis ply the route from Moulhoulé to Assab in Eritrea. It's about four hours from Obock to the border (DFr2000) and from the border to Assab another 3½ hours (Nfa300). At the time of writing there were about two weekly services, but there's no fixed schedule and taxis leave when they have enough customers.

Note that there's no formal Immigration Office on the Djiboutian side (there is talk of setting one up). If you can't get your passport stamped at the border, don't forget to do it either at the Police Office in Obock or at the **Police de l'Air et des Frontieres Office**

(☎ 350289; ✆ 24hr) inside the port area in Djibouti City. When leaving Djibouti City for Eritrea, it's also best to go first to the Police de l'Air et des Frontieres and ask for an exit stamp – unless they send you to the Police Office in Obock.

ETHIOPIA
Bus

There is a daily service between Dire Dawa and Djibouti City – a strenuous 10- to 12-hour ride on a gravel road. You'll take your first bus to the border town of Gelille, then another bus to Djibouti City; see p274.

From Djibouti City, buses leave at dawn from ave 26. The company is called **SPB** (☎ 826573, 828838). Buy your ticket at least a day in advance to be sure of getting a seat.

Hitching

Hitching is never entirely safe in any country, and we don't recommend it. Still, if you want to enter Djibouti from Ethiopia via the border town of Galafi, the only option is to hitch a lift (front seats only) with one of the legions of trucks that ply the route between Addis Ababa and Djibouti City via Awash, Gewane, Logiya and Dikhil (about three days). Prices are negotiable. This option is best avoided by women.

Train

Passengers can hop on the old Addis Ababa–Djibouti City train at Dire Dawa. The leg costs about Birr80 in '1st' class. The train leaves three times a week. From Djibouti City to Dire Dawa (via Ali Sabieh), it'll cost you DFr3900 in 1st class, minimum duration 13 hours. You're well advised to buy your ticket one day in advance at the **railway station** (☎ 358070; ave F. d'Esperey; ✆ 7am-noon Tue, Thu & Sat).

See p274 for more information.

GETTING AROUND

The road network links all major villages in the country with the capital. The Route de l'Unité, a good sealed road, covers the 174km from the capital around the Gulf de Tadjoura. From Tadjoura to Obock and on to Moulhoulé at the Eritrean border, there's a gravel road only passable by 4WDs.

There is pretty limited public transport. See the Getting There & Away section of Dikhil (p288), Ali Sabieh (p289) and Obock (p289) for details on the most useful routes.

Eritrea

Eritrea

Eritrea is a heartbreaker. It was once heralded as a good place for travelling and, with a bit of luck, it could soon be so again. But as long as the country is at odds with its neighbour Ethiopia (again!), its sworn enemy, tourism development won't be a priority. One of the most secretive countries in Africa, Eritrea seems doomed to remain a hidden gem.

On the bright side, unlimited opportunities for off-the-beaten-track exploration abound. Who knew that Asmara, the capital, boasts the most shining collection of colonial architectural wonders in Africa? It is like a set from an early Italian movie, with vintage Italian coffee machines and outstanding examples of Art Deco architecture. On the Red Sea coast, the sultry town of Massawa is redolent with Islamic influence. It is also the starting point for visits to the Dahlak Islands, one of the least-spoilt and least-known reefs in the Red Sea.

Southern Eritrea features a superb array of archaeological sites that tell volumes of history. The Sahel Mountains in the north, for a long time the home of the guerrilla fighters, have a wild and bleak quality. The apocalyptic wasteland of Dankalia, stretching to the south, is considered one of the most arresting places on Earth and has a desolate magnetism. Eritrea's nine colourful ethnic groups are diverse and individual, and are a major highlight.

Isn't that enough? Although the country faces numerous hardships, it also remains one of Africa's most peaceful, secure and welcoming destinations. Once you've set foot there, your heart will be broken. You've been warned!

HIGHLIGHTS

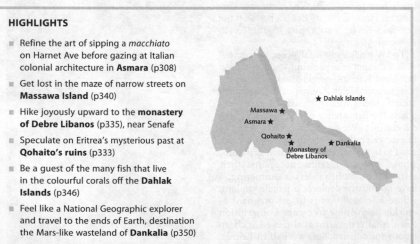

- Refine the art of sipping a *macchiato* on Harnet Ave before gazing at Italian colonial architecture in **Asmara** (p308)

- Get lost in the maze of narrow streets on **Massawa Island** (p340)

- Hike joyously upward to the **monastery of Debre Libanos** (p335), near Senafe

- Speculate on Eritrea's mysterious past at **Qohaito's ruins** (p333)

- Be a guest of the many fish that live in the colourful corals off the **Dahlak Islands** (p346)

- Feel like a National Geographic explorer and travel to the ends of Earth, destination the Mars-like wasteland of **Dankalia** (p350)

- Enjoy the smug feeling of having the whole country to yourself!

★ Dahlak Islands
Massawa ★
Asmara ★
Qohaito ★
★ Dankalia
Monastery of Debre Libanos

SNAPSHOT ERITREA

'I can't afford milk for my children.' 'Tef has become outrageously expensive.' 'We all ride bicycles because fuel is restricted and too expensive,' Eritreans confess in plaintive whispers. Today Eritrea is not exactly in wonderland. The country has one of the most restrictive economies on the planet, and it's in a morass. The state has taken control of all private companies. Power cuts, food shortages, skyrocketing prices and rationing of staples are the order of the day. Eritreans have refined the art of belt-tightening and suffer in near silence. In 2003, 1kg of meat cost Nfa20, 1kg of sugar was Nfa5, and they were easily available. Today they cost Nfa98 and Nfa20 respectively and Eritreans have to wait in queues at state-run stores to get their monthly ration or buy them on the black market.

As if that was not enough, freedom of speech is nonexistent. According to the US-based Committee to Protect Journalists, Eritrea is one of the world's leading jailers of journalists. A heroic guerrilla commander, President Isaias Afewerki has metamorphosed into a stereotypical dictator, quashing hopes for democracy in the name of 'protecting national security'. He has curbed civil liberties, shut down Eritrea's free press and jailed domestic dissenters. The end result? Eritrea has won the less-than-enviable sobriquet of 'the North Korea of Africa'.

Today reaching a final peace agreement with Ethiopia is a pressing issue but both President Isaias Afewerki and his Ethiopian counterpart Meles Zenawi can't relinquish their fighter's mentality, which partly explains the persistence of the senseless border conflict. 'We want peace, we're weary of this never-ending war with Ethiopia, we just want to live a normal life,' lament Eritreans, whose growing resentment against their intransigent, mulish rulers is simmering. 'I have no future,' deplores a female student, whose sole ambition is to get pregnant as quickly as possible to escape conscription (incidentally, the army is also used as cheap labour for construction works). In Eritrea, the buzz word has long been 'self-reliance'. At first, this meant a sense of responsibility. Now this has transformed into utter paranoia. Every outside influence is viewed with suspicion. Western NGOs and UN staff? 'Ants that undermine the stability of the country' – the nasty beasts were arbitrarily expelled in 2005. The BBC correspondent – the last Western journalist based in the country – is only tolerated. No wonder that the sense of isolation is overwhelming. Foreigners feel like they are setting foot on another planet.

Is it all that grim, though? Paradoxically, visitors feel very safe and most welcome as long as they don't interfere with politics. Eritreans show an exceptional resilience and have not abandoned their dreams of a renaissance. To top it off, they have not lost their appetite for life and Asmarans still surrender to the daily ritual of *passeggiata* (see p320). And they are still *macchiato* (espresso with a dash of milk) addicts. As one Eritrean realistically puts it: 'Governments come and go, but the people stay the same.' Eritrea will bounce back. The only question that haunts the minds is: when?

HISTORY

IN THE BEGINNING

Eritrea's earliest inhabitants are thought to have been related to the Pygmies of Central Africa. Later, they intermingled with Nilotic, Hamitic and finally Semitic peoples migrating from across Africa and Arabia. By around 2000 BC, close contacts had been established with the people of the Nubian lowlands to the west and those from the Tihama coast of southern Arabia to the east. Some ruins in Eritrea are thought to date from the pre-Aksumite Civilisation.

AKSUMITE CIVILISATION

Around the 4th century BC, the powerful kingdom of Aksum began to develop. Situated in Tigray, in the north of modern Ethiopia (around 50km from present-day Eritrea), Aksum lay just 170km from the Red Sea. Much foreign trade – on which Aksum's prosperity depended – was seaborne, and came to be handled by the ancient port of Adulis in Eritrea.

On the way to Adulis (a 12- to 15-day journey from Aksum) many exports, including rhinoceros horn, gold, hippopotamus hide, slaves, apes and particularly

ERITREA

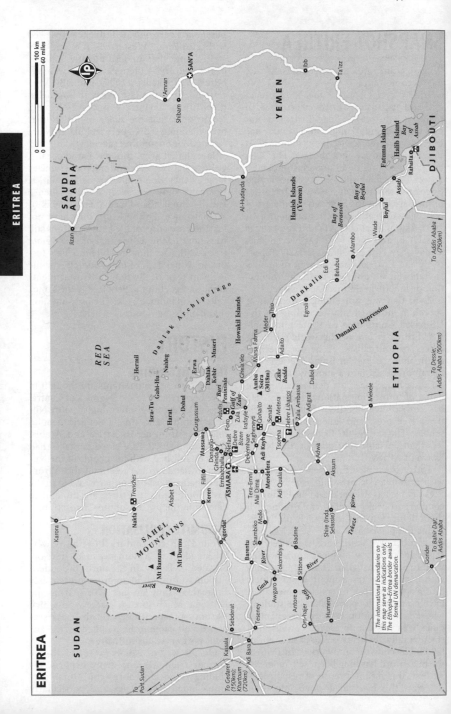

The international boundaries on this map serve as indications only. The Ethiopia-Eritrea border awaits formal UN demarcation.

FAST FACTS

- Population: 4.6 million (estimated)
- Area: 124,320 sq km
- GNI per capita: US$180
- Average life expectancy: 51 years (men), 55 years (women)
- Number of UN staff deployed at the Ethiopian border: 3500
- Number of Eritreans in uniform (male and female): 300,000
- Fine if you're caught changing money on the black market: Nfa2,000,000
- Number of journalists detained without charge: 14
- Average monthly income of a hotel receptionist: US$40
- Thickness of froth in a *macchiato*: about 1.5cm (estimated)

ivory, passed through Eritrean towns, including Koloe (thought to be present-day Qohaito in the south). Some of the goods exported were Eritrean in origin, including obsidian, a black volcanic rock.

ARRIVAL OF CHRISTIANITY

Christianity was undoubtedly the most significant 'import' into the region during the Aksumite period. According to the Byzantine ecclesiastical historian Rufinus, the religion was brought to the region by accident when Christian Syrian merchants travelling home from India were shipwrecked on the Red Sea coast. Whatever its origin, by the 4th century AD Christianity had become the Aksumite state religion. The new religion had a profound impact on Eritrea's culture, influencing much of the country's art and literature.

THE RISE OF ISLAM & THE DECLINE OF AKSUM

Islam, the arrival of which coincided with Christian Aksum's decline in the 7th century, was the other great influence on the region. Though not directly responsible for the empire's collapse, the expansion of the religion was concomitant with the increasing power of the Arabs, who fast became the new masters of the Red Sea. Aksum's

commercial domination of the region was over.

Islam made the greatest inroads in the Dahlak Islands. Muslims traders also settled in nearby Massawa on the mainland.

Aksumite authority had long been challenged by other forces too, with incursions, attacks, rebellions and even mass migration by neighbouring tribes, particularly the Beja tribe, a Cushitic people originating from present-day Sudan.

After the settlement of the Beja in the interior of the country, and the Arabs on the coast, the Ethiopians were unable to recover the influence the Aksumites had held over the region for another thousand years.

THE TURKISH & EGYPTIAN IMPRINTS

The Turks first arrived in the Red Sea at the beginning of the 16th century. For the next 300 years (with a few short-lived intervals) the coast, including the port of Massawa, belonged to the Ottomans.

By the middle of the 19th century, new powers were casting covetous eyes over the region. The Egyptians, under Ali Pasha (Mohammed Ali), invaded modern-day Sudan and occupied parts of Ethiopia. Soon after, the western lowlands of modern-day Eritrea were also taken, including the port of Massawa.

Under threat, the Ethiopian Emperor Yohannes eventually forced a battle. In 1875 at Ghundet, near Adi Quala in modern-day southern Eritrea, and later at Gura, near Dekemhare, Yohannes inflicted resounding defeats on the Egyptian armies.

The power vacuum left by the departing Egyptians was soon to be filled by yet another meddling foreign power – Italy.

THE RED, RED SEA

Eritrea is said to derive its name from the Greek word erythrea, meaning 'red'. It was coined from the famous Periplus of the Erythrean Sea, a trade or shipping manual written by a Greek-speaking Egyptian sailor or merchant around the 1st century AD. The erythrea (or 'red of the sea') is so named because the water turns a vermilion shade as a result of newly spored algae during certain periods.

ERITREA

THE LAND OF PUNT

Since the dawn of history, the Horn of Africa has been a source of fascination for the outside world. Lying on the African side of the Red Sea, the area provided a crucial trade link, connecting Egypt and the Mediterranean with India and the Far East.

However, this wasn't the region's only asset. Known to the Egyptian Pharaohs as 'Land of the Gods' or 'Land of Punt' (together with what is now Djibouti), the area yielded a seemingly limitless supply of precious commodities. Gold, frankincense, myrrh, slaves, ostrich feathers, antelopes, ebony and ivory were all loaded onto foreign ships jostling in the region's ports.

Egyptian accounts of this land accorded it almost legendary status and provide the earliest glimpse of the region. Expeditions are thought to date from the First or Second Dynasties (2920–2649 BC).

For scholars today, the Land of Punt retains its legendary aura. Thought to lie somewhere between the lands to the south of Nubia and those just north of present-day Somalia, no-one knows its exact location. Eritrea, Djibouti, Yemen, Somalia and even Kenya have all made claims to the title of the Land of Punt.

THE ITALIANS STEP IN

During the partition of the continent by the competing European powers in the second half of the 19th century, France grabbed Djibouti (which then became known as French Somaliland) and Britain snatched Aden in Yemen, as well as a stretch of Somali coastline. Italy wasn't going to miss out on a piece of the pie. Italian colonisation started in 1869 near Assab. In 1885 the Italians occupied Massawa.

Alarmed by further expansion and the threat it posed to his kingdom, Yohannes challenged the Italians, but was killed in battle with the Mahadists (Sudanese) in 1889.

As the struggle against the Mahadists preoccupied the Ethiopians, the Italians were left to get on with the realisation of their military ambitions.

Relations were at first good with the new Ethiopian emperor, Menelik, and in 1889 the Treaty of Wechale was signed. In exchange for granting Italy the region that was to later become Eritrea, the Italians recognised Menelik's sovereignty and gave him the right to import arms freely though Ethiopia. However, relations began to sour a few years later.

Towards the end of 1889 the Italians turned their attention to the south. In 1890, they took Adwa and Mekele in Ethiopian territory, as well as Aksum and Adigrat a few years later.

Following the Battle of Adwa in 1896, when the Ethiopians resoundingly defeated the Italian armies (for more details, see p143), new international boundaries were drawn up: Ethiopia remained independent and Eritrea became, for the first time, a separate territory – and an Italian colony.

ITALIAN RULE

Of all Italy's colonies (Eritrea, Libya and Italian Somaliland), Eritrea was considered the jewel in the crown. Apart from providing a strategic base for imperial ambitions (particularly against Ethiopia), it boasted vital access to the Red Sea, as well as potential for mineral and agricultural exploitation. For this reason, much effort was put into industrialising the little country, and major schemes began to be developed, including the building of the great railway between Massawa and Asmara in 1909 (which was later extended to Keren) and the construction of a national network of roads.

By the end of the 1930s, Eritrea was one of the most highly industrialised colonies in Africa. By 1930 Massawa had become the largest port on the East African coast.

The Italians initially governed Eritrea indirectly through local chieftains. Later, a series of provinces was created, administered by a large body of Italian civil servants, headed by a governor.

BRITISH TAKEOVER

In May 1936 Italy avenged itself for the defeat at Adwa and triumphed over the Ethiopians. In 1940, with the outbreak of WWII, Italy declared war on Britain, and soon became embroiled in conflicts in what was then Anglo-Egyptian Sudan. Though initially successful, Italian campaigns in this area were soon repulsed by reinforced British armies.

Soon British forces were giving chase to the Italians, pursuing them into Eritrea, and capturing Agordat. The year 1941 marked a turning point: the British took the strategically important town of Keren before defeating the Italians in Asmara. The colony became an Administration of the British.

The British attempted to maintain the status quo in the territory largely due to practical constraints. They left in place the old Italian administration, but the colony inevitably sank into a state of demoralisation and decline. When the course of WWII changed, the territory lost its strategic importance and in 1945 the British began a slow withdrawal.

By 1946 the country was in trouble. The economy was floundering, unemployment was soaring, and unrest was brewing.

ARRANGED MARRIAGE WITH ETHIOPIA

In 1948 Eritrea's fate was pondered by a fcommission consisting of the UK, the USA, France and the Soviet Union. Unable to reach a decision, the commission passed the issue on to the UN's General Assembly.

In 1947 a commission of inquiry found the population divided into three main factions: pro-Ethiopian Unionists (mainly Christian), anti-Unionists (mainly Muslims

in favour of a Muslim League) and members of a Pro-Italia party (many of them Italian pensioners). The commissioners, whose findings reflected the political interests of their respective governments, produced totally different conclusions and recommendations.

In 1950 the very contentious Resolution 390 A (V) was passed. Eritrea became Ethiopia's 14th province and disappeared from the map of Africa.

UNMATCHED COUPLE

This 'shotgun wedding', as it has been described, between Eritrea and Ethiopia was never a happy one. Little by little, Ethiopia began to exert an ever-tighter hold over Eritrea, as both industry and political control were shifted to Ethiopia's capital, Addis Ababa. The Eritrean economy stagnated and the province's autonomy dwindled. Eritrean politicians and leaders were soon ousted, Ethiopian Amharic replaced Tigrinya as the official language in schools, and protests against the regime were suppressed with brutality.

The repeated appeals by the Eritrean people to the UN fell on deaf ears. With the start of the Cold War in the 1950s, the Americans had set their sights on establishing a communications centre in Asmara. When, in the early 1960s, Ethiopia formally annexed Eritrea in violation of international law, Cold War politics ensured that both the US and the UN kept silent.

With no recourse to the international community, the frustration of the Eritrean people grew. In 1961 the inevitable happened. In the little town of Amba Adal in the western lowlands, a small group of men led by Hamid Idriss Awate assailed one of the much-resented Ethiopian police stations and stole some pistols. The fight for independence had begun.

TIME TO DIVORCE

The first resistance movements on the scene included the ELM (Eritrean Liberation Movement), the (Christian) People's Liberation Front (PLF), and the (Muslim) Eritrean Liberation Front (ELF). From the latter two, a splinter group emerged, the Eritrean People's Liberation Front (EPLF), which called for social revolution as well as national independence. It was only after

---

ITALIAN APARTHEID

From 1922 to 1941 a system of discrimination existed in Eritrea and Ethiopia that was remarkably similar to the apartheid system of South Africa.

Local and Italian children were educated at different schools; non-Italian adults were prevented from learning basic skills or professions; on buses and in cinemas, Italian passengers sat in the front, whereas locals were obliged to sit at the back; marriage between Italians and locals was forbidden by law, with a punishment of up to five years in prison for offenders.

Thousands of locals were evicted from their houses and resettled in reservations far from where the Italians lived. The best agricultural land was seized, rent for town houses was not paid and there were continual abuses of law; locals were punished, fined and even killed without cause.

ERITREA

A LONG, LONG WAR

The Struggle, as resistance to Ethiopian rule became popularly known, was a major event in the history of the Horn. Lasting for 30 years, it shaped – physically and psychologically – the Eritrean nation and its people. For the first time, a real sense of national identity was forged.

But the price of Eritrea's freedom was high. The war wrecked the country's infrastructure and economy, cost 65,000 lives and drove at least a third of the population into exile. It was not a story of vast armies, brilliant leadership and sweeping conquests. For three decades, a tiny guerrilla force (which numbered at most 40,000 during its last days) was able to thwart the might of a country 10 times its size, which was backed by two superpowers and had all the modern weaponry of the 20th century.

Initially a ragbag bandit force, the resistance fighters operated in tightly organised cells, taught their soldiers history, philosophy, political economy and to read and write, as well as guerrilla tactics. Equality of all people was advocated; soldiers had to respect the gender (many soldiers were women), ethnic group, religion and race of their fellow fighters.

In response to the devastating blanket bombing inflicted by the Ethiopians, whole villages were constructed underground, with schools, hospitals, factories, printing presses, mills, pharmacies, workshops and entertainment halls. The remains of these 'towns' can be seen today in the village of Nakfa in the north of Eritrea.

---

periods of bloody civil war and the defeat of the ELF in 1981, that the EPLF emerged as the leader of unified forces.

Nevertheless, the resistance continued to make progress, and in 1978 the Eritreans were on the brink of winning back their country. However, just on the point of victory, yet another foreign power decided to intervene.

In 1974 Colonel Mengistu Haile Mariam, a communist dictator, had come to power in Ethiopia. Three years later the Soviet Union began to arm his troops. In the face of massive aerial bombardment and an army bristling with modern weaponry, the EPLF was obliged to retreat. The famous 'Strategic Withdrawal', as it is known, later proved to be crucial to the movement's survival.

Eight major offensives were carried out against the Eritrean fighters from 1978 to 1986, all of which were repulsed. From 1988 the EPLF began to inflict major losses on the Ethiopian army, capturing first its northern headquarters in Afabet, then the large highland town of Keren. In 1990, amid some of the fiercest fighting of the war, the EPLF took the strategically important port of Massawa.

By this time, however, Mengistu's regime was threatened from within, and civil war had broken out in Ethiopia. In 1991 Mengistu was overthrown and fled to Zimbabwe. His 140,000 Ethiopian troops laid down their weapons and ran. The EPLF walked into Asmara without having to fire a single bullet.

FREEDOM, AT LAST!

In April 1993 the Provisional Government of Eritrea held a referendum on Eritrean independence. More than 99.81% of voters opted for full Eritrean sovereignty, and on 24 May 1993 independence was declared. Eritrea was back on the African map.

In early 1994 the EPLF dissolved itself and re-formed as the People's Front for Democracy and Justice (PFDJ) under the chairmanship of the head of state, President Isaias Afewerki. Some members of the old ELF were also invited to join the team.

After the war, the little nation worked hard to rebuild its infrastructure, repair the economy and improve conditions for its people. Wide-ranging laws, policies and constitutional rights were drawn up, from protection of the environment and positive discrimination towards people with disabilities at work, to the rights of women and the fight against AIDS. Eritrea was also at pains to establish good international relations with, among others, Ethiopia, the Gulf States, Asia, the USA and Europe.

However, this progress was seriously undermined in 1998, when war broke out with Ethiopia (see p39 for details).

ERITREA TODAY

It's still more or less the same (sad) story. The rancour between Eritrea and Ethiopia has not waned. The tensions peaked again late 2005, when the two enemies were poised on the brink of a new war. Frustrated by not seeing the enforcement of the Boundary Commission ruling (see p40), Eritreans shifted troops to the border and banned the UN from overflying its territory. The psychological war between the two countries is ongoing. For the tenacious Eritrean leaders, the enforcement of the Boundary Commission is a matter of life and death and they made it clear they would not compromise. Meanwhile, Eritrea's isolation is mounting, as is internal resentment against their despotic president, Isaias Afewerki. While Ethiopia has managed to nurture its ties with Western countries, the intransigent Eritrean government has lost the support of the international community and is growing notoriously dictatorial, threatening to expel the UN peacekeepers who are deployed on the border. Freedom of press and speech is nonexistent and any Western agency suspected of criticism against the regime runs the risk of being ousted.

The economy is in tatters, with food and oil shortages. Mass conscription has deprived many industries of manpower and there is no longer a private sector. In January 2005 the government introduced a currency declaration form to control all transactions, deterring foreign investments. Remittances from diaspora Eritreans is virtually the only source of income. As if that was not enough, for the four consecutive years to 2006, drought wreaked havoc on agricultural resources.

It has become vital to find a solution to the devastating conflict with Ethiopia and to come to terms with the stalemate. There were some signs of hope when this book went to print. The UN had just extended the stay of the UN Mission in Ethiopia and Eritrea (UNMEE). Whether it's enough to foster sustainable peace is anybody's guess.

THE CULTURE

THE NATIONAL PSYCHE

Who are the Eritreans? It's a question few foreigners would be able to answer with any confidence. Eritreans remains something of an enigma to most Westerners. All things considered, the lack of tangible international image and stereotypes about Eritrea and its people is a chance rather than a drawback.

Eritreans are different in temperament from their neighbours (which partly explains the bitter relations between the two countries). 'Rather die than surrender', could be their motto. Years of invasion have created a siege mentality and a sense of isolation. A deep-seated desire to protect the integrity of their nation, founded understandably by historic circumstances, has led to an attitude of self-preservation and, one would say, mulishness. Eritreans have a fierce pride in their own history, and their decades of struggle against the Ethiopians. Though impoverished, the nation has from the outset shown self-reliance, vigour and independence. Eritreans are not about to become anyone's vassal and this stoic attitude has elicited both passionate admiration and furious exasperation from visitors, aid workers and international organisations alike. Their ability to endure hardships without moaning – to a masochistic degree – is notorious. Tradition and a deep-rooted attachment to the land play an integral part in the national psyche too.

You'll soon realise that Eritreans are a withdrawn people who have to be coaxed into friendship, but if you succeed you'll discover a steely strength hidden beneath their stoic façade. Initially indifferent to strangers (at least by comparison with other African nations), Eritreans may appear somewhat taciturn at first meeting, but once the ice has broken you will find intense friendships. This guarded nature is hardly surprising, however, considering the country's history of oppression. This does not mean that they are standoffish or cold. Towards the traveller, Eritreans show exceptional politeness and hospitality. The inhospitability of the countryside in which most of the people live may well contribute to this keen sense of the importance of hospitality.

LIFESTYLE

The contrast in lifestyle between Asmara and elsewhere is stark. Asmara is a city with allure, where people take the art of living seriously no matter the state of the economy. Asmarans are notoriously *bon vivants* and take the dolce vita very seriously – a legacy of the Italian era. Nobody would miss

ERITREA

ERITREA

the daily ritual of a cup of *macchiato* at a pavement terrace during the evening *passeggiata*. Then there is the rest of Eritrea: a monochrome mix of provincial town and rural landscape, where poverty is about the only prevalent excess.

Sadly, both the economic turmoil and the hard line followed by Isaias' government have severely impacted lifestyles and standards of living. Scratch the surface and you'll soon realise how hard Eritreans are hit by the economic crisis and lack of freedom. Life's a struggle for many Eritreans. Households have been feeling the financial downturn in recent times, with the cost of commodities having more than doubled in three years. Eating out and holidays have been curtailed radically, and waiting queues in front of state-controlled stores are now a common sight in Asmara. Food rationing has become a fact of life. A certain weariness can be felt. Diaspora Eritreans who returned to the country and have invested in the country are in a bit less of a predicament – they understandably enjoy a better quality of life.

In a country where people have lost faith in their government, the family remains one pillar of society on which Eritreans continue to depend. Family ties remain fiercely strong. Religious occasions and public holidays are vigorously celebrated, as are more personal, family events, such as weddings.

POPULATION

The Eritrean people are a highlight of the country. The population is estimated to be 4.6 million. Eritrea might be a tiddler of a country by Africa's standards, but it hosts a kaleidoscopic range of tribes. Cultural diversity forms an integral part of the social fabric. There are nine ethnic groups, each with their own language and customs. It is estimated that about 1000 Italians live in Eritrea, mostly in Asmara.

Approximately 35% of the population are nomadic or seminomadic. About one million Eritreans live abroad.

Tigrinya ትግርኛ

The Tigrinya make up approximately 50% of the Eritrean population and inhabit the densely populated central highlands, extending over the provinces of Dubub, Central and the area of Adi Keyh. They are largely Orthodox Christian, with just a small minority of Muslims who are known as Jiberti. The very distinct plaited hairstyle of the women has for centuries been depicted in local art.

Their language, Tigrinya, is one of the country's official languages.

Tigré ትግሬ

The Tigré make up about 30% of the population, and inhabit the northern lowlands, from the Sudanese frontier to the western limits of the Danakil.

A heterogeneous people, the Tigré are divided into groups and clans. Most Tigreans are Muslim, and they are both sedentary and nomadic.

Tigrean society is traditionally hierarchical, with a small aristocracy known as *shemagille* ruling the masses. When the village leader dies, his power passes to his offspring.

Tigrean oral literature is rich. Fables, riddles, poetry, funeral dirges, war cries and supernatural stories colour the different elements of Tigrean life. The Tigré are also known for their love of singing and dancing, usually to the accompaniment of a drum and a guitar.

Saho ሳሆ

The Saho make up 5% of the population. They inhabit the coast and the hinterland south of Asmara and Massawa. Towards the end of April, when the rains stop in the lowlands, many Saho leave the coastal area and trek with their livestock up to the highlands near Adi Keyh. When the rains stop in September, they return for the wet season on the coastal lowlands.

WILES & WAYS

For weddings, religious festivals and special occasions, Tigré and Tigrinya women love to get their hair done. The mass of tiny plaits go right up to the scalp, and can take a whole morning to prepare.

Married women can additionally have the palms of their hands and their feet tattooed with curvilinear patterns of henna. Fashionable teenagers prefer to have their gums tattooed. Pricked until they bleed, the gums are rubbed with charcoal. The resulting blue colour sets off a dazzling set of teeth, and is considered a mark of great beauty.

FIGHTER'S SALUTE

Shoulder contact is used for greeting in Eritrea. When two male friends meet, they clasp hands, then lean towards one another and hit each other's right shoulders, usually three times. This sign of great comradeship is called the 'fighter's salute'. As a foreigner, you're not supposed to try this type of greeting – it's pretty hard to imitate, and you would probably look awkward!

The Saho people are predominantly Muslim, and feelings of ethnic identity are less strong among them than other groups. Known as great pastoralists, they fought for centuries with the highlanders over the pastures of the mountains. Today they often tend other people's cattle, including those of the Tigrinya, in exchange for grain. Many Saho children (up to the age of 16) wear little leather pouches around their neck, which are full of herbs and spices to ward off evil spirits.

Some Saho are farmers who have settled in the highlands south of the country. Honey is an important part of the Saho diet and they are known as good beekeepers. In the past they were also reputed as warriors, and were often enlisted to escort trade caravans between central Ethiopia and the port of Massawa.

Afar አፋር

The Eritrean Afars, also known as the Danakils, make up 5% of the population and inhabit the long coastal strip stretching from the Gulf of Zula into Djibouti. Predominantly nomadic pastoralists, the Afar people are Muslim, though elements of ancient ancestor-worship still persist.

Since early times the Afar territory has been divided into kingdoms and ruled by individual sultans who have always remained fiercely independent of any foreign power.

The sole inhabitants of one of the most inhospitable regions on Earth, the Afars have acquired a fearsome reputation among Western travellers and explorers during the last 100 years.

The men still carry the famous *jile* (curved knife), and some file their teeth to points. Afar oral literature reveals a high esteem for military prowess, with a whole repertoire of war chants. See also the boxed text, p222.

Hedareb ሃዳረብ

The Hedareb, along with their 'brother' tribes the Beni Amer and Beja, make up 2.5% of the population, and inhabit the northwestern valleys of Eritrea, straddling the border with Sudan.

Most Hedarebs are nomadic and travel great distances in search of pasture. They are Cushitic in origin (probably directly descended from the ancient Beja tribe) and speak mainly Tigré and an ancient Beja language (though this is in decline, as it is replaced by more dominant languages).

The Beni Amer are a strongly patriarchal, socially stratified, almost feudal people. Their skills as camel drivers and rearers are legendary. Many of the men scarify their cheeks with three short, vertical strokes – the Italians called them the '111 tribe'.

Bilen ብሌን

The Bilen inhabit the environs of Keren and make up approximately 2% of the population. Cushitic in origin, the Bilen are either settled Christian farmers or Muslim cattle rearers.

Bilen traditional society is organised into kinship groups. The women are known for their brightly coloured clothes and their gold, silver or copper nose rings which indicate their means and social status. Like the Beja language, Bilen is slowly being replaced by Tigré, Tigrinya and Arabic, due to intermarriage, economic interactions and because Arabic is taught in local schools. Henna tattoos that mimic diamond necklaces or little freckles are fashionable among the women.

Kunama ኩናማ

The Kunama inhabit the Gash Barka province in the southwestern corner of Eritrea, close to the Ethiopian and Sudanese border, and make up 2% of the population. Barentu is their 'capital'. The Kunama are Nilotic in origin, and very dark skinned. They are the original inhabitants of the region.

A few Kunama are Muslim, some are Christian, but the great majority are animist. According to their beliefs, the higher divinity, Anna, created the sky and the earth

ERITREA

but is largely indifferent to human fate. The spirits, by contrast, must be placated before every event, even ploughing a field.

The Kunanma only recognise the authority of the elders and the village assemblies. The community is closely knit, and many educated Kunama abandon the city to return to their traditional home.

Land is often farmed cooperatively and, after the work is finished, the village unites to celebrate with feasting and dancing. The Kunama are known for their dances, and have developed more than 25 dance forms, often re-enacting great historical events or victories.

Nara ናራ

The Nara, also known as the Baria, make up about 1.5% of the population and inhabit the Barka Valley near the Sudanese border. Along with the Kunama, they are the only Nilotic Eritrean tribe, and are mainly Muslim. They have three characteristic vertical scarifications on the cheeks, similar to those of the Hedareb.

The Nara practice mixed farming and share many customs with their neighbours, the Kunama. In the past, skirmishes and raids from other tribes have forced many of the people to flee.

Rashaida ራሻ ኢዳ

The Rashaida are the only true Eritrean nomads. Making up just 0.5% of the population, they roam the northern coasts of Eritrea and Sudan, as well as the southern reaches of the Nubian desert. Like their neighbours, the Beja (related to the Hedareb), they live by raising cattle and are Muslim.

The Rashaida were the last of the Semitic people to arrive in Eritrea in the middle of the 19th century. Their language is Arabic.

The magnificent Rashaida women are famous for their black-and-red geometrically patterned dresses, and their burkas (long, heavy veils) elaborately embroidered with silver thread, beads and sometimes seed pearls.

The Rashaida are known for their great pride; marriage is only permitted within their own clan. They are expert goat and cattle rearers, as well as merchants and traders along the Red Sea coasts.

SPORT

Bicycle races take place in many of the larger towns. Streets are cordoned off, and everyone comes to watch. The most popular cycling event is the annual Giro d'Eritrea, a 10-day race across the country. It is held in February or March.

MULTICULTURALISM

Eritrea is surprisingly and refreshingly multicultural. Since the beginning of time, Eritrea has attracted migrants, merchants and meddlesome foreign powers. Today these influences are reflected in the country's diverse ethnic population. With nine ethnic groups and languages as well as several religions, Eritrea is a model of cultural diversity. During the war, religious, ethnic and gender differences were set aside in favour of unity against the Ethiopians. In Asmara, the Great Mosque, the Orthodox church, the Catholic cathedral and the synagogue stand placidly in the same precinct. Intermarriage is common and there's no racial ghetto. The government ensures that each ethnic group has a voice in the decision-making process.

There's no immigration as such but diaspora Eritreans bring a refreshing influx of outside influence. More painful is the situation of the Eritrean returnees, from Sudan and Ethiopia, who live in refugee camps on the outskirts of frontier towns.

MEDIA

Freedom of the press in Eritrea? Dream on! There is no press freedom. Period. Isaias Afewerki has been battling the press for years, forcing many independent papers out of business and jailing free-speaking journalists without charge. More than 10 independent journalists have 'disappeared' these last years. The state-run Haddas Eritrea is the only newspaper in the country, often featuring headlines bellowing how the country is following the right path and how perverse the Ethiopian leaders are.

Surprisingly, there's no ban on satellite TV. The few Eritreans who can afford a satellite dish can tune to BBC, CNN or Euronews to get a more balanced vision of reality.

RELIGION

The population of Eritrea is almost equally divided between Christians and Muslims. Christians are primarily Orthodox; the

Eritrean Orthodox church has its roots in the Ethiopian one (see p50). There are also small numbers of Roman Catholics and Protestants, as a result of missionary activity. The Muslims are primarily Sunnis, with a Sufi minority.

Roughly speaking, the agriculturalist Orthodox Christians inhabit the highland region and the Muslims are concentrated in the lowlands, the coastal areas and towards the Sudanese border. Some animists inhabit the southwestern lowlands.

There are at least 18 monasteries in Eritrea. Following the raids of the famous 16th-century Muslim leader, Mohammed Gragn the Left-Handed, almost all of them were safely tucked away in very remote and inaccessible places. Three of the oldest and most important are Debre Bizen (near Nefasit), Debre Libanos (near Senafe) and Debre Sina (near Keren).

WOMEN IN ERITREA

Women enjoy far greater equality in Eritrea than in most other African countries. This refreshingly liberal attitude has been won by Eritrea's women, who themselves contributed more than one-third of troops in both the recent wars against Ethiopia. In Asmara, they can be seen wearing the latest fashion clothes. However, Eritrea remains a deeply conservative country and the 'double liberation' (for their country and for their gender) expected after independence has not been as forthcoming as some had hoped. In rural areas, prejudices remain deeply rooted.

In the towns, several active, well-organised women's groups have sprung up in the last few years.

The status of women is something to behold. Eritrean women have guaranteed representation in Parliament. They enjoy their own national holiday, equal property rights and the right to divorce, and also have equal rights to the custody of their children in any settlement. Eritrean women have attitude. In Asmara, women who were soldiers during the war can be seen wearing old jeans and T-shirts.

ARTS
Dance

Dance plays a very important social role in Eritrea. It marks the major events of life, such as births and marriages, and is used in celebrating special occasions and religious festivals. Dances traditionally permitted young girls and boys to meet, and warriors to show off their prowess.

The dances of the Kunama and Hedareb are particularly exuberant.

Music

Traditional musical instruments of Eritrea have their roots in Ethiopia. They include the *krar* and *wata*, both string instruments; the *shambko*, a type of flute; and the *embilta*, a wind instrument.

Though sharing some similarities, each of the nine ethnic groups has its own distinct melodies and rhythms.

Atewebrhan Segid is considered one of the leading traditional musicians and singers in Eritrea today. The famous Eritrean singer Yemane Gebremichael, known as the 'father of the poor', died in 1997.

Others singers, both traditional and modern, include Faytinga, Helen Meles, Berekhet Mengisteab, Osman Abdel Rahim, Idriss Mohammed Ali, Teklé Kiflemariam, Tesfay Mehari and Samuel Berhane.

Literature

Eritrea's oral literature – in the form of folk tales, ballads, poetry, laudations etc – is rich and diverse (for more on oral literature, see p55).

The Italians imposed their own language and literature (and Latin alphabet) on the country, as did the British and Ethiopians. Woldeab Woldemariam is especially venerated for his part in fighting the suppression of the local languages. His *Zanta Quedamot* is a collection of children's stories designed to make the Tigrinyan alphabet more easily understood by children.

During the Struggle for Independence from Ethiopia, writing in the vernacular was encouraged through such publications as the fighters' magazine *Mahta* (Spark) and *Fitewrrari* (Avant Garde).

Today Eritrean writers are publishing and producing increasing amounts of poetry, fiction and drama (mainly in Tigrinya and Arabic). Current novelists include Alemseged Tesfai, Solomon Drar and Bruk Habtemikael.

In recent times, the nine languages of the nine ethnic groups have adopted written scripts: six have adopted the Latin alphabet and one Arabic. The other two, Tigrinya and Tigré, have always used the Ge'ez-derived script of ancient Aksum.

Architecture

Eritrean vernacular architecture depends on both its ethnic and geographical origin. In the cool highlands, the traditional house is the *hidmo*. Built on a rectangular plan, the house is constructed with dry-stone walls topped with a thick, earthen roof, supported both inside and out with strong wooden pillars.

In the lowlands, where warmth is less of a concern, people traditionally live in huts. Depending on the ethnic group, the hut walls are made of adobe (sun-dried brick), wood or stone, and have thatched roofs.

In Asmara and many of the larger towns, such as Keren, Massawa and Dekemhare, the colonial heritage can be seen in the Italian-style buildings (see the boxed text, p317). Many of them, in Asmara and Massawa in particular, are remarkable historical and artistic pieces, but most of them are in urgent need of restoration. There are plans to protect and restore some of the buildings.

Painting

The country's ancient Orthodox church has long provided an outlet for painting. Most church walls are painted with colourful and dramatic murals. Canvas and parchment manuscripts, some several hundred years old, are illustrated with delightful and sometimes very beautiful biblical scenes.

Painters in various media today include Mikael Adonai, Tesfay Gebremikael, Ygzaw Mikael and Giorgis Abraham.

Theatre

Eritrean theatre is an ancient art and, like painting, has its roots in Ethiopia. Traditionally, it was staged to celebrate religious festivals, and involved music, singing, dance and acting.

During federation with Ethiopia, censorship was one of the principal constraints restricting the development of local theatre. With the emergence of the EPLF in the 1980s, new works began to appear. One of them, *The Other War* by Alemseged Tesfay, has appeared in an English anthology of contemporary African plays.

ENVIRONMENT

THE LAND

With a land area of 124,320 sq km, Eritrea is about the size of England or the state of Pennsylvania in the USA. The coastline measures around 1000km and off it there are over 350 islands.

Eritrea has three main geographical zones: the eastern escarpment and coastal plains, the central highland region, and the western lowlands.

The eastern zone consists of desert or semidesert, with little arable land. The people inhabiting the region are generally nomadic pastoralists or fishing communities.

The northern end of the East African Rift Valley opens into the infamous Dankalia region in the east, one of the hottest places on Earth. This semidesert lies in a depression up to 120m below sea level, and is home to several salt lakes.

The central highland region is more fertile, and it is intensively cultivated by farming communities.

The western lowlands, lying between Keren and the Sudanese border, are watered by the Gash and Barka Rivers. Farming is practised, but less intensively than in the highlands.

WILDLIFE

In the past, Eritrea was home to a large range of animals, including buffaloes, cheetahs, elephants, giraffes and lions. With the loss of the forests and the decades of civil war, many of these animals have disappeared.

Animals

BIRDS

Eritrea's range of habitats is surprisingly diverse, and its birdlife is correspondingly rich. A total of 537 species of birds have been recorded, including the rare blue sawwing.

The isolated and uninhabited Dahlak Islands, and the rich feeding grounds that surround them, attract large numbers of nesting sea birds from all over the Red Sea (and from the Mediterranean and the Gulf). Some 109 species have been recorded on the islands, including the Arabian bustard and osprey.

Eritrea also lies within a popular migratory fly way. Hundreds of species of wintering and migratory coastal and sea birds can be seen crossing between the continents of Africa and Arabia.

On the Buri Peninsula, the ostrich and Arabian bustard are commonly seen. Sea birds include gulls, terns, boobies and, on the coastline and islands, many species of wader.

In the lush, evergreen, tropical forests in the Semenawi Bahri area northeast of Asmara, birdlife is particularly abundant. Species include the near-endemic white-cheeked turaco and the Narina trogon.

MAMMALS & REPTILES
Mammals commonly seen today include the Abyssinian hare, African wildcat, black-backed jackal, common jackal, genet, ground squirrel, pale fox, Soemmering's gazelle and warthog. Primates include the vervet monkey and hamadryas baboon.

Lions, greater kudus and Tora hartebeests are said to inhabit the mountains of Gash-Barka province, north of Barentu. On the Buri Peninsula, dik-diks and dorcas gazelles can be seen. In the area between Omhajer and Antore, in the country's southwest, Eritrea's last population of elephants is said to roam around – buy a lottery ticket if you happen to spot one!

MARINE LIFE
Major Eritrean marine ecosystems include the coral reefs, sea-grass beds and mangrove forests.

In the Red Sea at least 350 species of coral are known to exist. Eritrea's coral is mainly found as 'patch reef' extending from the surface to a depth of around 15m to 18m; below this, coral development tends to be limited.

Eritrea is home to at least three species of mangrove, despite its location on the northerly limits of the mangrove ranges. They are found along the coast and on the Dahlak Islands.

Five species of marine turtle have been recorded. Most common are the green and hawksbill turtles. The green turtle is quite often spotted around the Dahlak Islands, as are dolphins and sharks.

The Eritrean and Sudanese coastlines are thought to be home to at least half the 4000 to 5000 endangered dugongs (sea cows) estimated to inhabit the Red Sea.

Collecting coral, shells or plant life from the beaches and waters is forbidden in the Dahlak Islands.

ENDANGERED SPECIES
The greatest threat to wildlife in Eritrea is the loss or degradation of habitat. Almost all of Eritrea's animals (with the exception of the baboon, ostrich and gazelle) are considered endangered within the country's own national perimeters. Internationally, the Nubian ibex (which has probably disappeared from Eritrea) is considered dangerously threatened. In recent years, concerns have also been expressed for Eritrea's elephant populations. A century ago, significant numbers inhabited Gash-Barka province. Today it is thought that no more than 100 elephants exist.

Plants
The landscape of eastern Eritrea is characterised by acacia woodland (several species), brushland and thicket, semidesert vegetation, riverine vegetation and mangrove swamp.

The highland region is dominated by an indigenous species of juniper *(Juniperus procera)* and wild olive *(Olea africana)*. Various species of acacia are also found. In degraded areas, various eucalyptus plantations have been established.

The Semenawi Bahri (Green Belt area) is in the northeast of Asmara, around the village and valleys of Filfil. It contains the last remnant of mixed, evergreen, tropical woodland in Eritrea. At an elevation of between 900m and 2400m, it stretches north to south for about 20km.

The landscape to the west is made up mainly of woodland savanna, brushland, thicket and grasslands *(Aristida)*. Around 50% of the firewood needed for the population of Asmara is collected from this area, resulting in serious deforestation. Species include the doum palm *(Hyphaenea thebaica)*, found particularly along the Barka River, eucalypts and various acacia species. Other species include baobab *(Adansonia digitata)*, toothbrush tree *(Salvadora persica)* and tamarisk *(Tamarix aphylla)*.

Endangered species of flora include the eucalypt *(Boswellia papyrifera)*, the baobab and the tamarind tree *(Tamarindus indica)*.

ERITREA

RESPONSIBLE TRAVEL: ENVIRONMENT & CULTURE

The country receives relatively few tourists, so their impact on the environment has so far been fairly minimal.

The beautiful coral reefs around the Dahlak Islands are perhaps most vulnerable to damage, and in addition receive more tourists (local and foreign) than many areas.

Eritrea is a party to Cites (Convention on International Trade in Endangered Species of Wild Fauna and Flora), and it is therefore illegal to export any endangered species or their products, such as turtle or ivory. You may find turtle and elephant souvenirs in shops (particularly in Asmara). It's best to avoid these, as all species of marine turtle are currently threatened. Coral and shell collection is now discouraged too.

Try to resist the temptation to buy any genuinely old artefacts, such as manuscripts, scrolls and Bibles, found in some of the shops in the capital. Eritrea has already lost a huge amount of its heritage, particularly during the Italian era. Such exports will soon be illegal anyway.

Water is an extremely precious and scarce resource in Eritrea. Take care not to waste it.

NATIONAL PARKS

There are no formal national reserves or parks in Eritrea, although their establishment is expected sooner or later.

There are no marine parks either, but several islands in the Dahlak group have been proposed, and research has been conducted to study the fragile ecosystem of these islands in greater detail.

ENVIRONMENTAL ISSUES

Eritrea's environment has been greatly impacted by war, famine and demographic pressure. Much of Eritrea's farming is still subsistence or semisubsistence, so land productivity is vital to the population's survival.

Today population growth is the biggest problem, placing increased demands on the land and leading to overgrazing and overcropping. Adding to woes is the practice of 'shifting cultivation' in the southwestern lowlands (in which whole areas of vegetation are burnt before planting), which is also seriously detrimental to the region's flora.

Deforestation poses a great threat to the country. Less than 1% of the country is covered by woodland, as compared with 30% a century ago – this says it all. During the war with Ethiopia, troops on both sides cleared forests for the construction of shelters, trenches and other fortifications. The traditional *hidmo* also requires large quantities of wood. In times of famine, trees provide emergency rations for the people and their livestock. Above all, the trees prevent soil erosion. Eritrea's current water shortages and low-yielding land are directly linked to the destruction of the forests. Measures to combat deforestation include a nationwide programme of tree planting and the establishment of nearly 100 nurseries nationwide, but it will take time before the results materialise.

FOOD & DRINK

Eritrea is not exactly the gastronomic capital of Africa but it's certainly better and more varied than you would expect, especially in Asmara. Cuisine-skip from Italian to traditional Eritrean and to the odd Indian or Chinese – you can't tire of dining in the capital. And nothing can beat a strong *macchiato* and a melt-in-your-mouth pastry at an outdoor table early morning or late afternoon.

Most types of food are reasonably priced, the only exception being imported food in some of the capital's supermarkets. A dinner for two comes to around Nfa180. People eat early in Eritrea (usually between 6.30pm and 8pm).

STAPLES & SPECIALITIES
Italian

Along with their roads, towns and bridges, the Italians left another legacy: *macchiato*, pizza and spaghetti. Italian dishes are available in all restaurants throughout Eritrea. Outside the capital, these may be limited to just one dish: lasagne or spaghetti bolognese. However, it fills the gap.

In the capital, the choice is much more extensive, with both *primi piatti* (first courses, usually pasta dishes, especially *penne, fusili,* tagliatelle) and *secondi piatti* (main dishes, usually fish or meat) on offer.

Traditional

Shiro, kitfo, zilzil, kwanta, fir fir, berbere… If you have visited Ethiopia, you'll soon realise that traditional Eritrean cuisine is almost the same as in Ethiopia; see p68 for a complete rundown of typical local dishes, ingredients and food etiquette, and a glossary of food terms. Most of the terms used are the same as in Ethiopia, except for *wat,* the fiery and ubiquitous sauce, which is known as *tsebhi* in Tigrinya; *injera* (large Ethiopian version of a pancake/plate), which is sometimes called *taita* in Tigrinya; *tibs* (sliced lamb, pan fried in butter, garlic, onion and sometimes tomato), known as *tibsi* in Tigrinya; and *kai wat* (lamb, goat or beef cooked in a hot *berbere* sauce), known as *zigni* in Tigrinya.

Eritrean food can sit heavily in the stomach but is no less mouthwatering one it. If you like hot food, try the delicious *silsi,* a peppery fried tomato and onion sauce served for breakfast. Another very popular breakfast dish is *ful* (based on chickpea purée), with *frittata,* omelette or scrambled egg jazzed up with a bit of pepper.

Capretto often features on menus. It's roast goat, sometimes served like a rack of lamb. Another succulent choice is *gored gored* (chunks of fresh beef cooked with seasoned butter and *berbere*).

Desserts aren't a traditional part of the diet and usually consist of fruit salad or synthetic crème caramel, but you could head for a pastry shop any time of day and gobble a heavenly *foret noire* (a cake with cocoa and cream) or croissant. Eritrean yogurt (served in a glass) and the mild local cheeses are a much better bet. The latter are sometimes served with bread and exquisite local honey, which makes for a terrific and easily prepared picnic.

In the western lowlands, look out for little boys selling *legamat,* a deep-fried dough sold hot in newspaper cones in the early morning; it's delicious for an early breakfast.

In the far west, food is heavily influenced by the proximity of Sudan. One popular and very tasty dish is *sheia,* lamb drizzled with oil and herbs then barbecued on very hot stones until it sizzles. It's delicious. It's usually served with *ades,* a lentil dish, and a stocklike soup known as *merek.*

In Massawa, the Arabic influence is evident. Kebabs and Yemeni-style charcoal-baked fish are both widely available.

DRINKS

Don't fear the heat, even in Massawa. There's no dearth of beverages to slake your thirst.

Alcoholic Drinks

In the capital and towns, all the usual favourites are available, including whisky, gin, vodka and beer. As many are imported, they tend to be expensive.

Local varieties include Asmara gin (also known as *ouzo*), which is a bit rough around the edges (as you will be the morning after drinking it), but it is soon knocked back. A shot of gin (about Nfa10) is only slightly more expensive than Coke or mineral water (Nfa6 to Nfa8).

The local beer, called Asmara Beer, is popular among both Eritreans and foreigners who are happy to guzzle it down with a pizza or a plate of tagliatelle. It's manufactured in Asmara, has a mild, quite smooth flavour and is very drinkable. It's also cheap at about Nfa10.

As for the red Asmara wine – it is no huge cause for celebration. Local wines are very reasonably priced in restaurants, usually between Nfa30 and Nfa60 per bottle. Imported wine starts at about Nfa120.

If you're not catching an early bus out of town the next morning, try the local *araki,* a distilled aniseed drink, a little like the Greek ouzo. *Mies* is a delicious local wine made from honey, and comes in varying degrees of sweetness (the drier it is, the more alcoholic). Don't miss it. If you're in Afar territory in Dankalia, try the delicious – but very powerful – *doma* palm wine (see p351).

Nonalcoholic Drinks

In Asmara and, to a lesser degree, the larger towns, innumerable little cafés and bars dot the centre. In true Italian style, frothy *macchiato*, espresso and fragrant cappuccino topped with delicate layers of foam are all served, along with a selection of pastries and cakes.

The Eritreans seem to get a fix from large amounts of sugar, which is copiously applied to all hot drinks and even fresh fruit juices. If you don't want sugar, you'll have to make that clear when you order. Ask for *beze sukkar.*

ERITREA

Outside the capital and in the country, sweet black tea is the most common drink. Following Islamic traditions, it is often offered as a gesture of welcome to guests. In the lowlands, cloves are often added. In the west, near the Sudanese border, coffee is sometimes spiced with ginger. If you don't want it, ask for *beze gingebel*.

The water in Asmara is considered safe to drink but, as in many places, new arrivals may experience problems with it. Various makes of bottled water (known in Tigrinya as *mai gas*) can be bought in all the towns and some villages. Local brands include Dongollo and Sarguma (which has a lighter fizz).

Fresh fruit juices (most commonly mango, papaya, pineapple and banana) are sold in Asmara and some of the larger towns.

Various fizzy soft drinks are widely available, even in Dankalia, where without refrigeration they are served at room temperature, which in some places is as warm as tepid tea.

Glass bottles are recycled; save them and you can exchange them for full ones.

WHERE TO EAT & DRINK

The capital is well endowed with restaurants, bars, cafés, fast-food and pastry shops. Unlike other African countries, there are no street eats. You will also find several supermarkets, some stocked with a good selection of European imports. Outside the towns, local shops have a very limited selection of food products for sale and the choice of dishes on offer in the restaurants is pretty limited. In Asmara, most restaurants have their menu translated into English.

Sadly, there were some food shortages throughout the country at the time of writing, and some staples were in short supply.

VEGETARIANS & VEGANS

Vegetarians will thank their lucky stars in Eritrea – they'll be pretty well catered for, at least by African standards. Most restaurants have several vegetarian options, especially on Wednesday and Friday, the traditional fasting days. If you're after vegetarian food, ask for *nai tsom,* a selection of vegetable dishes similar to the Ethiopian *beyainatu.* And of course, you can always order a plate of spaghetti.

HABITS & CUSTOMS

As important as the style or quality of the food is the ceremony. You won't forget your first meal, shared from a large plate with fellow diners and accompanied by *injera.* Tear off a piece of *injera* with your right hand and wrap it around the food served with it. Your host might even feed the tastiest morsel directly into your mouth – don't cringe, this is a mark of great friendship.

If you enjoyed your meal, express your satisfaction with a useful Tigrinya word that will please your host: *te-oom* (delicious).

ASMARA አስመራ

pop 1,062,000 / elev 2347m

If only all African capitals were as enchanting as Asmara! Hedonistic, seductive, civilised, unexpected, Asmara has charm in spades. By some kind of miracle, it has been spared the litter-strewn, sprawling ghettos of many developing-world cities, and the bleak high-rise office buildings of postcolonial Africa. Instead, think tree-lined avenues, peaceful neighbourhoods, pavement cafés with vintage Italian coffee machines, cheery pizza parlours and tantalising pastry shops. Bathed in glorious sunshine eight months of the year, it boasts a balmy and temperate climate that rejuvenates the soul and body. Its relaxed pace of life is infectious. In many ways you'll feel like you've been teleported to a southern Italian town. And there's the fabulous architecture: even jaded visitors can't help but be enthralled by its gobsmacking portfolio of unheralded architectural wonders from the Italian era. Where else could you find such a mix of rationalist, Art Deco, cubist, expressionist, futurist and neoclassical styles?

But that is just one facet of Asmara. The city also exudes an undeniably African and Arab atmosphere. In the morning you'll hear the sound of the cathedral bells and the footsteps of the Orthodox monks on their way to Mass, as well as the Muslim call to prayer. These sounds are symbolic of the remarkable harmony that reigns in the city and throughout the country among the different religious and ethnic groups.

The picture is not all that rosy, though. Sadly, Asmara's ability to dazzle has been marred over past years by the battered economy and the clampdown on civil liberties.

Gone is the dolce vita – belt-tightening is now the order of the day. Power cuts? Almost a fact of life. Waiting queues in front of food stores? Now a daily chore. During the day, business is slack. At night, streets are dark and deserted. The city that was buzzing at the turn of the century has vanished. It's now all whispers and subdued conversations.

One thing is sure, though: this diamond of a city will shine again. Meanwhile, nab a seat at one of the outside tables at Bar Impero and watch the world go by: gorgeous giggling girls, ex-fighters and old men in double-breasted suits. You'll find it hard to tear yourself away. This is the best way to start your Eritrean journey.

HISTORY

The town was settled in the 12th century by shepherds from the Akele Guzay region, in the southeast of the country. Encouraged by the plentiful supplies of water, they founded four villages on the hill that is now the site of the Orthodox church of Enda Mariam. The site became known as Arbate Asmere (Four Villages), from which the name Asmara is derived. Soon it developed into a small but bustling trading centre.

At the end of the 19th century, Ras Alula, the dashing Tigrinya *negus* (prince) made it his capital and the centre of a flourishing caravan trade.

The town then caught the eye of Baldissera, the Italian general, and in 1889 he took it over. Italian architects and engineers got to work and had soon laid the foundations of the new town: Piccola Roma, as it was dubbed, was born.

In 1897 the first governor of Eritrea, Governor Martini, chose Asmara (in preference to Massawa) as the future capital of the Italian East African empire. Amid dreams of great military conquests in Abyssinia during the Mussolini era, the town was greatly enlarged.

During the Struggle, Asmara was the last town held by the occupying Ethiopian army and, from 1990, it was besieged by the EPLF. By a fortuitous turn of events, the Ethiopian dictator Mengistu was overthrown in 1991, his troops fled Eritrea and a final confrontation in the capital was avoided. Asmara was left intact. It was one of the very few Eritrean towns to survive the war undamaged.

ORIENTATION

The centre encompasses the area on and just north of Harnet Ave (the main artery), marked by Bahti Meskerem Sq at the eastern end of Harnet Ave and the former Governor's Palace in the west. To the south of Harnet Ave was once the Italian residential quarter. The areas to the northeast and well outside the confines of the town centre are the residential quarters of the local population.

To the southwest, Sematat Ave leads to the Tiravolo District, where several midrange hotels and nightclubs are clustered. Further to the southwest you'll reach the airport, about 6km from the centre. See p326 for information on getting to/from the airport. The railway station is about 1.5km east of the centre.

Like most colonial towns, Asmara was built according to a strict urban plan. It's clearly laid out and is a breeze to navigate.

Maps

The Municipality of Asmara produces an excellent town map (Nfa20), *Asmara City Map & Historic Perimeter,* which covers the city in detail and pinpoints historic buildings. It's available in the bookshops.

INFORMATION
Bookshops

Awghet Bookshop (Map p311; Bahti Meskerem Sq; 8am-7pm Mon-Sat) Has a mediocre selection of books on Fritrea but stocks the very useful *Asmara City Map & Historic Perimeter.*

Ghirmay Bookshop (Map p313; Sematat Ave; 7am-noon & 2.30-8pm) Sells old copies of the *International Herald Tribune, Time* and *Newsweek.*

Cultural Centres

Alliance Française (Map p313; ☎ 201775; Nakfa Ave; 9-11.30am & 2-5pm Mon-Fri) In the same building as the French Embassy.

British Council (Map p313; ☎ 123415; 175-11 St) Has a respectable library as well as a reading room stocked with British newspapers and magazines.

Emergency

Ambulance (☎ 122244)
Police (☎ 207799)

Internet Access

Internet services have sprung up all over town in recent years, so it is not hard for webheads to get their regular hit. Be warned

ERITREA

ERITREA

ASMARA IN...

Two Days

Kick off the day with a *macchiato* at **Sweet Asmara Caffe** (p323). Confess your sins in the **Catholic cathedral** (p312), just across the street. Get your bearings over the urban sprawl you're going to embrace by climbing up the **bell tower** (p313). Next, wind your way to the nearby **Great Mosque** (p314) and delve into the jumble of streets of the **central market** (p314) area to soak up the atmosphere. Continue to **Medebar Market** (p314) for a salutary lesson in waste management.

Make your way to **Cafe Fiori** (p323) for a flaky croissant. Suitably re-energised, you can prepare yourself for the evening *passeggiata*. Stroll down Harnet Ave and watch the world go by at snazzy **Pasticceria Moderna** (p323). Is it dinner-time yet? Take your weary bones to **Hidmona** (p322) and treat yourself to a proper feed in traditional surrounds.

Start off day two with an educational hour at the **National Museum** (p315). Feeling peckish? Nothing will beat an alfresco lunch in the courtyard of **Casa degli Italiani** (p322), followed by a cake at **Modka Caffe & Pastry** (p323). Burn it off with our **city walking tour** (p316).

Return to your hotel to put on your glad rags, then hit the **Spaghetti & Pizza House** (p321) for a supertasty pizza. Drink at hip **Zara** (p323) before heading to **Mocambo** (p325) or **Green Pub** (p325), where you'll wind'n'grind the night away in good company.

---

that connections can be painfully slow; try early morning or late evening.

CIC Central Internet Cafe (Map p313; Harnet Ave; per hr Nfa10; 8am-10pm)

Double M Internet Cafe (Map p313; Harnet Ave; per hr Nfa10; 8am-10pm)

Tekseb Internet Cafe (Map p313; Adi Hawesha St; per hr Nfa10; 8am-10pm)

Laundry

Laundries are few and far between in Asmara. Ask at the reception of your hotel or your *pension*.

Zamay Laundry (Map p313; Mata St) Charges Nfa100 for a complete wash and dry (24 hours).

Medical Services

There's a profusion of pharmacies around town.

Cathedral Pharmacy (Map p313; Harnet Ave) Opposite the Catholic cathedral.

Sembel Hospital (150175; HDAY St) The most reputable hospital in town, on the road to the airport. The standard fee is US$30 per consultation. Also has dental services.

Money

Since the government took over the whole banking system, there are no longer private exchange bureaus. At least changing money won't be a cause of headaches: rates are fixed by the government and are the same everywhere in the country, whether for cash or travellers cheques. There's a foreign-exchange booth at the airport; it's open to

meet all arriving flights and changes cash only. All transactions must be registered on your currency declaration form. There's a black market, but it's illegal and the risks incurred are huge (see p360).

There are currently no ATMs in Asmara.

Commercial Bank of Eritrea (Map p313; 122425; Harnet Ave; 8-11am & 2-4pm Mon-Fri, 8-11am Sat) Changes cash and travellers cheques. Also acts as an agent for Western Union.

Himbol Bahti Meskerem Sq (Map p311; 120735; Bahti Meskerem Sq; 8am-8pm); Harnet Ave (Map p313; 123124; Harnet Ave; 8am-noon & 2-8pm Mon-Fri, 8am-noon & 2-7pm Sat, 8am-noon & 2-6pm Sun) Changes cash and travellers cheques, and can do cash advances on your credit card for a commission of 7%. The main office is on Bahti Meskerem Sq.

Post

Main post office (Map p313; 8am-noon & 2-6pm Mon-Fri, 8am-12.30pm Sat) Just north of the western end of Harnet Ave.

Telephone & Fax

Telecommunications building (Map p313; Harnet Ave; 8am-9pm Mon-Fri, 8am-7.30pm Sat & Sun) At the western end of the street. You can make international calls in the special cabins, or local calls. Phonecards are available. There's also a fax counter, to the left of the entrance of the building. You can also receive faxes here.

Tourist Information

In addition to the tourist office, the most reliable sources of information are the travel agencies (see following).

ERITREA

ASMARA

0 500 m
0 0.3 miles

Sandals.	21	B3
Selam Hotel.	22	B2
Tobacco Factory.	23	D3

SLEEPING
Africa Pension.	24	C3
Embasoira Hotel.	25	C3
Savanna International Hotel.	26	B4
Sunshine Hotel.	27	C4

EATING
Al Sicomoro Bar & Restaurant.	28	A4
Blue Nile Bar & Restaurant.	29	B3
China Star.	30	B3
Da Silla.	31	E2
Golden Fork Fast Food.	32	A4
Milano Restaurant.	33	D3
Rendez-Vous Restaurant.	34	B3
Roof Garden.	35	C4

DRINKING
Bar Aquila.	36	B4
Bar Zilli.	37	B4
Cinema Roma.	38	B2
Crispi Bar.	39	A2
Hakosea.	40	B3
Zara.	(see 12)	

ENTERTAINMENT
Cinema Roma.	(see 12)	

SHOPPING
African Curio Shop.	41	B3

TRANSPORT
Alpha Travel Agency.	42	E2
City Bus Terminal.	43	D2
EgyptAir.	44	E2
Leo Car Rental.	45	A4
Main Bus Terminal.	46	C1
Mai Khah Khah Fountain.	47	C1
Second Bus Terminal.	48	C1
Third Bus Terminal.		

SIGHTS & ACTIVITIES
Africa Pension.	(see 24)	
Asmara Piscina.	9	B3
Capitol Cinema.	10	B2
Central Market.	11	D2
Cinema Roma.	12	B3
Enda Maram Orthodox Cathedral.	13	E2
Fiat Tagliero Building.	14	A4
Former Governor's Palace.	15	B3
Greek Orthodox Church.	16	D2
Irga Building.	17	A4
Mai Khah Khah Fountain.	18	D3
Medebar Market.	19	E1
National Museum.	20	B3

INFORMATION
American Embassy.	1	C4
Awghet Bookshop.	2	E2
British Embassy.	3	B2
Department of Immigration.	4	B2
Djiboutian Embassy.	5	C4
Himbol.	6	E2
Italian Embassy.	7	B3
National Museum Office.	(see 20)	
Villa Roma.	8	C3

See Central Asmara Map (p313)

To Train Station (100m);
Asmara War Cemetery (1.5km); Debre Bizen
Monastery (28km); Nefasit (25km);
the Red Sea Coast

To German Embassy (400m);
Lufthansa (400m); Yemeni
Embassy (400m); Orthodox
Church Headquarters (700m);
Alla Scala Hotel (700m);
Bgoli Hotel (1km); Bologna
Hotel (1km); Sudanese Embassy
(1.1km); Expo Park (1km);
Hotel Inter-Continental Asmara
(2km); Berhe Alba (2.2km);
Sembel Hospital (3km);
Asmara Airport (4km)

To Ghidei - Eritrean
Cultural Centre (200m)

To Dekemhare (35km);
Mendefera (86km); Massawa;
the south

Sabi Stadium

Asmara University

Kiddus Yoseph Church

Fort

Kiddus Mikael Cemetery

Kiddus Mikael Church

Mekane Hiwot Hospital

St George's Episcopa Church

Kidane Mihret Church

Hadish Adi Quarter

Battu Mekerem Sq

Hamasien Sq

Warsay St
Meret St
DGSA St
Adai St
Bihat St
Kekese St
Beleza St
Fred Hollows St
Geleso Sudan St
Sem-bel Ave
Maran GMBI St
Denden St
Mienik St
Beirut St
Kohayto St
Marsa Fatuma St
Denkel Ave
Mata St
Felket Ave
Hamet Ave
Adi-Haweshi St
Nakfa Ave
Selam St
Baden St
Gonder St
Afabet St
Beno St
Sematat Ave
Mogolo St
Timnet Sq
Sudan Ave
Falket Seyb St
Fenengeya Ave
Keyh Bahri St
Adi Quala St
Hamasien St
Barka St
Selsenya St
Tesenay St
Eritrea Sq
Teseney St
Martaky Ave
Kuba Asahs Ave
BDHO Ave
St George's

Tourist Information Centre (Map p313; ☎ 124871; Harnet Ave; ☒ 7am-noon & 2-6pm Mon-Fri) Next to Sweet Asmara Caffe. Has some brochures and issues the compulsory travel permit.

Travel Agencies

The two main travel agencies in Asmara are listed here. For details of the sort of tours they offer, see p368. Flights can be booked through these agencies or through the various airline offices in Asmara.

Explore Eritrea Travel & Tours (Map p313; ☎ 125555, 120259; www.exploreeritrea.com; Adi Hawesha St) English-speaking staff offer a range of travel services throughout the country.

Travel House International (Map p313; ☎ 201881/2; www.travelhouseeritrea.com; 175-15 St; ☒ 8am-noon & 2-6pm Mon-Fri, 8.30am-noon & 3.30-6pm Sat) A well-regarded travel agency, opposite the Casa degli Italiani restaurant. Ask for Tedros, who knows the country very well and speaks very good English. All kinds of tours can be organised.

Travel Permits

To travel outside Asmara you'll need a travel permit, obtainable at the Tourist Information Centre. Keep it with you outside Asmara as you'll have to present it at checkpoints. Provided you're a tourist (and not a journalist or a NGO worker), it's a pretty straightforward affair, just a mere form to fill in and sign, listing all your intended destinations in Eritrea. A permit is also necessary to visit the monasteries. For more details on travel permits, see p363.

DANGERS & ANNOYANCES

Fear not! Asmara is fundamentally a very safe city, especially compared with other African cities. It's generally safe to stroll around day or night in the centre. However, women should use their common sense and avoid walking alone in deserted and dark streets.

Due to power cuts, very few streets are lit at night. It's a bit intimidating but there's no particular risk of getting mugged.

Begging is actively 'discouraged' by the government and it's still rare to see beggars in central Asmara.

SIGHTS

Asmara's greatest attraction is undoubtedly its gobsmacking collection of buildings revealing its colonial past (see the boxed text, p317). As you walk around the town, you will see splendid examples of the Art Deco,

international, cubist, expressionist, functionalist, futurist, rationalist and neoclassical architectural styles, that will enthral even the least culturally inclined travellers. How the buildings have managed to step viably into the 21st century without a complete restoration is a mystery. To top it off, viewing much of it doesn't cost a cent.

Most of Asmara's major sights are clustered in the centre or within easy distance from it.

Harnet Ave

The best place to start exploring is the **former Governor's Palace** (Map p311), which stands majestically at the western end of Harnet Ave. With its pediment supported by Corinthian columns, this architectural wonder is thought to be one of the finest neoclassical buildings in Africa. Unfortunately, it is not currently possible to visit it because it's an official building. So frustrating!

Within staggering distance of the Governor's Palace, the **Opera House** (Map p313) is sure to elicit strong reactions. One of Asmara's most elegant early-20th-century buildings, it was completed around 1920. This eclectic building combines a Renaissance scallop-shell fountain, a Romanesque portico supported by classical columns and inside, above multitiered balconies, a spectacular Art Nouveau ceiling.

By contrast, the adjacent **Ministry of Education** (Map p313) looks strikingly austere. Typically Fascist, indeed. Built during the 1930s as the Casa del Fascio (the Fascist Party headquarters), it mixes the classical (the right-hand section) with the monumental and Fascist. Its soaring tower has strong vertical elements, including three gun-slit windows. The steps, string courses (projecting bands of bricks) and mouldings give the building harmony.

Ambling down Harnet Ave you'll soon come across Asmara's most iconic monument, the elaborate, brick-walled **Catholic cathedral** (Map p313). Consecrated in 1923, it is thought to be one of the finest Lombard-Romanesque-style churches outside Italy – this says it all. The cathedral's lofty interior is an absorbing sight: the altar is made of Carrara marble and the baptistry, confessionals and pulpit are carved from Italian walnut. Masses are celebrated every Sunday at 6.30am (in Tigrinya), 9.30am (in Italian) and 11am (in English) in the cathedral. The tallest structure in Asmara, the narrow, Gothic **bell tower** (☻ 8-11am & 2-5pm) makes a useful landmark and offers smashing views over the town. Ask at the 'Ufficio Parrochiale' for the key. A donation is expected.

Another eye-catching building, the nearby **Cinema Impero** (Map p313) is part of a grand rationalist terrace built in 1938. The imposing cinema is made up of three massive windows that combine strong vertical and horizontal elements with 45 porthole lamps (which look like huge wireless buttons). In the lobby, all the marble, chrome and glass features are original. The cavernous auditorium seats 1800 people and is

CENTRAL ASMARA

0 — 200 m
0 — 0.1 miles

INFORMATION	
Alliance Française	1 A4
British Council	2 A4
Cathedral Pharmacy	(see 35)
CIC Central Internet Cafe	(see 35)
Commercial Bank of Eritrea	3 D4
Double M Internet Cafe	4 D4
Egyptian Embassy	5 A5
Explore Fritrea Travel & Tours	6 A4
French Embassy	(see 1)
Ghirmay Bookshop	7 A4
Himbol	8 A4
Main Post Office	9 A4
Tekseb Internet Cafe	10 A4
Telecommunications Building	11 A4
Tourist Information Centre	12 C4
Travel House International	13 A4
Zamay Laundry	14 C4

SIGHTS & ACTIVITIES	
Asmara's Synagogue	15 C4
Bar Impero	(see 18)
Bowling Alley	16 D5
Catholic Cathedral & Bell Tower AAA	17 B4
Cinema Impero	18 C4
City Park	19 A4
Garage	20 D5
Great Mosque (Kulafah Al Rashidin)	21 D4
Ministry of Education	22 A4
Municipality Building	23 C4
Odeon Cinema	24 A5
Opera House	25 A4

SLEEPING	
Albergo Italia	26 A4
Ambassador Hotel	27 B4
Asmara Central Hotel	28 C5
Bristol Pension	29 A5
City Center Pension	30 B4
Concord Pension	31 C4
Crystal Hotel	32 A5
Khartoum Hotel	33 C5
National Pension	34 C4
Pensione Pisa	35 B4
Pensione Stella	36 A4
Red Sea Pension	37 D4
Sheghay Hotel	38 C5
Top Five Hotel	39 D5

EATING	
Alba Bistro	40 A4
American Bar	41 A4
Bar Vittoria	42 A4
Bereket Fast Food	43 C4
Casa degli Italiani	44 A4
Cathedral Snack Bar	45 B4
Mask Place	46 A4
Pasticceria Moderna	47 C4
Pizza Napoli	48 A4
Portico Snack Bar	49 A4
Senay Supermarket	50 B4
Spaghetti & Pizza House	51 A4
Sun Pizza & Fast Food	52 A4
Wikianos Supermarket	53 D4

DRINKING	
Bar Impero	(see 18)
Bar Royal	54 B4
Cafe Fiori	(see 30)
Capri	55 C4
Casa degli Italiani	(see 44)
Damera Bar & Pastry	56 D4
Mask Place	(see 46)
Modka Caffe & Pastry	57 B5
Mona Lisa Snack Bar & Pastry	58 C4
Multi Sport Bowling	(see 16)
Odeon Cinema	(see 24)
Sweet Asmara Caffe	59 C4
Tre Stelle Bar	60 D4

ENTERTAINMENT	
Cinema Impero	(see 18)
Mocambo	61 A4

SHOPPING	
Aida Gift Articles Shop	(see 35)
Jolly Shop	62 A4

TRANSPORT	
Africa Rent Car	63 C5
Eritrean Airlines	64 B4
Explore Eritrea Travel & Tours	(see 6)
Fontana Rent a Car	65 C5
Saudia Arabian Airlines	66 B4
Travel House International	(see 13)
Yemenia Yemen Airways	67 D4

decorated with motifs such as lions, nyalas and palm trees depicted in Art Deco style. Next door, the **Bar Impero** (Map p313), where cinemagoers traditionally enjoyed an apéritif before the film, is also original. Look out for the bevelled-glass cake-and-fruit cabinet, the 'zinc' bar, the dark wood panels and the old cash machine.

Further east, it's impossible to miss the imposing **Municipality building** (Map p313). Though built in the 1950s, this monolith is firmly rationalist. The two geometric wings are 'stripped Palladian' in style, and are dominated by a soaring central tower. The windows are beautifully detailed. Look out for the 'crazy majolica' façade in green and beige.

South of Harnet Ave

A block south of the Municipality building, the **bowling alley** (Map p313; 194-4 St; ☻ 8am-8pm) is one of the few genuine 1950s alleys left in the world. It was probably built for US servicemen when they were manning military bases in the region. The reloading system is still manual. Look out also for the bowling motifs on the balustrades, the blue and white lockers and the carved wooden benches. The colourful early 'pop art' window is spectacular at sunset. Across the road from the bowling alley is a **garage** (Map p313; 194-4 St), possibly built in the 1950s. The roof of the building features zigzags.

Further south, you'll stumble across one of the most elegant pieces of architecture in Asmara, the **Mai Khah Khah fountain** (Map p311; Marsatekly Ave). It cascades down the hillside in a series of rectangular steps. Above the fountain is the attractive suburb of Gezzabanda, which is full of impressive villas.

Tucked away in a residential district further west, the **Africa Pension** (Map p311; Keskese St) is a gem of place. This huge cubist villa was built in the 1920s by a spaghetti millionaire. The villa is characterised by its elegant marble staircase and the ring of 40 marble urns. Today a solemn and slightly ludicrous bronze bust of Augustus Caesar stands guard in the once-formal garden. The villa is now a very affordable hotel (see p318). You like it? Book a room!

You can't but be dazzled by the gleaming **Villa Roma** (Map p311; 173-3 St) opposite the Africa Pension. This beautiful villa, built in 1919, epitomises the Roman style. The

marble staircases, louvred shutters, curving balustrades, shady portico, fountain, and loggia with cascading purple bougainvillea are typical features of the ideal Roman villa. Today it is the residence of the Italian ambassador. Lucky him!

Just off Harnet Ave, near the telecommunications building, the quirky **Odeon Cinema** (Map p313; Bihat St), with its authentic Art Deco interior, is attractive. The box office, bar, bevelled mirrors, black terrazzo and Art Deco strip lights are a good introduction to the large auditorium.

Heading downhill on Felket Ave, south of the centre, past a row of old shops and 1950s Formica bars with fly-bead doors, you'll see several attractive villas and buildings, including the **tobacco factory** (Map p311; Felket Ave). It is regarded as the most adventurous Art Deco building in Asmara.

North of Harnet Ave

The sprawling **central market** (Map p311; ☻ morning Mon-Sat), just north of Eritrea Sq, is one of Asmara's major attractions. The best time to visit is early on Saturday (from 7am), when people come in from all over the country. However, it was pretty tame when we visited because of the economic downturn in the country. Highlights include the spice market, filled with colourful women from different ethnic groups. The souvenir market is a great place to browse too, and is more interesting than the shops in the town. You can find, among other things, local basketwork, wooden masks, musical instruments, decorated gourds, warrior knives and skin paintings.

Duck up northeast to soak up the atmosphere of the **Medebar Market** (Map p311; Qelhamet St). No doubt you'll be awestruck the minute you enter this mind-boggling place. It is like an open-air workshop where absolutely everything is recycled. Moseying around the alleys of this market is a uniquely unforgettable experience. The air is filled with hammering, sawing and cutting; old tyres are made into sandals, corrugated iron is flattened and made into metal buckets, and olive tins from Italy are made into coffee pots and tiny scoopers.

Thread your way back to the south until you reach the **Great Mosque** (Kulafah Al Rashidin; Map p313; Selam St). Completed in 1938 by Guido Ferrazza, this grand complex combines rationalist, classical and Islamic styles. The symmetry of the mosque is enhanced by the minaret, which rises on one side like a fluted Roman column above Islamic domes and arches. The *mihrab* (niche indicating the direction of Mecca) inside consists of mosaics and columns made from Carrara marble. Ferrazza's style is also seen in the great square and market complex surrounding the mosque.

Another outstanding monument, the **Enda Mariam Orthodox Cathedral** (Map p311; Arbate Asmara St), to the east, was built in 1938 and is a curious blend of Italian and Eritrean architecture. Its central block is flanked by large square towers. Rather garish mosaics of stylised Christian figures are framed vertically above the entrance. Traditional elements of Aksumite architecture can be seen, such as the massive horizontal stone beams. The four objects that look like broken elephant tusks suspended on the northern side of the compound are century-old 'bells'. These make a surprisingly musical sound when 'rung' (beaten with a stick).

Asmara's synagogue (Map p313; Seraye St) is also worth a peek. Its pediment, Doric columns and pilasters make it very neoclassical. As is usual in Asmara, the wrought-iron gates are handcrafted.

If you haven't run out of stamina, head west of the central market to the **Greek Orthodox Church** (Map p311; Selam St). The church has frescoes, carved wood and candles.

West of Harnet Ave

If you need to recharge the batteries before tackling the western outskirts of the centre, the **city park** (Map p313; Sematat Ave; ⏱ 6.30am-10.30pm) makes a perfect transition point in which to unwind and to relish a well-deserved beer or fruit juice. Come here late afternoon, when it's full of life and chatter.

Then you can make your way to the **Capitol Cinema** (Map p311; Denden St), north of the Governor's Palace. It was built in 1937. The massive horizontal elements and sweeping curves are typical of the expressionist movement. Unfortunately the building looks rather scruffy and is in urgent need of a face-lift.

A five-minute walk from Capital Cinema, the **Selam Hotel** (Map p311; Mariam GMBI St), built in the 1930s, was one of a chain constructed by an Italian company. Interesting interior details include the Arts and Crafts serving cabinets and the 'disc'-type lamps in the dining room, the old murals and the purple 'beehive' lamps in the rear courtyard. It's still run as a hotel.

Asmara's strong point are its buildings, rather than its museums, but it's also worth popping your head into the **National Museum** (Map p311; Mariam GMBI St; admission free; ⏱ 9-11am & 3-5pm Thu-Tue), west of the Governor's Palace. It contains exhibits on the ethnic groups of Eritrea, giving a basic introduction to traditional life in the countryside, as well as various artefacts found in the main archaeological sites of the country. It's a bit disappointing in its present state but there are plans to upgrade it and to relocate it closer to the centre.

Fancy a dip? The 1930s **Asmara Piscina** (swimming pool; Map p311; Kohayto St; admission Nfa40; ⏱ 9am-8pm) will fit the bill. It is housed in a yellow building, off Sematat Ave. Even if you don't feel like emulating Ian Thorpe, take a peek inside this modernist building. Interior details include the 'Leonardo' sporting figures on the walls and a rather refreshing bluish colour scheme.

Back to the main thoroughfare, you can't miss the **Cinema Roma** (Map p311; Sematat Ave), across the avenue. It's another fine example of Italian architecture. The appealing exterior features four entrances with double doors and a magnificent marble-coated façade sporting the letters ROMA below four square windows.

Ambling down Sematat Ave, you can't avoid the **Sandals** (Map p311; Sematat Ave) rising over a roundabout. Just in case it should ever slip your mind that Asmara is Eritrea's patriotic heart, this is an eccentric replica of sandals (yes!). Note that the Eritrean soldiers are equipped with sandals, not combat boots. There's not much to say about it, save that this sculpture commemorates the victory of the Eritrean fighters in the Struggle.

Don't even think of leaving town until you've seen the **Fiat Tagliero Building** (Map p311; Sematat Ave), at the southern end of Sematat Ave. Perhaps the most outstanding in Asmara, this quirky monument is liable to make you wonder, 'What the hell is that?' It's another superb example of a futuristic building. Built in 1938, it is designed to look like a plane. The central tower with its glass 'cockpit' is similar to many structures in Miami, USA. Oddly enough, it's now a service station. A sandal's throw from the

ERITREA

Fiat Tagliero Building, the harmonious **Irga Building** (Map p311; Sematat Ave) is both neoclassical in its proportions and very modern.

East of Harnet Ave

On the road to Massawa on the periphery of Asmara (2km from the centre), is the beautifully tended **Asmara War Cemetery**, dating from 1941. Interred here are 280 men killed during the Ethiopian campaign. There is also a Hindu burial ground for the Indian soldiers who fought alongside the British.

WALKING TOUR

With its ideal weather, profusion of historic buildings, lack of hassle and unhurried pace of life, it's hard to imagine a better place than Asmara for a walking tour. This saunter covers the main sights in the centre.

Start at the magnificent **Opera House** (**1**; p312) and **Ministry of Education** (**2**; p312) at the western end of Harnet Ave. Keep striding east down the main artery, where you'll pass the well-proportioned building of the former **Bank of Eritrea** (**3**) on your right. Asmara's most obvious landmark, the lofty **Catholic cathedral** (**4**; p312) soon comes into

---

WALK FACTS

Start Opera House
Finish Albergo Italia
Distance About 4km
Duration Half a day

---

view. The stunning façade of the **Cinema Impero** (**5**; p313) is 150m to the east. Next door, **Bar Impero** (**6**; p314) is an ideal pit stop for a caffeine fix. Turn left into Senafe St and walk along until you reach the main junction with Nakfa Ave. Turn right into Nafka Ave then left into Adi Ebrihim St and you'll soon see the **Great Mosque** (**7**; p314) standing majestically. Follow Selam St for about 100m to the west, then take the first street on the right (Sarayi St). You'll enter the **market area** (**8**; p314). Explore it at leisure before heading to **Enda Mariam Orthodox Cathedral** (**9**; p315) that looms to the east. Walk down Arbate Asmera St until you emerge on Harnet Ave. Travel two blocks down Harnet Ave past the monumental **Municipality building** (**10**; p314). Continue west and turn left into Denkel St. Walk two blocks and turn right into Nora St.

The **Piazza Mai Cew** (**11**), which was once the heart of the Greek community, is a good place to unwind. On the corner on the east side you'll spy an old school that resembles a Greek temple. To the south, you can't miss the ochre building of the **Eritrean Election Commission** (**12**).

From the piazza, head west through the next square (which has a palm tree in the middle) and up the hill (173-3 St). Near the top of the hill you'll stumble across the **Africa Pension** (**13**; p318) and the lovely **Villa Roma** (**14**; p314). About 100m to the west, the conical roof of the quirky **Hamasien Hotel** (**15**) beckons. On the northern side of the

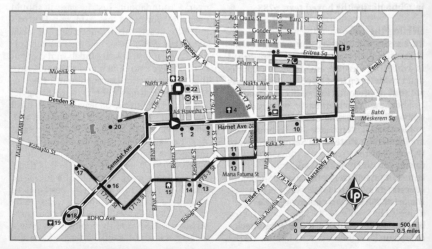

hotel, descend 171-10 St (there's a cul-de-sac sign). The steps lead you down to Bihat St. Take 171-3 St, which begins between the Dutch embassy and the Crystal Hotel, then turn right into 171-4 St, which will bring you to Sematat Ave. On the corner have a look at **Cinema Roma** (16; p315). Cross Sematat Ave and walk down Kohayto St until you reach the **Asmara Piscina** (17; p315).

If you haven't run out of stamina, backtrack to Sematat Ave and mosey south along the avenue until the **Sandals** (18; p315) monument. Decide whether you're in the 'love it' or 'hate it' camp. After a tipple at historic **Bar Zilli** (19; p324), proceed back to Harnet Ave. Have a peek at the **Governor's Palace** (20; p312) that sprawls on your left (it's impossible to go near). Then head back to Harnet Ave and turn left into 175-15 St, which starts opposite the telecommunications building. Walk two blocks and you'll see a cluster of historic buildings, including the **main post office** (21; p310), the former building of the **Commercial Bank of Eritrea** (22) and the glamorous **Albergo Italia** (23; p320). Book a room here if you can afford it – you've really earned it!

ASMARA FOR CHILDREN

Frankly, there aren't many attractions geared to little tackers, but the unhurried pace of life and the pervading safety make Asmara a nonetheless agreeable city for children. Understandably most of the colonial buildings will leave the little 'uns cold. If your five-year old has lost interest in rationalist architecture, you can still head to the child-friendly City Park (p315) at the western end of Harnet Ave, where they can rest safely while sampling an ice cream. They can also have a (refreshing) dip at Asmara Piscina (p315) or try their hands at the bowling alley (p314).

Climbing towers is usually a winner. Try the bell tower at the Catholic cathedral (p312), but be cautious – the stairs are steep.

FESTIVALS & EVENTS

Asmara hosts many religious and secular festivals throughout the year. For more information, see p359.

SLEEPING

Asmara boasts a cluster of accommodation options, from very affordable, homy guesthouses and good-value midrange options to

---

COLONIAL ARCHITECTURE: FRAGILE BEAUTIES

Another litter-strewn African capital disfigured with concrete eyesores? Not here. Asmara is one of the most entrancing cities in Africa. It usually comes as a surprise to many travellers to discover a slick city crammed with architectural gems harking back to the city's heyday as the 'Piccolo Roma' (small Rome). Isolated for nearly 30 years during its war with Ethiopia, Asmara escaped both the trend to build postcolonial piles and the push towards developing-world urbanisation. Thus, it has kept its heritage buildings almost intact and is refreshingly low-rise. Wander the streets in the centre and you'll gaze upon a showcase of the Art Deco, international, cubist, expressionist, functionalist, futurist, rationalist and neoclassical architectural styles. No need to be an architecture buff – they all stand out.

When Mussolini came to power in Italy in 1922, he nursed two ambitions relating to Italy's role in the Horn: to avenge Italy's defeat at Adwa (see p143) and to create a new Roman Empire in Africa. To realise these dreams he needed a strong industrial base. Labour, resources and lire were thus poured into the new colony and, by the 1930s, it was booming. By 1940 Eritrea had become the second-most industrialised country in sub-Saharan Africa. At the same time – and encouraged by il Duce – a new and daring architectural movement called rationalism was springing up in Italy. Eritrea, in common with many colonies, became an experimental architectural laboratory in which new and exciting ideas could be tested. Asmara, or Piccola Roma, soon came to epitomise the new philosophy: it was not just beautiful, but was well planned, well built and, above all, functional. Today Asmara remains a model Art Deco town.

Not everything is perfect. A number of buildings are decaying for lack of funds. It is hoped that some of them will be rehabilitated in the near future. The city could also be declared a World Heritage site. But peace with Ethiopia must come first.

The best way to see Asmara's built heritage is to walk around town (see opposite). *Asmara – Africa's Secret Modernist City*, by Edward Denison, is the most comprehensive book on the subject.

luxury hotels. Most places rate zero on the charm scale but are usually well equipped and fairly comfortable. However, power cuts were common at the time of writing.

Most of Asmara's accommodation is concentrated in and around the centre, but there are several good midrange places further afield on the road to the airport in the Tiravolo district.

Budget beds are not too much of an endangered species in Asmara, but avoid the cheapies dotted around the marketplace. Most of them can't be seriously recommended. Much better are those just off Harnet Ave.

Some hotels in the midrange price bracket and most top-end hotel quote their prices in US dollars but accept local currency, provided you have your currency declaration form. If you pay in hard currency, the transaction must be registered on your form.

Top-end hotels all offer rooms with bathroom.

Harnet Ave
BUDGET
Pensione Pisa (Map p313; ☎ 124491; Harnet Ave; s with shared bathroom Nfa60, d with shared bathroom Nfa95-120) This welcoming *pension* is housed in an apartment, just opposite the (functioning) bell tower of the Catholic cathedral. Earplug alert for some, atmospheric and thrilling for others. Take into account the unbeatable location and the clinical cleanliness of the rooms. Bathroomwise, don't even think of gesticulating in the diminutive cubicles (bring a straitjacket!). If you're solo, there's only one single room. Sizzling-hot value for what you get.

Midrange
Ambassador Hotel (Map p313; ☎ 126544; fax 126365; Harnet Ave; s Nfa255-420, d Nfa430-575) This faded glory is still a contender in the featherweight division of midrange and wears its worn atmosphere as a badge of honour. Cleanliness pervades throughout and there's a good restaurant on the 1st floor, with European and Eritrean specialities on offer. It's right in the thick of things, opposite the Catholic cathedral.

South of Harnet Ave
BUDGET
Africa Pension (Map p311; ☎ 121436; Keskese St; s/d with shared bathroom Nfa150/200) Backpackers

gravitate towards this mellow *pension* in a converted villa for good reason. You won't be tripping over your backpack in the generous-sized rooms, and the setting is really alluring, with a neatly manicured garden and a bronze bust. Angle for a room with a view of the Italian ambassador's residence (Villa Roma) but steer right away from room 13 at the back (Nfa100) – very shoddy. The *pension* is in a residential neighbourhood, a jaunt from Harnet Ave. Considering bathrooms are shared and hot water is sketchy at times, this place is a tad overpriced, but the historic aura that shrouds the place sweetens the deal.

Bristol Pension (Map p313; ☎ 121688; 175-4 St; s/d with shared bathroom Nfa110/165) A short stagger from the telecommunications building, the Bristol is a fine example of classic rationalist design, with a stunning central stairwell tower surmounting geometric designs. An architectural gem it may be, but we were not blown away by the quality of the rooms. This is what we scribbled on our notepad when we passed through: 'dull, plain but OK'. Enough said.

MIDRANGE
Khartoum Hotel (Map p313; ☎ 128008; 176-13 St; s with shared bathroom Nfa200-250, d with shared bathroom Nfa250-300, s/d Nfa300/350) The Khartoum has been smartened up and is now heralded as one of the best venues in this price bracket. One block south of Harnet Ave, it offers superclean rooms and the shared bathrooms are probably the cleanest-smelling this side of the Rift Valley. The rooms with bathroom are unsurprisingly more cheerful and have satellite TV. If you need to sate a

sweet tooth any time of the day, there's a pastry shop just round the corner.

Crystal Hotel (Map p313; ☎ 120944; www.crystal hoteleritrea.com; Bihat St; s incl breakfast US$42-56, d incl breakfast US$56-75) An excellent addition to Asmara's sleeping scene, this professionally run outfit is kept in top nick, featuring a fine selection of cheerful rooms with all the creature comforts and a working lift for easy access. If you're feeling peckish and don't fancy venturing out, there's an on-site bar and restaurant.

Top Five Hotel (Map p313; ☎ 124922/19; fax 124931; Marsatekly Ave; s/d Nfa200/360) It's impossible to go wrong at this great-value option not far from the centre. Rooms are in good shape and the atmosphere is friendly. An added bonus is the restaurant (mains Nfa60 to Nfa100), featuring excellent local and European specialities in an attractive setting.

Asmara Central Hotel (Map p313; ☎ 120041, 120446; fax 122023; Mata St; r Nfa300-370) As the name suggests, the Asmara Central boasts an enviable position in the heart of town. After a much-needed face-lift, this senior citizen looks decidedly youthful. The rooms and communal areas now feature modern fixtures, sleek bathrooms, new tiles and carpeting. It has a handful of suites for those seeking a bit more space. Brilliant value.

Embasoira Hotel (Map p311; ☎ 123222, 120233; fax 122595; Beleza St; s incl breakfast US$40-48, d incl breakfast US$57-68) It's an overpriced government-run pile, but the Embasoira remains a solid choice, with sizable rooms, squeaky-clean bathrooms and glorious gardens at the back. Bag a room with a view. Credit cards are accepted, but there's an 8% commission.

Sheghay Hotel (Map p313; ☎ 126562; Baka St; s/d Nfa180/200) No frills, flounces or phones here, but this typical middling hotel just spitting distance from the cathedral still does the trick if you're watching the pennies. If only the bathrooms were smartened up! The roof terrace proffers great views over the town.

TOP END

Sunshine Hotel (Map p311; ☎ 127880/2; fax 127866; BDHO Ave; s/d incl breakfast US$69/87; 🖳) Discerning travellers will find that the Sunshine is a reliable middle-of-the-road option. The rooms are a bit on the small side but the room scent is the smell of clean rather than cover-up air freshener. And the green-filled garden at

the back looks like a mini oasis – an instant elixir to a long day's sightseeing.

Savanna International Hotel (Map p311; ☎ 202143; fax 202146; Geregr Sudan St; s incl breakfast US$40-70, d incl breakfast US$55-85) Tired of flabby beds? Here's the antidote. We won't forget the well-sprung mattresses in the rooms we visited – so bouncy you could use them as trampolines. Overall it's shiny-clean, light-filled and well organised. That said, the architecture is dull, the carpets tatty and the furniture mismatched in some rooms. Not exactly central but within walking distance of the centre. There's a bar and restaurant.

North of Harnet Ave

BUDGET

National Pension (Map p313; ☎ 121466, 126920; Adi Ebrihim St; s with shared bathroom Nfa100-110, d with shared bathroom Nfa165-245, d Nfa220) A safe choice in this price range, with a mixed bag of rooms: ask to see a few before you make a decision to stay here, as some are pokey and have no natural light. Overall it's well maintained, clean and secure, if a bit charmless.

City Center Pension (Map p313; ☎ 201875; 176-3 St; r with shared bathroom Nfa200, r Nfa250-300) Another reliable stand-by, a skip from the post office. It has an apparent dearth of character and a few more lights would cheer things up, but the tariff is attractive and the place will never be far away when you decide to call it a night. Ask for a more expensive room if you want more breathing space.

Pensione Stella (Map p313; ☎ 120731; Adi Hawesha St; s/d with shared bathroom Nfa80/100) Off the western end of Harnet Ave, this *pension* is not exactly decked out for honeymooners but the crude rooms are acceptable and the shared bathrooms passed the schoolmarm's cleanliness inspection. It's very central and a good base if you want to spend your nights carousing at the nearby Mocambo (p325), which you will certainly do during your stay.

Red Sea Pension (Map p313; ☎ 126778; Nakfa Ave; s with shared bathroom Nfa100, d with shared bathroom Nfa120-150) Off the eastern end of Nakfa Ave, this average *pension* is slightly frayed around the edges but does the trick for budgeteers or architecture buffs: its sweeping façade is typical of the modernism style. Some rooms smell a bit musty, so sniff a few before committing. The hot communal showers are passable but the roof terrace is agreeable.

ERITREA

ERITREA

PASSEGGIATA

Times are hard in Eritrea, but good-natured hedonism has not vanished in Asmara, as testified by the *passeggiata*. Don't miss this daily ritual. As in Italy, join the evening event (between 5pm and 6.30pm), when the whole town promenades up and down Harnet Ave and the adjacent streets to see what's new, catch up with friends, hear the latest gossip, flirt, window-shop, and generally take things easy. It's when Asmara emerges from its torpor and is at its lively best. All terraces and cafés fill up with chattering locals sampling a cappuccino. Grab a seat at a well-positioned café and watch the world strut by. Believe us, it's hard not to gape slack-jawed at the gorgeous women dressed to kill and the elegant, classy elderly gentlemen wearing well-cut suits, sunglasses and Borsalino hats. You're not in Africa, but in a Fellini film!

TOP END

Albergo Italia (Map p313; ☎ 120740; fax 126993; Nakfa Ave; r incl breakfast US$150-250) Wow! If one day we are offered fringe benefits, we will park our grungy backpack in this boutique-ish hotel housed in an old Italian villa. Offering a fine sense of individuality, the Albergo features cushy rooms decorated with period furniture, communal areas awash with heritage aesthetics, including polished wood, elegant furnishings and marble, and beds so plump you could pop them. Oh, and the bathrooms are quite blissful. If, like us, you haven't graduated to luxury class, you can still soak up the ambience in one of the two classy restaurants. Sadly, the hotel was empty when we visited.

Tiravolo District

MIDRANGE

Alla Scala Hotel (☎ 151540; fax 151541; Warsay St; s incl breakfast US$30, d incl breakfast US$48-55; 🖳) It's not straight out of the pages of *The 1001 Nights* but at least this high-rise, located about 4km from the centre on the road to the airport, is perfectly serviceable. Standards are more than acceptable, with 28 well-appointed rooms with crisp linen, scrupulously clean bathrooms, a bar and restaurant. To round things off, Internet access is free.

TOP END

Expo Hotel (☎ 182708, 186695; fax 186686; Embahara St; s incl breakfast US$27-63, d incl breakfast US$63-88; 🖳) In the vicinity of the Alla Scala Hotel, the Expo is a smart place to rest your head. Rooms are well kept and come equipped with satellite TV and balconies, and there's not a speck of dirt to be found. Facilities include a sauna to soothe aching bones, a restaurant and a bar. Rooms and beds vary in size and shape, so scope out a few. It's in Tiravolo, a five-minute taxi ride from the centre.

Bologna Hotel (☎ 186690, 181360; fax 186686; Embahara St; s US$24-36, d US$48) If fancy décor is out of the question but hygiene and absolute quiet are high on your list, then the Bologna could be worth it. This modernish establishment features bright and well-appointed rooms with satellite TV, a bar and a restaurant. It's almost next door to the Expo.

Hotel Inter-Continental Asmara (☎ 150400; inter con@eol.com.er; Warsay St; s incl breakfast US$160-180, d incl breakfast US$180-200; 🖳 🖳) This five-star bigwig sits at the very top of the country's hotel hierarchy – an easy distinction given the lack of competitors. Lying 4km from the town centre on the airport road, this muscular building won't appeal to fans of minimalism but it has all the bells and whistles your platinum card will allow for, including conference rooms, a brace of bars and restaurants, a business centre, a nightclub and a sparkling swimming pool (Nfa200 for nonguests) – not to mention the well-equipped fitness centre to keep off those extra pounds graciously added by too many pastries. Credit cards are accepted.

EATING

Asmara has the best selection of restaurants in the country and will refreshingly seem like a gourmet haven if you're returning to the city after time spent elsewhere in Eritrea. Most places serve both Eritrean and Italian dishes, but some specialise in either traditional food or Italian specialities. Many Asmara restaurants – particularly the more upmarket ones – add a tax of up to 15% to bills. Unless otherwise specified, most places are open every day for lunch and dinner. Note that most of the larger restaurants close around 10pm. Given food shortages, not everything was available on the menu when we visited.

Apart from the smart places, most restaurants charge about the same for drinks with your meal: Nfa25 to Nfa50 for local wine or Nfa90 to Nfa150 for imported wine. Beer costs around Nfa10.

Some of the smarter hotels have their own restaurants and serve average to excellent local and international food, though at more expensive prices than elsewhere.

Harnet Ave
BUDGET

American Bar (Map p313; Harnet Ave; mains Nfa20-50) This snazzy fast-food joint with polished surrounds serves up decent burgers and explosively fruity cocktails. The streetside terrace allows for a dash of people-watching panache – unless you prefer to ponder over the harmonious proportions of the Ministry of Education building, just opposite.

Bereket Fast Food (Map p313; ☎ 120383; Harnet Ave; mains Nfa25-70) Near the Municipality building, this modernish, bustling outfit churns out fresh lunches, filling breakfasts and delicious yogurts with honey (when available). Unfortunately there's no outdoor seating.

Portico Snack Bar (Map p313; Harnet Ave; mains Nfa2-25) Opposite the theatre, this popular spot fills its crevices with coffee-sipping 20-somethings without being pretentious. The menu boasts fairly standard fare (burgers, snacks and juices) but it's the buzz that most come to ingest.

Wikianos supermarket (Map p313; ☎ 200789; Harnet Ave; ⏰ 8am-1pm & 3.30-9pm Mon-Fri, 8am-1pm Sat) Opposite the Municipality building. It has the best selection of products. Most food is imported, so prices are much higher than in local supermarkets.

MIDRANGE
Spaghetti & Pizza House (Map p313; ☎ 122112; Harnet Ave; mains Nfa50-120; ⏰ Tue-Sun) This sophisticated trattorialike venue wouldn't be out of place in Roma and gets top marks for flawlessly prepared Italian specialities. It's hard to choose between the wide range of salads, bruschetta, pasta and pizza. Wash it all down with a glass of Italian or South African wine – it can't get better than this.

South of Harnet Ave
MIDRANGE
Roof Garden (Map p311; ☎ 202625; BDHO Ave; mains Nfa80-110; ⏰ Mon-Sat) If you think the time has

come to give your tastebuds something new to sing about, this is the place. The only Indian restaurant in Eritrea, this upmarket joint on the 5th floor of the NICE building gets kudos for its lip-smacking biriyani, tandoori, fish masala, naan and chapati. The service is as smooth as its divine lassis and the décor is refreshingly cosy, if not exempt from cheesy touches (those fake Greek columns…). Definitely worth the splurge.

Milano Restaurant (Map p311; ☎ 120422; Felket Ave; mains Nfa50-90) It may look unpromising from the outside but fear not, you can't go wrong at this long-standing favourite if you're after Eritrean fare. It has two dining rooms; head for the one at the back, wrapped in incense smell, where local food is served in a traditional setting. The one at the front is a more conventional option in unexceptional surrounds with standard Italian dishes.

North of Harnet Ave
BUDGET
Mask Place (Map p313; ☎ 117530; Adi Hawesha St; mains Nfa40-80) Don't expect culinary revelations in this snappy joint, just snacks and burgers honestly prepared and served by sexy waiters. Grab a steak and satisfy the inner animal. And yes, there are African masks hanging on the walls.

Pizza Napoli (Map p313; ☎ 123784; Adi Hawesha St; pizzas Nfa30-50) Well, this unpretentious yet authentic joint is not exactly straight out of Naples, but it's regarded as one of the best places in town for a fresh pizza. After having vacuumed up the ricotta, served on a

---

EATING OUT IN ASMARA

The impact of the economic crisis in Eritrea can be measured in the restaurants, among other places. Asmara has excellent dining options but life has become so hard for cash-hungry Eritreans that they can't really afford a proper meal in these venues. In less than three years, prices have almost tripled and food shortages are common. Don't be surprised if you are the only customer who actually eats – most patrons just sit and ask for a *mai gas* (bottle of water), an Asmara Beer or a cup of coffee. True, it's a bit indecent. In posher restaurants it's less of an issue as they are patronised by wealthier diaspora Eritreans on holiday and diplomats.

wooden plate, we won't argue. Oh, and the painting on the wall is cheesy too!

Senay Supermarket (Map p313; ☎ 122593; 176-5 St; ☽ 8am-1pm & 3.30-9pm Mon-Sat, 7am-1pm Sun) A cheaper option than Wikianos.

MIDRANGE

Casa degli Italiani (Map p313; 175-15 St; mains Nfa20-60; ☽ closed dinner Sun) It's the setting that's the pull here, more than the food. Swimming in a blithe, balmy atmosphere, this haven of peace is blessed with a faaabulous courtyard, which is a perfect spot for a relaxed feed at lunchtime or a tipple any time of the day. Try the well-presented *piatto del giorno* (dish of the day: osso bucco, lasagne, cannelloni…). It is also a good place for a restorative morning fry-up (frittata, omelette…).

Alba Bistro (Map p313; ☎ 202421; Adi Hawesha St; mains Nfa45-90) Brimming with good cheer, this place is an ideal refuelling stop after a walking tour in the area. Its energetic staff serve up pasta, meat and fish dishes, as well as tempting ice creams. There's a picture menu to facilitate your choice. It's also a good place to start the day: hoe into a scrumptious brekky and you'll leave with a smile on your face.

West of Harnet Ave
MIDRANGE

Blue Nile Bar & Restaurant (Map p311; ☎ 117965; Sematat Ave; mains Nfa80-100) The Blue Nile is heralded as one of the best restaurants in town. Judging by the *zilzil tibs* (strips of beef, fried and served slightly crunchy with *awazi* sauce) or *kwanta fir fir* (strips of beef rubbed in chilli, butter, salt and *berbere* then usually hung up and dried; served with torn-up *injera*), this reputation is not exaggerated. Be warned, the servings are voluminous, so bring an empty tum. If you want to stick to Western-style food, there is also a good

---

THE AUTHOR'S CHOICE

Sun Pizza & Fast Food (Map p313; ☎ 07 116391; Seraye St; mains Nfa40-130) Nancy, the English-speaking owner, knows her classics. Pasta offerings span creamy *carbonara* through to faultless spaghetti with seafood (a whopping Nfa130), but the pizzas are equally scrumptious. And all this within a warm setting that wouldn't be out of place in Roma. A winning formula.

---

selection of Italian dishes. It's patronised by expats and upper-crust locals, and the waiters are cute in their traditional garb.

Rendez-Vous Restaurant (Map p311; ☎ 126307; Sematat Ave; mains Nfa50-90) This newish operation (we could still smell the paint when we popped in) carries a modest nautical theme with a blue colour scheme. Foodwise it cooks up creative dishes, including fish (grilled, poached, curried, Provençal), pasta, soups and local specialities that will put a smile on your face.

China Star (Map p311; ☎ 125853; Beirut St; mains Nfa45-100; ☽ closed lunch Sun) Growing weary of *capretto* or *injera*? Take a seat amid the typical ho-hum Chinese interior, overhung with the mandatory reddish Chinese lanterns, and choose from the extensive menu. Results can be a little patchy. On the bright side it gives your palate some needed diversity.

East of Harnet Ave
MIDRANGE

Da Silla (Map p311; ☎ 121909; mains Nfa50-100; ☽ Mon-Sat) Owned by a well-travelled, English-speaking lady, Da Silla is a bit out of the way, 200m east of Bahti Meskerem Sq, but is well worth the detour for its delectable fare served in snug décor. The menu (with a good English translation) covers enough territory to suit all palates, including Italian and Eritrean specialities, all flawlessly cooked. If you want to blow your tastebuds, but not your arteries, opt for the *piatto tradizionale vegetariano* (traditional vegetarian plate).

Tiravolo District
BUDGET

Golden Fork Fast Food (Map p311; ☎ 202477; Warsay St; mains Nfa30-60) An excellent-value stomach filler for those in need of some serious Western snacking: burgers, pizzas and pastries. In warm weather, the voluminous interior spills out onto the terrace. It's a good place to make eye contact with Eritrean students.

MIDRANGE

Hidmona (☎ 07 111955; Expo Park; mains Nfa70-90) There's no question about this being one of the best places in town for traditional food and décor. Hidmona is an eclectic mix of restaurant, café, bar and live-music venue. With its lush interior and ethnic knick-knacks, scattered low tables and various indoor spaces, the snug Hidmona brings an unexpected dash of African exoticism to Expo Park. Snaffle a plate of *zilzil tibs* if you want to look local. Of course, the waiters are in national costume.

Al Sicomoro Bar & Restaurant (Map p311; ☎ 207826; 189-6 St; mains Nfa70-90) Ease a belt hole at this upscale venture and feast on palate-blowing Eritrean or Italian dishes, such as *kilwa assa* (fish with *injera*), gnocchi, penne or roast lamb. The tiramisu washed down with coffee is a victory for humanity. The wine list is ably administered to complement the food. The location, on the 2nd floor of a modern high-rise, is a bit off-putting, but that's our only gripe.

Banifer (☎ 189200; Expo Park; mains Nfa50-100; ☼ Mon-Sat) This quirky, trattorialike venue has a tempting menu showcasing the classics of Italian cuisine. Drool over a plate of *fusili* or nosh on well-prepared veal cutlet. The spiffing rooftop terrace is an unbeatable place to linger over a meal and whisper sweet nothings into your sweetheart's ears.

DRINKING

Asmara prides itself on its atmosphere-laden cafés. Most of the time they are packed with Asmarans sipping the ubiquitous *macchiato*, prompting many a visitor to wonder if anyone works in this city. Sometimes it's hard to distinguish between a café and a bar as you can drink just about anywhere and any time.

Cafés & Pastry Shops

See the boxed text on p324 for a list of our 10 favourite places. The following ones are also good places to get jazzed.

Most places listed in this section serve pastries (usually made on the premises), fruit juices and beers, and are also great for breakfast. Most are open by 7am, some earlier, and close around 9pm.

Sweet Asmara Caffe (Map p313; Harnet Ave) Almost opposite the Catholic cathedral, this sleek pastry shop is a treasure-trove for the sweet tooth, with a tempting array of diet-busting little things. And, of course, coffee. Ah, the coffee. Leaving Sweet Asmara minus a cappuccino is, quite simply, a crime.

Cafe Fiori (Map p313; 176-3 St) With an appetising selection of croissants and other delicacies that any chef in Rome would be proud of, this pastry shop should be carb-lovers' first port of call on this side of Harnet Ave.

It is usually packed to the rafters with students in the late afternoon.

Modka Caffe & Pastry (Map p313; ☎ 118382; 173-3 St) A little corner of peace, a block south from the grinding pace of Harnet Ave. Keep up your strength with a *macchiato* and a delectable pastry.

Mona Lisa Snack Bar & Pastry (Map p313; Mata St) Ignore the two tacky pillars at the entrance and grab a chair in the vast, vivacious room. Tempting pastries and good coffee.

Cathedral Snack Bar (Map p313; Harnet Ave; mains Nfa20-50) Just opposite the Catholic cathedral, this ambient spot dishes up good fare at wallet-friendly prices.

Capri (Map p313; Mata St; juices Nfa7-15) This place is famous for one thing and one thing only: fresh fruit juices. See the heap of bananas on the counter and the rows of papaya on the shelves? They are just waiting to be squeezed and blended with milk or ice cream – mmm! Pity about the large, neon-lit interior – it is as charming as a hospital waiting room.

Pasticceria Moderna (Map p313; Harnet Ave) This humming, comfortably sexy venue on the main drag concocts some of the most melt-in-the-mouth croissants we've ever surrendered to – the perfect spot to start the day. Thank your lucky stars if you can nab an outdoor table during *passeggiata*.

Damera Bar & Pastry (Map p313; Harnet Ave) Another perennial fave, with the usual winning offerings: squidgy cakes, good coffee and fresh beer. The upstairs lounge is a slightly more intimate place to imbibe.

Bars

See the boxed text, p324 for a rundown of the not-to-be-missed places. The following places are also worth considering, and usually stay open longer: until 10pm or 11pm during the week, and until at least 2am at the weekend. Music in the bars is for the most part local (Tigrinya and Amharic pop), which, like the food, takes a bit of getting used to. Western music and some reggae are also played.

Zara (Map p311; Sematat Ave) Ease into low gear sinking a cocktail at this atmospheric lounge bar. It's genteel and civilised, and a popular hang-out for well-heeled diaspora Eritreans on holiday and foreigners alike. When not on stalks gawking at the gorgeous things, expat eyes stare into rapidly

ERITREA

TOP TEN SPOTS FOR A CAFFEINE FIX (OR A TIPPLE)

Forget your good old days in Rome or Florence – Asmara is packed with cafés oozing soul and character, some of which are housed in heritage buildings. Note that the distinction between café and bar is a bit blurred; they all serve coffee, beer and local gin (aargh!). They are open every day from around 7am to 9pm or later. You'll certainly be the only foreigner in these places – be prepared to be the focus of attention for a couple of minutes. Take your pick!

■ There's something delightfully timeless about the old-fashioned, hanky-sized **Tre Stelle Bar** (Map p313; Nakfa Ave) at the eastern end of Nakfa Ave. Old regulars wearing Borsalino hats sip wonderful *macchiatos* in lively surrounds. Look at the vintage Gaggia coffee machine. So Asmarino!

■ We'll never forget the evening we spent in the super atmospheric **Bar Aquila** (Map p311; Fred Hollows St). With its vintage *billiardo* (pool table), faded football posters plastered on the walls, chequered floor, Art Deco bar and its old Campari advertisements *('un sorso di benessere')*, Bar Aquila looks like it's come straight out of a Fellini film. You'll probably be greeted with a *'buena sera'* when you enter, as if you were a member of the family.

■ The **Odeon Cinema** (Map p313; Bihat St) is a very inspiring place. The Art Deco bar on the south side of the lobby features on the cover of the *Asmara – Africa's Secret Modernist City* book, and no wonder: it is one of Asmara's finest historic interiors, with a melange of vertical and horizontal lines, and two spherical ceiling lights made of glass 'petals'. Oh, and the beer is dangerously cheap (Nfa7).

■ Inside the bowling alley complex (see p314), the laid-back **Multi Sport Bowling** (Map p313; 194-4 St) is a great place. You can while away the hours trying your hand at *billiardo* with old men wearing double-breasted suits, or even having the odd drink or two.

■ The cafeteria in the lobby area of **Cinema Roma** (Map p311; Sematat Ave) is a killer. It's high on personality, with dark wood fixtures and an impressive old projection camera. And the coffee kicks like a mule, too. The retro feel is offset by the loud TV tuned to BBC.

■ Boasting one of the most intact modernist interiors of the city, **Crispi Bar** (Map p311; Denden St) has got soul to boot. Revive your spirits with a *macchiato* or an Asmara gin if you dare, and marvel at the soothing, earth-toned '30s décor. The rounded chrome bar is a stunner, and the stools would not look out of place in a design museum. Very Asmarino.

■ Wax nostalgic in the heritage-style **Bar Zilli** (Map p311; Sematat Ave) while swilling a draught beer or an incendiary Asmara gin. This real earthy hang-out can become rough-and-ready, but that's part of the fun.

■ Almost next door to Cinema Impero, **Bar Impero** (Map p313; Harnet Ave) is another endearing café with a more traditional feel. Enjoy a treat or sip a *macchiato* while watching the sophisticated swagger of beautiful young things passing by at *passeggiata* (see p320).

■ **Casa degli Italiani** (Map p313; Harnet Ave) is the perfect salve after a day spent exploring the city on weary feet. The palm-shaded courtyard is a great place to retreat with a new friend. It's also popular at lunchtime (see p322).

■ Mmm! We can still smell the scent of freshly baked cakes and the aroma of coffee wafting from the door of **Bar Vittoria** (Map p313; Adi Hawesha St). The crowd ranges from chattering old men in well-cut suits to courting students, depending on the time of the day. Irresistible cakes and a cappuccino you'll want to bathe in.

emptying wallets: you'll have to cough up Nfa90 to Nfa120 for a glass of spirits or a high-octane cocktail. The 'Grand Screwdriver' kicks like a mule. It's a good place to warm up before hitting the clubs.

Bar Royal (Map p313; Harnet Ave) Towards the western end of Harnet Ave. It feels a bit too Westernised but it's congenial and buzzing in the late afternoon.

Hakosea (Map p311; 174-1 St) The Hakosea is housed in a nondescript 'conference hall' not far from Crispi Bar. It usually features live bands in the evening and is a great place to meet students.

Mask Place (Map p313; Adi Hawesha St) Is it a busy restaurant with a great bar, or a funky bar that does decent food? Spacious, luminous and snazzy, this bar/restaurant has a happening buzz.

Banifer (Expo Park, Tiravolo District; ☺ Mon–Sat) In the basement of the eponymous restaurant, this piano-bar pulls in a smart crowd from 7pm until late.

Berhe Aiba (Warsay St) A good venue in the city for those who prefer a straightforward, uncomplicated vibe, albeit sometimes cramped and a little sweaty. Come to this bar-disco on your own, as you can easily blend in with the crowd and get chatting if the music is not too deafening. It's on the road to the airport, about 100m past the Hotel Inter-Continental.

The bars of the larger hotels are also worth a try (see the midrange and top-end sections under Sleeping, p317).

ENTERTAINMENT

Most of the country's facilities for leisure and entertainment are in Asmara. Here you'll find decent cinemas (showing films in English and sometimes Italian) and nightclubs.

There's good potential for partying in the capital but it was very quiet when we visited. The economy was in such a shambles that few Asmarans could afford to go out. The ones who do are mostly moneyed diaspora Eritreans who have returned to the country or who are on holiday.

Nightclubs

Locals love to dance, but Asmara was not particularly awake when we visited – the economic crisis also reflects on nightlife. Still, you'll find a couple of places for whooping, whistling, sweating and jigging. Places are scattered in various parts of the city and are fairly safe for single women travellers (at least in comparison with other African cities), but expect to be the focus of attention. Men should be aware that most of the women in the smaller bars and nightclubs are prostitutes.

Iskista (traditional dancing) features a lot of shaking of body parts (some of which is hard to imagine, until you see it). It's certainly unique in style. If you can give it a go, you'll win a lot of friends, however inept and awkward you may feel.

Most clubs open only on Friday and Saturday (from around midnight to 5am). Entrance costs between Nfa50 and Nfa100, depending on the venue and on the day, and local beer costs between Nfa20 and Nfa40. Transport is not a problem; taxis usually line up outside the nightclubs.

Mocambo (Map p313; Adi Hawesha St) With its modern black-and-white décor, Mocambo is regarded as one of the most hip nightclubs, and exhilarates dance junkies every weekend with live music, both traditional and Western. It doesn't pick up until after midnight, but once it does, it rocks.

West End (Expo Park, Tiravolo District) It can get packed at weekends, mostly with wealthy Eritreans and adventurous expats. Cool, edgy and favouring both Eritrean and international tunes, with sometimes a live band on stage for good measure.

Green Pub (Hotel Inter-Continental Asmara, Warsay St; admission Nfa50) In the Hotel Inter-Continental Asmara, this Westernised pub-disco is heaving on Wednesday, Friday and Saturday. It is one of the favourite haunts of expats in search of fun and company. No doubt they are lured by the pack of gorgeous Eritrean women strutting on the dance floor.

Hidmona (Expo Park, Warsay St) The most authentic place in town. It gets frantic at weekends, with a live band knocking out Eritrean tunes and plenty of drinks flowing. Here you won't see expats spooning with local girls but only Eritreans indulging in *iskista*. It's also a bar-restaurant (see p322) where you can chill your danced-out bones.

Cinemas

The historic décor is as much fun as the flicks. It costs about Nfa10.

Cinema Impero (Map p313; Harnet Ave) One of the best places in town. It shows action-packed American and Indian films (in the original language).

Cinema Roma (Map p311; Semat Ave) Another well-known cinema, with a superb auditorium.

SHOPPING

The number of souvenir shops in Asmara is limited. For variety and colour, your best bet is to head to the central market (p314).

Aida Gift Articles Shop (Map p313; Harnet Ave) In the same building as Pensione Pisa. Has a bit of everything, but nothing outstanding.

ERITREA

Jolly Shop (Map p313; ☎ 121062; Adi Hawesha St) One block north of Harnet Ave. Items range from traditional paintings to carved figures, jewellery and pottery.

African Curio Shop (Map p311; ☎ 121109; Sematat Ave) Just off the Sandals. A good place to stock up on *mesob* (hourglass-shaped woven tables), pottery, woodcarvings and traditional clothing.

Ghidei – Eritrean Cultural Centre (☎ 124950; Rahayta St) An authentic place cheerfully decorated with Eritrean artefacts that are sometimes on sale. It's southwest of the centre.

There are goldsmiths and leather shops in the street running parallel to Harnet Ave, a block north. Gold goes for Nfa250 to Nfa300 per gram; silver is Nfa100 per gram.

GETTING THERE & AWAY
Air
Eritrean Airlines (Map p313; ☎ 125500; www.flyeritrea .com; Harnet Ave) flies three times a week to Assab (Nfa1110/2220 one way/return). Note that this flight is operated by the military and you'll be issued an open ticket only; the return flight has to be reconfirmed once in Assab. The army is given priority over civil passengers.

For details of international flights to/from Asmara airport, see p364.

Bus
The **city bus terminal** (Map p311; Eritrea Sq) lies next to the central market.

The long-distance bus station is about 10 minutes' walk due north of Harnet Ave, and is split into three different terminals. The ticket office at the main bus terminal is open from 5am to 6pm daily.

Buses to Nefasit or Ghinda (Nfa12, one hour), Massawa (Nfa28, 3½ hours), Assab (Nfa190, two days), Agordat (Nfa45, five hours), Barentu (Nfa57, six hours) and Teseney (Nfa85, one day) leave from the **main bus terminal** (Map p311; off Afabet St). There are numerous buses to Massawa until late in the afternoon. For the other destinations, buses leave early in the morning. Tickets to Barentu, Teseney and Assab should be bought one day in advance. For Assab, there are three buses per week.

Buses to Keren (Nfa22, three hours) leave every half hour from the **second bus terminal** (Map p311; Falket Sayb St). If you want to continue to Nakfa, you must change at Keren.

Southbound buses to Dekemhare (Nfa10, one hour), Mendefera (Nfa15, two hours), Adi Quala (Nfa22, three hours), Adi Keyh (Nfa27, four hours) and Senafe (Nfa32, six hours) leave from the **third bus terminal** (Map p311; Fengaga St). There is no fixed schedule for these buses. Most buses leave early in the morning and when they are full. Tickets are sold on the bus.

Train
An old train trundles along a remarkable railway line constructed during the Italian era (see the boxed text, below). The line runs between Asmara and Nefasit. Using this train is way more than a means of getting from Asmara to Nefasit – it's a thrilling experience. It leaves every Sunday from the **train station** (☎ 123365) at 8am and arrives in Nefasit at 9am, before returning to Asmara at 10am (arrival time: noon). It costs US$50 or Nfa750. Seats must be booked in advance, as a minimum of 10 passengers is needed.

For groups, it's possible to charter the train down to Massawa.

GETTING AROUND
Central Asmara is so small that almost all places can be reached within 20 minutes on foot.

To/From the Airport
A taxi to/from the airport should cost around Nfa150 (Nfa300 at night).

You can also take the city buses 0 and 1, which pass in front of the cathedral on

---

THE REBIRTH OF THE OLD RAILWAY

The old Italian railway, which climbed from Massawa 2128m up the escarpment to Asmara, passing through three climate zones, 30 tunnels and 65 bridges, is a masterpiece of civil engineering. At independence, Eritrea appealed for help to rehabilitate the old line. 'Impossible,' said most. 'Too expensive,' said some; 'It depends,' said others. Undeterred, the Eritreans pulled the old railway workers, metal forgers and blacksmiths out of retirement, called for volunteers and set to work. The great line reopened in 2003 and ranks among the world's great scenic railways. Each year it attracts a fair share of train buffs from all over the world.

Harnet Ave; they cost Nfa1.50. Buses normally come every 20 to 25 minutes, but the service is erratic and you can wait up to 40 minutes.

To catch the bus from the airport, bear left at the airport exit; the bus stop is a two-minute walk to the far end of the airport compound. The bus service runs from 6am to 8pm.

Bicycle
It's not a bad idea to navigate around the city by bicycle. Traffic is limited and the roads are in good shape. Riding a bike is forbidden on Harnet Ave and Sematat Ave. The **Travel House International** (Map p313; 201881/2; www.travelhouseeritrea.com; 175-15 St; 8am-noon & 2-6pm Mon-Fri, 8.30am-noon & 3.30-6pm Sat) can organise bike rental for about Nfa80 per day.

Bus
The red Mercedes buses you'll see around serve all parts of the town, as do smaller white buses ('Coaster'). It costs Nfa1 for journeys within town with the big bus and Nfa1.50 by minibus. Buses 0 and 1, which run along Harnet Ave and out to the airport, passing Tiravolo District and the Hotel Inter-Continental, are probably the most useful for travellers.

Car & Motorcycle
Asmara is the obvious base from which to rent a car. See p367 for details on the most reliable car-hire companies.

Taxi
If you hire the taxi for yourself, or take it off the main routes, it will cost about Nfa40. There are no meters, so you should always agree on a fare in advance. At night, fares usually double. On Harnet Ave, taxis can be found 24 hours a day.

AROUND ASMARA

Asmara is a good base to explore the country, and there are some excellent places within a day's trip of Asmara, such as Filfil, renowned for its superb landscape, and Debre Bizen monastery, which gives an enlightening glimpse of the religious heritage of the country.

FILFIL ፍልፍል
Forests, vegetation, greenery…hallelujah! Asmarans swear by Filfil (so do we), and for good reason. North of Asmara, the area around Filfil is Eritrea's 'Green Belt' and is home to Eritrea's last remnant of tropical forest. Amid the arid starkness of the surrounding landscape, Filfil rises up oasislike before you, cool, lush and verdant – a magical sight. There are also plantations of coffee and fruit trees. The forest is evergreen, so it's good to visit any time of year, but it's particularly lush from October to February, after the heavy rains.

Filfil is one of the best places in Eritrea to see birds and mammals. Vervet monkeys and hamadryas baboons are easily seen, and gazelles, duikers, bushbucks, klipspringers and even leopards have been reported.

Unfortunately, Filfil was off limits to travellers at the time of writing, due to obscure strategic reasons. Check out the situation while in Asmara.

Getting There & Away
Filfil lies 61km due north of Asmara and is now accessible by a good tarred road. There's no public transport so you'll have to hire a car (ideally with a driver to guide you). The journey should take around two hours (one way) from Asmara, and makes a great half-day trip. There are exceptional views along the way.

DEBRE BIZEN MONASTERY ደብረ ብዜን ገዳም
If you need an escape hatch, there's no better site than the monastery of Debre Bizen. The monastery lies 2400m above sea level, near Nefasit (east of Asmara). It was founded in 1368 by Abuna Philippos. The library at the monastery contains over 1000 manuscripts as well as various church relics, including crowns, robes and incense burners. On a clear day, the view from the monastery is breathtaking: you can see the Dahlak Islands in the Red Sea. The birdlife is good in the woodlands around the monastery.

As with many Orthodox monasteries, Debre Bizen is not open to women (or any female creatures, including hens and female donkeys!). But even if you can't enter the monastery, the journey still makes a great hike.

ERITREA

THE MOST SCENIC ROAD IN ERITREA

A tip: from Asmara, consider following the tarred road to Filfil and then south all the way down to the coastal plain (instead of backtracking directly to Asmara), where it joins the road from Massawa to Asmara. It's certainly the most scenic loop in Eritrea, with innumerable hairpin bends (hair-raising, *really*!), jaw-dropping vistas, cool air and sometimes a veil of mist which adds a touch of the bizarre. The whole circuit takes around six to seven hours (without a stop). This route, known as the Pendice Orientali, takes you through some of the most dramatic and diverse landscape in Eritrea. It makes a great day excursion. Unfortunately the road was off limits to foreigners at the time of writing (but not at the time of research, lucky us!). This is very frustrating, but the situation can change in the twinkling of an eye; check with the Tourist Information Centre in Asmara.

Men need to obtain a permit (see p363) to visit the monastery or they will be turned back. Bring lots of water (only rainwater is available). You will be welcomed with *sewa* (home-brewed beer) and bread when you arrive.

Men are welcome to stay at the simple monastery guesthouse (with just a bed or goatskin) for a couple of days. There's no charge but it's normal to make a contribution to the upkeep of the monastery. Simple gifts are a good idea too (sugar, coffee, candles etc).

Getting There & Away

To get to Debre Bizen, take the bus to Ghinda and get off at Nefasit (Nfa8, about 45 minutes). A taxi costs around Nfa400. From Nefasit, it's a 1½- to two-hour steep walk. A local will show you the start of the path up to the monastery.

NORTHERN ERITREA

Welcome to a secretive world. Bar the well-known town of Keren, northern Eritrea still remains *terra incognita* for foreigners. At the time of writing, the highly symbolic town of Nakfa was off limits to travellers. Once it becomes accessible again, don't miss the ride to reach this middle-of-nowhere town, set in the remote and wild province of Sahel. The journey alone is a lesson in Eritrean history. During the Struggle for Independence, every inch of the road was fought over, and the carcasses of the tanks that line the road testify to the ferocity of the fighting. Like the site of a pilgrimage, Nakfa is worth the long, demanding journey.

Easily accessible from Asmara, Keren is a definite must-see. This market town offers a fascinating glimpse into provincial Eritrea.

KEREN ከረን
pop 75,000 / elev 1392m

Set on a small plateau and surrounded by mountains, Keren is one of Eritrea's most attractive towns. It boasts an enticing mishmash of architectural styles – mosques, churches, colonial buildings from the Italian era – and has a vibrant feel that you won't experience elsewhere in the country bar Asmara. Though austere and arid, the surrounding landscape has a peculiar appeal. Ancient baobab and acacia trees dot the plains, and at dusk, the ruggedly good-looking mountains turn a shade of blue. Camels – sometimes making up huge caravans – far outnumber vehicles. Around Keren the beautiful Bilen women, adorned with large gold rings in their noses and henna tattoos on their necks and faces, can be seen squatting in the shade of acacia trees.

Trade blossomed once Keren was connected to Asmara by the old Italian railway, and the little town grew rapidly. Today it is the third-largest town in the country and is still an important centre of commerce.

Nevertheless Keren remains firmly small-town in flavour, and this is largely its attraction. Since Italian colonial days, the town has been a popular weekend retreat for the inhabitants of Asmara.

Orientation & Information

The centre of Keren is marked by the Giro Fiori (Circle of Flowers) roundabout.

Commercial Bank (✆ 8am-noon & 2-4.30pm Mon-Fri, 8-11am Sat) Changes cash and travellers cheques.

Post office (8am-noon & 2-6pm Mon-Fri, 8am noon Sat) About 100m off the Giro Fiori.

Sarina Hotel (per hr Nfa10; Asmara Rd; 8am-9pm) Has Internet access.

Telecommunications office (8am-8pm Mon-Sat) Next door to the post office.

Sights & Activities

There are enough sights to keep you busy for a day or two – nothing outstanding, but a bit of everything, like a kaleidoscope.

Because of its strategic position, Keren was the scene of bitter fighting between the Italians and the British during WWII. This past is conjured up at the **British War Cemetery**, off the Agordat road, about 2.5km northwest of the centre. In it, 440 Commonwealth troops lie buried, including the Hindu soldier Subadar Richpal Ram of the Sixth Rajputana Rifles, who was posthumously awarded the Victoria Cross, Britain's highest military decoration for bravery.

Just past the cemetery, a small **statue of the Madonna** watches over the road from Agordat in the west.

Keren's markets are some of the most interesting in the country and are great for an afternoon's exploration. The **covered market** immediately behind Keren Hotel sells fruit, vegetables, baskets and other household objects. Branching off the covered market are narrow alleyways, columns and low porticoes filled with the whirring machines of tailors and cloth merchants. Beyond, descending towards the well-tended **Italian cemetery**, lies the **grain market**.

If you continue on foot a further 30 minutes, you come to the shrine of **St Maryam Dearit** (see the boxed text, right), 2.3km out of town. On 29 May every year, there's a pilgrimage to the site, and hundreds of people congregate to dance and sing; if you're in the region at this time, don't miss it.

The old Italian **railway station** (now a bus station) and the old **residential area** testify to Keren's Italian heritage. As in Asmara, some of the architecture is exceptional for the period. Several Italian Roman Catholic churches dot the town, including **St Antonio** and **St Michael**.

Overlooking the town to the northeast is the **Tigu**, the Egyptian fort at 1460m, dating from the 19th century. At its foot lie the ruins of the old Imperial Palace, which was destroyed during the Struggle in 1977. There are good views from the top of the fort.

In another quarter off the covered market, the workshops and boutiques of the **silversmiths** can be found. Keren is traditionally the place to buy silver. Although it's a little cheaper than in Asmara (Nfa60 to Nfa80 per gram), the choice may not be as good.

There's also a picturesque **wood and camel market** in the riverbed, usually on Monday. You can expect up to several dozen camels. If you want to get up close and personal with one of these beasts, this is your chance!

Sleeping & Eating

If you're after a romantic hideaway, you won't be spoilt for choice in Keren. It has a couple of bland places for budget and midrange travellers, but desperately lacks upscale options.

Sarina Hotel (400230; fax 402685; Asmara Rd; s incl breakfast Nfa225-325, d incl breakfast Nfa325-425;) The ritziest of a meagre brood, this newish venture, about 2km from the centre on the road to Asmara, gives substantial bang for minimal buck. Stay here if you want functional facilities, bright rooms and prim bathrooms, but don't expect airs and graces – its institutional layout makes it a bit sterile.

Shege Hotel (401971; Agordat Rd; s/d Nfa132/187) On the outskirts of town on the Agordat

---

MADONNA OF THE BAOBAB

Close to Keren's market area there stands an ancient and gnarled baobab tree. Long venerated by the locals, it is believed to mark the spot from which fertility springs.

In the late 19th century, the Sisters of Charity built a small chapel in the tree, in the place where the city's orphans played, and it became known as St Maryam Dearit – the Madonna of the Baobab.

In 1941 some Italian soldiers took refuge in the tree from British planes. Though the tree was hit, it, the Italians and the shrine survived.

Today, according to Tigrinya tradition, if a woman desires a husband or a child, she must prepare coffee in the shade of the tree. If a traveller passes by and accepts a cup, her wish will be granted.

road, this is a no-fuss hotel with unadorned yet cleanish rooms. Best asset is the flower-filled garden at the back.

Yohannes Hotel (☎ 401422; Agordat Rd; s with shared bathroom Nfa77, d with shared bathroom Nfa88-132, s/d Nfa132/200) A Frisbee throw from Albergo Sicilia, this concrete pile offers 22 neat but rather cramped rooms with mosquito nets. Upstairs, the more expensive ones receive more sun and have firmer mattresses.

Albergo Sicilia (☎ 401059; Agordat Rd; r with shared bathroom Nfa55-80, r Nfa100) If you're in a good mood, you may find that this time-warped colonial house with a leafy courtyard has a grungy appeal. Plug your nose before using the shared bathrooms, though. Overall it's spartan but acceptable, at a pinch.

Senhit Hotel – Aregay Restaurant (☎ 401042; mains Nfa50-60) Ignore the hotel section – one look at the pongy communal toilets and your bladder will be on leave for a few days. Still, the restaurant has garnered high praise for its *capretto*. The setting is not exactly eye candy but it has a ramshackle charm. It's off Giro Fiori.

Heran Pastry (cakes Nfa4; ◷ 7am-8pm) Yogurt yogurt yogurt, get us our lactose fix please! Off Giro Fiori, this is our favourite refuelling stop for stodgy pastries accompanied by a fresh yogurt.

Mackerel Seafood Restaurant (mains Nfa45-65) Not far from the Giro Fiori, this eatery unsurprisingly focuses on fish dishes. The dining room upstairs is as sexy as an operation ward but there's outdoor seating. It also has a pastry shop.

Drinking
The veranda of Estifanos Bar (near the post office) is a good place for a sundowner while watching the world go by.

Red Sea Hotel (Giro Fiori) Another popular watering hole with a shady outdoor area.

The terrace at Keren Hotel (near the post office) is also an ideal place to sip a beer or a juice. The interior is so frumpy that it's almost charming!

Getting There & Away
Keren lies 91km northwest of Asmara. The road is in good condition.

For Nakfa, one bus leaves each morning at 5am (Nfa57, eight to nine hours). To Asmara, nearly 30 buses depart daily

(Nfa22, three hours). For Massawa, change at Asmara. For Barentu, three to five buses leave each morning (Nfa35, four hours). For Teseney, two to four buses depart each morning (Nfa64, eight hours); for Agordat there are six daily buses (Nfa20, three hours).

AROUND KEREN
There are a couple of monasteries around Keren, including the **Debre Sina monastery**, thought to date from the 6th century. The older, inner part of the church (which unlike many monasteries in Eritrea is open to both men and women) is hewn from the rock and, according to local tradition, is 2100 years old. The troglodyte dwellings of the 60 nuns and priests who live there can also be visited. The monastery lies around 35km east of Keren. You'll need a 4WD, then it's a 15-minute walk to the monastery.

NAKFA ፍችፊ
elev 1780m
Mention Nakfa to any Eritrean, and they will immediately refer to the Eritrean Resistance. This tiny, remote village lying some 221km from Asmara has achieved cult status among the whole population, and no wonder. In 1978, after the famous 'Strategic Withdrawal', Nakfa became the EPLF's centre of resistance. Located on a strategic supply route to Sudan, it received some of the most intense and continuous assaults of the entire war.

At first sight, the corrugated-iron shacks of the village are hard to reconcile with the legendary Nakfa so venerated by Eritreans. However, Nakfa has become the symbol of the Eritrean independence, and even gave its name to the country's new currency.

With a little exploration, the town's special history soon reveals itself. Nakfa is a poignant place, even for those who are not normally military-minded.

Unfortunately, the town was off limits to travellers at the time of writing, for obscure reasons – 'because of road works', we were told. Check with the tourist office in Asmara.

Sights
Should Nakfa be again accessible to travellers, plan on at least half a day's touring with a good local guide.

On the approach to Nakfa, look out for the distinct twin-peaked mountain known as **Den Den**. It was from here that the fighters broadcasted news of the Struggle every day. You can climb to the top of the mountain (around 1½ hours), from where the views are great.

In the centre, the **Nakfa mosque** is unmissable. For many Eritreans, it symbolised the unwavering faith of the fighters throughout the Struggle. After the continual Ethiopian bombardments, the mosque was the only building left standing with more than two walls. It is currently undergoing reconstruction.

Around the trenches (see below), constructed underground, and carefully camouflaged from the Ethiopian planes, were a series of buildings: the famous **underground towns**. The functions of these buildings ranged from manufacturing weapons to printing literature (see the boxed text, p298). At the time of writing, many of these sites were closed because of lack of access.

The **Tsa'abraha Underground Hospital**, 12.5km north of Nakfa, is accessible. Between 1973 and 1991, at least 100 patients a day were treated in the hospital by five doctors working full time. The wounded were brought here by donkey, mule or camel, and important medical equipment was smuggled in from Sudan. Though little more than the dug-out foundations of two hospital buildings and a pharmacy remain, the site is still worth a visit.

Around 1.5km from the hospital lie the remains of some school buildings. The **Winna Technical College** was another installation dug into the mountainside.

Sleeping & Eating

Come prepared: Nakfa doesn't exactly suffer from an embarrassment of riches when it comes to accommodation and dining options.

Apollo Hotel (s/d Nfa120/175) The only proper hotel in town, with adequate rooms. The rooms have balconies with beautiful views over the whole town.

You'll find several cheap eateries in the centre of town.

Getting There & Away

There's a daily bus from Keren to Nakfa (Nfa47, eight hours). Although it's just about 110km from Keren, the ride is nonetheless tiring. The road after Afabet is very rough in parts and winds through the mountains. However, it's not all bad news: the road was being upgraded and sealed at the time of writing. When it's completed, getting to Nakfa should be more straightforward.

SOUTHERN ERITREA

Discovering this part of Eritrea is a time-travel adventure. For history and archaeology buffs, it offers an unparalleled chance to step back in time. Ancient cities, monasteries cut into cliffs and interesting ruins all testify to former flourishing civilisations and vie for your attention. It's like a vast, open-air archaeological site. Though less spectacular than the more famous ruins found to the south in Ethiopia, some ruins are no less important. It is hoped that Qohaito and Metera will eventually be declared Unesco World Heritage sites.

THE TRENCHES

The shoulder-deep trenches that run warrenlike all over the southern ridges of the Den Den mountain give a vivid idea of the daily life of the fighters. Take a peek at the underground bunkers. In these tiny holes, measuring no more than 1m by 2m, five to six fighters ate, slept and fought their war for up to 18 months at a time without a break. Stretching for over 25 miles, the trenches meander across the hillside in an apparently random manner. In fact, these irregular patterns made accurate targeting by Ethiopian long-range artillery almost impossible.

Until quite recently, the trenches were littered with the bleached bones of soldiers from both sides. Most have now been buried. Shells of every type do still litter the landscape: rockets, mortar bombs, bullets...even napalm casings.

To the north of the trenches, on a peaceful spot overlooking the hillside, lies Dig Dig, the fighters' cemetery. Graves are marked with simple painted metal plaques, with the fighter's name and date of death given in Tigrinya.

This interweaving of past and present, along with the mystery that still surrounds Eritrea's ancient past, makes the south a fascinating place to explore. If more funds were allocated to the promotion and restoration of the ancient sites, this area could easily be a magnet for tourists – which it will eventually be when peace with Ethiopia is achieved.

What about nature? If you're after dramatic landscapes, jagged peaks and vertigo-inducing gorges, southern Eritrea has it all.

DEKEMHARE ደቀምሓረ
pop 26,000 / elev 2060m

Despite not being an especially charming destination, Dekemhare's past keeps it on the tourist map, with a handful of colonial buildings from the Italian era. The Italians had planned to make it the industrial capital of Eritrea, and Dekemhare became an important industrial centre where offices, warehouses and factories were concentrated. During the war of independence, however, the town suffered much damage, and today just two of the old factories still operate. Other remains of colonial days include the old market with its iron roof to protect the fruit, vegetables and grain, as well as several notable buildings in the centre.

That aside, there's nothing to lure the casual visitor.

Information

Commercial Bank of Eritrea (8-11.30am & 2-5pm Mon-Fri, 8-11.30am Sat) Cannot change travellers cheques, but does change cash.

Post office (8am-noon & 2-5.30pm Mon-Fri, 8am-noon Sat)

Telecom office (8am-noon & 2-7pm)

Sleeping & Eating

Dekemhare is surprisingly well endowed with places to stay and you won't have to look far to find a decent pile to rest your head. Avoid the scruffy cheapies in the centre. Safer bets are listed here. And food? There's no dearth of holes in the wall in the centre, but the hotels mentioned here have better restaurants.

Park Hotel (☎ 641304; fax 641959; Mendefera Rd; s Nfa100-200, d Nfa200-300) Opened late 2005, this monolith lies conspicuously on the outskirts of town. It's not exactly for fans of minimalism but at least you can walk barefoot on the clean tiles and jockey comfortably on the toilet seats. Oh, and the pinkish bedcovers, sporting lovely brocaded hearts (see room 103), are the tackiest we've ever seen. The restaurant (mains Nfa30 to Nfa70) has an eclectic menu with good Eritrean and Italian fare that will have you walk out belly-first.

Fika Hotel (☎ 641435; Asmara Rd; r with shared bathroom Nfa25-60, r Nfa80) On the northern edge of the town, near the bus station. It has sparse but clean rooms with furniture you would be happy to find at a flea market. Rooms vary in size, layout and plumbing quality so scope out a few before committing yourself.

KM Hotel (☎ 641812; Asmara Rd; r with shared bathroom Nfa50) Almost next door to the Fika, this more recent player stands its ground with luminous rooms and shared bathrooms that you won't dread using.

Castello Bakery & Pastry If you want to treat yourself, this place in the centre, opposite the cinema, has tempting pastries – provided flour is available. There's an adjacent bar.

Other recommendations:

Bana Hotel (☎ 641696; main street; r Nfa50) A decent place for a night's snooze, with 10 well-kept rooms arranged around a plant-filled courtyard at the back.

Paradise Hotel (☎ 641316; main street; r Nfa100) A very optimistic description but it's well maintained and there's hot showers.

Getting There & Away

Dekemhare is 37km from Asmara. For Asmara there are about 40 buses a day (Nfa10, one hour); Adi Keyh has about three buses daily (Nfa17, two hours); for Senafe, you'll need to change at Adi Keyh.

There's a rough road that winds from Dekemhare to just north of Mendefera. Three buses travel to Mendefera daily (Nfa14, around two hours).

AROUND DEKEMHARE

At the exit from a gorge, at the approach to some experimental agricultural nurseries, is the village of **Segheneyti**, about 20km from Dekemhare. It is dominated by the huge Catholic Church of St Michael and two forts from which there are good views.

In season (mid-June to mid-September), Segheneyti and the surrounding area is known for the delicious and surprisingly thirst-quenching *beles* (prickly pear fruit). Watch out for the skins – they're notorious for their almost invisible thorns.

Continuing south of Segheneyti, the road traverses the plain of Deghera, known popularly as the **Valley of the Sycamores** for the magnificent sycamore figs that march across the plain. At dusk, the trees make one of the most beautiful natural sights in all of Eritrea. Many are at least 300 years old. Village assemblies, community debates and advisory sessions from the elders still take place under their branches.

ADI KEYH ዓዲ ቀይሕ
pop 23,000 / elev 2390m

The dust-swirling city of Adi Keyh, 104km from Asmara, boasts one green mosque, a nice Catholic church and an afternoon market that should be chaotic if the economy was not in the doldrums. Unfortunately, it was almost deserted when we visited. Otherwise it is little more than a staging post for visiting the archaeological ruins of Qohaito.

Information
Commercial Bank of Eritrea (8-11am & 2-5pm Mon-Fri, 8-11.30am Sat) Close to the Central Hotel. Changes cash (euros and US dollars) and travellers cheques.
Post office (8am-noon & 2-5pm Mon-Fri, 8am-noon Sat) A small building near the police station.
Telecom office (8am-8pm) On the northern edge of the town.

Sleeping & Eating
Central Hotel (650632; s/d Nfa100/150) Opened late 2005, this is the most commendable option in town. 'Mod cons' here mean that bathrooms are well kept and functional, and that rooms are tidy and spacious.

Midre Ghenet Hotel (650188; s/d with shared bathroom Nfa50/80) Northwest of the centre, near the hospital. Decent fall-back but the shared toilets are a tad skanky. Bucket showers only.

Garden Hotel (650065; r with shared bathroom Nfa50) The best you can say about this budget hotel is that it has yawn-inspiring but acceptable rooms. It's one block behind the Commercial Bank of Eritrea.

Most of these hotels serve local food on request, with limited choice. The Central Hotel is a notch up, but don't expect culinary revelations. You'll pay around Nfa50 for a dish.

Getting There & Away
Around one to three buses leave daily for Senafe (Nfa6, 45 minutes), and only one

to two buses were running daily to Asmara (Nfa26, four hours) at the time of writing.

QOHAITO ቆሓይቶ
Shrouded in peaceful solitude amid a vast, barren plateau, the archaeological site of Qohaito is a must-see for anyone with an interest in Eritrea's ancient past. Don't expect colossal monuments, though – the scant finds of this site are not exactly gripping. Instead, come here to ponder over its former grandeur and you'll leave happy.

To top it off, the scenery is captivating on a clear day: the air is pure, the surrounding mountains make a perfect backdrop and there's a special kind of beauty in the barrenness of the plateau.

History
According to some specialists, the ancient town of Qohaito flourished at the time of the great Aksumite kingdom and provided a staging post between the ancient port of Adulis in the north and the capital of the kingdom, Aksum, in the south. Even if it was not the case (some modern scholars favour Metera), Qohaito's importance in the ancient world during this time is obvious.

Very little is known about the exact history of the settlement. A few ancient chronicles record that Qohaito was still flourishing in the 6th century AD. However, like Adulis and Metera, it then vanished very suddenly in the next one or two hundred years.

At an altitude of 2700m, Qohaito lies high above the port of Adulis and the baking lowlands, and may also once have served as a summer retreat for the Aksumite merchants. The traces of cultivated areas found between the buildings have led to the belief that Qohaito was once a garden city.

Orientation & Information
Lying some 121km south of Asmara, Qohaito's impressive ruins are spread over a large area measuring 2.5km wide by 15km long. You'll need a good half day to see all the sites. As much as 90% of the ruins remain unexcavated, and information – even the age of the sites – remains scarce. Admission is free but you will need to get a permit from the National Museum office in Asmara (see p363).

If you want to visit the rock art sites or the great canyon, you should ask at the village of

Qohaito for a guide. One guide who speaks passable English is Ibrahim. He'll check your permit and will expect a small tip.

Sights

GREAT CANYON

Wow! Be prepared to run out of superlatives. A short walk from Qohaito takes you to the edge of a vast canyon that plummets dramatically. Come here on a clear day (get there early in the morning, as it tends to cloud over later) and you'll be rewarded by truly orgasmic views.

A word of warning: don't stand too close to the edge of the canyon – it's easy to feel dizzy, and there's no fence.

TEMPLE OF MARIAM WAKIRO

ማሪያም ዋቺሮ ቤተ - መቅደስ

Although it does not play in the same league as Macchu Picchu, the Temple of Mariam Wakiro ranks among Qohaito's most important ruins. Four columns rise out of a mass of stones and fallen pillars. One of the columns is topped by an unusual four-sided capital. The temple was built on a rectangular plan on a solid platform, and may have been the site of a very early Christian church or even a pre-Christian temple. Nearby, other pilasters and platforms attest to the existence of at least half a dozen other temples.

EGYPTIAN TOMB

ሓወልቲ መቓብር ግብጻውያን

To the north, a little less than a kilometre from the ruins of Mariam Wakiro, lies an ancient underground tomb dug out of sandstone. Discovered in 1894, the tomb faces east, overlooking the Hedamo River. Rectangular and built with large blocks of stones, its most distinctive features are the two quatrefoil (flower-shaped) crosses carved on the inside walls; go inside otherwise you won't see them.

SAPHIRA DAM ሳፊራ ግድብ

This structure, lying beyond the new village mosque, measures 67m long and 16m deep and is constructed of large rectangular blocks of stone. For around 1000 years, it has served the local Saho people as the main source of water. It's supposedly Qohaito's greatest claim to fame, although it's pretty boring from a visual point of view – it's just a pool, after all.

A team of German archaeologists has suggested – amid hot controversy – that the structure may actually be a water cistern dating to the Aksumite period, and not a dam dating to the pre-Aksumite period as had previously been thought.

ADI ALAUTI CAVE & GORGE

There are several rock art sites scattered in the area. The most easily accessible and the best-preserved one is the cave of Adi Alauti. Getting there is half the fun. It involves a beautiful 30-minute walk along a mule path down the edge of a vertiginous gorge. The views of the surrounding mountains, including Mt Ambasoira (3013m) to the south (the highest peak in Eritrea), are stunning. Far below, you can make out the terraced fields and tiny *tukuls* (thatched conical huts) of a seemingly inaccessible Saho settlement. In the cave, a close inspection reveals a large number of animals, including camels, giraffes, hyenas and gazelles, depicted in ochre and white.

It's definitely worth the sweat, if only for the jaw-dropping vistas.

Getting There & Away

From Adi Keyh, it's an 11km drive south until you reach the left-hand turn-off from the main road, marked by a signpost; then it's a further 10km along a dirt road to the village of Qohaito. A 4WD is essential to cover the latter stretch. Public transport being almost nonexistent, your best bet is to book a tour with one of the travel agencies in Asmara or to rent a 4WD with driver.

AROUND QOHAITO

If you have time to kill in Adi Keyh, it's worth having a peek at the modest Aksumite ruins of **Toconda**, 4km south of Adi Keyh in a wide valley (it's signposted). The ground is littered with potsherds, broken pillars and chiselled stones. Close to the dirt road there are two pillars: a small one with a pedestal and a larger one measuring about 2m in height. Toconda is unexcavated and very little is known about it.

SENAFE ሰንዓፈ

Shelled-out buildings, heavy military presence, refugee camps on the outskirts of town, disorganised infrastructure: at first glance, Senafe, the last Eritrean town of any size before the Ethiopian border, 139km from Asmara, is not exactly reminiscent of *Alice in Wonderland*. The town suffered an extreme battering during the conflict with Ethiopia, and the scars of the tragedy are still conspicuous. With the ongoing tension with Ethiopia, Senafe is still in a bit of a mess. This shouldn't stop you visiting, though. Locals will offer you a warm welcome and the not-to-be-missed ancient city of Metera is just 2km south of Senafe.

Information
There are few facilities in Senafe. The town has no bank and the telecom office was not in operation at the time of writing.

Immigration office (main street) Opposite the temporary hospital, about 100m past the bus station. It's housed in a crumbling, concrete building, behind a ruined house, and it's staffed by the military. If you have your travel permit delivered by the Tourist Information Centre in Asmara and the permit from the Orthodox Tewahdo Church Headquarters (see p363), and provided there's no tension at the border, it will issue on the spot the permit to visit Metera and the monastery of Debre Libanos.

Post office (☷ 8am-noon & 2-6pm Mon-Fri)

Sights & Activities
Apart from the archaeological site of Metera, Senafe is known for the huge rocky outcrops that dominate the plain. You can hike to the top of **Amba Metera**, one of the outcrops, in about an hour, though there are several routes with varying degrees of difficulty. Local boys soon appear and will guide you for a small tip. The most popular route takes 45 to 60 minutes and is in parts a scramble over boulders; in one place, a fixed rope helps you up a short section in which grooves are chiselled into the rock. Heavy or bulky camera equipment should be left behind. From the top there is a dizzying view that recalls Senafe's name, which is supposedly derived from the Arabic: 'Can you see San'a?'

Make sure you go early in the morning, as it gets very hazy later on.

The **grain and vegetable market**, located just over a kilometre outside town, is worth a peek, particularly on Saturday, the major market day.

Sleeping & Eating
Star Hotel (main street; s/d with shared bathroom Nfa40/80, r Nfa60) Rooms with private bath-

room and running water, arranged around a flowery courtyard for this price? Don't ask questions – just take the room! There's an attached restaurant. This newish venture is at the southern fringe of town, just past the temporary hospital.

Senafe Hotel (main street; r with shared bathroom Nfa35) Near the main intersection, the Senafe has spartan, hanky-sized rooms and the mattresses sink like hammocks, but at this price we're not complaining.

Momona Hotel (main street; mains Nfa30-45) Was the only decent hotel before the war but was destroyed by the Ethiopians. The restaurant at the back of the compound is open, though. It serves *capretto*, pasta, *zigni* (meat cooked in a hot sauce) and sandwiches at puny prices, but the service is painfully slow.

Getting There & Away
Buses from Senafe go to Adi Keyh at least every hour (Nfa6, 45 minutes). To Asmara (Nfa30, four hours), four buses were plying the route every morning at the time of writing.

When the border with Ethiopia was open, there were regular buses to Zala Ambessa, the first village after the border.

AROUND SENAFE
Monastery of Debre Libanos
It takes a certain amount of decisiveness and a sense of adventure to come to the monastery of Debre Libanos (also known as Debre Hawariyat) but it's well worth every effort. Debre Libanos is the oldest church in Eritrea, and is accessible from the very remote village of Hamm, perched dramatically on a high plateau, with sweeping views all around.

Embedded into a steep cliff, the monastery is thought to date from the 6th century. It is open only to men (a rule that is strictly enforced) but other parts on the other side of the valley can be visited by women, including a collection of 60 mummified bodies (supposed to date from the 4th century).

Hamm can be reached in less than two hours by foot from the village of Haaz. The walk from Haaz is worthwhile for its scenery of dramatic peaks and valleys and vertiginous views south into Ethiopia. There is a guesthouse some 10 minutes from the monastery where you can stay for free (on a goat skin on the floor). Remember to leave

ERITREA

a contribution for the monastery. You'll be offered bread and *sewa*.

To get to Haaz from Senafe, follow the road to the south for about 15km until you reach a turn-off. Then take a dirt track on the right for about 9km; a 4WD is essential. In Haaz, you'll need a guide to show you the way (about Nfa50). From Hamm, a steep and fairly difficult descent takes you down to the monastery (around 50 minutes down). From the monastery, it's a one-hour walk across the valley to reach the site of the mummified bodies. From there your guide can show you a quicker way back to Hamm (about one hour), but expect a steep ascent. Altogether, it's a six-hour loop (minimum) from Haaz.

A fun alternative is to approach Debre Libanos from Tsorena, about 30km to the northwest.

Public transport is virtually nonexistent. To get there, your best bet is to hire a 4WD with driver in Asmara.

To be allowed to access the monastery, you'll need a permit obtainable at the Orthodox Tewahdo Church Headquarters in Asmara (see p363), on top of your travel permit. If you have both, the military based in Senafe will let you proceed to Debre Libanos, provided there's no tension at the border. At the time of writing, the Orthodox Tewahdo Church did not issue permits to foreigners – allegedly for security reasons. The situation is very versatile so check when you're in Asmara.

METERA መተራ

While it will never be mistaken for the Acropolis, the site of Metera is a definite must-see if you're serious about history or archaeology. Visually, it's fairly underwhelming, but it has a high historical significance. If you happen to be here late afternoon on a clear day, the truly magnificent setting adds a touch of poignancy and eeriness to the site.

History

Like Qohaito, Metera flourished around the time of the ancient civilisation of Aksum. The scattered ruins testify to the existence of a once large and prosperous town.

Metera is important for three main reasons: for its age – some of it, from about the 5th century BC, actually pre-dates Aksum;

for its huge size – it spreads over at least 20 hectares, making it the largest Aksumite site after Aksum itself and Aksum's port, Adulis; and for its unusual character – it is the only place in the Aksumite civilisation where a large bourgeois community is known to have thrived.

If you've visited Aksum in Ethiopia, you'll soon recognise the typical Aksumite architectural features present at Metera, such as construction in tiers. There are also big differences from Aksum, such as the plan and layout of the buildings. Nevertheless, it is clear that there were very strong cultural ties between Aksum, Adulis and Metera, not just during the Aksumite period, but earlier too.

Orientation & Information

The site lies about 2km south of Senafe. Admission is free but you'll need a permit from the National Museum office in Asmara (see p363).

If you want to do full justice to this site, your best bet is to visit it with a knowledgeable guide. Contact one of the travel agencies in Asmara (see p312).

Sights

THE STELE ሓወልቲ - ሕል፯ እም'ነ መ፮'ብር
One of Metera's most important objects is its enigmatic stele. Unique in Eritrea, the stele is known for its pagan, pre-Christian symbol of the sun over the crescent moon, engraved on the top of the eastern face. Like the famous Aksum stelae, it faces eastward.

Standing about 5m tall, the stele has an inscription near the middle in Ge'ez. An unknown king dedicates the stele to his ancestors who had subjugated the 'mighty people of Awanjalon, Tsebelan'.

Inexplicably, the stele was uprooted from its original position on the hill, and was at one time broken into two pieces. Today it is at the foot of the hill Amba Saim, in front of the open plain.

EXCAVATIONS

Metera was 'discovered' in 1868, when Frenchman Denis de Rivoire reported its existence. In 1959 the Ethiopian Institute of Archaeology began major excavations under the French archaeologist Francis Anfray. From 1959 to 1965 Anfray excavated various sites. A large mound 100m northwest of the stele revealed a large central building – perhaps a **royal palace** or a villa – attached to an annexe of living quarters. A huge wall surrounds the whole complex. Excavations revealed several burial chambers in the larger building; in one of them, the skeleton of a chained prisoner was discovered.

Between 1961 and 1962, two additional mounds were investigated. Excavations exposed a large, square, multiroomed complex, built on a sturdy podium. A **tomb chamber** was also unearthed – but, curiously, it was empty.

In the middle of the ruins, one of the building structures, made from finely chiselled, large blocks of limestone, contains a stairway that descends into a corridor. Though collapsed, the remains of what seems to be an **underground tunnel** are visible. According to local legend, this tunnel dates from the time of King Kaleb, and leads all the way to Aksum, hundreds of kilometres to the south. Curiously, a similar entrance is said to exist in Aksum, but it is blocked by a large boulder. A more modern hypothesis – and almost as exciting – is that the 'tunnel' is a deep burial chamber containing great sarcophagi.

Objects unearthed at Metera in the last 50 years include some beautiful and amazingly well-preserved gold objects – two crosses, two chains, a brooch, necklaces and 14 Roman coins dating from between the 2nd and 3rd centuries AD – found in a bronze vase. Bronze coins minted by the great Aksumite kings have also been found, as have many 'household' items.

Only a tiny part of Metera has been excavated. Big mounds lie tantalisingly untouched all around. The ancient people's tombs – hidden somewhere among the rocks – still await exploration, and may yield remarkable finds.

Getting There & Around
Metera lies just 2km from Senafe, so is easily reached on foot.

MENDEFERA መንደፈራ
pop 65,000 / elev 1980m
Mendefera is a city with something up its sleeve. Glamorous it may not be, but Mendefera has managed to retain a lively ambience despite Eritrea's economic woes. The capital of Dubub province, it's refreshingly active.

Reflecting an old rivalry, the town is dominated by two churches: the Orthodox San Giorgio and the Catholic church school, situated on hills opposite one another.

The town's name refers to the hill around which the town grew up. Mendefera (literally meaning 'No One Dared') is a reference to the fierce resistance put up by the local people against Italian colonialisation. The hill was never taken.

Mendefera also makes a convenient stop-off point on your way to or from the south.

Information
Commercial Bank (8am-noon & 2-5pm Mon-Fri, 8-11am Sat) Can change cash (euros and US dollars) and travellers cheques.
Paul & Peter Internet Cafe (per hr Nfa10; 8am-9pm) One block behind the post office, near the grain market.
Post office (8am-noon & 2-6pm Mon-Fri, 8am-noon Sat) On the main roundabout.
Telecom office (8am-8pm) On the main roundabout

Sleeping & Eating
Mendefera has several places to stay. Most hotels are scattered along the road to Adi Quala, on the southern outskirts of town. Most places have their own restaurant and welcome nonguests.

Mereb Hotel (611443, 611636; Adi Quala Rd; r Nfa200-280) The Mereb shines out like a diamond in the dust and has well-maintained rooms. OK, it's a tad pricey for Mendefera but it's churlish to quibble when the rates include amiable, English-speaking staff (ask for the lady who runs the place), hot showers, toilets that are a complete joy and the odd chance of scoring a room with garden views at the back. Throw in a good restaurant (mains Nfa35 to Nfa65) with an extensive menu featuring Eritrean and Italian specialities and you're laughing. It's the southernmost place to stay, about 800m from the post office.

Semhar Hotel (611356; Adi Quala Rd; r with shared bathroom Nfa50) This popular haunt boasts a pleasant setting with an enticing leafy courtyard. It features nine sparse yet cleanish rooms with shared bathrooms that shouldn't make you squirm. Another plus is the on-site restaurant (mains Nfa30 to Nfa50) with dishes that will fill your grumbling tummy without emptying your wallet.

Awet Hotel (611063; Adi Quala Rd; r with shared bathroom Nfa50) Almost a carbon copy of the

Semhar (same architect?), this relatively well-maintained place, with 19 shoebox-sized rooms clustered around a courtyard enlivened by papaya trees, is worth considering. And the shared bathrooms (cold water) will have you sighing with relief.

Kangaroo Pastry (☎ 611226; Asmara Rd; ✆ 8am-9pm) No, it's not owned by an Aussie expat... No matter, it's time to say goodbye to those pastry cravings! It's almost next door to the Mobil petrol station.

N Bar-Restaurant (Asmara Rd; mains Nfa20-45) On the road to Asmara, 100m from the Mobil petrol station, this modest eatery won't leave you everlasting memories but it knocks out local and Italian dishes and a few snacks at criminally low prices.

Getting There & Away

Mendefera's bus station lies around 20 minutes' walk from the town centre, off the road to Asmara. If your bus is continuing south, ask to be dropped off at one of the hotels on the main street.

To Adi Quala, around 20 buses leave daily (Nfa9, 1½ hours); for Barentu, you'll have to hop between towns: first to Mai Dima (Nfa21, three hours), then to Shambiko (Nfa25, three hours), then to Barentu (Nfa25, two hours). It's impossible to cover this stretch in one day; you'll have to overnight in Mai Dima or Shambiko. To Dekemhare, five buses go daily (Nfa12, three hours); to Asmara, around 50 buses depart daily (Nfa15, two hours).

The road west to Barentu is a gravel track, and there's just one fuel station, at Shambiko. If you're driving, make sure you fill up before setting off.

ADI QUALA ዓዲ ቋላ
elev 2054m

Adi Quala functions as a frontier town (it's the last town of any size before the Ethiopian border). The status of frontier town can be either a blessing or a damnation. In the case of Adi Quala, it's more a damnation. With the border with Ethiopia being indefinitely closed, this town is another casualty of war – it has lost much of its vitality and *raison d'être*. Polite observers might call it languid and peaceful, others would simply call it a depressed outpost, the fate of which is closely linked to geo-politics. But when the border crossing with Ethiopia reopens, be sure that Adi Quala will resurrect and get the most out of its proximity with Ethiopia.

At the time of writing there was no bank in Adi Quala.

Visitors come here to see the attractive **tukul church** on the southern edge of the city. The church has some interesting frescoes, including a depiction of the battle of Adwa. It's a good place to see traditional Eritrean religious painting if you haven't already; if you want a guided tour of the frescoes, ask for the resident priest Gebremichael. He'll expect a small tip.

If you plan to stay overnight, the **Gash Hotel** (s/d with shared bathroom Nfa30/50) should fit the bill. It's in a side street off the main road, close to the bus station. If Gash Hotel is full, try the **Tourist Hotel** (r with shared bathroom Nfa20, r Nfa30), on the main road. Meals are available on request at both places.

Getting There & Away

To Mendefera, around 10 buses leave daily (Nfa9, 1½ hours); to Asmara, about 10 buses run daily (Nfa22, 4½ hours). When the border with Ethiopia reopens, there will be regular services to Adwa.

THE RED SEA COAST

Say 'Red Sea Coast' and images of sprawling resorts, concrete eyesores disfiguring the land, built-up coastline and horrendous crowds spring to mind. But don't mistake Eritrea for Egypt. Luckily, the Eritrean coast has remained wild, pristine and untouched. There's a lot to love about this area: hundreds of miles of beach, luscious coastline, a historic city and a fantastic archipelago. This is an idiosyncratic, largely unspoilt region where tourism development is still in its infancy. Sure, Massawa boasts a number of well-organised facilities but it retains a refreshingly humble scale, with a distinct atmosphere. It looks not west towards Asmara but east across the water towards Arabia.

As for the Dahlak Islands off Massawa, they give access to Eritrea's thriving coral reefs. Snorkelling and diving are possible there, although the logistics are not easy to organise. Seekers of peace and solitude will experience nirvana in these sparsely populated islands, where the environment is both harsh and unique. A couple of days sailing around them or camping on their beaches makes for a memorable experience.

However, one thing is sure: when the country is back on its feet, the Eritrean Red Sea coast will face a boom in tourism and construction. The Massawa area is due to become another 'resort area' in the Red Sea, and foreign investors will be most welcome. So far, the political situation has prevented any development on the coast. Before it gets trendy, be a pioneer. Discover this region before everyone else does.

ASMARA TO MASSAWA

Be prepared for a dizzying downhill trip. The journey from Asmara to Massawa is one of the most dramatic in Eritrea. In just 115km, the road descends nearly 2500m, plummeting through mountains often clad in mist, around hairpin bends and over old Italian bridges. Built by the Italians in 1935–36, the road was the most important in the country, linking the capital with the coast. You'll find several good viewpoints along the way. Don't forget your camera!

After leaving Asmara, the first village you come to is **Sheghrini**. Meaning roughly 'I've got a problem' in Tigrinya, these were supposedly the words uttered during the colonial era by an Italian whose car, like so many other vehicles, finally gave out at the top of the steep climb from Massawa.

Three kilometres further on from the Seidici Restaurant (near Sheghrini) is the little village of **Arborobu**. Its name means 'Wednesday-Friday' after its market days. The town is known for its *beles*, in season from mid-June to mid-September.

Around 25km east of Asmara lies the little town of **Nefasit**, the starting point for trips to the Debre Bizen Monastery (p327). The monastery, perched high above the town, is just visible from the road.

Ghinda is 47km from Asmara and halfway to Massawa. It lies in a little valley that traps the warm, moist air from the coast. Rainfall is much higher than normal here and its green, terraced hillsides supply the fruit and vegetable markets of Asmara and Massawa. The Jiberti (Tigrinya Muslims) inhabit the area. Prohibited in the past from owning and cultivating land, they became instead great craftspeople, artists and scholars.

Dongollo and the springs of **Sabarguma**, 15km towards Massawa from Ghinda, are the sources of the Eritrean mineral waters that bear their names.

Nearby, across the River Dongollo, is the triple-arched **Italian bridge** with the inscription in Italian Piedmontese *Ca Custa Lon Ca Custa* (Whatever It Costs), said to be a reference to the Italian purchase of the Bay of Assab in the late 1860s.

Getting There & Away

Take any bus or minibus plying the route from Asmara to Massawa and ask to be dropped at the town of your choice.

There's also a weekly train service from Asmara to Nefasit (see p326).

MASSAWA ባጽዕ
pop 35,000

Massawa is a real gem that oozes ambience and soul and should definitely be on your itinerary. Entering Massawa Island, you could be forgiven for thinking you're in Zanzibar or Yemen, and it's pure joy to explore the alleyways and streets flanked by low, whitewashed buildings, porticoes and arcades.

Though only about 100km to the east of Asmara, Massawa could not be more different from the capital. The history, climate, architecture and atmosphere of the town seem to come from another world. Massawa has a more Arab feel to it, reflecting its centuries-old connection with Arabia across the other side of the Red Sea. The town boasts some remarkable Islamic architecture but, like an old museum, the exhibits are covered in dust and gradually disintegrating. It is hoped that in the future funds will be found to restore these historic buildings.

Although Massawa now far from warrants its former accolade of 'Pearl of the Red Sea', it retains an engaging, exotic character, which makes it an interesting place to explore. It's also hassle-free and pretty safe – no mean feat for a modern, international port. One major drawback is the heat. The average annual temperature is 29.5°C, though it often far exceeds that, sometimes reaching 46.5°C. With the high coastal humidity, the town can seem like a furnace, and there's marginal variation between day- and night-time temperatures.

ERITREA

The best time to visit Massawa is from October to May.

History

Massawa's natural deep harbour and its position close to the mouth of the Red Sea and the Indian Ocean have long made it the target of foreign powers. It was occupied by the Portuguese, Arabs, Turks and Egyptians; finally, the British held it for a time before they all but handed it over to the Italians in 1885. Trade in Massawa flourished throughout these occupations; everything – slaves, pearls, giraffes, incense, ostriches and myrrh – passed through the port.

Massawa's buildings reflect its history of occupation. The Ottoman Turks, who occupied the city for nearly 300 years, had the biggest influence on the architecture. Their successors, the Egyptians, also left a legacy of buildings and public works, including the elevated causeways, an aqueduct and the governor's palace. In 1885 the Italians occupied Massawa, and the town became their capital until it was superseded by Asmara in 1897. During this time, many of the fabulous villas were built.

Once one of the most beautiful cities on the Red Sea, Massawa was all but flattened during the Struggle for Independence. Around 90% of the town was blitzed by Ethiopian blanket bombing, and great scars are still visible. Many visitors are shocked by the derelict state of a number of historic buildings. Rehabilitation has started but the process is slow for lack of funds. Various restoration schemes are under investigation and there should be decisive changes in the forthcoming years due to the financial support of various international organisations.

Orientation

The town of Massawa consists of two islands, Taulud and Massawa, and a mainland area. The mainland area, called Massawa, is largely residential, and a long causeway connects it to Taulud Island. Taulud is home to some old Italian villas, the administrative buildings, and a few of the town's smarter hotels.

A shorter causeway connects Taulud to the second island, known simply as Batsi or Massawa Island. This is the oldest part of town and in many ways its heart. The port is here, along with most restaurants and bars.

Information

Note that business hours in Massawa differ from those in the rest of the country. Government offices open from 6am to 2.30pm Monday to Friday from June to September and from 8am to noon and 4pm to 6.30pm Monday to Friday from October to May. Private businesses open from 6am to noon and 3pm to 6pm Monday to Friday the whole year.

Commercial Bank of Eritrea (mainland; ☽ 7-11.30am & 4-5.30pm Mon-Fri, 7-10.30am Sat) Changes cash and travellers cheques (US dollars and euros).

Internet Training Centre (Massawa Island; per hr Nfa15; ☽ 7am-10pm) Under the arcades on the seafront.

Post office (Massawa Island, ☽ 7am-noon & 4-6pm Mon-Fri, 7am-noon Sat)

Telecommunications office (Massawa Island; ☽ 7am-10pm) In the same building as the post office.

Sights

MASSAWA ISLAND

Even if many buildings are in a very bad shape, they boast a dilapidated charm that is uniquely unforgettable. Start your exploration with a cup of coffee and delve into the maze of little streets. Fear not, you're never lost for long.

As you come over the causeway from Taulud Island, a broad sweep of white, arcaded *palazzi* (palaces) stretches out before you. On the corner, opposite the transport office, you'll see the **Hotel Savoiya** with its long gallery.

Near the port entrance there is a good example of a 17th-century **coral-block house**. For centuries, coral was the local building stone. Heading back towards the causeway, you'll pass the **Banco d'Italia**, an exact copy of its 1920s original and a mishmash of styles, including Gothic windows and towers. Unfortunately, the building is dilapidated and awaits restoration. In a square beyond the Banco is a rare example of a **Turkish house** with a domed roof, now partially restored. Turn back towards the port entrance, passing by the **Shaafi Mosque**. Founded in the 11th century but rebuilt several times since, it's worth a quick look.

As you keep heading towards the port, you'll come across the ancient **house of Mammub Mohammed Nahari** with soaring Ottoman-style windows on every side. Unfortunately, they are particularly decrepit. Around this area are some large and ornate

18th-century Armenian and Jewish **merchant houses**.

On your right, about 150m from the port entrance, is the **house of Abu Hamdum**, with its *mashrabiyya* (trellised) balcony, which allowed cool breezes to enter and the air inside to circulate. It's a remarkable example of Turkish Ottoman architecture, but it is almost crumbling and needs urgent restoration. Continue on until you get to the Piazza degli Incendi (meaning 'Square of the Fire', after it was the scene of a great fire in 1885), in the centre of which is the **Sheikh Hanafi Mosque**. At over 500 years old, this mosque is one of the oldest surviving structures in the city. Sheikh Hanafi was a great teacher, who funded his students' studies in Egypt. The walls of the courtyard are decorated with stuccowork and inside hangs a remarkable chandelier from the glassworks of Murano near Venice in Italy.

Passing through the piazza, notice the small group of **coral-block houses** with finely detailed façades on your right. Then turn left into the **Campo**, a huge square lined on all sides by houses with trellised balconies, finely carved wooden doors and shutters of Turkish or Egyptian origin.

To the north of the Campo is the **covered market**. Behind and to the north of the market lies the Massawa Hotel, bringing you into the main commercial artery of the town. Turn right towards the heart of the old town then take the first left. This area was the old **covered bazaar**. Its ancient roof – in the Turkish style – was beamed like an upturned boat; at the time of writing, there was only a very small section remaining. There are plans to rebuild it.

TAULUD ISLAND

Just north of the gates of the Dahlak Hotel is the **Imperial Palace**, overlooking the harbour. The palace was badly damaged during the Struggle for Independence. In its present state, it gives a very vivid idea of how all Massawa looked shortly after the war. The original palace was built by the Turkish Osdemir Pasha in the 16th century. The present building dates from 1872, when it was built for the Swiss adventurer Werner Munzinger. During the federation with Ethiopia, it was used as a winter palace by Emperor Haile Selassie, whose heraldic lions still decorate

the gates. It's usually possible to wander around the grounds.

Back on the causeway road, you'll see to your right the old Italian municipal buildings. Head south down the tree-lined road, past the Dahlak Hotel. Hotels and villas line the eastern shore. Some of the villas are exceptionally beautiful, combining elements of Art Deco style with traditional Moorish arcades and huge *mashrabiyya* balconies. After about 500m you'll find yourself at the Orthodox **St Mariam Cathedral**, which is at the end of the causeway from the mainland. Opposite the cathedral is the massive **monument** to the Eritrean Struggle for Independence. Three huge tanks are preserved where they stopped in the final assault on the town in 1990, and now stand on a black marble base which is lovingly cleaned each morning.

South of the cathedral is the famous **Red Sea Hotel**, scene of many glamorous balls in the 1960s and 1970s. Devastated in the war, it has been rebuilt and is now a reputable hotel.

At the southern tip of the island is the beautiful 1930s **Villa Melotti**, built by the owners of the Asmara brewery. With its stunning setting on the seafront, gardens and swimming pools, it has the decadent grandeur of a Fellini film set. Unfortunately, it's not possible to go near the building.

From the villa, take the road on the western side of Taulud and head north, passing by the causeway leading to the mainland. Look out for birds in the mud flats around the causeway. Pelicans are quite common visitors. Continuing north, you'll pass the **old railway station**, built during the Italian occupation, with its columns and elegant façade. There is access to the *sambuk* (dhow) **docks** just south of the train station, and it's worth taking a look at these beautiful traditional boats. There are always at least a couple around; the boats require a lot of maintenance (see the boxed text, p343).

Activities

DIVING

Massawa is the starting point for trips to the Dahlak Islands, Eritrea's main diving destination. Trips to the islands and equipment hire can be organised in Massawa. For details on boat and equipment hire, see p348.

If you want to learn to dive, you can contact the **Eritrea Diving Center** (☎ 552688, 07 120145; fax 551287) on Taulud Island. Ask for the

ERITREA

MASSAWA

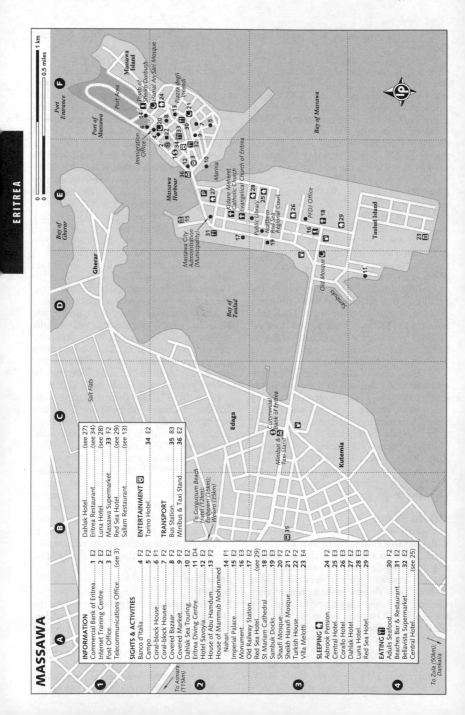

INFORMATION	
Commercial Bank of Eritrea........1	E2
Internet Training Centre............2	E2
Post Office.............................3	E2
Telecommunications Office........(see 3)	

SIGHTS & ACTIVITIES	
Banco d'Italia.........................4	F2
Campo..................................5	F2
Coral-block House....................6	F1
Coral-block Houses..................7	F2
Covered Bazaar.......................8	F2
Covered Market.......................9	E2
Dahlak Sea Touring..................10	E2
Eritrea Diving Centre................11	D4
Hotel Savoyia.........................12	E2
House of Abu Hamdum.............13	F2
House of Mammub Mohammed	
Nahari................................14	F1
Imperial Palace.......................15	E3
Monument............................16	E3
Old Railway Station..................17	E3
Red Sea Hotel........................(see 29)	
St Mariam Cathedral................18	E3
Sambuk Docks........................19	E3
Shaafi Mosque........................20	F2
Sheikh Hanafi Mosque..............21	F2
Turkish House........................22	F2
Villa Melotti..........................23	E4

SLEEPING	
Ashrook Pension.....................24	F2
Central Hotel.........................25	E3
Corallo Hotel.........................26	E3
Dahlak Hotel.........................27	E2
Luna Hotel............................28	E3
Red Sea Hotel........................29	E3

EATING	
Adulis Seafood.......................30	F2
Beaches Bar & Restaurant..........31	E2
Bellavista Supermarket.............32	E2
Central Hotel.........................(see 25)	

Dahlak Hotel.........................(see 27)	
Eritrea Restaurant...................(see 34)	
Luna Hotel............................(see 28)	
Massawa Supermarket..............33	F2
Red Sea Hotel........................(see 29)	
Sallam Restaurant...................(see 13)	

ENTERTAINMENT	
Torino Hotel..........................34	E2

TRANSPORT	
Bus Station...........................35	B3
Minibus & Taxi Stand................36	E2

To Asmara (115km);

ERITREA

0 .... 1 km
0 .... 0.5 miles

Massawa Island

Port Entrance

Port of Massawa

Port Area

Tomb of Sheikh Durbush
Hamal An Sari Mosque
piazza degli Incndi

Immigration Office

Bay of Gherar

Gherar

Massawa Harbour

Marina

Kidane Meheret Catholic Church
Evangelical Church of Eritrea
Public Library
Northem Red Sea Regional Court
PFDJ Office

Massawa City Administration (Municipality)

Old Mosque

Sembuks

Bay of Taulud

Taulud Island

Bay of Massawa

Salt Flats

Edaga

Kutemia

Commercial Bank of Eritrea

Minibus & Taxi Stand

To Gurgussum Beach Hotel (12km); Embeen (15km); Wekiro (35km)

To Zula (50km); Dankalia

ERITREA

INDEFATIGABLE DHOWS

Since the 15th century, the ancient trading vessel, the dhow, has provided a link between Africa and Asia. Unmistakable on the sea for its single lateen (triangular) sail, the dhow is painted with multicoloured patterns, particularly around the castellated stern. Today many dhows are also fitted with engines.

Three types of dhow are found in Eritrea: sizes range from the *zaroug* (the largest), to the *zeima* and the *sambuk* (the smallest). The boats are traditionally constructed (without the aid of a plan) entirely from the expertise and memory of the master craftspeople who make them. Many Yemeni builders have inherited the art directly from the legendary builders of Mukallah (on the east coast of the Gulf of Aden, in Yemen). A *sambuk* takes around three months to build.

The vessel is lined with large planks of teak, impregnated with shark oil to prevent rot. A mixture of shark fat and lime is boiled together to make an extremely efficient, airtight filler, which still outperforms any modern equivalent. Weighing between 30 and 500 tonnes and measuring from 15m to 40m, the boats ply the waters between Eritrea, Djibouti, Sudan, Somalia, the Arabian Peninsula and the Gulf. The boats attain a maximum speed of only about 5 to 6 knots, even with a favourable wind.

The holds of the boats are crammed with every merchandise imaginable, from salt, cigarettes, animal hides and coffee, to dates, shark fins, electronic goods and dried fish. Even vehicles have been loaded – with the help of a lorry. Stories and rumours still abound of dhows filled with other cargo: smuggled goods, arms and even slaves.

Navigation is always without maps. Most sailors have plied the sea routes since their childhood days. The boats' captains continue to fear the storms of the Red Sea – the dhows, though beautiful, are notoriously unstable. Pirates are also said to scour the seas.

---

helpful English-speaking Nasreddin Osman, who can organise the usual Professional Association of Diving Instructors (PADI) courses. Open-water courses (US$360) can usually be completed in four days. For those who just want a taste of Eritrea's underwater world, there's a 'Scuba Diving Introduction' for US$50, which runs over a half day.

FISHING

If you want to go fishing, you can hire a boat and a captain and set off. A half-day's rental of a small boat in the Bay of Massawa costs about Nfa2000 for one to three people, including the boat captain. Contact **Dahlak Sea Touring** (☎ /fax 552489; Massawa Island).

SNORKELLING

Green Island (also known as Sheikh Saïd Island) is 10 to 20 minutes from Massawa and is the most accessible place for decent snorkelling and tolerable beaches. To be frank, it ain't Bora Bora, but it can make an excellent retreat if you need some hush and a place to rest your sightseeing-abused feet. Dahlak Hotel organises day trips to Green Island (Nfa600 per boat). You can also contact Dahlak Sea Touring (see p349 for contact details and prices).

SWIMMING

Don't expect porcelain sand and translucent waters lapping your toes – beaches are *not* Massawa's forte. If you really fancy a dip, try the stretch of sand at the Gurgussum Beach Hotel (p344) on the mainland. It's OK, though it suffers a bit from litter and algae due to tidal fluctuations. It can get crowded at weekends. You could also head to Green Island (see left).

Sleeping

It's best to avoid the hotels on Massawa Island bar the one we've included. They are noisy and decrepit and none of them can be seriously recommended. Though less central, Taulud is much quieter and offers better standards in more polished surroundings, but prices are fairly high for Eritrea. A brief reminder: though most hotels are close to the shore, there's no beach where you can cool off.

TAULUD ISLAND

Red Sea Hotel (☎ 552839; fax 552544; s/d Nfa420/480; ⌘) This Italian-designed hotel is regarded as one of the best options in Massawa. It is well arranged and has 50 tidy rooms with air-con, satellite TV, balcony and sea views.

Freshen up in the big bathrooms after a dreamy slumber in the comfy beds. Facilities include a restaurant and well-tended gardens in which to curl up with a book.

Corallo Hotel (☎ 552406; r with shared bathroom Nfa180, r Nfa250; ✕) A good safe bet well worth bookmarking, with a ramshackle charm. There are three kinds of rooms to suit most budgets. Though very simple, the cheaper rooms are good value. The more expensive ones have bathroom, air-con and balcony with sea views. The on-site restaurant is an added bonus.

Central Hotel (☎ 552002, 552218; r Nfa240-485, ste Nfa485; ✕) Soothingly positioned by the shore, the well-managed Central Hotel won't start a revolution but it offers three kinds of well-kept rooms, with air-con and TV. The more expensive ones face the sea and are more spacious. If your wallet is plump, upgrade to a suite. There's a restaurant on the premises.

Luna Hotel (☎ 552272; r with shared bathroom Nfa130, r Nfa250; ✕) While the unexceptional rooms don't set hearts aflutter, the Luna is a decent option if the bottom line counts. There's a good restaurant on the premises.

Dahlak Hotel (☎ 552818; fax 551282; s/d Nfa250/ 325; ✕) The Dahlak was undergoing a major revamp and extension at the time of writing but construction works were progressing slowly because of the economic slump. When it's completed, it should feature excellent facilities, including a dive centre, a swimming pool and a marina – insh allah. The owner has also launched the construction of a new hotel on Dissei Island, which will likely be called Dahlak Village Resort.

MASSAWA ISLAND
Ashrook Pension (☎ 552535; r with shared bathroom Nfa110) After a ruthless inspection of all accommodation options on Massawa Island, we were left with this unpretentious guesthouse, a short bag-haul from the port entrance. It's a little dowdy if you look too closely and the shared bathrooms are a tad dank but at this price it would be churlish to quibble. There's no air-con but fans will save your night. Ibrahim, the owner, speaks good English.

MAINLAND
Gurgussum Beach Hotel (☎ 551901/4; fax 551902; r Nfa252-756; ✕) On the mainland, 12km from Massawa on a moderate stretch of beach.

This sprawling venue is the closest thing Massawa has to a resort, though 'resort' is an optimistic description. At least it's fronted with an acceptable beach. It's very popular with Eritrean families at the weekend and the beach is usually crowded at that time (and almost empty during the week). The rooms vary in size, shape and atmosphere, but overall it's clean. If your purse strings are a bit relaxed, opt for the more comfortable and spacious family cottages. There's a decent restaurant and an open-air bar on the premises. To get there from Massawa Island, hire a taxi (Nfa100) or take a minibus on Saturday or Sunday (Nfa10).

Eating
Most restaurants, except the ones at the big hotels, are on Massawa Island.

MASSAWA ISLAND ባጽዕ ደሴት
You'll find a handful of cheap eateries on and around the main street. The following ones are the pick of the crop.

Sallam Restaurant (fish dishes around Nfa80; ✕ dinner) It doesn't look like much from the outside and actually looks worse inside but, believe it or not, it is a culinary gem. Here you can relish the Yemeni speciality of fresh fish sprinkled with hot pepper and baked in a tandoori oven. The fish, served with a chapatti flat bread, is served in two sizes: medium and big. It's absolutely superb! Ask also for the mokbusa, the traditional accompaniment made with honey, butter and either dates or bananas. It's deservedly popular with holidaying Asmarans and gets crowded at weekends. While eating you'll be surrounded by plenty of cats expecting a tidbit.

Adulis Seafood (fish dishes around Nfa70; ✕ dinner) Opposite the mosque. Adulis also specialises in seafood. It enjoys better outdoor seating than the Sallam but the fried shrimps were utterly disappointing and service was lackadaisical the day we stopped by. Alcohol is not served.

Eritrea Restaurant (☎ 552640; mains Nfa50-80) This used to be the best place for Italian food on Massawa Island but these days the Eritrea has seemingly lost much of its appeal, with a thin menu and a general lack of motivation.

Self-catering is a doddle with a smattering of well-stocked supermarkets that are easily found.

Massawa Supermarket (☎ 552480) The best stocked if you're preparing for a picnic, a trip to the islands or an expedition through Dankalia.

Bellavista Supermarket (☎ 552986) Opposite Massawa Supermarket. Another worthwhile option if you need to load up on food.

TAULUD ISLAND

Rumbling tummies won't go hungry on Taulud Island. Most hotels have an on-site restaurant and welcome nonguests. They won't win any Michelin awards but serve the usual suspects at reasonable prices. Ease a belt hole at the following favourites.

Central Hotel (mains Nfa50-100) Chequered tablecloths bring a touch of colour to this bright but impersonal dining room. Seafood, meat dishes and pasta are available.

Dahlak Hotel (mains Nfa60-120) The circular dining room proffers good views of Massawa Island. The stomach-grumbling menu includes fish and meat dishes, as well as pasta. Undecided tastebuds should go for seafood, including crabs or lobster. The indulgent wine list yields some good quaffs.

Red Sea Hotel (mains Nfa60-110) If you can forgive the plain dining room, the food is generally good quality.

Luna Hotel (mains Nfa40-60) The most affordable option. The setting is nothing flash but the food has garnered hearty recommendations for the copious servings. It's deservedly popular with weekending Eritreans, which is not a bad sign.

Beaches Bar & Restaurant (☎ 552940; mains Nfa50-95) Found at the back of the prominent, Soviet-style greyish building, this is the only independent restaurant on Taulud Island. What it lacks in style – the dining room is about as cosy as a dentist's waiting room – it makes up for with tasty dishes and a seaside terrace from where you can watch the *sambuks*. Italian and Eritrean specialities feature equally on the menu.

Drinking

There's a host of lively little bars on Massawa Island. Don't expect subdued sophistication, elaborate cocktails and nifty décor: they're rather boisterous, down-at-heel affairs serving only Asmara Beer, Eritrean gin (good luck!), sodas and coffee. Single male travellers will soon find they have plenty of local female company. Most bars have large terraces in which to idle away hours in the late evening. Just follow your nose.

Entertainment

Torino Hotel (admission Nfa30; Massawa Island; ☽ 10pm-3am) Don't come to Massawa to wallow in revelry but if you want to find a dance partner head to this hotel. It has an airy roof terrace as well as a dancing area inside with the obligatory mirror ball. Depending on the day and the clientele, the atmosphere can vary from fun and relaxed to rather seedy.

Getting There & Away
BOAT
At the time of writing, there was talk of launching regular cargo services between Massawa and Assab, in the country's south. Check while you're in Massawa.

BUS
There are frequent buses leaving from the bus station on the mainland for Asmara (Nfa28, 3½ to four hours). The last bus departs at about 5pm. For Assab, you will have to go to Asmara and catch the bus there, as the buses pass through Massawa but don't take passengers as they are usually full. For Foro (to visit Adulis) in the south, one bus leaves daily, at noon (Nfa20, two to 2½ hours).

CAR
The road to Massawa is sealed and in good condition. A normal car can make the journey from Asmara in around three hours.

TRAIN
The old Italian train linking Massawa to Asmara began functioning again in 2003, and at the time of writing only offered charter services to groups; check with travel agencies in Asmara (see p312).

Getting Around
MINIBUS
The town minibuses (with 'Taxi' written on the front) are plentiful, fast and efficient. They can be flagged down anywhere, and are great for hopping between the islands and getting to Gurgussum Beach Hotel (Nfa10) at weekends. Short journeys around town cost Nfa2.

TAXI
A taxi ride costs about Nfa60. To the Gurgussum Beach Hotel a taxi costs Nfa100.

An unofficial taxi stand can be found at the entrance of Massawa Island.

AROUND MASSAWA

North of Massawa, stretching along the sandy coast into Sudan, lies the traditional territory of the enigmatic Rashaida people (see p302). Around 4km out of Gurgussum, a track branches right off the Massawa road. A few Rashaida camps are visible between the villages of **Emberemi** and **Wekiro**. A peek into their world is as fascinating as ever, but you'll need a 4WD and a local guide who speaks Arabic. It's essential to show respect towards the people and not attempt to take any photos until you have clear permission. It's a good idea to bring some simple gifts, such as tea and sugar. You may well be expected to buy something, such as the traditional silver jewellery, and it's normal to haggle over the prices.

DAHLAK ISLANDS ዳህላክ ደሴት

It sounds like another tropical paradise on Earth but it's certainly not. Don't be confused: the Dahlak Islands are not the Bahamas. Those searching for room service, fully fledged resorts, all-night carousing and luxurious pampering were badly advised by their travel agent. The only superlatives that spring to mind are 'austere', 'rough', 'desolate'. If you come prepared, you'll enjoy this sense of austerity.

Some 350 islands lie off the Eritrean coast, the majority – 209 – of which make up the Dahlak Archipelago. Largely arid, barren and flat, the islands have a maximum altitude of 15m. Fresh water is very scarce, and very few of the islands are inhabited (only three within the Dahlak Archipelago).

Information

You need a permit to visit any of the Dahlak Islands, except Green Island. The permit costs US$20 per person for the first three days, then US$10 for each day after that. The fee has to be paid in US dollars (cash) or in nakfa. If you're joining a tour or hiring a boat, the permit should be organised for you. Don't forget your passport.

There's only one (basic) hotel on the islands. Another was being constructed when we visited. Independent travel is not really possible. You'll have to go through a boat rental operation or a travel agent in Asmara.

Sights

DAHLAK KEBIR ዳህላክ ከቢር

This is the largest island (over 650 sq km) in the archipelago, with nine villages and a population of 2300. The island has been inhabited for at least 2000 years and is known for its archaeological ruins. The islanders speak their own dialect, Dahalik, guard their own customs and traditions, and seem to use the same centuries-old building techniques as their ancestors. Most islanders make a living from the sea, either fishing in village cooperatives or collecting sea cucumbers and shark fins for the Middle East, India, the Philippines and China.

The Luul Hotel, the only hotel in the archipelago, is on this island. There's a post office on the island not far from the hotel, and a wonderful old wind-up Italian telephone, which even does for international calls (via Asmara).

On the southern coast of the island, 300m southeast of the village of Dahlak Kebir, lie some of Eritrea's most ancient relics, including 360 or so **underground cisterns**, cut from the madreporic (coral) limestone. According to local tradition, there was a different well for every day of the year. The cisterns catch rainwater and are the main source of water for the islanders, though the water from some is not drinkable now.

Around 50m southwest of the cisterns lies a huge and ancient necropolis, with literally thousands of **tombs** marked by small, upright basalt stones, beautifully inscribed with Kufic (ancient Arabic) script. The tombs are thought to date from at least AD 912 to the 15th century. Look out for the fossils scattered everywhere. Needless to say, nothing should be removed from the site.

Adel አደል

This is a fascinating and totally unexcavated site near the village of **Selawit**, around 30km north of Dahlak Kebir village, on the journey back to the Luul Hotel. Very little is known about the mysterious ruined buildings, but the site may be even older than Dahlak Kebir, possibly dating from pre-Islamic times. The buildings are beautifully constructed, with very straight, thick walls, arches and some columns.

Currently the only way of getting to the sites is by hiring a car from the Luul Hotel. From the hotel, it's a 44km journey (around

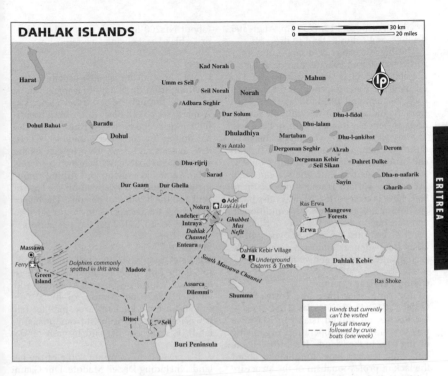

DAHLAK ISLANDS

1½ to two hours) to the village of Dahlak Kebir, along a bumpy road. It's polite to stop at the village (before or after a visit to the ruins), where you'll be offered tea and biscuits. You should leave a tip. Though not expected, any income is much appreciated – life is tough here for the islanders.

A fishing trip on a traditional *sambuk* can usually be arranged through the Luul Hotel.

DISSEI

There's a small settlement on this island, the destiny of which should change quite rapidly in the forthcoming years. The owner of the Dahlak Hotel in Massawa has launched the construction of 42 comfortable bungalows, due to open in 2007.

Activities

DIVING & SNORKELLING

There's huge potential for diving in the Dahlak Islands, but they shouldn't be mistaken for Egypt or the Bahamas. Diving in Eritrea is still in its infancy because of lack of facilities and tourists; don't expect state-of-the-art dive outfits and top-notch gear.

One of the very few positive effects of the Struggle for Independence is that Eritrea's reefs have been allowed to flourish. The reefs were also spared pollution from industry and marine traffic, and the invasions of tour boats and divers. As a result, the fish population has grown to an incredibly dense level and the reefs may well be home to one of the last pristine subaquatic coral environments in the Red Sea. The variety of wreck diving around the Dahlak Islands is also good, ranging from well-preserved Ethiopian cargo boats and WWII Italian warships to rusting Russian tankers.

To really appreciate the reefs, you need to bear a few things in mind. Because the reefs lie on a shallow continental shelf, there are no vertical drop-offs or 'deep blues' around the Dahlak Islands, and the coral growth is not as profuse here as in the northern Red Sea. During the summer, the water temperatures on the plateau rise to the upper limit of coral tolerance. Dense algae, plankton spore and sediment are also thought to inhibit growth. Most coral is found as fringing 'patch' reefs, ranging from the surface to a depth of around 15m to 18m. At greater depths, coral colonies tend to drop off.

The biggest cause of disappointment – particularly for underwater photographers – is visibility, which is notoriously erratic. The clarity of the water depends on the influx of cooler waters and plankton and nutrients from the Indian Ocean. Visibility frequently drops to between 10m and 13m, or even less. The best time for water visibility seems to be during the summer months (end of June to end of August), when temperatures outside touch 45°C. At this time, the sea can seem like a bath: surface temperatures of up to 36°C have been reported. Many cruise boats are not, or not adequately, air-conditioned, and sleeping on deck is the only option.

All divers must be certified (you will be asked for evidence), and each dive must be accompanied by a local dive master.

Diving Services

At the time of writing, the **Eritrea Diving Center** (☎ 552688, 07 120145; fax 551287; Taulud Island, Massawa) on Taulud Island in Massawa was the only diving operation organising diving trips to the islands. It's fairly reliable but some readers have complained about the lack of professionalism of the structure and its lackadaisical safety procedures.

When the extension of the Dahlak Hotel is completed, the hotel will have facilities for diving.

If you want to hire snorkelling gear, check also with the Eritrea Diving Centre

(about Nfa200 for mask, fins and snorkel) or Dahlak Sea Touring (see opposite).

Tours

Cruises around the islands, usually lasting anything from three days to a week, can be organised through the best travel agencies in Asmara (see p312). Boats range from beautiful Turkish *caiques* with private cabins and bathrooms to converted *sambuks*. Chefs, dive masters and crew are provided, as are air cylinders (boats have their own compressors). Some have diving and fishing equipment for hire. Prices depend on the type of boat and the number of persons. The bigger the group, the cheaper it is. Be prepared to spend at least US$150 per day per person.

Sleeping

Luul Hotel (bungalows US$50) On Dahlak Kebir, this is the only hotel on the islands. There are small bungalows, as well as suites. Add another US$20 per person for food. You can also use the kitchen for a small fee (all provisions must be brought from the mainland). Prices must be paid in cash in US dollars.

It's possible to camp on some of the islands, including Dissei, Madote, Dur Gaam and Dahlak Kebir. Some boat operators hire out full camping equipment; fresh water for showering is included in the price. Dissei (the east or north of the island) and Madote are probably the best for camping. Bring plenty of mosquito repellent.

THE JOYS OF DIVING IN ERITREA

The southern waters of the Red Sea around Eritrea are known principally for four things: the huge shoals of fish, the large size of individual specimens of fish, the fishes' apparent lack of fear of humans and the significant number of unusual species, even by Red Sea standards.

Snappers, jackfish, sweetlips, unicorn fish and fusiliers all form enormous schools. Giant specimens of groper are quite frequently seen, and large Napoleons, bumphead parrotfish and lyretail cod are common sightings.

The southern Red Sea was once famous for its shark population but shark life is not as abundant as it once was due to commercial shark fishing. However, reef, grey, hammerhead and nurse sharks, turtles, stingrays and dolphins are all common. Manta rays and dugongs are occasionally seen.

Divers should be aware that the reef is a very fragile ecosystem. Avoid touching living organisms or dragging equipment across the reef. Polyps can be damaged by even the gentlest contact. Maintain proper buoyancy control. Resist also the temptation to collect or buy corals or shells, and ensure that you take home all your rubbish, especially plastics.

Water temperatures range from 27°C to 29°C, so a swimskin or 3mm tropical wetsuit offers more than adequate protection.

For more information, refer to Lonely Planet's *Diving & Snorkeling Red Sea*.

Getting There & Away

Unless you've got your own boat, you'll need to hire one. The journey from Massawa to most of the islands takes between 1½ and two hours by motorboat.

Boats can be hired for picnic excursions, fishing, snorkelling or diving trips to the islands. It's worth shopping around, as prices vary from company to company and also depend on the season (low season is from October to February). If you come in the low season, you should be able to get a discount. Boat operators advise reservations of one week to 10 days in advance. However, if you just turn up, something can almost always be organised within 24 hours. If a boat is available, it takes about an hour to get it ready. The services of a boat captain are always included in the price. You may be offered cheaper deals for *sambuks;* check that they look reasonably seaworthy (some are very rickety) and are carrying sufficient life jackets and supplies of water. Most are infested with mice and cockroaches.

No boats are currently fitted with compressors. A maximum of 10 air cylinders can be carried at one time.

Eritrea Diving Centre (☎ 552688; fax 551287; Taulud Island) charges Nfa1000 for a trip to Green Island, and from Nfa1300 to Nfa11,000 for the other islands.

Dahlak Sea Touring (☎/fax 552489; Massawa Island), run by Btzuamlak Gebre Selassie who is better known as 'Maik', has various boats for hire. A trip to Green Island costs Nfa700 for one to three people. Boats to all the other islands cost between Nfa9000 and Nfa11,000. Bigger boats (for up to 10 people) can also be organised. Maik also has ice boxes, gas stoves, cutlery and dishes for hire.

Most travel agencies in Asmara (see p312) offer tours to the islands. Prices depend on the number of islands visited and on the number of people.

Getting Around

Boats can be hired from the Luul Hotel for trips to the surrounding islands and cost between Nfa1500 and Nfa6000 (depending on the distance) for round trips with up to two hours spent on an island.

A couple of village cars can usually be hired on Dahlak Kebir Island for about Nfa900 per day, including driver, petrol and mileage. The villagers have a monopoly so they can ask what they like but you can try bargaining. You'll need to give two to three days' notice to organise a car.

ADULIS አዶሊስ

To be frank, we're at a loss as to why this site has such a name. Lying 59km to the south of Massawa, near the village of **Foro**, the ancient Aksumite ruins of Adulis have a high historical significance but visually it's not particularly exciting. Adulis' present condition belies its former grandeur, and many travellers are disappointed. It remains around 98% unexcavated; almost everything is still underground. If you're not an archaeology fiend, it's probably not worth the hassle to go there.

History

Once numbering among the greatest ports of the ancient world, Adulis was the site of large and elegant buildings and a bustling international port. Inhabited since at least the 6th century BC, the site is the oldest in Eritrea.

Like modern-day Massawa, Adulis' importance lay in its port, and by the 3rd century AD the port had grown to become one of the most important on the Red Sea. Trade at this time flourished from the Mediterranean all the way to India.

Adulis' fortunes waxed and waned with the ancient kingdom of Aksum. Like Aksum, its heyday came during the 3rd and 4th centuries AD. It then went into decline, before a brief revival in the 7th century. The town supplied all sorts of foreign goods, including gold, myrrh and frankincense, to all the major Aksumite towns of the interior: Aksum, Qohaito, Metera and Keskese.

Orientation & Information

To visit Adulis, it's best to pick up a guide at Foro. Try asking for Salhé, who has long accompanied the archaeologists working on the site. He speaks quite good Italian and Arabic, and passable English; ask for him at one of the cafés or bars. From Foro it's around 7km to Adulis, in the direction of Zula.

Don't forget that you need a permit from the National Museum Office in Asmara to visit the site (see p363).

ERITREA

ERITREA

Sleeping

Assab Hotel (Foro; r with shared bathroom Nfa15) The only acceptable option in Foro, just in case you get stuck there. You guessed it – it's ultrabasic.

Getting There & Away

The road from Massawa as far as Adulis is quite good. If you're driving, you can usually find a guide at Foro.

From Massawa, one bus leaves daily for Foro at noon (Nfa20, two hours). You'll need a guide to take you to the ruins, which lie about 7km northeast of Foro. To return to Massawa, there's a bus from Foro at 6am. Chartered bush taxis can also make the journey (Nfa50). Ask around at Foro.

DANKALIA ደንካሊያ

Dankalia is the sort of place that has writers lunging for their thesauruses in search of superlatives: 'dramatic, stunning, overwhelming' will do. Dankalia is the name given to the narrow strip of land about 50km wide that stretches south of Massawa down to Djibouti (about 600km), along the coastline. You can't miss it on the map: it looks like a long peninsula protruding from the south of the country. It's a volcanic desert where you'll be struck in awe by otherworldly, lunar landscapes. It is known as one of the hottest and most inhospitable places on Earth: there's little to see, nothing to do, and no great destination awaiting you at the other end. The journey is hot, tiring and demanding; few travellers come here. But the sense of exploration is real, even on the rickety old bus. If you drive, the journey is likely to be one of the most memorable of your trip. If there's one place in Eritrea where travel is for travel's sake, it's Dankalia.

As if that was not enough, Dankalia is the territory of the legendary Afar people, described as one of the fiercest tribes on Earth (see p46). A journey into Dankalia gives a fascinating glimpse into their way of life.

The best time to go is from November to December or from March to April. At the height of summer, the heat is unbearable; in winter, the sparse rain can quickly turn the tracks and wadis (valleys) into a mire.

SOUTH TO ASSAB

Most villages on the Danakil coast survive from a mixed economy of fishing, salt mining and animal husbandry. The millennia-old trading contact with the Arabian peninsula still thrives; in some places smuggling with Yemeni merchants has proved a more lucrative means of income. If your time and budget are limited, an excursion as far as Thio will give you a good idea of the region.

Irafayle

The little fishing village of Irafayle (meaning 'Place of Elephants' – slim chance now) lies 87km from Massawa and marks the boundary between the provinces of Akele Guzay and Dankalia. Here Afar territory and its desolate landscape begins. The village offers simple refreshments and accommodation.

The bay around the **Gulf of Zula** has good sandy beaches and snorkelling, and birdlife is plentiful along the shore. The British General Sir Robert Napier landed here in 1868 to rescue the hostages held by the Emperor Tewodros.

The **Buri Peninsula** is probably one of the best places in Eritrea for wildlife. Ostriches, hamadryas baboons and gazelles (Soemmering's and Dorca) are all quite frequently seen. The wild ass is also reported, though it's now very rare. Mangroves, good beaches and huge salt flats also characterise the area. If you have the time, a detour into the peninsula is worthwhile. Ask for a guide (about Nfa50) at Ghela'elo, some 70km from Zula.

Marsa Fatma ማርሳ ፋጥማ

Marsa Fatma, 158km from Massawa, is the starting point for a visit to the crater lake known as **Lake Badda**, around two hours (43km) west of the village of **Adaito**. Lying below sea level, seasonal water from the Tigré Mountains collects here, feeding the agricultural plantations. Unless you have lots of time, it's probably not worth a special excursion.

South of Marsa Fatma, fishing village **Thio** (245km from Massawa) offers food and accommodation. The village, with its brightly painted wooden huts, is worth a stroll.

Edi ዕዲ

Edi, 130km from Thio, is another Afar fishing village and also offers food and accommodation. Some 70km south of Edi, the **Bay of**

DOMA, ANYONE?

Road-weary? Take a break and heighten your spirits in the village of Wade, around 70km southeast of Afambo. Situated on a large plain dotted with *amba* (flat-topped mountains), the village is the site of an oasis of *doum* palms. The whole area from Wade to Beylul is known for its production of the very alcoholic *doum* palm 'wine', called *doma*. You'll see old lemonade bottles in the villages frothing over with a milky liquid.

Don't miss the chance to try some; you may be invited into one of the local 'pubs': discreet enclosures made from the wood and palms of the *doum* palms. A litre bottle costs between Nfa1.50 and Nfa7, depending on the quality.

In Wade, the drink has become almost a village addiction, and the authorities have tried to ban consumption! Fines of up to Nfa100 have been introduced.

Beraesoli features a stunning lunar landscape. There are several islands off the coast.

Some 60km further south, you'll reach the village of **Beylul** (515km from Massawa), surrounded by palms. You'll be offered the *doma*, a local palm wine. From Beylul, it is another 61km until Assab.

ASSAB ዓሰብ

pop 75,000

Depending on your mood, you'll find Assab either somniferous or a ghost town. Around the middle of the day, you could pretty safely fire a gun along the main streets and not hit anyone. Assab, Eritrea's largest port, is hot, windy and industrial, and has none of the charm of small-town Massawa. Lying less than 100km from Ethiopia, at the southern extremity of the desolate and inaccessible Dankalia region, it has always been a bit of an outpost. Tourism facilities are almost totally lacking. For centuries up until recently, it was Ethiopia's principal port of access to the Red Sea. However, the dispute with Eritrea in 1998 ended that. The deviation of all Ethiopian commerce via Djibouti has made Assab even more of a backwater, and a feeling of dereliction emanates from the town. It's not as desperate as that, though. When the conflict with Ethiopia is settled, it could resurrect and again be used by the Ethiopians.

Come prepared: Assab's average annual temperature is 29.5°C, though it can reach 46.5°C. Annual rainfall is just 58mm. The coolest time is between November and February.

Orientation & Information

The town can be divided into three parts. To the northeast lies Assab Seghir (Little Assab), home to the large Yemeni community with their many restaurants, fruit sellers and small shops. In the centre lies Assab Kebhir (Big Assab), which makes up the administrative centre and includes the port. Most of the hotels are located here. To the west lies Campo Sudan, formerly the residential quarter for many of the town's Ethiopians and the main area for 'nightlife'.

There is no tourist office in Assab. The post office, in front of the Municipality of Assab, keeps regular business hours.

Note: if you come from Djibouti, you'll have to get a travel permit at the **Immigration Office** (8am-noon & 4-6pm Mon-Fri) – in the centre, not far from the Bank of Eritrea – to journey on. You'll be asked to show this permit at the various checkpoints on the road to Massawa.

Commercial Bank of Eritrea (🕒 7am-noon & 4-6.30pm Mon-Fri, 7am-11.30am Sat) Changes cash and travellers cheques.

Telecom office (🕒 7am-1pm & 4-6pm Mon-Fri, 7am-1pm Sat) Next to the Commercial Bank of Eritrea. International calls are possible from here.

Dangers & Annoyances

There are significant red-light districts, requiring vigilance, around both Campo Sudan and the port. These are poorer areas with many bars and the atmosphere can get rough and ready at times.

Heat rash is a common problem here and is best relieved by cold showers. There are also electrical power cuts.

Sights & Activities

The pleasant and sandy **Bayeta beach** lies 4km to 5km from town on the airport road. A contract taxi to here costs around Nfa120.

Sleeping & Eating

In most of the hotels in Assab, the showers are cold.

Kebal International Hotel (☎ 661700, 660229; fax 661708; r Nfa75-185; ⊠) Often still known by its old name, the Nino. It's a bargain, with three types of spacious and well-kept rooms to suit most budgets. The more expensive ones are fairly bright and comfortable and come with air-con, TV and fridge. It's in the town centre.

Assab Pension (r with shared bathroom Nfa45, d Nfa50-110; ⊠) Opposite Kebal International Hotel, this old colonial place is a reasonable option for budget travellers.

Ras Gembo Hotel (☎ 661114; s Nfa75-140, d Nfa95-175; ⊠) This faded glory, near St Michael's Church outside the main port area, lacks atmosphere and customers. Still, it remains presentable with decent rooms amid a leafy compound. Its greatest advantage is its beach.

Aurora Restaurant (mains Nfa40-80) The best place to assuage hunger pangs. Pasta and grilled fish are available. It's in the town centre.

As Assab Seghir is a Muslim area, no alcohol is served at restaurants.

Drinking

You could have a sundowner at your hotel. If you're after something more authentic, head for Campo Sudan, where local joints and outdoor 'beer gardens' (usually a gravel or cement courtyard plus a single tree decorated with Christmas lights) abound. It is a lively area at night, though you'll need to take care: bring with you the minimum amount of money, and women should be accompanied.

Getting There & Away

AIR

The airport, about 5km from town, is little more than a shack with a few wooden tables set up inside. **Eritrean Airlines** (☎ 660028, 660665), in the town centre, is closed Wednesday and Sunday. There are three flights a week to Asmara (Nfa1110/2220 one way/return).

BUS

Incredibly, a bus service connects Assab to Massawa (and on to Asmara). The track between the two cities has been improved and the service is now relatively reliable, though

still tiring and uncomfortable. After heavy rain, when the track becomes too muddy, services might be cancelled. The journey usually takes at least one day. Bring all the food and water you can carry.

Three buses a week (usually Monday, Thursday and Saturday) depart for Asmara (Nfa190) at 4am; the journey takes approximately two days. Tickets should be bought one day in advance. There is no bus station, but the bus departs from the Shell petrol station, near Kebal International Hotel.

Djibouti

The border between Eritrea and Djibouti is open but there are no buses between Assab and Djibouti. Before the recent Ethiopia–Eritrea War, the best option for Djibouti was to hitch a lift with a truck towards Addis Ababa and get off at the junction to Galafi on the border between Ethiopia and Djibouti; from there, it was an easy hitch to Djibouti City.

The alternative route via Rahaita (around 112km from Assab) in the south is possible, though traffic between the two towns is limited. From Assab, shared taxis sometimes go as far as Moulhoulé in Djibouti to pick up passengers coming from Obock. Check the situation while in Assab, as this service is unreliable. Another option is to hire a 4WD to the border and then try and hitch to Obock; from there, you can take a dhow or a speedboat to Djibouti City. In any case, there's no fixed schedule. Be ready to get stuck for a couple of days in Assab.

Ethiopia

At the time of writing the border with Ethiopia was indefinitely closed. Before the conflict with Ethiopia, many trucks ran from Assab port to Addis Ababa (1½ days).

BOAT

At the time of writing there was talk of establishing a line between Massawa and Assab.

Currently it's not possible to hitch a ride on boats to Yemen.

Getting Around

TO/FROM THE AIRPORT

Ignore the taxis jostling for custom at the exit; you can take a minibus, which costs Nfa30, into town.

MINIBUS

The yellow minibuses serve as taxis about town. Journeys cost between Nfa2 and Nfa4 depending on the distance. You can also hire the whole bus (Nfa60).

WESTERN ERITREA

Historic sites and must-see attractions? Nope. Attractive cities? Virtually nonexistent. Superb scenery? Not really. Tourist infrastructure? Poor. At first sight, western Eritrea doesn't have much to promote itself; it's easy to see why it is overshadowed by the Red Sea coast or the much-lauded south.

Time seems to have stood still in this part of the country. It lacks the development and bustle of the densely populated south or east, and tourists are an almost nonexistent species – you'll probably have the whole place to yourself. Yet it's here, in these often forgotten lowlands, where you can experience a slice of quintessential Eritrea. A bit like the Australian outback, western Eritrea seduces with wild expanses and empty spaces. All things considered, the region seeing so few travellers is a major part of its attraction. Not to mention its fascinating inhabitants: some of the ethnic groups that populate the west – such as the Kunama – are among the more enigmatic in Eritrea. In climate, geography, religion, industry, people and way of life, Eritrea's Muslim lowlands could not be more different from the Christian highlands. The more you forge west, the more you can feel a Sudanese flavour.

Very few people know that this area is also famed for its birdlife. The current state of the economy hampers any development, but this area will attract twitchers from around the globe as soon as the country is back on its feet.

During the Struggle, many towns in the west witnessed some bloody fighting. The relics of war are visible everywhere: tank carcasses, blown-up bridges, rubble and bullet holes – poignant remnants of a not-so-distant past.

With your own 4WD, the west is a great place to explore; you can also travel relatively easily by bus. The road is now entirely sealed between Asmara and Teseney. Be prepared for searing heat, pesky mosquitoes and basic accommodation.

AGORDAT ኣቍርደት

pop 25,000 / elev 615m

Lying 160km west of Asmara, Agordat is not particularly engaging. The town seems to have been severely hit by the transfer of the administration of the Gash Barka province to Barentu. The sickly state of the economy does not help and business was particularly slack when we stayed here.

There's a post office and a telecom office. The **Commercial Bank** (8am-noon & 4-5.30pm Mon-Fri, 8-11.30am Sat) changes cash and travellers cheques (US dollars and euros).

Like most towns in the west, Agordat has an overwhelmingly Arab feel to it – even the colonial governor's **palace** is Moorish-inspired. Other major Muslim landmarks include the **mosque** – the second-largest in Eritrea – and the **marketplace**, one of the most important in the lowlands.

Sleeping & Eating

Beilul Hotel & Restaurant (711228; r with shared bathroom Nfa70) A little out of town, near the main junction, this bare-bones option can fit the bill should you decide to overnight in Agordat. The rooms with ceiling fan and mosquito net are Spartan, to say the least. Meals are served in a migraine-inducing dining room but the food is surprisingly varied and tasty (fresh salad, pasta, *shiro* or chickpea purée, yogurt, roast beef).

You'll find several cheap eateries around the market and the bus station. Most places have a small terrace where you can unwind and have a drink in the evening.

Getting There & Away

Buses leave from the main square, close to the ticket office. One to three buses depart early each morning for Asmara (Nfa48, five hours); about four buses travel daily to Keren between 6am and 4pm (Nfa20, three hours); one minibus goes to Barentu (Nfa16, 1½ hours). For Teseney, you should go to Barentu and change buses there.

If you have your own vehicle, you must be off the roads outside the town by 6pm for the night curfew.

BARENTU ባረንቱ

pop 16,200 / elev 980m

Barentu is a peaceful, sprawling town that sees few visitors. Heading west, it's a relaxed place to hang out and a convenient spot to

ERITREA

break a journey to Teseney or Sudan. There's not much to see or do here, but the town exudes a congenial ambience without being overwhelming. The new seat of the regional Gash Barka administration, Barentu does not have the forlorn atmosphere that you can feel in Agordat. In the evening, the main street fills up with college students in blue shirts – a superb sight in its own right.

Barentu is also the heartland of the Kunama people, one of the most fascinating of Eritrea's ethnic groups (see p301). If you want to mingle with locals, delve into Barentu's colourful market on Thursday or Saturday, the two market days. Fantastic!

Information

The following are all located off the main square.

Commercial Bank of Eritrea (7-11.30am & 4-6pm Mon-Fri, 7-10am Sat) Changes cash and travellers cheques.
Post office (7am-2.30pm Mon-Sat, 7am-2pm Sat)
Telecom office (8am-6pm) Same building as the post office.

Sleeping & Eating

There's a bevy of slipshod cheapies located in the centre, but none can be seriously recommended.

Unite Family Hotel (731073; Teseney Rd; r with shared bathroom Nfa80) At the southern edge of town, spitting distance from the bus station, the Unite was the only reliable pile at the time of writing, and the lack of competition shows. Beds are a bit of the 'ye olde' variety but rooms come equipped with mosquito net and fan. There's a central compound where you might catch the breeze (if any) and a restaurant that serves cheap but filling staples, including pasta, *capretto* and *shiro*. Overall it's simple but not at all depressing.

Merhaba Hotel (731101; Teseney Rd) A short hop from the Unite, the Merhaba was undergoing a major overhaul when we visited and should hit the mark with well-appointed, modern rooms with all mod cons. Stay tuned.

Sahel Cafeteria (main street; mains Nfa10-20) Munch on a tasty *ful* and get stuffed for minimal coinage at this modest eatery, about 250m from the main square (don't look for signage – it's so worn out that it's illegible). The delicious yogurt goes down a treat too. There's a congenial terrace at the rear.

You'll find other cheap eateries in the centre.

Getting There & Away

The bus station is on the outskirts of the town, on the road to Teseney. For Mendefera, you'll have to hop between towns: first go to Shambiko (Nfa25, three hours, four daily) and then take a minibus to Mai Dima (Nfa25, three hours, three daily) and another to Mendefera (Nfa21, two or three daily, three hours). It's impossible to cover this stretch in one day; you'll have to overnight in Mai Dima or Shambiko. The road east to Mendefera is a gravel track, and there's just one fuel station, at Shambiko. If you're driving, make sure you fill up before setting off.

For Asmara, four buses leave daily (Nfa57, six hours). Four buses go daily to Keren (Nfa35, four hours). To Teseney, five buses leave daily (Nfa29, three hours). For Agordat (Nfa16, one hour), there are regular minibus services.

If you have your own vehicle, the night curfew comes into effect here too: be off the road by 6pm.

TESENEY ተሰነይ

pop 15,000 / elev 585m

Teseney is a large frontier town, just 45km from the Sudanese border. The status of border town usually does not bode well but Teseney is unexpectedly vibrant and thrives on trade and smuggling with neighbouring Sudan. Coming from Agordat, you'll find it refreshingly dynamic.

At first sight the town seems like a large, sprawling, rubble-strewn conglomeration, devoid of trees, beautiful architecture or anything of interest. But Teseney has an intriguing atmosphere and is unlike any other town in Eritrea.

A crossroads between Eritrea and Sudan, the town has long been a meeting place for various ethnic groups from both countries. Feel like dabbling in contraband? You can visit the various Rashaida markets on the outskirts of the town, where the Rashaida people sell virtually everything from petrol to satellite dishes.

Information

Commercial Bank (7.30-11.30am & 3.30-5pm Mon-Fri, 7-10.30am Sat) Cash can be changed here. It's in the centre.

Immigration & Nationality (☎ 721011; ☒ 8am-noon & 2-4pm Mon-Fri) Stop here to get the latest on border crossing with Sudan, as the situation is volatile. It's near the Housing & Commerce Bank, in the centre.
Post office (☒ 7.30am-noon & 3-5pm Mon-Fri, 8am-noon Sat) In the centre.
Telecom building (☒ 7am-noon & 2-5pm) Diagonally opposite the post office.

Sleeping & Eating

There are a number of cheapies in Teseney. They all offer spartan accommodation, with cold showers, fans, mosquito nets and saggy beds. And air-con? Forget it – you're in Teseney, darlings. Pick of the crop are listed. In summer, it's too hot to sleep inside; your best bet is to opt for a bed outside. A new hotel was under construction when we visited.

Luna Hotel (☎ 721037; r with shared bathroom Nfa45, r Nfa66) A good pick. Try to snaffle a room upstairs; they have more generous proportions and come equipped with private bathrooms. There's a leafy courtyard where you can hang out and relax.

Khartoum Hotel (s/d Nfa150/200) The Khartoum has the best rooms but prices are inflated and tend to vary according to the owner's mood.

Sabrina Hotel (☎ 721231; s/d Nfa66/91) The Sabrina is nothing to write home about but the rooms pass the cringe test and are more than OK for a night's kip.

For cheap and tasty fare in the evening, nothing beats the souq area, known locally as 'Shuk al Shab' ('Market of the Masses' in Arabic). It is straight out of Sudan. It's home to a huge open-air restaurant; you just join the rabble (most of them truck drivers from Sudan) at the long wooden tables and wait to be served. It's lively and fun and the evening air fills with the smoking and sizzling of the *sheia*. Beer is not available, but you can swallow delicious yogurts or guzzle exquisite orange juices. It's also a good place to start the day.

From June to August, watermelons are sold by the roads around the town.

Getting There & Away

Teseney is situated 119km west of Barentu. The road is entirely tarred from Asmara.

Teseney's bus station lies about 500m east of Shuk al Shab. Six buses run daily to Barentu (Nfa29, three hours). Two buses

go every morning to Asmara (Nfa85, one day).

Teseney is a jumping-off point to Sudan and the border was open at the time of writing. A handful of minibuses and shared taxis leave every morning to Adi Bara, at the border (Nfa30, one hour), from where you can find transportation to Kassala, the nearest Sudanese town of substance.

With your own vehicle, you must be safely off the roads by 6pm.

ERITREA DIRECTORY

ACCOMMODATION

Tourism is still in its infancy in Eritrea, and accommodation is limited.

Camping

Alas, there are no official camping facilities in Eritrea.

Hotels

There's a stark contrast between Asmara and the rest of the country. The capital boasts hotels of all categories that will suit all wallets. The real shame though is the lack of imaginative and different places to stay. Most places, including top-drawer options, rate zero in the charm department. Elsewhere the hotel scene is much more modest, except maybe in Massawa, and accommodation is quite humdrum and no cause for great excitement. Lack of investment is the main explanation. In Asmara, you should find someone who can speak English at the reception.

Many budget hotels also have cold water only (not a worry in the lowlands). Though breakfast is provided by some, you will usually be charged extra for it. Unless otherwise stated, all rooms have private bathroom facilities. Towels and soap are usually not provided in budget hotels. Power cuts are common.

All the small towns have hotels. They're often pretty basic affairs. Often rooms contain up to six beds (though you can pay for the whole room) and many lack running water (you get a bucket shower instead).

In the torrid lowlands, including Massawa, many people sleep on beds in the courtyards and on the verandas or rooftops. The cheap hotels, which do not have any

---

PRACTICALITIES

■ Eritrea uses the metric system for weights and measures.

■ Eritrea predominantly uses the 220V system, and most sockets take European continental two-round-pin plugs. Bring a universal adaptor if you need to charge your phone or run other appliances. Power cuts are frequent, especially at night.

■ The only local publication is *Hadas Eritrea* (New Eritrea), a newspaper published six days a week in both Tigrinya and Arabic. It's the voice of the government. It has an equivalent in English, *Eritrea Profile*, which is published twice weekly by the Ministry of Information. It is available from roaming street vendors (Nfa1.50). Don't expect breaking news – press freedom is a thing of the past in Eritrea.

■ Eritrean national radio, known as 'Voice of the Broad Masses', broadcasts three times a day in the nine Eritrean national languages (on 945 kHz medium wave and 41 and 49 metre bands short wave). The BBC World Service can be picked up on short-wave radios.

■ BBC World, Euronews and CNN can be received on satellite TVs.

■ Eritrea, like Italy, uses the PAL system. It differs from France (which uses the SECAM system), and the USA, Canada and Japan (which use NTSC). The three systems are not compatible.

■ The government-controlled EriTV has two national TV channels. EriTV 1 broadcasts every evening from around 4pm in Tigray, Arabic, Tigrinya and English. You can tune in to the English programmes at 9.30pm. EriTV2 broadcasts only in Asmara.

---

air-conditioning or ceiling fans, usually have similar arrangements.

In the rural areas, accommodation is sometimes little more than a bed in a hut, without running water, electricity or even washing facilities.

In Eritrea, a room with a double bed is usually called a 'single', and a room with twin beds a 'double'. In our reviews we've used the Western interpretation of singles, doubles and twins. Prices for one and two people are often the same.

Where appropriate, accommodation options are split into budget, midrange and top-end categories. In general, lodging won't wreak havoc on your budget. Prices for budget accommodation average US$7 to US$10 for singles and US$8 to US$15 for doubles. For midrange hotels, you'll pay about US$15 to US$30 for singles and US$20 to US$60 for doubles. A five-star place to stay will set you back up to US$200. These prices apply to hotels in the capital. In the rest of the country, rates are usually cheaper.

Few hotels accept credit cards. The ones that do charge a hefty commission. In Asmara, some midrange and top-end hotels quote their prices in US dollars. Payment can also be made in local currency, but at the official rate, and you may be asked to show your currency declaration form.

ACTIVITIES

Action seekers, be prepared to grit your teeth: Eritrea has great potential for outdoor pursuits but there are no proper facilities. Because of the war and the lack of funds, nothing has been really developed yet. Be patient: when the situation stabilises, Eritrea will probably catch up and you'll be offered the full slate of outdoor pursuits.

Bird-Watching

Eritrea is heaven for bird-watchers (see p304). The best bird-watching opportunities can be found around the Semenawi Bari area (Filfil), around Massawa and in the Gash Barka area. Sadly, there's no infrastructure yet. There's potential but it's still embryonic and much has to be done to promote this activity. The owner of Travel House International in Asmara (see p312) is passionate about bird-watching and may organise tailor-made bird-watching trips on request.

Diving & Snorkelling

Eritrea's best-known activity is diving in the Red Sea. The Dahlak Islands off the coast near Massawa are currently the only place where organised diving and snorkelling takes place. A word of warning, though: it has absolutely nothing to do with the northern Red Sea. Diving in Eritrea is still on a very low-key scale. At the time of writing, there was only one operator based in Massawa. When the country is back on its feet, you can expect many more outfits as there's great potential off the Dahlak Islands.

Again, don't expect too much. If you have dived, say, in Egypt, you might be slightly disappointed. Visibility is far from exceptional and most sites require a tedious (and expensive) boat ride from Massawa. Though the islands are opening up, access is still limited, monopolised by a few boat companies charging very high prices. At the moment, most destinations are out of the reach of budget travellers. To make it worthwhile and affordable, a minimum of eight divers is usually required – a condition which, in practice, is not easy to meet.

But if you can afford a trip – even just snorkelling – the opportunity is not to be missed. The sites are absolutely pristine and there are absolutely no crowds – you'll feel like a pioneer.

For more information, see p347.

Hiking & Camel Trekking

In theory hiking is possible in the various hills and mountain ranges in the east of the country, but unfortunately there are no sign-posted paths and you should consider hiring a local guide because some areas are still not cleared of land mines.

Some travel agents in the capital can organise treks into the hinterland by camel (for contact details see p368).

BUSINESS HOURS

Private businesses, shops and post offices keep various hours. In general, most open from 8am to noon and 2pm to 6pm Monday to Friday, and on Saturday morning. Many shops in the capital stay open until 7.30pm.

Most banks open from 8am to 11am and from 2pm to 4pm Monday to Friday, and from 8am to 11.30am on Saturday.

In Massawa and Assab, government offices open from 6am to 2.30pm Monday to Friday during the hot season (June to September) and from 8am to noon and 4pm to 6.30pm Monday to Friday the rest of the year. Private businesses open from 6am to noon and 3pm to 6pm Monday to Friday the whole year.

In Muslim areas, business hours are shorter during Ramadan, and cafés and restaurants may be closed during the day.

Normal opening hours for restaurants are 7.30am to 10pm, cafés 7.30am to 8pm and bars 8am till late.

Reviews won't list business hours unless they differ from the standards given here.

CHILDREN

Eritreans are very welcoming and open towards children, and travelling here with young ones is unlikely to present any major problems. However, many useful facilities for children are almost totally lacking. Other concerns include the presence of malaria in certain areas, the stifling heat in summer, the scarcity of good medical facilities outside Asmara, and the length involved in many road journeys. Not to mention the dearth of basic staples, including milk, in small towns.

Items such as nappies and mineral water are available only in the expat supermarkets of Asmara, but they are quite expensive.

When it comes to sights specifically geared towards children, it's true to say that they are rare. The beaches along the Red Sea coast are not supervised, and the Dahlak Islands are almost devoid of infrastructure.

For more information on family travel generally, see Lonely Planet's *Travel with Children* by Cathy Lanigan.

CLIMATE CHARTS

Eritrea's climate corresponds to its geography. The low, eastern zone is by far the hottest area. Temperatures range from a torrid 30°C to 39°C during the hot season (June to September) and from 25°C to 32°C during the cooler season (October to May). During the rains from July to September, the roads north can become impassable.

Rainfall on the coast is less than 200mm per year, and occurs mostly from December to February. The high humidity in the coastal region makes temperatures seem much higher than those further inland.

In the Dankalia region, temperatures can reach 50°C in the shade! Rainfall is practically zero.

In the highland zone, the average annual temperature is 18°C (17°C in Asmara). May is the hottest month, when daily temperatures can reach around 30°C. The coldest months are from December to February, when lows can approach freezing point. Temperatures can vary by up to 20°C between day and

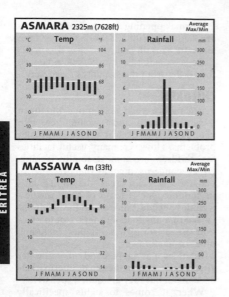

night. Light rains fall from March to April, with heavy rains from the end of June to the beginning of September.

In the western zone, temperatures range from 30°C to 41°C in the hot season (April to June). December is the coolest month (13°C to 25°C). Rainfall mirrors that in the highland zone.

See also p14.

CUSTOMS

On arrival at the airport, any major electronic items (such as expensive cameras, laptops, video cameras) must be registered at customs. This is to deter black-market business. On departure the items will be signed off. If anything is stolen during your stay in Eritrea, make sure you immediately obtain a police statement registering the loss.

Duty-free allowances include 1L of alcohol and 200 cigarettes.

Since January 2005 any person entering the country must fill in a foreign currency declaration form. The declaration form is mandatory for changing money so don't lose it. You'll have to hand it in upon departure and an official will check your statement.

It is strictly forbidden in theory to export any nakfa from Eritrea. In practice, an allowance of up to Nfa50 is permitted to allow for any problems or needs.

DANGERS & ANNOYANCES
Checkpoints

There are army checkpoints at the entrance and exit of each major town. They are pretty straightforward and foreigners never get hassled or asked for bribes; just show your passport and your travel permit (see p363) and you'll be OK.

Crime

Eritrea is a very safe country in which to travel. Muggings are unheard of, pickpocketings rare, corruption not visible and everyone lets everyone else get on with their business.

Asmara is an extremely peaceful city and the crime rate is incredibly low, but minor incidents of street crime are occasionally reported. With the economy squeezed ever tighter by the war with Ethiopia, such incidents will inevitably become more common. Markets all over the world attract pickpockets, and no less so in Asmara, so take some basic precautions. Outside the capital, the crime rate is even lower.

In the far western and northern areas bordering Sudan, a few incidents of bandit and terrorist attacks against Eritrean civilians were reported in the late 1990s but the situation was back to normal when we visited. It's still wise to keep your ear to the ground.

Land Mines

After 30 years of war, the biggest threat outside the capital is the risk of land mines and unexploded munitions. Despite the government's best efforts, thousands still litter the countryside; they continue to sporadically kill and maim the population.

Most mines are confined to the sites of major battle fronts but there is some element of risk anywhere fighting has occurred. Areas north and west of Keren and around Ghinda are still thought to be heavily mined.

Check with local government and local village officials before travelling in less-frequented areas. Never stray off the road.

EMBASSIES & CONSULATES
Eritrean Embassies & Consulates

The Eritrean embassy in Addis Ababa, Ethiopia, was closed when this edition went to print. Eritrean embassies and consulates include the following:

> **MAIMING MINES**
>
> During the Struggle, two million land mines were laid, which works out at almost one for every Eritrean inhabitant. However, the guerrillas quickly learnt to turn the deadly weapons against those who had laid them. Replanted up to 10 or 12 times, the mines accounted for 30% of all Eritrean People's Liberation Front (EPLF) victories.
>
> Since independence, the government has tried hard to rid the land of mines, but thousands still remain. Between 1995 and 1998, 3500 antitank and antipersonnel mines exploded. Almost all victims were children.

Australia (☎ 02-6282 3489; fax 02-6282 5233; 26 Guilfoyle St, Yarralumla, ACT 2606)
Canada (☎ 613-234 3989; fax 613-234 6213; Suite 610, 75 Albert St, Ottawa K1P 5E7)
Djibouti (☎ 354961; fax 250212; Le Heron District, Djibouti City)
Egypt (☎ 20-2-303-3505; fax 20-2-303-0516; 6 El Fallah St, Al Muhandesein, PO Box 2624 Cairo)
France (☎ 01 43 06 15 56; fax 01 43 06 07 51; 1 rue de Stael, 75015 Paris)
Germany (☎ 30-446 74 60; fax 30-446 74621; Stavanger Str 18, 10439 Berlin)
Italy (☎ 06-4274 1293; fax 06-4208 6806; Via Boncompagni No 16 Int 6, 00187 Roma)
Kenya (☎ 2-443164; fax 2-443165; 2nd fl, New Rehema House, Raphta Rd, Westlands, PO Box 38651, Nairobi)
Sudan (☎ 11-483834; fax 483835; Khartoum 2-St 39, PO Box 1618)
UK (☎ 207-713 0096; fax 207-713 0161; 96 White Lion St, London N1 9PF)
US (☎ 202-319 1991; fax 202-319 1304; 1708 New Hampshire Ave, NW Washington DC 20009)
Yemen (☎ 1-209422; fax 1-214088; Western Safia, Algeria St, Bldg No 68, PO Box 11040 San'a)

Embassies & Consulates in Eritrea

All embassies and consulates are based in Asmara. They are open from Monday to Friday and keep regular business hours. Visa applications are usually received in the morning.
Djibouti (Map p311; ☎ 125990; Saro St)
Egypt (Map p313; ☎ 120056; Marsa Fatuma St)
Ethiopia Closed at the time of writing.
France (Map p313; ☎ 126599, 127615; Nakfa Ave)
Germany (☎ 186670; Saba Bldg, Warsay St)
Italy (Map p311; ☎ 120160; 171-1 St)
Sudan (☎ 189595; Tiravolo District)

UK (Map p311; ☎ 120145; Mariam GMBI St)
USA (Map p311; ☎ 120004; 171-9 St)
Yemen (☎ 181399; Agamet St, Tiravolo District)

FESTIVALS & EVENTS

The best festivals and celebrations in Eritrea are linked to religious and secular holidays. See below .

FOOD

For a rundown of the culinary delights in Eritrea, see the Food & Drink section (p306). The restaurant scene is fairly low-key except in Asmara, and prices won't make you cringe. Given the state of the economy, there are severe food shortages in the country, even in Asmara, and not everything is available on the menus.

GAY & LESBIAN TRAVELLERS

Homosexuality is severely condemned by traditional and religious cultures and is a topic of absolute taboo. Eritrea's penal code concerning homosexuality is currently still based on Ethiopian law (see p262). Although homosexuality obviously exists in Eritrea, local gays behave with extreme discretion and caution. Gay and lesbian travellers are advised to do likewise.

HOLIDAYS
Public Holidays

Eritrea's public holidays can be divided into three categories: national (secular) holidays, Christian Orthodox holidays and Islamic holidays.

The country follows the Gregorian (European) calendar, with 12 months to the year. However, the Eritrean Orthodox church, which is derived from the Ethiopian Orthodox church, follows the Julian calendar, which has 13 months (see p268). Some events, therefore, trail those of the Gregorian calendar by around one week. Muslim holidays are based on the Hejira calendar, which is 10 or 11 days shorter than the Gregorian calendar, so these holidays fall 10 or 11 days earlier each year. The precise dates of these holidays are determined by the sighting of the moon.

National holidays include the following:
New Year's Day 1 January
International Women's Day 8 March
Workers' Day 1 May
Liberation Day 24 May

ERITREA

Martyrs' Day 20 June
Start of the Armed Struggle 1 September

The main Christian Orthodox holidays:
Leddet (Christmas) 7 January
Timkat (Epiphany) 19 January
Tensae (Easter) March/April (variable)
Kiddus Yohannes (Orthodox New Year) 11 September
Meskel (Finding of the True Cross) 27 September

Islamic holidays include Lailat al-Miraji, Eid al-Fitr, Eid al-Adha Arafa (the Muslim New Year), Al-Ashura, and Eid Mawlid al-Nabi (the Prophet's birthday).

For more information on the religious holidays listed in this section, see p261.

INSURANCE

A travel insurance policy covering all medical problems is essential for travel in Eritrea, while one to cover theft and loss really is helpful but not vital. For information on medical insurance, see p369.

INTERNET ACCESS

In Asmara, you'll never be far from an Internet café. Fees are usually around Nfa10 per hour. All Internet cafés have English keyboards. Unfortunately, connections were pretty slow at the time of writing. Outside the capital, Internet access is harder to find. There are a few outlets with Internet access in Massawa and Mendefera.

If you're travelling with a notebook, a couple of midrange and top-end hotels in Asmara have dataports in the rooms. However, your modem may not work once you leave your home country; for more information, see www.teleadapt.com.

LEGAL MATTERS

Foreign visitors are subject to the laws of the country in which they are travelling. Penalties for possession, use or trafficking of illegal drugs are strictly enforced in Eritrea. Convicted offenders can expect long jail sentences, fines and possible confiscation of personal property.

Note that consumption of the mildly intoxicating leaf *chat* isn't permitted in Eritrea.

Exchanging money at the black market (outside the banks) is strictly illegal. If you do indulge, be aware that you're taking a big risk: a two-year imprisonment sentence and a fine of up to Nfa2 million.

MAPS

A country map is useful, but not vital, given that most travellers rent a car with driver.

The best map currently available is the one produced by ITMB Publishing in Canada (1:9,000,000). Most map suppliers should stock it, including **Stanfords** (☎ 020-7836 1321; www.stanfords.co.uk), in London. For those planning a longer trip in the Horn, Michelin's 1:4,000,000 map 11745 *(Africa North and East – Arabia)* is very useful.

At the time of writing, no maps of the country were available in Eritrea. Your best bet is to get one before leaving home.

MONEY

The unit of currency is the nakfa (Nfa). It was introduced in November 1997 to replace the old Ethiopian birr. It is divided into 100 cents, and is available in 5, 10, 25, 50 and 100 cent pieces, and in 1, 5, 10, 20, 50 and 100 nakfa notes.

For exchange rates, see the table on the inside front cover of this guide. For information on costs, see p15.

ATMs

There are currently no ATMs in Eritrea.

Black Market

Oops, this is a very touchy issue in Eritrea since the government took drastic measures to eliminate the black market. Changing money on the black market still exists but is no longer widespread due to the heavy penalties incurred. However, it's tempting to change money on the black market because official rates massively overvalue the nakfa (up to 30%, which can make a big difference). But if you do indulge, you're taking a very big risk. Always conduct your transaction very discreetly, with somebody you know. US dollars and euros are the hot favourites. Note that the government introduced a currency declaration form in 2005, which makes changing money on the black market more complicated to handle.

Cash

While most major currencies are accepted in Asmara, US dollars (cash or travellers cheques) are the best currency to carry, followed a distant second by euros. Not only are US dollars easier to exchange outside the capital, but you have to pay for certain things in US dollars, including some hotels, visa extensions, some air tickets and the departure tax.

Credit Cards

The larger hotels in the capital, some airlines and, increasingly, some travel agents accept credit cards but they usually charge an additional 5% to 7% commission; check in advance.

Himbol in Asmara can do cash advances on your credit card but the commission exacted is a ludicrous 7%.

Moneychangers

You can change cash with a minimum of hassle at the Commercial Bank of Eritrea in all major towns and cities. Himbol exchange office in Asmara also changes money. Each transaction must be registered on your currency declaration form. Don't lose time shopping around and comparing rates; they are fixed nationwide by the government and there is no commission.

Travellers cheques can also be changed without fuss in Asmara, as well as in the bigger branches of the Commercial Bank of Eritrea outside the capital.

INTERNATIONAL TRANSFERS

If you need to wire money, **Western Union** (www.westernunion.com) transfers can be made at the Commercial Bank of Eritrea in Asmara. Using the service of this global money-transfer company is a handy way of receiving money in Eritrea. The sender pays all the charges. Contact Western Union to find out the location of their nearest agency.

Tipping

The practice of tipping is expected in the towns only. In the rural areas, you may even have your tip returned to you.

In the smaller restaurants in the towns, service is included, and Eritreans don't tip unless the service has been exceptional (in this case, Nfa2 to Nfa5 would be an appropriate amount to leave). In bars and cafés, loose coins are sometimes left. However, in the larger restaurants accustomed to tourists, at least 10% will be expected, and in the larger hotels, staff will expect a bare minimum of Nfa10.

Travellers Cheques

It's not a bad idea to carry travellers cheques in Eritrea since the exchange rates are the same as cash and no commission is applied. Moreover, the process is pretty straightforward.

As with cash, travellers cheques are best carried in US dollars, although most major currencies can be exchanged in the banks in the capital and some banks in the bigger towns.

Don't forget to list your travellers cheques on your currency declaration form upon arrival, otherwise you won't be able to cash them.

PHOTOGRAPHY & VIDEO

Decent print film is quite widely available in the capital and costs around Nfa70 for a 36-exposure Kodak film. Some slide film is also available, but only in the capital. Outside Asmara, it's difficult to find film except in the larger towns, and it may not always be within its use-by date.

Asmara has plenty of one-hour film-processing labs. Depending on the print size, processing and printing costs about Nfa130 for a 36-exposure film. Don't count on transferring digital images onto CD; consider yourself lucky if you find an Internet café that is equipped to do it.

For information and technical tips on photographing in the Horn of Africa, see the boxed text, p266.

Photographing People

In some areas, people such as the colourful Rashaida and enigmatic Afars are more accustomed to photographers and understandably want to benefit by it too. They may ask for money. The fee should always be agreed in advance. In some places, you may be charged a fee for video cameras, though this seems to be randomly applied.

Restrictions

After 30 years of war, certain subjects in Eritrea are still considered 'sensitive'. Avoid military and police installations and personnel, and even airports and bridges. Civil engineering and government buildings are off limits too.

Outside the capital, it's fine to take pictures of war relics.

ERITREA

POST

The Eritrean postal service is considered quite reliable, albeit not the speediest. Postage for the first 20g is Nfa7 worldwide, except for neighbouring countries, which are cheaper. Postcards cost Nfa6 worldwide. Courier services are available in Asmara.

There is a free poste restante service in the capital; you'll need to show your passport to collect mail. Address mail to Poste Restante, Post Office, Asmara, Eritrea.

SHOPPING

Eritrea's tourism industry is not yet greatly developed, and you won't find many shops catering to tourists. Most curios are imported from other countries (such as the wooden carvings and sculptures from Kenya).

Shops sell intricate silver and gold jewellery (priced by weight), fabrics, ceramics and basketware. Quality (and some might say taste) is variable, so it's worth taking a good look around before you buy.

More unusual and interesting souvenirs include little pewter crosses, which are often crudely fashioned.

Gabi, the equivalent of a toga worn by the local men, are also available. They are quite bulky, but can be turned to a multitude of uses – blankets, ground sheets, pillows and wraps – while you're travelling.

In some of the shops along Harnet Ave, ivory carvings and turtle shells are still available. Apart from the environmental arguments against buying these, it is also illegal to import them into most Western countries.

Outside the capital, simple pottery, basketware and combs can be found in local markets.

Bargaining

Unlike in other places in Africa, corruption is not the norm in Eritrea. Overcharging of tourists is very rare in the country, and prices are usually firmly fixed; haggling can offend Eritreans. However, all the usual discounts apply, and it's always worth asking for them for long stays in hotels, extended car hire and the like.

The one exception where haggling is almost expected is in the local shops and markets; there are no fixed prices. In shops, prices are rarely displayed.

SOLO TRAVELLERS

As the level of day-to-day harassment is negligible, solo travellers will find travelling alone a breeze. You may be a minor curiosity in rural areas, but that's part of the fun, after all. However, it is an advantage to join a group (if any) if you want to hire a car so you can share costs.

TELEPHONE & FAX

For the international dialling code, see the inside front cover of this book. International calls are best made from the telecommunications office found in all the main towns. International rates are the same all day, and costs are calculated per minute: about Nfa20 for Italy, Germany, Sweden, the UK and the USA; and Nfa25 for Australia, Canada and New Zealand. National calls cost between Nfa1.15 and Nfa5.45 (Nfa0.40 within Asmara). Telephone cards are available in denominations of Nfa34, Nfa59 and Nfa109 but are useful only in Asmara.

Mobile (cell) phones are becoming more widespread. The expanding network covers major towns throughout the country. Mobile phone numbers use eight digits: a two-digit number starting with 0, followed by six-digits. To reach a mobile phone from outside Eritrea, dial the country code, then the mobile number without the initial 0. At the time of writing, foreign mobile phones were not functioning in Eritrea for lack of roaming agreements with foreign countries. Check with your own company.

Faxes can be sent and received from some of the telecommunications offices. It costs between Nfa24 and Nfa35 for one minute's transmission, depending on the destination. It is also possible to make calls and send or receive faxes from the larger hotels, but rates are much more expensive than from telecommunications offices.

TIME

Eritrea is three hours ahead of GMT/UTC. There is no daylight saving time. See the World Time Zone map, pp402-3.

TOILETS

Both the sit-down and squat types of toilet are found in Eritrea, reflecting Italian and Arab influences respectively.

In the highlands, the sit-down type tends to prevail. In the Muslim lowlands such as in Massawa, the squat style is more commonly found (but only in the cheaper hotels). Toilet paper is very rare in either, so carry your own.

In the small villages of the lowlands, you'll be lucky to find a bush. The inhabitants simply demarcate an area outside the village, point you in that direction, and off you trot.

If you're caught short in the towns, the hotels are the best places to head, and unlike in Europe, wouldn't dream of turning you away in your moment of need. Some of the Italian-designed cafés also have toilets.

TOURIST INFORMATION

Eritrea's tourist facilities are fairly woeful, with little literature and only one tourist office, in Asmara. On the bright side, it's usually staffed by English-speaking students as part of their military service, but don't expect esoteric tips. However, it's a mandatory stop because it issues travel permits for foreign visitors. You could also approach one of the two privately run travel agencies in Asmara (see p312). They are a fount of useful information, but their interests obviously lie in selling you a tour.

Outside Eritrea, the Eritrean embassy or consulate in your home country (the few that exist) is your best bet, but tourist literature is generally limited.

In France contact the **Association France-Erythrée** (asmaraparis@hotmail.com; 6 rue Charles Bassée, 94120 Fontenay-sous-Bois).

TRAVELLERS WITH DISABILITIES

Taxis are widely available in towns and are good for getting around, though none have wheelchair access. Car hire with a driver is easy to organise, if expensive. In Asmara, at least one hotel (Hotel Inter-Continental) has facilities for travellers with wheelchairs. A few hotels have lifts.

Eritrea's Struggle for Independence left many of its inhabitants disabled. Land mines continue to maim the population. Disabled visitors can expect to find a sympathetic and accommodating attitude from Eritreans.

VISAS & DOCUMENTS

All foreign nationals require visas for entry to Eritrea. Visas should be obtained from the Eritrean embassy or consulate before you leave your home country. If there isn't any diplomatic representation in your home country, obtain a visa from the nearest one. If this is inconvenient, you can contact one of the travel agencies in Asmara (see p312). They can offer a tourist visa service for about US$20. You'll need to fax them details of your passport pages and give them at least 10 days to organise the visa. They will fax the details back to you and you'll then be issued with the visa upon arrival at the airport (US$40).

If you're planning to visit neighbouring countries first, including Djibouti, it might be easier to get a visa there, although it's not possible in Ethiopia.

For visa applications, you'll need your passport (valid for at least three months) and one passport photo. Some embassies also require you to show proof of an onward ticket before they'll issue a visa. Most embassies require you to possess a certificate as evidence of yellow-fever vaccination if you will be arriving in Eritrea within six days of visiting an infected area.

The visa application form may require an address in Eritrea and a 'reference'. If you don't have any, find a hotel and tour operator in this chapter, and use these names. Applications can be made by post, and normally take 48 hours to process.

You usually have to travel within three months of the date of issue of the visa.

Tourist visas are for single entry only, and are valid for 30 days from the date of arrival in Eritrea. They cost between US$40 and US$50.

Travel Permits

Due to the ongoing tension with Ethiopia, travelling in Eritrea has become pretty bureaucratic. But there's nothing too irksome; getting permits is pretty straightforward.

Head first to the Tourist Information Centre (p312) in Asmara, where you'll fill in a form and list all the places you intend to visit in the country (be extensive). The form is then signed on the spot by the staff. Then you'll be asked to make a copy and keep one for yourself. Keep this travel permit at all times outside Asmara, as you'll be asked to show it at checkpoints, along with your passport. If you travel overland and come from Djibouti, you'll need to go to the Immigration Office in Assab to get this permit, otherwise you won't be allowed to journey on.

ERITREA

Eritrea's 'national treasures' are protected by paperwork. To visit any of the archaeological sites of Eritrea, you'll need to get a special permit from the **National Museum office** (Map p311; ☎ 112318; Mariam GMBI St, Asmara; ☽ 8.30am-noon & 2.30-6pm Mon-Fri), on the 1st floor of the National Museum building. You'll need your passport and Nfa150 per site (or US$10). The paper can be issued immediately; the staff are helpful and efficient. If you're taking a tour, your agency should do this for you. Bring your passport.

You'll also need a permit to visit the Dahlak Islands, but this should be handled by the travel agency or the owner of the boat that takes you there. It costs US$20.

To visit the monasteries obtain a permit from the **Orthodox Tewahdo Church Headquarters** (☎ 182098; Warsay St; ☽ 8am-noon & 2-4.30pm Mon-Fri) in Asmara (ask for the 'monastery tour application'). It's about 300m past the Lufthansa office, across the street. It costs Nfa150 or US$10 per monastery.

At the time of writing, Nakfa and Filfil were off limits to travellers.

Visa Extensions

In Asmara, the **Department of Immigration** (Map p311; ☎ 200033, ext 204; Denden St; ☽ 7-11.30am & 2-5pm Mon-Fri) will extend your visa twice for a further 30 days. This costs US$40 (except for US citizens, who pay US$25) and you will need one photo, photocopies of your passport details and visa page, and a 20¢ stamp. Payment must be made in cash and with exact change. It takes about three days to process. Applications must be made before the old visa expires.

Visas for Onward Travel

For contact details of embassies and consulates in Eritrea, see p358.

Djibouti One-month entry visas cost US$30 or €25, require two photos, and are issued within 24 hours.
Sudan You'll need two photos and a copy of your passport pages. Then the application is sent to Khartoum (Sudan). Expect a long processing time (about three weeks). If the answer is favourable, you'll pay US$60 (US$160 for US citizens) and you'll have to take a medical examination at Sembel Hospital. The embassy is tricky to find; it's tucked away in a side street about 500m north of Alla Scala Hotel.
Yemen One-month entry visas cost US$55, require two photos, a valid return air ticket and a medical examination at Sembel Hospital. They are processed within 24 hours.

WOMEN TRAVELLERS

With a very low national crime rate and an unusually liberal policy towards women, Eritrea must be one of the safest and least restrictive countries on the continent for women travellers. Use your common sense, though; all the usual precautions apply, such as safety in numbers.

ERITREA TRANSPORT

GETTING THERE & AWAY

Although Eritrea's conflict with Ethiopia has taken a heavy toll on its international land, sea and air links, Eritrea is by no means isolated and is still connected to the outside world. Flying is by far the most convenient way to enter the country. A few adventurous souls also travel overland to Eritrea from Djibouti.

Entering Eritrea

As long as you have a visa (p363) or have made arrangements to pick up your visa on arrival at the airport, entering Eritrea should be no sweat. You will be asked to fill out a currency declaration form (see p358).

PASSPORT

Other than needing a visa, there are no entry restrictions for any nationalities bar Ethiopians.

Air

Travel during the months of July and August, and over Easter, Christmas and New Year should be booked well in advance. Eritreans living abroad tend to visit their families during this time and most flights are more expensive.

THINGS CHANGE...

The information in this section is particularly vulnerable to change. Check directly with the airline or a travel agent to make sure you understand how a fare (and ticket you may buy) works and be aware of the security requirements for international travel. Shop carefully. The details given in this section should be regarded as pointers and are not a substitute for your own careful, up-to-date research.

AIRPORTS & AIRLINES

Eritrea's one international airport lies 6km from the capital. Eritrean Airlines is the national carrier and has a good safety record.

The following are airlines flying to and from Eritrea, with offices in Asmara:

EgyptAir (airline code MS; Map p311; ☎ 127034; www
.egyptair.com.eg; Marsa Fatuma St) Hub Cairo.

Eritrean Airlines (airline code B8; Map p313;
☎ 125500; www.flyeritrea.com; Harnet Ave) Hub Asmara.

Lufthansa (airline code LH; ☎ 186904; www.lufthansa
.com; Warsay St) Hub Frankfurt.

Saudi Arabian Airlines (airline code SV; Map p313;
☎ 120166; www.saudiairlines.com; Harnet Ave) Hub
Jeddah.

Yemenia Yemen Airways (airline code IY; Map p313;
☎ 121035; www.yemenia.com; Harnet Ave) Hub Sanaa.

AFRICA & MIDDLE EAST

Before the war, Ethiopian Airlines had daily flights from Addis Ababa to Asmara. These should resume eventually, but it is difficult to predict when.

EgyptAir has two flights a week between Asmara and Cairo for US$550/680 one way/return.

Saudi Arabian Airlines has three flights a week between Asmara and Riyadh via Jeddah (US$570 return).

Yemenia has three flights weekly between Asmara and Sana'a (US$285 return).

Eritrean Airlines flies twice a week to Djibouti (US$215/285 one way/return) and on to Dubai (US$275 return). It also flies to Jeddah (US$255/375 one way/return).

At the time of writing there was talk of starting services between Asmara and Nairobi (Kenya). The flight would be operated by Kenya Airways on a twice-weekly basis. Check with your travel agent.

ASIA

The best connections from Asia are via Dubai (United Arab Emirates), from where there are connections to Asmara with Eritrean Airlines.

AUSTRALIA & NEW ZEALAND

There are no direct flights from Australia and New Zealand to Eritrea. The best routing is through Cairo (via Singapore) or via Sana'a (Yemen). You can also fly to Dubai (United Arab Emirates), and then continue to Eritrea via Djibouti with Eritrean Airlines. Plan on from about A$2500 return.

> **DEPARTURE TAX**
>
> International departure tax is US$20 or €20, paid in cash after check-in.

UK & EUROPE

Eritrean Airlines flies to Frankfurt, Rome, Milan and Amsterdam, on a twice-weekly basis in high season, and on a once-weekly basis in low season. Expect to pay around €750 return to/from Frankfurt, €820 return to/from Amsterdam, Rome or Milan.

Other international airlines connecting Asmara to Europe include Lufthansa, which currently flies three times a week from Frankfurt for around €980 return; Egypt-Air, which flies to Asmara (via Cairo) from London or Paris twice a week for around €850; and Yemenia Yemen Airways, which has flights from Paris, Frankfurt and Rome to Asmara (via San'a) for around €820.

USA

United Airlines and Lufthansa fly on a code-share basis three times a week from various US cities to Asmara (via Frankfurt), and a return trip will set you back anything from US$2000 to US$2300.

Eritrean Airlines, in conjunction with either Northwest Airlines, Delta Airlines or United Airlines, operates flights to/from the USA via Amsterdam or Frankfurt. Return trips cost from US$1500 to US$1800 (depending on which US city you depart from).

Land

BUS

There are no bus services between the neighbouring countries and Eritrea.

DJIBOUTI

There's only one border crossing, at Rahaita/Moulhoulé, about 110km south of Assab. Travel overland to/from Djibouti is possible but traffic is fairly limited and public transport far from reliable. Only dirt roads lead south of Assab to Djibouti.

From Djibouti, there are infrequent pick-ups and Land Cruisers that ply the route between Obock and Moulhoulé, the last Djiboutian settlement before the border (about four hours); from there, in theory, Eritrean bush taxis go to Assab (four hours). Be

ERITREA

warned: there's no fixed schedule, so stock up on travel literature and CDs and be prepared to hang around for a few days either in Obock or in Assab before setting off.

Coming from Djibouti, you'll have to go to the Immigration Office in Assab to get your travel permit. You'll need it to journey on in Eritrea.

Leaving Eritrea, it's still advisable to register at the Immigration Office in Assab, even if there's an Immigration Office at Rahaita (the Eritrean border town).

For more information on this border crossing, see p290.

ETHIOPIA
As long as the conflict with Ethiopia remains unresolved, the borders between the two countries will remain closed. The most convenient way to get to Ethiopia is to go through Djibouti (p284).

When the situation between the two countries improves, you'll be able to use one of the three sealed roads connecting Eritrea with Ethiopia: the first goes from Asmara via Mendefera and Adi Quala to Aksum in Ethiopia; the second route goes from Asmara via Dekemhare and Adi Keyh in Eritrea to Adigrat in Ethiopia; and the third route connects Assab in the south with Addis Ababa in Ethiopia.

SUDAN
At the time of writing, it was possible to cross the border from Eritrea to Sudan but not the other way. Check the current situation when you get there.

The road is now sealed from Asmara to Teseney, near the border. From Teseney, there are bush taxis to Adi Bara at the Sudanese border. From there you should find transportation to Kassala (Sudan).

Sea
Eritrea has two ports, Massawa and Assab. There are no scheduled passenger services, but many cargo ships from other Red Sea countries use the ports, particularly the one at Massawa. It is sometimes possible to hitch lifts.

GETTING AROUND
While the conflict with Ethiopia remains unresolved, travel around Eritrea may be slightly restricted. A travel permit is necessary

to travel outside Asmara. Fear not, it's quite an unfussy affair (see p363). At the time of research, Nakfa and Filfil were declared off limits to foreigners for unknown reasons. However, this might change in the twinkling of an eye, so check the situation when you get to Asmara.

Air
AIRLINES IN ERITREA
Eritrean Airlines (☎ 125500; www.flyeritrea.com), the national carrier, flies to just one domestic destination: Assab.

Bicycle
If you're ready to sweat it out, it's not a bad idea to get around by bicycle. Given the outrageous price of petrol, traffic is minimal. The only real problem is the steep roads, except in the western lowlands where you can expect more flat terrain. Oh, and there's the heat too. After a couple of weeks, you'll be ready for the Tour de France!

Asmara is also a great city in which to cycle. It's possible to hire bikes in one place only, see p327.

Boat
At the time of writing there were no regular boat services between Massawa and Assab on the Red Sea, but there's speculation that ferry transport may resume on this route. Ask in Massawa.

Bus
The bus service in Eritrea is reasonably efficient and extensive, but few would call it comfortable – expect something resembling a battered school bus. Coverage of Keren, Massawa, Mendefera and Dekemhare is excellent. Services thin out the further away from the capital you get. There are usually at least two buses a day between the larger towns (Asmara, Massawa and Keren), and in principle one bus a day between the smaller ones.

Fares used to be very cheap, but with the soaring fuel prices and shortages it's become a bit less economical. However, the bus still remains the best mode of transport

---

DOMESTIC DEPARTURE TAX

The domestic departure tax is Nfa20.

CYCLING IN ERITREA *Tom Hall*

Eritreans love their cycling. At weekends races are cheered by enthusiastic, ululating crowds and the annual Giro d'Eritrea in February is the country's biggest sporting event. If this gets your legs twitching, here are a few pointers on two-wheeled travel in Eritrea.

Bike hire isn't common in Asmara. Your hotel can probably arrange a mountain bike for a morning, but they won't know what to charge you so be ready to negotiate. For anything more serious consider bringing your own wheels. Workshops in the market area of Asmara can fix most problems but lack sophisticated spare parts. If you think you might need a titanium screw or a specialised pedal clip, bring one with you.

Lots of the day excursions from Asmara in this book could be done by bicycle, at least one way. If your brakes are in good order the ride from Asmara to Nefasit, complete with hairpin bends and baboons for company, is thrilling. At the bottom simply flag down a passing bus and ask them to put your bike on the roof for the ride back up. One bus I travelled on had two live goats on the roof for most of the journey, so a bike won't pose a problem! The area around Massawa is flat, hot and windy so cycling is best limited to local exploring. Always take as much water as you're likely to need and keep protected from the sun. Seek local advice before setting out.

If you do any cycling, remember to keep your passport with you for going through checkpoints when leaving and entering towns. Cycling isn't allowed on the main streets of downtown Asmara – a hangover from pre-independence days when cyclists played a prominent role in agitating against Ethiopian targets.

for budgeteers. Services run between 6am and 4.30pm or 6pm but it's wise to start your journey early in the morning. For long-distance journeys (those taking three hours or longer), buses usually leave between 5.30am and 6.30am.

The major drawback of bus travel is that it's time-consuming. Progress on the road is often slow. Additionally, buses don't adhere to fixed timetables; they depart when they're full. For long-distance journeys, you need to be at the bus station by 6am to buy a ticket and be guaranteed a seat. It's not usually possible to buy tickets in advance, except for the journey between Asmara and Teseney and between Asmara and Assab.

Car & Motorcycle

Over long distances in Eritrea, cars can be twice as quick as buses. It gives you freedom of movement and it's a great way to visit the country at your own pace.

BRING YOUR OWN VEHICLE

If you're taking your own car or motorcycle into Eritrea, you should always carry your passport, a valid international driving licence, the vehicle ownership papers and proof of insurance (third-party insurance is mandatory) covering all the countries you are visiting. Cars can be imported duty-free for a period of four months.

DRIVING LICENCE

To hire a car, you must have a valid international driving licence and be over 25 years old.

FUEL & SPARE PARTS

Ouch! At the time of research, petrol was in short supply in Eritrea and prices were exorbitant. In Asmara petrol was Nfa38 per litre and diesel Nfa17. Fortunately, distances between most destinations are quite short.

HIRE

Vehicle hire is expensive in Eritrea. If you're just planning on travelling on the main routes between towns, a 2WD vehicle is sufficient. But some sights, including Qohaito, are only accessible by 4WD.

Fortunately, the country is small and, with your own wheels, most of its attractions can be seen in quite a short period. If you're travelling solo, or as a couple, you can reduce the cost by joining up with other travellers to hire a car plus a driver/guide. Most vehicles accommodate around five passengers.

A deposit of around Nfa2000 is required to rent a 4WD; for a car it's around Nfa1000.

A driver is usually provided for your 4WD, which is a great help. Having someone who speaks Tigrinya and knows the

---

FUEL CRISIS

There were major diesel and petrol short-ages in Eritrea at the time of writing, as a result of the country's lack of hard currency to buy petrol. This might affect bus sched-ules and vehicle hire.

---

roads is absolutely priceless. Sometimes there's an additional charge if you want the driver to work more than eight hours in a day; check in advance.

Cars cost Nfa350 to Nfa550 per day; a 4WD costs Nfa1500 to Nfa1900 per day, including third-party insurance. The first 50km to 90km are free, and each additional kilometre costs between Nfa1.50 and Nfa3. For Assab, there's usually a surcharge of Nfa500 per day. If you want to hire a car with a driver, add Nfa100 per day. Not all rental agencies accept credit cards. If they do, they add an extra commission (usu-ally 7%).

Cars can be rented from the following agencies in Asmara:

Africa Rent Car (Map p313; ☎ 121755; fax 202597; Nora St)

Alpha Travel Agency (Map p311; ☎ 201355; fax 121668) Off Bahti Meskerem Sq.

Fontana Rent a Car (Map p313; ☎ 120052; fax 127905; Mata St)

Leo Car Rental (Map p311; ☎ 125859, 202307; dilorenzo@cts.com.er; Sematat Ave)

ROAD CONDITIONS

There's a small but surprisingly good net-work of sealed roads connecting Asmara to the north (until Keren), south (until the Ethi-opian border), east (until Massawa) and west (until Barentu). Recent projects include the construction of sealed roads between Keren and Nakfa (under progress), Massawa and Nakfa and, eventually, Massawa and Assab in the south (sealing works had begun on the southern edge of Massawa at the time of writing).

The track between Massawa and Assab has been much improved.

ROAD HAZARDS

The road hazards that exist in Ethiopia also apply in Eritrea: precipitous roads, curfews, children playing, livestock wandering, land

mines and roads that are impassable in the rainy season. For more detailed informa-tion see p280.

ROAD RULES

Driving is on the right-hand side of the road.

Hitching

Hitching is never entirely safe in any coun-try, and we don't recommend it. Given the scarcity of traffic, hitching is not really an option in Eritrea anyway.

Local Transport

Taxis are plentiful in Asmara and can also be easily found in Massawa, Keren and Mendefera.

Tours

In Asmara there's a handful of reputable travel agencies that organise tours around the country. Tours can be tailored to your time, means and interests; from one-day bird-watching excursions from Asmara or weekend trips to the beach in Massawa, to boat trips to the Dahlak Islands or six-day expeditions through the Dankalia region to Assab. They also offer hotel and flight reservations and car hire, as well as visa services. The following ones get good re-ports from travellers and have plenty of experience in guiding foreigners:

Explore Eritrea Travel & Tours (Map p313; ☎ 120259, 125555; www.exploreeritrea.com; Adi Hawesha St, Asmara)

Travel House International (Map p313; ☎ 201881/2; www.travelhouseeritrea.com; 175-15 St, Asmara)

Train

The old Italian railway that stretched be-tween Massawa, Asmara, Keren and Agor-dat was another casualty of war. Many of its tracks were pulled up to reinforce trenches. See also p326.

However, a section of the stretch has been repaired and there's now a regular service on Sunday morning between As-mara and Nefasit (US$50 or Nfa750 return, one hour). It leaves Asmara at 8am and is back at noon. If there's a group of you (say, eight to 10 people), the train can also be chartered until Massawa. Contact the **train station** (☎ 123365) in Asmara.

Health

CONTENTS

One who hides his illness has no medicine; one who hides his problem has no remedy.

Ethiopian proverb

As long as you stay up to date with your vaccinations and take some basic preventive measures, you'd have to be pretty unlucky to succumb to most of the health hazards covered in this chapter. Africa certainly has an impressive selection of tropical diseases on offer, but you're much more likely to get a bout of diarrhoea (in fact, you should bank on it), a cold or an infected mosquito bite than an exotic disease such as sleeping sickness.

BEFORE YOU GO

A little planning before departure, particularly for vaccinations or if you have a pre-existing illness, will save you a lot of trouble later. Before a long trip get a checkup from your dentist, and from your doctor if you have any regular medication or chronic illness, eg high blood pressure or asthma. You should also organise spare contact lenses and glasses (and take your optical prescription with you); get a first-aid and medical kit together; and arrange necessary vaccinations.

It's tempting to leave it all to the last minute – don't! Many vaccines take several doses over a period of up to six weeks, so you must visit a doctor six to eight weeks before departure. Ask your doctor for an International Certificate of Vaccination (otherwise known as the yellow booklet), which will list all the vaccinations you've received. This is necessary as proof of yellow-fever (and possibly cholera) vaccination is mandatory in Ethiopia.

Travellers can register with the **International Association for Medical Advice to Travellers** (IMAT; www.iamat.org). Its website can help travellers to find a doctor who has recognised training. Those heading off to very remote areas might like to do a first-aid course (contact the Red Cross or St John's Ambulance) or attend a remote medicine first-aid course, such as that offered by the **Royal Geographical Society** (www.wildernessmedical training.co.uk).

If you're bringing medications with you, carry them in their original containers, clearly labelled. A signed and dated letter from your physician describing all medical conditions and medications, including generic names, is also a good idea. If carrying syringes or needles be sure to have a physician's letter documenting their medical necessity.

How do you go about getting the best possible medical help? It's difficult to say; it really depends on the severity of your illness or injury and the availability of local help. If malaria is suspected, seek medical help as soon as possible or begin self-medicating if you're off the beaten track (see p373).

INSURANCE

Medical insurance is crucial, but many policies differ. Check that the policy includes all the activities you want to do. Some specifically exclude 'dangerous activities' such as white-water rafting, rock climbing and motorcycling. Sometimes even trekking is excluded. Also find out whether your insurance will make payments directly to providers or will reimburse you later for overseas health expenditures (in Ethiopia and Eritrea many doctors expect payment in cash). Ensure that your travel insurance will cover the emergency transport required to get you to

HEALTH

a hospital in a major city, to better medical facilities elsewhere in Africa, or all the way home, by air and with a medical attendant if necessary. If you need medical help, your insurance company might be able to help locate the nearest hospital or clinic, or you can ask at your hotel. In an emergency, contact your embassy or consulate.

Membership of the **African Medical & Research Foundation** (Amref; www.amref.org) provides an air evacuation service in medical emergencies in many African countries, including Ethiopia, Eritrea and Djibouti. It also provides air ambulance transfers between medical facilities. Money paid by members for this service goes into providing grassroots medical assistance for local people.

RECOMMENDED VACCINATIONS

The **World Health Organization** (www.who.int/en) recommends that all travellers be covered for diphtheria, tetanus, measles, mumps, rubella and polio, as well as for hepatitis B, regardless of their destination. The consequences of these diseases can be severe, and outbreaks of them do occur.

According to the **Centers for Disease Control & Prevention** (www.cdc.gov), the following vaccinations are recommended for all parts of Africa: hepatitis A, hepatitis B, meningococcal meningitis, rabies and typhoid, and boosters for tetanus, diphtheria and measles. Proof of yellow-fever vaccination is mandatory for travel to Ethiopia and Eritrea. Depending on where you've travelled from, cholera vaccination may also be required.

MEDICAL CHECKLIST

It's a very good idea to carry a medical and first-aid kit with you, to help yourself in the case of minor illness or injury. Following is a list of items you should consider packing.

- Acetaminophen (paracetamol) or aspirin
- Acetazolamide (Diamox) for altitude sickness (prescription only)
- Adhesive or paper tape
- Antibacterial ointment (eg Bactroban) for cuts and abrasions (prescription only)
- Antibiotics (prescription only), eg ciprofloxacin (Ciproxin) or norfloxacin (Utinor)
- Antidiarrhoeal drugs (eg loperamide)

- Antihistamines (for hayfever and allergic reactions)
- Anti-inflammatory drugs (eg ibuprofen)
- Antimalaria pills
- Bandages, gauze, gauze rolls
- DEET-containing insect repellent for the skin
- Iodine tablets (for water purification)
- Oral rehydration salts
- Permethrin-containing insect spray for clothing, tents, and bed nets
- Pocket knife
- Scissors, safety pins, tweezers
- Sterile needles, syringes and fluids if travelling to remote areas
- Steroid cream or hydrocortisone cream (for allergic rashes)
- Sunblock
- Syringes and sterile needles
- Thermometer

Since falciparum malaria predominates in Ethiopia, consider taking a self-diagnostic kit that can identify malaria in the blood from a finger prick.

INTERNET RESOURCES

There's a wealth of travel health advice on the Internet. For further information, **LonelyPlanet.com** (www.lonelyplanet.com) is a good place to start. The World Health Organization publishes a superb book called *International Travel and Health*, which is revised annually and is available online at no cost at www.who.int/ith. Other websites of general interest are **MD Travel Health** (www.mdtravelhealth.com), which provides complete travel health recommendations for every country, updated daily, also at no cost; the Centers for **Disease Control and Prevention** (www.cdc.gov); and **Fit for Travel** (www.fitfortravel.scot.nhs.uk), which has up-to-date information about outbreaks and is very user-friendly.

It's also a good idea to consult your government's travel health website before departure, if one is available.
Australia (www.dfat.gov.au/travel)
Canada (www.hc-sc.gc.ca/english/index.html)
UK (www.doh.gov.uk/traveladvice/index.htm)
USA (www.cdc.gov/travel)

FURTHER READING

- *A Comprehensive Guide to Wilderness and Travel Medicine* by Eric A Weiss (1998)

- *Healthy Travel* by Jane Wilson-Howarth (1999)
- *Healthy Travel Africa* by Isabelle Young (2000)
- *How to Stay Healthy Abroad* by Richard Dawood (2002)
- *Travel in Health* by Graham Fry (1994)
- *Travel with Children* by Cathy Lanigan (2004)

IN TRANSIT

DEEP VEIN THROMBOSIS (DVT)

Blood clots can form in the legs during flights, chiefly because of prolonged immobility. This formation of clots is known as deep vein thrombosis (DVT), and the longer the flight, the greater the risk. Although most blood clots are reabsorbed uneventfully, some might break off and travel through the blood vessels to the lungs, where they could cause life-threatening complications.

The chief symptom of DVT is swelling or pain of the foot, ankle or calf, usually but not always on just one side. When a blood clot travels to the lungs, it could cause chest pain and breathing difficulty. Travellers with any of these symptoms should immediately seek medical attention.

To prevent the development of DVT on long flights you should walk about the cabin, perform isometric compressions of the leg muscles (ie contract the leg muscles while sitting), drink plenty of fluids, and avoid alcohol.

IN ETHIOPIA & ERITREA

AVAILABILITY & COST OF HEALTH CARE

Health care in Ethiopia and Eritrea is varied: Addis Ababa and Asmara have good facilities with well-trained doctors and nurses, but outside the capitals health care is patchy at best. Medicine and even sterile dressings and intravenous fluids might need to be purchased from a local pharmacy by patients or their relatives. The standard of dental care is equally variable, and there's an increased risk of hepatitis B and HIV transmission via poorly sterilised equipment. By and large, public hospitals in the region offer the cheapest service, but will have the least

up-to-date equipment and medications; mission hospitals (where donations are the usual form of payment) often have more reasonable facilities; and private hospitals and clinics are more expensive but tend to have more advanced drugs and equipment and better trained medical staff.

Most drugs can be purchased over the counter in the region, without a prescription. Try to visit a pharmacy rather than a 'drug shop' or 'rural drug vendor' as they're the only ones with trained pharmacists who can offer educated advice. Many drugs for sale in Africa might be ineffective: they might be counterfeit or might not have been stored under the right conditions. The most common examples of counterfeit drugs are malaria tablets and expensive antibiotics, such as ciprofloxacin. Most drugs are available in larger towns, but remote villages will be lucky to have a couple of paracetamol tablets. It's strongly recommended that all drugs for chronic diseases be brought from home. Although condoms are readily available (sometimes boxes – yes boxes! – are in hotel rooms), their efficacy cannot be relied upon, so bring all the contraception you'll need. Condoms bought in Africa might not be of the same quality as in Europe or Australia, and they might have been incorrectly stored.

There's a high risk of contracting HIV from infected blood if you receive a blood transfusion in the region. The **BloodCare Foundation** (www.bloodcare.org.uk) is a useful source of safe, screened blood, which can be transported to any part of the world within 24 hours.

INFECTIOUS DISEASES

It's a formidable list but, as we say, a few precautions go a long way…

Cholera

Cholera is usually only a problem during natural or artificial disasters, eg war, floods or earthquakes, although small outbreaks can also occur at other times. Travellers are rarely affected. It's caused by a bacteria and spread via contaminated drinking water. The main symptom is profuse watery diarrhoea, which causes debilitation if fluids are not replaced quickly. An oral cholera vaccine is available in the USA, but it's not particularly effective. Most cases of cholera could be avoided by close attention to good drinking water and by avoiding potentially contaminated food. Treatment is by fluid replacement (orally or via a drip), but sometimes antibiotics are needed. Self-treatment isn't advised.

Dengue Fever (Break-bone Fever)

Spread through the bite of the mosquito, dengue fever causes a feverish illness with headache and muscle pains similar to those experienced with a bad, prolonged attack of influenza. There might be a rash. Mosquito bites should be avoided whenever possible. Self-treatment: paracetamol and rest. Aspirin should be avoided.

Diphtheria

Found in all of Africa, diphtheria is spread through close respiratory contact. It usually causes a temperature and a severe sore throat. Sometimes a membrane forms across the throat, and a tracheostomy is needed to prevent suffocation. Vaccination is recommended for those likely to be in close contact with the local population in infected areas. More important for long stays than for short-term trips. The vaccine is given as an injection alone or with tetanus, and lasts 10 years.

Filariasis

Tiny worms migrating in the lymphatic system cause filariasis. The bite from an infected mosquito spreads the infection. Symptoms include localised itching and swelling of the legs and/or genitalia. Treatment is available.

Hepatitis A

Hepatitis A is spread through contaminated food (particularly shellfish) and water. It causes jaundice and, although it's rarely fatal, it can cause prolonged lethargy and delayed recovery. If you've had hepatitis A, you shouldn't drink alcohol for up to six months afterwards, but once you've recovered, there won't be any long-term problems. The first symptoms include dark urine and a yellow colour to the whites of the eyes. Sometimes a fever and abdominal pain might be present. Hepatitis A vaccine (Avaxim, VAQTA, Havrix) is given as an injection: a single dose will give protection for up to a year, and a booster after a year gives 10-year protection. Hepatitis A and typhoid

vaccines can also be given as a single dose vaccine, hepatyrix or viatim.

Hepatitis B

Hepatitis B is spread through infected blood, contaminated needles and sexual intercourse. It can also be spread from an infected mother to the baby during childbirth. It affects the liver, causing jaundice and occasionally liver failure. Most people recover completely, but some people might be chronic carriers of the virus, which could lead eventually to cirrhosis or liver cancer. Those visiting high-risk areas for long periods or those with increased social or occupational risk should be immunised. Many countries now give hepatitis B as part of the routine childhood vaccinations. It's given singly or can be given at the same time as hepatitis A (hepatyrix).

A course will give protection for at least five years. It can be given over four weeks or six months.

HIV

HIV, the virus that causes AIDs, is an enormous problem throughout Ethiopia and Eritrea. The virus is spread through infected blood and blood products, by sexual intercourse with an infected partner and from an infected mother to her baby during childbirth and breastfeeding. It can be spread through 'blood to blood' contacts, such as with contaminated instruments during medical, dental, acupuncture and other body-piercing procedures, and through sharing used intravenous needles. At present there's no cure; medication that might keep the disease under control is available, but these drugs are too expensive for the overwhelming majority of Africans, and are not readily available for travellers either. If you think you might have been infected with HIV, a blood test is necessary; a three-month gap after exposure and before testing is required to allow antibodies to appear in the blood.

Leishmaniasis

This is spread through the bite of an infected sandfly. It can cause a slowly growing skin lump or ulcer (the cutaneous form) and sometimes a life-threatening fever with anaemia and weight loss. Dogs can also be carriers of the infection. Sandfly bites should be avoided whenever possible.

Leptospirosis

It's spread through the excreta of infected rodents, especially rats. It can cause hepatitis and renal failure, which might be fatal. It's unusual for travellers to be affected unless living in poor sanitary conditions. It causes a fever and sometimes jaundice.

Malaria

Malaria is a serious problem in Ethiopia and Eritrea, with one to two million new cases reported each year. Though malaria is generally absent at altitudes above 1800m, epidemics have occurred in areas above 2000m in Ethiopia. The central plateau, Addis Ababa, the Bale and Simien Mountains, and most of the northern historical circuit are usually considered safe areas, but they're not risk-free.

For short-term visitors, it's probably wise to err on the side of caution. If you're thinking of travelling outside these areas, you shouldn't think twice – take prophylactics.

The disease is caused by a parasite in the bloodstream spread via the bite of the female Anopheles mosquito. There are several types of malaria; falciparum malaria is the most dangerous type and makes up 70% of the cases in Ethiopia and Eritrea. Infection rates vary with season and climate, so check out the situation before departure. Unlike most other diseases regularly encountered by travellers, there's no vaccination against malaria (yet). However, several different drugs are used to prevent malaria, and new ones are in the pipeline. Up-to-date advice from a travel health clinic is essential as some medication is more suitable for some travellers than others. The pattern of drug-resistant malaria is changing rapidly, so what was advised several years ago might no longer be the case.

Malaria can present in several ways. The early stages include headaches, fevers, generalised aches and pains, and malaise, which could be mistaken for flu. Other symptoms can include abdominal pain, diarrhoea and a cough. Anyone who develops a fever in a malarial area should assume malarial infection until a blood test proves negative, even if you have been taking antimalarial medication. If not treated, the next stage could develop within 24 hours, particularly if falciparum malaria is the parasite: jaundice, then reduced consciousness and coma (also known as cerebral malaria) followed by death. Treatment in hospital is essential, and

the death rate might still be as high as 10% even in the best intensive-care facilities.

Many travellers are under the impression that malaria is a mild illness, that treatment is always easy and successful, and that taking antimalarial drugs causes more illness through side effects than actually getting malaria. In Africa, this is unfortunately not true. Side effects of the medication depend on the drug being taken. Doxycycline can cause heartburn, indigestion and increased sensitivity to sunlight; mefloquine (Larium) can cause anxiety attacks, insomnia and nightmares, and (rarely) severe psychiatric disorders; chloroquine can cause nausea and hair loss; and atovaquone and proguanil hydrochloride (malarone) can cause diarrhoea, abdominal pain and mouth ulcers.

These side effects are not universal, and can be minimised by taking medication correctly, eg with food. Also, some people should not take a particular antimalarial drug, eg people with epilepsy should avoid mefloquine, and doxycycline should not be taken by pregnant women or children younger than 12.

If you decide that you really do not wish to take antimalarial drugs, you must understand the risks, and be obsessive about avoiding mosquito bites. Use nets and insect repellent, and report any fever or flulike symptoms to a doctor as soon as possible. Some people advocate homeopathic preparations against malaria, such as Demal200, but as yet there's no conclusive evidence that this is effective, and many homeopaths don't recommend their use.

People of all ages can contract malaria, and falciparum causes the most severe illness. Repeated infections might result eventually in less serious illness. Malaria in pregnancy frequently results in miscarriage or premature labour. Adults who have survived childhood malaria have developed immunity and usually only develop mild cases of malaria; most Western travellers have no immunity at all. Immunity wanes after 18 months of nonexposure, so even if you have had malaria in the past and used to live in a malaria-prone area, you might no longer be immune.

If you're planning a journey through a malarial area, particularly where falciparum malaria predominates, consider taking standby treatment. Emergency stand-by treatment should be seen as emergency treatment aimed at saving the patient's life and not as routine

HEALTH

THE ANTIMALARIAL A TO D

- A – Awareness of the risk. No medication is totally effective, but protection of up to 95% is achievable with most drugs, as long as other measures have been taken.

- B – Bites – avoid at all costs. Sleep in a screened room, use a mosquito spray or coils, sleep under a permethrin-impregnated net at night. Cover up at night with long trousers and long sleeves, preferably with permethrin-treated clothing. Apply appropriate repellent to all areas of exposed skin in the evenings.

- C – Chemical prevention (ie antimalarial drugs) is usually needed in malarial areas. Expert advice is needed as resistance patterns can change, and new drugs are in development. Not all antimalarial drugs are suitable for everyone. Most antimalarial drugs need to be started at least a week in advance and continued for four weeks after the last possible exposure to malaria.

- D – Diagnosis. If you have a fever or flulike illness within a year of travel to a malarial area, malaria is a possibility, and immediate medical attention is necessary.

---

self-medication. It should be used only if you'll be far from medical facilities and have been advised about the symptoms of malaria and how to use the medication. Medical advice should be sought as soon as possible to confirm whether the treatment has been successful. The type of stand-by treatment used will depend on local conditions, such as drug resistance, and on what antimalarial drugs were being used before stand-by treatment. This is worthwhile because you want to avoid contracting a particularly serious form such as cerebral malaria, which affects the brain and central nervous system and can be fatal in 24 hours. As mentioned earlier, self-diagnostic kits, which can identify malaria in the blood from a finger prick, are also available in the West.

The risks from malaria to both mother and foetus during pregnancy are considerable. Unless good medical care can be guaranteed, travel throughout Africa when pregnant – particularly to malarial areas – should be discouraged unless essential. Self-treatment: see stand-by treatment (earlier) if you're more than 24 hours away from medical help.

Meningococcal Meningitis

Meningococcal infection is spread through close respiratory contact and is more likely in crowded situations, such as buses. Infection is uncommon in travellers. Vaccination is recommended for long stays and is especially important towards the end of the dry season. Symptoms include a fever, severe headache, neck stiffness and a red rash. Immediate medical treatment is necessary.

The ACWY vaccine is recommended for all travellers in sub-Saharan Africa. This vaccine is different from the meningococcal meningitis C vaccine given to children and adolescents in some countries; it's safe to be given both types of vaccine.

Onchocerciasis (River Blindness)

This is caused by the larvae of a tiny worm, which is spread by the bite of a small fly. The earliest sign of infection is intensely itchy, red, sore eyes. Travellers are rarely severely affected. Treatment in a specialised clinic is curative.

Poliomyelitis

Generally spread through contaminated food and water. It's one of the vaccines given in childhood and should be boosted every 10 years, either orally (a drop on the tongue) or as an injection. Polio can be carried asymptomatically (ie showing no symptoms) and could cause a transient fever. In rare cases it causes weakness or paralysis of one or more muscles, which might be permanent.

Rabies

Rabies is spread by receiving the bites or licks of an infected animal on broken skin. It's always fatal once the clinical symptoms start (which might be up to several months after an infected bite), so postbite vaccination should be given as soon as possible. Postbite vaccination (whether or not you've been vaccinated before the bite) prevents the virus from spreading to the central nervous system. Animal handlers should be vaccinated, as should those travelling to remote areas where a reliable source of post-bite vaccine isn't available within 24 hours. Three preventive injections are needed over a month. If you have not been vaccinated you'll need a course of five injections starting 24 hours or as soon as possible after the injury. If you have been vaccinated, you'll need fewer postbite injections, and have more time to seek medical help.

Schistosomiasis (Bilharzia)

This disease is spread by flukes (minute worms) that are carried by a species of freshwater snail. The flukes are carried inside the snail, which then sheds them into slow-moving or still water. The parasites penetrate human skin during paddling or swimming and then migrate to the bladder or bowel. They're passed out via stool or urine and could contaminate fresh water, where the cycle starts again. Paddling or swimming in suspect freshwater lakes or slow-running rivers should be avoided. There might be no symptoms. There might be a transient fever and rash, and advanced cases might have blood in the stool or in the urine. A blood test can detect antibodies if you might have been exposed, and treatment is then possible in specialist travel or infectious disease clinics. If not treated the infection can cause kidney failure or permanent bowel damage. It's not possible for you to infect others.

Tuberculosis (TB)

TB is spread through close respiratory contact and occasionally through infected milk or milk products. BCG vaccination is recommended for those likely to be mixing closely with the local population, although it gives only moderate protection against TB. It's more important for long stays than for short-term stays. Inoculation with the BCG vaccine isn't available in all countries. It's given routinely to many children in

---

TAPE WORMS

These parasites are relatively common in Ethiopia and the Horn. Eating Ethiopian traditional food like *kitfo* and *tere sega* (raw meat dishes) in rural areas is usually the cause. Consider having your stool tested when you get home to avoid future health problems.

---

developing countries. The vaccination causes a small permanent scar at the site of injection, and is usually given in a specialised chest clinic. It's a live vaccine and should not be given to pregnant women or immunocompromised individuals.

TB can be asymptomatic, only being picked up on a routine chest X-ray. Alternatively, it can cause a cough, weight loss or fever, sometimes months or even years after exposure.

Trypanosomiasis (Sleeping Sickness)

Spread via the bite of the tsetse fly. It causes a headache, fever and eventually coma. There's an effective treatment.

Typhoid

This is spread through food or water contaminated by infected human faeces. The first symptom is usually a fever or a pink rash on the abdomen. Sometimes septicaemia (blood poisoning) can occur. A typhoid vaccine (typhim Vi, typherix) will give protection for three years. In some countries, the oral vaccine Vivotif is also available. Antibiotics are usually given as treatment, and death is rare unless septicaemia occurs.

Yellow Fever

Yellow fever is spread by infected mosquitoes. Symptoms range from a flulike illness to severe hepatitis (liver inflammation) jaundice and death. The yellow-fever vaccination must be given at a designated clinic and is valid for 10 years. It's a live vaccine and must not be given to immuno-compromised or pregnant travellers.

Travellers must carry a certificate as evidence of vaccination to obtain a visa for Ethiopia and Eritrea, though Eritrea only requires one if you're arriving within six days of visiting an infected area. You may also have to present it at immigration upon arrival. There's always the possibility that a traveller without a legally required, up-to-date certificate will be vaccinated and detained in isolation at the port of arrival for up to 10 days or possibly repatriated.

TRAVELLERS' DIARRHOEA

Although it's not inevitable that you'll get diarrhoea while travelling in Ethiopia and Eritrea, it's certainly very likely. Diarrhoea is the most common travel-related illness:

HEALTH

figures suggest that at least half of all travellers will get diarrhoea at some stage. Sometimes dietary changes, such as increased spices or oils, are the cause. To help prevent diarrhoea, avoid tap water (see opposite). You should also only eat fresh fruits or vegetables if cooked or peeled, and be wary of dairy products that might contain unpasteurised milk. Although freshly cooked food can often be a safe option, plates or serving utensils might be dirty, so you should be highly selective when eating food from street vendors (make sure that cooked food is piping hot all the way through). If you develop diarrhoea, be sure to drink plenty of fluids, preferably an oral rehydration solution containing water (lots), and some salt and sugar. A few loose stools don't require treatment but, if you start having more than four or five stools a day, you should start taking an antibiotic (usually a quinoline drug, such as ciprofloxacin or norfloxacin) and an antidiarrhoeal agent (such as loperamide) if you're not within easy reach of a toilet. If diarrhoea is bloody, persists for more than 72 hours or is accompanied by fever, shaking chills or severe abdominal pain, seek medical attention.

Amoebic Dysentery

Contracted by eating contaminated food and water, amoebic dysentery causes blood and mucus in the faeces. It can be relatively mild and tends to come on gradually, but seek medical advice if you think you have the illness as it won't clear up without treatment (which is with specific antibiotics).

Giardiasis

This, like amoebic dysentery, is also caused by ingesting contaminated food or water. The illness usually appears a week or more after you have been exposed to the offending parasite. Giardiasis might cause only a short-lived bout of typical travellers' diarrhoea, but it can also cause persistent diarrhoea. Ideally, seek medical advice if you suspect you have giardiasis, but if you're in a remote area you could start a course of antibiotics.

ENVIRONMENTAL HAZARDS
Heat Exhaustion

This condition occurs following heavy sweating and excessive fluid loss with inadequate replacement of fluids and salt, and is particularly common in hot climates when taking unaccustomed exercise before full acclimatisation. Symptoms include headache, dizziness and tiredness. Dehydration is already happening by the time you feel thirsty; aim to drink sufficient water to produce pale, diluted urine. Self-treatment: fluid replacement with water and/or fruit juice, and cooling by cold water and fans. The treatment of the salt-loss component consists of consuming salty fluids as in soup, and adding a little more table salt to foods than usual.

Heatstroke

Heat exhaustion is a precursor to the much more serious condition of heatstroke. In this case there's damage to the sweating mechanism, with an excessive rise in body temperature; irrational and hyperactive behaviour; and eventually loss of consciousness and death. Rapid cooling by spraying the body with water and fanning is ideal. Emergency fluid and electrolyte replacement is usually also required by intravenous drip.

Insect Bites & Stings

Mosquitoes might not always carry malaria or dengue fever, but they (and other insects) can cause irritation and infected bites. To avoid these, take the same precautions as you would for avoiding malaria (see p373). Use DEET-based insect repellents. Excellent clothing treatments are also available; mosquitos that land on treated clothing will die.

Bee and wasp stings cause real problems only to those who have a severe allergy to the stings (anaphylaxis). If you're one of these people, carry an 'epipen': an adrenaline (epinephrine) injection, which you can give yourself. This could save your life.

Scorpions are frequently found in arid or dry climates. They can cause a painful bite that is sometimes life-threatening. If bitten by a scorpion, take a painkiller. Medical treatment should be sought if collapse occurs.

Fleas and bed bugs are often found in cheap hotels. Fleas are also common on local and long-distance buses and in the rugs of some remote churches. They lead to very itchy, lumpy bites. Spraying the mattress with crawling insect killer after removing bedding will get rid of them.

Scabies is also frequently found in cheap accommodation. These tiny mites live in the skin, particularly between the fingers. They cause an intensely itchy rash. The itch is easily treated with malathion and permethrin lotion from a pharmacy; other members of the household also need treating to avoid spreading scabies, even if they do not show any symptoms.

Snake Bites

Basically, avoid getting bitten! Do not walk barefoot, or stick your hand into holes or cracks. However, 50% of those bitten by venomous snakes are not actually injected with poison (envenomed). If bitten by a snake, do not panic. Immobilise the bitten limb with a splint (such as a stick) and apply a bandage over the site, with firm pressure, similar to bandaging a sprain. Do not apply a tourniquet, or cut or suck the bite. Get medical help as soon as possible so antivenin can be given if needed.

Water

Never drink tap water unless it has been boiled, filtered or chemically disinfected (such as with iodine tablets). Never drink from streams, rivers and lakes. It's also best to avoid drinking from pumps and wells: some do bring pure water to the surface, but the presence of animals can still contaminate supplies.

Bottled water is available everywhere, though it's better for the environment if you treat/filter local water. If bottled water is obtained, always crush the bottle to minimise waste.

Language

CONTENTS

ETHIOPIAN AMHARIC

Amharic is Ethiopia's national language. It belongs to the Afro-Asiatic language family, in the Semitic language sub-group, which includes Arabic, Hebrew and Assyrian.

While regional languages such as Oromo, Somali and Tigrinya are also important, Amharic is the most widely used and understood language throughout the country. It is the mother tongue of the 12 million or so Amhara people in the country's central and northwestern regions, and a second language for about one third of the total population.

Amharic word endings vary according to the gender and number of people you're speaking to. Gender is indicated in this guide by the abbreviations 'm' (to a male), 'f' (to a female) and 'pl' (to more than one

---

THE ETHIOPIC SYLLABARY

The unique Ethiopic script is the basis for the alphabets of Amharic, Tigrinya and Tigré. The basic Ethiopic syllabary has 26 characters; Amharic includes another seven, and Tigrinya another five characters to cover sounds that are specific to those languages.

The alphabet is made up of root characters representing consonants. By adding lines or circles (representing the vowel sounds) to these characters, seven different syllables can be generated for each consonant (eg **ha**, **he**, **hë**, **heu**, **hi**, **ho**, **hu**). As with Roman script, the characters are written from left to right on a page.

---

person, regardless of gender). There are also general modes of address that can be either informal or polite, indicated by the abbreviations 'inf' and 'pol' respectively.

For a more comprehensive guide to the language, get a copy of Lonely Planet's *Ethiopian Amharic Phrasebook*. It has useful introductory sections on pronunciation and grammar, and includes Amharic script throughout.

PRONUNCIATION

While many of the sounds of Amharic will be familiar to you, there are some sounds for which there are no English equivalents. Keep your ears tuned to the way Ethiopians pronounce their language – this will be a good start in mastering pronunciation.

In general, stress falls equally on each syllable. Like English, a raised tone at the end of a sentence signifies a question.

Vowels

a   as in 'mamma'
e   as in 'let'
ë   as the 'a' in 'ago'; shorter and flatter than **eu** below
eu   as the 'e' in 'her', with no 'r' sound
i   as in 'bit'
o   as in 'hot'
ō   a cross between the 'oa' in 'coat' and the 'au' in 'haul'

u	as in 'flute' but shorter
ay	as the 'ai' in 'bait'
ai	as in 'aisle'

Consonants

ch	as in 'church'
g	as in 'get'
gw	as in 'Gwen'
h	as in 'hit'; at the end of a sentence it's like a short puff of breath
kw	as the 'q' in 'queen'
j	as in 'jump'
s	as in 'plus' (never a 'z' sound)
sh	as in 'shirt'
z	as in 'zoo'
ny	as the 'ni' in 'onion'
r	a rolled 'r'
'	a glottal stop, ie a momentary closing of the throat, like the 'tt' in the Cockney pronunciation of 'bottle'

You should also be aware of the Amharic consonant sounds that have no English equivalents – 'glottalic' or 'explosive' variants of some consonants, made by tightening and releasing the vocal chords. To explain these sounds in any depth would take more space than we have here so they haven't been included in this guide. Instead, their nearest English equivalents have been used.

ACCOMMODATION

Where is a ...?	... yet nō?
hotel	hotel
good hotel	tēru hotel
cheap hotel	rēkash hotel
bed	alga
room	kēfēl

Do you have ...?/	... alleu?
Is there ...?	
a room/bed	alga
a single room	and alga
a room with two beds	baleu huleutt alga
a quiet room	seut yaleu kēfēl
showers	shaweur
water for bathing	meutateubiya wuha
hot water	muk wuha

How much is the room/bed for ...?	alga leu ... sēntē nō?
one night	and mata
one week	and samēnt

Does it include breakfast?	kursēnēm yicheumēral?
I'd like to see the room.	kēflun mayet ēfeullēgallō
Can I see a different room?	lela kēfēl mayet ēchēlallō?
I leave tomorrow.	neugeu ēhedallō

CONVERSATION & ESSENTIALS

Hello/Greetings.	tenastēllēn (lit: 'may you be given health')
Hello.	seulam (lit: 'peace be with you')
Hello.	tadiyass (inf)
How are you?	deuhna neuh? (m)
	deuhna neush? (f)
	deuhna not? (pol)
	deuhna nachu? (pl)
I'm fine.	deuhna
Good night.	deuhna deur (m)
	deuhna deuri (f)
	deuhna yideuru (pol)
	deuhna deuru (pl)
Goodbye.	deuhna seunbēt (m)
	deuhna seunbēch (f)
	deuhna yiseunbētu (pol)
	deuhna seunbētu (pl)
Goodbye/See you.	chow (inf, as in Italian ciao)
Have a nice trip.	meulkam guzo
Yes.	awo
OK.	ēshi
No. (not the case/not so)	ai (pronounced 'eye')
No. (not there/not available)	yeulleum
Maybe.	mēnalbut
Please.	ēbakēh (m)
	ēbakēsh (f)
	ēbakon (pol)
	ēbakachu (pl)
Thank you.	ameuseugēnallō
Thank you very much.	beutam ameuseugēnallō
Don't mention it.	mēnēm aideuleuhm
Excuse me.	yikērta
Sorry.	aznallō
What's your name?	sēmēh man nō? (m)
	sēmēsh man nō? (f)
	sēmēwot man nō? (pol)
My name is ...	sēme ... nō
What country are you from?	keu yet ageur neuh? (m)
	keu yet ageur neush? (f)
	keu yet ageur not? (pol)
I'm from ...	keu ...
Are you married?	ageubtēhal? (m)
	ageubtēshal? (f)

LANGUAGE

I'm married.   agëbëchallö
I'm not married.   alageubahum
May I take your   (anteun/anchën/ërswön) foto
  photograph?   mansat yichalal? (m/f/pol)

DIRECTIONS
Where is ...?   ... yet nö?
I want to go to ...   weudeu ... meuhed ëfeullëgallö
How do I get to ...?   weudeu ... ëndet ëhedallö?
Is it near/far?   kërb/ruk nö?
Can I walk there?   beugër yaskedal?
Can you show me   kartaw lai yasayunyal? (pol)
  on the map?
Turn ...   beu ... beukul tateuf/tateufi (m/f)
Go straight ahead.   beukeutëta hid (m)/hij (f)
on the (left/right)   beu (gra/keuny) beukul
at the next corner   yeumikeutëllö meutateufiya
to the north   weudeu seumen
to the south   weudeu deubub
to the east   weudeu mësrak
to the west   weudeu më'ërab
in front of/behind   fit leu fit/beuholla
highway   awra godana
main road   wanna meungeud
street   meungeud
village   meuneudeur

SIGNS – ETHIOPIAN
Open   ክፍት ነው-
Closed   ተዘግቷል
Entrance   መግቢያ
Exit   መውጫ
Information   ማስታወቂያ
Danger   አደገኛ
No Smoking   ማጨስ ክልክል ነው-
Toilets   ሽንት ቤት
  Men   የወንዶች
  Women   የሴቶች

HEALTH
I'm sick.   amonyal
I need a doctor.   hakim ëfeullëgallö
doctor   hakim
hospital   hospital
medical centre   yeu hëkëmëna tabiya

I'm allergic to ...   ... ais-mamanyëm
  antibiotics   antibiotiks
  penicillin   peunisillin

I have ...   ... alleubëny
  diabetes   sëkwar beushëta
  nausea/vomiting   yasmeulëseunyal
  stomachache   hoden yameunyal

EMERGENCIES – AMHARIC
Help!   ërduny!
It's an emergency!   aschëkwai nö!
There's been an   adeuga neubbeur!
  accident!
Thief!   leba!
Go away!/Leave me   teumeulleuss!
  alone!
I'm lost.   meungeud teuftobënyal
Where is the toilet?   shënt betu yeuht nö?

Call ...!   ... tëra/tëri! (m/f)
  the police   polis
  an ambulance   ambulans

LANGUAGE DIFFICULTIES
Do you speak ...?   ... tëchëlalleuh? (m)
                              ... tëchëyalleush? (f)
                              ... yichëlallu? (pol)
  English   ënglizënya
  Amharic   amarënya

Yes, I speak (English).   aow, (ënglizënya) ëchëlallö
I don't speak   (amarënya) alchëllëm
  (Amharic).
Do you understand?   geubbah? (m)
                              geubbash? (f)
                              geubbawot? (pol)
I don't understand.   algeubanyëm
I understand.   geubëtonyal
Do you have/Is   asteurgwami alleu?
  there a translator?
Does anyone here   ënglizënya yeumichël alleu?
  speak English?
Please speak slowly.   ëbakëh keuss bëleuh
                                teunageur (m)
                              ëbakësh keuss bëleush
                                teunageuri (f)
                              ëbakon keuss bëlö
                                yinageuru (pol)
Please write it in   ëbakon beu ënglizënyaalfabet
  Roman script.   yisafuliny

NUMBERS
Although there are Amharic script numerals, Arabic numerals (ie those used in English) are now commonly used throughout Ethiopia. Amharic is used when referring to numbers in speech.

½   gëmash
1   and
2   huleutt

3	sost
4	arat
5	amëst
6	sëdëst
7	seubat
8	sëmënt
9	zeuteuny
10	assër
11	assra and
12	assra huleutt
13	assra sost
14	assra arat
15	assra amëst
16	assra sëdëst
17	assra seubat
18	assra sëmënt
19	assra zeuteuny
20	haya
21	haya and
30	seulassa
31	seulassa and
40	arba
50	hamsa
60	sëlsa
70	seuba
80	seumanya
90	zeuteuna
100	meuto
101	meuto and
200	huleutt meuto
1000	and shi
2000	huleutt shi
100,000	meuto shi

SHOPPING & SERVICES

Where is a/the ...?	... yet nö?
bank	bank
church	beteu kërëstëyan
city centre	meuhal keuteuma
... embassy	yeu ... embassi
market	geubeuya
mosque	meusgid
pharmacy	farmasi/meudhanit bet
police station	polis tabiya
post office	posta bet
public toilet	shënt bet
restaurant	mëgëb bet
tourist office	yeu turist biro
university	yuniveursiti

What time does it open/close?
  sënt seu'at yikeufeutal/yizzeugal?
I want to change money/travellers cheques.
  geunzeub/travleurs cheks meukeuyeur ëfeullëgallö

I want to make a (local/international) call.
  (ageur wëst/wëch ageur) sëlk meudeuweul ëfeullëgallö

Where is a/an ...?	... yet nö?
bakery	dabbo bet
bookshop	meusëhaf bet
clothes shop	yeu lëbs suk
general store	sheukeuta sheukeut meudeubër
market	geubeuya
stationers	stesheunari
shop	suk

Where can I buy ...?	... yet yigeunyal?
I'm just looking.	ëyayo nö
I want a (larger/	(tëllëk yaleu/anneus yaleu) ...
smaller) ...	ëfeullëgallö
How much is it?	sëntë nö?
That's (very)	(beutam) wëdd nö
expensive.	
Do you have	rëkash alleu?
anything cheaper?	

TIME & DAYS

When?	meuche?
What time is it?	sënt seu'at nö?
It's (one) o'clock.	(and) seu'at nö
It's a quarter past	(and) seu'at keurub nö
(one).	
It's half past (one).	(and) seu'at teukul nö
the morning	tëwatu
the evening	mëshëtu
the night	lelitu

now	ahun
today	zare
tonight	zare mata
tomorrow	neugeu
yesterday	tënantëna

Monday	seunyo
Tuesday	makseunyo
Wednesday	rob
Thursday	hamus
Friday	arb
Saturday	këdame
Sunday	ëhud

TRANSPORT

Where is the ...?	yet ... nö?
airport	awroplan mareufiyaw
bus station	awtobës tabiyaw
bus stop	awtobës makomiyaw
taxi stand	taksi makomiyaw
ticket office	tiket biro/tiket meushchaw
train station	babur tabiyaw

LANGUAGE

Which bus goes to ...?	yetënyaw awtobës weudeu ... yihedal?
Does it go to ...?	weudeu ... yihedal?
Please tell me when we get to ...?	ëbakon ... sënëdeurss yinëgeuruny?
I want to get off here.	ëzzih möreud ëfeullëgallö

What time does the ... arrive/leave?	... meuche yideursal/yineusal?
boat	jeulba
bus	awtobës
car	meukina
minibus	wëyëyët
plane	awroplan
train	babur
truck	yeu chëneut meukina

next	yeumikeutëllö
How much is it to ...?	weudeu ... sënt(ë) nö?
I'd like to reserve a ticket to ...	weudeu ... tiket beukëd miya meugzat ëfeullëgallö
I'd like a one way ticket to ...	weudeu ... meuheja tiket ëfeullëgallö
I'd like a return ticket to ...	weudeu ... deurso meuls tiket ëfeullëgallö

I want to rent a ...	... meukeurayeut ëfeullëgallö
bicycle	bësklet
car	meukina

TIGRINYA

Tigrinya is the principal language of Eritrea and is also widely spoken in Tigray province in Ethiopia. It belongs to the Ethiopic branch of the Semitic language family. Like Amharic, it uses the syllabic alphabet of classical Ethiopic or Ge'ez (see The Ethiopic Syllabary on p378).

Tigrinya word endings vary according to the gender of the person you are speaking to; this is indicated in this guide where relevant by the abbreviations 'm' (to a male) and 'f' (to a female).

PRONUNCIATION
Vowels

a	as in 'mamma'
e	as in 'men'
ee	as in 'heed'
i	as in 'bit'
o	as in 'or', with no 'r' sound
oo	as in 'cool'
u	as in 'put'
ay	as in 'bait'
ai	as in 'aisle'
ō	a cross between the 'oa' in 'coat' and the 'au' in 'haul'

Consonants

Most consonants are pronounced as per their English counterparts but, like Amharic, there are some consonant sounds not found in English. The transliterations in this guide are designed for ease of use and are not meant as a detailed phonetic representation of all the consonant sounds of Tigrinya. By pronouncing the words and phrases clearly you should be able to make yourself understood. Listening to the everyday speech of the people is the best way to master some of the more complex sounds of the language.

ch	as in 'church'
g	as in 'get'
h	as in 'him'
j	as in 'jump'
ny	as the 'ni' in 'onion'
q	like a 'k' from far back in the throat
r	as in 'run'
s	as in 'plus' (never a 'z' sound)
sh	as in 'shirt'
ts	as the 'ts' in 'its'
z	as in 'zoo'

ACCOMMODATION

hotel	hotel
guesthouse	maeref agaysh/albeirgo
youth hostel	nay mena-esey hostel
camping ground	metkel dinquan/teinda bota

Do you have any rooms available?	medekesi kiflee alekado?
How much is it per night/person?	neha-de leiti/seb kenday yikifel?
Is breakfast included?	kursi mesoo hisub d'yu?

single bed	kelete arat
double bed	hadde arat
for one/two people	neha-de/kelete seb
for one/two nights	neha-de/kelete leiti

CONVERSATION & ESSENTIALS

Hello.	selam
Welcome.	merhaba

Good morning.	dehaando hadirka/hadirkee (m/f)
Good afternoon.	dehaando weelka/weelkee (m/f)
Good evening.	dehaando amsika/amsikee (m/f)
Good night.	dehaan hideru
Goodbye.	dehaan kun (also Italian ciao)
Yes.	u-we
No.	aykonen
Please.	bejaka/bejakee (m/f)
Thank you.	yekanyeley/yemesgin
That's fine, you're welcome.	genzebka/genzebkee (m/f)
Excuse me.	yikrai-ta
I'm sorry.	aytehazeley
How are you?	kemay aleka/alekee? (m/f)
I'm fine, thanks.	tsebuk, yekeniyeley
Pleased to meet you.	tsebuk afleto/leila yigberelna
What's your name?	men semka/semkee? (m/f)
My name is ...	shemey ... iyu
Where are you from?	kabey metsika/metsikee? (m/f)
I'm from ...	a-nne kab ... iye
Are you married?	temereka dikha? (m)
	temerekee dikhee? (f)
How many children do you have?	kenday kolu-oot (deki) alowuka/ ulowukee? (m/f)
I don't have any children.	deki yebeleyn.
I have a son.	wedi aloni
I have a daughter.	gual alatni
May I take your photograph?	kese-alekado?

DIRECTIONS

Where is ...?	abey alo ...?
I want to go to ...	nab ... kikeid delye
How do I get to ...?	kemey geire naboo ... yikeid?
Is it far/near?	rehooq/kereba diyu?
Can I walk there?	baegrey kikedo yikealdo?
Can you show me the direction?	ket-hebreni tikealdo?
Go straight ahead.	ket elka kid
Turn left/right.	netsegam/neyeman tetewe

HEALTH

I need a doctor.	a-nne hakim/doctor yedliyeni a-lo
Where is the hospital?	hospital/beit hikimina abey alo?
I have a stomachache.	a-nne kirtset aloni
I'm diabetic.	a-nne shikor/shikoria himam aloni
I'm allergic to penicillin.	a-nne nay pencillin kute-at aloni
diarrhoea	witse-at
medicine	medhanit/fewsi
nausea	egirgir/segedged

LANGUAGE DIFFICULTIES

Do you speak (English)?	(engiliznya) tezarebdo/ tezarebido? (m/f)
I don't speak Tigrinya.	a-nne tigrinya ayzareben
I understand.	yirede-anee iyu/teredioonee
I don't understand.	ayeterede-anen

NUMBERS

1	hadde
2	kelete
3	seleste
4	arba-ate
5	hamushte
6	shedushte
7	shewate
8	shemonte
9	tesh-ate
10	aserte
20	isra
30	selasa
40	arba-a
50	hamsa
60	susa
70	sebe-a
80	semanya
90	tese-a
100	mi-eetee
1000	sheh

SHOPPING & SERVICES

I'm looking for ...	ne ... yenadi alekoo
a bank	bank
the hospital	hospital/ beit hikmena
the market	idaga/shooq
a pharmacy	farmacha/beit medhanit
the post office	beit busta
a public telephone	nay hizbi telefon
the tourist office	nay turist haberaita beit tsihfet
What time does it open?	saat kenday yikifet?
What time does it close?	saat kenday yi-etso?
Do you have ...?	... alekado?

LANGUAGE

LANGUAGE

How many/much?	kenday?
this/that	eizee/etee
How much is it?	kenday iyu waga-oo?
I'm just looking.	nikeree tirah iye
That's too expensive.	aziyu kebiruni
bookshop	mesheta metsahifti
clothes shop	mesheta kidawenti
market	idaga/shouq
local products	nay kebabi etot/firyat

TIME & DAYS

What time is it?	saat kenday koynoo?
today	lomee/lomee me-altee
tomorrow	tsebah
yesterday	timalee
morning	niguho
afternoon	dehri ketri
night	leytee
Monday	senui

Tuesday	selus
Wednesday	reboo
Thursday	hamus
Friday	arbi
Saturday	kedam
Sunday	senbet

TRANSPORT

Where is the ...?	abey alo ...?
airport	aryaporto/maerefi nefarit
bus station	maerefi autobus
bus stop	autobus tetew tiblelu
When does the next	tikitsil ... saat kenday
... leave/arrive?	tinekel/te-atu?
boat	jelba
bus (city)	autobus (ketema)
plane	auroplan/nefarit
taxi	taksi
train	babur

Also available from Lonely Planet:
Ethiopian Amharic Phrasebook

Glossary

Ethiopian and Eritrean culinary terms are found under Eat Your Words on p73.

For information on the languages of Ethiopia and Eritrea, see p378.

abba – a prefix used by a priest before his name; means 'father'

abuna – archbishop of the Ethiopian and Eritrean Orthodox church, from the *Ge'ez* meaning 'our father'

adaï – evergreen shrub used as toothbrush

agelgil – round, leather-bound 'lunch boxes' carried by locals

amba (also *emba*) – flat-topped mountain

Ato – literally 'sir'; equivalent of 'Mr'

azmari – itinerant minstrel (Ethiopia)

beat – Amharic word meaning 'place', which is attached to the end of other words, eg *buna beat*, *shint beat* (Ethiopia)

buluko – heaviest type of *shamma*, used in cold areas such as the Bale Mountains (Ethiopia)

buna – coffee (Ethiopia)

chat – mildly intoxicating leaf that's consumed primarily in eastern Ethiopia; it's illegal in Eritrea

contract taxi – private, or nonshared, taxi

dejazmach – title (usually of nobility though given to any outstanding male) equivalent to duke or prince; lower ranking than *ras*

Derg – Socialist military junta that governed Ethiopia from 1974 to 1991; derived from the *Ge'ez* word for 'committee'

dhow – see *sambuk*

dula – wooden staff carried by many Ethiopian highlanders

emba – see *amba*

enset – false-banana tree found in much of southern Ethiopia, used to produce a breadlike staple also known as *enset*

EPLF – Eritrean People's Liberation Front; victorious guerrilla army in the 'Struggle for Independence'

Falasha – Ethiopian Jew

faranji – foreigner, especially Western ones (Ethiopia)

gabeta – ancient board game

gabi – slightly thicker version of the *shamma*, worn by men

gada – age system of male hierarchy among the Oromo

gari – horse-drawn cart used for transporting passengers and goods in the towns

Ge'ez – a forerunner of modern Amharic

gegar – a rectangular, two-storey structure with a flat roof

gommista – tyre repair shop (Italian)

gotera – granary with a little thatched roof (Ethiopia)

Injera – a unique pancake upon which sits anything from spicy meat stews to colourful dollops of boiled veg and cubes of raw beef; see p68 for more details

jellabia – hooded cloak with wide sleeves (Eritrea)

jile – the curved knife that is carried by Afar nomads

kemis – white cotton dress worn by Ethiopian highland women

Kiddus – Saint, eg Kiddus Mikael translates to St Michael

maqdas – inner sanctuary of a church (Holy of Holies)

mesob – hourglass-shaped woven table from which traditional food is served (Ethiopia)

mies – see *tej*

natala – women's equivalent of a *shamma*, but with a decorated border *(tibeb)*

negus – king (Ethiopia)

negus negast – king of kings; the traditional and official title of Ethiopian emperors

ras – title (usually of nobility but given to any outstanding male) similar to duke or prince

sambuk – traditional Arab vessel (or *dhow*) rigged with a lateen (triangular) sail, plying the Red Sea and Indian Ocean (Eritrea)

sewa – see *tella*

shamma – a white, light cotton toga; see also *gabi*, *natala* and *buluko*

shifta – traditionally a rebel or outlaw; today a bandit or roadside robber

shint beat – toilet (Ethiopia)

shirit – saronglike wrap worn by men in Eritrea and Ethiopia's eastern lowlands

tabot – replica of the Ark of the Covenant, kept in the *maqdas* of every Orthodox church

tankwa – traditional papyrus boat used on Lake Tana and elsewhere (Ethiopia)

tef – an indigenous grass cultivated as a cereal grain; the key ingredient of *injera* (p68)

tej – wine made from honey, popular in Ethiopia; known in Eritrea as *mies*

tella – home-brewed beer made from finger millet, maize or barley, popular in Ethiopia; known in Eritrea as *sewa*

tibeb – the decorative border of a woman's shawl (Ethiopia)

tukul – traditional cone-shaped hut with thatched roof; like South Africa's rondavel

wadi – a river that is usually dry except in the rainy season

Weizerit – equivalent of 'Miss' (Ethiopia)

Weizero – literally 'lady', now equivalent of 'Mrs' (Ethiopia)

Behind the Scenes

THIS BOOK

Frances Linzee Gordon wrote the 1st edition of *Ethiopia, Eritrea & Djibouti*. The 2nd edition, *Ethiopia & Eritrea*, was updated by Frances (Ethiopia), and Jean-Bernard Carillet, who wrote the Addis Ababa and Eritrea chapters. This 3rd edition was updated by Matt Phillips (Addis Ababa, Northern, Southern and Western Ethiopia) and Jean-Bernard (Eastern Ethiopia, Eritrea and Transitting Through Djibouti). This guidebook was commissioned in Lonely Planet's Melbourne office, and produced by the following:

Commissioning Editors Will Gourlay, Marg Toohey, Lucy Monie
Coordinating Editors Charlotte Orr, Kyla Gillzan
Coordinating Cartographer Ross Butler
Coordinating Layout Designer Jacqui Saunders
Managing Cartographer Corinne Waddell
Assisting Cartographers James Ellis, Joshua Geoghegan, Sophie Richards
Cover Designer Wendy Wright
Project Manager Rachel Imeson
Language Content Coordinator Quentin Frayne
Talk2Us Coordinator Raphael Richards

Thanks to David Burnett, Sally Darmody, Jennifer Garrett, Mark Germanchis, Nancy Ianni, Katie Lynch, Kate McDonald, Celia Wood

THANKS
MATT PHILLIPS

Thanks to my amazing finacée George. Her love, understanding and support carried me over the highlands and through the trenches of write-up. Thanks to Will Gourlay for his kind support and for sending me back to Africa for the third time this year – it has been a crazy ride! Marg Toohey, who took over Will's reigns near the end of the project, was also incredibly helpful – thanks! Thanks Jean-Bernard for the coffee in Paris and for your passion on this region. Thanks Mum and Bernie for your smiles and laughter, and Dad and Vikki for teaching me to dream big. Thanks to Pam and Dave for always looking out for me. Thanks also to Margaret and Eunice, and their kids Alex, Bonnie, Lizzy and Rose, for always keeping me in their thoughts. Although now separated by a continent and ocean, I'd like to thank my wonderful friends in Vancouver for continually bringing home back to me each time they call. I'd also like to thank Stefano Spaggiari for laughs in Gonder and Addis. Particularly helpful on the road were Terje Ostebo, Cathy Braid and Martin Rack. And lastly, thanks to Messeletch Tsige at Addis Ababa's Tourist Information Centre for your patience.

JEAN-BERNARD CARILLET

Heaps of thanks to Lonely Planet's Will for his constant trust and encouragements since the beginning of this fantastic African adventure. I'd also like to express my deepest gratitude to Matt, the ideal author-coordinator whose commitment is second to none – not to mention his patience, *bonne humeur* and efficiency. To share the same passion was a pleasure throughout. A big thanks also to the carto team for their great job!

At home, I'd like to thank my little Eva, who helps give meaning and direction to my otherwise gypsy life. And I won't forget my Mum for

THE LONELY PLANET STORY

The story begins with a classic travel adventure: Tony and Maureen Wheeler's 1972 journey across Europe and Asia to Australia. There was no useful information about the overland trail then, so Tony and Maureen published the first Lonely Planet guidebook to meet a growing need.

From a kitchen table, Lonely Planet has grown to become the largest independent travel publisher in the world, with offices in Melbourne (Australia), Oakland (USA) and London (UK). Today Lonely Planet guidebooks cover the globe. There is an ever-growing list of books and information in a variety of media. Some things haven't changed. The main aim is still to make it possible for adventurous travellers to get out there – to explore and better understand the world.

At Lonely Planet we believe travellers can make a positive contribution to the countries they visit – if they respect their host communities and spend their money wisely. Every year 5% of company profit is donated to charities around the world.

her generous care and support. In the Horn and in France, several people helped with tips, pointers and logistics, including Gerard Neveu and Dominique Lommatzsch in Paris; Mulugheta in Addis Ababa; Brudo Pardigon and his family, Vicente, Ali Liaquat, Daoud, Ermano, Mahammed Abdullahi Wais, Ikram, Yasmina and the whole bunch of friends in Djibouti; Solomon Abraha, Tedros Kebbede, Tekle, Rahel and Gerard Sambranna in Eritrea. Lastly, to all the Africans I met while on the road – thanks for your fabulous zest for life, which is always a great lesson of hope.

OUR READERS

Many thanks to the travellers who used the last edition and wrote to us with helpful hints, useful advice and interesting anecdotes:

A Raf Aerts, Dan Alton, David Anden **B** Fabio Barros, Linda Battaglia, Susan & Ken Batten, Jacinta Beehner, Maria Grazia Benedetti, Andre Bes, Marlies Beschorner, Colin J Biggs, Roland Brandenburg, Anthony Buckwell **C** Emily Churchman, Piet Convents **D** Ake Dahllof, Judy Daniel, Marina D'Arco, John Davidson, Valerie de Graffenried, Barrie Dennett, Richard Desomme, Dinqa Dhugassa, Frederic Dichtel, Ekkehard Doehring **E** Abraham Ebisa, Ole Botnen Eide, Tim Eyre **F** Jacek Fraczek, Kathy Freeman **G** Brett Gardner, Orin Gensler, Nicole Giordino, Efrem Girmay, Nicolas Gizardin, Dee Griffin, Richard Griffith **H** Larry Hallock, Amelia Hanslow, Mulle Harbort, Donal Hickey, Emma Holmbro **I** Richard Iles **J** Clark Jemetha, Iris Jenkins, Robert Jenkins, Da-eul Jeong, Graham Jones **K** Will Kenney, Boris Kester, Andrew Knowles, Joanna Knowles, Catherine Koch, Marian Korecek **L** Mark Langdale, Susan Lee, Dieter Leonhard, Francesc Lopez, Christine Lutz **M** Sarah Mackie, Harald Mark, Colin McKenna, Van Mejia, Anne Meyer, Urs Michalke, John Bernard Miller, David Morawetz, Sandra Mos **N** Ryszard Niedzielski, Nienke Nijhoff, Charles Notcutt, Eva November **O** Christopher O'Connell, Jostein Olseng **P** Elspeth Paterson, Allen Perrel, Andrew Phillips **Q** Mark Quaid **R** Hussny Rabat,

SEND US YOUR FEEDBACK

We love to hear from travellers – your comments keep us on our toes and help make our books better. Our well-travelled team reads every word on what you loved or loathed about this book. Although we cannot reply individually to postal submissions, we always guarantee that your feedback goes straight to the appropriate authors, in time for the next edition. Each person who sends us information is thanked in the next edition – and the most useful submissions are rewarded with a free book.

To send us your updates – and find out about Lonely Planet events, newsletters and travel news – visit our award-winning website: **www.lonelyplanet.com/feedback**.

Note: We may edit, reproduce and incorporate your comments in Lonely Planet products such as guidebooks, websites and digital products, so let us know if you don't want your comments reproduced or your name acknowledged. For a copy of our privacy policy visit www.lonelyplanet.com/privacy.

Cosgrove Robert, Marci Roberts, Edu Romero, Shimon Rumelt, Ian Rutherford **S** Mark Sadler, Claude Saubusse, Dirk Singer, Karin Sjöstrand, Caroline Skelton, Ben Smart, Stephen Smolar, Peter Southon, Benjamin Sternthal, Wolfgang Stoephasius, Nancy Strider, Anders Svensson **T** Michael Turner **V** Gea Van Egmond, René Van Slooten, Detlev Vreeken **W** Laszlo Wagner, Dirk Wierich, Martin Willoughby-Thomas **Y** Tim & Beryl Yeadell

ACKNOWLEDGMENTS

Many thanks to the following for the use of their content: Globe on back cover ©Mountain High Maps 1993 Digital Wisdom, Inc.

Index

INDEX

000 Map pages
000 Photograph pages

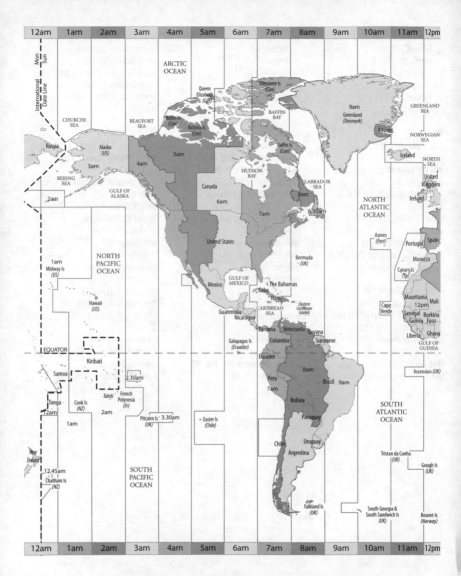

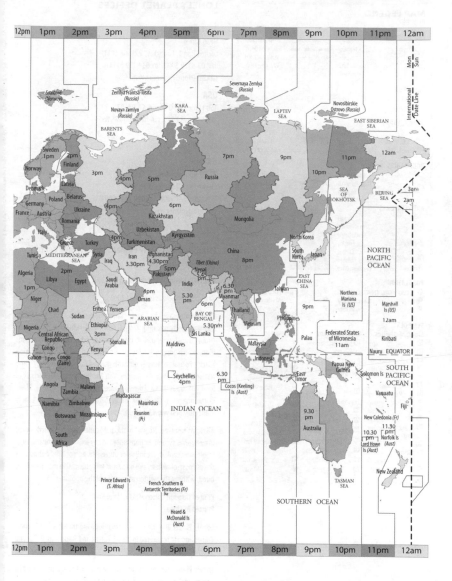

404

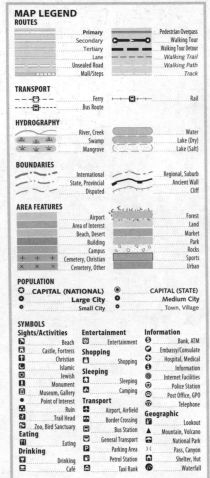

MAP LEGEND

ROUTES
- Primary
- Secondary
- Tertiary
- Lane
- Unsealed Road
- Mall/Steps
- Pedestrian Overpass
- Walking Tour
- Walking Tour Detour
- Walking Trail
- Walking Path
- Track

TRANSPORT
- Ferry
- Bus Route
- Rail

HYDROGRAPHY
- River, Creek
- Swamp
- Mangrove
- Water
- Lake (Dry)
- Lake (Salt)

BOUNDARIES
- International
- State, Provincial
- Disputed
- Regional, Suburb
- Ancient Wall
- Cliff

AREA FEATURES
- Airport
- Area of Interest
- Beach, Desert
- Building
- Campus
- Cemetery, Christian
- Cemetery, Other
- Forest
- Land
- Market
- Park
- Rocks
- Sports
- Urban

POPULATION
- CAPITAL (NATIONAL)
- Large City
- Small City
- CAPITAL (STATE)
- Medium City
- Town, Village

SYMBOLS

Sights/Activities
- Beach
- Castle, Fortress
- Christian
- Islamic
- Jewish
- Monument
- Museum, Gallery
- Point of Interest
- Ruin
- Trail Head
- Zoo, Bird Sanctuary

Eating
- Eating

Drinking
- Drinking
- Café

Entertainment
- Entertainment

Shopping
- Shopping

Sleeping
- Sleeping
- Camping

Transport
- Airport, Airfield
- Border Crossing
- Bus Station
- General Transport
- Parking Area
- Petrol Station
- Taxi Rank

Information
- Bank, ATM
- Embassy/Consulate
- Hospital, Medical
- Information
- Internet Facilities
- Police Station
- Post Office, GPO
- Telephone

Geographic
- Lookout
- Mountain, Volcano
- National Park
- Pass, Canyon
- Shelter, Hut
- Waterfall

LONELY PLANET OFFICES

Australia
Head Office
Locked Bag 1, Footscray, Victoria 3011
☎ 03 8379 8000, fax 03 8379 8111
talk2us@lonelyplanet.com.au

USA
150 Linden St, Oakland, CA 94607
☎ 510 893 8555, toll free 800 275 8555
fax 510 893 8572
info@lonelyplanet.com

UK
72-82 Rosebery Ave,
Clerkenwell, London EC1R 4RW
☎ 020 7841 9000, fax 020 7841 9001
go@lonelyplanet.co.uk

Published by Lonely Planet Publications Pty Ltd
ABN 36 005 607 983

© Lonely Planet Publications Pty Ltd 2006

© photographers as indicated 2006

Cover photographs by Lonely Planet Images: Two Karo people with elaborate body painting, Kolcho, Ethiopia, Ariadne Van Zandbergen (front); Lunch wrapped in *injera* and carried in an *agelgil*, a traditional lunch box, Simien Mountains, Ethiopia, Frances Linzee Gordon (back); Portrait of Hamer girl with painted face and jewellery, Omo National Park, Ethiopia, Ariadne Van Zandbergen (p23); Portrait of local girl, Gash Barka, Eritrea, Frances Linzee Gordon (p291). Many of the images in this guide are available for licensing from Lonely Planet Images: www.lonelyplanetimages.com.